CRIMINAL JUSTICE IN IRELAND

Criminal Justice in Ireland

Edited

with seven introductory essays

by

PAUL O'MAHONY

IPA

INSTITUTE OF PUBLIC
ADMINISTRATION

First published 2002
by the Institute of Public Administration
57–61 Lansdowne Road
Dublin 4

ISBN 1 902448 71 5 hbk
ISBN 1 902448 67 7 pbk

British Library Cataloguing-in-Publication Data
A catalogue record for this book is available from the British Library.

Cover design by Butler Claffey Design, Dún Laoghaire
Origination by Carole Lynch, Dublin
Printed by ColourBooks, Dublin

Table of Contents

Acknowledgements

The publication of this book has been made possible by funding from the Department of Justice, Equality and Law Reform. The grant from the Department's Research Committee is gratefully acknowledged. The book, however, has been produced from beginning to end and in all its phases with total editorial freedom. Since the chapters represent the independent views of the various authors and the editor, nothing in this book should be taken as representative of the official views or policies of the Department of Justice, Equality and Law Reform. Nor can it be inferred that any views expressed in the book receive the official endorsement of the Department of Justice, Equality and Law Reform.

The editor wishes to acknowledge the tremendous efforts and the whole-hearted co-operation of the many authors who have contributed to the book, especially those who wrote commissioned chapters specifically for the book, often on previously neglected topics that required a pioneering approach. The editor is grateful for the assistance of Susan Crilly and Orla Kenny of the Department of Justice, Equality and Law Reform and greatly appreciates the patience, professionalism and cheerfully constructive approach of Tony McNamara, the Publisher at the Institute of Public Administration, the excellent and meticulous editorial assistance of Tom Turley, and the support of Patricia Whittle of the School of Occupational Therapy, Trinity College. The editor gratefully acknowledges the permission to republish chapters granted by the following publishers: Round Hall Sweet and Maxwell (Dublin); Studien Verlag (Innsbruck); Hart Publishing (Oxford); and the IPA (Dublin).

Finally, in respect of his own contributed chapters and seven introductory essays, the editor wishes to thank his wife, Dr Sheila Greene of Trinity College, for her astute critical reading of his work and for her always pertinent and constructive suggestions for improvement – which were almost always followed!

Paul O'Mahony

Notes on Authors

Sean Aylward is director general of the Irish Prison Service since July 1999. A career public servant, his previous position was assistant secretary in the Department of Justice, Equality and Law Reform where he worked in various capacities from 1986. In his earlier career Sean served in the Departments of Defence, Taoiseach and Industry and Commerce.

Ivana Bacik, LLB, LLM (Lond), practises at the Irish Bar and is Reid Professor of Criminal Law, Criminology and Penology at Trinity College Dublin. She is co-author (with James Kingston and Anthony Whelan) of *Abortion and the Law* (1997) and co-editor (with Michael O'Connell) of *Crime and Poverty in Ireland* (1998). She was co-ordinator of an EU-funded study on rape law in different European jurisdictions (*The Legal Process and Victims of Rape* 1998). She is co-author (with Stephen Livingstone) of *Towards a Culture of Human Rights in Ireland* (2001), and has been the editor of the *Irish Criminal Law Journal* since 1997. She writes and researches on human rights law, criminal law and criminology.

Eamonn M. Barnes is a barrister and was appointed to be Ireland's first Director of Public Prosecutions in 1975. He remained in this post until 1999 through a period of great change in Irish society and in criminal justice. He has written widely on legal and especially criminal law topics. He was president of the International Association of Prosecutors from 1996 to 1999.

Robert Barr is a judge of the High Court. He was called to the Bar in 1957 and to the Inner Bar in 1972. He was elected a bencher of King's Inns in 1984. He has been a judge of the High Court since 1985 and of the Special Criminal Court since 1987. As both a prosecutor, a defender and a judge, he has specialised in criminal law.

Shane Butler, PhD, is a senior lecturer in Social Work at Trinity College Dublin and co-chair of Trinity's Addiction Research Centre. He is currently a member of the National Advisory Committee on Drugs, and he also co-ordinates the MSc in Drug and Alcohol Policy at TCD.

Pat Byrne is the current commissioner of An Garda Síochána. He joined the force in September 1965 and in 1972 undertook detective duties at Dublin Castle. In 1985 he was transferred to the Crime and Security Section at garda headquarters at the rank of inspector. Upon promotion to superintendent in 1988, he took charge of the Tipperary District. He returned to garda headquarters in 1989 and has served in a number of positions including assistant commissioner (Human Resource Management and Research) and as deputy commissioner (Operations). He was appointed commissioner in July 1996. Commissioner Byrne graduated from the FBI Academy in Quantico, Virginia, USA in 1986.

Paul Carney is a judge in the Irish High Court and presiding judge of the Central Criminal Court, which is the criminal division of the High Court. Justice Carney has delivered judgements in many landmark cases in the area of criminal law. He is president of the Irish Association for the Protection of Financial Interests of the European Union. As president of that association Justice Carney has been intensively involved in the drawing up of the Corpus Juris which is designed to combat fraud against the European Commission budget.

Johnny Connolly is a consultant and researcher with the Dublin North Inner City Drugs Task Force and the Community Policing Forum. He is currently completing a PhD at Edinburgh University entitled Popular Justice and Police Reform in Northern Ireland. He is author of *Beyond the Politics of Law and Order* (1997).

James Donovan BSc, PhD, FICI, CChem, FRSC, Eurchem, is director of the State Forensic Science Laboratory. After completing his research in UCC, he joined Erin Foods and then worked as a chemist in the State Laboratory specialising in Forensic Toxicology and Explosives. In 1975, he was appointed by the Department of Justice to establish a forensic science laboratory in order to provide a service in scientific analysis in crime investigation.

P.J. Fitzpatrick is a career public servant who has served in four health boards as personnel officer, industrial relations officer, deputy chief executive and programme manager. He served as chief executive officer of the Eastern Health Board prior to his appointment as CEO designate of the Courts Service in November 1998. In the first two years of service as chief executive of the now independent Courts Service he has overseen a sea change in the administration of the Irish courts.

Bill Lockhart, PhD, is a chartered forensic psychologist and chief executive of Extern, a voluntary organisation which provides services for people affected by crime and social exclusion. He has written widely on criminal justice but has a special interest in restorative justice. He was an independent member of the Criminal Justice Review set up under the Good Friday Agreement in Northern Ireland. He is co-author (with J. Brewer and P. Rogers) of *Crime in Ireland, 1945-1995: Here be Dragons* (1997).

Ciaran McCullagh is a statutory lecturer in the Department of Sociology, University College Cork. He has written extensively on the issue of crime and is the author of *Crime in Ireland: A Sociological Introduction* (1996) and co-editor (with M. Tomlinson and T. Varley) of *Whose Law and Order: Aspects of Crime and Social Control in Irish Society* (1988).

Paul Anthony McDermott, BCL, LLM (Cantab), PhD, BL, is a practising barrister-at-law. He is also a lecturer in criminal law at UCD. He is author of *Res Judicata and Double Jeopardy* (1999), *Irish Criminal Law* (co-written with Peter Charleton and Margaret Bolger 1999) and *Irish Prison Law* (2000). He has written a textbook on *Contract Law* (2001). He is author of numerous articles on criminal law and other legal topics and writes a quaterly "Evidence and Procedure Update" for the *Irish Criminal Law Journal*.

Lillian McGovern has been employed by Victim Support as chief executive officer since July 1998. She took up this position at a time of significant progress in the development of victim services in Ireland. Since then she has developed the organisation on a national basis and currently represents Victim Support on the National Crime Council and the newly appointed Parole Board. She is also actively involved with the European Forum of Victim Services.

Aogán Mulcahy, PhD, teaches sociology at University College Dublin. His main areas of interest are criminology and the Northern Ireland conflict, and he has published several articles on these topics. He is currently engaged in research on policing and social change in Ireland.

Paul Murphy is a clinical psychologist with the Department of Justice, Equality and Law Reform. He has extensive experience in working with a wide variety of offender groups. For the last seven years he has been involved in setting up and operating dedicated sex offender programmes in Arbour Hill and Curragh Prison.

Tim Murphy lectures in Jurisprudence and Constitutional Law at University College Cork. He has also lectured in law in the United Kingdom, France and India. He is the author of *Rethinking the War on Drugs in Ireland* (1996) and co-editor (with Patrick Twomey) of *Ireland's Evolving Constitution, 1937-1997: Collected Essays* (1998).

Michael O'Connell PhD is lecturer in Social Psychology at University College Dublin. His research interests include crime and social deprivation, inter-group relations and media representations. Along with the publication of journal papers he has co-edited *Cultivating Pluralism* (2000) and *Crime and Poverty in Ireland* (1998).

Patrick O'Dea has worked as a probation and welfare officer since 1984. He has been Press Officer of the Probation and Welfare Officer Branch of IMPACT since 1992. In that role he has contributed to public debate, especially on the issues of community sanctions and the place of rehabilitation programmes in prisons. He is the author of *"A Class of our Own", Conversations on Social Class in Ireland* (1994), and *"Dear Frankie", Correspondence on the nation's life* (1998).

Hugh O'Flaherty was called to the Bar in 1959 and became a senior counsel in 1976. He was appointed to the Supreme Court in 1990 and served as a Supreme Court judge until 1999. He is author of *Justice, Liberty and the Courts* (1999). He is a past chairman of the National Archives Advisory Council.

Paul O'Mahony, PhD, is a senior lecturer in Psychology and Head of the School of Occupational Therapy, in Trinity College Dublin. He was formerly a forensic psychologist in the Irish prison system and research psychologist in the Department of Justice. He was a member of the National Crime Forum and is author of *Crime and Punishment in Ireland* (1993), *Criminal Chaos: Seven Crises in Irish Criminal Justice* (1996), *Mountjoy Prisoners: A Sociological and Criminological Profile* (1997) and *Prison Policy in Ireland: Criminal Justice versus Social Justice* (2000).

Eoin O'Sullivan, PhD, is a lecturer in Social Policy in the Department of Social Studies, Trinity College Dublin. He is the co-author (with Robbie Gilligan) of *No School, No Future* (1997), (with Helen Buckley and Caroline Skehill) of *Child protection practices in Ireland: a case study* (1997), (with Mary Raftery) of *Suffer the Little Children: the inside story of Ireland's industrial schools* (1999) and (with Ian O'Donnell) of *Crime Control in Ireland; The Politics of Intolerance* (2001).

Philip Pettit is professor of Social and Political Theory at the Research School of Social Sciences at Australian National University in Canberra. He is the author of *The Common Mind: An Essay in Psychology, Society and Politics* (1993), *Republicanism: A Theory of Freedom and Government* (1997) and co-author (with John Braithwaite) of *Just Deserts: A Republican Theory of Criminal Justice* (1990).

Marian Quinn has previously worked directly with young people at risk and managed a national crime prevention programme for five years. She is currently director of Child and Family Services for the East Coast Area Health Board. She has published widely in the areas of early school leaving and juvenile justice, in particular on the subject of inter-agency approaches to youth crime prevention.

Eugene Regan, BL, is an economist and practising barrister. He is a former member of the cabinet of Commissioner Peter Sutherland in the European Commission and is chairman of the Institute of European Affairs European Lawyers' Group. He is author of a number of articles on legal issues relating to European integration and editor of *The New Third Pillar: Cooperation against Crime in the European Union* (2000).

Patrick Riordan, SJ, has lectured in philosophy at The Milltown Institute of Theology and Philosophy since 1985. His main areas of interest are political philosophy and ethics, including punishment and penal policy. He is author of *A Politics of the Common Good* (1996). His most recent book, *Philosophical Perspectives on People Power*, was published in the Philippines in 2001. He was visiting professor there in 2000/01, and he has also lectured and published in the Philippine debate about the death penalty.

Dermot Walsh is the chair of Law and the director of the Centre for Criminal Justice at the University of Limerick. He formerly lectured in University College Cork and the University of Ulster and is a former secretary and president of the Irish Association of Law Teachers. He is a member of the Northern Ireland Bar, the National Crime Council and the Committee to Review the Offences against the State legislation. His primary research interests lie in the areas of criminal justice, European law and human rights. Major recent publications include *The Irish Police: a Legal and Constitutional Perspective* (1998) and *Bloody Sunday and the Rule of Law in Northern Ireland* (2000).

Kevin Warner co-ordinates prison education in Ireland. He studied in Cork, Liverpool (MEd) and the LSE (MScEcon) and taught in schools and adult education in Ireland and England. He was main author of the Council of Europe report, *Education in Prison* (1990), first chairperson of the European Prison Education Association and a Fulbright scholar to California in 1995.

Foreword

This remarkable book presents an incisive and multi-faceted survey of the Irish criminal justice system and its social and political environment. In his earlier works Paul O'Mahony looked with a fresh and enquiring eye at crime, criminals and punishment. In this new book he has, as editor, assembled a series of contributions from writers reflecting their profound practical experience of the criminal justice system and their study of the roots of crime in personality and in society. They analyse society's reaction to crime, and the underlying philosophies of punishment in the penal system.

The contributors include lawyers, judges, police, civil servants, academics and researchers. Personal reflections are provided by, among others, the former director of public prosecutions, the garda commissioner and the presiding judge of the Central Criminal Court.

Each of the book's seven sections is prefaced by an introduction by Paul O'Mahony. These introductions are themselves full of insight and innovative ideas. One of the themes of the book, both in the editor's own work and in a number of the contributions, is the complex interaction between the media, the public, politicians, government and the development of the criminal law. I found Michael O'Connell's essay on "The Portrayal of Crime in the Media – Does It Matter?" fascinating, with its analysis of the treatment of crime in different newspapers, culminating in interviews with leading crime correspondents.

Philip Pettit's "Prisons, Politicians and Democracy" looks in a new way at our extraordinarily high level of imprisonment as "the principal response to crime". "Not much knowledge", Professor Pettit points out, "is required to see that prisons are brutalising and stigmatising institutions that deepen the alienation of offenders from the general society. And not much reflection is needed to see that they are likely to serve as recruiting and organising networks for those of dedicated criminal intent".

Many of the judges who preside on a regular basis over the criminal courts will share some of the views of the contributors to this valuable work. Frequently prison is used as a punishment because no real alternative is available. Judges value highly the work of the probation service and positively seek to have its remit extended and its personnel increased; yet at a time when there has been a steep increase in the number of prison places the development of the probation service has been slow. There has been a general judicial welcome for the introduction of the pilot Drug Court; judges had already tried to operate a similar system on an unofficial basis. Mr Justice Barr in his contribution notes and welcomes what he describes as "a reawakening of interest in rehabilitation", particularly in connection with young offenders.

There is so much that is valuable in this book that it is impossible to mention all its aspects in a brief foreword such as this. I can only express the hope that it will be widely read by those who are professionally involved in the criminal justice system, by those who frame and enact our criminal law, and by the wider public.

Catherine McGuinness
Judge of the Supreme Court

Preface

This book is aimed at third-level students with an academic or vocational interest in criminal justice, including students of law, sociology, psychology, politics and other cognate disciplines and people studying to become police officers, probation officers, social workers, child care and youth workers, prison officers and others. It is hoped that the book, as a compendium of contemporary Irish writing on a broad spectrum of criminal justice topics by authors from many different professions and disciplines, will also be of interest to the inquiring citizen and of value to the many professionals working in or connected with the field, from judges to journalists and politicians.

The book gathers together between two covers a selection of some of the best writing on criminal justice in Ireland of the last ten years. In addition many chapters have been specially commissioned in order to provide coverage of previously neglected topics or to present the perspective of holders of important offices in the criminal justice system. The authors of both original and republished chapters are either leading figures in the criminal justice system or academics, practitioners and analysts with an established expert reputation in the fields on which they write.

The book is divided into seven sections which deal with 1) the criminal law, 2) the phenomenon of crime, 3) crime and society, 4) the police, 5) the courts, 6) the penal system and 7) crime prevention, crime reduction and the treatment of offenders. This is a comprehensive and ambitious agenda, which seeks to provide, on the one hand, an introduction to most of the important facets of the Irish criminal justice system, as it operates at the beginning of the twenty-first century, and, on the other, some discussion of many of the significant and controversial dilemmas that confront the system. Some of the chapters focus almost exclusively on the presentation of factual information, some describe the organisations that constitute the criminal justice system and the vision that motivates these organisations, and some are issue-driven and so more analytical and argumentative. Inevitably the various authors draw on their own professional and academic backgrounds and employ a wide variety of styles of writing and divergent theoretical perspectives.

The chapters do not dialogue with each other; rather each chapter stands alone and so can be read in isolation. However, within the seven sections, chapters have been carefully selected to complement each other. The aim is to reflect in some measure the variety of structures, activities, events, ideas, evidence, interpretations, constructs and opinions relevant to the particular topic. In order to provide a further modicum of coherence, the editor has also contributed an introduction to each section. This is intended, without referring to the section chapters, to provide a brief factual and analytical overview of the area, on occasion touching on significant issues that are not covered in the section.

While the approach is inclusive and wide-ranging, it is explicitly not the claim of this book to provide an exhaustive and definitive coverage of criminal justice in Ireland. On the contrary, the book is inspired by the notion that crime and criminal justice are inexhaustibly multifaceted social issues; they are such immensely complicated issues and so inextricably tied into other social issues that it is effectively impossible to reach definitive conclusions or exhaust all potentially fruitful paths to understanding.

Indeed, it is an aim of the book to demonstrate the urgent need for both practitioners and theorists to abandon their often fragmented, professionally guarded and insular approaches to criminal justice issues and seek a more holistic understanding. This is an area where philosophers and statisticians, policemen and rehabilitation experts, sociologists and lawyers need to talk to each other and learn from each other. The multiple perspectives and conflicting ideologies that surround the difficult problems of crime and society's response to it will never be fully reconciled, but all the different actors in the complex mosaic of criminal justice and all the various interested disciplines have valuable and highly relevant insights to share. While respecting the inevitable constraints imposed by different professionals' roles and points of view, it is hoped that this wide-ranging book will stimulate the kind of cross-fertilisation of ideas that can improve the understanding of crime and criminal justice.

Paul O'Mahony

SECTION 1

THE CRIMINAL LAW

1

Introduction

Paul O'Mahony

Ireland is an ancient nation with a long and troubled history which for the last eight hundred years has been inextricably interwoven with the history of the neighbouring island, Britain. Contempory Ireland, including its political structures and its system of criminal laws and procedures, can only be understood against the background of its history, in particular: a) its colonisation by the English and the long struggle for independence; b) the experience over many centuries by the majority of the population of almost total exclusion from the processes of government; c) the savage trauma of the terrible famines of the 1840s; and d) the long-established pattern of emigration to Britain, America, and Australia, where very substantial proportions of the current populations claim Irish ancestry.

Furthermore, following the War of Independence, the partition of Ireland in 1922 into an independent nation, Ireland, with a population of almost 3.8 million, occupying 26,000 square miles (or 26 of the total 32 administrative counties of the island), and Northern Ireland, which is a constituent part of the United Kingdom of Great Britain and Northern Ireland, continues to have immense consequences for Irish political, social and economic life.

The criminal justice system of Ireland (frequently but incorrectly termed the Republic of Ireland) is the subject of this book. Ireland is a parliamentary representative democracy with a written Constitution, a President as head of state, and a bicameral parliament. The President, whose term of office is seven years, is head of state only and does not have executive powers. The sole power of making laws for the state is vested in the Oireachtas, the Houses of Parliament. Government policy and administration may be critically examined in both the

Dáil and the Seanad, the lower and the upper houses, but, according to the Constitution, the government is responsible and accountable to the Dáil alone.

The Dáil also has superior powers in respect of law-making and indeed in the amendment or repeal of past legislation. An ordinary Bill passed by the Dáil is sent on to the Seanad, which has ninety days to consider it (the role of the Seanad in regard to Money Bills is more restricted). The Seanad may suggest amendments or even reject a Bill but if, after a period of 180 days, the Dáil wishes to proceed with the Bill in its original form it may resolve to do so and declare the Bill to have passed both Houses of the Oireachtas. In this event, if a majority of the Seanad and a third of the Dáil agree that a matter of national importance is at issue, they may petition the President not to sign the Bill and to refer the matter to the people by way of referendum. The Seanad has in fact never exercised this power. The Constitution is the basic law of the country and it may only be amended by means of a referendum, that is by a majority vote in favour of amendment by the people of Ireland. Bills to amend the Constitution can only be initiated in the Dáil.

The history of the Irish criminal justice system is, like Irish political history, intimately linked with that of Britain. The current Irish system is the direct successor to the English legal system, which from 1169, the date of the Anglo-Norman invasion led by "Strongbow", the Earl of Pembroke, began to be imposed on the then prevailing native system of law known as Brehon law. The Brehon system was based on custom and is named after the travelling justices of the Celtic Christian period, who were called Brehons (Byrne and McCutcheon 1996). The Brehons are thought to have evolved from, and to have undertaken a similar social role to, the pre-Christian Celtic druids. Brehon law was a quite extensive, well-developed and sophisticated body of law, which, as far back as the seventh and eighth centuries, was carefully documented in the Irish language. There has been a relatively recent publication, in six annotated volumes (Binchy 1978), of all the extant Brehon laws.

Within the island, there was a long period of coexistence, but not commingling, of English and Brehon law. This period began at the King's Council of 1171 at Waterford, when the feudal Anglo-Norman King, Henry II, asserted his overlordship over the territory of Ireland and proclaimed that "the laws of England were by all freely received and confirmed". However, it was more than 400 years before this over-optimistic claim became a reality. Brehon law persisted and predominated in many areas. It was active and influential, particularly in the North and West, until the early seventeenth century when it was finally supplanted by English law throughout the island.

Poyning's Law which dates from 1494 marks an important turning point in Irish political and legal history. Poyning's Law was clearly designed to address the growing tendency for English colonists and their descendents in Ireland, many of whom adopted the Irish language and Irish customs, and native Gaelic Irish alike to assert more and more autonomy from the English Crown by means of legislation at local Irish parliaments. Poyning's Law curtailed the powers of Irish parliaments, proclaiming the precedence of English legislation over Irish legislation and affirming the supremacy of English law in Ireland. Even so, for a considerable period after Poyning's Law, English law actually held sway only within the Pale, the eastern part of the country that was under close control of the English.

This situation prevailed until the Tudor monarchs finally extended and consolidated English hegemony over the whole island. Henry VIII was the first English monarch to declare himself King of Ireland in 1541, but it was not until the 1800 Act of Union that Ireland was fully absorbed into the Westminster political system under the British Crown, and became an integral part of the United Kingdom of Great Britain and Ireland.

Until 1922, then, Ireland was an integral part of the United Kingdom, sending its own representatives to Westminster. The Irish criminal justice system was, therefore, in this period, no more than a regional branch of the general British system. The court and legal systems were largely similar to the English with some local modifications, which reflected the political and social realities on the ground. For example, it was considered useful to have a corps of salaried professional judges called resident magistrates in the lower courts in Ireland rather than to rely on the more communitarian English system of non-professional local magistrates. Policing was more distinctive. There was a separate police authority for Dublin but elsewhere a national armed police force called the Royal Irish Constabulary. The concept of the unarmed, courteous English policeman was born, in the early nineteenth century, out of the need to persuade and appease British voters, who were none too sure that they required to be policed at all, while, as Reiner (1994) tells us, "a more militaristic and coercive model was from the outset exported to the colonial situation, including John Bull's other island (ie Ireland)".

In general, following the course of development in Britain, the criminal justice system in Ireland in the nineteenth century and the early twentieth century evolved slowly without dramatic or sudden change. Throughout the nineteenth century, more and more specific legislation was passed by Westminster defining and setting out penalties for criminal behaviour throughout the United Kingdom, including Ireland. This active process of creating law limited the scope of the common law. However, it is important to remember that in Ireland there were considerable additional tensions within and pressures upon the criminal justice system, arising from the fact that the system was very frequently used to suppress nationalist activists, landless peasant agitators and the victims of famine and extreme poverty, all of whom had special reason to reject the authority of the law. The courts, the police and the penal system continued to be perceived by large sectors of the population as the coercive arm of an alien colonial power.

Despite this history, there is in the modern Irish legal system a remarkable continuity with the British era in Ireland. Although distinctive structures and legal frameworks have emerged, there is still a strong similarity to the British system. This does not simply reflect the legacy of the past but also the fact that many of the innovations introduced in Ireland since partition, for example the penalty of a Community Service Order, have been closely modelled on similar initiatives previously undertaken in Britain.

One interesting historical note is that during the War of Independence, between 1920 and 1922, the revolutionary government set up its own courts, called the Dáil courts. This led to a brief, partial revival of Brehon law (Kotsonouris 1993). In a highly symbolic gesture, clearly signalling an ardent desire to reject everything associated with the colonial past and the imperial masters, English law textbooks were not to be cited in the Dáil courts. Brehon and European civil law decisions, on the other hand, could be used as persuasive precedents.

However, this experimental attempt to resurrect the ancient native Irish system of law was short-lived. After the Treaty of 1922, establishing the Irish Free State, the Dáil courts were abolished and the court system reverted to its previous form. Brehon precepts and rules have no place in the contemporary Irish legal system. Indeed, it is one of the ironies of the modern, independent state of Ireland that some Westminster legislation of the last century is still law, although the same legislation has long ago been repealed or revised in England and Wales

The Irish legal system, then, is firmly rooted in the English common law tradition and many statutes passed by the British parliament before 1921 continue to have the force of law, because they have not been repealed by the Irish parliament. On the other hand, the current Irish legal system has been termed by Rottman and Tormey (1985) "a hybrid, combining basic features of both the American and the British models as well as some distinctive native innovations".

The common law as the source of law has been described by Byrne and McCutcheon (1996) as "consisting of the hundreds of thousands of decisions which have been delivered by the courts over the centuries and which, by virtue of the demands of the doctrine of precedent, enjoy binding force of law ... To this day significant areas of Irish law are governed by common law rules unaffected by rules derived from other sources". The principal further sources of Irish Law are legislation and the Constitution of 1937, and these take precedence over common law.

Indeed, the provisions of the Constitution supersede both the common law and legislative rules (Forde 1987). It is with respect to the central role of the Constitution that the Irish system can be described as having a strong affinity to the American model. An important aspect of this is the doctrine of the separation of powers between the legislature, the executive and the judiciary. Since the function of interpreting the provisions of the Constitution, which is the basic law of the country, is entrusted by the Constitution itself to the courts, the judiciary have come to play a major role in defining the actual operation of the criminal justice system (Hogan and Whyte 1994).

There is one further source of Irish law and that is European Community law. The Court of Justice of the European Communities, sitting in Luxembourg, presides over this legal system, which takes precedence over national law both as a matter of Community law and national law. On Ireland's accession to membership of the European Community in 1973 an amendment to the Irish Constitution acknowledged this precedence. The European Court of Justice is mainly active in the economic and social areas.

In accordance with the Constitution of 1937, justice in Ireland is administered in public in courts established by law. In serious criminal matters, there is, with a few notable exceptions, a constitutional right to trial by jury. Judges are appointed by the President on the advice of the government and are invariably senior practising members of the legal profession. Under the constitutional doctine of the separation of powers, the judiciary is guaranteed independence in the exercise of its functions. A judge can only be removed from office for misbehaviour or incapacity and removal can only be achieved by resolution of both Houses of the Oireachtas (ie the Dáil and the Seanad).

There are four levels of ordinary courts, including, in order of importance, three courts of first instance – the District Court, the Circuit Court and the High Court – and one court of final appeal – the Supreme Court. The High Court has original and full jurisdiction in matters criminal and civil and also has the power to rule on the constitutionality of legal rules. The High and Circuit Courts hear appeals from lower courts. There is also a Court of Criminal Appeal, which hears certain criminal appeals. This court is composed of one Supreme Court judge and two High Court judges. It decides by majority and only one judgement is given. Since 1993 this court has the power to issue a certificate of miscarriage of justice which renders the state liable to pay damages to the individual treated unjustly.

The Supreme Court does not have original jurisdiction but exercises appellate and consultative jurisdiction, most significantly on constitutional matters. The High and Supreme Courts, therefore, play an immensely important role in shaping the legal framework of Irish life and in particular in deciding criminal justice principles and procedures.

The Special Criminal Court is a rather anomalous court in the context of the Irish Constitution and is quite controversial. The Special Criminal Court is contentious because it is a non-jury court that tries serious criminal cases despite the general provision in the Constitution that the accused should have the right to trial by jury.

The Special Criminal Court was set up in 1972 by proclamation of the government, invoking the Offences Against the State Act of 1939 and as envisaged by the Constitution at Article 38.3.1, which allows for the establishment of non-jury special criminal courts, whenever the government deems that the "ordinary courts are inadequate to secure the effective administration of justice, and the preservation of public peace and order".

The relatively serious political terrorist problem in 1972, which spilled over from Northern Ireland, was the spur for the establishment of the Special Criminal Court. Defendants charged with offences scheduled under the Offences Against the State Act (including membership of illegal organisations, handling of explosives, possession of firearms etc) were to be tried by a non-jury court composed of three judges, one each from the District, Circuit and High Courts.

However, there is also provision for the Director of Public Prosecutions to have accused persons tried before the Special Criminal Court on charges relating to non-scheduled offences, ie ordinary, non-political criminal offences. In recent years, this has resulted in the use of the Special Criminal Court to try a number of defendants charged with involvement in organised crime, especially drug-related crime. Some critics of the system (ICCL, IPRT, ICJP 2000) consider that the current level of political unrest and terrorist danger no longer justify the continuation of a Special Criminal Court and that accused persons are unnecessarily being deprived of their constitutional right to a jury trial. The main argument for continuation of the Special Criminal Court and its extension to cover non-terrorist type cases centres on the serious danger of intimidation and subornation of witnesses and jury members in cases involving organised criminal gangs.

While for most of the twentieth century the attitude to the criminal law has been conservative and traditional, criminal justice structures have remained largely untouched, the last years of the century have witnessed a more activist, revisionist and innovative political orientation towards criminal justice and a consequent quickening pace of reform. For example O'Donnell (1999) identifies 1998 as a watershed year in which there were legislative and operational developments that together "comprise the most thorough reconsideration of the structure and operation of the criminal justice system since the foundation of the state". In March 2001, the Chief Justice, Ronan Keane (*Irish Times* 2001) publicly argued for a remodelling of the courts system to include a merging of the District and Circuit Courts and the establishment of a two-tier appellate court system with separate criminal and civil branches.

Amongst new legislation enacted in recent years have been the Bail Act 1997, which gave effect to the sixteenth amendment of the Constitution by allowing a court to refuse bail to a person charged with a serious offence where it is reasonably considered necessary to prevent the commission of a serious offence by that person; the Criminal Law Act 1997, which abolished the distinction between felonies and misdemeanours; the Non-Fatal Offences against the Person Act 1997, which created new offences relating to criminal conduct involving syringes and stalking; the Offences against the State (Amendment) Act 1998, which increased powers of detention, enabled the court to draw inferences from certain refusals by suspects to provide information, and provided for unlimited fines and the forfeiture of property where that property is used for storage of firearms or explosives; the Criminal Justice Act 1999, which abolished the preliminary examination of a case against a suspect at the District Court level, allowed the giving of certain evidence by certificate, and provided for mandatory minimum sentences of ten years imprisonment for possession and supply of illegal drugs worth more than £10,000.

This legislation and other initiatives, like the expansion of the judiciary, the movement towards independent management structures for the courts and the prisons, and the establishment of computer crime and money laundering investigation units within the Garda Síochána and, most especially, the creation of the Criminal Assets Bureau, represent a considerable effort to modernise and improve the efficiency of law enforcement and the courts. The Criminal Assets Bureau, established in 1996, is a particularly important innovation because it is a multi-agency, statutory body, involving the Garda, Customs, Revenue Commissioners and Department of Social, Community and Family Affairs and is empowered to investigate illegal financial and property gains and to freeze or confiscate such gains through court proceedings. The Bureau has been effective against organised criminals, especially those involved in the importation and distribution of drugs, but it has also been used against corrupt public officials.

While much of the innovation of recent years has been an attempt to strengthen the arm of the law it could, from the civil liberties perspective, be seen as repressive and open to justified criticism. This is especially true in regard to changes, like the curtailment of the right to silence, preventative refusal of bail to suspects and the extension of police powers of detention, all of which impact on due process and the presumption of innocence.

However, this general "get tough" approach has been tempered by other initiatives with a more progressive orientation. For example, structures for consultation have been put in place such as the National Crime Forum (1998), the National Crime Council and mechanisms for garda-community liaison; a pilot Drugs Court has been established that will provide for sentences to drug rehabilitation treatment outside the prison system for non-violent addict offenders; and, most crucially, a Children Act 2001 has been passed that will potentially revolutionise the area of juvenile justice. The Children Act raises the age of criminal responsibility to twelve years from seven years, puts the Juvenile Diversion Scheme on a statutory footing, introduces elements of restorative justice into the system, including Family Group Conferencing, and places considerable emphasis on preventative and early intervention measures and on the diversion of young offenders from prosecution. There is a distinct possibility that some of the preventative and alternative to custody approaches, if they prove effective in the juvenile area, may in time be extended to the criminal justice system more generally.

REFERENCES

Binchy, D. 1978, *Ancient Irish Law Extracts,* Dublin: Institute of Advanced Studies

Byrne, R. and McCutcheon, P. 1996, *The Irish Legal System,* Dublin: Butterworths

Forde, M. 1987, *Constitutional Law of Ireland,* Cork: Mercier

Hogan, G. and Whyte, G. 1994, *Kelly: The Irish Constitution,* 3rd Edition, Dublin: Butterworths

ICCL, IPRT, ICJP 2000, *Shadow Report under the International Covenant on Civil and Political Rights,* Dublin: Irish Council for Civil Liberties, Irish Penal Reform Trust and Irish Commission for Justice and Peace

Keane, Chief Justice Ronan, Report of Speech at UCC, *Irish Times,* 27 March 2001

Kotsonouris 1993, *Retreat From Revolution: The Dáil Courts 1920-1924,* Dublin: Irish Academic Press

National Crime Forum 1998, *Report,* Dublin: Stationery Office

O'Donnell, I. 1999, "Criminal Justice Review", *Administration* 47, 2 175-211

Reiner, R. 1994, *"Policing and the Police",* in *Oxford Handbook of Criminology,* Oxford: Clarendon Press

Rottman, D. and Tormey, P. 1985, "Criminal Justice System: an Overview", in *Report of the Committee of Inquiry into the Penal System,* Dublin: Stationery Office

2

The Legal Framework of the Criminal Law

Paul Anthony McDermott

The purpose of this chapter is to set out the basic framework of the Irish criminal justice system. The chapter will commence by identifying the different sources of Irish law and will explain the structure of the criminal courts. Recent reforms in Irish criminal law will then be listed and consideration will be given to whether more law reform is necessary. Next, an examination will be made of the way in which criminal liability is constructed. This will involve a discussion of the burden of proof and the presumption of innocence. The basic ingredients of a criminal offence will then be explored in detail, and this will involve looking at the act committed by the accused, his mental state whilst committing that act and whether or not he can raise a defence. Next the rapidly developing concept of corporate criminal liability will be explained. Finally the extent to which Irish courts have jurisdiction over crimes committed abroad will be discussed. By the end of the chapter the reader should have a broad overview of the Irish criminal justice system. Of course, the success or failure of a criminal prosecution can depend as much on the rules of evidence and procedure as on the rules of substantive criminal law. Thus, the following chapter will examine the rules of evidence and procedure that are applied by Irish criminal courts.

THE SOURCES OF CRIMINAL LAW

There are several sources of criminal law in this jurisdiction. The first one is the Oireachtas. Article 15.2 of the Constitution provides that the sole and exclusive power for making laws for the state is vested in the Oireachtas. As a result Irish judges are powerless to intervene by declaring a perceived common mischief to be a criminal offence. Unless particular conduct is proscribed by the Oireachtas no person can be charged with it before a criminal court. Nor can the Oireachtas declare acts to be infringements of the law which were not so at the date of their commission.[1]

The criminal law must be sufficiently certain so that citizens may regulate their conduct accordingly. A good example of a case where the requirement for certainty was an issue is the treatment of the offence of blasphemy by the Supreme Court in *Corway v Independent Newspapers*.[2] In the wake of the divorce referendum the *Sunday Independent* published a cartoon which depicted three well-known politicians waving goodbye to a plump and comic caricature of a priest. At the top of the cartoon were printed the words '*Hello progress – bye bye father*'. This was clearly a play upon the '*Hello divorce – bye bye daddy*' slogan which had been used by some anti-divorce campaigners during the referendum. The applicant sought leave of the court to bring a prosecution for blasphemy against the newspaper. In the Supreme Court Barrington J focused on the fact that there was no clear definition of the offence to be found anywhere and concluded that this uncertainty was fatal to any attempt to prosecute the offence. He stated:

> In this state of the law, and in the absence of any legislative definition of the constitutional offence of blasphemy, it is impossible to say of what the offence of blasphemy consists. As the Law Reform Commission has pointed out neither the *actus reus* nor the *mens rea* is clear. The task of defining the crime is one for the Legislature, not for the Courts. In the absence of legislation and in the present uncertain state of the law the Court could not see its way to authorising the institution of a criminal prosecution for blasphemy against the respondents.[3]

OTHER SOURCES OF CRIMINAL LAW AND PROCEDURE

Since 1972 another source of summary criminal law has existed, namely the European Union. The European Communities Act 1972 provides that

2. From the 1st day of January, 1973, the treaties governing the European Communities and the existing and future acts adopted by the institutions of those Communities shall be binding on the State and shall be part of the domestic law thereof under the conditions laid down in those treaties.

---

[1] Article 15.5 of the Constitution
[2] [2000] 1 ILRM 426
[3] [2000] 1 ILRM 426 at 436-437. Note that the *actus reus* is the physical component of an offence and the *mens rea* is the mental component. These concepts are fully discussed below

3. (1) A Minister of State may make regulations for enabling section 2 of this Act to have full effect.

(2) Regulations made under this section may contain such incidental, supplementary and consequential provisions as appear to the Minister making the regulations to be necessary for the purposes of the regulations (including provisions repealing, amending or applying with or without modification, other law, exclusive of this Act).

(3) Regulations under this section shall not create an indictable offence.

(4) Regulations under this section may be made before the 1st day of January, 1973, but regulations so made shall not come into operation before that day.

This has resulted in a large number of summary criminal offences being created by secondary legislation. For example, under s 10(5) of the European Communities (Unfair Terms In Consumer Contracts) Regulations 1995[4] "A person who obstructs or impedes an authorised officer in the exercise of a power under this Regulation, or does not comply with a requirement under this Regulation shall be guilty of an offence. A person guilty of an offence under this Regulation is liable on summary conviction to a fine not exceeding £1,500."

A second potential new source of law is the European Convention on Human Rights. The Minister for Justice, Equality and Law Reform has announced that he "is currently giving serious consideration" to incorporating the Convention into Irish law.[5] It is likely that the Convention would have a significant impact if incorporated in domestic law, despite the fact that in theory it is already taken into account by Irish courts in reaching decisions. The jurisprudence built up by the European Court of Human Rights would affect not only substantive criminal law but also police investigation, trial procedures, evidence, sentencing and the prison system. It would have a particular impact on prisoners, which is appropriate given that modern international human rights treaties grew up out of revulsion at the way prisoners were treated during the Second World War.

It should be noted that the Convention sometimes requires positive measures to be taken. For example in *X and Y v Netherlands*[6] a sixteen-year-old mentally handicapped girl was sexually assaulted by an adult male of sound mind. Due to a loophole in Dutch law he could not be prosecuted. This was because under Dutch law only the victim of the crime could register a criminal complaint, a rule that applied even where the victim was incapable of doing so due to her handicap. The European Court found that the absence of an effective criminal procedure was a violation by the Netherlands of its duty to secure respect for the victim's private life under Article 8. The Court stated that Article 8

---

[4] S.I. No. 27 of 1995

[5] *The Irish Times*, 29 February, 2000

[6] (1985) Series A/91

... does not merely compel the State to abstain from ... interference: in addition to this primarily negative undertaking, there may be positive obligations inherent in an effective respect for private and family life. These obligations may involve the adoption of measures designed to secure respect for private life even in the sphere of the relations of individuals between themselves.[7]

Now that England has passed the Human Rights Act 1998 (the principal sections of which were implemented in October, 2000), Ireland remains one of the few states in Western Europe not to have incorporated the Convention.[8] Incorporation is necessary to protect the Convention from its own success. From its inception up to the end of 1997, the Commission registered over 39,000 applications. It has been calculated that it takes on average five years for an individual to get a case into the European Court of Human Rights once all domestic remedies have been exhausted, and costs an average of £30,000.[9]

Unless otherwise determined by the Oireachtas, international human rights treaties are not part of domestic law and so cannot be directly relied upon by litigants.[10] This was established in *Re Ó Laighléis*[11] where Maguire CJ stated:

The Oireachtas has not determined that the Convention of Human Rights and Fundamental Freedoms is to be part of the domestic law of the State, and accordingly this Court cannot give effect to the Convention if it be contrary to domestic law or purports to grant rights or obligations additional to those of domestic law.

One concern about incorporation is that the courts would immediately be inundated with challenges to every aspect of Irish criminal law. This was the experience of Canada where a flood of litigation followed the passing of the Charter of Rights and Freedoms in 1982. Nobody could be sure that an offence or procedure still applied until it had been tested against the Charter. For example in *MS*[12] the accused argued that the criminalisation of incest was unconstitutional as

---

[7] (1985) Series A/91 at 11

[8] For a discussion of the Human Rights Act 1998 see Cheney and Others, *Criminal Justice and the Human Rights Act 1998* (1999)

[9] White Paper, *Rights Brought Home* (1997) (Cm 3782), p. 6

[10] See generally Lester "The Challenge of Bangalore: Making Human Rights A Practical Reality" [1999] EHRLR 273; Hunt, *Using Human Rights Law in English Courts* (1997); Hogan, "The Belfast Agreement and the Future Incorporation of the European Convention on Human Rights in the Republic of Ireland" (1999) 4, *Bar Review* 205

[11] [1960] IR 93 at 125. See also *Norris v The Attorney General* [1984] IR 36 at 67 where O'Higgins CJ said "Neither the Convention on Human Rights nor the decision of the European Court of Human Rights in *Dudgeon v United Kingdom* is in any way relevant to the question which we have to consider in this case". Similarly in *O'B v S* [1984] IR 316 at 338 Walsh J stated that a case of the ECtHR to which he had been referred "can have no bearing on the question of whether any provision of the Act of 1965 is invalid having regard to the provisions of the Constitution".

[12] (1997) 111 CCC (3d) 467

consent was not a defence and there was no age limit appended to the definition of 'child' in the offence. He also claimed that the offence breached his right to freedom of association, equality and religious freedom. Needless to say the British Columbia Court of Appeal rejected all of these claims.

Of course a flood of litigation that tested our often outdated criminal laws against international human rights standards would not necessarily be a bad thing. As a result of litigation under the Charter, Canada now has a highly developed and sophisticated criminal law jurisprudence. For example at common law the defence of duress is not available if the threats were not immediate and the threatener was not present when the offence was committed. In *Ruzic*[13] the Ontario Court of Appeal held that this limitation on the defence was in breach of the Charter as it failed to take into account the human frailties of the accused.

THE CRIMINAL COURT SYSTEM

An offence is termed summary or indictable by the statute that creates it. A summary offence is generally a minor one and is less serious than an indictable offence. An example of a summary offence is assault contrary to s 2 of the Non-Fatal Offences Against the Person Act 1997. Summary offences are heard in the District Court by a judge sitting without a jury. The District Court is generally limited to imposing a maximum sentence of one year in jail. An example of an indictable offence is murder. Indictable offences are tried in front of a jury either in the Circuit Criminal Court or, in the case of murder or serious sexual offences, in the Central Criminal Court. Certain offences are triable "either way". In other words, the prosecutor can decide to bring summary charges or charges on indictment. An example of an offence triable either way is assault causing harm contrary to s 3 of the Non-Fatal Offences Against the Person Act 1997. In the case of certain indictable offences, the accused can waive his right to trial by jury and elect to have the matter heard in the District Court. However this may only be done where the District Judge is satisfied that the offence is a suitable one to be heard in the District Court, and serious offences will invariably be sent forward to a higher court.

All indictable offences commence in the District Court before being sent forward to a higher court. The District Court determines such matters as bail and the service of a book of evidence on the accused (ie a book containing the evidence that the prosecution intends to call at the trial). Until recently the District Court also conducted a preliminary examination of the evidence to determine if a reasonable jury, properly directed, could convict on it. However Part III of the Criminal Justice Act 1999 has abolished the preliminary examination. Instead, at

---

[13] (1998) 165 DLR (4th) 574

any time after he has been sent forward for trial, the accused may apply to the trial court to dismiss one or more of the charges against him. If it appears to the trial court that there is not a sufficient case to put the accused on trial for any charge it must dismiss that charge. In addition, at any time after the accused has been sent forward for trial, the prosecutor or the accused may apply to the trial court for an order requiring a person to appear before the District Court to give a sworn deposition. This is a useful mechanism whereby the accused or the prosecutor can test the credibility of a potential witness before the criminal trial begins. At the time of writing, a commencement order for Part III of the 1999 Act has yet to be signed by the Minister for Justice, Equality and Law Reform.

Where a person has been convicted of a criminal offence various avenues of appeal will be open to him. The appeal may be against conviction or sentence or both. Appeals from the District Court are to the Circuit Court which sits without a jury for this purpose. Appeals from the Circuit Criminal Court, the Central Criminal Court and the Special Criminal Court are to the Court of Criminal Appeal. There is no automatic right of appeal to the Court of Criminal Appeal and the accused must obtain leave from the trial judge or, if he refuses, from the Court of Criminal Appeal itself. The Court of Criminal Appeal sits with three judges. Its decision is final unless the Court or the DPP certifies that the decision involves a point of law of exceptional public importance, in which case an appeal may be taken to the Supreme Court. A person convicted in the Central Criminal Court may appeal directly to the Supreme Court as an alternative to appealing to the Court of Criminal Appeal.

It is not open to the DPP to appeal an acquittal, save in the case of an acquittal by the District Court. However s 2 of the Criminal Justice Act 1993 empowers the DPP to apply to the Court of Criminal Appeal to review a sentence which he regards as unduly lenient. This only applies to sentences imposed on conviction on indictment, and thus excludes sentences imposed by the District Court. The Court of Criminal Appeal may quash the sentence and replace it with a new one or it may refuse the application. The onus of proof in such a case is on the DPP to show that the sentence was lenient and great weight will be given to the trial judge's reasons for imposing the sentence. The power given to the DPP to appeal a sentence is intended to be used sparingly and to date sentences have been increased by the Court of Criminal Appeal in only a handful of cases.

Indictable offences prosecuted in the Circuit Criminal Court or the Central Criminal Court are tried by a jury. However, in the Special Criminal Court, cases are heard by three judges who sit without a jury.[14] Some explanation of why this is so is necessary. The Constitution of 1937 contemplated that special courts

---

[14] See generally Charleton and McDermott, "From Diplock Courts to Jury Courts", 8 CIJL Yearbook 99 (2000)

would continue to be provided for. Thus, on serious criminal charges the Constitution permits certain accused persons to be deprived of the ordinary right to jury trial guaranteed by Article 38. Section 35 of the Offences Against the State Act 1939 provides that where the government is satisfied that the ordinary courts are inadequate to secure the effective administration of justice and the preservation of public peace and order, it may make and publish a proclamation bringing the Special Criminal Court into force. All offences scheduled in the Act must come before the Special Criminal Court for trial unless the Director of Public Prosecutions certifies that the ordinary courts are adequate in that regard. The Schedule includes firearms, explosives and subversive offences under the 1939 Act. Under the Act, where the Director of Public Prosecutions is satisfied as regards an ordinary offence, such as murder or robbery, that the ordinary courts are inadequate to secure the effective administration of justice he may require that someone should be tried before the Special Criminal Court. The High Court has never set aside the Director's opinion either that the ordinary courts are adequate, or that they are inadequate[15]. Unless an applicant can put forward a prima facie case of a serious irregularity which amounts to an impropriety he cannot obtain judicial review[16]. While the court was set up to deal in essence with the threat of insurrection, it has been acknowledged many times by the Supreme Court that the court can be legitimately used in other respects. In this context Walsh J. has observed:

> It is common knowledge ... that what was envisaged were cases or situations of a political nature where juries could be open to intimidation or threats of various types. However, a similar situation could well arise in types of cases far removed from what one could call 'political type' offences. There could well be a grave situation in dealing with ordinary gangsterism or well-financed ... drug dealing or other situations where it might be believed or established that juries were for some corrupt reason, or by virtue of threats, or illegal interference, being prevented from doing justice.[17]

TREASONS, FELONIES AND MISDEMEANOURS

At common law a crime was classified either as a treason, a felony or a misdemeanour. The original distinction between a felony and a misdemeanour was that between a major and a minor crime (the former attracting different and more serious penalties). However over the years this distinction had become blurred. Finally, the Criminal Law Act 1997 abolished the felony/misdemeanour distinction and provided that on all matters where such a distinction had

---

[15] *O'Reilly v DPP* [1984] ILRM 224
[16] *Foley v DPP, Irish Times,* 25 September, 1989
[17] *The People (DPP) v Quilligan and O'Reilly (No. 1)* [1986] IR 485

previously been made, the law and practice would henceforth be the law and practice applicable at the commencement of the Act to a misdemeanour.

THE NEED FOR REFORM

There is no doubt that much of our criminal law is outdated and in need of reform. An example that has recently provoked debate in the media is the law relating to bribery and corruption. Many of our laws were made during the reign of Queen Victoria (1837-1901) and have remained almost unaltered since that time. Little of the law was then written down because the prevailing view was that it was better to trust to the wisdom of judges, in interpreting their prior decisions, rather than stating the law in the form of an all-embracing code. The result of this is that we have left undefined the most fundamental concepts of criminal liability. For example the Oireachtas has never provided a legislative statement on the foundation of criminal liability and the various mental elements of crime. In addition, only one defence, namely the lawful use of force, has ever been codified. Even proscribed conduct is often described in imprecise language. For the most part, legislators have abrogated the responsibility of codifying our law, save where a particular topic either forces itself upon them or commends itself to their attention due to public interest.

RECENT REFORMS

Compared to previous decades, the last ten years have witnessed a comparatively large amount of criminal law reform. What follows is a brief list of the major developments of the last decade.

(1) The Criminal Justice (Public Order) Act 1994 abolished certain common law offences relating to public order and replaced them with new statutory offences.

(2) Law Reform has been particularly active in the area of sexual offences. The Criminal Law (Sexual Offences) Act 1993 decriminalised buggery between parties of seventeen years or more and codified the law against prostitution. In addition, it reformed the hopelessly outdated law on the protection of mentally impaired persons from sexual exploitation. The Criminal Law (Incest Proceedings) Act 1995 dealt with the vexed question of how to balance the right of the victims of incest to anonymity with the right of the press to report on criminal proceedings. The Sexual Offences (Jurisdiction) Act 1996 made it possible to prosecute in Ireland child sex tourists who commit their offences against children abroad. The Child Trafficking and Pornography Act 1998 was the first Act in the history of the state to specifically target child pornographers and was

carefully drafted so as to bring paedophiles who use the internet within its scope. The Sex Offenders Bill 2000 has proposed a scheme for the post-release monitoring and supervision of those convicted of sexual offences.18 It will also provide for limited legal representation for victims in trials of sexual offences.

(3) The Criminal Law Act 1997 finally abolished the outdated distinction between felonies and misdemeanours. It also repealed a large number of obsolete criminal statutes, such as the Garrotters Act 1863 and the Whipping Act 1862. It had been a long time since anyone had been charged with garrotting in Ireland.

(4) The Non-Fatal Offences Against The Person Act 1997 codified the law as to assault, as well as dealing with syringe attacks, poisoning, endangering others and false imprisonment. It also made harassment a criminal offence. Most interestingly of all, the Act codified the defence of self-defence. This is the first time since the founding of the state that a defence has been codified and as such is a very welcome development. It is to be hoped that similar treatment will soon be given to other defences.

(5) The other main developments centred around attacking the proceeds of crime. The Criminal Law Act 1994 outlaws money laundering and provides for the forfeiture of criminal assets after a conviction. The more radical Proceeds of Crime Act 1996 permits the seizure of the proceeds of crime even if no conviction has been recorded. It has proved very effective in damaging the operations of the so called "godfathers" of crime who had previously believed themselves to be untouchable.[19]

Whilst this harvest of criminal legislation is to be welcomed compared to the famine of previous years, one worrying aspect has been the tendency to rush through far-reaching legislation in response to a particular event. Thus the Proceeds of Crime Act 1996 was enacted in direct response to the murder of Veronica Guerin and the Offences Against the State Act 1998 followed the Omagh bombing. A more considered approach to law making in the criminal field is desirable.

CONSTRUCTING LIABILITY[20]

Criminal law is built upon the idea that people should be punished by the state when they are to blame for conduct involving, or causing, certain wrongs. Before being stigmatised as a criminal a citizen should be blameworthy in respect of that

---

[18] For a discussion of the Bill see Bacik, "The Sex Offenders Bill, 2000", (2000) 5 *Bar Review* 387

[19] See generally McDermott, "The Proceeds of Crime Act 1996: A Review of the Past Twelve Months", (1999) 4 *Bar Review* 413

[20] See generally Charleton, McDermott and Bolger, *Criminal Law* (1999), chapter 1

for which he stands accused. That blameworthiness is a consensus of the ideas of right-thinking citizens. Historically the moral law, as interpreted by various religions, indicated the behaviour that was proscribed. In modern times a layer of moral order is still clearly discernible in our law, particularly in those areas where human conduct has not been assisted or altered by technological advance. Thus it has always been a crime to deliberately kill someone or to sexually assault someone. New methods lead to new mischief and often the law lags behind in describing as crimes what the people regard as grave social wrongs.

PROOF OF GUILT

At the heart of the Irish criminal justice system is the principle that a person is presumed to be innocent until the jury finds him guilty. It is only where each element of the crime is proved against the accused, beyond reasonable doubt, that he may be found guilty.[21] The accused is under no obligation, in the absence of a special statutory provision, to give evidence in his own defence. He may simply test the evidence proffered by the prosecution by cross-examination and may call on the judge at the end of the prosecution's case to rule that there is insufficient material on which a reasonable jury, properly instructed, could find him guilty. This is called an application for a direction. It may be granted in cases where there is a gap in the evidence tendered on behalf of the prosecution or where some vital link in the chain of proof is missing. It can also arise in cases where an apparent link in the chain of proof is so tenuous that it would clearly be perverse for a jury, properly directed as to the onus of proof which rests upon the prosecution, to act upon it[22]. Should the accused choose to raise a defence the prosecution bears the onus of disproving it beyond reasonable doubt.[23] The sole exception to this is the defence of insanity, where the accused has the burden of proving this defence on the balance of probabilities.

It is instructive to compare the criminal standard of proof to the civil standard. In a civil case, the plaintiff has to prove what he alleges on the balance of probabilities. In other words, he must show that what he alleges is more likely to have happened than not to have happened. In a criminal case the prosecution must prove its case beyond reasonable doubt.

The most recent case to consider the burden of proof is *DPP v Kelly*.[24] The accused had been convicted of various sexual offences against boys in a particular

---

[21] *Woolminton v DPP* [1935] AC 462

[22] *The People (DPP) v O'Shea (No 2)* [1983] ILRM 592

[23] *The People (A-G) v Quinn* [1965] IR 366

[24] Unreported, Court of Criminal Appeal, 13 December, 1999. In *Ching* [1976] 63 Cr App R 7 the English Court of Criminal Appeal showed some impatience with the attempts being made by English judges to elaborate upon what "beyond reasonable doubt" means and stated that "[i]f

institution. The Court of Criminal Appeal quashed the conviction on the grounds that the jury might have seen the trial judge's direction as an indication that if they accepted the prosecution evidence they should find the accused guilty. The jury were given no assistance as to the manner in which they were to deal with the accused's own evidence. In addition, the jury should not have been told that they could convict if they did not believe the accused. The direction should have gone further and told the jury that they had to be satisfied of the guilt of the accused beyond all reasonable doubt, notwithstanding that they did not accept his evidence.

Determining that the accused has, or has not, been proven guilty is a matter for the jury alone. A reasonable doubt is the kind of doubt which may affect the mind of a person in the conduct of important affairs. In explaining that standard, the trial judge will often contrast the degree of proof in a criminal case with that in a civil case, where a jury need only be satisfied before finding in favour of a plaintiff or defendant, that a version of events is the more probable. Achieving the standard of beyond reasonable doubt requires that the prosecution should be able to present evidence from which the inference of the accused's guilt is inescapable. They may do this by presenting either direct evidence or circumstantial evidence as to his guilt. Direct evidence would indicate that the accused is guilty from testimony available to the prosecution. For example, in a narcotics case, the accused may be caught inside a house weighing ounces of heroin on a set of scales. The obvious inference to draw from such evidence is that he is a drug dealer. Where the proof is by circumstantial evidence it must be consistent with the guilt of the accused and must be inconsistent with any other rational hypothesis consistent with innocence.[25] For example, the evidence might be to the effect that a woman asked a number of men to kill her husband in a particular way shortly before he was found dead after having been killed in that same manner. She may claim that she was only joking when she asked the men to kill him and that she bore him no ill-will. It will be for the jury to determine whether or not they believe her. Juries tend to be sceptical of extraordinary coincidences. In practice one suspects that juries are most motivated to acquit where the gardaí are shown to have been, apparently, less than fully professional or honest. Such an acquittal may occur notwithstanding that the accused is, apparently, obviously guilty. This phenomenon is known as jury nullification.

---

judges stopped trying to define what is impossible to define there would be fewer appeals". The Court suggested the following guidelines:

i) the issue of the burden of proof should be dealt with at the start of a summing-up
ii) it is advisable not to explain "beyond all reasonable doubt" as doing so usually confuses the jury
iii) an appeal court should look at the whole effect of a summing up when considering whether it was correct or not

[25] *The People (A-G) v McMahon* [1946] IR 267

LIMITATIONS ON THE PRESUMPTION OF INNOCENCE[26]

In exceptional circumstances the prosecution has been assisted by the legislature in discharging the burden of proof by provisions which require that a mental state should be inferred on the proof of certain external factors. The constitutionality of such presumptions[27] has recently been vigorously, but unsuccessfully, challenged in a trilogy of cases. This is a controversial area of Irish law and the cases merit careful consideration.

The first case in the trilogy was *O'Leary v The Attorney General*[28], where two provisions were challenged. Section 24 of the Offences Against the State Act 1939 provides that

> On the trial of a person charged with the offence of being a member of an unlawful organisation, proof to the satisfaction of the court that an incriminating document relating to the said organisation was found on such person or in his possession or in lands or in premises owned or occupied by him or under his control shall, without more, be evidence until the contrary is proved, that such a person was a member of the said organisation at the time alleged in the said charge.

By virtue of s 2 of the Act of 1939 an incriminating document is defined as "a document of whatsoever date, or bearing no date, issued or emanating from an unlawful organisation or appearing to so emanate or purporting or appearing to aid or abet any such organisation or calculated to promote the formation of any unlawful organisation". Section 3(2) of the Offences Against the State (Amendment) Act 1972 provides that

> Where an officer of the Garda Síochána, not below the rank of Chief Superintendent, in giving evidence in proceedings relating to an offence under the said section 21, states that he believes that the accused was at a material time a member of an unlawful organisation, the statement shall be evidence that he was then such a member.

The accused had been convicted of two counts of membership of an unlawful organisation after thirty-seven posters containing the words "IRA calls the shots" were found in his possession and a chief superintendent gave evidence that the accused was a member of the IRA. In the High Court Costello J accepted that every accused in every criminal trial enjoys a constitutionally protected right to the presumption of innocence and that any statute which permitted a trial to be held

---

[26] See generally Ní Raifeartaigh, "Reversing the Burden of Proof in a Criminal Trial: Canadian and Irish Perspectives on the Presumption of Innocence", (1995) 5 ICLJ 135

[27] Trying to find a definition of the word "presumption" is not easy and a lot of academic writing exists on the issue. Essentially, a presumption permits the jury to draw a certain conclusion unless the accused takes steps to make that conclusion unwarranted. The accused can do this either through cross-examination of prosecution witnesses or by giving evidence himself

[28] [1993] 1 IR 102 (HC), [1995] 1 IR 254 (SC)

otherwise than in accordance with this presumption would be unconstitutional. However, he concluded that, although the legal burden of proof (ie the duty to prove all the elements of the offence beyond reasonable doubt) remained on the prosecution throughout a criminal trial, there was nothing unconstitutional about shifting an evidential burden onto the accused in respect of certain matters. Shifting such an evidential burden onto the accused did not discharge the legal burden on the prosecution. Thus the accused could elect not to call any evidence and would still be entitled to an acquittal if the evidence adduced by the prosecution did not establish his guilt beyond all reasonable doubt. Costello J concluded that the 1972 Act simply made admissible in evidence certain statements of belief which would otherwise be inadmissible and the Act of 1939 merely shifted an evidential burden onto the accused. On appeal, the Supreme Court upheld this judgment. In respect of the incriminating document provision O'Flaherty J held that

> It is clear that such possession is to amount to *evidence* only; it is not to be taken as proof and so the probative value of the possession of such a document might be shaken in many ways: by cross-examination; by pointing to the mental capacity of the accused or the circumstances by which he came to be in possession of the document, to give some examples. The important thing to note about the section is that there is no mention of the burden of proof changing, much less that the presumption of innocence is to be set to one side at any stage.[29]

The second case was *Hardy v Ireland*[30], where s 4 (1) of the Explosive Substances Act 1883 was unsuccessfully challenged. The section provides that where a person makes, possesses or controls an explosive substance in circumstances such as to give rise to a reasonable suspicion that he is not making, possessing or controlling it for a lawful object it shall be an offence unless he can show that he made it or had it in his possession or under his control for a lawful object. The Supreme Court held that there was nothing unconstitutional about placing an evidential burden of this sort on the accused. Such a burden could be discharged by the accused on the balance of probabilities. Murphy J concluded:

> ... I do not see that there is any inconsistency between a trial in due course of law as provided for by Article 38, s.1 of the Constitution and a statutory provision such as is contained in s 4 of the Explosive Substances Act, 1883, which affords to an accused a particular defence of which he can avail if, but only if, he proves the material facts on the balance of probabilities.[31]

Hederman J examined the constitutional right to a trial in due course of law and concluded that it did not prevent inferences being drawn from certain established facts:

---

[29] [1995] 1 IR 254 at 265
[30] [1994] 2 IR 551
[31] *Id.* at p. 568

It protects the presumption of innocence; it requires that the prosecution should prove its case beyond all reasonable doubt; but it does not prohibit that, in the course of the case, once certain facts are established, inferences may not be drawn from those facts and I include in that the entitlement to do this even by way of documentary evidence. What is kept in place, however, is the essential requirement that at the end of the trial and before a verdict can be entered the prosecution must show that it has proved its case beyond all reasonable doubt.[32]

The final case in this trilogy is *Rock v Ireland*.[33] This time the provisions under scrutiny were s 18 and s 19 of the Criminal Justice Act 1984. Section 18 permits an inference to be drawn from the accused's failure to account for any object, substance or mark found on his person, clothing or in his possession or in any place where he is at the time of his arrest. Section 19 permits an inference to be drawn from the failure of an accused to explain his presence at a particular place if a member of the garda reasonably believes that the presence of the person at that place and at that time may be attributable to his participation in the commission of an offence. The High Court rejected the challenge to the two sections and the Supreme Court upheld this decision on appeal. Hamilton CJ held that although the Act permitted the court to draw inferences from an accused's failure to offer an explanation, the court was not obliged to draw any such inference. In deciding whether or not to draw such an inference the court would be obliged to act in accordance with the principles of constitutional justice and thus would be under a constitutional obligation to ensure that no improper or unfair inferences were drawn. The sections in question did not interfere in any way with the accused's right to the presumption of innocence or the obligation on the prosecution to prove his guilt beyond all reasonable doubt:

If inferences are properly drawn, such inferences amount to evidence only; they are not to be taken as proof. A person may not be convicted of an offence solely on the basis of inferences that may properly be drawn from his failure to account; such inference may only be used as corroboration of any other evidence in relation to which the failure or refusal is material. The inferences drawn may be shaken in many ways, by cross-examination, by submission, by evidence or by the circumstances of the case.[34]

Any interference with the right to silence was proportional to the duty of the state to protect the life, person and property of all its citizens.

It remains to be seen whether this trilogy of cases is compatible with the European Convention on Human Rights. In *Murray v UK*[35] the court held that

---

[32] *Id.* at p. 565
[33] High Court, Murphy J, 10 November 1995; [1997] 3 IR 484 (SC)
[34] [1997] 3 IR 484 at 498
[35] (1996) 22 ECHR 29

where a *prima facie* case was established and the burden of proof remained on the prosecution, adverse inferences could be drawn from a failure to testify. In the earlier case of *Salabiaku v France*[36] the court held that presumptions against the accused must be confined within reasonable limits which take into account the importance of what is at stake and which respect the rights of the defence. The most recent case was *Averill v United Kingdom*[37] where the European Court rejected the applicant's claim that the drawing of an adverse inference against him rendered his trial unfair. However the court did hold that the complete denial of any access to a solicitor for the first twenty-four hours of interrogation had breached the applicant's right to legal representation under Article 6 of the Convention.

It is instructive to consider some of the provisions of the Offences Against the State (Amendment) Act 1998 in the light of the existing case law on inferences and presumptions. Section 2 of the 1998 Act permits an inference to be drawn from the failure of the accused to answer material questions in relation to an offence under s 21 of the Offences Against the State Act 1939. The wording of s 2 is similar to the wording of s 18 of the Criminal Justice Act 1984 which was upheld in *Rock v Ireland*.[38] Section 4 of the 1998 Act amends s 3 of the Offences Against the State (Amendment) Act 1972 by extending the meaning of conduct which an accused may be asked to explain at risk of an adverse inference to include a refusal "to deny published reports that he was a member of an unlawful organisation, but the fact of such denial shall not by itself be conclusive". Section 3 of the 1972 Act was upheld in *O'Leary v The Attorney General*.[39] Nonetheless, it is submitted that making a failure to deny published newspaper reports presumptive evidence is constitutionally suspect. For example, how is the evidential weight of a tabloid assertion that someone is a member of a terrorist group to be assessed without calling the journalist to give evidence and to reveal his sources? Is an individual expected to purchase a newspaper every day to see if he has been "outed" as a terrorist, or is the section limited to reports that are brought to his attention, perhaps by a newspaper being pushed across the interview table by a garda in the middle of an interview? Under s 5 of the 1998 Act an inference may be drawn from the failure of an accused to mention any fact when questioned that he later relies on in his defence, being a fact which in the circumstances existing at the time he could reasonably have been expected to mention when so questioned. This is a broad sweeping provision, but again would seem to come within the scope of the decided cases.

---

[36] (1988) 13 EHRR 379
[37] Unreported, ECtHR, 6 June, 2000
[38] [1997] 3 IR 484
[39] [1993] 1 IR 102 (HC), [1995] 1 IR 254 (SC)

CONCLUSIVE CERTIFICATES

Whilst shifting an evidential burden onto the accused may be permissible, any attempt to conclusively prove all the ingredients of a criminal prosecution by means of a certificate will be unconstitutional. In *O'Callaghan v Clifford* [40] the tax provisions contained in the Finance Act 1967 as amended were considered. These made the failure knowingly or wilfully to make a return of income within a limited time as required by notice from the inspector of taxes an offence which could be proved by a certificate. In the Supreme Court Denham J stated that:

> The only method by which the Court may conclude on the State's case that the necessary *mens rea* exists is by inferring from the said certificate (which does not mention *mens rea*) that a notice was duly given to the appellant and that the appellant refused knowingly or willfully to make the return.
>
> The burden of proof in criminal matters is higher than that in civil matters and thus whereas a particular certificate may be adequate in a civil matter it may not be so in a criminal matter.

THE ELEMENTS OF LIABILITY [41]

In Ireland criminal responsibility depends on

(a) a law making the specified act or omission criminal at the date when it is performed
(b) an act or omission by the accused covered by the definition of the offence (this is known as the *actus reus*)
(c) a state of mind accompanying the act which is of sufficient gravity to come within the definition of the offence (this is known as the *mens rea*)
(d) the absence of a defence.

PROSCRIBED CONDUCT

The rule is that there must be a law outlawing the particular activity or conduct alleged against the accused. Under Article 15.2.1 of the Constitution of 1937 "The sole and exclusive power of making laws for the State is hereby vested in the Oireachtas: no other legislative authority has power to make laws for the State". However in the controversial case of *A-G (SPUC) v Open Door Counselling Limited* [42] the High Court followed English authority to the effect that the

---

[40] IV Irish Tax Reports 478. See also *In the matter of Article 26 of the Constitution and In the matter of the Employment Equality Bill*, 1996 [1997] 2 IR 321

[41] See generally Charleton, McDermott and Bolger, *Criminal Law* (1999), chapter 1

[42] [1988] IR 593; [1987] ILRM 477

protection of certain public interests could require judges to retain a legislative function. On this basis the High Court recognised the existence of an offence of "conspiracy to corrupt public morals". In the absence of any legislation, what amounts to public morals will of course be a matter entirely for the trial judge. It is submitted that an offence as vague as conspiracy to corrupt public morals should only exist, if at all, in a statute passed by the Oireachtas clearly setting out the ingredients of the offence.

Article 15.5 of the Constitution provides that "The Oireachtas shall not declare acts to be infringements of the law which were not so at the date of their commission". In *Magee v Culligan*[43] the Supreme Court held that the Article constitutes

> … an expressed and unambiguous prohibition against the enactment of retrospective laws declaring acts to be an infringement of the law, whether of the civil or the criminal law. It does not contain any general prohibition on retrospection of legislation, nor can it be by any means interpreted as a general prohibition of that description.

CONDUCT OF THE ACCUSED

There must be a proscribed physical act before a crime can be committed. A simple example will illustrate this point. Suppose I am about to walk home from a party in a friend's house and notice that it looks like raining. Making sure that no-one is looking I surreptitiously remove an umbrella from the coat stand and slip out the door. When I get home I discover that my name is on the umbrella and realise that I must have left it at my friend's house by mistake on some previous occasion. I have committed no crime. I may have intended to steal an umbrella and may have believed that I was stealing one, but in fact no theft has actually occurred as I simply removed my own property. Nor may a person be held guilty merely because another person receives injuries through a mistaken apprehension of his intentions. For example, suppose a woman has been hitchhiking and is given a lift by the accused. During the journey the woman jumps out of the car because of its high speed and her fear that the driver is going to take her to a place where he can assault her. If this apprehension of bodily injury is grounded in the girl's own mind and not in any intentional act or misconduct or words of the accused, he is not guilty of any crime.[44]

The accused must commit the criminal act or omission by reason of his voluntary conduct. This concept of voluntary conduct has developed into the defence

---

[43] [1992] 1 IR 233. For further reading see White "The Present Prosecution of Abolished Offences", (1998) 8 ICLJ 196

[44] See *Kissick* (1937) 14 CCC (2d) 505

of automatism. Where the accused acts as a mere body, disengaged from, and not subject to, the control of the mind he is not criminally responsible. Thus, if a swarm of bees flies in through a car window and causes the driver to lose control, he would not be liable for dangerous driving causing death if he struck a pedestrian. The concept of voluntariness is fundamental to criminal liability. A person cannot be responsible for an act or omission which he has not contributed to by some voluntary action or omission. There is one exception to this. The law will ignore the absence of voluntary conduct if it has its origin in a state brought on by the voluntary consumption of alcohol or other drugs.

HOW LIABILITY IS CONSTRUCTED

The typical situations on which criminal liability is constructed fall into the following seven categories.

1) Possession-based offences

Possession based offences are fundamental to the prohibition on the use of dangerous articles and have been resorted to because the proof of this kind of relationship is far easier than the proof of an ulterior intent to use the article in a dangerous way, or the proof that it was so used, or the proof that the accused had such an article in order to attempt a crime with it. In such cases possession may be established by proving that the accused bears a relationship of physical control to an object which is

    i)   close at hand, or
    ii) in a place to which he can resort when he has need of it, or
    iii) is with a person subject to his control.

2) Assault-based offences

In most assault-based offences the accused is required to have struck at, or moved towards striking at, some other person. The majority of offences against the person are based on the concept that it is wrong to strike another person, or to put them in fear of being immediately struck. Murder and manslaughter had their origin in this concept but are now analysed in terms of the result of the accused's conduct being death to the victim caused by a voluntary act of the accused, which, in the case of murder, was intentional or which, in the case of manslaughter, was criminally negligent, was criminal and dangerous or was an assault. A range of offences based on assaults that do not result in the death of the victim are to be found in the Non-Fatal Offences Against the Person Act, 1997. These offences include assault (s 2), assault causing serious harm (s 3), causing serious harm (s 4), threats to kill or cause serious harm (s 5), syringe attacks (s 6, 7 & 8), coercion (s 9), harassment (s 10), demands for payment of debt causing alarm (s 11), poisoning (s 12), endangerment (s 13), endangering traffic (s 14), false imprisonment (s 15) and abduction of children (s 16 and 17).

3) Liability for omissions

In exceptional cases, where the accused bears a relationship giving rise to a duty to protect the welfare of another, he may be criminally liable for failing to act. Traditionally, such a relationship was based on a duty arising from a contract (such as employment) or on ties of blood or family. For example, in the famous English case of *Gibbins and Procter*[45] a man and a woman with whom he was co-habiting withheld food from the man's child as a result of which it died. They were convicted of murder. By living with the man and receiving money from him for food the woman had assumed a duty towards the child. Similarly, a niece living with her aunt who fails to give the aunt any food or to procure any medical attendance for her when the aunt becomes ill may be found guilty of manslaughter if such neglect accelerated the aunt's death.[46] In *Miller*[47] the accused went to an unoccupied house to sleep for the night. He lay down on a mattress and later woke up to find it smoldering from a cigarette he had dropped before going to sleep. Instead of trying to put the fire out, he simply moved to another room and promptly fell asleep again. The house was badly damaged and the accused was charged with arson. It was held by the House of Lords that the accused's omission to put the fire out did amount to arson on the facts of the case. Once the accused became aware that the mattress was on fire he had a legal responsibility to act to prevent the rest of the house being damaged by fire.

Some minor offences proscribe a failure to act when requested by authority. Examples include failure to co-operate with gardaí when exercising their statutory functions. In the circumstances of an arrest under s 30 of the Offences Against the State Act 1939, a person in custody commits a criminal offence for which the penalty is six months imprisonment, if he fails, on request by a garda, to give an account of his movements or actions (s 52). The constitutionality of s 52 was upheld by both the High Court and the Supreme Court in *Heaney v Ireland*.[48] However, the European Court of Human Rights has recently held that, on the facts of *Heaney*, a conviction under s 52 amounted to a breach of the applicant's right to silence and his privilege against self-incrimination.[49]

---

[45] (1918) 13 Cr App Rep 134
[46] *Instan* [1893] 1 QB 450
[47] [1983] 2 AC 161
[48] [1994] 3 IR 593 (HC), [1996] 1 IR 580 (SC)
[49] *Heaney and McGuinness v Ireland*, unreported, ECtHR, 21 December 2000

4) Property offences

It is an offence for anyone to deprive another of his or her property. If it were otherwise commerce could not function and violence would flow from disputes based on the use of force to seize goods. Most property offences are to be found in the outdated and hopelessly complicated Larceny Act 1916. At the time of writing a new Fraud Bill is in the process of being drafted.

5) Crimes of ulterior intent

In addition to a voluntary action the definition of an offence sometimes requires a further ulterior intent to perpetrate a particular consequence. For example in murder the accused must intend to kill or to cause serious injury by his actions.[50]

6) Incohate offences

There are three inchoate offences (ie offences where the planned crime does not need to have been actually carried out in order for criminal liability to arise): attempt, conspiracy and incitement. The word "inchoate" may be misleading in this context, for an incitement, conspiracy or attempt is a completed offence in itself, even if the projected harm has not materialised. It would be an ineffective system of criminal law that had to sit back and wait for a planned crime to materialise before it could act.

7) Aiders and abettors

Persons who do not themselves perpetrate an offence, or who cannot be proved to have perpetrated an offence, are considered separately under the rules relating to aiding and abetting an offence, and the rules imposing liability for a common design to commit an offence. Common law rules in relation to complicity are designed to deal with those who assist or encourage others to commit crime. The rules are a recognition that criminal liability extends beyond the party who appears to be the principal perpetrator. The policy of the law requires that those who knowingly assist in the commission of an offence, whether mentally, by encouraging it, or physically by supplying the means for its commission, will equally be guilty of that crime. For example, in the case of *The People (DPP) v Paul Ward*[51] the prosecution proceeded to prove the murder of the victim, notwithstanding the fact that the accused's only involvement was in making himself and his property available pursuant to a pre-arranged plan to dispose of the murder weapon and motorcycle in the immediate aftermath of the killing.

---

[50] Criminal Justice Act 1964, s. 4
[51] Unreported, Special Criminal Court, 27 November, 1998

THE MENTAL ELEMENT

Criminal liability depends on the coincidence of a mental element appropriate to the offence together with the commission of the external elements of that offence. Different crimes call for different mental elements. These mental elements fall into six main categories:

(1) intention (often expressed in the statutory form as requiring that the accused should act "knowingly")
(2) recklessness
(3) criminal negligence
(4) negligence
(5) strict liability subject to a defence of reasonable mistake
(6) absolute liability.

Only the first two categories could truly be said to require subjective mental states. These are the categories most often employed in serious crimes. Criminal negligence is limited to the commission of manslaughter. Crimes of negligence are essentially regulatory in nature. The final two classifications are concerned with the less serious crimes which are truly regulatory in nature, such as measures designed to prevent pollution.

It is instructive to compare the concepts of recklessness and negligence. In order to be reckless the accused must have foreseen the risk of harm but decided to continue with his conduct anyway. Thus, it is a purely subjective test. In order to be negligent a person must simply fall below the standards expected of a hypothetical reasonable person. Thus, it is an objective test.

LEGAL VERSUS MORAL GUILT

The mental element of a crime is concerned with legal, not with moral, guilt. Thus many acts which are generally regarded as immoral, for example adultery, are not crimes. An example will illustrate the point. Suppose that C, a man with paedophiliac inclinations, intentionally indecently assaults a young boy. He claims that he would not have given way to his inclinations and committed the offence but for drugs secretly administered to him by D. D secretly administered the drugs to C and to the boy so that he could obtain some compromising photographs of C for the purposes of blackmail. The drug did not render C insane nor did it render him an automaton. Its sole effect was to reduce his ability to resist temptation. As C had intended to assault the boy he will be properly convicted of the assault even though the intent arose out of circumstances for which C says he bears no moral blame.[52] Of course it is never possible

---

[52] *Kingston* [1994] 3 WLR 519

to completely separate legal and moral guilt and one may take the view that C's failure to exert control over himself in the above example evinces a moral weakness.

INTENTION

The mental state is normally proved by an irresistible inference from the circumstances in which the accused committed the external elements of the crime. In many criminal trials there will be no dispute as to the mental element but the issue will be as to whether the right person is before the court, in other words, was it the person in the dock who committed the murder? If a drug dealer shoots one of his couriers, whom he suspects of stealing a consignment of his drugs, through the head and dumps the body in a field, few people would seriously entertain an argument that he had no intention to kill or to cause serious injury to his victim. This is the mental state for murder required by s 4 of the Criminal Justice Act 1964. Intention is a simple word which, when it is used in the definition of a criminal offence, requires that a person be proved to have acted with the purpose of causing the harm or circumstance outlawed. In other words, that he meant to do what he did. Irish juries seem quite comfortable with the concept of intention and appear to have no difficulty in applying it. This can be contrasted with the position in England, where a lot of judicial and academic ink has been spilt agonising over the precise meaning of intention. The current English definition of intention runs as follows.[53]

(1) A result is intended when it is the actor's purpose.

(2) A court or jury may also infer that a result is intended, though it is not desired, when:
   (a) the result is a virtually certain consequence of the act, and
   (b) the actor knows that it is a virtually certain consequence.[54]

Motive can be an item of evidence which assists the prosecution in proving the crime. Its absence can assist the accused in pointing to material which the jury may consider raises a reasonable doubt in his favour. Motive is never part of the mental element of a crime. It is the underlying impetus which may lead to the commission of the crime. For example, a drug dealer may wish to extend his territory and may kill a rival in order to achieve that end. In the celebrated case of *Chandler v DPP*[55] the accused were charged with conspiracy to enter an RAF base for a purpose prejudicial to the safety or interests of the state. They claimed that their actions had

---

[53] See *Hancock and Shankland* [1986] AC 455 *Nedrick* [1986] 3 All ER 1
[54] For an interesting discussion of this topic see Norrie "Oblique Intention and Legal Politics" [1989] *Crim LR* 793
[55] [1964] AC 763

been for the purpose of drawing the public's attention to their cause so that nuclear weapons could be abolished. In their opinion reducing the risk of a nuclear holocaust was not something which could be described as being prejudicial to the safety and interests of their country. A majority of the House of Lords held that the offence had been proven. A certificate issued by the Ministry of Defence under the royal prerogative stating that the act of obstructing the runway was prejudicial to the safety and interests of the state was conclusive and the court could not look behind it. The appellants' desire to prevent a nuclear holocaust may have been their motive in conspiring to do the act, however a person's motive is irrelevant in determining his or her intention. What was important was whether it was that person's purpose to bring about the external element of the offence.

RECKLESSNESS

Recklessness is a less culpable mental state than intent. In general, intent and recklessness are alternative mental elements for most offences. Examples are rape and assault. Recklessness can be simply defined as the conscious running of an unjustifiable risk. The definition of recklessness in Ireland is that the accused must have foreseen the risk but have proceeded with his conduct nonetheless.[56] An example of recklessness would be where a man sees a woman drunk on a bed. He decides to have intercourse with her but, although he can see that she is in no state to resist his advances, he does not bother to ask her consent. The next morning when she wakes up and discovers what has happened she makes a complaint of rape. It is right that the man should be convicted. A person who has a faint suspicion that the woman with whom he is having sexual intercourse is not consenting to the act, can remove that suspicion by the simple expedient of an enquiry; to fail to do so involves a high degree of moral culpability and so is equivalent to taking a serious risk.

CRIMINAL NEGLIGENCE

Where the mental element of a crime is cast in terms of criminal negligence the prosecution is relieved of the burden of proving that an individual accused was aware that his conduct might result in the harm constituting the external element of the offence. The general effect of the decisions on criminal negligence has been that the degree of carelessness required to fulfil the definition is such that almost no normal person would ever be unaware of the danger that they are creating. Criminal negligence applies only in the case of manslaughter. In *The People (DPP) v Culagh*[57] the accused, who owned and operated a "chair-o-plane" ride

---

[56] *The People (DPP) v Murray* [1977] IR 360
[57] Unreported, Court of Criminal Appeal, 15 March 1999

was convicted of manslaughter after a passenger was killed when a chair became detached. The "chair-o-plane" had been in a deplorable state of repair.

NEGLIGENCE

Negligence consists of a failure by an accused person to exercise that degree of care in the conduct of his affairs, where they affect others, which would be exercised by a reasonable or ordinary person performing the task in question. Some statutes create simple offences of negligence. These are mostly summary offences which are dealt with in a trial before a judge, without a jury, in the District Court. Prior to the reforms introduced by the Road Traffic Act 1961, situations where death was caused in road traffic accidents could only be dealt with by charging manslaughter. Where serious injury was caused there was no offence designed to deter and punish even those offenders who had behaved in a criminally culpable fashion. Two new offences were created by sections 52 and 53 of the Road Traffic Act 1961 and later amended by s 51 of the Road Traffic Act 1968. These were the offences of dangerous driving and careless driving. Section 52 indicates that careless driving is an offence and s 53 indicates that dangerous driving is an offence. The mode of prosecution of an offence under s 53 will depend the result of the dangerous driving. If death or serious bodily harm is caused to another, then trial is by way of indictment, ie with a jury. Otherwise, it is a summary trial. The following standard direction on the meaning of dangerous driving was given by O'Brien J: "… driving in a manner which a reasonably prudent motorist, having regard to all the circumstances, would clearly recognise as involving a direct and serious risk of harm to the public".[58]

STRICT AND ABSOLUTE LIABILITY

Offences of negligence and of strict liability are always created by statute; they are unknown to the common law. This is because at common law there is a presumption that a mental element is required for all crimes. To find that an offence is one of strict liability it is necessary to consider both the wording of the statute creating the offence and the subject matter with which it deals. The subject matter should deal with a regulatory matter and the manner in which the offence works should be such that putting the defendant under strict liability assists in the enforcement of the law. There must be something that he can do, directly or indirectly, by supervision or inspection, by improvement of his business methods or by exhorting those whom he may be expected to influence or control, which

---

[58] Reported (1963) 97 ILT 219 and referring back to and varying slightly the definition given earlier and reported at (1962) 96 ILT 123. Referred to as *The People (AG) v Quinlan,* in R. Pierse, *Road Traffic Law in the Republic of Ireland,* Butterworths (1989) p. 157

will promote the observance of the law. The English courts have laid down the following rules in relation to strict liability.[59]

(1) There is a presumption of law that *mens rea is* required before a person can be held guilty of a criminal offence.

(2) The presumption is particularly strong where the offence is "truly criminal" in character.

(3) The presumption applies to statutory offences, and can be displaced only if this is clearly, or by necessary implication, the effect of the statue.

(4) The only situation in which the presumption can be displaced is where the statute is concerned with an issue of social concern, and public safety is such an issue.

(5) Even where a statute is concerned with such an issue, the presumption of *mens rea* stands unless it can also be shown that the creation of strict liability will be effective to promote the objects of the statute by encouraging greater vigilance to prevent the commission of the prohibited act.

In the leading Irish case of *Maguire v Shannon Regional Fisheries Board*[60] the appellant was convicted under s 171(1)(b) of the Fisheries (Consolidation) Act 1959, which provides that any person who "throws, empties, permits or causes to fall into any waters any deleterious matter" shall be guilty of an offence unless such act is done under licence. The appellant was proprietor of a piggery where a PVC pipe had fractured causing whey to flow into a river. The district judge found as a fact that the appellant had taken all reasonable steps to prevent the accident and to prevent the flow of whey into the river. The judge stated a case to the High Court as to whether the offence was one of strict liability. Lynch J held that as s 171 was regulatory in character and did not create an offence that would be regarded as truly criminal it was a strict liability offence. The pollution of rivers was a public nuisance and strict liability would encourage greater vigilance on the part of potential polluters. Lynch J concluded that if a mental element had to be proved in these sort of cases "… it would be very difficult ever to establish an offence."[61]

VICARIOUS LIABILITY

Ordinarily a person can only be convicted of a criminal offence committed by another if he or she is a party to the offence. This distinguishes criminal law from the law of tort. An employer cannot generally be convicted of a criminal offence

---

[59] *Gammon Ltd v A-G of Hong Kong* [1985] 1 AC 1 at 14

[60] [1994] 3 IR 580

[61] *Id.* at p. 589. The same conclusion was reached in *Shannon Regional Fisheries Board v Cavan* [1996] 3 IR 267

which his or her employee committed in the course of his employment. This is because the employer will lack the requisite mental element. The principle has existed since at least 1730, when it was held in *Huggins*[62] that a prison warden could not be vicariously liable for a murder committed by a deputy goaler. The warden had neither ordered the murder nor encouraged it nor in any way participated in it. However, there are some limited exceptions to this principle in the context of regulatory offences.

In *Allen v Whitehead*[63] the defendant was the owner of an all-night café which was run by a manager whom he employed. The police had warned the defendant about harbouring prostitutes in his café. Despite warnings from the defendant, the manager continued to permit prostitutes to gather in the café. The defendant was charged with knowingly permitting prostitutes to congregate in a refreshment shop. It was held that the defendant's ignorance of his manager's continuing disobedience was no defence because he had delegated the management of the café. When someone delegates the performance of certain duties which have been imposed by statute, the acts and mental states of the delegate can be imputed to the principal person. If this were not so the statute would be ineffective.

The leading Irish decision on vicarious liability is the judgment of the Supreme Court in *The Employment Equality Bill 1996*[64]. The Court held that vicarious liability could only be imposed if the following conditions were met:

1) the provision is essentially regulatory in character, and
2) the defendant has a particular privilege (such as a licence) or a duty to make sure that public standards as regards health and safety or the environment or the protection of the consumer, and such like, are upheld, and
3) it might be difficult, invidious or redundant to seek to make the employee liable.

THE DEFENCES

The behaviour of a person may fit precisely within the definition of a crime yet he may be blameless, or have his culpability reduced to a lesser crime, by reason of some further circumstance which amounts to a defence at law. The most obvious example is where a person is approached by an intending mugger and, on being threatened, punches him in the face. Because the action of the person was inspired by the need for self-defence, and as no more force was used than was reasonable in the circumstances, he is entitled to be acquitted on a charge of assault. The defences available in Irish law are

---

[62] (1730) 2 Stra 883
[63] [1930] 1 KB 211
[64] [1997] 2 IR 321

i) the lawful use of force (often known as 'self-defence')
ii) provocation
iii) necessity and duress
iv) insanity and automatism
v) intoxication
vi) mistake.

The scope of these defences may only be ascertained by trawling through a large volume of case law in which a number of common law principles are established. In only one case, namely the lawful use of force, has the Oireachtas provided a statutory scheme.[65]

CORPORATE CRIMINAL LIABILITY[66]

Traditionally when one speaks of criminal law, one imagines a man or a woman standing in the dock and facing the twelve members of the jury. However as the affairs of corporate entities impact more and more on peoples' lives the prosecution of companies may become a familiar part of the Irish criminal landscape. New developments in corporate criminal liability have emerged in other jurisdictions. For example, in England two directors of a haulage firm were found guilty of corporate manslaughter after ignoring the excessive working hours of one of their drivers who fell asleep at the wheel and caused a fatal crash.[67] A jury at the Old Bailey concluded that the directors were responsible for the crash in which two people died. The directors had been accused of being grossly negligent in allowing their driver to spend more than sixty hours a week at the wheel in breach of the law on driving hours. The prosecution had described the driving habits of the driver as "an accident waiting to happen" and had alleged that the directors were grossly negligent because they knew or ought to have known the state that their driver was in. Whilst litigation following the sinking of the Herald of Free Enterprise in Zeebrugge had established that companies could in theory be convicted of corporate manslaughter,[68] until recently successful prosecutions had been the exception rather than the rule.

The prosecution of companies is likely to increase over the next few years. Where a company benefits from the crimes of its senior employees there is no good reason why it should not face a jury alongside those employees. Charging companies opens up the prospect of recovering larger fines and hence hurting shareholders who will then demand higher standards from their company. The

---

[65] See the Non-Fatal Offences Against the Person Act 1997
[66] See generally McDermott "Defences to Corporate Criminal Liability" (2000), 5 *Bar Review* 170
[67] *The Times*, November 20, 1999
[68] *R v P & O European Ferries (Dover) Ltd* (1991), 93 *Cr App R* 72

Canadian Supreme Court has explained why prosecutors have turned their attention to companies:

> ... the corporate vehicle now occupies such a large portion of the industrial, commercial and sociological sectors that amenability of the corporation to our criminal law is as essential in the case of the corporation as in the case of the natural person.[69]

The most common method of imposing corporate criminal liability is to locate it in the conduct of the company's senior officers when acting in the course of their duties. A distinction is drawn between persons whose acts may incur liability and those whose acts will not. In practice this distinction can be difficult to draw. The question is who represents the directing mind and will of the company and controls what it does.

In the leading English case of *Tesco Supermarkets v Natrass*[70] the issue before the House of Lords was whether the actions of a regional manager of one of the company's supermarkets could incur criminal liability for the company. Lord Diplock stated the legal test in the following terms:

> ... what natural persons are to be treated as in law as being the company for the purpose of acts done in the course of its business, including the taking of precautions and the exercise of due diligence to avoid the commission of a criminal offence, is to be found by identifying those natural persons who by the memorandum and articles of association or as a result of action taken by the directors, or by the company in general meeting pursuant to the articles, are entrusted with the exercise of the powers of the company.[71]

The Supreme Court of Canada has explained this method of attributing criminal liability to a corporation as follows.

> The identification theory was inspired in the common law in order to find some pragmatic, acceptable middle ground which would see a corporation under the umbrella of the criminal law of the community but which would not saddle the corporation with the criminal wrongs of all its employees and agents.[72]

Religious bodies may be made amenable to the criminal law on the same basis. For example in *R v Church of Scientology of Toronto*[73] the defendant Church was convicted on two counts of breach of trust and fined $250,000. The evidence established that it had planted persons in government agencies to obtain confidential information. The charges arose from activities carried out by the Intelligence Bureau

---

[69] *Canadian Dredge & Dock Co v The Queen* [1985] 1 SCR 662 at 692
[70] [1972] AC 153
[71] *Id.* at p. 199-200
[72] *Canadian Dredge & Dock Co v The Queen* [1985] 1 SCR 662 at 701
[73] (1997) 116 CCC (3d) 1

within the "Guardian's Office", which was a management arm of the defendant. Scientologists had gained employment in government agencies perceived to be enemies of the Church and in breach of their oaths of office then took copies of confidential documents from the agencies that employed them. The Church was convicted and on appeal argued that corporate criminal liability had no application to a non-profit religious corporation. Rosneberg JA, giving the judgment of the Ontario Court of Appeal, rejected this argument as being based on a misunderstanding of how and why corporate criminal liability arises:

> ... the identification doctrine is fully applicable to non-profit organisations without share capital. The rationale for the imposition of criminal liability on corporations is not that they make a profit or are engaged in commerce, or even that they have shareholders. Rather, since corporations occupy such a central role in society, it would be unacceptable to have them operating outside the criminal law.

Whilst such a conclusion might mean that any economic penalty imposed would be borne by innocent parishioners, this was simply a risk or cost associated with the privilege of operating through the corporate vehicle. Given the proliferation of charities in Canada and the fact that Canadian taxpayers donated almost $3 billion to them, to leave such organisations outside the purview of the criminal law would be "intolerable".

JURISDICTION

The general principle is that jurisdiction in criminal matters is territorial. This means that jurisdiction is limited to offences committed within the territory of the state regardless of the nationality or domicile of the accused. An offence committed on an Irish ship is committed within the jurisdiction of the state.[74] Similarly, an act taking place on board an Irish controlled aircraft also takes place within the jurisdiction of the Irish courts.[75] Murder and manslaughter constitute an exception to the general principle that criminal jurisdiction is territorial. The Irish courts have jurisdiction over murders and manslaughters committed outside Ireland, provided the accused is an Irish citizen.

The Extradition (European Convention on the Prevention of Terrorism) Act, 1987 also gives an extremely wide jurisdiction. It is an offence contrary to s 5 of the 1987 Act to do or attempt an act in a convention country which if done in Ireland would have constituted an offence[76] involving

---

[74] *Gulf Oil* [1973] ILRM 163. Generally see Air Navigation and Transport Act 1973
[75] Air Navigation and Transport Act 1973, s. 2
[76] In the case of subsection (I) a serious offence

(1) an attack against the life, physical integrity or liberty of an internationally protected person or

(2) kidnapping, the taking of a hostage or serious false imprisonment or

(3) the use, to the endangerment of persons, of an explosive or automatic firearm.

The nationality of the offender is not relevant in this context.

The Criminal Law (Jurisdiction) Act 1976 essentially provides a mechanism whereby persons who commit certain terrorist-type crimes in Northern Ireland may be tried in this jurisdiction, as an alternative to extradition. The Act of 1976 was passed, in essence, as an alternative to extradition. It was considered, at the time, that the Constitution forbade the extraction of political offenders from this jurisdiction. Where a person does in Northern Ireland an act which, if done in Ireland, would constitute an offence scheduled under the Criminal Law (Jurisdiction) Act 1976 he is guilty of an offence contrary to s 2 of that Act and is liable to the same penalty as if the act had been committed in the state.[77] The offences which are scheduled include the common law offences of murder, manslaughter, arson, kidnapping and false imprisonment. In addition offences contrary to specified provisions of the Offences Against the Person Act 1861, the Explosive Substances Act 1883, the Larceny Act 1916 and the Firearms Act 1925 are included.

Exceptional jurisdiction is also conferred by the Sexual Offences (Jurisdiction) Act 1996 which permits prosecutions to be brought in Ireland against citizens of the state or persons ordinarily resident in the state who commit sexual acts involving children outside of the state. The Act is aimed at so called "child sex tourists".

CONCLUSION

One of the themes in this brief overview of the Irish criminal justice system has been the need for reform. It is of fundamental importance that every citizen has easy access to the criminal law. This is impossible so long as it is contained in a combination of case law and statutes, many of which are out of date. In addition, we have left undefined the most fundamental concepts of criminal liability. What is required is nothing less than a complete codification of the criminal law. This would mean that every member of the public could turn to a single book in order to discover what the criminal law is. In a reflection on his twenty-four years as Director of Public Prosecutions, Eamonn Barnes was critical of this legacy of inaction.

---

[77] References to doing an act include references to the making of an omission; s. 2(1). Liability does not depend on the accused being a national of any particular state. For an analysis of the working of the Act see *The People (DPP) v Campbell and Others* (1983) 2 Frewen 131

In a system in which ignorance of the law is no excuse, it is inexcusable that it is so inaccessible to members of the public. Even criminal lawyers have the utmost difficulty in finding and ascertaining it with any confidence or authority. Countries all around the world with much smaller resources than ours have long since codified their laws. Anyone familiar with the French system will recognise the two little red books, the penal code and the code of criminal procedure, which you can slip into your jacket pocket. As a matter of social justice, I think the Irish public is entitled to an accessible code in which they can easily ascertain their potential liabilities. The Irish criminal lawyer is entitled to no less. It could I believe be done relatively easily and quickly.[78]

It is to be hoped that if the European Convention of Human Rights is adopted into domestic law it will finally provide the necessary impetus for this change to occur.

---

[78] Barnes "Reflections on the past 24 years as Director of Public Prosecutions" (1999), 4 *The Bar Review* 389 at 394

3

Criminal Procedure and Evidence

Paul Anthony McDermott

In the previous chapter we examined the basic framework of the criminal justice system. We also examined the main elements of a criminal offence. The purpose of this chapter is to focus on the rules of evidence and procedure that govern criminal trials in Ireland. The chapter commences with a brief examination of why we have rules of evidence and procedure in the first place. It then examines the functioning of the jury with particular emphasis on how a jury is selected for a criminal trial. Two aspects of police investigation are then considered, namely the issuing of search warrants and the powers of arrest and detention. This will also involve an examination of the rights of detained persons and the right to bail. Pre-trial issues are considered under the headings of pre-trial publicity, delay and disclosure. The burden of proof has already been introduced in the previous chapter and some more attention will be given to it in this chapter. The chapter then examines a number of rules of evidence in some detail. These are the rules relating to circumstantial evidence, visual identification evidence, accomplice evidence, confession evidence, unconstitutionally obtained evidence, hearsay evidence and character evidence.

"The rules of evidence should not be allowed to offend common-sense." So proclaimed Barron J in the Court of Criminal Appeal in December of 1999.[1] Yet to many persons, our outdated and often incoherent rules of evidence do offend common sense. As with substantive criminal law the problem is usually one of lack of reform. The main sources of our rules of evidence and procedure are a

---

[1] *DPP v Kelly*, unreported, CCA, 13 December, 1999 at p. 28. For a detailed discussion of the rules of criminal evidence in Ireland see Charleton, McDermott and Bolger, *Criminal Law* (1999), chapter 2

variety of statutes and the common law. The European Convention on Human Rights is also an increasing source of basic standards of fairness in criminal trials. Save for one Act in 1992[2] little has been done by the Oireachtas to codify the diverse rules of the common law that currently govern the admissibility of evidence. The position is somewhat better as regards procedure. As we saw in the previous chapter, the Criminal Justice Act 1999 has abolished the right of preliminary examination of indictable offences in the District Court. Instead the accused can now apply to the trial judge in advance of his trial to have one or more of the charges against him dismissed.

Contrary to popular perception, the success or failure of a prosecution case depends as much on the rules of evidence and procedure as on the rules of substantive criminal law. In some criminal cases more time is spent arguing over the admissibility of evidence than is spent on establishing the guilt of the accused. There are good reasons for the existence of many of the rules of evidence. However sometimes these rules lack justification. They have grown up in a piecemeal fashion and do not appear to be based on any identifiable fundamental premise. If one subscribes to the view that the fundamental purpose of a criminal trial is a search for the truth, it must be a matter of some concern that there are instances where the rules of evidence stand in the way of that search.

There are three main reasons why we have a special set of rules for the admissibility of evidence.[3] First it is to avoid the risk of irrational jury verdicts. For example, if there were no restrictions on introducing material about the bad character of the accused the jury might be irrationally prejudiced against him by such material and might therefore not determine the charges before the court on the merits. Secondly it is to avoid the infringement of the basic constitutional rights of persons suspected of crimes. A jury should not be allowed hear a confession of guilt extracted by the use of force by an accused's interrogators, regardless of whether the confession might be true or not. This is in order to discourage the torture or cruel and oppressive treatment of persons in custody. Thirdly, experience has revealed the inherent unreliability of certain kinds of evidence, for example that which consists of "forced" confessions.

THE JURY

A randomly selected jury who may deliberate in secret forms the basis of the Irish criminal justice system. Article 38(5) of the Constitution provides that "... no person shall be tried on any criminal charge without a jury". The Article is fleshed out by the Juries Act 1976. Section 20 provides that the prosecution and each

---

[2] Criminal Evidence Act 1992
[3] See Seabrook and Sprack, *Criminal Evidence and Procedure* (2nd ed., 1999), para. 1.1

accused person may challenge *without cause shown* (ie without having to give any reason) seven jurors and no more. Section 21 provides that the prosecution and each accused person may challenge for cause shown any number of jurors. Whenever a juror is challenged for cause shown, such cause must be shown immediately upon the challenge being made and the trial judge then allows or disallows the challenge as he thinks proper.

In *de Burca v The Attorney General*[4] Henchy J held that the jury envisaged by the Constitution is comprised of a group of persons "chosen at random" and that "the jury must be drawn from a pool broadly representative of the community so that its verdict will be stamped with the fairness and acceptability of a genuinely diffused community decision". For his part Griffin J stated that "the jury should be a body which is truly representative, and a fair cross-section of the community". He emphasised that this did not entitle an accused person to "a jury which is tailored to the circumstances of the particular case, whether relating to the sex or other condition of the defendant or to the nature of the charges to be tried, provided that the jury be indiscriminately drawn from those eligible in the community for jury service ..." This concept of a "random" jury has recently been fleshed out in two cases.

In *MacCárthaigh v Ireland*[5] the question arose as to whether the applicant, was entitled to a jury consisting solely of fluent Irish speakers. In rejecting this claim O'Hanlon J placed particular emphasis on the fact that it would effectively exclude at least 75% (and possibly 90%) of the population of Dublin City from serving on the trial. He stated that "It should be capable of being said of any jury in every criminal case that they represent every category of the public in the area in which the action is to be heard". O'Hanlon J quoted from the *Taylor v Louisiana*[6] where the US Supreme Court held that

> Restricting jury service to only special groups or excluding identifiable segments playing major roles in the community cannot be squared with the constitutional concept of a jury trial.

The Supreme Court concurred with O'Hanlon J, and Hamilton CJ noted that if one excluded non-Irish speakers "... most of the people of Ireland would be excluded. That would amount to a violation of Article 38.5 of the Constitution."

In *DPP v Judge Haugh*[7] the issue arose as to whether a trial judge has jurisdiction to send out a questionnaire to potential jury members. The case arose out of the prosecution of former Taoiseach Charles Haughey on two charges of obstructing the McCracken Tribunal. Previously the accused had unsuccessfully

---

4 [1976] IR 38
5 [1999] 1 IR 200
6 (1975) 419 US 522 at 530
7 [2001] 1 IR 184

sought an adjournment of his trial on the ground that adverse pre-trial publicity had rendered it impossible for him to obtain a fair trial. In the course of his judgment on the issue of publicity the learned trial judge stated that he would be prepared to give consideration to what additional safeguards or procedures might be adopted in the manner of selecting persons to serve on a jury, "… perhaps even questioning individual potential jury members before either party is expected to exercise a right of challenge …". The learned trial judge invited submissions from counsel on the issue and after hearing such submissions he drew up a list of questions to be sent to potential jury members. The purpose of this exercise was to assist the accused to challenge any jurors whom he felt might not be able to try the case in a dispassionate manner. A Divisional Court held that the trial judge had no jurisdiction to issue such a questionnaire. The court noted that Mr Haughey could not be distinguished from any other criminal defendant. Carney J pointed out that if in a future case a gangland figure was permitted to send out a questionnaire "It would strike terror into the jury panel to receive such a questionnaire in such a case".[8] The court noted that s 15 of the Juries Act 1976 expressly requires the judge to invite any person connected with the case or who has an interest in it to communicate that fact to him. This provided an effective mechanism for filtering out any person who could not try the case dispassionately.

A couple of final points may be noted about the jury system. Some concerns have been expressed that the truly representative nature of the jury is undermined by the ease with which jury service can be evaded. A majority of the persons who actually turn up for jury service appear to be students, housewifes, retired persons or persons in non-professional occupations. Of course, such people all make perfectly competent jurors, but can it be said that Irish juries are truly random when one almost never sees the managing directors of large companies appearing on a jury panel? The jury system is not something which should be taken for granted. The non-jury trials held in the Special Criminal Court have already been discussed in chapter 1. In addition, the jury system periodically comes under attack in the media. The temptation to see the jury as a scapegoat for all of the problems in the criminal justice system should be resisted. Lord Devlin has suggested that we are too ready to dispense with the jury system in times of crisis of confidence in the criminal justice system:

> There is in some minds a tendency to think that, if anything goes wrong or is thought likely to go wrong with the criminal process, the first thing to do is to get rid of the jury. Jury exclusion seems to have the same appeal as bleeding the patient had to the medicos of the seventeenth century.[9]

---

[8] [2001] 1 IR 184 at 194
[9] Foreword to Greer and White, *Abolishing the Diplock Courts* (1986, The Cobden Trust)

Blackstone defended the jury system in the following terms:

> Trial by jury ever has been, and I trust ever will be, looked upon as the glory of English law ... the liberties of England cannot but subsist so long as this palladium of liberty remains sacred and inviolate, not only from all open attacks (which none will be so hardy to make), but also from all secret machinations, which may sap and undermine it by introducing new and arbitrary methods of trial, by justices of the peace, commissioners of the revenue and courts of conscience.[10]

The advantages of jury trial over non-jury trial are as follows.

i) Trial by jury bestows upon ordinary people the democratic right and duty to directly participate in decisions which gravely affect the rights of others.

ii) Trial by jury maintains contact between the criminal justice system and ordinary people and sustains their confidence in it.

iii) In a trial by judge alone the vital distinction between the admissibility of evidence and the weight which should be attributed to it is all but lost. In a jury trial the question of admissibility of evidence is decided in the absence of the jury. Thus, if the evidence is ruled to be inadmissible, the jury will never be exposed to it. However, in a non-jury trial, the judge cannot determine the question of admissibility without hearing, or at least being aware of, the evidence on which he has to rule. If he determines that the evidence is inadmissible, he must then attempt to put it out of his mind as he takes on the role of trier of fact.

iv) The separation of powers between judge and jury is particularly valuable in testing the credibility of witnesses. In the words of Greer and White, "[w]hereas a judge's legal training will lead him or her to concentrate on inconsistencies or the lack of them, a jury will take an overall view of a witness, bearing in mind his or her demeanour, attitude and so on.[11]

SEARCH WARRANTS

At some stage, most serious criminal investigations will involve a search of the premises of those suspected of perpetrating the crime. Ever since the famous English decision of *Entick v Carrington*[12] in 1765 the rule has been that in order to be valid a search warrant must have a clear basis in law and the conditions attached to such basis must be strictly adhered to. In *Entick* Camden CJ stated the principle in the following terms:

---

[10] *Commentaries,* Book IV, p. 350
[11] "A Return to Trial by Jury", in Jennings, *Justice Under Fire* 54 (Pluto Press, 1988)
[12] [1765] 2 Wils 275

Our law holds the property of every man so sacred, that no man can set his foot upon his neighbour's close without his leave: if he does he is a trespasser, though he does no damage at all: if he will tread upon a neighbour's ground he must justify it by law.

In addition to the common law, the Constitution also places limits on the power of the state to search private property. For example, no act by the government which infringes the rights of a citizen can be pursued in an irrational manner.[13] Thus any search mechanism must be conducted in a fair manner and must not be used as an instrument of oppression. Authority for this proposition is to be found in *Hanahoe v Hussey*[14] where Kinlen J suggested that there is a constitutional aspect to the issuing of a search warrant and stated that

In the case of serious invasion of constitutional rights, the judge must be satisfied on the facts that the appropriate statute would apply and must seek to ensure that the constitutional rights of the citizen are protected.

In *DPP v Owens*[15] the Supreme Court held that a search warrant is a document which may affect constitutional rights and thus in a criminal trial its validity must be proved by calling oral evidence (ie of the person who sought the warrant and the person who granted it). Thus the Supreme Court concluded that a Circuit Court judge had been correct to direct the jury to find the accused not guilty because there was no evidence of the state of mind of a peace commissioner who signed the relevant search warrant. In that case the peace commissioner was very elderly and at the time of trial was too ill to give evidence.

The leading Irish case on the validity of search warrants is the decision of the Supreme Court in *Simple Imports v The Revenue Commissioners.*[16] This case concerned the question as to whether the failure of a search warrant to show jurisdiction on its face renders it invalid. The case arose out of the following facts. Customs officers had raided the applicants' premises pursuant to search warrants and seized materials said to be indecent and/or pornographic. The applicants alleged that the warrants showed a lack of jurisdiction on their face. The warrants failed to relate on their face that the district judge had satisfied himself that there was *reasonable* cause or grounds for the suspicion of the officer concerned that there were uncustomed or prohibited goods in the premises. The relevant legislation made it clear that before issuing the warrant the district judge "must have come to the conclusion, from the information on oath of the customs officer, not merely that the officer suspects that there are uncustomed or prohibited goods on the particular premises but that his suspicion is reasonable. In other words, it

---

[13] *The State (Keegan) v Stardust Compensation Tribunal* [1986] IR 642
[14] [1998] 3 IR 69 at 93
[15] [1999] 2 IR 16
[16] [2001] 2 IR 184 243

was not sufficient that the district judge was satisfied that the officers simply had grounds or a cause for their suspicion. The judge had to go further and be satisfied, on the basis of the information supplied by the officer that, viewed objectively, the cause or ground relied on by the officer for his suspicion was reasonable."[17] The recital in the warrants in question failed to show that this statutory precondition for the exercise of jurisdiction had been satisfied. The question the Supreme Court had to determine was what the consequence of this omission should be. It concluded that the warrant was invalid. Keane J stated:

> I am satisfied that the submission on behalf of the respondents that, in a case where the warrant itself states that it is being issued by the District Judge on a basis which is not justified by the statute creating the power, the invalidity of the warrant can be cured by evidence that there was in fact before the District Judge evidence, which entitled him to issue the warrant within the terms of the statute is not well founded. That proposition seems to me contrary to principle and unsupported by authority. Given the necessarily draconian nature of the power conferred by the statute, a warrant cannot be regarded as valid which carries on its face a statement that it has been issued on the basis which is not authorised by the statute. It follows that the warrants were invalid and must be quashed.[18]

The judgment in *Simple Imports* is important because Keane J confirmed that a test of strict scrutiny applies to the validity of search warrants:

> These are powers which the police and other authorities must enjoy in defined circumstances for the protection of society, but since they authorise the forcible invasion of a person's property, the courts must always be concerned to ensure that the conditions imposed by the legislature before such powers can be validly exercised are strictly met.[19]

He held that when parliament conferred the power to issue search warrants to judges "It must be presumed that it was envisaged that the judges would, in no sense, permit themselves to be treated as ciphers, but would conscientiously satisfy themselves that the relevant preconditions had been satisfied".[20]

ARREST

Neither a garda, nor anyone else, has a general power to arrest for crime. The Criminal Law Act 1997 provides for powers of arrest in respect of arrestable offences. An arrestable offence is defined as an offence which carries a maximum

---

[17] [2001] 2 IR 243 at 251
[18] [2001] 2 IR 243 at 255
[19] [2001] 2 IR 243 at 250
[20] [2001] 2 IR 243 at 250-251

term of imprisonment of at least five years. A member of the Garda Síochána who reasonably suspects that an arrestable offence has been committed, and that the suspect is a perpetrator, may arrest such a person.

The most contentious statutory power of arrest is contained in section 30 of The Offences Against the State Act 1939. The power of arrest exists in respect of any offence committed under the Offences Against the State Acts 1939-1998 and in respect of any offence that is scheduled under the Act. These include firearms and explosive offences. The powers under section 29 and 30 of the Offences Against the State Act 1939 are often used in the investigation of armed robbery and murder offences. As with any power of arrest, section 30 must be exercised in good faith for the purpose for which it was given. It is easy to think of a tenuous connection between the commission of a serious, but not scheduled offence, and an offence which is scheduled for the purposes of section 30. Criminal damage is no longer scheduled, but it was up to 1991. In *The People (DPP) v Walsh* [21] the accused was arrested at a time when malicious damage was a scheduled offence. The accused was arrested for maliciously damaging the clothing in which the victim was clad when a knife penetrated the victim's body resulting in his death. Earlier, in *The State (Bowes) v FitzPatrick* [22] the justification for the use of section 30 was the malicious damaging of a knife which had occurred while it was being plunged into the victim's skull. Since murder was not, and is not now, a scheduled offence these justifications were questionable devices to make the powers under section 30 available to the gardaí.

Further draconian powers of detention are contained in the Criminal Justice (Drug Trafficking) Act, 1996. Section 2 provides that where a member of the Garda Síochána arrests without warrant a person whom he, with reasonable cause, suspects of having committed a drug trafficking offence, the arrested person may be taken to a Garda Síochána station. If the member of the Garda Síochána in charge of the station has, at the time of the arrested person's arrival there, reasonable grounds for believing that his detention is necessary for the proper investigation of the offence, the person may be detained in that station. The provisions of Act have again re-introduced seven day detention, but extensions beyond two days are only given on the authorisation of a judge.

The rights of arrested persons

While in custody the accused's rights are protected by the Criminal Justice Act 1984 (Detention of Persons by Garda Síochána) Regulations 1987. The Regulations require the member in charge to keep, or to cause to be kept, a custody record. [23] This

---

[21] (1989) 3 Frewen 260
[22] [1987] ILRM 195
[23] Regulation 6

will indicate the date, time and place of arrest, the time of arrival at the station, the nature of the offence for which the accused was arrested and relevant particulars relating to his physical and mental condition. The detention of such a person can only be authorised where, on reasonable grounds, the member in charge, or the garda officer delegated in that regard, believes that such detention is necessary for the proper investigation of the offence.[24] The arrested person is entitled to information as to what he is being arrested for, as to his right to consult a solicitor and as to other matters which have now been reduced to a standard form which is read over and explained to an accused person on his arrival.[25] Where a detained person is under seventeen years of age, he is entitled to the fact of his custody being notified to his parent or guardian, or other responsible adult and such a detainee can only be questioned with that person present.[26] The garda officer in charge of overseeing the custody of the accused is obliged to ensure that the circumstances of his custody has due respect for his personal rights and his dignity as a human person. This particularly applies to people who have any physical or mental disability.[27] Force can only be used against a person in custody where that force is reasonable in self defence, to secure compliance with lawful directions, to prevent escape or to restrain the prisoner from injuring himself or others, damaging property or destroying or interfering with evidence. The use of that force must be reported in writing. A complaint made by a prisoner must also be recorded in writing.[28] An interview is to be conducted in a fair and humane manner. The arrested person is entitled to know the name and rank of the person interviewing him. Not more than two people may interview an accused, though up to four may be present with the accused at any one time. The interview should not last for more than four hours and then it must be adjourned for 'a reasonable time'. This is generally taken to mean a reasonable period for rest and refreshment of about an hour.[29] There are elaborate provisions guaranteeing the right of access to a solicitor. These regulations allow a person "reasonable access to a solicitor of his choice".[30] Where an arrested person asks for a solicitor he should not be asked to make a written statement in relation to an offence until a reasonable time for the attendance of his solicitor has elapsed.[31] An arrested person is not to be kept in isolation. Apart from a right to medical and legal visits, he also has the right to receive a supervised visit from a relative, friend or other person with an interest in his welfare if he so wishes.

---

[24] Regulation 7
[25] Regulation 8
[26] Regulation 8, Regulation 9, Regulation 13
[27] Regulation 3
[28] Regulation 20
[29] Regulation 12
[30] Regulation 11
[31] Regulation 12(6)

The visit may take place provided that the member in charge "is satisfied that the visit ... will not hinder or delay the investigation of crime".[32] This generally means that where a relative is reasonably suspected of complicity the visit is not allowed.

Where an arrested person is under the influence of drink or drugs so that he is unable to appreciate the significance of questions put to him or his answers, he is not to be questioned while he is in that condition without express authority of the member in charge who must have reasonable grounds for believing that to delay questioning the person would involve a risk of injury to persons, serious loss of or damage to property, the destruction of, or interference with, evidence or the escape of accomplices.[33] The accused also has a right to medical treatment where he is injured, under the influence of drugs or drink and cannot be roused, fails to respond normally to questions (except through drink), appears to be suffering from a mental illness or otherwise appears to need medical attention. Where a person claims to need medication he should be allowed to take it or a doctor should be called.[34] The custody record must include the time and date of the interviews and who was present; the time when the interview commenced and ended and any relevant occurrences should be brought to the attention of the member in charge.[35] The custody record should be preserved.

A breach of these regulations does not mean that the evidence obtained thereby cannot be used in a subsequent prosecution. Section 7(3) of the Criminal Justice Act 1984 provides that a failure on the part of any member of the Garda Síochána to observe any provision of the regulations shall not of itself affect the lawfulness of the custody of the detained person or the admissibility in evidence of any statement made by him. This leaves it as a matter for the court's discretion as to whether or not to admit such evidence. For example, in *The People (DPP) v Reddin & Butler*[36] the Court of Criminal Appeal admitted a statement where the period of interrogation had exceeded four hours with the consent of the accused.

BAIL

Until recently bail could only be refused on the basis that the accused would not turn up for trial or would interfere with witnesses. This principle had been clearly

---

[32] Regulation 11(4)

[33] Regulation 12(7), (9)

[34] Regulation 21

[35] Regulation 12(11), (12)

[36] [1995] 3 IR 560. See also *The People (DPP) v Francis McCann* unreported, Court of Criminal Appeal, 11 March 1998. The applicant began to make a confession in the presence of his solicitor. Half way through the confession he was informed that his period of detention had expired and he was free to leave. He left, but then returned a couple of minutes later and recommenced the confession with the same parties present in the room. The Court of Criminal Appeal held that the confession had been correctly admitted into evidence by the trial judge

established by the Supreme Court[37] but has now been significantly modified by the Sixteenth Amendment of the Constitution in 1996 which added the following provision as Article 40.4.7:

> Provision may be made by law for the refusal of bail by a court to a person charged with a serious offence where it is reasonably considered necessary to prevent the commission of a serious offence by that person.

Section 2 of the Bail Act 1997 now provides:

> (1) Where an application for bail is made by a person charged with a serious offence, a court may refuse the application if the court is satisfied that such refusal is reasonably considered necessary to prevent the commission of a serious offence by that person.
>
> (2) In exercising its jurisdiction under subsection (1), a court shall take into account and may, where necessary, receive evidence or submissions concerning –
>
> (a) the nature and degree of seriousness of the offence with which the accused person is charged and the sentence likely to be imposed on conviction,
>
> (b) the nature and degree of seriousness of the offence apprehended and the sentence likely to be imposed on conviction,
>
> (c) the nature and strength of the evidence in support of the charge,
>
> (d) any conviction of the accused person for an offence committed while he or she was on bail,
>
> (e) any previous convictions of the accused person including any conviction the subject of an appeal (which has neither been determined nor withdrawn) to a court,
>
> (f) any other offence in respect of which the accused person is charged and is awaiting trial,
>
> and, where it has taken account of one or more of the foregoing, it may also take into account the fact that the accused person is addicted to a controlled drug within the meaning of the Misuse of Drugs Act 1977.
>
> (3) In determining whether the refusal of an application for bail is reasonably considered necessary to prevent the commission of a serious offence by a person, it shall not be necessary for a court to be satisfied that the commission of a specific offence by that person is apprehended.

A 'serious offence' means an offence specified in the Schedule for which a person of full capacity and not previously convicted may be punished by a term of imprisonment for a term of five years or by a more severe penalty.

---

[37] See *Ryan v DPP* [1989] IR 399. See generally O'Higgins, "Bail – A Privilege or a Right?" (1998), 3 *Bar Review* 318

PRE-TRIAL ISSUES

Before a criminal trial commences it is open to the accused to attempt to stop it on the grounds that it is not possible for him to obtain a fair trial. He may base such a claim on, *inter alia,* adverse pre-trial publicity, delay or non-disclosure by the prosecution of relevant information. These three grounds will now be considered in turn. It will be seen that whilst non-disclosure is treated as a very grave matter, it is very difficult to stop a prosecution on the grounds of publicity or delay.

Adverse Pre-Trial Publicity

Where the defence forms the view that its client cannot receive a fair trial due to adverse publicity it has a duty to raise that matter before the court. It is extremely difficult to stay a trial on the grounds of adverse publicity. This became clear after the decision of the Supreme Court in *The People (DPP) v Z*[38] where a man accused of unlawful carnal knowledge and sexual assault against the girl in the *X* case failed to prohibit his trial despite the fact that the relevant events had become the focus of national and international political, judicial and public attention. The claim of *Z* was based on the fact that in his case there had been widespread publicity surrounding the taking of DNA from the alleged victim and media references to the sample having rendered conclusive proof of the guilt of the accused.

A recent example will illustrate the principles involved in claims of adverse publicity. In *The People (DPP) v Charles J. Haughey*[39] the accused faced trial by jury in the Circuit Criminal Court on two charges of obstructing the McCracken Tribunal contrary to the Tribunals of Enquiry (Evidence) Act 1921 as substituted by the Tribunals of Enquiry (Evidence)(Amendment) Act 1979 . He sought an adjournment of his trial until some reasonable period after the report of the Moriarty Tribunal had been delivered. The essence of his complaint was that in the current climate of public opinion, because of the publicity which had been generated by the McCracken and Moriarty Tribunals, his reputation and standing had become so damaged and public passions had been so inflamed against him that there was a real risk he would not receive a fair trial. In addition he alleged that any trial should await the outcome of the Moriarty Tribunal at which point his reputation would have been fairly judged after he had had an opportunity to present his side of the story. The prosecution strongly opposed this application and warned that trial by jury would have to be consigned to history if juries were deemed to be unable to give fair trials to persons of "general bad public reputation".[40]

---

[38] [1994] 2 IR 476
[39] Unreported, Circuit Court, December 17, 1999
[40] It should be emphasised that the prosecution made this as a theoretical point and did not claim that the accused in the present case was a person of "general bad public reputation".

Haugh J commenced his judgment in the Circuit Criminal Court by reiterating the general principle that a person facing trial on a criminal charge is entitled to a fair trial. This means that where a trial by jury is proposed

> … it should not proceed where the minds of the persons to be selected to make up a jury are so inflamed against the accused or where they may be so biased against him that there is a real or serious risk that the jury selected for the trial will not try the case objectively and dispassionately so that they leave aside views or opinions formed from extraneous sources and stimuli and so that they, as required by their oath, render a true verdict in accordance with the evidence.

He observed that the media also has rights, which include the right to disseminate information and to express views freely. In addition, the public has a right to information from the media, including a specific right to information in relation to trials of criminal charges. However, where these two rights are in conflict, the rights of the media and the public right to information must yield to the accused's right to a fair trial.

Haugh J accepted that the accused had been exposed to, in the traditional wording of the defamation suit, "hatred, ridicule and contempt". He gave the example of an edition of the Late Late Show where a phone call by a member of the public to the effect that "Charlie is alright" was received by the studio audience with "a deafening and a chilling silence". Haugh J also accepted the prosecution's contention that the issues raised in the obstruction charges could be described as being relatively narrow and readily identifiable. He also noted that the prosecution intended to base its case mainly on documentary evidence. But he rejected a claim by the prosecution that the accused had failed to take reasonable steps to vindicate his own reputation. He held that there was no onus or duty on the accused to do so and in any event the accused's applications to the Moriarty Tribunal to either postpone its sittings or to hold them in camera until the criminal proceedings were over were as much as could be reasonably expected from him.

Haugh J concluded that at that time there was not a real or serious risk that the accused would receive an unfair trial. He believed that "persons empanelled to serve on a jury take their oath seriously and conscientiously go about their deliberations in a manner directed by a trial judge's charge". He concluded:

> I accept that the offences with which the accused stands charged concern narrow and clearly identifiable issues and I believe that they can be considered and determined by a jury not irremediably prejudiced by the publicity given by much wider and in my opinion more serious allegations. I do not accept that the accused has in effect been denied the totally proper and legitimate right of answering the charges by relying solely on deficiencies or alleged deficiencies in the prosecution case nor that he will in effect be compelled to go into evidence nor do I believe that should he wish to go into evidence that his reputation has been so damaged that his evidence would not be other than fairly and properly considered and evaluated.

Ultimately the issue comes down to one's belief in the ability of juries to compartmentalise issues in their minds and the ability of trial judges to assist them in this process. As Haugh J noted in *Haughey*, there are two schools of thought about the resilience of juries. At one extreme there is the school which believes that juries can be relied upon virtually no matter what the circumstances. At the other extreme is the belief that "the naïve assumption that prejudicial effects can be overcome by instructions to the jury, all practising lawyers know to be unmitigated fiction". Depending on which school one subscribes to, one will either support or condemn the judgments in *Z* and *Haughey*. Haugh J stated that in his opinion the true position "probably lies somewhere in between" the two schools.

Subsequently, a second application was made by Mr Haughey to have his trial stayed on the basis of further pre-trial publicity. This application was successful.[41] Haugh J focused on the effect of remarks made by the Tanaiste (in which she had apparently called for Mr Haughey to be jailed) and on flyers which had been distributed around Dublin for a "jail the corrupt politicians" rally. Haugh J stated "I … believe that the very existence of the plan to hold this rally and the stated reasons for the purpose thereof is probably symptomatic of the depth of feeling which exists in a percentage of the population of Dublin against the accused and this further causes me concern". An attempt by the DPP to judicially review the decision of Jaugh J proved unsuccessful.[42]

Delay

Where the defence forms the view that its client cannot receive a fair trial due to excessive delay it has a duty to raise that matter before the court. In *The State (Healy) v Donoghue*[43] Murphy J stated:

> It seems to me, therefore, that the authorities have established that the Constitution guarantees to every citizen that the trial of a person charged with a criminal offence will not be delayed excessively or to express the same proposition in positive terms that the trial will be heard with reasonable expedition.[44]

There are two separate issues which must be distinguished; pre-complaint delay and post-complaint delay. Pre-complaint delay occurs where the victim of a crime delays for weeks, months or even years before reporting the alleged offence to the authorities. Post-complaint delay is delay that occurs after the authorities have received a complaint from the victim. Pre-complaint delay usually arises in the case of sex offences committed against children. Due to fear instilled by their attacker, who will often be a person of authority over them such as a parent,

---

[41] *The People (DPP) v Charles J. Haughey* unreported, Circuit Court, 26 June, 2000
[42] *DPP v Judge Kevin Haugh and Charles J. Haughey*, unreported, High Court, Carroll J, 3 November
[43] [1976] IR 325
[44] [1976] IR 325 at 349

relative, teacher or religious minister, the child may feel unable to report the offence until years or even decades later. In the leading case of *B v The DPP* [45] Denham J stated that the following factors had to be taken into account when a claim of pre-complaint delay was made.

    i) the delay in the case
    ii) the reason for the delay
    iii) the accused's actions in relation to the events in issue
    iv) the accused's assertion of his constitutional rights
    v) actual prejudice to the accused
    vi) pre-trial incarceration
    vii) anxiety and concern
    viii) impairment of defence
    ix) circumstances which may render the case into a special category
    x) the community's right to have offences prosecuted.

A recent case which examined the issue of delay is *J.L. v DPP.* [46] Here the accused sought to restrain his prosecution for an alleged rape and buggery which occurred between June 1979 and September 1980. At the time of the assault the complainant would have been about seven or eight years of age and the accused would have been a young adult. The assault was alleged to have occurred in the accused's caravan which was located on a building site. The complainant alleged that the accused had instructed her not to tell anyone about what he had done to her. It was not until 1994 that she finally told an adult about what had happened. The accused admitted that he had a caravan on the site in question but claimed that he had sold it to a couple some three months prior to the earliest date on which the offence was alleged to have been committed. He claimed that whilst he could remember the first names of the couple he had been unable to trace them due to the lapse of time.

In rejecting the accused's application Geoghegan J observed that an age disparity between the complainant and the accused may, of itself, have the effect of inhibiting the child from reporting. He held that there is no requirement of a relationship of trust between the complainant and the accused in order for the court to disregard delay. Geoghegan J noted that the mere fact that the offence charged is of a sexual nature is not of itself a factor which would permit the court to disregard delay. He stated that the relevant statement of the law on delay is to be found in the following passage by Keane J in *P.C. v DPP*:

> There are cases, however, of which this is one, where the disparity in age between the complainant and the person accused is such that the possibility arises that the failure to report the offence is explicable, having regard to the reluctance of young

[45] [1997] 3 IR 140
[46] Unreported, High Court, 8 June, 1999

children to accuse adults of improper behaviour and feelings of guilt and shame experienced by the child because of his or her participation, albeit unwillingly, in what he or she sees as wrongdoing.[47]

Geoghegan J was satisfied on the evidence of a clinical psychologist that if the complainant's allegations were true then there were sound psychological reasons why she did not make an earlier complaint. It would have been "an off-shoot of the applicant's own alleged misconduct which would have inhibited an earlier complaint". Geoghegan J proceeded to consider whether the accused's ability to defend himself at the trial had been so impaired that the trial should not be allowed to go ahead. He accepted that "a serious alibi defence which could no longer be availed of for some reason or other might well be a ground on which a court would prevent a trial going ahead". However on the facts of the case he was satisfied that there was no risk of an unfair trial. Whilst the accused enjoyed a presumption of innocence he nevertheless had to discharge a certain onus of proof in the judicial review application in order to satisfy a court that "as a matter of probability there would be a serious danger of an unfair trial". Geoghegan J observed that it was very easy to invent a dead or lost alibi and was not impressed with the bald statement in the accused's affidavit that he had been unable to trace the couple to whom he claimed to have sold his caravan. As no details had been furnished of any attempt to locate the couple there was no reason to believe that any such attempt had in fact been made. If the applicant really had moved into a house on a particular date as he claimed then it should be easy to corroborate that with title documents and other documentary evidence. He concluded that "a jury would be well capable of sorting all of this out and I cannot see that there is any risk of an unfair trial".

In the summer of 2000 a number of Supreme Court decisions on pre-complaint delay were delivered and revealed that some of the members of that court take very different approaches to the issue.[48]

Disclosure

The prosecution is obliged to disclose to the defence all relevant evidence which is within its possession. Relevant evidence includes information which may reasonably be regarded as providing a lead to other information that might reasonably assist the accused in either attacking the prosecution case or making a positive case of his own. The prosecution is under no obligation, however, to disclose irrelevant material to the defence. The prosecution is exempted from disclosure where the information consists of confidential statements made by a garda informer or where such statements would otherwise identify a garda

---

[47] Unreported, Supreme Court, 28 May, 1998
[48] See *J.O'C v DPP* unreported, Supreme Court, 19 May 2000; *J.L. v DPP* unreported, Supreme Court, 6 July 2000 and *P.O'C v DPP* unreported, Supreme Court, 6 July 2000

informer. The prosecution is further exempted from disclosure where revealing the identity of a potential witness, or a party who has simply assisted the gardaí without ever intending to be a witness, would place that person in peril. These exemptions do not apply where failing to disclose the material could reasonably be regarded as a failure to disclose to the accused material which establishes, or might reasonably be regarded as helping to establish, his innocence of the offence charged. This is known as the innocence at stake principle.

These rules were clarified in the litigation arising out of the murder of Veronica Guerin and the trial of Paul Ward for that offence.[49] Veronica Guerin was an investigative journalist whose attention had turned, for some time prior to her death, to the affairs of a particular criminal gang. She had sought to interview the alleged leader of that gang about his activities but had, apparently, been seriously assaulted. A charge of assault was brought by her against that member of the gang, but shortly before it came to trial she was murdered on the Naas to Dublin dual carriageway on 26 June, 1996. Subsequent to the murder a member of the gang who had apparently co-operated with the gardaí had the house in which he was living burnt to the ground. His girlfriend was threatened with death. The prosecution had argued that undisclosed material in their possession should not be disclosed to the defence. They asserted privilege against disclosure on two bases. The first was that some of the witnesses fell within the classic exception to disclosure as being police informers. The second privilege asserted was related to the need to preserve the life and bodily integrity of persons who had co-operated with the gardaí and might never give evidence in the trial of any member of the criminal gang. Carney J in the High Court upheld the existence of a privilege arising in both these circumstances. The Supreme Court agreed. The reason for the litigation was that the Special Criminal Court had made a ruling that the lawyers acting on behalf of the accused would be entitled to view the privileged material and then to make submissions to the court as to whether they needed to use this material in the trial of their client. After a comprehensive review of the authorities Carney J in the High Court quashed the decision of the Special Criminal Court. The Supreme Court upheld the decision of Carney J.

BURDEN AND STANDARD OF PROOF

The accused is presumed to be innocent unless and until the jury find him guilty. It is wrong to charge a jury so as to imply there is an onus on an accused. Except where expressly otherwise provided, the burden of proof is always on the prosecution at every stage of a criminal trial. That burden is discharged by the

---

[49] *Ward v Special Criminal Court* [1998] 2 ILRM 493; *DPP v Special Criminal Court*, High Court, Carney J unreported, 13 March, 1998

prosecution proving beyond reasonable doubt that the accused is guilty of the offence. A judge should not tell a jury that if they reject the explanation, if any, given by the accused that they are thus automatically entitled to convict. It is wrong to state or imply that if a defence is likely or probable the accused should be acquitted: the test always is; has the prosecution disproved the defence beyond all reasonable doubt. Because the burden of proof remains at all times on the prosecution, even if the jury reject the accused's version of events, which in law means that they do not have a reasonable doubt as a result of a consideration of his version of events, they must return and consider the entirety of the prosecution case and ask the question as to whether it proves the guilt of the accused beyond reasonable doubt. The dictum of Lord Sankey in *Woolmington v DPP*[50] has been expressly approved in Ireland:[51]

> Throughout the web of English criminal law one golden thread is always to be seen, that it is the duty of the prosecution to prove the prisoner's guilt ... if at the end of and on the whole of the case, there is a reasonable doubt, created by the evidence by either the prosecution or the prisoner, as to whether the prisoner killed the deceased with a malicious intention, the prosecution has not made out the case and the prisoner is entitled to an acquittal.

Once the prosecution has adduced evidence upon which a reasonable jury, properly instructed, could find the accused guilty of the crime charged, the case should be left to their consideration.[52] If, however, such proof does not exist at the close of the prosecution case it is the duty of the trial judge to withdraw the case from the consideration of the jury; and the jury have no option but to abide by his direction to acquit the accused.

CIRCUMSTANTIAL EVIDENCE

A jury may convict on purely circumstantial evidence, but to do this they must be satisfied, not only that the circumstances were consistent with the prisoner having committed the act, but also that the facts were such as to be inconsistent with any other rational conclusion than that he was the guilty person. It is the function of the jury to first consider the weight to be attached individually to each piece of circumstantial evidence and then to consider all the evidence in the case as a whole. If the weight of the cumulation of evidence is such as to prove to their satisfaction beyond reasonable doubt that the accused committed the crime, then the jury may convict.

---

[50] [1935] AC 462
[51] *The People (AG) v Oglesby* [1966] IR 162; *The People (AG) v Quinn* [1965] IR 366
[52] *Dublin, Wicklow and Wexford Railway Company v Slatter* (1878) 3 App cas 1155; 10 Ir CLR 256

VISUAL IDENTIFICATION

Miscarriages of justice have occurred by reason of a witness mistakenly identifying the accused as the perpetrator of the crime. Extreme errors have been made in the past. Influenced by such errors, in *The People (AG) v Casey (No. 2)*[53] the Court of Criminal Appeal required a mandatory warning of juries in cases where the prosecution is relying substantially or wholly on the visual identification of the accused as the person who perpetrated the crime:

> We are of opinion that juries as a whole may not be fully aware of the dangers involved in visual identification nor of the considerable number of cases in which such identification has been proved to be erroneous; and also that they may be inclined to attribute too much probative effect to the test of an identification parade. In our opinion it is desirable that in all cases, where the verdict depends substantially on the correctness of an identification, their attention should be called in general terms to the fact that in a number of instances such identification has proved erroneous, to the possibilities of mistake in the case before them and to the necessity of caution.

It would be a mistake to assume that identification parades are a foolproof method of overcoming the dangers inherent in visual identification. At the majority of such parades the witnesses pick out nobody, or an uninvolved person.[54] It is wrong to suppress the fact that a witness had previously identified a person incorrectly and this fact should be disclosed to the defence. There should be a full disclosure at the trial of all the circumstances of identification, so as to enable a jury to find whether it has been established beyond reasonable doubt that the correct person has been picked out and not merely a person who comes closest to a general description.[55]

The circumstances of identification should conform with fundamental standards of fairness of procedure. If, however, a suspect refuses to go on an identification parade he cannot complain about his later identification in less than satisfactory circumstances.[56] Whether the circumstances of an identification are satisfactory or not goes to the weight to be attached to such evidence. Dock identifications carry very little weight but may, subject to a stringent warning, be regarded as adequate.[57] Informal identification parades are not completely satisfactory, as where an accused, while remanded on bail, is identified by a witness in the precincts of the District Court. They are, however, admissible in evidence.[58] The identification of a suspect by means of photographs can also be subject to error. When the witness is shown the photographs, he is likely to pick on the face that

---

[53] [1963] IR 33
[54] Glanville Williams, *The Proof of Guilt* (3rd ed. 1963) 120
[55] *The People (AG) v Fagan* (1974) 1 Frewen 375
[56] *The People (AG) v Martin* [1956] IR 22
[57] *The People (DPP) v Cooney* [1997] 3 IR 205. See also *The People (AG) v Bond* [1966] IR 215
[58] *The People (DPP) v O'Reilly* [1991] ILRM 10

best accords with his recollection of the culprit. Thereafter, his recollection of the culprit and recollection of the photograph are likely to be so merged that he can no longer separate them, even though in fact his identification was mistaken.[59] It is permissible for a garda who has received a description of an offender to show photographs to the describing witness. The proper course is to use a series of photographs, not merely one or two, and to leave it to the unaided recollection of the witness as to whether any are identified. The trial judge should direct the jury's attention to the fact that the identification at a later identification parade may have been coloured by the witness having seen such a photograph.[60] The defence may introduce the fact that such photographs were official garda photographs, but the prosecution, for fear of prejudicing the trial, may not do so.

ACCOMPLICES

A person who participates in a crime is an accomplice. Very often the prosecution will have no option but to call evidence from those who have been involved in the commission of a crime. This is particularly so in the case of organised crime where those most responsible for the perpetration of criminal activity will hide behind a wall of silence and distance themselves through having subordinates commit the crime. No accomplice to crime is likely to be blameless. The accomplice should have pleaded guilty or the Director of Public Prosecutions should have made a decision not to charge him, prior to his giving evidence.[61] Where the trials for a co-accused are separated one should not be called to give evidence against another until the state witness's case has been disposed of.[62] Where an accused has pleaded guilty it is generally thought desirable that he should have been sentenced before being called on behalf of the prosecution

An accomplice is both a competent and a compellable witness against any accused, including a former co-accused or co-conspirator in a crime. The jury may convict on the uncorroborated testimony of an accomplice, but they should consider with particular care the nature of the evidence against the accused and the possibility that the accomplice may be acting out of reasons of revenge, spite or ill-will towards a former criminal confederate in giving his evidence.

SEXUAL OFFENCES

Formerly it was the law that where the offence alleged was any form of rape or sexual assault, the judge should warn the jury in clear and unmistakable terms that

---

[59] Glanville Williams, *The Proof of Guilt* (3rd ed. 1963) 121-122
[60] *The People (AG) v Mills* [1957] IR 106
[61] *Conti* (1973) 58 Cr App R 378; *Richardson* (1967) 51 Cr App R 381
[62] *Pipe* (1967) 51 Cr App R 15

it was dangerous to convict on the uncorroborated testimony of the complainant. This law has been abolished. Currently, the judge may give a warning at his discretion, but the form and content of the warning, if given, are a matter for the judge.

CONFESSIONS

The rules relating to confessions by accused persons to members of An Garda Síochána are stricter than any other branch of the law of evidence. Often the trial within the trial as to the admissibility of confession material, held in the absence of the jury, takes as long as the trial of the issue of whether the prosecution has proved its case beyond reasonable doubt in front of the jury. Close investigation of the circumstances of the taking of a confession is carried out by the courts. Occasionally stringent criticism of garda methods has emanated from judges trying cases depending substantially on confession evidence.[63]

Where an accused person has made allegations of harassment and sustained oppression in the process of interrogation, it is essential for the trial judge to put these matters before the jury in a very clear and unqualified form, indicating to the jury in accordance with the onus of proof that if such allegations should raise in their minds any doubt as to the truth of the admissions alleged to have been made, that the accused should be acquitted. The Oireacteas has also intervened with s 10 of the Criminal Procedure Act 1993 which provides

(1) Where at a trial of a person on indictment evidence is given of a confession made by that person and that evidence is not corroborated, the judge shall advise the jury to have due regard to the absence of corroboration.

(2) It shall not be necessary for a judge to use any particular form of words under this section.

Many of the major cases which come before Irish courts allege the guilt of the accused on the crime charged at least partially on the basis of a confession. A confession is any admission of the accused tending to show guilt. To be admissible in evidence, the trial judge must be satisfied that a confession was a free and voluntary emanation of the accused's mind and not obtained from him by a threat or inducement or by oppressive questioning. The burden of proof is on the prosecution to establish beyond reasonable doubt that a confession was not obtained in a manner which would render it inadmissible. However, there is an obligation on the accused to identify, at least in outline form, the nature of the contest which he raises against the admissibility of an alleged confession statement.

---

[63] See the judgment of the Special Criminal Court in *The People (DPP) v Paul Ward*, unreported, 27 November, 1998

The admissibility of a confession is a matter of law for the trial judge in the absence of the jury. Even if admitted in evidence the accused is entitled to challenge the weight that the jury might attach to the confession in the presence of the jury by asking, in essence, the same questions again.[64] If the issue raised is as to whether a confession was not made by the accused, but invented by the gardaí, this is an issue of fact for the jury.[65] Often, however, such a case is run on the basis that a combination of oppression and inducements left the accused in a state where he is unable to recall definitively what he said, if anything. It is necessary to establish that the involuntary nature of the confession emanated from the threat, inducement or oppression in question. The burden of proof remains with the prosecution and if they are unable to disprove beyond reasonable doubt the causal effect of same, the doubt must be exercised in favour of the accused by excluding the confession.

Voluntariness

A confession may not be admitted for the consideration of the jury if the prosecution, on being challenged, failed to prove that it was a voluntary statement in the sense that it was not obtained from the accused either by fear of prejudice or hope of advantage, excited or held out by a person in authority.[66] Essentially there are two questions. First was something said or done which in law would render the statement involuntary? If the answer to this question is yes, did the confession result from what was said or done? The only legal test to determine the admissibility of a confession is whether any action or words on the part of the gardaí, or other party in authority such as the Customs or Criminal Assets Bureau, caused a confession through offering or exciting hope of advantage or fear of prejudice.[67] A statement which is not voluntary is never admissible in evidence against the accused.[68]

Oppression

Apart from an inducement, a confession must be excluded if it is obtained by oppression. More subtle forms of manipulation than physical beatings are complained of in the current climate.[69] A custody record is kept by a garda independent of the interrogators and its purpose is to establish the pattern of questioning, eating, sleeping, and legal and medical attention during a period of detention. This should operate as an independent check in relation to the circumstances alleged against the gardaí by the accused. A better check might be the tape or

---

[64] *The People (AG) v Ainscough* [1960] IR 136
[65] *Ajodha* [1982] AC 204
[66] *Ibrahim v R* [1914] AC 599 at 609
[67] See Cole, *Irish Cases on Evidence* (2nd ed. 1982) 61-69
[68] *The People (AG) v Cummins* [1972] IR 312
[69] For an example see *The People (DPP) v Ward,* Special Criminal Court, unreported, 27 November, 1998

video recording of confession statements. Section 27 of the Criminal Justice Act 1984 allows the Minister for Justice to make regulations providing for the recording of interviews in garda stations. Facilities for the recording of interviews are currently being introduced in garda stations on a widespread basis.

Lord McDermott in a lecture defined oppression in the following terms which have since been accepted by the Court of Criminal Appeal:

> Questioning which by its nature, duration or other attendant circumstances (including defective custody) excites hopes (such as the hope of release) or fears, or so affects the mind of the subject that his will crumbles and he speaks when otherwise he would have remained silent.[70]

In *The People (DPP) v Breathnach*[71] the accused had been almost constantly interrogated for forty hours following his arrest; he had been denied access to legal advisers and to friends and his confession was made after he had been awakened from a few hours of much needed sleep and brought down at 4.00 am. for further interrogation into the passage way of the Bridewell Garda Station in Dublin. The Court of Criminal Appeal reversed the ruling of the Special Criminal Court and excluded the confession. In *The People (DPP) v Pringle*[72] the accused was intensively interviewed over a period of three days. In admitting the confession particular emphasis was laid by the Court of Criminal Appeal on the nature of the accused's work and what the court of trial had found to be the toughness of his character. The court stated:

> In this case the accused was a man of forty-two years of age, in good health, who for some time prior to his arrest had been a fisherman in the Galway area. He was apparently an experienced man of the world not unused to conditions of physical hardship. It was clearly open to the court of trial to hold that the will of such a man would not have been undermined by the interviews he had experienced and by lack of sleep and that he spoke the inculpatory words when otherwise he would have remained silent.[73]

Fairness

Evidence may be excluded if it falls below the required minimum standard of fairness. In *The People (DPP) v Shaw*[74] Griffin J explained this principle in the following terms:

---

[70] Adopted by the Court of Appeal in *Prager* [1972] 1 All ER 1114, 56 Cr App R 151 and approved by the Court of Criminal Appeal in *The People (DPP) v McNally and Breathnach* (1981) 2 Frewen 43 and *The People (DPP) v Pringle* (1981) 2 Frewen 57

[71] (1981) 2 Frewen 43

[72] (1981) 2 Frewen 57

[73] Per O'Higgins CJ at 82. For the subsequent history of the case see *The People (DPP) v Pringle [No. 2]* [1997] 2 IR 225

[74] [1982] IR 1 at 61

... because ... our Constitution postulates the observance of basic or fundamental fairness of procedures, the judge presiding at a criminal trial should be astute to see that, although a statement may be technically voluntary, it should nevertheless be excluded if, by reason of the manner or the circumstances in which it was obtained, it falls below the required standard of fairness. The reason for exclusion here is not so much the risk of an erroneous conviction as the recognition that the minimum or essential standard must be observed in the administration of justice.[75]

The passage has been approved many times in rulings in the Central Criminal Courts. An example of its application is *The People (DPP) v Paul Ward*.[76] There a finding by the trial court that the accused's mother and girlfriend had been brought to see him without his request led to the exclusion of alleged verbal admissions made by him on the ground that these visits constituted an unfair procedure deliberately engineered by the gardaí to put pressure on him. Thus, even short of finding oppression a confession may be excluded if the circumstances of taking it fall below fundamental standards of fairness.

The Judges' Rules

The Judges' Rules established at common law constitute the basic guide to police conduct.

1) When a police officer is endeavouring to discover the author of a crime there is no objection to his putting questions in respect thereof to any person or persons, whether accused or not, from whom he thinks that useful information may be obtained.

2) Whenever a police officer has made up his mind to charge a person with a crime, he should first caution such a person before asking him any questions, or any further questions as the case may be.

3) Persons in custody should not be questioned without the usual caution being first administered.

4) If the prisoner wishes to volunteer any statement, the usual caution should be administered. It is desirable that the last two words of such caution should be omitted, and that the caution should end with the words 'to be given in evidence'.

5) The caution to be administered to a prisoner when he is formally charged should therefore be in the following words: "Do you wish to say anything in answer to the charge? You are not obliged to say anything unless you wish to do so, but whatever you say will be taken down in writing and

---

[75] It should be noted that this passage was used by the majority judgment of the Supreme Court in *The People (DPP) v Healy* [1990] ILRM, [1990] 2 IR 73 to postulate a constitutional right of access in a detained person to a solicitor, whether requested by him or on his behalf

[76] Special Criminal Court, unreported, 27 November, 1998

may be given in evidence". Care should be taken to avoid the suggestion that his answers can only be used in evidence against him, as this may prevent an innocent person making a statement which might assist to clear him of the charge.

6) A statement made by a prisoner before there is time to caution him is not rendered inadmissible in evidence merely because no caution has been given, but in such a case he should be cautioned as soon as possible.

7) A prisoner making a voluntary statement must not be cross-examined, and no questions should be put to him about it except for the purpose of removing ambiguity in what he has actually said. For instance, if he has mentioned an hour without saying whether it was morning or evening, or has given a day of the week and day of the month which do not agree, or has not made it clear to that individual of what place he intended to refer in some part of his statement, he may be questioned sufficiently to clear up the point.

8) When two or more persons are charged with the same offence and their statements are taken separately, the police should not read these statements to the other persons charged, but each of such persons should be given by the police a copy of such statements and nothing should be said or done by the police to invite a reply. If the person charged desires to make a statement in reply the usual caution should be administered.

9) Any statement made in accordance with the above rules should, whenever possible, be taken down in writing and signed by the person making it after it has been read to him and he has been invited to make any corrections he may wish.

A breach of the Judges' Rules will not lightly be excused. The Judges' Rules are not rules of law. They are rules for the guidance of persons taking statements. However, they have stood up to the test of time and will be departed from at peril.

UNCONSTITUTIONALLY OBTAINED EVIDENCE

Any infringement of the constitutional rights of an accused person to the inviolability of his dwelling, his personal liberty, his privacy or any of his personal constitutional rights may result in the exclusion of all evidence that results from it. The fundamental focus, therefore, of virtually every criminal trial on indictment is an attempt by the accused to assert such rights and by the state to justify the actions of the gardaí within the parameters of an express legal authority authorising such invasion. In consequence, the rules of substantive criminal law have been either ignored or overlooked in favour of this process.

In the leading case of *The People (AG) v O'Brien*[77] the accused was indicted on various charges of larceny. Stolen goods were the main evidence at the trial. These had been identified by their owners after having been found by the gardaí in the dwelling house of the accused at No. 118, Captain's Road, Crumlin. The search warrant, however, described the address to be searched as "118, Cashel Road, Crumlin". In fact, this was an adjoining street. The search warrant was therefore invalid and members of the Garda Síochána were trespassers in the accused's house. They had violated the dwelling of the accused as guaranteed by Article 40.5 of the Constitution. On investigation it turned out that the illegality in question was in the nature of a mere oversight which was in no way deliberate. The court of trial, the Court of Criminal Appeal and the Supreme Court all accepted that the gardaí had done their best to comply with the law. Unanimously, the Supreme Court ruled in favour of admitting the evidence. They held that no argument could be advanced that this factual error amounted to a deliberate invasion of the accused's constitutional rights. Since the mistake had only been noticed after the search had been completed, it could not have been argued that their unauthorised presence on the accused's property took place in deliberate disregard of the law. The Supreme Court was anxious to stress the community's interest that crime should be detected and punished, which principle was not to be defeated by an unintentional and accidental illegality. The principle of not excluding evidence which was obtained by an accidental and unintentional infringement of the Constitution was followed in many subsequent cases.[78]

The accused is entitled only to assert his own rights in aid of the exclusionary rule and not those of any other person. In *The People (DPP) v Lawless*[79] a garda search of a flat resulted in the discovery of seventeen paper packs of heroin. The search warrant was defective. The accused, however, did not live in this flat, but gave evidence that he was merely waiting there for the return of his brother from a nearby flat. The Court of Criminal Appeal held that as he could not assert any right to the inviolability of a dwelling which was not his he could not plead the exclusionary rule as against the state[80].

Evidence obtained in breach of the Constitution may be admitted if it was obtained out of the need to rescue a victim in peril, or the need to rescue vital evidence. In *The People (DPP) v Shaw*[81] the accused was detained for three days and extensively questioned. The accused were suspected of being involved in the abduction and murder of two young women, E and M. M had disappeared only four days prior to the arrest of the accused. The purpose by the gardaí to discover

---

[77] [1965] IR 142

[78] *The People (DPP) v Lawless* (1985) 3 Frewen 31

[79] (1985) 3 Frewen 30

[80] See also *Wong Sun v US* (1963) 371 US 471 and *Jones v US* (1960) 362 US 257

[81] [1982] IR 1

if M might still be alive was accepted by the trial judge as being the motive of the gardaí in continuing to detain the accused illegally. The Supreme Court ruled that in seeking to save the life of M, at the cost of discounting the right to liberty of the accused, the gardaí had endeavoured to protect the more important of two conflicting rights under the Constitution and, in consequence, had not acted unlawfully in continuing to detain the accused without bringing him before a court at the first reasonable opportunity. In *The People (DPP) v Lawless*[82] the gardaí, in unknowing possession of a defective search warrant entered the flat in which the accused was staying somewhat earlier than they otherwise would have, by reason of a person rushing up the stairs towards a toilet. In fact, heroin flushed down the lavatory was retrieved by another detective garda. The Court of Criminal Appeal commented that the need to prevent the imminent destruction of vital evidence would have excused such an unlawful entry.[83]

THE HEARSAY RULE

A statement other than one made by a witness while giving oral evidence in the proceedings is inadmissible as evidence of any facts stated. In other words, the court should only accept as evidence the account of witnesses who have themselves perceived the events in issue, and not an account which depends upon what the witness knows from information supplied by other people. The hearsay rule is subject to many exceptions. One of the most important is a confession made by an accused of his complicity in the offence, or some admission which connects him to the commission of the offence. A statement by a party to proceedings as to a matter material to those proceedings is admissible in evidence as an exception to the rule against hearsay and may be proved by someone who witnessed such an admission.[84] Further, since *Christie* in 1914[85] it has generally been held that statements made in the presence of an accused are always admissible in evidence. The facts were that a small boy accused Christie, in the presence of the boy's mother and a police officer, of having indecently assaulted him. It was held that although the accused denied the charge the accusations by the boy might be proved by his mother and the police officer. The case does not mean that a mere statement in the presence of a party is evidence of the facts stated. The issue is the accused's reaction to the statement and as to whether it is suggestive of rejection or a possible acceptance of the truth. In consequence the decision in the case is that the reaction of an accused to what is said in his presence may or may not amount to acceptance, and therefore to an admission. A

---

[82] (1985) 3 Frewen 30
[83] See also *Palumbo v US* (1984) 53 LW 3329
[84] *Erdheim* [1896] 2 QB 260 at 270. Further see Phipson on Evidence (13th ed., 1982) Chapter 19
[85] [1914] AC 545

number of other exceptions to the hearsay rule also exist.

1) The utterances of the words may itself be a relevant fact, quite apart from the truth or falsity of anything asserted by the words spoken. To prove, by the evidence of a witness who heard the words, that they were spoken, is direct evidence, and in no way encroaches on the general rule against hearsay.

2) Where an act or transaction is in issue declarations which accompany or explain the act or transaction are generally admitted under the somewhat vague principle that they form part of the *res gestae*. Insofar as the evidence of the words spoken is offered merely to explain or qualify the nature of the act, there is no breach of the hearsay rule.

3) The statements accompanying an act may be offered as showing the mind of the actor at the time of the doing of the act.

Other exceptions to the hearsay rule may be briefly noted. These include statements in a public document and dying declarations[86]. Other exceptions include declarations against proprietary or pecuniary interest, declarations as to dissent or relationship, declarations as to public rights, statements appropriately recorded in a public document[87], declarations by testators as to the contents of their wills, after they have been made and declarations made in the course of duty.

WITNESSES

Generally speaking all citizens and persons subject to the jurisdiction of the court are both competent and compellable witnesses. The court is entitled to the benefit of the evidence of every person who can assist it in the determination of an issue before it.[88] Since the Criminal Justice (Evidence) Act, 1924 the accused, and the wife or husband of same, is a competent witness for the defence. Section 21 of the Criminal Evidence Act 1991 provides that in any criminal proceedings the spouse or a former spouse of an accused shall be competent to give evidence at the instance of the prosecution, and of the accused or any person charged with him in the same proceedings. Section 22 provides that in any criminal proceedings the spouse of an accused shall be compellable to give evidence at the instance of the prosecution only in the case of an offence which involves violence, or the threat of violence, to the spouse, a child of the spouse or of the accused, or any person who was at the material time under the age of seventeen years. The spouse of an accused is also compellable to give evidence at the

---

[86] *Mooney* (1851) 5 Cox CC 318; *Jenkins* (1869) LR 1 CCR 187; *Pike* (1829) 3 C and P 598
[87] *Sturla v Freccia* (1880) 4 App Cas 623
[88] *The People (DPP) v JT* (1988) 3 Frewen 141

instance of the prosecution in the case of a sexual offence alleged to have been committed in relation to a child of the spouse or of the accused, or any person who was at the material time under the age of seventeen years. Section 23 provides that in any criminal proceedings the spouse or a former spouse of an accused is compellable to give evidence at the instance of the accused.

A witness is never entitled to give evidence as to the ultimate issue before the jury. Thus, a witness may never be asked "and do you say that the accused is guilty?" Witnesses are entitled to depose to what they saw, but the interpretation of the facts, and the inferences to be drawn from such facts as are proven is exclusively one for the jury. A witness cannot act as a thirteenth juror.

Evidence of opinion is admissible on questions of art and science outside the competence of ordinary members of the community, from which jurors are drawn, provided that opinion is given by an expert in the relevant field. It is for the judge to decide whether a witness is sufficiently qualified or experienced to express an opinion in an expert field. This is usually attested to by the giving of evidence of relevant qualifications, as in the case of a pathologist, or evidence as to courses of study followed as in the case of a fingerprint expert or a scenes of crime examiner.

CHARACTER EVIDENCE

Every accused has the right to call evidence as to his good character. This might be adduced by asking questions of a garda witness as to whether the accused has previous convictions. The accused may also call positive evidence from character witnesses to indicate that his past life has been so blameless, and exemplary in terms of good works, that it makes it unlikely that he would commit the crime charged.

The general rule is that the prosecution may not introduce evidence of the previous bad character of the accused. However, an accused may be cross-examined as to his credit when the accused has caused questions to be asked of witnesses for the prosecution with a view to establishing his own good character, or has called evidence as to that character. If the conduct of the defence goes beyond the testing and examination of prosecution witnesses and instead involves an actual imputation on the character of a prosecution witness then the trial judge may, at his discretion, in the absence of the jury, give leave to the prosecution to cross-examine the accused as to his prior bad character. Section 1(f) of the Criminal Justice (Evidence) Act 1924 provides:

> A person charged and called as a witness in pursuance of this Act shall not be asked, and if not asked, shall not be required to answer, any question tending to show that he has committed or been convicted of or been charged with any offence other than that wherewith he is then charged, or is of bad character, unless

(i) the proof that he has committed or been convicted of such other offence is admissible evidence to show that he is guilty of the offence wherewith he is then charged; or

(ii) he has personally or his advocate asked questions of the witnesses for the prosecution with a view to establish his own good character, or has given evidence of his own good character, or the nature or conduct of the defence is such as to involve imputations on the character of the prosecutor or the witnesses for the prosecution; or

(iii) he has given evidence against any other person charged with the same offence ...

CONCLUSION

Just as is the case with our substantive criminal law, the rules of criminal evidence and procedure would benefit greatly from reform and codification. It is bizarre to say the least that a prosecution for a complex computer crime might stand or fall on the interpretation of a 200 year old case on a rule of evidence that was invented for a very different age and for very different crimes. One interesting suggestion for reform has come from former Director of Public Prosecutions, Eamonn Barnes.

> I believe that there is an unanswerable case for at least one long overdue change in the system of trial procedure which as a nation we inherited from our former masters. I refer to the procedure whereby various legal issues, notably those regarding admissibility of evidence and legality of detention, are debated at great and often inordinate length at what has become known as the trial within a trial while a jury is retired, often for very lengthy periods. I believe all such questions should be judicially determined as preliminary issues before the proceedings involving the jury are commenced. Such determinations should be appealable by both sides to an appropriate appellate court, again before the main trial begins. This would be greatly in ease of unfortunate jury persons who, under current procedures, can have their freedom of movement curtailed for weeks on end and secondly would enable them to concentrate on the evidence in a coherent manner without lengthy interruptions.[89]

Ultimately it comes down to the importance which the Oireachtas attaches to having a coherent and up-to-date system of criminal justice in Ireland.

---

[89] Barnes "Reflections on the past 24 years as Director of Public Prosecutions" (1999) 4 *The Bar Review* 389 at 392

4

The Constitution and Criminal Justice[*]

Paul O'Mahony

THE PURPOSE OF THE CONSTITUTION

The primary function and the chief achievement of any Constitution is the fashioning of the institutional infrastructure for the administration of government and the law. There are two other vital tasks. First, there is the issue of the character and quality of the society envisioned by the Constitution. A Constitution will explicitly and implicitly embody a set of fundamental principles and ideals that express an ordering of values for society and are intended to shape the type of society that emerges. Second, there is the more immediately practical issue of the relationship between the state and its powers, vested in its officers and institutions, and the citizen.

The Constitution of a modern parliamentary democracy must be concerned to curb the potentially immense, coercive powers of the state and make them subject to the law in a manner that both promotes the liberties of the individual citizen and protects him or her from possible abuses and injustices. This chapter will briefly examine some aspects of the role of the Constitution in shaping criminal justice procedures, controlling the exercise of the state's coercive powers, and defining, realising, and protecting the civil liberties of the citizen.

The essential task of the 1937 Constitution of Ireland was to define the organisational structures and the basic ground rules for the exercise of political

---

[*] In *Ireland's Evolving Constitution 1937–1997*, T. Murphy and P. Twomey (eds.), Oxford: Hart, 1998

and legal power in the state. Few would argue with the proposition that it succeeds admirably in this task. Many might question the quality, utility, and even the rationality of much of the political and judicial activity in this country, but few harbour serious dissatisfactions with the actual structures of government or of the legal system as laid down by the Constitution. In particular, the separation of the powers of the executive, the legislature, and the judiciary and the critically important function of the Supreme Court in interpreting the Constitution itself and in testing the constitutionality of legislation have proven to be enduring and, arguably, effective mechanisms for the creation and maintenance of democracy.[1]

It is likely that the Constitution of the US was an important model for de Valera and the other framers of the Irish Constitution[2] and both Constitutions are most obviously successful at the work of fashioning governmental structures. The most obvious flaws in both Constitutions, on the other hand, relate to the value ordering function and the manner in which the Constitutions were partially shaped by unresolved political and ethical dilemmas arising directly from the political and cultural context at the time of drafting.

Just as it is possible to discern in the US Constitution the influence of specific historical imperatives, most obviously the need to win over some reluctant states who were fearful of the strength of federal government and concerned to protect their slave-owning traditions, the Irish Constitution can be seen to have been written from a particular political, historical and religious perspective with an anxious weather eye on Westminister and the Unionists in the six counties and with a deferential, indeed in places subservient, nod to the Roman Catholic Church.[3]

The original US Constitution of 1787 was concerned to create a federal nation which could survive the fact that some states permitted and others strongly disapproved of and were moving towards prohibition of slavery. Article 4ii stated that "No Person held to Service or Labour in one State, under the Laws thereof, escaping into another, shall, in consequence of any Law or Regulation therein be discharged from such Service or Labour, but shall be delivered up on Claim of the

---

[1] J.M. Kelly in the introduction to his first edition of *The Irish Constitution*, reproduced in G. Hogan and G. Whyte (eds.), *The Irish Constitution* (3rd ed., Dublin, Butterworths, 1994) p. xcii, expressed the view that the average liberal observer would probably say the overall impact of the courts on modern Irish life, in their handling of constitutional issues, "had been beneficial, rational, progressive, and fair ..."

[2] The US Constitution of 1787, according to J.M. Kelly, *A Short History of Western Legal Theory* (Oxford, Clarendon Press, 1992), at 278, was "virtually a world novelty" and as a successful model in English undoubtedly exerted some influence over the framers of the Irish Constitution, particularly with respect to the central doctrine of the separation of powers, which finds clear expression in the US Constitution, although as B. Chubb states in *The Government and Politics of Ireland* (London, Longman, 1970), Britain was the chief model for governmental structures

[3] See N. Browne, "Church and State in Modern Ireland"; G. Whyte, "Some reflections on the Role of Religion in the Constitutional Order"; and D.M. Clarke, "Education, the State and Sectarian Schools", in *Ireland's Evolving Constitution 1937–1997*, T. Murphy and P. Twomey (eds.), Oxford: Hart, 1998

Party to whom such Service or Labour may be due". This article, which would later allow for the infamous fugitive slave laws, was from the beginning considered by many to be inconsistent with the Declaration of Independence and inimical to the core values of the United States, but was also considered necessary to gain the compliance of the southern slave-owning states. It represented compromise and troublesome, unfinished business that was not finally resolved until the American Civil War and the inclusion in the Constitution in 1866 of the 13th, 14th, and 15th amendments which, among other things, abolished slavery and conferred citizenship on former slaves.

There is, clearly, also much compromise and unfinished business lurking menacingly in the articles of the Irish Constitution.[4] A prime example has been the territorial claim of Articles 2 and 3 which, until the Good Friday agreement[5], remained to taunt Unionist opinion in Northern Ireland and Britain and to reinforce aggressive nationalism in the whole of Ireland.[6] The Constitution's patronising view of women[7] and its increasingly irrelevant endorsement of religiously inspired values regarding the family, marriage, and other aspects of personal morality have been challenged and undercut by amendment, as in the case of the 15th amendment permitting divorce, and even more obviously by social evolution and by developments in national and international law. But for the fact that the Irish people are generally so satisfied with the form of government defined by the Constitution, it is likely that the deficiencies of the Constitution in its value ordering function would have by now led to its demise and replacement by a more modern, realistic and pluralist alternative.

THE CONSTITUTION AND THE CRIMINAL JUSTICE SYSTEM

There is less disquiet expressed about the provisions of the Constitution governing criminal justice procedures. However, the general satisfaction or lack of dissatisfaction with this area of the Constitution can hardly be fully justified by reference to the explicit enumeration of rights within the text itself, since these are relatively few and sometimes far from unequivocal.

The important Articles are the following: Article 13.6 which endows the President with the power to commute or remit punishments imposed by the courts (significantly, some of these powers can be conferred by law on executive

---

[4] An All-Party Oireachtas Committee on the Constitution is currently attempting to address some of the anachronisms and anomalies by preparing a report on suggested amendments to the Constitution

[5] As agreed under the Belfast Agreement a referendum was held in May 1998 and the Nineteenth Amendment to the Constitution was duly passed with the effect of deleting the territorial claim

[6] See A. Carty, "The Irish Constitution, International Law and the Northern Question – The Need for Radical Thinking", in Murphy and Twomey (eds.) *op. cit.*

[7] See D. Dooley, "Gendered Citizenship in the Irish Constitution", in Murphy and Twomey (eds.) *op. cit.*

authorities, in particular the Minister for Justice); Article 15.5 which prohibits retrospective criminalisation; Article 34.1 which provides that justice be administered in public by courts; Article 35.2 which provides that judges are independent and subject only to the law and the Constitution; Article 38.1 which provides that no person shall be tried on any criminal charge except "in due course of law"; Article 40.4.1 which provides that no person shall be deprived of personal liberty except in accordance with law – with further subsections setting out specific procedures for taking a *habeas corpus* case to the High Court; Article 40.1 which provides that that every person should be held as equal before the law; Article 38.5 which provides that, except for certain specified exceptions, no person should be tried on a criminal charge without a jury; and Article 40.5 which provides that a person's home is inviolable and shall not be forcibly entered except in accordance with the law. The Sixteenth Amendment (1996), incorporated in Article 40.4.7, which allows for the refusal of bail on the grounds of reasonable suspicion that the accused might commit a serious offence if set free on bail, and the Twenty-First Amendment (2001), which prohibits the re-introduction of the death penalty, add to the constitutional provisions directly related to criminal justice.

Even before taking account of the qualifications that have been built into the Constitution severely to constrain some of these rights and of the Offences Against the State Act 1939, which is a part of permanent legislation and provides mechanisms for the suspension of normal constitutional rights, it must be admitted that the Constitution is a disappointingly vague legal framework on which to base the protection of individual liberty from state power and on which to construct fair and just criminal procedures. Compared to the Bill of Rights in the American Constitution and more recent European Constitutions, such as the Spanish, the Irish criminal justice provisions appear to be spare and minimalist. There is little of a concrete or definitively affirmative nature apart from the right to a jury trial, the openness of the process, the independence of the judiciary, and the more general principle of equality before the law and all of these have been subjected to certain unfortunate limitations by the Constitution itself.

By contrast, the American Bill of Rights enunciates quite specific liberties (eg. in the Fourth Amendment, from searches and seizures without probable cause) and procedural rights (eg. in the Sixth, the right of an accused to a speedy trial and to "have compulsory process for obtaining witnesses in his favor" or in the Fifth, the right not to be "compelled in any criminal case to be a witness against himself"). The Spanish Constitution, as a modern European example, is also more explicit than the Irish Constitution and stipulates the abolition of the death penalty and the principle of proportionality of punishment as well as actively supporting the principle of rehabilitation of offenders.

However, the Twenty-First Amendment to the Irish Constitution, passed with the support of 62% of voters in the referendum of June 2001, emulates the stand of the Spanish Constitution on capital punishment. This amendment removes all previous references to the death penalty from the Constitution and lays down that "the Oireachtas shall not enact any law providing for the imposition of the death penalty". Capital punishment was abolished by statute through the Criminal Justice Act (1990) and this amendment now makes the abolition a matter of constitutional principle, disallowing the re-introduction of the death penalty by statute even in time of war or armed rebellion.

The focus of the criminal justice provisions that do appear in the Irish Constitution is firmly on the criminal process itself and the areas of law enforcement and police powers are not covered in any detail. Most especially, the crucial area of punishment, apart from capital punishment, is almost completely ignored. In contrast, the Eighth Amendment to the US Constitution addresses this area directly declaring that: "Excessive bail shall not be required, nor excessive fines imposed, nor cruel and unusual punishments inflicted".

THE RULE OF LAW AND THE EMERGENCE OF A "META-CONSTITUTION"

The most obvious general point to make about the criminal justice provisions in the Irish Constitution is that several of the articles simply invoke the concept of "the law", allowing certain state interventions in individuals' lives only "in accordance with the law". In this manner the Constitution establishes, as it were, the rule of law. Two things flow from the minimalist approach of the Constitution and its reliance on the concept of the rule of law. First, it is clear that the actual quality of justice and of protection of individual rights must be determined more by the statute laws already in place and to be developed in the future, by the tradition of the common law and all the principles on which it is based, and increasingly by international conventions to which Ireland is a signatory, such as the European Convention on Human Rights[8], than by the Constitution itself. All of these three sources of law are influential so long as they do not contradict the Constitution. Second, the approach implicitly, but perhaps unwittingly, recognises the contingent, evolutionary, and fluid nature of the law and, consequently, advances and ensures the critical role of the judiciary in interpreting the Constitution and the law and in, effectively, creating a "meta-Constitution" based on judge-made law that arises out of the actual Constitution like the genie out of Aladdin's lamp.

In practice this has meant that the High and Supreme Courts, in exercising their interpretative powers, have fleshed out the Constitution and plugged many

---

[8] The Supreme Court has repeated that, with regard to international agreements, Article 29.6 means that in the absence of incorporation the Convention is not part of domestic law: In *Re O Laighleis* [1960] IR 93. Nevertheless, the Convention and other international agreements have had a significant indirect effect in domestic law: see generally G. Hogan and G. Whyte, *supra* n. 1, at 295-301. The government has announced that it intends to incorporate the European Convention on Human Rights into domestic law by means of legislation

of its obvious gaps, particularly in the area of criminal justice procedures. The judiciary has 'read into' the Constitution a whole set of safeguards, which come close to the American Bill of Rights not just in content but also in comprehensiveness and effectiveness. One Article in the Constitution has played a vital and positive role in the discovery, definition and protection of rights. This is Article 40.3.1 in which the "State guarantees in its laws to respect, and, as far as practicable, by its laws to defend and vindicate the personal rights of the citizen" (in particular, the life, person, good name, and property rights). Article 45 has also played an auxiliary, if more indirect, role in the process of constructing a "meta-Constitution". Article 45 is known as the Directive Principles of Social Policy and is intended exclusively for the guidance of the Oireachtas in its law-making function – especially at 45.1, which provides that "The State shall strive to promote the welfare of the whole people by securing and protecting as effectively as it may a social order in which justice and charity shall inform all the institutions of the national life". Nevertheless, judicial interpretation has inevitably been influenced by this high-minded aspiration.

Judicial interpretation and argument, leaning on these and other Articles and sometimes deriving principles from them, have led to the doctrine of unenumerated rights through which certain rights, such as of access to the courts, to privacy, to bail, to legal counsel, and to fair procedures in decision-making, have been granted constitutional status. In this way the framework of constitutional safeguards has been extended and reinforced to an extent that might make the minimalist and often equivocal provisions in the actual Constitution appear irrelevant or, some might argue, even beneficial, since they have given rise to such an efflorescence of important civil rights.

However, this is not the case. The vagueness and the deficiencies of the Constitution in the area of criminal justice have had a very definite negative impact at both the theoretical and practical levels. The special exemptions built into the Constitution which in certain circumstances allow for the suspension or curtailment of the rights, which the Constitution simultaneously brings to life, have been a major and growing problem through the years. The judiciary has extended the Constitution in many positive ways, delineating individual rights, but this process has coexisted with an acquiescence in the way in which success-ive governments have chosen to use the special and emergency powers, allowed to them by the Constitution, and with a tendency to interpret the law and the Constitution in certain key areas relating to special and emergency powers in a manner that appears to undercut rather than bolster civil liberties. In recent years, this has meant that the Constitution has not provided the kind of clear, un-ambiguous guidance that has been needed to temper the growing momentum of the political hardline agenda on criminal justice, an agenda which seems irrevocably wedded to a programme of increasing "toughness on crime" and ever more repressive measures.

THE RHETORIC-REALITY GAP

Before looking at some of the key areas more closely, it is worth making two
general points. First, the vagueness of the Constitution on criminal justice and its
reliance on the concept of the rule of law and the consequent need for extensive
judicial interpretation have meant that this crucial area of law has become almost
impossibly complex and arcane. For example, the low level of public and political
debate prior to the 1996 bail referendum[9] can be related to the inherent legal
complexity of the issue, which manages to baffle many lawyers as well as the
general public. The convoluted ramifications of the law in many areas of the
"meta-Constitution" on civil liberties ensures that these matters remain the
preserve of a handful of specialists. Because of this, there is a lack of information
and understanding amongst citizens about their constitutional rights and, even
more crucially, no sense of personal ownership of the Constitution. In some
countries like the US the guarantees of the Constitution are widely known and
have a significant psychological impact on the general population and the way
they relate to the state and civic authorities. The remoteness of Irish people from
their Constitution in this critical area is a real loss.

Secondly, it is worth emphasising that, in the final analysis, what counts is the
day-to-day practice within the courts and the wider criminal justice system. The
most eloquent declaration of rights and the noblest of ethical principles, even when
embodied in a Constitution, mean little, if in practice the police harass the innocent
and guilty alike, the courts punish disproportionately and the prisons oppress,
degrade, and alienate the convicted. The important questions are how well on a
day-to-day basis is the liberty of the ordinary citizen protected from unwarranted
interference by the state and how effective are the controls on the authorities as
they go about their crime prevention, investigation, prosecution, judicial, and penal
business. Are suspects, detainees, and convicts treated with justice and charity? To
what extent can a citizen expect equality of treatment before the law?

A substantial degree of discretion, in the courts, the prosecution service, the
prisons, and police operations is inevitable in the process of translating the
principles of any Constitution into daily practice. It is also inevitable that vested
interests within the system, such as the police, will employ the full latitude of
their discretionary powers and will exploit legal grey areas and constitutional
ambiguities to advance their own activities. Even perfectly explicit and un-
ambiguous constitutional guarantees require a panoply of practical measures and
mechanisms to ensure that rights are not infringed or at least not infringed
regularly and with impunity.

---

9   See the editorials "Bail Reform: Expediancy before Principle" (1995) 13 ILT 233 and "Bail
    Reform: Might We Think before We Leap" (1996) 14 ILT 29; also C. McCullagh "Asking the
    Wrong Questions: A Note on the Use of Bail in Irish Courts" (1990) 38 *Administration* 271-279

In this regard, the American experience is a salutary lesson. The American Bill of Rights is undoubtedly a far superior instrument for the governing of criminal justice procedures than the Irish Constitution. However, the reality of the US criminal justice system is an object lesson in the yawning gulf between the rhetoric of the law and the reality of law enforcement.

Despite the impressive constitutional safeguards, many Americans today experience their society as little better than a police state. As the Rodney King case[10] demonstrated, in some areas of the US the illegal use of violence by officers of the law has become institutionalised and widespread.[11] The justice system was in this case shown to be so skewed that, even when a savage and unwarranted beating was captured on video and seen throughout the world, the police perpetrators were found innocent in a criminal trial. This disaster for American civil liberties was made possible mainly by moving the jury trial to an outlying suburb, which, it so happened, was home to many Los Angeles policemen but to very few Afro-Americans.

The fact that, by comparison with the US, there is relatively little systematic abuse of civil liberties in Ireland and few clearcut cases of miscarriage of justice should not blind us to the deficiencies in our system and the potential for a substantial escalation of problems in this area. There is at present in Ireland a serious lack of effective and adequate control mechanisms within the criminal justice system. For example, the Irish system allows an accused to be convicted on the basis of a retracted, uncorroborated confession, yet, despite the lessons of the Sallins Train Robbery[12] and the Kerry Babies[13] cases and the more recent Pringle, Connell and Lyons cases,[14] the recommendations of the 1990 Martin Committee[15] to have interrogations videotaped have yet to be fully implemented. However, in August 1999, the Minister for Justice announced that in the near

---

[10] *Koon v United States*, 116 SC 2035, 1996 US LEXIS 3877; L Ed 2d 392

[11] See eg C. Pope and L. Ross, "Race, Crime and Justice: The Aftermath of Rodney King" (1992) 17 The Criminologist 1-10 and R McNeely and C. Pope (eds.) *Race, Crime and Criminal Justice* (Beverly Hills, Calif., Sage 1981)

[12] *Kelly v Ireland* (1986) IR 757

[13] See *Report of the Tribunal of Inquiry into the Kerry Babies Case* (Dublin, Stationery Office, 1995), and for a discussion of the inadequacies of the official response to the implications of the case regarding police interrogation see P. O'Mahony, "The Kerry Babies Case: Towards a Social Psychological Analysis" (1992) 13 *Irish J of Psychology* 223-38

[14] For a brief overview of both the Pringle and Connell cases and for an examination of their implications with respect to Garda interrogation methods see P. O'Mahony, "The Garda Síochána and the Ethics of Police Interrogation" (1996) 6 *Irish Criminal Law J* 46-54; also, for a brief discussion of the Lyons case and the importance of having a solicitor for the accused present during interrogation, see P. O'Mahony "The Psychology of Police Interrogation: The Kerry Babies Case" in this volume

[15] *Report of the Committee to Enquire into Certain Aspects of Criminal Procedure* (Dublin Stationery Office, 1990). This report recommended routine taping of interrogations in all relatively serious criminal cases

future all interrogations relating to serious crime would be videotaped and a commitment was made to provide taping facilities at all major garda stations within eighteen months[16]. A strong case can be made that taping, although a valuable safeguard, is not an entirely adequate protection against false admissions and consequent miscarriage of justice and that the sitting in on interrogations of a solicitor for the accused is a necessary further protection[17].

Nor has there been action on the recommendation of the European Committee for the Prevention of Torture[18] to reform the Garda Complaints Board in order to make it more independent of the Garda Síochána. The Committee has expressed concern about the possibility of frequent physical abuse of suspects during detention in Dublin police stations. Nor has there been action on the sixteen year old recommendation of the Whitaker Committee[19] to establish an independent inspectorate of prisons to monitor one of the most secret and neglected areas of state criminal justice activity. In these and other areas the Irish criminal justice system is weak and ineffectual at the essential, coal face work of practical vindication of undisputed constitutional rights.

Turning, then, to some of the key areas of concern arising from the ambiguities of the Constitution itself and judicial interpretation of it, I will briefly discuss emergency powers, the system of petitions, and the question of the refusal of bail as a form of preventative detention as defined by the amendment to the Constitution, passed by referendum in November 1996.

THE OFFENCES AGAINST THE STATE ACT 1939

Broadly speaking it is the area of emergency powers, special criminal courts, and special criminal procedures that gives most direct cause for concern with respect to civil liberties today in Ireland.[20] In 1937, Ireland was a young nation led by Eamon de Valera, the chief framer of the Constitution, who was himself a former rebel against the "legitimate" government of the country and a former active protagonist in a bitter and bloody civil war. It is perhaps not surprising that de Valera would have been sensitive to the dangers of armed rebellion and would, in his Constitution, have made provision for the suspension of normal civil rights in

---

[16] Unfortunately, at the expiry of the eighteen months period in February 2001, only eleven, out of over a hundred garda stations requiring them, had the necessary facilities installed

[17] See White J.P.M. (2000), "The Confessional State – Police Interrogation in the Irish Republic: Parts I and II, *Irish Criminal Law Journal* 10, 1,17-20 and 10, 2, 2-6

[18] European Committee for the Prevention of Torture and Inhuman or Degrading Treatment or Punishment, *Report on Irish Places of Detention*, December 1995, Strasbourg: Council of Europe

[19] *Report of the Committee of Enquiry into the Penal System* (Dublin, Stationery Office, 1985). More recently, a recommendation for a part-time, independent Inspector of Prisons was made in the Department of Justice paper, *Towards an Independent Prisons Board* (Dublin, Stationery Office, 1997)

[20] See generally J. Casey, *Constitutional Law in Ireland* (London, Sweet and Maxwell, 1992), at 149-56; G. Hogan and G. Whyte, *supra* n. at 236-48

the event of active attempts to subvert the Irish government. In any event, such emergency provisions for the suspension of normal constitutional safeguards in a time of war or armed rebellion are normal features of most Constitutions. However, the relative ease with which the normal safeguards can be set aside under the 1937 Constitution is, to put it mildly, unfortunate and the way that these special provisions have been used in Ireland gives cause for real concern.

Indeed, there is, in Article 28.3.3 of the Constitution, a power bestowed on the Oireachtas to, in effect, suspend the Constitution itself in a time of national emergency. Such powers were used in 1976 to introduce seven day detention.[21] However, this legislation was only implemented for a year and in practice the most obviously problematical article has been 38.3.1, which allows for the establishment of non-jury special criminal courts, whenever the government deem that the "ordinary courts are inadequate to secure the effective administration of justice, and the preservation of public peace and order".[22]

The present Special Criminal Court was established in 1972 by way of a governmental proclamation under Section 35 of the Offences Against the State Act 1939 and as envisaged by the Constitution. The Offences Against the State Act is part of permanent legislation and has been referred to the Supreme Court and found by it to be consistent with the Constitution.[23] It is, therefore, highly significant that as well as providing an instrument for the setting up of the Special Criminal Court, it provides for the suspension of certain normal legal safeguards in the area of police detention and admissible evidence.

The High Court has struck down as unconstitutional one section of the Act, which provided that anyone convicted before the Special Criminal Court could be barred from public service employment for a seven-year period.[24] However, Section 52 of the Offences Against the State Act, which requires a person to account for his movements, and so is a clear infringement on the right to silence, and Section 12, which permits possession of a pro-IRA poster to be used along with the word of a senior police officer to convict a person of IRA membership, and so breaches the normal precepts of admissible evidence, have both received the seal of approval of the Supreme Court.[25] Challenges to the constitutionality of the Special Criminal Court itself and of the powers of the Director of Public Prosecutions to refer non-subversive offenders to it have failed.

---

[21] See D. Clarke, "Emergency Legislation, Fundamental Rights and Articles 28.3.3" (1977) 12 *Ir Jur* 217)

[22] See M. Robinson, *The Special Criminal Court* (Dublin, Dublin University Press, 1974)

[23] *In re Article 26 and the Emergency Powers Bill 1976* (1977) IR 159; D. Gwynn Morgan, "The Emergency Powers Bill Reference – Part 1" (1978) 13 *Ir Jur* 67 and "The Emergency Powers Bill Re ference – Part II" (1978) 14 *Ir Jur* 253

[24] *Cox v Ireland* (1992) 12 IR 167

[25] *Heaney and McGuiness v Ireland and The Attorney General* (1994) 3 IR 593 (H/Ct); 1 IR 586 (S/Ct) and *O'Leary v The Attorney General* (1993 1 IR 102 (H/Ct); (1995) 1 IR 254 (S/Ct)

Of the special police powers, conferred by the Offences Against the State Act, Section 30, which allows a person to be detained without charge for up to forty-eight hours, is the most important, partly because it is so frequently used. Significantly, this section was upheld by the Supreme Court in 1992 in a case that involved clearly "non-subversive" type offences. Section 30 has come to be used routinely by the gardaí to investigate serious crime generally.[26] It is used in preference to the normal powers of detention for the period subsequent to arrest but before charge, under the Criminal Justice Act 1984, which permits detention for only up to twelve hours and only of persons suspected of having committed an offence that carries a sentence of at least five years imprisonment.

Normal civil rights are clearly curtailed for anyone detained under Section 30 and it is a matter of concern that only a small minority of those detained are actually charged with offences. This suggests that the gardaí may be using these special legal powers routinely in an intimidatory fashion and as a questionable means of collecting criminal intelligence. Between 1975 and 1985, 14,000 people were arrested under Section 30, but only 500 of these were charged and less than 300 were eventually convicted under the Act.

Although the annual number of cases dealt with by the Special Criminal Court has declined dramatically from 286 in 1974 to 29 in 1994, more than 2,000 non-scheduled offences cases have come before the court and non-subversive cases continue to be tried there. For example, in 1993, Fr Patrick Ryan was tried on charges of receiving a stolen caravan and its contents and, in 1994, Rossi Walsh was convicted for arson, despite no evidence of a paramilitary dimension to the crime. In the High Court in 1995, Joseph Kavanagh, apparently an "ordinary, common or garden criminal", who was alleged to have kidnapped Jim Lacey, the chief executive of the Northern Bank, sought an order prohibiting his trial before the Special Criminal Court.[27] This was in effect an attempt to ensure he be granted his constitutional right to trial by jury. This was refused. Laffoy J in the High Court held that the proclamation setting up the Special Criminal Court was not unconstitutional and that the certification by the Director of Public Prosecutions stands even if "the true factual situation is that the alleged offences ... have no subversive or paramilitary connection".

There are three important points to be made here. First, while some provision for special arrangements in a time of war or rebellion is probably necessary and sensible, in Ireland, the use of special powers, most especially the Offences Against the State Act (which does not rely on a state of emergency), has crossed the line between the suspension of normal rights when warranted by extraordinary circumstances and the expedient use of special provisions to establish a quasi-

---

[26] *The People (Director of Public Prosecutions) v Quilligan* (1986) IR 495
[27] *Kavanagh v Ireland* (1996) 1 ILRM 133

permanent, alternative and, potentially, more repressive criminal justice system. A complacent judiciary, political establishment, and general public have become habituated to the presence of the Special Criminal Court and there appears to be no will to abolish it and no sense of urgency about subjecting the rationale for its existence (ie that the ordinary courts are inadequate to secure the effective administration of justice and the preservation of public peace and order) to any form of reality-testing. Indeed, there is some political pressure to extend its operations to cover organised crime and drug dealing and, alarmingly, a majority of the Constitution Review Group, reporting in 1996, supported this view.[28]

However, looking at the level of crime and terrorism in Ireland in recent years, many countries would be astonished at the continued existence of the Special Criminal Court and at the public tolerance of or indifference to the suspension of the fundamental constitutional right to a jury trial (for other than a minor offence). Similarly, the normalisation of special police powers is to be decried, even though it should be noted that many European countries allow similar forty-eight hour detention as a matter of normal police powers. It is to be decried most of all because it compromises the Supreme Court, setting up a system of double standards, whereby the Supreme Court both continues to maintain that the constitutional guarantee of personal liberty means that a person should not be detained for questioning for more than twelve hours and, simultaneously, allows the routine use of forty-eight hour detention at the wide discretion of the police.

Second, while the Special Criminal Court and special powers under the Offences Against the State Act have become a normal, unremarkable part of the criminal justice system, it is clear that the remit of the court has also been broadened by judicial rulings and practice, to include non-scheduled offences and non-subversive offenders. This creeping net-widening is most regrettable and further attentuates the basic constitutional principle of equality before the law.

Third, the continued reliance on special powers has served as a negative model and a kind of bridgehead for the introduction of more repressive "ordinary" legislation. The widespread insensitivity to the seriousness of suspending normal rights on spurious or weak grounds creates an ethos which is conducive to the extension of such alternative arrangements to cover more and more cases. In particular, recent legislation targeting drugs dealers has resurrected the concepts of seven-day detention for interrogation and restrictions on the right to silence and made them applicable to a specific group of non-subversive suspects, thereby

---

[28] *Report of the Constituition Review Group* (Dublin Stationery Office, 1996) at 283. The group recommended that Art. 38.3 be amended to provide that special courts may be established only for a fixed period but they argued that, because of the existence of organised crime in Ireland, changes were appropriate which would allow the use of special courts where it appeared that ordinary courts with trial by jury, were "inadequate to secure the administration of justice"

severely eroding the principles of equality before the law and of the presumption of innocence.[29] Judicial rulings in cases relating to similar provisions in the Offences Against the State Act have meant that this can be done without change to the Constitution and with little fear of legal challenge.

These matters are not just of concern to Irish civil libertarians, since there is growing evidence of international disapproval of the Irish use of the Special Criminal Court and the Offences Agsinst the State Act. Two recent cases could be interpreted as an invitation to the Supreme Court and the legislature to rethink their attitude towards emergency powers and to reinforce the constitutional protections for accused people. In December 2000, the European Court of Human Rights[30] held that a conviction under section 52 of the Offences Against the State Act violated the accused's right to silence and privilege against self-incrimination. On 4 May 2001 the UN Committee on Human Rights ruled that Ireland had in effect violated the right of Joseph Kavanagh to a jury trial. In their judgment it was not sufficient for the Director of Public Prosecutions to simply issue a certificate that Kavanagh could be tried before the Special Criminal Court without also providing reasonable and objective grounds for the decision.

THE PETITIONS SYSTEM

Even the apparently straightforward and reasonable provision in Article 13.6 of the Constitution to grant the right of pardon to the President and to extend it to the Minister for Justice has had highly regrettable consequences for justice in Ireland. This area is a graphic illustration of how the intentions of the Constitution can be distorted when translated into actual practice and how a measure directed at leniency rather than at repression can become a source of inequity and injustice in the system.

Over the years, until the 1994 High Court challenge in *Brennan v. Minister for Justice*,[31] the questionable system of petitions to the Minister for Justice had expanded to such an extent that over 6,000 people per annum were petitioning the minister. The majority of these convicted people were successful in having their fines or even sentences of imprisonment commuted. This clearly amounted to an alternative system of justice firmly under political control. It had become a system for second-guessing and sometimes overturning the legitimate, supposedly independent, judicial process of sentencing. As such it was clearly open to abuse and a potential source of inequity and unfair advantage in a criminal justice system which, according to its own traditional and constitutional principles, should always be totally fair and even-handed. The very fact that some

---

[29] Criminal Justice (Drug Trafficking) Act 1996
[30] *Heaney and McGuinness v Ireland*, unreported ECtHR, 21 December, 2000
[31] Unreported, 28 April, 1995

citizens do not know that you can have your fine reduced by petitioning the Minister for Justice and that others would not demean themselves to make such a petition means that the system must operate unfairly.

The system was also essentially secret. In the District Court, Judge Brennan cited the response to a recent Dáil question on the reduction of fines, in which the Minister for Justice conveyed no information whatsoever except to say, in effect, that no details would be given. The judge said of this: "In other words, a Minister for Justice can do what the minister likes with fines and is not accountable to anyone, not even the Dáil".[32] Because of this secrecy it is impossible to judge the extent to which the system has become not only a source of inequality before the law but a politically motivated system of favoritism. For example, two highly pertinent but unanswered questions are: do the constituents of Ministers for Justice petition more frequently than other citizens? and are the constituents of ministers more frequently successful in their petitions than other people?

In *Brennan*, the High Court expressed considerable disquiet at the petitions system as then operated and held that it should be used more sparingly and only for clearcut humanitarian reasons. However, it felt constrained by the Constitution itself at article 13.6 to conclude that the system was not unconstitutional. As a consequence, the system has continued, if at a much reduced level. Recent figures suggest that petitions are currently running at about a quarter of their former level.[33] This is an improvement but the system remains shrouded in secrecy and to an extent open to abuse.

THE 1996 BAIL REFERENDUM [34]

The bail issue has recently taken on immense importance with respect to the role of the Constitution in civil liberties in Ireland. The referendum of November 1996, passed an amendment allowing for preventative detention. The amendment, which read "Provision may be made by law for the refusal of bail by a court to a person charged with a serious offence where it is reasonably considered necessary to prevent the commission of a serious offence by that person", was passed by a 3 to 1 majority. However, there was a very low turnout of around 30% and so the Constitution was in fact amended by the pro-amendment votes of only 22% of the electorate.

The origins of this referendum were in genuine disquiet about the failings of the bail system, but its motive force was a political belief that here was a surefire proposal that would gain overwhelming popular support and would triumphantly demonstrate the government's determination to be "tough on crime".

---

[32] District Judge Patrick Brennan, quoted in an article in *The Sunday Press,* 16 May, 1993

[33] Minister for Justice Nora Owen in response to a Dáil Question on the petitions system, 30 April, 1997

[34] See Law Reform Commission, *An Examination of the Law of Bail* (Dublin, Stationery Office, 1994) and P. O'Mahony, "The Proposed Constitutional Referendum on Bail: An Unholy Grail?" (1995) 13 ILT 234-39

The proposed amendment was specifically designed to counteract Supreme Court judgements in the *The People (Attorney General) v O'Callaghan*[35] and *Director of Public Prosecutions v Ryan*[36] cases, relating to the Articles in the Constitution which protect the personal freedom of the individual. These judgements concluded that there is an esssential and crucial difference between depriving suspects of freedom by denying them bail in order to ensure that they face justice and depriving them of freedom in order to prevent them from committing crimes while on bail. The latter was seen by the Supreme Court as unacceptable because, in effect, it punishes people for a future offence, of which, in reality, they could never be guilty. In *O'Callaghan*, Chief Justice O'Dalaigh ruled that "The courts owe more than verbal respect to the principle that punishment begins after conviction, and that everyone is deemed to be innocent until tried and duly found guilty".[37] More recently, in *Ryan*, Chief Justice Brian Walsh stated that "The criminalising of mere intention has been usually a badge of an oppressive or unjust system".[38]

This amounts to a vigorous reiteration and defence of the concept of the presumption of innocence. The Supreme Court has, through its rulings, firmly established a right to bail within the "meta-Constitution" and placed severe limits on the grounds on which bail can be refused. In contrast to other countries where preventative refusal of bail of the type envisaged by the amendment has long been in place and also in contrast to the Supreme Court's more tentative positions on other civil liberties issues like the right to silence, this approach represents a highly principled and even purist vindication of the citizen's right to liberty.

In this context the political decision to seek to amend the Constitution must be seen as an extraordinary attack not just on the formerly very liberal Irish bail laws but also on the system by which the Supreme Court acts as the ultimate guardian of our civil liberties. Of course, it is right that the will of the people, expressed in a referendum, should override even the deeply considered opinion of the Supreme Court, but it is extremely disquieting that this can happen on foot of an inadequate and ill-informed public debate fuelled by exaggerated perceptions of the crime problem, by unwarranted expectations of benefit from the proposed changes, and by politicians vying with each other to appear the toughest on crime. The Supreme Court in its rulings was alert to the fact that the presumption of innocence is an essential protection for all citizens but it is likely that many of the voters for the amendment thought that the question of bail is rarely if ever of any relevance to the innocent and that refusal of bail will only ever impact on the guilty. The public

---

[35] (1966) IR 501
[36] (1989) IR 399
[37] *Supra* n. 30, at 509
[38] *Supra* n. 31, at 407

was certainly encouraged in such a narrow and misguided view by the campaigns of the political parties, who resorted to simplistic slogans like "Jail not bail" and "Tougher bail for safer streets".

The Supreme Court, having taken perhaps its most principled civil libertarian stance on the bail issue, now finds itself forced to interpret as best it can a Constitution which allows preventative detention in a potentially wide range of circumstances, yet which, according to its former scrupulously considered view, disallows it as a matter of fundamental principle. The less than harmonious end result must be both an erosion of the fundamental principle of the presumption of innocence and a diminution of the Supreme Court's ability to uphold such fundamental principles. There also results an unfortunate increase in the uncertainty and vagueness surrounding the constitutional provisions for civil liberties and in the general level of tolerance for double-thinking and for parallel standards of justice characterised by ever greater use of discretion. In short, the bail referendum represents a triumph of populist, pragmatic politics and sloganising hardline rhetoric over principled concern for fairness and civil liberties.

There are many other key issues, which have hardly been touched upon, such as police interrogation, tacit forms of plea-bargaining, prisoners' rights and prison conditions, and – perhaps most significant of all – the manifest tendency of the criminal justice system to target certain types of crime (property theft) and certain types of offender (those from socially, educationally, and economically disadvantaged backgrounds) and to largely ignore the undoubtedly fairly widespread crimes of dishonesty and exploitation committed by the privileged and powerful classes. However, the issues that have been discussed do clearly indicate that the 1937 Constitution has been a mixed blessing. It has not always afforded the clear and definitive guidance that one might wish for in this sensitive and vital area. While there has been much progress in terms of the construction of a "meta-Constitution", vindicating important civil rights, the bail amendment and Supreme Court rulings in recent years have muddied the waters and to an extent justify a sense of disillusionment about the role of the Constitution in upholding "just and charitable" criminal justice procedures and institutions.

At a conference in Galway in 1995, Professor Ralph Steinhardt of George Washington University has argued[39] that a slow revolution was proceeding by which the distinction between domestic constitutional law and international law, as exemplified in the Universal Declaration of Human Rights and the European Convention on Human Rights, was increasingly perceived as unworkable and irrelevant. Clearly, the time is now ripe in Ireland, as the government has recently recognised, to give serious consideration to the incorporation within Irish domestic

---

[39] Speaking at a conference entitled "The role of the Judiciary in Liberal Democracies" at University College, Galway in October, 1995

law of the European Convention on Human Rights.[40] In relation to the operation of the criminal justice system, this initiative would provide a lucid, coherent, and easily comprehended set of basic minimum standards, which could be harmonised with the more stringent protections that already exist in certain areas in Irish law.

---

[40] For some discussion of the issues see L. Heffernan (ed.) Human Rights; a European perspective, Dublin, Round Hall Press, 1994, and for an interesting application of European and international instruments to the Irish prisons situation, see Irish Commission for Justice and Peace, Human Rights in Prison, Dublin, Irish Bishops' Commission for Justice and Peace, 1994

5

Reflections on Twenty-Five Years as Ireland's First Director of Public Prosecutions[*]

Eamonn M. Barnes

Undoubtedly the workload of the Director of Public Prosecutions (DPP) has been extraordinarily heavy from its inception in 1975, frequently stretching the resources of the Office almost to breaking point. That stated however, the last quarter century has been extremely stimulating and I would not have missed a day of it, even the very bad ones. It has also of course been an extraordinary honour to have been the state's first DPP and it would be churlish of me to complain about the difficulties or responsibilities of the position. Indeed had it not been complex and demanding it would have been boring and I suspect I would have turned to something else many years ago.

Let me start by saying, without any apology, that I am personally very proud of the record and the quiet achievements of the Office since its inception. I do not make this statement with any sense of self congratulation. The credit is due to the expert and dedicated (and seriously overworked) staff with whom I have been blessed from the start. It has been, I am glad to be able to say, a happy Office and together we have been able to identify the principles necessary for the discharge of our duties and gradually to weld them into a prosecutorial philosophy. It is worth repeating, in an age where suspicion and cynicism are all pervasive, that

---

[*] This chapter was originally an address on 11 March, 1999, to the Law Graduates' Association of the National University of Ireland, Galway

there are thousands of public servants who quietly and conscientiously discharge their duties to the public without seeking any special recognition. I know the calibre and the dedication of the people who work in my former Office and the care which is taken in all sections of it to ensure that justice is done. Many decisions are taken each day, some of which are of great importance to the public and all of which are of great importance to someone directly affected by them. They are never taken lightly.

The beginning is often not a bad point at which to start a story. I was made aware of my appointment as Director of Public Prosecutions on 7 January 1975. The statutory instrument bringing the Prosecution of Offences Act 1974 into operation on 19 January had already been made. I had accordingly twelve days in which to organise a prosecution service, including staff, premises, telephones, stationary and other mundane but essential matters. It was also necessary within that time at least to initiate the functional relationship with the investigative service of the state, the Garda Síochána. In my view the subsequent development of that relationship has been a matter from which both services can justifiably take considerable satisfaction. However some of the consequences of that highly pressurised beginning persist to this day. In particular the inability to identify and establish the structures necessary for the creation of an efficient and cohesive prosecution service before the prosecutorial functions were transferred to the DPP resulted in those structures never being established and in the matter not being addressed at all until recently. While much was, in the event, achieved with the very limited resources which were available, I consider that it was a pity and a great loss to the public that a proper modern prosecution service with adequate structures such as exists in every other common and civil law jurisdiction, whether wealthy or underdeveloped, was not provided from the beginning. I am very glad that the Public Prosecution System Study Group has now been established to make recommendations in this context and that it is currently considering all relevant aspects of this issue. I hope that as a result of the Group's deliberations, a future DPP will be in a position to direct a more cohesive and unified prosecution service than is currently possible. Such a service is no longer a luxury, if indeed it ever could properly have been regarded as such. It is essential to the proper security of the citizen and the community and the effective enforcement of the criminal law.

It may be helpful to put the establishment of the Office in its historical context. The 1960s were years of relative tranquillity in which serious crime was low in the register of public and social concerns. This changed with the 1970s, perhaps partly because of the outbreak of violence in Northern Ireland, perhaps partly for other social reasons not peculiar to Ireland. Whatever the reasons, serious and violent crime rapidly became a feature of our society. This development, together with our accession to the European Communities and the resultant pressures on the resources of the Attorney General, constituted one of the reasons for the creation of a new, separate and independent prosecution authority. The year 1974 had seen, among many atrocities in the island of Ireland, the appalling carnage caused by the Dublin and Monaghan bombs. The Office's first year, 1975, saw the murder of a very brave garda, Michael Reynolds, in St Anne's Park in Raheny and the kidnapping of the prominent Dutch industrialist, Tiede Herrema. The year 1976 saw the murder of the British Ambassador to Ireland. It also saw murders of two young women, one in Wicklow and one in Connemara, for both of which two persons were subsequently convicted. Although these particular events in the first two years of the DPP's Office were exceptionally shocking to the community, they were unfortunately part of a very wide pattern of murders, armed and violent robberies and other serious offences against person and property which were almost commonplace. The Office could hardly have come into existence in more turbulent circumstances. The years since 1975 have seen several more members of the Garda Síochána die in the line of duty, many other outrages such as the murders of Earl Mountbatten and his companions in 1979 and the emergence of new problems for the law enforcement agencies such as the dramatic increase in sexual crime, particularly the sexual abuse of children. As an Office we have rarely had the benefit of periods of calm during which we could consider the broad issues of policy and of standards which would normally be to the forefront of the thinking of public service agencies and particularly of those involved in the administration of justice. Despite the difficulties created by the environment within which we had to develop our service, I think we have succeeded in establishing high standards both of prosecutorial ethics and of efficiency comparable to any I know on the international scene.

I would not wish to create the impression that standards were low before our Office was established. The scope in practice of the functions performed by Attorneys General pre-1975 was somewhat different to that now obtaining, particularly in relation to the division of prosecutorial functions between the Attorney General and the Garda Síochána, but the ethical principles applied by the Office of the Attorney General were, as I personally know, very high indeed. Equally I would not wish to convey the impression that the Garda Síochána, when exercising prosecutorial functions pre-1975, were less than conscientious in seeking to do justice. I will deal with some aspects of this matter in the context of my own former Office but again I am personally aware of the very high standards and concern for justice which have been exercised by the Garda Síochána when prosecuting criminal cases both at that time and since then.

High on our list of priorities in the early period of the Office was the necessity to reinforce and demonstrate the constitutional and statutory independence of the Office. The necessity for that independence, and what must at times have appeared to be our obsession with it, have often been misunderstood. I do not propose to deal here with the subject in any detail. To do so would require a paper devoted entirely to it. I merely state, as I have done many times, that the functional independence of a public prosecutor, like that of a judge, does not exist for its own sake or to boost the importance of the office or office holder. It is necessary, indeed essential, to enable the prosecutor to take decisions in an objective and impartial manner on matters which involve very important issues of justice for those affected by them. In a very real sense the independence of the DPP is of far greater importance to the public than it is to him or her. The necessity for prosecutorial independence is now generally accepted, though not always fully implemented, around the world. The jurisdictions in which it is not fully applied tend to be those in which problems regarding miscarriages of justice and breaches of human rights most often arise.

Another early priority was the need to reject, and be seen to reject, any attempt at political or other inappropriate influence in the discharge of the functions of the office. Section 6 of the Prosecution of Offences Act 1974 proved to be an invaluable aid in this process. I can say that at a very early date the making of representations prohibited by Section 6 ceased to be a problem for the Office. In this connection it may be worth mentioning, because it does not appear to be widely known, that the provisions of Section 6 have been extended to the DPP's functions under Section 2 of the Criminal Justice Act 1993 (appeals against sentences considered by him to have been unduly lenient) and that accordingly the DPP cannot entertain any communication to him made for the purpose of influencing the making of a decision under Section 2, other than communications by one of the persons specified in Section 6. I would be glad if this were more widely known.

Unfortunately Section 6 does not prohibit or discourage attempts to pressurise the Office into prosecuting and some very inappropriate calls are publicly made from time to time either to initiate or to continue particular prosecutions or to increase perceived prosecution rates in relation to particular types of offence. Here the independence of the office is of particular importance. Prosecutorial decisions must of course always be taken on the particular merits of each individual case and on that basis only. To do otherwise would be to risk a dreadful injustice to the persons concerned.

The turbulence which existed when the DPP's Office was established was not confined to criminal activity. It is difficult in 1999 to appreciate fully the jurisprudential revolution which occurred in the 1970s and the 1980s, especially in the area of criminal justice. It started I suppose somewhat earlier with the *People v O'Brien* 1965 IR 142. That was a somewhat unlikely vehicle for major constitutional pronouncements on exclusionary rules and admissibility of evidence. The core of the case was the admissibility or otherwise of evidence relating to stolen goods found in the course of a search of premises pursuant to a search warrant which had contained a typographical error in specifying the address of the premises. The judgement of the Supreme Court, after ranging widely over the common law principles theretofore thought to apply to such situations, homed in on the constitutional considerations involved and promulgated the doctrine that evidence obtained in breach of a constitutional, as opposed to a common law, right of an accused was for virtually all practical purposes absolutely inadmissible. The decision, given at a time when, as I have said, serious crime was not a major problem in the country, had relatively little immediate impact on the criminal justice system other than to engender greater care when typing draft search warrants. Another seminal case however, though reported in the Irish Reports as early as 1930, was then, like Gray's country churchyard flower, blushing unseen and waiting to be rediscovered. It is hard now to comprehend the impact which *Dunne v Clinton* (incidentally a civil action for damages for false imprisonment) had on the investigation, prosecution and trial of offences after it was applied to the legality of a suspect's custody and therefore to his constitutional right to freedom in the course of his trial for capital murder in the mid 1970s. Theretofore, while occasionally the matter might have been debated over hot whiskies by criminal lawyers as a theoretical rather than a practical problem, the general right of the Garda Síochána to "hold" or "detain" a suspect while they pursued their enquiries had not been seriously or generally challenged. The absence of any statutory power of detention for questioning or other investigation (apart from Section 30 of the Offences against the State Act 1939 or, briefly, Section 2 of the Emergency Powers Act 1976, neither of which applied to criminal offences generally) while often commented upon by prosecution lawyers and by gardaí, had not up to then constituted in practice a major obstacle to the successful investigation of crime. This changed dramatically in the late 1970s. The situation was reasonably well covered by the 1939 Act as far as crimes involving firearms or explosives were concerned, although doubts were from time to time voiced as to the applicability of Section 30 to non-subversive crime. Indeed it was held by the Central Criminal Court (*People v Quilligan*) that it did not so apply. Exercising a hard won prosecution right of appeal to which I will refer later, the DPP appealed that decision to the Supreme Court, which reversed the decision of the Central Criminal Court (1986 IR 495). As far as all crimes other than those scheduled under the 1939 Act were concerned – virtually the entire spectrum of crime including murder unless the crime involved the use of a firearm or explosive or, until repealed, malicious damage under the Malicious Damage Act 1861 – there was frequently no power of arrest and never a power of detention until the enactment of the Criminal Justice Act 1984. Even that measure, extremely limited though it is by international standards in relation to powers of detention and detailed though it is in its provision of safeguards for persons in detention, encountered considerable opposition to its enactment and did not become law until several years after the necessity for it had become pressing and obvious. A graphic example of the difficulties encountered by my Office, and by the Garda Síochaná, arising from the absence of a general power of detention is to be found in the *People v Shaw* 1982 IR 1, a prosecution arising out of the Connemara murder to which I have already referred. At least in that case it proved possible to prosecute and ultimately to have the conviction upheld in two appeal courts, though it must be said with the utmost difficulty. In very many others we were unable either to initiate prosecutions or, where we could prosecute, to obtain convictions.

The principles in the *O'Brien* case were developed over the ensuing decades in a great number of decisions of the Superior Courts. I should stress that I am not in any way criticising any of the judgements in the cases to which I have referred or to which I will now refer. Indeed given the *ratio decidendi* the *O'Brien* case, there was a logical inevitability to what followed. That *ratio* owed more to the United States Constitution and the jurisprudence in relation to constitutional rights developed in that country than it did to the common law tradition in these islands. That the courts here would look for persuasive precedents to a country having a written Constitution rather than to jurisdictions not so endowed is not surprising. Whether one agrees with that approach or not, whether one accepts the underlying principle of *O'Brien* or not and whether the consequences of applying rigidly that principle were foreseen or not is at this stage entirely irrelevant. The constitutional principles involved are now well settled and would require a constitutional amendment to alter them.

I list the following cases as representative of the decisions which flowed from the *O'Brien* case (and in some cases from *Dunne v Clinton*) and which were given by the superior courts during the period since my Office was established.

People (DPP) v Madden 1977 IR 336
People (DPP) v Farrell 1978 IR 13
People (DPP) v O'Loughlin 1979 IR 85
People (DPP) v Walsh 1980 IR 294
People (DPP) v Lynch 1982 IR 64
People (DPP) v Conroy 1986 IR 460
People (DPP) v Byrne 1987 IR 364
People (DPP) v Healy 1990 2 IR 73
People (DPP) v Boylan 1991 1 IR 472
People (DPP) v Connell 1995 1 IR 244

Each of these cases was of importance for our criminal justice system. Some, such as *Madden, Farrell, Lynch, Byrne* and *Healy* could properly be described as milestone cases on the jurisprudential road since 1975. Perhaps *Healy* in particular, which established the constitutional nature of the right of access to legal advice and assistance when in custody and held that a denial of that right invalidated an otherwise lawful detention, stands out as being particularly important. Each of those cases required a great investment of time and resources by my Office. All of them show a clear commitment by the courts to protecting and vindicating the legal and constitutional rights of persons suspected of serious crime.

In the *People (DPP) v O'Shea* 1982 IR 384, my Office achieved what we regarded as being and what briefly proved to be a most valuable judgement by the Supreme Court. In essence it was that the People had a right of appeal to the Supreme Court under Article 34.4.3 of the Constitution from a decision of the Central Criminal Court acquitting a defendant. We worked very hard indeed to secure that judgement. We did so not with a view to appealing any jury verdict, however much we might disagree with it, rendered after a properly conducted trial in which all admissible evidence was placed before the jury. In fact no such appeal was ever brought. The right of appeal was seen by us as important mainly to enable the Supreme Court to decide important questions of law on which a ruling considered to be erroneous in law had been rendered by the trial judge and which, in the absence of an appeal, would remain binding on lower courts and persuasive in the Central Criminal Court. The case of *Quilligan* to which I have referred was an excellent example of the importance of the right. Without it the only possible remedy would have been legislation. Inexplicably, and without consultation with my Office, the Supreme Court decision in *O'Shea* was effectively reversed by Section 11 of the Criminal Procedure Act 1993 which in fact went farther and abolished the right of appeal which lay, independently of *O'Shea*, against awards of costs following criminal trials in the Central Criminal Court. I have to say respectfully that the summary abolition of this hard-won right was seriously mistaken. It was a most valuable right designed and intended to give access to the Supreme Court only on rulings of law. I got the impression that the *O'Shea* ruling was opposed by certain ultra conservative legal persons who felt the fabric of civilisation would shatter if the slightest exception were to be made or appear to be made to the rule of double jeopardy. I suggest this view is erroneous in a number of respects. First, a major exception to *non bis in idem* has existed since 1857. Section 2 of the Summary Jurisdiction Act of that year, as extended by Section 51 of the Courts (Supplemental Provisions) Act of 1961, enables prosecution appeals against acquittals in cases of summary jurisdiction to be taken by way of case stated and it has long been settled that the jurisdiction of the superior courts to set aside a verdict of acquittal and remit for further trial extends to the issue of whether or not the prosecution evidence had warranted a conviction. Secondly it was never contended that the right of appeal contested for in *O'Shea* would extend to an appeal on the merits of a jury acquittal. The parameters of the right of appeal pronounced in *O'Shea* are very clearly stated in the judgements of O'Higgins CJ and Walsh J. Until the right was abolished, my Office adhered rigidly to those parameters. Some very valuable statements of law

were as a result obtained from the Supreme Court, not all of them by the way
favourable to the contentions made by the prosecution. I believe of course that both
as a matter of individual justice and of finality and certainty in the administration
of the law, a jury verdict of acquittal arrived at after a trial conducted in due course
of law, including the admission of all properly admissible evidence and accurate
rulings of law by the trial judge, should be final and unchallengeable. I would hold
that view even in relation to suggestions now being made that the discovery
subsequent to an acquittal of incontrovertible evidence of guilt should be a ground
for re-opening the case. But I believe that the proposition that all jury verdicts,
however arrived at, are sacrosanct is untenable. In this connection I would quote
the following words of Walsh J in his judgement in *O'Shea*:

> Jury trial in criminal cases, which is made mandatory by the Constitution save in the
> exceptions provided for, is a most valuable safeguard for the liberties of the citizen.
> It must, therefore, be permitted to operate properly. It would be totally abhorrent if a
> conviction which had been obtained by improper means, such as the corruption or
> coercion of a jury, should be allowed to stand. It should be equally abhorrent if an
> acquittal obtained by the same methods should be allowed to stand. If attempts to
> sway the verdicts of jurors by intimidation or other corrupt means were allowed to
> go unchecked, they could eventually bring about the destruction of the jury system
> of trial. Persons who are tempted to do so would think twice about it if they were
> faced with the possibility that such efforts on their part could negative results which
> they had corruptly achieved. All prosecutions on indictment are, by virtue of the
> Constitution, brought in the name of the people and it is of fundamental importance
> to the people that the mode of trial prescribed by the Constitution should be free to
> operate, and be seen to operate, in a manner in which the law is respected and upheld.
>
> The examples of intimidation and corruption which I have taken are extreme
> examples, but it is necessary to take extreme examples to test the validity of the
> proposition that all acquittals by a jury in the High Court are unimpeachable.

I am strongly of the view that not alone should *O'Shea* have been allowed stand
but that a clear system of prosecution appeals, albeit limited to issues of law,
admissibility of evidence and procedure and possibly including the type of
intimidation and corruption referred to by Walsh J, should be adopted. At present
all appellate rights, apart from the case stated procedure, are vested in the
defendant. I believe more balance in our procedures is required.

In the same context, I believe that there is an unanswerable case for at least one
long overdue change in the system of trial procedure which as a nation we
inherited from our former masters. I refer to the procedure whereby various legal
issues, notably those regarding admissibility of evidence and legality of detention,
are debated at great and often inordinate length in what has become known as a
trial within a trial while a jury is retired, often for very lengthy periods. I believe

all such questions should be judicially determined as preliminary issues before the proceedings involving the jury are commenced. Such determinations should be appealable to an appropriate appellate court, again before the main trial begins. This would be greatly in ease of unfortunate jury persons who under current procedures can have their freedom of movement curtailed for weeks on end and secondly would enable them to concentrate on the evidence in a coherent manner without lengthy interruptions.

I should state that the views I have expressed regarding rights of appeal and trial procedures are not new. They are the product of our experience over the past twenty-four years and during that time have been stated by me on many occasions in various fora. I think the time is now opportune for them to be the subject of full debate and hopefully of action.

I might add that I think that criminal trials are very often inordinately long. There is a strong case to be made for pre-trial conferences or other procedures where non-contentious issues and evidence could be agreed or admitted. Much time and enormous expense is incurred by the necessity to call evidence which without any risk to the interests of justice could be admitted pursuant to Section 21 and 22 of the Criminal Justice Act 1984. It has proved almost totally impossible for some reason to get the co-operation of defence lawyers to the use of those sections which for all practical purposes have remained inoperative since their enactment. The result is, for instance, the necessity for the attendance of often large contingents of gardaí simply to prove the preservation intact of the scene of a crime, and the prolongation of the trial consequent on that attendance. At a time when criminal trial judges are struggling vainly to keep their lists reasonably up to date, this is a matter which requires urgent attention.

There has been much legislative innovation in the areas of the substantive criminal law and of criminal procedure, most of it representing very significant improvement on what had gone before. In this regard very great credit is due to the Law Reform Commission and to the Department of Justice, Equality and Law Reform. The area of criminal activity now most urgently in need of law reform is that of fraud, theft and dishonesty and related offences against property. I am particularly pleased that a Dishonesty Bill dealing with this most difficult and complex area will be processed through the Oireachtas in the very near future. Many relevant offences, notably those involving commercial fraud and financial malpractice, cause immense suffering and damage, often to persons least able to withstand the blow. Until now we have sought to counter such activities under legislation conceived in a very different era. The main statute dealing with most of these matters remains the Larceny Act 1916, the draftsmen whereof were unlikely to have had any conception of the electronic world in which we live and through which those with fraudulent intent and a modest proficiency in automated procedures can roam with impunity. We have been deeply frustrated on many occasions over the past twenty-four years at our inability to prosecute many cases of obvious fraud, very often because there was no criminal offence to match the particular fraudulent activity. That aspect of the problem will I believe largely disappear with the enactment of the Dishonesty Act. It will not however solve all the problems in this area.

We live in an age of tribunals of enquiry. Needless to say I will make no comment on recent or current tribunals or on their remits or work. I would however like to say a few words on the legislative framework within which they conduct their search for truth. I do so in the context of statements, repeated by me many times over the years, that in relation to at least certain types of criminal offence, an inquisitorial system of criminal investigation is much superior to an accusatorial one as a means of ascertaining truth with reasonable certainty. One such type of criminal offence is fraud.

Tribunals of enquiry operating under the Act of 1921 as amended by the Acts of 1979 and 1997 have certain distinctive characteristics, two in particular. The first is that they can compel, on pain of criminal sanctions, the co-operation of any person considered to possess information relevant to the particular tribunal's remit. The second, which is complementary to the first, is that any such person is immune by statute (Section 5 of the 1979 Act) from criminal proceedings arising from his or her evidence to the tribunal other than for knowingly giving false evidence. With these characteristics a tribunal of enquiry is in a very strong position in which to get at the truth. There is I believe a clear message in this for anyone concerned with the efficiency of the criminal process. My former Office has been the target of much criticism for perceived failures to prosecute in cases of fraud. Invariably the failure has been either the lack of an offence to fit the fraud or the inability to compel the evidence necessary to prove an offence.

I would stress that I am not here talking about the right to silence of a suspect. I am talking about the current inability to compel non-suspects, or even minor suspects to whom criminal immunity could be extended, to co-operate in a criminal investigation. This is an inability not widely appreciated by the public. It is often fatal to an investigation. Under our purely accusatorial system, prosecutions based upon a suspicion as to what someone might say or as to what it is hoped the person would say are not permitted. If a witness refuses to co-operate with the gardaí, there is usually little or nothing which can be done about it. Very often the item of evidence involved is simultaneously both innocuous and vital. It may be as simple as establishing from company records a link between a debit in one area and a credit in another. It may nevertheless be an essential proof without which a fraudster cannot even be charged, still less convicted.

I would be in favour of retaining, subject to certain purely procedural changes such as I have suggested above, our current accusatorial and adversarial system for the trial of offences. For criminal investigations however, I believe the case for compellability of witnesses as distinct from suspects is daily becoming more and more obvious. For this purpose I see no necessity whatever for the introduction of any form of examining magistrate. The function could be perfectly well performed by members of the Garda Síochána.

I would like to make a few short and entirely inadequate observations regarding the Garda Síochána. Wearing a hat other than that of DPP I have, particularly in recent years, had the opportunity to observe other criminal justice systems, prosecutorial services and police forces in many countries around the world. I do not think that the Irish people appreciate properly the standard of our police force and of the service which they provide for us. I can assure you that it is second to none in my experience. My Office has to deal at arm's length with the Garda Síochána. That is how it should be. The independence of the Garda Commissioner and his force in the exercise of the investigative function is every bit as important as the prosecutorial independence of my Office. This does not mean that there are not numerous areas of close co-operation between the two functions and in those areas I have and have always had the highest opinion of their expertise and commitment to justice. In the early days of the Office I was asked to supervise the investigation of a very important and sensitive matter. The then commissioner assigned to me a very high powered and expert team. I quickly realised that, while remaining available to offer advice on request, I should not attempt to intervene in the investigation in any way but confine my activities to a prosecutorial judgement on the result. It is a practice we have followed ever since. I am aware that it is not the practice in other countries and that increasingly prosecutors are becoming involved in the investigation. Personally I consider our division of function to be much healthier and in the long run much more efficient.

One matter which has caused public comment from time to time and about which I have never, I think, spoken publicly is what is commonly but very inaccurately called plea-bargaining. In the forms in which it is to be found in other jurisdictions, plea-bargaining does not exist in this country. It may be helpful for me to clarify a few matters which are often the subject of misunderstanding.

First, the practice of the prosecution and defence attending in a judge's chambers to ascertain what sentence would be imposed in the event of a particular plea of guilty being offered and to enter into an agreement about the matter does not happen here. It is quite common in other countries, notably in the United States of America. I believe that if such a practice were to be introduced here, appropriate legislative sanction for it would be at least desirable if not actually essential. Some time ago I discovered that the practice had begun to grow of prosecution counsel accompanying defence counsel to the judge's chamber for the purpose of expressing a view, if asked by the judge, on a sentence which might be imposed. As I felt that in the absence of legislation such a practice was thoroughly undersirable and should be stopped, I issued a circular instruction to that effect. Prosecution counsel are not authorised to enter into any bargain or agreement about sentences and as far as I know they do not now ever do so.

Secondly, the prosecution does not bargain in any real sense of that word with the defence regarding the offer or acceptance of a plea to a less serious offence. It never solicits such a plea or initiates a bargaining session regarding it.

Thirdly, our firm policy is never to over-charge. Again unlike some other countries, we do not prefer a more serious charge than the evidence warrants in order to secure a plea or conviction to a less serious offence.

Fourthly, it follows that a plea to a less serious offence would not normally be appropriate or generally be accepted in the absence of some material change of circumstance such as the death of an important witness. An exception to this might very occasionally arise if for some humanitarian reason it was decided that the public interest and the interests of justice would be served by acceptance of the less serious plea.

Fifthly, when there is such a material change of circumstance which renders the book of evidence no longer an accurate reflection of the evidence to be led by the prosecution, the defence would be informed and if at that stage a plea to a less serious offence were offered it would be considered, the guiding principle always being the public interest and the interests of justice. Again prosecution counsel should not invite the offer of such a plea.

I would make just one final point. Reform of our criminal law is at a very advanced stage and will shortly be complete. I believe it should now be codified both as to substantive law and criminal procedure. Even after reform it is spread over very many years and statutes. In a system in which ignorance of the law is no excuse, it is inexcusable that it is so inaccessible to members of the public. Even criminal lawyers often have the utmost difficulty in finding and ascertaining it with any confidence or certainty. Countries around the world with much less resources than ours have long since codified their laws. Anyone familiar with the French system will recognise the two little red books, the penal code and the code of criminal procedure, which you can slip into your jacket pocket. As a matter of social justice, I think the Irish public is entitled to an accessible code in which they can easily ascertain their potential liabilities. The Irish criminal lawyer is entitled to no less. It could I believe be done relatively easily and quickly.

SECTION 2

THE PHENOMENON OF CRIME

6

Introduction

Paul O'Mahony

THE DARK FIGURE OF CRIME, INVISIBLE CRIME AND POLICE-DEFINED CRIME

It is difficult to give a comprehensive and accurate account of the nature, prevalence and seriousness of crime in Ireland. The difficulty stems in part from the inadequacy and inconsistency of official statistics on crime and from the existence of the "dark figure" of crime, that is the immense amount of crime that escapes official notice, either because it is not reported to the police or because it is reported but not officially recorded. But a complete picture of crime is also elusive because of common misrepresentations of the reality of crime and because of conflicting views of what is to be counted as criminal.

Victimisation studies in Britain (eg Mayhew et al 1994) and Ireland (O'Connell and Whelan 1994; Central Statistics Office 1999) have provided useful evidence on the disparity between official crime figures and the reality of crime. Studies have compared large representative samples of victims' accounts of crimes they have experienced with official figures for those crimes. The comparison indicates that, in the case of certain offences, such as vandalism and sexual assault, only a minority of instances are reported to the police and, in the case of others, such as theft from the person or robbery, about as many of the instances actually reported to the police go unrecorded by them as are recorded.

With some crucial exceptions, such as sexual assault and certain types of white-collar crime, the more clearcut, certain and intrinsically harmful the offence, the more likely it is to be both reported and recorded. So, almost all homicides are both reported and recorded. However, according to Mayhew et al's figures, while 95% of actual motor thefts identified by victims in the British

Crime Survey were reported to and recorded by the police, only 29% of attempted motor thefts were eventually officially recorded, whether reported or not. It is reasonable to conclude that, for a variety of reasons, victims frequently lack sufficient incentive to report certain types of crime and that the police exercise considerable discretion when deciding whether or not to record certain types of crime reported to them.

The area of drug offences provides a telling example of the importance of police "discovery" of crime, especially so-called victimless crime, which lacks a complainant. Discovery in this sense extends beyond the failure to record reported offences into the areas of discretionary failure to target or lack of capacity to target large numbers of crimes that certainly occur. Speeding offences are another clearcut example of essentially police defined offences, since it is obvious that only a small minority of such offences come to official attention.

The number of drug offence charges has increased exponentially over recent decades in Ireland. In 1965, there were only two such charges, undoubtedly reflecting the lack of a serious street drugs problem. But, at the height of the original heroin epidemic in 1983, there were just over 2,000 drugs charges, the vast majority of which related to cannabis. In 1993 there were a little over 4,000 drugs charges and, in 1999, 7,137. More than 4,000 of the 1999 figures related to cannabis and more than 1,000 to ecstasy, but only 887 to heroin. This breakdown of charges by drug type is extraordinary given that research (Comiskey 1998) indicates that perhaps as many as 13,000 people in Dublin have a heroin habit and given that heroin is the most serious drug of abuse in Ireland because of its multiple linkages with crime and because of the intrinsic dangers of the drug and of its most common mode of use, intravenous injection. Since possession of heroin is a criminal offence, it is manifestly obvious that different garda policies and practices, targeting heroin possession and use, could lead to the "discovery" of drug offences in numbers that would have a very significant impact on annual crime figures.

But the term the "dark figure" of crime also refers to "invisible" forms of crime that are customarily ignored by the criminal justice system or are, for the most part, successfully hidden by perpetrators. "Invisible" crime encompasses certain types of financial, so-called white-collar crime, occupational crime and corporate crime. The category also includes types of crime that are currently gaining in visibility yet remain largely unreported, such as domestic violence, pollution and degradation of the environment and child sex abuse. More people have been convicted of these kinds of crime in recent years and public awareness of them has risen but, because of their inherent secrecy, many occurrences still go unnoticed by the criminal justice system. The widespread existence of these types of crime, which can be very serious and extremely damaging, and their relative absence from official figures and from the conventional discourse on crime complicates the picture of crime immeasurably.

Defining what is criminal: legality, morality and intention

Beyond these concerns about the "dark figure" of crime, including "invisible" crime, lies the equally challenging, definitional problem of what conduct is to be judged criminal and by what criteria. Much of the discourse on crime simply evades these difficult philosophical issues, instead assuming the existence of an entirely unproblematic social consensus about what is criminal. However, there are often very real ambiguities surrounding the definition of actions as criminal and genuine difficulties in drawing distinctions between the criminal, the immoral, the anti-social, and the merely undesirable or unfortunate.

Lying is a good example of a complex behaviour that, depending on the circumstances and motives of the lier, can be deemed variously as benevolent, necessary, courteous, expedient, immoral, harmful or frankly criminal. Magicians use deception to intrigue and entertain, three card tricksters and other conmen use deception to criminally deprive the gullible of their money. One can deceive by omission, that is by withholding information or by wilful equivocation; the phrase "economical with the truth" points to a popular political method for misleading without committing an obvious lie. On the other hand, lying under oath during a criminal trial is legally defined as perjury and is a clearcut, punishable criminal offence. Many behaviours that are generally regarded as immoral or harmful, such as marital infidelity, bullying or excessive use of alcohol, are not normally in the Irish system categorised as criminal.

But even in the case of actions, such as homicide or theft, which are almost always unambiguously classed as criminal, the detailed context of an action and the state of mind of the actor can in some significant ways alter the definition of the act as a crime. In the Latin terminology of the law, the key distinction is between the *actus reus* and the *mens rea*, ie the concrete wrongful act and the guilty mind of the perpetrator. In the trial process, the freedom of the actor to choose, which can be influenced by factors such as mistake, accident, provocation, duress and automatism, and the intentions of the actor are often crucial to the perpetrator's legal defence. If it can be shown that the perpetrator lacked an understanding of right and wrong or acted involuntarily, then he or she can be acquitted at trial and fully exonerated of blame for the "criminal" act. In other words, the criminality of an event, at least as far as the perpetrator's role is concerned, does not only reside in the concrete facts of the event. The questions of moral responsibility and degree of culpability as well as the question of guilt – that is whether the accused was in actual fact the perpetrator of the prohibited action – are matters for active dispute in the criminal courts. Possible reasons for mitigation of punishment, which normally also relate to factors deemed to lessen culpability, can be raised at the sentencing stage.

THE AGE OF CRIMINAL RESPONSIBILITY AND OTHER FORMS OF EXCUSING CRIME

Most importantly, the offences of children and the mentally disturbed are treated as special cases. In 2001 the Irish legislature raised the age of criminal responsibility from seven to twelve years by way of the Children Act. A child below twelve will now be considered not capable of crime and even the obviously criminal acts he or she commits will, in one meaningful legal sense, be deemed not crimes. People with manifestly limited intellectual capacity or with serious psychiatric illness can also be treated by the law as if they were children and incapable of criminal responsibility. These exceptions are sensible and pragmatic, insofar as they merely pay due regard to the maturational process in children, the retarded development of the learning disabled, and the effects of thought-disordering mental illness. Ordinary adult levels of understanding, judgement, intellectual skill and self-control cannot be expected of children, the learning disabled and the psychotically ill. Crimes committed by children, the insane and those acting without *mens rea* will still appear in official statistics and the damage they inflict on victims is, obviously, unchanged by their eventual legal status. However, these crimes are in a special category; they are essentially crimes without a guilty perpetrator and might be regarded as tragic mishaps rather than crimes in the fullest sense. Doolan (1991), for example, states "insanity exempts from criminal responsibility a person who commits an act which otherwise would be criminal".

This already convoluted picture is further complicated by the existence of certain categories of crime which are dealt with under the principle of strict liability. With respect to a wide range of offences, usually relatively minor offences punishable by fine, the law does not concern itself with issues of intent or gradations of moral responsibility. For these offences, the mere fact of guilt, that is proven authorship of the offending action, is sufficient cause for punishment. For example, in a case of drunk-driving or speeding it is irrelevant to the criminality of the act and to the process of punishment how or why the guilty person came to be drunk-driving or speeding and what they might have intended. Ignorance of the law is also irrelevant in these cases and does not excuse the perpetrator.

It is clear,then, that purely positivistic, legal definitions of crime, such as that crime is an act or omission punishable by law, are in the final analysis unsatisfactorily simplistic. Such definitions do not capture the many complexities and subtleties that govern interpretation and decision-making in this area. Can a crime that cannot have a guilty perpetrator be truly regarded as a crime? In Britain, the age of criminal responsibility is ten and in the Bulger child-killing case the perpetrators, Thompson and Venables, were, at age ten, effectively prosecuted for murder as if they were adults. If the two boys had been a few months younger, they could not have been prosecuted because they would have been deemed entirely incapable of crime by the law. The age of criminal responsibility in Ireland has just been raised to twelve and other European countries set the age of criminal responsibility at fourteen or sixteen years. Since an enormous proportion of offending can be attributed to teenagers, the implications of the age of criminal responsibility for the discovery or the obscuring of crime are profound and wide-ranging.

THE SOCIAL CONSTRUCTION OF CRIME

A purely legal definition of crime is also unsatisfactory because crime is a social more than a legal construction. Crime undoubtedly existed in primitive societies before the creation of formal legal codes; so, crime is a social reality before it becomes a legal concept. Indeed it is reasonable to conjecture that formal criminal law originated as a means for the social collective to deal with the disruption caused by pre-existing, that is pre-legally defined, forms of crime (Fattah 1997). Rules for making certain forms of conduct punishable follow from rather than give birth to the actual occurrence of that conduct. Crime is not the product of society's creation of law, rather law is the product of society's need to respond to crime. It is, therefore, circular and fatuous, although perhaps essential in the everyday work of the policeman, the judge and the lawyer, to define crime as that behaviour which is outlawed by the criminal law.

Social value systems, including collective patterns of disapproval and tolerance, are continuously shifting. Public attitudes undoubtedly influence the practice of law enforcement agencies and both social attitudes and official practices often anticipate and actively promote change in the criminal law. For example, for many years prior to the decriminalisation of homosexuality in Ireland, laws outlawing homosexual acts by consenting adults remained in place but were rarely enforced. Currently, attitudes to a variety of behaviours are undergoing substantial change. For example, domestic violence is more and more seen as a matter for state intervention by way of the criminal law rather than as an issue of private morality. Similarly, society is moving towards the criminalisation of physical chastisement of children. The physical punishment of schoolchildren, which in the past was regarded by many as a useful and integral element in the socialisation process, is already prohibited. "Invisible" crime is invisible partly because it is well hidden but partly also because of society's failure to look. Some forms of offence such as white-collar financial dishonesty, drunk-driving, tax evasion, sexual crime, and crime against the environment have until recently largely escaped attention because of this reluctance to look and see. In other words, not only do the criminal law and the police take an active role in defining and discovering crime but society in general, and especially powerful elites within it, also make a major contribution to the process.

The relativity of crime definitions between jurisdictions and over time within jurisdictions, which is especially obvious in the wildly varying treatment of psychotropic drugs by different criminal justice systems and in different eras, contradicts universalistic, absolutist notions such as the natural law. There is no Platonic ideal code of behaviour that is or is ever likely to be universally acknowledged and respected by mankind. While, as Bean (1981) states, "the law is an institution designed to give people artificial motives for respecting the interests of others", the law always operates in a specific, concrete socio-cultural context and so varies from place to place and time to time, both in its precepts and in its operation. Criminal law relates to a set of locally approved forms of co-operative behaviour, conformity and self-restraint. These forms are normative and variable, precisely because they are positively and intensively promoted by a society's unique socialisation process. The law is, therefore, always a relative, historical construct, shaped by current, local norms and socio-cultural context.

THE SEPARATE DOMAINS OF MORALITY AND CRIMINAL LAW

There is considerable overlap between the domains of morality and criminal law and, in the past, the criminal law has adopted an unabashed religious moral outlook and has endeavoured to enforce a specific religious moral code. Indeed, even today in some Islamic countries, the criminal law is basically a theocratic system, enforcing a specific religious moral code. In Iran and Afghanistan a woman can be stoned to death for adultery or severely punished for exposing her arms in public.

However, in the West, the criminal law is far more limited in its scope than morality. The criminal law works by prohibiting and punishing defined forms of behaviour, most usually those that threaten property and the personal security of the individual. Morality, on the other hand, is concerned with broad duties and promotes a vision of how we *ought to* live and treat other people. So, the criminal law is highly selective in the "interests of others" that it chooses to protect, whereas morality is all-encompassing, proactive and relentless in its demands.

The criminal law focuses on preventing determinate, harmful actions from happening (although it does this mainly by punishing harmful actions that have actually occurred), whereas morality focuses on positively and endlessly encouraging indeterminate forms of righteous behaviour. For example, the law does not attempt to enforce key moral injunctions, such as "love thy neighbour as thyself".

The present Irish criminal law system is a "mixed economy" reflecting its current secular philosophy, but also its historical roots in a religiously based moralistic view of the law. Recognising the need to construct *ab initio* a criminal code not founded on religious or other moral codes, the Law Reform Commission of Canada (1976) has produced a set of criteria that could possibly serve as the basis for decisions about criminalising specific behaviours:

1   does the act seriously harm other people?
2   does it in some other way so seriously contravene our fundamental values as to be harmful to society?
3   are we confident that the enforcement measures necessary for using criminal law against the act will not themselves seriously contravene our fundamental values?
4   given that we can answer yes to the previous three questions, are we satisfied that criminal law can make a significant contribution in dealing with the problem?

The Law Reform Commission of Canada clearly contends that harm should be the primary criterion for criminalisation, either serious harm to others or, in the case of seemingly victimless personal behaviour, such as drug-taking, harm to the fabric of society. But it also believes that the criminal legal approach should be minimalist and that society should avoid criminalising behaviours when that approach would have little impact in terms of preventing those behaviours or may damage other important rights and freedoms.

These criteria provide a non-moralistic rationale for defining crime within a framework that recognises the need to balance preventing and punishing harm to others and society with the maximal maintenance of personal freedoms and human rights, such as privacy. This approach is beneficial because it acknowledges the arbitrary nature of morality-based legal systems and the immense diversity of moral codes to which people sincerely adhere. The legitimacy of the criminal law is open to serious challenge, if the law is founded on a particular moral code and thereby tends to devalue all other codes. The Canadian approach, by focusing on the relatively concrete issue of harm, seeks a consensus that will transcend differences in moral outlook without offending followers of any particular moral code. It seeks to identify a basic core of behaviours that should be prevented by state intervention and state punishment.

However, this approach is by no means the ultimate solution to the many difficulties surrounding the definition of crime. The Canadian criteria offer no direct guidance on the tricky questions of criminal responsibility, on when perpetrators should be excused and found not deserving of punishment. The concept of what is serious harm is itself problematic, contestable and susceptible to gradual evolution as popular attitudes, values and conventional practices change. The adoption of the Canadian framework is not likely to eliminate the problem of "invisible" crime, nor to clarify the ambiguities and ambivalences surrounding it, especially the collusive failure of society to look and see "invisible" crime. Most importantly, the kind of major moral dilemmas that currently haunt the Irish criminal law, such as the vexed debates about criminalising abortion and decriminalising drug use, would not disappear in a purely harm-based system for defining crime. Arguments would undoubtedly rage on in forms essentially indistinguishable from moral debate. Indeed, it is arguable that it is impossible to talk about what harms are serious and what private behaviours are damaging to society without resorting to the language of morality and without addressing the issue of how things *ought to* be. Indeed, the Canadian criteria admit as much themselves when they make reference to the central importance of society's fundamental values.

EXAGGERATED PERCEPTIONS AS A BARRIER TO UNDERSTANDING CRIME

There are some further formidable barriers to a complete understanding of the nature and extent of crime. These barriers are created by widely prevalent, highly influential social representations of crime. In recent years, skewed media representations, hyperbolic political rhetoric, and consequent excessive fear of crime have taken a dominant role in conditioning the public's understanding of crime. Extravagant representations of crime have also helped mould the practical legal and institutional response to crime, particularly through the political and legislative process. It is always necessary, when discussing crime, to be alert to the distinction between the media-generated mirage of crime, however widely publicised and believed, and the lived social reality of crime, however widely ignored. It is necessary to see beyond clichés and stereotypes and to deconstruct and deflate exaggerated, alarmist discourse.

These thorny issues surrounding the understanding of crime, that is the "dark figure" of crime, the valid excusing of crime, the uncertainty and inconstancy of the definition of certain crimes, and the wide credence given to exaggerated representations of the crime situation, mean that it is always essential to carefully qualify any analysis based on the official statistical picture of crime. However, it would be foolish to dismiss the official picture as altogether uninformative or misleading. After all, for some important categories of crime, such as arson, homicide and car theft, official figures are a very accurate reflection of the reality. The frequency of reporting and recording tends to increase in proportion to the seriousness of the offence and to the lack of doubt concerning its occurrence and to lack of ambiguity about its interpretation as a crime. These influences on reporting and recording are fairly consistent across most developed countries and appear to lead to a similar shaping of official crime statistics. It is, therefore, useful to make comparisons of official crime statistics across jurisdictions, when definitions are equivalent or approximately so.

Most crucially, however, the official picture of crime must be treated with respect because it provides a description of the processed "product" of the criminal justice system and its law enforcement agencies. While it is obviously important that there is a great deal of crime that goes unnoticed and unpunished, it is equally important to address what the police, the courts and the prisons do accomplish. It is an informative exercise in its own terms to study the levels of crime that are recorded, detected, prosecuted and punished. It is also useful and generally justifiable to use official statistics in order to track trends in criminal justice over the years.

THE OFFICIAL PICTURE OF CRIME

Accordingly, the most readily available and most important source of information on the nature and extent of crime in Ireland is the Annual Crime Report of the Garda Síochána. This report gives a statistical accounting of indictable, that is more serious, crime, broken down into four main categories of offences: 1) against the person, such as murder, rape, and assault; 2) against property with violence, such as arson, robbery and burglary; 3) against property without violence, such as petty larceny, embezzlement and forgery; and 4) a catch-all category, covering miscellaneous offences such as indecent exposure, misuse of drugs and poaching. The Crime Report chronicles, in less detail, non-indictable, summary offences, which normally number about 500,000 in a year. These offences are police defined, in the sense that they are only recorded if a culprit is caught and proceeded against. The majority of summary offences are Traffic Acts offences, such as speeding, drunken driving and being without insurance. However, the category also covers a large variety of relatively serious criminal offences such as minor assaults, taking a car for the purpose of joy-riding and public order offences.

In 1947, there was a total of 15,000 indictable crimes recorded (429 crimes per 100,000 of population). By 1970, this figure had doubled to a total of 30,000 indictable crimes and the following decades have seen an even more rapid increase in crime. The figures for 1983 were more than 3 times greater than those for 1970. Indeed the increase in indictable crimes in the one year from 1980 to 1981 was greater than the total figure for 1947. In 1995, indictable crime reached an historic peak of 102,000 (2,684 per 100,000 of population), but then declined in each of the following four years, standing at 81,274 in 1999.

However, even the peak official crime figures for Ireland suggest that it is, comparatively speaking, a low crime country. The Irish recorded indictable crime rate per capita (2,200 per 100,000 in 1999) is less than half that for the US (5,060 per 100,000 – FBI 1992) and a less than a quarter of that for both England and Wales (9,620 per 100,000 – Home Office 1995) and Denmark, a similarly sized Northern European country (9,960 per 100,000 – Danish Statistical Abstract 1995). The average rate for the EU countries in 1996 was, at 6350 per 100,000, almost three times the Irish rate. While these particular comparisons are quite reliable because of the broad similarity in the methods of classifying and recording of crime in these countries, there are inevitably definitional and equivalence problems with international comparisons, and inferences that can be drawn are inevitably tentative.

Recorded indictable crime in Ireland is overwhelmingly dominated by property crimes. The largest single category is burglary, which normally accounts for about 30% of all crime.The various kinds of larceny account for about a further 55% of all indictable crime, with larcenies from unattended vehicles the single largest category in this group (12,377 in 1998). Robbery is also a relatively common crime accounting for about 3% of the total, but armed robbery and armed aggravated burglary are comparatively rare and currently decreasing quite significantly, numbering about 481 in 1996, but only 221 in 1998.

The most serious crimes are offences against the person and these are, according to official statistics, relatively rare. In 1998, there were 1,907 such crimes. In that year there were 51 homicides, which is a rate of about 13.7 per million. This represents a recent increase from a fairly constant average of about 9 per million over the previous 20 years. Thus, the Irish homicide rate is currently at about the same level as that in England and Wales (Home Office 1995) but can still be regarded as low by international norms. By comparison, the Italian rate is close to 30 per million (Dooley 1995) and the US rate is about 98 per million (FBI 1992).

Another category of offence against the person that has seen dramatic increases in the level of reported crime is that of rape and other serious sex assaults (Department of Justice 1997). In the 1980s there was an average of about 60 reports of rape per annum and an average of about 160 other serious sex assaults. In 1998, the figures were 292 for rape of females and 687 for other serious sex assaults (79 and 186 per million respectively). This marked increase is thought to be mainly due to: the increased willingness of victims to come forward, report and prosecute cases; changed attitudes of the police and the prosecution service towards such offences; and changed sentencing practice and new legislation governing punishment for sex offences.

Accordingly, given these plausible explanations, there may well have been no real increase in the underlying incidence of serious sex offending. Indeed, consistent with this view, many of the crimes, for which sex offenders have been convicted in recent years, date back many years and in some cases several decades. However, sexual offending is clearly one area where official figures have only a tenuous relationship with the actual prevalence of crime. Information from rape crisis centres, for example, indicates that even the subset of rape victims who report to such centres do not necessarily report to the police. Indeed, only about one third of them do so. The current Irish figures for reported sex crime are, nonetheless, still low by international comparison. For example, in the US there are annually over 400 reported rapes per million of population (FBI 1992) and in England and Wales over 100 per million (Home Office 1995), five times and one and a half times the Irish rate respectively.

CONTEXTUALISING AND INTERPRETING THE FIGURES

A very significant development in Irish criminal justice in the last ten years is the exposure of a hitherto unacknowledged level of child sexual abuse by people in positions of trust, such as parents, clergy, sports coaches and care workers. Revelations in this area, often relating to offences dating back several decades, have led to many trials, convictions and long prison sentences. Public, institutional and criminal justice attitudes have been profoundly influenced by these revelations.

Another major influence on the actual nature and the perception of Irish crime has been the growth of hard drug abuse and its interconnection with crime. Heroin and other hard drug use was almost unknown in Ireland before 1979. However, there are now somewhere between 10,000 and 13,000 heroin addicts in Ireland, who are based mainly in the socially deprived areas of Dublin (Comiskey 1998). A recent study (Keogh 1997) indicated that heroin addicts are responsible for about two-thirds of all indictable crime in Dublin.

The advent of serious levels of drug abuse has impacted on the nature of crime in various ways. Individual addicts, who finance their habit through crime, often tend to be reckless, desperate and indifferent to victims. This has translated into a growth in the violence of crime and in the breaking of previously well-established taboos against victimising the vulnerable. Old people and women have been targeted to an unprecedented degree. Another new phenomenon is robbery using a syringe as a weapon. This involves the direct threat of infection with AIDS or hepatitis, which are rife amongst the drug-using population. In 1996 there were 1,100 such robberies in Dublin (and these were, incidentally, at that time not categorised as offences against the person).

The involvement of organised criminal gangs in the importation and distribution of drugs has also had a major negative effect. These gangs have made huge illegal profits and introduced a climate of violence and intimidation new to the Irish crime scene. In June 1996, one such gang organised the murder of the well-known investigative journalist, Veronica Guerin, who was working to expose their operations. There was a huge public outcry at this killing and it led directly to a period of more resolute policing and intense legislative activity. Most of those involved in the killing had been identified and arrested by 1998 and presently two people are serving life sentences for the murder. However, in the year before Guerin's murder, there were twelve gangland assassinations of criminally involved victims. None of these cases has been solved and there have been about twenty similar cases since.

While current Irish crime rates are not high by international comparison, the Irish public's perception of the crime problem does not by any means reflect this relatively favourable position. Recent changes in the Irish crime scene do undoubtedly justify public concern, but it can be argued that the small size of the

Irish community and its still fairly intimate scale and cohesive character play a powerful role in amplifying the climate of fear and creating exaggerated perceptions of crime. Saturation coverage in the media of gruesome murder cases or ghastly sex crimes resonates throughout Irish society and often provokes an enormous amount of interest and intense emotional reaction in the general public. The fear-mongering tone and selective, frequently sensational emphasis of the media are undoubtedly influential.

In 1983, American criminologist Freda Adler included Ireland in her study of ten nations around the world with particularly low crime rates. She called this study "Nations not obsessed with crime" (Adler 1983). This title now appears ironic since, in recent years, the Irish media and general public have become greatly preoccupied with what they believe to be a severely deteriorating crime situation. The political response to crime, driven by public perceptions of crime, has, arguably, been over-heated and disproportionate. For instance, the 1997 general election campaign made crime the number one issue and the victorious political parties in that election are thought to have gained a considerable advantage at the polls by promising to introduce a "zero tolerance" policy on crime and to almost double available prison places. Many of the recent reforms and much new legislation in the criminal justice area has been inspired by a hardline, "get tough" ideology (Fennell 1993; O'Mahony 1996).

Researchers from Queen's University Belfast (Brewer et al 1997) have shown that the growth of crime since the forties has been very similar in the Republic and Northern Ireland. However, they also show that in the forties and early fifties per capita crime rates were almost identical South and North of the border but that from the sixties on this changed so that crime rates, over most categories and not just terrorist-related crimes, were consistently worse in Northern Ireland. This difference has been maintained to the present day and, on average in recent years, crime rates in the Republic have been about 60% of those in Northern Ireland, including those for non-terrorist homicides.

The International Victimisation Study (Van Dijk et al 1990), which looked at victimisation rates in Western Europe and in other developed nations such as Canada, the US, Australia, and Japan, covered Northern Ireland as a separate jurisdiction but did not include Ireland. According to this well-controlled, systematic scientific survey, Northern Ireland "has been found to have the lowest rate of victimisation of all fourteen participating countries over a range of personal and property offences". This line of evidence strongly suggests that Ireland with about 60% of the crime of Northern Ireland is one of the lowest crime rate countries in the developed world.

Paradoxically, then, two seemingly opposed propositions are true of contemporary Ireland. On the one hand, crime is not out of control in most areas; the extent of crime is seriously exaggerated by occasional media-generated "moral panics"; and the political response to crime is often over-emotive and lacking in reasoned deliberation and any sense of balance or coherence. On the other hand, there has been, over the last thirty years, a severe deterioration both with respect to the quantity and quality of crime in Ireland; people's sense of personal security has been substantially diminished; and there is a new and disturbing awareness of previously hidden crime of a particularly vicious and damaging nature, although much of this, especially in the white-collar area, continues to go unrecorded and unpunished.

REFERENCES

Adler, F. 1983, *Nations not obsessed with crime* Littleton, Colo: Fred B. Rothman

Bean, P. 1981, *Punishment: A Philosophical and Criminological Inquiry,* Oxford; Martin Robertson

Brewer, J, Lockhart B. and Rodgers, P. 1997, *Crime in Ireland : 1945-1995* Oxford: Clarendon Press

Central Statistics Office 1999, *Quaterly National Household Survey: Crime and Victimisation September-November 1998,* Dublin: Stationery Office

Comiskey, C. 1998, *Prevalence estimate of opiate use in Dublin Ireland during 1996,* Dublin: Institute of Technology Tallaght

Doolan B. 1991, *Principles of Irish Law* (3rd ed.,) Dublin : Gill and Macmillan

Dooley, Enda 1995, *Homicide in Ireland 1972-91,* Dublin: Department of Justice

Danish Stastitical Abstract 1995, Copenhagen: Government Publications Office

FBI (Federal Bureau of Investigation) 1992 *Crime in the United States 1991,* Washington DC: US Government Printing Office

Fattah, E. 1997, *Criminology : Past, Present and Future,* New York: St Martin's Press

Fennell, C. 1993, *Crime and Crisis in Ireland: Justice by Illusion,* Cork: Cork University Press

Garda Síochána, *Report on Crime (annually),* Dublin: Garda HQ

Home Office 1995, *Digest 3 Information on the Criminal Justice System in England and Wales,* London: HMSO

Keogh, E. 1997, *Illicit Drug Use and Related Criminal Activity in the Dublin Metropolitan Area,* Dublin: Garda Headquarters

Law Reform Commission of Canada 1976, *Our Criminal Law,* Ottawa: Information Canada

Mayhew P. Mirlees-Black C. and Aye Maung N. 1994 *Trends in Crime: Findings from the 1994 British Crime Survey* London: HMSO

O'Connell, M. and Whelan A. 1994, "Crime Victimisation in Ireland", in *Irish Criminal Law Journal* 4, 1, pp 85-112

O'Mahony, P. 1996, *Criminal Chaos: Seven Crises in Irish Criminal Justice,* Dublin: Round Hall Sweet and Maxwell

Van Dijk, J., Mayhew, P. and Killias, M. 1990, *Experiences of Crime across the World,* Deventer: Kluwer Law

7

Assessment of the Crime Rate in Ireland – Issues and Considerations[*]

Michael O'Connell

IRELAND'S POSITIVE CRIME PROFILE

Crime is often perceived as a shocking, and worsening, problem in Ireland. This is not surprising given the prominent coverage of atypical and extreme offences in the Irish media (see O'Connell 1999). However, it is also known among many commentators that the Garda Síochána *Annual Report on Crime*, the official record of the volume of reported crime, paints a less pessimistic picture of the situation here. For a developed society like Ireland, the levels appear to be less worrying when compared to other EU member countries. McCullagh (1996: 12) noted that while there were some worrying increases in certain types of offences, "Ireland is still a country with a low crime rate" in a European context. O'Mahony (1993) has suggested that the official crime rate compares favourably with our European neighbours and also with the separate jurisdiction of Northern Ireland.

In a detailed analysis, Brewer et al (1997) compare the recorded crime levels of the Republic of Ireland (ROI) and Northern Ireland (NI) and provide more support for the ROI's relatively low crime profile. Using a number of sources for multiple confirmation, the authors were able to conclude that Northern Ireland's crime rate is substantially lower than that of England and Wales, as is shown by comparisons of the official statistics (Chief Constable's Report, Northern Ireland and Crime

---

[*] An earlier version of some of the material covered in this chapter appeared in the *Irish Criminal Law Journal* 10, 2000, 7–11

Statistics, England and Wales) as well as survey data (the Continuous Household Survey, Northern Ireland and the British Crime Survey). A comprehensive cross-national victimisation survey, the 1989 International Crime Survey (reported in Van Dijk et al 1990) included Northern Ireland along with thirteen other juris-dictions in North America and Western Europe. The survey identified Northern Ireland as having the lowest rate of victimisation overall for a combined number of offences and below average on all offences except for theft of cars and motorcycles. The authors compared the levels for NI with the ROI and note that the trajectory of crime growth is similar in both countries but while the rate of increase in crime in the ROI between 1945 and 1995 was five-fold, it was ten-fold in NI (and was about nine-fold in England and Wales). Paradoxically, the rate of growth of crime in an already industrialised and urbanised Northern Ireland began to exceed the growth rate of the ROI as the ROI began to industrialise in the late 1950s, a process that usually leads to a very rapid acceleration in crime rates.

Besides the views of those expert commentators on the situation in the ROI, and the relatively positive comparison of the ROI with NI, another low crime jurisdiction, there are two further reasons for reassurance with regard to the volume of crime in Ireland, at least in terms of official statistics. The first and major reason is the drop in the numbers of indictable offences recorded in very recent years. The year 1995 represented a high point with a count of 102,484 offences (see p 55 of the 1998 Garda Síochana *Annual Report on Crime*, the most recently available at the time of writing) while the 1998 figures had dropped to 85,627 offences, the second lowest level recorded in the previous seventeen years. In Figure 1a below, the annual recorded figures for most of the last two decades are presented. Thus, the comforting downward spiral in frequency in the last few years can be noted.

Figure 1a: recorded indictable crime (1981-1998)

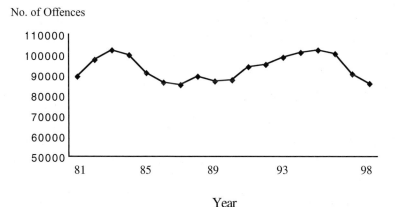

STANDARDISING THE CRIME LEVEL

There is a second positive angle in relation to these crime figures which is that, at least in one way, they overestimate the proportion of offending in Ireland. The reason for this is that the figures are generally presented (in the garda report and elsewhere) as a raw figure, with the annual number of offences for any new year displayed and compared against any other. But this takes no account of demographic changes occurring in Ireland over this time. Year to year, the population change will be minor but over two decades, especially the last two decades, the change is more substantial. The experience of first a sharp recession in Ireland with high levels of emigration followed by an economic boom and substantial immigration from the mid-90s onwards may mean that raw figures are no longer comparable. While it is in no way as misleading as comparing the number of actual offences recorded in two countries with very different populations, nonetheless the differences in the Ireland of 1981 and of 1998 should be controlled for. Just as one might contrast the level of crime in Ireland with that, say, of Denmark by looking at the rate of crime per 100,000 population, temporal changes should also be examined with a standardised rate.

The Central Statistics Office (CSO) provides census figures and annual population estimates. In Figure 1b, the indictable crime rate per annual population is provided (the lower line connected by circles) in contrast to the previous measure, number of offences per annum (the higher line connected by dark diamonds). For ease of comparison, the 1981 measure for both has been fixed at 100 and the subsequent change portrayed relative to that score for both sets. (Appendix 1 displays the three sets of figures used to construct Figure 1b – the CSO census figures or population estimates in 1,000s, the number of indictable offences and the crime level divided by the population for the years 1981-1998).

Figure 1b: two measures of trend in indictable crime

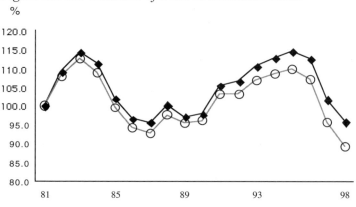

◆ % of 1981 total of recorded crime   ○ % of 1981 total adjusted for population change

As can be seen in Figure 1b, the crime rate reduction is even sharper. Because the population has been slowly increasing since 1981, the lowest crime rate per 1,000 population was recorded in 1998, the year for which the most recent figures are available. Even the high point of 1995 looks less extreme once the somewhat larger population size has been incorporated.

HOMICIDES IN IRELAND

Crime trends are assessed, in the section above, using the rate of offending standardised by population size. But one must have serious reservations about this measure. In the next section below, the major reservation, the accuracy of official statistics, is discussed. However, another issue which needs to be raised is the number of very serious offences contained among the thousands of indictable crimes recorded per annum. Studies examining the ratings that the public attribute to different offences conclude that violent offences are perceived more seriously than property offences (see O'Connell and Whelan 1996 for a discussion of public perceptions of crime seriousness in an Irish context). And at the top of the scale in terms of public concerns is murder. In other words, all crimes are not equal in the eyes of the people (and the courts). If Ireland's overall indictable crime rates were relatively low but the murder rate relatively high, then to describe the society as a low crime one would only be correct in a literalist, not a meaningful way. Indeed, murders in a country like Ireland, with its small population and cultural homogeneity, may create very intense levels of concern since people can empathise with the plight of the victims.

In 1995, Dooley at the Department of Justice in Ireland published a report containing a detailed analysis of the homicide rates in Ireland for the twenty-year period 1972-1991. Specifically, the category of offences analysed was "felonious homicide" and was composed of murder, manslaughter, infanticide and "psychiatric cases" (where the offender was unfit to plead). Dooley carried out a global assessment of the figures for the period. Sensibly, he also included analysis of averages for the five periods of four years in the twenty year span in order to lessen the effect of extreme results in any given year. The average rate of homicides per million was 9.9 in Ireland for that time period. The rate for 1990 was 8 per million. Italy's comparable figure was 27 per million, 21 per million in France and 11 per million in Norway. Dooley concluded that "in the context of figures from other European jurisdictions, it is apparent that Ireland has a lower rate of homicide than all of the other countries surveyed" (p 24). An independent assessment by Wilbanks (1996) also concluded that Ireland's murder rate in the modern era is low relative to other countries as well as to Irish society in the past. However, O'Mahony (1996), while welcoming these studies as a sober and useful response to more hysterical and sensational media accounts of murders, warns against complacency and notes that the rates of murder have increased in very recent years. Dooley provided summary homicide figures for five periods between 1972 and 1991. In Table 1, these figures (standardised to mean per annum) are placed beside the figures of murders and manslaughters (other than traffic fatalities) for the periods 1992-94 and 1995-98.

Table 1: homicide rate (averaged per annum) in Ireland over seven different time periods

Time Period	Homicide Rate
1972 - 1975	34.75
1976 – 1979	31.50
1980 - 1983	34.75
1984 – 1987	34.25
1988 – 1991	32.00
1992 – 1995*	38.75
1995 – 1998*	50.75

* Data for 1999 not available so 1995 data are used in two time periods

The last number of years have seen a worrying increase in the homicide rate, as Table 1 shows, and its impact on public fears should not be underestimated. Interestingly, on p 43 of the Garda Síochána *Report* for 1997, there is a comparative analysis of Ireland's homicide rate for that year along with some other selected countries. While no other country has a lower rate, Ireland now shares its safest position of 12 per million with Belgium. And it is much closer to England and Wales with their level of 13 per million, the same as in 1990.

FLAWS IN OFFICIAL STATISTICS

The analysis so far has relied on official statistics and the relative situation in Ireland with relation to crime can be said to be positive (with some caveats in relation to very recent murder trends). However, at this point, one is obliged to raise questions about the official crime statistics and their reliability as measures of the "real" levels of crime in society. It is not uncommon for researchers to note the potential flaws in official statistics and the pitfalls in relying on them before then going on to use them as "good enough" measures of the underlying phenomenon of crime. To a certain degree, such an approach is inevitable since in the absence of any other data, garda figures clearly represent the best estimate of crime prevalence. But one senses a lingering suspicion that these figures, rather than being a flawed but "good enough" measure of crime, seriously and consistently distort the real level of crime in Ireland. And by distortion, the suggestion is that crime is massively under-represented and the optimistic interpretation from international comparisons is extremely misleading.

In what ways might the official statistics of crime underestimate the actual number of offences? Criminologists have studied the two ways in which this might occur and these are outlined in Lea and Young (1984), O'Mahony (1993) and Walker (1971) and summarised in O'Connell and Whelan (1994). The first is the failure to report and the second is the failure by the police to record. (There are other reasons for a discrepancy – eg in England and Wales, the police must only notify the Home Office of so-called notifiable offences and these exclude offences like common assault – but this situation is relatively minor.) There are many reasons why people might not report being a victim of crime. The offence may be "victimless" (eg drug-use) or the victim may be unaware of being victimised (eg fraud). They may not know that a particular event is criminal (eg physical child abuse) or they may know but never be asked in an appropriate context or by the right person. Victims may regard the offence as too trivial. They may fail to recall that they have been victims of a crime due to injury or intoxication. Alternatively persons may feel that the police will not be able to provide realistic help or may fear reprisal from the offender. Sometimes they themselves may feel implicated in the offence or in certain circumstances the very definition of the offence may make reporting by the victim impossible (eg murder). Therefore, "fluctuations in police crime figures may reflect changes in reporting patterns by the public (and in police surveillance practice) as much as altered social behaviour" (O'Connell and Whelan, 1994: 86). For example, the degree to which the public tolerates anti-social public behaviour and the context in which that behaviour occurs are certainly important predictors of the reporting levels of at least some offences. Similarly, the degree to which victims of certain sex offences may be partially blamed and stigmatised by the criminal justice system and the public reveals the link between widespread social attitudes and reported crime.

Even if a crime is reported, it may not be recorded by the police. They may deem it to be a falsification, or it may be recorded incorrectly (eg theft as lost property). The police may try to deal with it informally (eg warning the offender) or by conciliation, such as in domestic disputes. The victim may subsequently decide not to press charges and the police in turn may not wish to record this offence. They may also be selective about recording offences involving drunkenness or motor vehicles. Historians have also shown that some police forces have "cuffed"or removed particular offences from their records in order to look more efficient or at other times have exaggerated the volume of crime in order to apply for more resources. Decisions have to be made on the way in which offences are classified and the manner in which a set of acts involving many victims may be labelled as a single offence, or many offences (or both), has serious implications for the recorded crime rate.

In each country, the population has its own tradition in dealing with crime and the police and there are undoubtedly societies with cultures promoting greater levels of reporting. The police force will also have its own style and habits of offence recording. Returning to Ireland's relatively low crime rate, is there any reason for thinking that factors other than the "real" crime level, such as rates of recording and reporting, might be responsible? For example, perhaps the crime situation is so bad and the population so sceptical about the usefulness of reporting any crime that the low crime figures represent an indictment of the criminal justice system and the efficacy of the police? (In economics, the negative correlation of official figures and good news is not unknown, eg increasing levels of forgery are sometimes welcomed as a sign that a currency is actually worth reproducing. In the same way, higher recorded crime figures might represent increased faith in the police.) Is there any way of confirming that Ireland's official figures relating to crime tell the observer something about the actual crime rate rather than the behaviour of the recorders and the beliefs of the victims?

CRIME SURVEYS

Crime surveys are a commonly used tool to obtain estimates of crime prevalence independent of the official police figures. In 1999, the results of a CSO 1998 Quarterly National Household Survey (QNHS) with a crime victimisation module were published and provided an alternative measure of the crime level in Ireland. These data did support suspicions that Irish crime is under-reported. The inconsistencies between the CSO findings and official data will be outlined in greater detail below but it is worth noting that other victimisation surveys in Ireland had reached similar conclusions. Unfortunately because of the dearth of Irish research – so many dragons on the criminological cartogram, to (clumsily) paraphrase Brewer et al 1997 – the few studies available are either now dated or rather small scale. The landmark work was that carried out by the ESRI in 1982-3 (Breen and Rottman 1985) where a sample of 8,902 respondents were asked about their experiences of six offences (burglary, theft of property around a dwelling, vandalism, theft from person, car theft, and theft from inside car). An analysis of the findings suggested that levels of these offences were far in excess of those reported in the official garda statistics. For example, Breen and Rottman estimated that 35,642 burglaries took place while the garda *Report* presented the figure of 16,558 for that year. These differences held for the five other offence categories also. Breen and Rottman's work raised some serious doubts over Ireland's claim to be a relatively low crime society. The results of a smaller survey of a national sample of 1,316 individuals by Irish Marketing Surveys in 1983 tallied with the ESRI data, with corresponding rates of criminal victimisation much greater than those published in the official garda report.

In the mid-1990s, two smaller victimisation studies were carried out. Murphy and Whelan's (1995) work was based on a national sample of 938 respondents and found that 14% of respondents recalled being victimised in the previous three years with higher rates, unsurprisingly, reported in Dublin. The Dublin Crime Survey (DCS), carried out by O'Connell and Whelan (1994), found a similar profile of offence categories reported by their respondents (n = 623) to that recorded in the garda data for Dublin. However there was a disparity in the level of offending, with the DCS recording 170 cases of victimisation per 1,000 population per annum against 49 per 1,000 in the garda statistics for the Dublin metropolitan area. Unfortunately, the comparison may be misleading since the garda figures refer only to indictable offences whereas the DCS recorded all criminal victimisation.

It may be protested anyway that police statistics and crime surveys are too different in their aims and methods to permit meaningful comparisons. Certainly there is scope for arguing that these methods provide separate, or at best complementary, sets of figures. The garda figures are provided on an annual basis while the CSO survey is a one-off measure. Garda data can be broken down into six regions or twenty-four sub-regions and provide an indicator of their workload. Crime surveys on the other hand do not measure crime at the small area level very well and being based on households will exclude crime against institutions as well as commercial and public sector establishments. Crime surveys also provide little or no information about fraud or victimless crimes. Mirrlees-Black et al (1998), Aye Maung (1995) and Lynn (1997) have written very detailed and thorough accounts of the difficulties in comparing crime survey data (with special reference to the now biennial British Crime Survey) with police data. Some of the problems they have noted are as follows:

1) crime surveys, like all surveys, suffer from non-response and non-respondents tend to have slightly lower crime risks

2) police data are a census of all crime recorded while the survey is a sample and subject to sampling error. Estimates are necessarily imprecise and this is a problem especially with relatively rare events

3) surveys tend to undercount crimes where victims and offenders know each other and respondents may wish to protect the offenders or may not think of them as "real" crimes

4) surveys require respondents to recall events and there may be errors in remembering whereby people may think an event happened within the frame of reference when it didn't or vice versa or they may simply forget the event. Overall, Mirrlees-Black et al (1998) suggest that response biases probably work to undercount survey-defined offences

5) surveys will include events perceived by the public as criminal and while police and public views generally coincide, there may be differences in agreement where the moral consensus on the event is weak.

However, while there are serious differences between crime surveys and official data in their method, purpose of collection and identity of collector, this does not mean that all comparison between both sets of figures is impossible. (O'Connell and Whelan (1994) suggested that it is like comparing apples and oranges but on reflection the situation is perhaps more analogous to comparing different types of apples.) Both methods have as one principal aim the desire to measure the extent of certain crimes. The challenge then is to choose the areas where meaningful comparison is possible rather than simply counting the total number of all offences offered by both. The methodology used in the CSO survey acknowledges this and rather than trying to count all offences, it measured the experience of the sample respondents with regard to a number of specific offences or comparable subset. The specific set of offences were either at the household level – household burglaries, car thefts, thefts from cars, vandalism – or at the individual level – personal thefts with violence and personal thefts without violence and physical assaults.

THE CSO NATIONAL HOUSEHOLD SURVEY

The National Household Survey collects information continuously throughout the year. Three thousand households are surveyed each week to give 39,000 households surveyed per quarter. In the quarter September-November 1998, a crime module was included and respondents were asked about crimes against themselves or their household which had taken place in the previous twelve months. A two-stage sample design was used and the 39,000 selected to represent the Irish population. The CSO estimates the number of households in the state as 1,237,400. The multiplier to estimate number of specific offences for household offences therefore is 31.73 (1237400/39000). The questions regarding "Individual" crimes were presumably asked only of the 39,000 respondents and the CSO estimates the number of individuals, eighteen years or older, as 2,686,600 and the multiplier here is 68.89 (2686600/39000).

The experiences of the representative sample were expanded or multiplied to generate estimates of the comparable subset of offences for the entire state. Some commentators (and not the CSO in their summary document) used these numbers in the comparable subset as a basis for commenting on the reliability of the official data. Below, in this paper, this same type of analysis is pursued with each crime in the survey matched to the garda definitions. The barchart in Figure 2 contrasts the estimates made by both systems. The definitions of the descriptions used for offences by the gardaí and the CSO are given in appendix 2. It is clear that an additional problem arises with the fairly archaic definitions and categories inherited by the gardaí which are not necessarily ideal for today's crime profile. (For example, "Other larcenies" reported in the summary section of indictable offences on page 58 of the garda report includes ten separate types of larcenies such as "larceny of copper, lead etc", and more confusing, a section called "other larcenies". A different category "Other – Criminal Damage" includes "killing and maiming cattle" along with "malicious damage to schools" and "other malicious injury to schools" and cattle-maiming/killing only counts for one occurrence – having a separate category in official records for a fairly obscure contemporary offence probably reflects older concerns and events.) The comparisons are then more fuzzy than precise because of definitional differences and ambiguities but by and large should still be broadly valid. For ease of comparison, the CSO estimate for each offence is treated as 100% in Figure 2. (The raw figures are presented in appendix 2.)

Figure 2: comparison of CSO survey estimates (standarised to 100%) with garda figures for seven offences

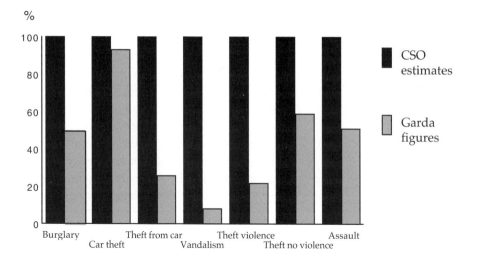

While there appears to be a close correspondence in the number of car thefts recorded by both methods, Figure 2 reveals very large divergences in the crime counts of both methods for other offences (perhaps where the issue of insurance is less salient). Theft from cars, Theft with violence and Vandalism are especially discrepant but Assaults and Burglaries are also quite different. In four of the seven cases, the garda figure is less than half that provided by the CSO and it is only marginally above 50% in two of the remaining three cases. Of course, as was noted above, one important reason for these differences is reporting rates and official statistics underestimate levels of crime because people often do not report their experience of victimisation to the gardaí. The CSO survey asked people, if they had experienced victimisation, whether they had reported it to the gardaí. Figure 3 below shows, along with the previous information on CSO estimates and garda figures of crime, the proportion in the CSO survey who reported their victimisation.

Figure 3: comparison of CSO survey estimates (standarised to 100%) with % victims reporting and garda figures for seven offences

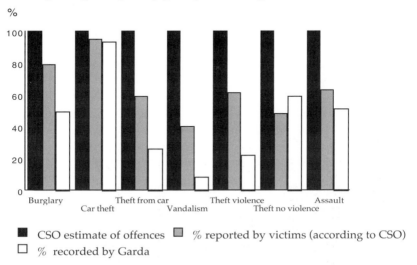

- ■ CSO estimate of offences
- ■ % reported by victims (according to CSO)
- □ % recorded by Garda

The inclusion of reporting rates explains some of the discrepancies especially for Car theft and Theft-no violence as well as Assault to a good degree.

However, there remain substantial gaps between the garda figures and the proportion of respondents who say they did report their crimes.

THE CHALLENGE TO IRELAND'S LOW CRIME STATUS

So is this the real reason for Ireland's low international crime rate? Does a sometimes apathetic and disheartened public unwilling to report an offence conspire and combine with a police force who lose or "cuff" crimes to generate a falsely and overly optimistic picture of the crime pattern in Ireland, relative to other countries? The answer must be in the negative. It is true that the figures presented above do suggest that the official figures do not capture many of the criminal events in our society. But this is true elsewhere and under-reporting and under-recording is not a unique Irish phenomenon. In fact, the studies available suggest that the Irish reporting rate may be higher than elsewhere – Breen and Rottman (1985), O'Connell and Whelan (1994) and Whelan and Murphy (1994) have all suggested Irish reporting rates are generally high in comparison with other European countries.

In order to place the contrast between the survey estimates and the police figures in context, it is important to examine the results of such contrasts elsewhere. The British Crime Survey (BCS) measures crime against people living in private households in England and Wales and has been conducted by the UK Home Office since its first sweep in 1982. The 1998 report measured crime in 1997 and allows comparison of a number of offences with the official police rate. Figure 4a below presents the contrast between the British survey estimate, the proportion who say they reported their victimisation, and the official police figures. (These data are derived from Table 4.1 of Mirrlees-Black et al 1998.)

Figure 4a: comparison of BCS estimates (standarised to 100%) with % victims reporting and police figures for seven offences (1997)

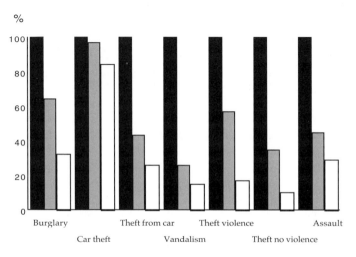

■ BCS estimates of offences ☐ % reported by victims (according to BCS)

☐ % recorded by police

The contrast between official figures and survey estimates is actually greater in the England and Wales data for 1997. For every offence except vandalism, the discrepancy between the measures is smaller, in Ireland's favour, and only with car theft is the reporting rate (marginally) higher for any offence. Figure 4b contrasts the percentages of survey estimates for each of the seven offences that makes its way into the police figures in Ireland (black bar) and Britain (grey bar).

An analysis of Figure 4b suggests that for most offences, the Irish crime figures represent the victimisation rates more accurately (or maybe less inaccurately).

If the patterns in Figure 4b were repeated and Ireland also had a favourable record in terms of recording and reporting its offences relative to other countries, it suggests that international comparisons using official data might in fact be overestimating the rate of crime in Ireland. While there are serious discrepancies between the CSO estimates and the garda figures, the gap is clearly far greater in England and Wales and there is no evidence that Ireland's low level of crime by international standards is an artifact. It might be objected that the concern is ultimately the crime rate in Ireland and that learning that the situation is worse elsewhere is no relief if the crime rate here is truly appalling. That approach firstly does not challenge Ireland's *relatively* good international crime level. And secondly and more importantly, understanding a frequent, complex but also routine phenomenon like crime is an inherently relative task – inevitably, we want to know how things stand compared to last year or ten years ago and also how this country performs relative to elsewhere. To take the figures of any one year in isolation offers us very little way of tracking the changes in society and the efficacy of responding to crime. Maguire (1997: 139) has written about the "predominance of numbers as a descriptive medium" in criminological discourse and the obsession with "volume, extent, growth, prevalence, incidence and trends" of offences, but in reality it is difficult to capture the phenomenon of crime without "painting by numbers".

Figure 4b: comparison of Irish and British police figures as percentages of their respective survey estimates (at 100%) for seven offences

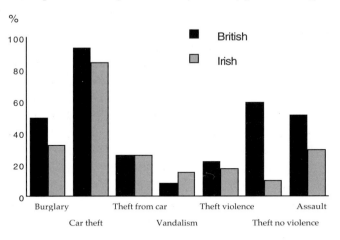

Interpreting the results of crime surveys is clearly complex and many qualifications must be made but the surveys are of great use to the researcher, analyst and policy-maker. Offence-specific comparisons seem the most reasonable way to operate when judging the official figures in the light of survey data but it is clear that the optimal comparison is between one crime survey and another at a different point in time. The BCS now offers tremendous complementarity to observers of crime in Britain, since it allows trends identified in the official figures to be checked against the corresponding crime surveys. This continuity in crime measurement by survey at a national level in Ireland would provide a very useful tool to appraise changes in official rates of crime. However, while they are clearly not independent of one another, it now seems unlikely that identical survey estimates and police figures for an offence will ever arise. The amount of time and energy it takes to "crime" an event or to turn an occurrence, which may be much more ambiguous or complex than expected or which may be perceived by potential reporter or recorder as trivial, into an officially-labelled offence is often too demanding for either, or both, police organisation and victim.

VICTIM SURVEYS

No review of crime assessment would be complete without the inclusion of victim survey data. Unlike crime surveys, victim surveys do not provide estimates of the "dark figure" of crime, the offences which go unreported or unrecorded. While crime surveys seek out the victimisation experiences of as representative a sample of the general public as possible, the respondents of victim surveys all have in common their experience of victimisation. The disadvantage is the loss of comparability to a non-victimised but equivalent group. The advantage however is that victim surveys can provide much more information on the impact of victimisation, on victim characteristics associated with higher levels of risk, on victims' relationship with offenders and their perception of the police. Watson (2000) has analysed these issues around a recent survey of 959 victims of crime in Ireland. A disproportionate stratified random sample was used. Ten crime categories were selected and these varied by property loss plus threat of violence (eg aggravated theft from person), property loss with no violence (eg theft of vehicle), no property loss but with threat of violence (assault) and no property loss and no threat of violence (vandalism). The sample was drawn from garda records of those reporting a crime between November 1994 to October 1995.

Watson found that repeat victimisation was a serious issue in Ireland and that about 80% of the institutions (businesses or organisations) in the survey had been victimised in the previous three years. The phenomenon of multiple victimisation meant that there were less (discrete) victims than incidents – Watson estimates 62 victims per 100 incidents. About one fifth of all victims of recorded crime are institutions in Ireland and about one third of all incidents of victimisation are against institutions – because institutions suffer more multiple victimisations. While crime against individuals shows the expected "Dublin concentration", this discrepancy is lower for crimes against institutions. The "Dublin concentration" was particularly high for violent crime involving theft with 80% of victimisation by aggravated theft and burglary recorded in the capital. About a sixth of the incidents involved some level of violence and threat. Along with its violent side, crime's routine or opportunistic aspect was also visible with three quarters of all incidents occurring in what individuals regarded as their own area. Watson's comparison of victim characteristics with those of the general population (p 103) suggest males are significantly more likely to be victims except for the categories of aggravated theft from person and theft from person where the victim is more likely to be female. Young males are most likely to suffer assault while those aged between 35-49 suffer a disproportionate level of victimisation especially of property offences. In terms of relationship of victim to offender, assault was the only offence category where the victim knew the offender in more than half the cases. Most respondents were satisfied with the immediate garda response to their situation but levels of satisfaction fell when asked about their follow-up activity and feedback provided.

CONCLUDING SUMMARY

The official statistics in Ireland continue to present a positive representation of crime levels, relative to other European countries. This is true of indictable crime generally (where recent years have shown marked progress, especially when population changes are accounted for) as well as for the most serious and fear-provoking offence, that of murder. However, there is evidence of a worrying upturn in murder levels which, while maintaining the Republic of Ireland as one of the lowest safest countries, is drawing it closer to more typical European levels. While it is reasonable to have concern over the accuracy and completeness of official crime data, and crime surveys point to a substantial unrecorded and unreported level of crime, there is no evidence that this proportion is any greater in Ireland than elsewhere. Indeed, a comparison of the results of the British Crime Survey with the recent CSO household survey in Ireland suggests that if anything the recorded data are capturing a greater proportion of crime in this country than in England and Wales. Finally, the reader should be aware of the importance of using surveys to complement official censuses of crime and also to obtain information on victim characteristics and experiences that can inform policy and practice.

REFERENCES

Aye Maung, N. (1995), "Survey design and interpretation of the British Crime Survey", in Walker, M. (ed.), *Interpreting Crime Statistics*, Oxford: Oxford University Press

Breen, R. and Rottman, D. (1985), *Crime Victimisation in the Republic of Ireland*, Dublin: Economic and Social Research Institute, paper no. 121

Brewer, J., Lockhart, B. and Rodgers, P. (1997), *Crime in Ireland 1945-95: Here be Dragons*, Oxford: Clarendon Press

Central Statistics Office (1999), *Quarterly National Household Survey: Crime and Victimisation*, CSO on the Web: *http://www.cso.ie*

Dooley, E. (1995), *Homicide in Ireland 1972-1991*, Dublin: Department of Justice

Garda Síochána, *Annual Report on Crime 1998*, Dublin: Stationery Office

Irish Marketing Surveys Ltd 1983, *The I.M.S. Poll*, Vol. 1, No. 4, April

Lea, J. and Young, J. (1984), *What is to be done about Law and Order?*, Harmondsworth: Penguin

Lynn, P. (1997), *Collecting Data about Non-Respondents to the British Crime Survey*, Report to the Home Office, London: Social and Community Planning Research

Maguire, M. (1997), "Crime statistics, patterns, and trends: Changing perceptions and their implications", in M. Maguire, R. Morgan and R. Reiner, *Oxford Handbook of Criminology* (2nd ed.), Oxford: Clarendon Press

McCullagh, C. (1996), *Crime in Ireland: A Sociological Introduction*, Cork: Cork University Press

Mirrlees-Black, C., Budd, T., Partridge, S. and Mayhew, P. (1998), "The 1998 British Crime Survey", *Home Office Statistical Bulletin*, 21/98

Murphy, M. and Whelan, B. (1994), "Public attitudes to the Gardaí", *Communique: An Garda Síochána Management Journal*, No. 1, pp 15-18

O'Connell, M. (1999), "Is Irish public opinion towards crime distorted by media bias?", *European Journal of Communication*, 14; 191-212

O'Connell, M. and Whelan, A. (1996), "Taking wrongs seriously: Public perceptions of crime seriousness", *British Journal of Criminology*, 36; 299-318.

O'Connell, M. and Whelan, A. (1994), "Crime victimisation in Dublin", *Irish Criminal Law Journal*, 4; 85-112

O'Mahony, P. (1996), *Criminal Chaos: Seven Crises in Irish Criminal Justice*, Dublin: Round Hall, Sweet and Maxwell

O'Mahony, P. (1993), *Crime and Punishment in Ireland*, Dublin: Round Hall Press

Van Dijk, J.J.M., Mayhew, P. and Killias, M. (1990), *Experiences of Crime across the World*, Deventer: Kluwer Law

Walker, N.D. (1971), *Crimes, Courts, and Figures: An Introduction to Criminal Statistics*, Harmondsworth: Penguin

Watson, D. (2000), *Victims of Recorded Crime in Ireland*, Dublin: Oak Tree Press.

Wilbanks, W. (1996), "Homicide in Ireland", *International Journal of Comparative and Applied Criminal Justice*, 20; 14-30

APPENDIX 1 – CENSUS FIGURES AND POPULATION ESTIMATES IN 000S,
NUMBER OF INDICTABLE OFFENCES RECORDED AND NUMBER OF INDICTABLE
OFFENCES/POPULATION IN 000S BY YEAR

Year	Population Estimate (from CSO, in 000s)	Indictable Offences (from Garda Síochána Annual Report)	Indictable Offences/ Population Estimate (000s)
1981	3443.4	89400	25.963
1982	3480.0	97626	28.053
1983	3504.0	102387	29.220
1984	3529.0	99727	28.259
1985	3540.0	91285	25.787
1986	3540.6	86574	24.452
1987	3546.5	85358	24.068
1988	3530.7	89544	25.361
1989	3509.5	86792	24.731
1990	3505.8	87658	25.004
1991	3525.7	94406	26.776
1992	3554.5	95391	26.837
1993	3565.9	98979	27.757
1994	3585.9	101036	28.176
1995	3601.3	102484	28.457
1996	3626.1	100785	27.794
1997	3660.6	90875	24.825
1998	3704.9	85627	23.112

APPENDIX 2 – CSO AND GARDA OFFENCE CATEGORIES

CSO offences 1998		Garda offence categories 1998	
Name	**Estimated Number**	**Name**	**Number**
Burglaries	52900	Burglaries	25730
Car Thefts	16500	Larceny of MPVs	1500
		Unauthorised Taking of MPVs	13793
Thefts from cars	47200	Larceny from unattended vehicles	12377
Vandalism	99000	Other malicious injury to property	7902
Personal thefts with violence	17700	Robbery	1831
		Larceny from persons (muggings)	1986
Personal thefts without violence	30000	Larceny from person	3202
		Other larcenies	14530
Assaults	17200	Assaults – wounding	646
		Assaults (non-indictable)	8077

8

Women and the Criminal Justice System

Ivana Bacik

INTRODUCTION

The subject of women and crime was neglected, or at least relatively neglected, by criminologists until the late twentieth century, but a significant body of research has been generated by feminist criminologists in the last thirty years.[1] In this chapter it is intended to examine the development of theories on women and crime, focusing on women both as offenders and as victims, on sex difference and sex discrimination within criminal justice systems, and on contemporary writing on gender and crime.[2] The small body of literature on women and crime in Ireland will be reviewed in the context of comparative literature.

WOMEN IN THE IRISH CRIMINAL JUSTICE SYSTEM

By way of context, it is useful to provide a statistical overview of women within the Irish criminal justice system. There is great discrepancy between the numbers of men and women who come into contact with the system. For example, in 1996 a total of 5,202 persons were convicted of indictable offences in Ireland; of these,

---

[1] See Heidensohn, F., "Gender and Crime" in Morgan, R. and Reiner, R., *Oxford Handbook of Criminology*. Oxford: OUP, 1997, at p.762

[2] For the purpose of this chapter, "sex" is taken to mean the biological category of "male" or "female", while "gender" refers to the socially constructed characteristics attributed to each sex

only 476, or less than 10%, were women. In 1998, 4,281 indictable convictions were recorded, and women accounted for 553 (12.9%). In the first nine months of 1999, out of 53 convictions of persons for indictable offences against the person, only 4 convictions (7%) were of women. Out of a total of 2,261 convictions for offences against property, 303 (13.4%) were of women. From an overall total of 2,341 convictions for indictable offences in 1999, women offenders accounted for 309 (13%), and their convictions were overwhelmingly for crimes against property (98%). A total of 7,844 juvenile offenders were included in the Garda Juvenile Diversion Programme in 1999, of whom 83% were male and only 17% female; no breakdown by type of offence is provided in respect of this programme.[3]

An analysis of homicide figures in Ireland over the four-year period 1992-96 showed that out of a total of 205 incidents of homicide during that period, the gender of the perpetrator was known in 200 cases. In 180 cases the perpetrator was male, with a female perpetrator in the remaining twenty. Out of the total 205 cases, in 151 (73.7%) the victim was also male, while in the remaining fifty-four (26.3%) of cases, the victim was female. In forty-six cases, a male perpetrator killed a female victim. In fifteen out of the twenty cases committed by women, the victim was male. According to the report, female perpetrators are significantly more likely than males to kill a spouse or family member; female perpetrators killed a spouse in 35% of cases, and in only a single case did a woman kill a stranger. By contrast, male perpetrators killed spouses in 10.2% of cases, and in 26.6% of cases the victim of a male perpetrator was a stranger.[4]

When further statistics on gender of victims are examined, it may be seen that in 45% of the forty-two murders recorded in 1996, the victims were female. Women accounted for 34% of murder victims in 1997, 24% of murder victims in 1998, and 21% in 1999.[5] Three of the nine manslaughter victims recorded in 1999 were female. By contrast, 68% of indictable sexual assault victims in 1999 were female, but of the 218 rapes recorded in 1999, 100% of victims were female. By contrast, men made up 82% of victims of indictable wounding and assault cases. There were 10,110 domestic violence incidents recorded in 1999, which represents an increase of 20% on the previous year; the offenders were overwhelmingly male (92%), and the complainants predominantly female (89%).

Unfortunately, no breakdown by gender is provided in the Garda Annual Reports in respect of most non-indictable offences.[6] The only exception relates to those drugs offences which are prosecuted before the District Court, and of a total

---

[3] *An Garda Síochana Annual Reports 1996-1999*, Dublin: Government Publications. Most figures supplied for 1999 related only to the first nine months of that year, due to a replacement of the Garda crime recording computer system in September 1999

[4] *Homicide in Ireland 1992-96*, Dublin: Government Publications

[5] *An Garda Síochana Annual Report 1999, op. cit.*

[6] that is, those dealt with summarily in the District Court

of 6,022 persons prosecuted before this court for drugs offences in 1999, 542 were female (9%).

In 1999, women therefore represented 13% of those convicted of indictable offences, and 9% of those convicted of drugs offences. However, women make up only 3% of the Irish prison population, indicating that even when convicted, women are less likely to go to prison than men.[7] The apparent anomaly in the treatment of women in sentencing has been the focus of a great deal of research elsewhere.

The statistics also show that the only category of indictable offence for which the proportion of women offenders comes anywhere close to the male figure is the category described as "larceny from shops or stalls" (shoplifting). The 1999 figures show that, out of a total of 367 convictions for shoplifting, 145 of those convicted were women (39.5%). In 1998, women accounted for 256 out of 600 convictions in this category (42.6%), and in 1996, 36.7% of those convicted of this type of larceny were also women. The consistently higher figures for women's participation in shoplifting offences, compared to the exceedingly low figures for female partici-pation in other types of crime, particularly crimes of violence, bears out contemporary research into female offending in other jurisdictions.

WOMEN OFFENDERS: EARLY THEORIES

The invisibility of women offenders within criminological study until the 1960s is typically attributed to the fact that across different legal systems, including Ireland, they universally make up only a very small proportion of all offenders. As Heidensohn writes, "'Women commit much less crime than men do' is a statement that has achieved the status of a truth universally acknowledged."[8] This fact alone should not have rendered women criminals invisible, however. Such a proportionately small and self-contained group of offenders could have been seen instead as offering great potential to criminological research, but this has only been recognised in the last thirty or so years. Before then, women were either ignored by criminologists, or else it was assumed that theories based on studies of male criminality could also explain female participation in crime.

As Dorie Klein[9] writes, women were thus "factored out" of criminology, and those few theorists who did refer to women criminals focused on the biological factors that they believed would turn a woman towards criminal activity. The founder of the Italian school of positivism, Cesare Lombroso, well-known for his

---

[7] Statistics provided by the website of the Irish Prisons Service, www.irishprisons.ie, in November 2001

[8] Heidensohn, F., *ibid.* at p. 764

[9] Klein, D., "The Etiology of Female Crime: a Review of the Literature" in Beirne, P. (ed.), *The Origins and Growth of Criminology*, Aldershot: Dartmouth, 1994

theories of biological determinism, was unusual in that he devoted a whole work to the study of women criminals.[10] In *La Donna Delinquente (The Female Offender)*, he described female criminality as being caused by a biological atavism in women, and argued that women make more ruthless criminals than men because their evil tendencies are more numerous and more varied. These tendencies usually remain latent, but when awakened, produce proportionately more terrible results. Despite the criminogenic characteristics he identified in women, Lombroso had to accept that they had a consistently lower crime rate than men. By way of explanation, he suggested that women had higher rates of undetected crime than men, mostly manifest as sexual crime.

It is notable that while Lombroso's research on male offenders has long been discredited, his work on female criminals still casts a long shadow over studies of women and crime. In particular, his focus on the sexual deviance of women was taken up by other writers, and has remained a dominant theme in this field until relatively recently. Some later variations on Lombroso's theme have similarly emphasised biological considerations as causal factors in female offending. In 1934, the Gluecks used physiological characteristics to explain women's crime,[11] and in 1968, Cowie, Cowie and Slater identified certain physical traits common to girls who had been classified as delinquent, claiming that "bigness" in girls can cause aggression.[12] In more modern instances, pre-menstrual syndrome has been used as an explanation for violent behaviour in women, and the condition known as "battered women's syndrome" has been put forward to explain violent crime perpetrated by women upon their abusive partners.[13]

Just as biological factors have been a dominant theme in research on female criminality, psychological theories too have assumed greater significance in studies of women criminals than in those of men. In the early twentieth century, Freud and others asserted theories based upon the belief that women shared universal psychological traits. Like Lombroso, Freud saw sexuality as the foundation of women's being, and thus the root cause of female criminality.[14] Under the influence of these ideas, prostitution became seen as the "typical female crime", since the view prevailed that women, defined as sexual beings, could only express deviance through their sexuality.

---

[10] Lombroso, C. and Ferrero, W., *The Female Offender*, London: Fischer Unwin, 1895
[11] Glueck, E. and S., *Four Hundred Delinquent Women,* NY: Alfred Knopf, 1934, cited in Klein, D., *op. cit.*, p. 37
[12] Cowie, J., Cowie, V. and Slater, E., *Delinquency in Girls*, London: Heinemann, 1968
[13] See *R v Smith* (1982) *Crim LR* 531 – a case in which pre-menstrual tension was put forward as a defence; and *R v Ahluwalia* [1992] 4 All ER 889 – where battered women's syndrome was used as a defence. For a discussion of the way in which defences in criminal law operate for women, see for example McColgan, A., *Women under the Law*, Harlow: Pearson, 2000, chapter 8
[14] Cited in Klein, D., *op. cit.*, at p. 49

Otto Pollak, in a major work on the criminality of women published in 1950, confirmed Lombroso's view of hidden deviance, arguing that most female crime goes undetected, because of women's inherent physiological capacity for deceit. While men cannot, in Pollak's view, make any pretence about their sexual performance, "Woman's body ... permits such pretence to a certain degree and lack of orgasm does not prevent her ability to participate in the sex act".[15] Much female crime, he suggested, takes the form of sexual deviance or prostitution, hidden from public view by deceitful methods.

Later theorists developed this idea, placed within a social structural framework. Parsons[16] and Cohen[17] asserted that since the focal concern of girls is sexual and marital, women are more likely to violate sexual mores than to express deviance in the more traditionally male delinquent activities. In his analysis of prostitution, Kingsley Davis[18] also argued that women must depend on sex for their social position much more than men. Taking a structural-functionalist perspective, he saw prostitution as a structural necessity whose roots lie in the sexual nature of men and women.

A number of common themes may therefore be identified in the writings of those few criminologists who had actually conducted any research on female offenders prior to the 1960s. Their work for the most part is based upon four assumptions; that women have lower rates of offending than men; that women's (mainly hidden) deviance is essentially different to men's; that women express deviance primarily through sexuality; and that prostitution is thus the typical female crime.

WOMEN OFFENDERS: FEMINIST PERSPECTIVES

A change in approach, and an overturning of these assumptions, came about in the 1960s and onwards, with the emergence of second-wave feminism, and an increased number of women working as practitioners and academics in criminal law and criminology. From a range of different perspectives within feminism, theorists challenged biologically determinist explanations for female offending.

Marie-Andree Bertrand,[19] Frances Heidensohn, and Carol Smart[20] were

---

[15] Pollak, O., *The Criminality of Women*, NY: Barnes, 1950, at pp. 10-11, quoted in Klein, *op. cit.*, at p. 52-3

[16] Parsons, T. and Bales, R., *Family, Socialization and Interaction Process*, Glencoe, Ill: Free Press, 1955

[17] Cohen, A., *Delinquent Boys*, London: Free Press, 1955

[18] Davis, K., "Prostitution", in Merton, R. and Nisbet, R. (eds.), *Contemporary Social Problems*, NY: Harcourt Brace, 1961

[19] Bertrand, M., "Self-image and Delinquency: A Contribution to the Study of Female Criminality and Women's Image" (1969), *Acta Criminologica*

[20] Smart, C., "The New Female Criminal: Reality or Myth?" (1979) 19 *B.J.Crimin.* 50-59

perhaps the first to tackle the question of female offending from a feminist view-point. Heidensohn[21] criticised the relative neglect of this topic, the stereotyped distortions of women criminals, and the tendency to sexualise all female deviance. She and others sought to have women included within empirical studies of crime, and to examine the impact upon women of the criminal law.

Indeed, the early feminist writers all emphasised the need for more empirical work on women's crime, but subsequently feminist approaches to criminology have gone through a series of stages. In her assessment of the development of feminist criminology, Smart[22] uses Harding's conceptual framework, which describes feminist theory as having gone through three conceptual positions: feminist empiricism, standpoint feminism and postmodern feminism.[23] In the first phase, feminist empiricism, the study of female offenders was facilitated in order to fill the gaps in pre-existing knowledge. No challenge to the methodology of criminology was made, so that men could go on studying men as offenders, once they did not make false claims about the universality of this research.

In the second stage of feminist knowledge, however, a different epistemo-logical basis was used – that of experience. Studies using experiential methodology aimed at expressing the experience of, for example, victims of rape and domestic violence. At this stage, the focus of research became the role of the victim within the criminal justice system, and this generated a great deal of change in the law to make it more responsive to women's needs and to the needs of victims of crime generally.

Finally, much feminist theory now takes a postmodernist stance, although Smart disputes the depiction of feminist postmodernism as a "third stage" in the development of feminist criminological theory. She argues that feminist postmodernism does not follow on neatly from earlier theories, but represents a recognition that women do not share a universal experience of oppression or victimhood. It involves a rejection of the concept of any unitary truth or objective knowledge about any knowable or fixed subject "crime", or any identifiable group "women". Theorists in this field now often focus upon discourses or processes, rather than on objects of study. They examine the way in which meanings are constructed through the workings of the criminal law; and how the law acts to en-gender both women's and men's bodies.

Postmodernist theorists often dismiss the early feminist empiricist studies with their modest aim of making up for the omission of women from previous

---

[21] Heidensohn, F., "The Deviance of Women: A Critique and an Enquiry" (1968) 19 *British Journal of Sociology* 160-75

[22] Smart, C., "Feminist Approaches to Criminology, or Postmodern Woman Meets Atavistic Man", in Gelsthorpe, L. and Morris, A. (eds.), *Feminist Perspectives in Criminology*, Bucks: Open University Press, 1990

[23] Harding, S., *Feminism and Methodology*, Milton Keynes: Open University Press, 1987

criminological theory. Indeed, some strange hypotheses emerged from these empirical studies. For example, during the mid-1970s, a thesis that "women's liberation causes women's crime" gained a certain prominence. One proponent of this view, Freda Adler, predicted that as women became more emancipated, they were likely to become more aggressive, more like men, and their crime rates would increase.[24] At the same time, Rita Simon asserted that as women's legitimate opportunities in the workplace expanded, so too would their opportunities to engage in property crime.[25] Both theses were strongly refuted by other writers on a number of grounds and lack credibility now; statistical trends since then have not borne them out.[26]

But aside from the potential for misinterpretation, empirical studies on women and crime provided vitally important information that was to assist greatly in later theoretical development. They confirmed that women's crime rate is lower than that of men's across different societies, and that women's crimes tend to be less serious and in particular less violent than those of men. Importantly, they challenged fundamentally the assertion that prostitution is the "typical female crime" by showing conclusively that the majority of crimes committed by women are crimes against property. The empirical work demonstrated that if any crime can be described as "typically female", it should be shoplifting, not prostitution.[27]

In terms of explaining low rates of female offending, some feminist theorists continued to adhere to the "iceberg" theory; that women's deviance is largely hidden or undetected, or not labelled criminal in the same way as men's behaviour. But socialisation theories also gained prominence, based on the idea that women are more controlled by social norms than men through childhood conditioning, so that criminal sanctions are not required to prevent women from engaging in deviance. Other theories were put forward to explain the differential treatment of those women who do enter the criminal justice system, and these are explored further below.

The work of the feminist empiricists and standpointists undoubtedly made a significant contribution to criminological thought. But Smart, for instance, argues that although feminist theory has revitalised the problematic discipline of criminology, criminology has done nothing for feminism in return.[28] Like her, Heidensohn has also become cynical about the project and purpose of a feminist

---

[24] Adler, F., *Sisters in Crime: The Rise of the New Female Criminal*, NY: McGraw Hill, 1975

[25] Simon, R., *Women and Crime*, Toronto/London: Lexington, 1975

[26] See eg Austin, R., "Liberation and Female Criminality in England and Wales" (1981) 21 *B. J. Crimin* 371-4 and Box, S. and Hale, C., "Liberation and Female Criminality in England and Wales" (1983) 23 *B. J. Crimin* 35-49

[27] See for example Carlen, P., *Women, Crime and Poverty*, Milton Keynes: Open University Press, 1988

[28] Smart, C., *op. cit.* (1990)

criminology. She argues that while feminist criminology used to possess the "falklands factor" (remote, unvisited and ignored), it now suffers from the "shetlands factor"; it has become nearer to the "mainland" of criminological thought than before, but remains more distant than it is presented on maps of the region.[29]

This is a clever notion, but other feminist writers do not subscribe to such a pessimistic view of the future of feminist theory within criminology. Carlen, for example, sees value in the feminist and postmodernist tool of deconstruction. She has not given up on the potential for a "grand theory" like left realism, as advanced by Jock Young, for rescuing criminology.[30] She points out that left realism takes crime seriously, uses empirical strategies and also has a strategy of democratisation. Thus, victims' experiences of crime are taken into account together with a continued adherence to economic causal theories, complementing the feminist project.

A relatively optimistic view of the future is also taken by Maureen Cain, who advocates an approach she calls "transgressive criminology".[31] This is both deconstructive and reconstructive, seeing maleness as well as femaleness in the criminological gaze. Other theorists similarly see hope in applying the postmodernist method to theories of gender, overturning the notion of "women criminals" as a unified category. They see challenge in the recovery of the "fragmented subject" and the adoption of more humble projects in criminology.[32]

In an influential demonstration of the application of postmodernist method, Frug for example discussed the way in which laws contribute to the "gendering" of women's bodies.[33] She argued that the criminal law plays a significant part in the creation and maintenance of gender stereotypes, describing how the law works to "terrorise", "sexualise" and "maternalise" women. Laws on prostitution and on rape, in particular, penalise women who do not conform to a particular mode of dress and a particular type of behaviour. In this way they contribute to

---

[29] Heidensohn, F., "Feminist Perspectives and their Impact on Criminology and Criminal Justice in Britain", in Hahn Rafter, N. and Heidensohn, F. (eds.), *International Feminist Perspectives in Criminology*. Bucks: Open University Press, 1995, at p. 66-7. Heidensohn explains that on maps of Britain, the Shetland islands "are usually represented in a box which separates them and also reduces the distance between them and the rest of the country."

[30] Carlen, P., "Women, Crime, Feminism and Realism", in Naffine, N. (ed.), *Gender, Crime and Feminism*. Aldershot: Dartmouth, 1995. For an account of Young's theory, see Young, J., "Writing on the Cusp of Change: A New Criminology for an Age of Late Modernity", in Taylor, I. and Young, J. (eds.), *The New Criminology Revisited*. Basingstoke: Macmillan, 1998

[31] Cain, M., "Towards Transgression: New Directions in Feminist Criminology", in Naffine, N. (ed.), *ibid.*

[32] See for example, Carrington, K., "Postmodern and Feminist Criminologies: Fragmenting the Criminological Subject", in Taylor, I. and Young, J. (eds.), *The New Criminology Revisited, op. cit.*, at p. 93

[33] Frug, M., "A Postmodern Feminist Legal Manifesto (an unfinished draft)" (1992) *Harvard Law Review* 105

the conceptualisation of "woman" as weak, sexy and nurturing. Frug's work demonstrates the potential of postmodernist methodology for feminist theory, and indeed for criminology.

So new directions in criminology have been opened up with the growing interest in exploring the gendering effect of the law, and the relationship between gender and crime. Particular focus is now placed upon analysing the construction of masculinity, and its potentially criminogenic effect. The original feminist empiricist question has been reversed. Instead of continuing to ask "why do so few women commit crime?", we are beginning to ask "why do so many men commit crime?" As the gendered nature of crime, its "maleness", becomes apparent, male offending can be seen through the prism of gender, just as female offending has always been. A new approach to crime, which analyses the social construction of gender rather focusing upon sex difference, has opened up exciting new possibilities within criminology. As Messerschmidt writes, "Rather than conceptualising gendered crime simplistically in terms of ... 'males commit violence and females commit theft', new directions in feminist theory enable us to explore which males and which females commit which crimes, and in which social situations."[34]

While theories about women and crime have developed through many different stages, in Ireland much basic empirical information about sex difference in the criminal justice system is still lacking. It is therefore important to review comparative literature on differential treatment of women offenders, and to examine the small number of Irish studies in this area, before moving to consider other aspects of the experience of women as offenders and as victims within the criminal justice system.

WOMEN OFFENDERS: DIFFERENTIAL TREATMENT

Those who appear before the courts as offenders in every society are not representative of the general population, but are disproportionately male, young and working-class (and in many societies, disproportionately drawn from ethnic minorities). Studies suggest that discrimination at different stages may contribute to this feature; class bias in the designation of certain conduct as criminal, for example, or bias in the policing and processing of offenders. Such bias is not necessarily seen as intentional or deliberate, but rather as being structurally located within the criminal justice system.

---

[34] Messerschmidt, J., "From Patriarchy to Gender: Feminist Theory, Criminology and the Challenge of Diversity", in Hahn Rafter, N. and Heidensohn, F., *op. cit.*, at p. 185. See also Messerschmidt, J., *Masculinities and Crime*, Maryland: Rowman and Littlefield, 1993; and Collier, R., *Masculinites, Crime and Criminology*, London: Sage, 1998

In order to explain the disproportionate over-representation of men in crime statistics, some studies have focused on gender bias in policing strategies. In one American study, for instance, Chesney-Lind noted that in the treatment of women, a chivalry ethos was sometimes expressed where the police let women off with certain offences.[35] However, this ethos was not found to extend to women from ethnic minorities, with the police more likely to make an arrest of them than of white women. In a British context, Ashworth also found that women were more favourably treated by the police, with a cautioning rate of 46% for adult women in 1993, compared to a 26% cautioning rate for men.[36]

Many more studies have pointed to differential treatment of women at the sentencing stage.[37] Generally, women are shown to be more leniently treated than men for most offences, although research has shown more severe treatment in particular cases. A number of different explanations have been advanced for these findings. The "chivalry" or "paternalism" factor explains more lenient sentencing, positing that judges (mostly male) are simply less willing to lock women up than they are to imprison men, particularly for crimes against property. Conversely, the "evil woman" thesis explains more severe sentencing of women for crimes that are more stereotypically "male" (such as crimes of violence), or where the offender has departed from the social role conventionally expected of women. This is also known as the "double deviance" theory; in being violent, women are transgressing against both the criminal law and the feminine stereotype, and so are doubly punished.

Farrington and Morris offer another explanation for the apparent discrepancy in sentencing between men and women. They found that gender seemed to have little or no independent effect upon sentence, but factors such as marital status, family background and parenthood were given greater consideration in the sentencing of women than of men, leading to differential outcomes. For example, divorced and separated women in their study received relatively more severe sentences than married women.[38]

Eaton's study of practices in an English Magistrate's Court revealed further that the family life of men and women was drawn upon equally as part of the decision-making process in sentencing, but as she pointed out, "By judging both male and female defendants in the context of their families, the court displays not

---

[35] Chesney-Lind, M. and Bowker, L., *Women, Crime and the Criminal Justice System*, US: Lexington, 1978

[36] Ashworth, A., *Sentencing and Criminal Justice*, London: Butterworths, 1995

[37] See, for example, Hedderman, C. and Hough, M., *Does the Criminal Justice System Treat Men and Women Differently?* London: HMSO, 1994 and Moxon, D., *Sentencing Practice in the Crown Court*, London: HMSO, 1988

[38] Farrington, D. and Morris, A., "Sex, Sentencing and Reconviction" (1983) 23 *B. J. Crimin.* 229

only impartiality or equality of treatment, but its role of preserving difference based on sexual inequality".[39]

Fewer studies have focused specifically on the treatment of violent women offenders. Indeed, Motz argues that there is a widespread denial of female violence, partly because it is usually committed in the private or domestic arena; but also due to the continuing idealisation of motherhood.[40] In her research on offenders convicted of filicide (the killing of a child by a parent or parent-substitute), Wilczynski concluded that the English criminal justice system responds differently to mothers who kill their children than to fathers in such a position, at all stages of the legal process.[41] She found that women were less likely to be prosecuted in the first place, but once before the courts were more likely to use "psychiatric" pleas, such as diminished responsibility and infanticide, and to receive psychiatric or non-custodial sentences. Men, on the other hand, were more likely to use "normal" pleas and receive prison sentences.

This confirms Allen's earlier study of the use of psychiatric reports by courts in sentencing, based on the empirical evidence that women are twice as likely as men to be dealt with by the court through the use of psychiatric treatment.[42] Allen's analysis showed that while reports on male defendants focused on their actions, the reports written about women depicted them as passive agents to whom things had just happened. In short, they were not seen as being responsible for their own behaviour.

These findings complement Worrall's thesis that the criminal justice system seeks to make women "treatable", since this neutralises the effect of their criminality and protects the gender stereotypes upon which social order is based.[43] Carlen describes the social stereotypes to which women must conform as the "gender contract".[44] The effect of the contract is that a woman's life must be "represented primarily in terms of its domestic, sexual and pathological dimensions".[45] Thus, if women engage in criminal acts, their behaviour will symbolically breach the contract, unless their deviance can be portrayed as "mad not bad".[46] So deviance

---

[39] Eaton, M., *Justice for Women? Family, Court and Social Control*, Milton Keynes: Open University Press, 1986, at p. 143

[40] Motz, A., *The Psychology of Female Violence: Crimes Against the Body*, Sussex: Brunner Routledge, 2001, p. 4

[41] Wilczynski, A., "Mad or Bad? Child-killers, Gender and the Courts" (1997) 37 *B. J. Crimin.* 419-36

[42] Allen, H., *Justice Unbalanced: Gender, Psychiatry and Judicial Decisions*, Milton Keynes: Open University Press, 1987

[43] Worrall, A., *Offending Women*, London: Routledge, 1990

[44] Carlen, P., *Women, Crime and Poverty, op. cit.*

[45] Worrall, *op. cit,* at p. 35

[46] Worrall, *op. cit,* at p. 35

that may be criminalised in boys or men is often represented as evidence of psychiatric illness, where expressed by girls or women.[47]

However, as Walklate comments, responses by the courts and the sentencing process to male defendants are also gendered. Law enforcers and courts make equally stereotypical assumptions concerning their masculinity, so that men are more likely to be imprisoned for lesser crimes, and less likely to receive medical or psychiatric treatment where they really need it.[48]

In an Irish context, only limited work has been done on differential treatment of men and women in the criminal justice system. In a study of 1979 District Court and Garda larceny records for the Dublin Metropolitan Area, Lyons and Hunt analysed the effects of gender upon sentence.[49] They examined the records relating to 108 women and 120 men, and found that, when other variables were excluded, women were still treated more leniently in 70% of cases. They concluded, like Farrington and Morris, and Eaton, that District Court judges were placing more weight on factors such as marital status, family background and parenthood in the sentencing of women.

A later study conducted by Bacik *et al* into Dublin District Court sentencing practice also showed evidence of differential sentencing practices for men and women.[50] While there was less discrepancy between men and women whose sentences were suspended, or who were sentenced to do community service or to pay fines, a marked variation was noted at each end of the sentencing spectrum. A significantly higher proportion of women received no conviction (62.8% of women as against only 42.8% of men); while only 14.6% of women defendants were sentenced to prison, as against 29% of male offenders.

WOMEN OFFENDERS: PRISON

Where women are sentenced to prison, again they are likely to receive significantly differential treatment to male prisoners. As noted earlier, women make up only 3% of all prisoners in Ireland.[51] This is a particularly low figure for female imprisonment by international standards, although in England and Wales,

---

[47] See for example Ussher, J., *Women's Madness; Misogyny or Mental Illness?* Harvester Wheatsheaf, 1991

[48] Walklate, S., *Gender, Crime and Criminal Justice*, Devon: Willan, 2001

[49] Lyons, A. and Hunt, P., "The Effects of Gender on Sentencing: a Case Study of the Dublin Metropolitan Area District Court", in Tomlinson, M. *et al* (eds.), *Whose Law and Order*, Belfast: Sociological Association of Ireland, 1983

[50] Bacik, I., Kelly, A., O'Connell, M. and Sinclair, H., "Crime and Poverty in Dublin: An Analysis of the Association Between Community Deprivation, District Court Appearance and Sentence Severity", in Bacik and O'Connell (eds.), *Crime and Poverty in Ireland*, Dublin: Round Hall Sweet and Maxwell, 1998

[51] This is approximately 90 prisoners, out of a prison population of 3,000 on any given day in 2001

similarly, women make up only 5% of the prison population.[52] Because very few women's prisons are therefore needed, many women may be held in prisons at considerable distance from their homes and families, and may often be held in secure prisons because no open or semi-open facilities are available. These are just some features that may distinguish the imprisonment of women; others relate to the differential and often more "domestic" conditions that tend to prevail in women's prisons.

In her review of studies on women in prison, Walklate comments that the concessions that are often made to women prisoners in comparison to men may create an "imagery of women's prisons being akin to a boarding-school", but that this comparison is far too superficial.[53] Studies she cites show that women in fact experience imprisonment as a "brutalising process". Women's experience of prison is compounded because they are drawn overwhelmingly from economically disadvantaged communities, have often spent childhood in care, and many have experienced sexual and physical abuse. In addition, they are likely to have significant health problems, both physical and psychological, often exacerbated by drug or alcohol addiction.

Carlen has described how the process of imprisonment renders women disciplined, infantilised, feminised, medicalised, and domesticated.[54] She argues that the social meanings and jurisprudential implications of women's imprisonment are significantly different to those of men, and has long argued for an alternative to imprisonment for women. She has devised a strategy for reducing the imprisonment of women, suggesting that sentencers should have to justify to a sentencing council what they hope to achieve each time they imprison a woman. Ultimately, she argues that it would be possible to release from prison all but a very small number of women serving time for serious violent crime, and to make extensive use of community service and probation groups for women offenders.[55]

Eaton has examined the ways in which women respond to imprisonment, by withdrawal, retaliation, self-mutilation, and in some cases by being drawn or incorporated into the system. While men may respond in similar ways to imprisonment, self-mutilation is a response particularly notable among women prisoners.[56]

There is little contemporary research on women in Irish prisons.[57] While two

---

[52] Figures for 1999 cited in Walklate, S., *Gender, Crime and Criminal Justice, op. cit.*, at p. 169

[53] Walklate, S., *ibid*

[54] Carlen, P. *et al, Criminal Women*, Oxford: Blackwell, 1985

[55] Carlen, P., *Alternatives to Women's Imprisonment*, Buckingham: Open University Press, 1990; *Sledgehammer: Women's Imprisonment at the Millennium*, Basingstoke: Macmillan, 1998

[56] Eaton, M., *Women After Prison*, Buckingham: Open University Press, 1993

[57] There are some historical accounts of women in Irish prisons, eg McCoole, S., *Guns and Chiffon: Women Revolutionaries and Kilmainham Gaol 1916-23*, Dublin: Heritage Service. In 1985, a sociological study comparing Swedish and Irish women prisoners was also published: Lundstrom-Roche, F., *Women in Prison: Ideals and Reals*, Stockholm: University of Stockholm, 1985

major studies of male prisoners in Mountjoy prison have been published,[58] there exists no comparable publication on women's imprisonment here. Some support for the findings produced by studies in other jurisdictions may however be found in a study on the health of women prisoners in Mountjoy conducted by Carmody and McEvoy, two women prison doctors, in 1996. They interviewed 100 women detained in Mountjoy, 26 of whom were between 17-20 years old (average age: 27.6 years), and 75 of whom had been in prison before.[59] The majority of crimes they had committed were theft and drug related offences; only 10 had been committed for offences of violence. They were likely to be from poor social backgrounds in Dublin's inner city, not to be in a relationship, and to have an average of two to three children each.

The focus of the study was on the drug and alcohol use, and health and psychiatric status of the women. The researchers found that 56 of the women were chronic drug users; 13 were known to have the HIV virus (although only half had been tested, so the incidence could have been higher); 49 had a history of psychiatric treatment, and 34 had attempted suicide.

The study also examined the incidence of self-mutilation among the women, finding that 20 had cut themselves at some time, and of that group, 11 had done so while in prison; 16 were drug users, and all but two had been in prison before. The researchers observed some of the women cut themselves to find an emotional release, rather than to express a genuine suicidal intent. The study clearly shows that women prisoners are a most vulnerable group, which possesses many special needs not catered for in the prison at the time.

In her sociological analysis of women in Mountjoy Prison, McCann James examined the forms of management in the prison, finding that the prison regime parallelled and intensified the social structures in Irish society which oppress women.[60] Her research shows that the practices in the prison institutionalised the transfer of social disadvantage from the larger society to the prison society, and served to sustain the oppression of women.

A new women's prison in Dublin (the Dóchas Centre) opened in 1999, replacing Mountjoy women's prison and providing seventy places for women prisoners.[61] The prison is designed so that small numbers of prisoners can live together in "houses", to encourage greater autonomy. Greatly improved physical

---

[58] O'Mahony, P., *Crime and Punishment in Ireland*, Dublin: Round Hall Press, 1993; and O'Mahony, P., *Mountjoy Prisoners: A Sociological and Criminological Profile*, Dublin: Government Publications, 1997

[59] Carmody, P. and McEvoy, M., *A Study of Irish Female Prisoners*, Dublin: Government Publications, 1996

[60] McCann James, C., *Recycled Women: Oppression and the Social World of Women Prisoners in the Irish Republic*, PhD Thesis for NUI Galway, 2001, unpublished

[61] Numbers of women held in the prison regularly exceed the specified limit of places

facilities are provided, including a theatre, gymnasium, creche and sports grounds. It is not yet possible to predict the effect, if any, these improvements have had upon the experience of women prisoners. Before it opened, the Irish Penal Reform Trust was critical of the decision to build one large prison in Dublin, rather than a series of small units around the country to facilitate greater family contact.[62] The Trust also noted an excessive emphasis on security in the new prison, and called for semi-open conditions to be provided instead.

Since the prison opened, an internal study conducted by PACE, the prisoners' support group, in May 2000 found that despite the improved conditions within the prison, no basic support services existed for the women upon release.[63] There were 72 women held in the prison on 1 May, 2000, 32 of whom were from Dublin, most serving sentences of between 12 months and two years. Of the total number, 23 classified themselves as homeless. All 11 inmates due for release said they wished to stay in the new jail rather than face homelessness upon their release. Concerning social factors, the study found that 42 women were aged 25 or younger, and 43 had children; only 8 had received third level education, and 38 were drug addicts.

WOMEN VICTIMS OF CRIME: RAPE

The focus of much feminist research into the experience of women as victims of crime, in Ireland and elsewhere, has been the law on rape. Rape is historically the archetypal gendered crime. While it is well-established that men can also be and often are victims of sexual violence, statistics show that rape victims are predominantly female and perpetrators overwhelmingly male. Feminists have campaigned for many years to change those features of the rape trial process that can make it particularly traumatic for the victim, but studies show victims' continued reluctance to report crimes of sexual violence to the police, for reasons including fear of unfair treatment by the legal system.[64] This fear is strengthened by reports that the proportion of convictions for rape is falling, despite increases in the number of reported rapes.[65]

---

[62] *Policy Statement: Women and the Penal System*, Dublin: Irish Penal Reform Trust, 1998

[63] PACE Study, 2000, unpublished and conducted for internal information purposes. Reported in O'Kelly, B., "Women Prisoners Want to Remain on the Inside", *Sunday Business Post*, October 8, 2000

[64] See for example, Temkin, J., *Rape and the Legal Process*, London: Sweet and Maxwell, 1987, at p.11, and US Dept of Justice, Bureau of Justice Statistics, *Criminal Victimization in the United States*, US Dept of Justice, Washington, DC, 1994

[65] Source: Home Office, *Speaking Up for Justice. Report of the Interdepartmental Working Group on the Treatment of Vulnerable of Intimidated Witnesses in the Criminal Justice System*, London: HMSO, 1998

In Ireland, as Leon writes, the incidence of recorded sexual offences has increased dramatically over the last decade, although there is no evidence to show that the prevalence of sexual victimisation has increased.[66] Rather, she attributes the growth in reporting levels to increased openness in Irish society, influenced by extensive media discussion about sexual abuse. Recent research by Leane *et al* has highlighted the high attrition rate that applies to sexual assault offence cases in Ireland, and has concluded that attrition or slippage can occur at multiple points in the legal process, including the pre-reporting stage.[67] The authors considered that numerous changes should be made to the processing of reports of rape, in order to improve upon this situation. While significant substantive and procedural reforms have already been instituted as a result of feminist campaigns, the law on rape remains problematic in many respects.

A 1998 Irish study by Bacik *et al* which sought to analyse different legal practices in rape trials throughout the EU and their impact on victims of rape found that significant difficulties remained, particularly with the definition of rape and with the rules applied to the victim's testimony at trial.[68] Historically, rape was only deemed to have occurred where there had been emission of semen within the vagina, thus putting the paternity of any child born to the woman into question. The requirement to prove emission was abolished in most jurisdictions in the nineteenth century, although the emphasis on penile-vaginal penetration has persisted until recently in European systems, showing continued evidence of what Carol Smart describes as "the dominant phallocentric perspective" on rape.[69]

Recent changes to the definition of rape throughout Europe have meant that it is now generally defined as a gender-neutral offence, capable of perpetration upon men and by women, but the Irish reform is unique. Here, the gender-specific offence of "common-law rape" has been retained, defined as non-consensual sexual intercourse by a man with a woman where he either knows that she does not consent, or is reckless as to whether or not she consents (the *mens rea* or mental element of the offence).[70] In 1990, however, a new and additional gender-neutral offence of "rape under section 4" was also introduced. This prohibits non-consensual penetration of the anus or mouth by the penis, or penetration of the vagina by an object.

---

[66] Leon, C., "Recorded Sexual Offences 1994-1997: An Overview" (2000) 10 *Irish Criminal Law Journal* 2-7

[67] Leane, M., Ryan, S., Fennell, C. and Egan, E., *Attrition in Sexual Assault Offence Cases in Ireland: A Qualitative Analysis*, Dublin: Government Publications and Cork: NUIC, 2001

[68] Bacik, I., Maunsell, C. and Gogan, S., *The Legal Process and Victims of Rape*, Dublin: Rape Crisis Centre, 1998. See also Bacik, I., "Rape and the Law: The Quest for a Best-Practice Rape Law Model" (2000) 4 *Irish Journal of Feminist Studies* 17-30

[69] Smart, C., "Law's Power, the sexed body and feminist discourse" (1990) 17 *Journal of Law and Society*, 194-210

[70] Criminal Law (Rape) Act, 1981, section 2, as amended

Thus, two separate rape offences now exist in Irish law, each carrying the same maximum penalty of life imprisonment. It is difficult to identify a rationale for maintaining a distinct offence of common-law rape, other than the traditional premise that penile-vaginal intercourse should be regarded differently in law than other forms of penetration because it may result in pregnancy. Feminist activists had called for all forms of sexual penetration to be included within one broadly-defined rape offence, and remain dissatisfied with this compromise approach to reform.[71]

Apart from problems with the legal definition of rape, two issues pertaining to the testimony of the victim at trial have been particularly contentious. The first is the use by the defence of evidence that the victim has had sexual intercourse with others, or with the defendant, at some time in her life prior to the rape. The second is the warning traditionally given by the judge to the jury that it is dangerous to convict on the uncorroborated evidence of a rape victim ("the corroboration warning"). Both rules are based upon the persistent "rape myth" that women are liable to make false allegations about rape.[72]

Despite reforms of these rules through legislation, it remains possible in Ireland for the defence to introduce evidence of a complainant's prior sexual history,[73] and judges continue to issue corroboration warnings to the jury in rape trials.[74]

It may therefore be seen that gendered rules continue to apply to rape law and the conduct of rape trials. Reform is ongoing in most European jurisdictions, but changes in the law alone are not sufficient to address the causes of rape in the relations between men and women. A better approach should emphasise the vital role of education in changing attitudes and challenging the prevailing myths about rape, and the aggressive construction of masculinity, in order to reduce the incidence of violence against women.

WOMEN VICTIMS OF CRIME: "DOMESTIC" VIOLENCE

Apart from the literature on rape, much research has also been done by feminist criminologists on women's experiences of "domestic" violence. The term itself is

---

[71] See Fennell, C., "Criminal Law and the Criminal Justice System: Woman as Victim", in Connelly, A., *Gender and the law in Ireland*, Dublin: Oak Tree Press, 1993, and the *Report of the Working Party on the Legal and Judicial Process for Victims of Sexual and Other Crimes of Violence Against Women and Children*, Dublin: National Women's Council of Ireland, 1996, at pp. 79-80

[72] For a discussion of this and other prevailing myths around rape, see eg Leonard, M., "Rape: Myths and Reality", in Smyth, A., *Irish Women's Studies Reader*, Dublin: Attic Press, 1993

[73] Although the victim is now entitled to have legal representation to enable her to argue against the introduction of such evidence, under sections 34-5 of the Sex Offenders Act, 2001

[74] Section 7 of the Criminal Law (Rape) (Amendment) Act 1990 gave the judge the discretion not to do so; but the Court of Criminal Appeal in *DPP v Molloy*, CCA, July 28, 1995, held that it would be "prudent" to continue to warn the jury where a rape victim's evidence is uncorroborated

regarded as unsatisfactory, since it hides the gendered nature of such violence, and trivialises its seriousness. Edwards has advocated that apostrophes should be placed around the word "domestic" where that is used.[75] The word does however signify the particular nature of this type of offence. As Stanko has written, for most of society the locus of danger is constituted in the threat from strangers in the street, and the home is seen as a safe haven.[76] But the statistics on abuse upon women by male partners show for many women, the home may be the most dangerous place.

Again, only limited data on "domestic" violence exist in Ireland; a recent report reviewing the literature in this jurisdiction recommended the establishment of a national system for the collection of statistics, in order to ascertain true levels of abuse.[77] A 1995 survey by Women's Aid found that 18% of respondents had been subjected to a form of violence, and concluded that "the rate of reported violence is likely to underestimate the true level of violence".[78] Meanwhile, recorded instances of "domestic" violence have increased dramatically over the past few years, from 3,986 incidents recorded in 1995 to 10,110 incidents in 1999.[79]

Aside from difficulties with the language used, and with establishing the extent of such violence, feminist writing has also focused on the low levels of criminal law enforcement in this area. The Women's Aid study found that despite a garda initiative on "domestic" violence adopted in 1994, gardaí would not usually arrest for such violence except in cases of aggravated assault. The law was strengthened with the passing of the Domestic Violence Act 1996, which extended protection beyond spouses to non-marital relationships, and gave enhanced powers of arrest to gardaí. This approach was supported by the Report of a Task Force on Violence Against Women, which advocated that "police should make arrests unless there are good reasons not to do so".[80]

The pro-arrest policies inherent in the 1996 Act have been criticised, somewhat controversially, by Vaughan.[81] He argues that such policies do not recognise that arresting the perpetrator may exacerbate violence in certain situations, and that victims may sometimes wish to warn off an abusive partner, but may not want him arrested or locked up. The danger with a "less-arrest" approach, however, is that

[75] Edwards, S., *Policing "Domestic" Violence*, London: Sage, 1989

[76] Stanko, E., "Fear of Crime and the Myth of the Safe Home: a Feminist Critique of Criminology", in Yllo, K. and Bograd, M. (eds.), *Feminist Perspectives on Wife Abuse*, London: Sage, 1988

[77] *Report of the Working Party on the Legal and Judicial Process for Victims of Sexual and Other Crimes of Violence Against Women and Children, op. cit.*, p. 57

[78] Kelleher and Associates with O'Connor, M., *Making the Links: Towards an Integrated Strategy for the Elimination of Violence Against Women in Intimate Relationships with Men*, Dublin: Women's Aid, 1995

[79] Garda Siochana Annual Reports

[80] *Report of the Task Force on Violence Against Women*, Dublin: Government Publications, 1997, p. 43

[81] Vaughan, B., "Selecting Responses to Domestic Violence" (2001) 11 *Irish Criminal Law Journal* 23-8

when the State appears reluctant to invoke legal procedures to protect women, it then "symbolically condones male violence and creates and reproduces a wider cultural climate ... in which violence against partners, unless it is of the most appalling gravity, is perpetuated".[82]

WOMEN IN PROSTITUTION

Having reviewed some of the literature on women offenders and victims of crime, it is useful to conclude with a brief discussion of the position of women involved in prostitution. Although such women are regarded as offenders within the criminal justice system, some feminists have argued that they might more properly be treated as victims. Catherine MacKinnon, for example, describes prostitution as another form of sexual violence against women: "rape, battery, sexual harassment, sexual abuse of children, prostitution, and pornography ... form a distinctive pattern: the power of men over women in society".[83] Bridgeman and Millns argue further that the "privatised nature" of prostitution ensures that prostitutes have to work out of public view, and in conditions where they are constantly in danger of sexual violence; when they make allegations of abuse, they are frequently distrusted by the criminal justice system.[84]

Although on a theoretical level prostitution is no longer regarded as the "typical female crime", the criminal law continues to operate and be applied in a gendered way. Typically, only those working as prostitutes (mostly women) are penalised, while the (mostly male) customers remain outside the controls of the criminal law. The law also promotes a double standard, in prohibiting the public display of prostitution, but not the act of selling sex itself. The focus is on controlling, containing and above all concealing the sale of sex.

Frug argued that laws controlling public display of prostitution have the effect of terrorising women's bodies, because they perpetuate among all women the fear of being mistaken for prostitutes.[85] This view is supported by Lorna Ryan's analysis of newspaper stories on prostitution in the British and Irish broadsheet press, in which she found that recognisable descriptions of "the prostitute" are constructed on the basis of appearance, time and place of presence.[86] Once a woman has been identified thus, legal evidence exists of her "intent to prostitute"; so the law facilitates and contributes to the stereotyping of all women.

---

[82] Edwards, S., *Sex and Gender in the Legal Process*, London: Blackstone Press, 1996, p. 226
[83] MacKinnon, C., *Feminism Unmodified: Discourses on Life and Law*, Cambridge MA: Harvard University Press, 1987, p. 5
[84] Bridgeman, J. and Millns, S., *Feminist Perspectives on Law: Law's Engagement with the Female Body*, London: Sweet and Maxwell, 1998, p. 737-8
[85] Frug, M., *op. cit.*
[86] Ryan, L., *Reading the Prostitute: Appearance, Place and Time in British and Irish press stories of prostitution*, Aldershot: Brookfield, 1997

In Ireland, the Criminal Law (Sexual Offences) Act 1993 created gender-neutral offences of loitering and soliciting for the first time, but retains the traditional terms of "loitering" and "soliciting" as the basis for prosecution.[87] Thus, in practice predictive identifying evidence by police must still be used to convict for prostitution. Increased penalties are also imposed for both soliciting and loitering, so that women are effectively forced to commit further criminal acts to pay their fines.

Since the Act came into force, the Women's Health Project (WHP), which provides medical services to Dublin sex workers, has commissioned a number of reports on female prostitution.[88] Its first report found that the new law had produced a more confrontational relationship between women and police, as the women were constantly being moved on. In a second report, women described an increasing reluctance to report attacks, because of their negative experiences with the gardaí under the new law. This perception was challenged by the Department of Justice, which claimed that "there is no evidence ... to support [prostitutes'] fear of prosecution when reporting assaults".[89]

Whatever the effects of the legislation, the dangers present for those engaged in prostitution remain even where a good relationship has developed between women and gardaí. In a further study in which thirty women working as street prostitutes in Dublin were interviewed about their experience of the criminal law, the participants again spoke of their fear of violence;[90] 80% of them had been subjected to violence of one form or another. They generally expressed confidence about police responses to complaints of violence. However, over 50% of them had already been prosecuted under the Act, while the others felt it was only a matter of time before they too were arrested; most recommended some form of decriminalisation.

Feminists disagree over what form prostitution laws should take, but one point is clear; while the public sale of sex remains unlawful, legislation is enforced far more vigorously against women than against male clients. Laws based upon a political concern to protect neighbourhoods and "respectable" women from harassment envisage that prostitution must be hidden from public view. The law

---

[87] Under section 7 of the Act, it is an offence to solicit or importune another person in a public place for the purposes of prostitution. Under section 8, a garda may direct a person to leave a public place if he or she believes they are loitering in order to solicit or importune another person for prostitution. Failure to comply with the garda's direction is an offence

[88] O'Connor, A., *The Health Needs of Women Working in Prostitution in the Republic of Ireland*, Dublin: Women's Health Project, 1994; and O'Connor, A., *Women Working in Prostitution: Towards a Healthier Future,* Dublin: Women's Health Project, 1996

[89] *The Law on Sexual Offences: A Discussion Paper*, Government Publications, 1998, p. 95

[90] Haughey, C. and Bacik, I., *Final Report: A Study of Prostitution in Dublin*, unpublished: Law School, TCD/Department of Justice, Equality and Law Reform, 2000

targets only the most visible manifestations of prostitution, not the private exploitation of women. But, as with rape, whatever form prostitution takes, no solution to its causes will be found in the law alone. Until women have social and economic equality, prostitution of one kind or another will continue to provide an obvious economic alternative for many women.

CONCLUSION

This brief overview of literature on women within the criminal justice system can provide only a glimpse of the criminological work that has been done by feminist researchers. As Heidensohn writes, "There has been a significant shift in the study of crime because of feminist perspectives on it".[91] Research carried out from a feminist point of view has enabled the development of new ideas about crime and criminology. Perhaps the most important of these is the idea that all crime is gendered. Feminist theory can offer significant insights into the gendering process; the social discourses through which masculinities are constructed. This in turn can provide useful information on the pathways into crime for many boys and young men. Criminology is now beginning – at last – to address how boys and men "do gender", and to engage critically with the "maleness of crime".

But while the development of research into masculinity and crime is a fast-growing and challenging new area for criminology, there is a danger that the feminist focus on women within the criminal justice system will be lost. In an Irish context, insufficient empirical research on women as offenders and victims has been conducted to enable us to address basic questions about women and crime. It is vital that feminist criminologists do not lose sight of these questions, in seeking to insert a gendered perspective into criminological research in Ireland.

---

[91] Heidensohn, F., "Gender and Crime", *op. cit.*, p. 791

9

How Dirty is the White Collar?
Analysing White-Collar Crime

Ciaran McCullagh

1 THE NOTION OF WHITE-COLLAR CRIME

The topic of white-collar crime has always had a somewhat uneasy relationship to the study of crime generally. There are a number of reasons for this. One is the complexity of what passes for white-collar crime. Another is the inability of some criminologists to deal with situations in which the offenders do not fit into categories of deprivation and powerlessness. But it has also quite a lot to do with the lack of political will in many societies to respond to the deviance of the middle and upper class. In this chapter I will deal with this issue. The discussion is divided into two sections. The first reviews the issues that arise in the study of white-collar crime and corporate misbehaviour. The second applies this analysis to the Republic of Ireland. This section will be the least satisfactory, reflecting the absence of sustained research on this kind of crime in Ireland, and reflecting also its relatively recent "discovery" as an issue worthy of political and social analysis.

The origin of the term

The term white-collar crime has its origins in the writings of Edwin Sutherland (1949). He was an American criminologist who did some of his most significant work in the 1930s and 1940s. At that time criminologists were concerned largely with street crime and with the crime committed by gangs of the adult type such as that run by Al Capone or the juvenile type, of which, Thrasher (1927) claimed, there were over a thousand in Chicago alone. Sutherland noted how this approach ignored the activities of other gangs, like the so-called "robber barons". These were rich businessmen, in areas such as railways and the meat industry, who abused the laws under which they were regulated, in order to destroy competitors and create cartels. Although Al Capone and his associates earned the title "the untouchables", the robber barons could have given them lessons in invisibility.

Sutherland coined the term "white-collar crime" to cover the activities of the "robber barons". The term was intended to refer to a crime "committed by a person of respectability in the course of his occupation" (Sutherland 1949:9). As such Sutherland used the term to include a diverse range of activities such as tax evasion, stock exchange manipulation, breaches of anti-trust legislation, false advertising and price-fixing between companies. What these actions had in common, he contended, was that their purpose was profit for the employer. On the basis of his studies he concluded that such crimes were frequent, widespread and routine in the world of business in the United States.

From white-collar crime to crimes of the powerful

Sutherland's work did not fully succeed in finding its audience until the 1960s and 1970s. This was a period of radical political change, most potently symbolised by the protest movement against the Vietnam War and the Watergate scandal. Crucially, Presidents of the United States were accused of collusion in criminal offences in both the Watergate scandal and the Vietnam War. In the former case, it was claimed, President Nixon was guilty of, among other things, burglary against his political opponents and, in the latter, several presidents were accused of the illegal bombing of civilian targets. The attempt to encompass these kinds of activities within the rubric of criminology led to a widening of the term, white-collar crime, to embrace what have been designated as "crimes of the powerful" (Pearce 1976).

This term covered four kinds of crime. The first was crime committed by business corporations, most notably the bribery by multi-nationals of both their own and foreign governments. In the latter case this was often to facilitate the acceptance in less developed countries of polluting and otherwise dangerous industries. The second was crime committed by governments. This included the use of state agencies against their political opponents and war crimes contrary to the Geneva Convention. The Watergate case, the illegal bombing of Cambodia by the United States and the murderous attack by the French government on *Rainbow Warrior*, a ship belonging to the environmental organisation Greenpeace, are cases in point. A more stark illustration is the participation of governments in genocide, the most recent examples of which include Rwanda in 1994.

The third was crime committed by state officials. This includes accepting bribes for political favours, for favourable decisions on industrial location, and for ignoring violations of health and safety or environmental protection legislation. The fourth was crime committed by the police, most notably the use of violence against suspects or the unnecessary use of lethal or brutal force. This latter type of offence was most dramatically illustrated by the assault by the Californian police on Rodney King, but others in many countries (see Box 1983) have documented the generally disproportionate use of force by the police, especially against minority populations.

The significance of the term

What sociologists and criminologists were trying to do with this work on white-collar crime was to direct attention to the nature of the offenders involved and in that way to counterbalance the common bias in criminology which locates the causes of crime in the working or lower class experience. Most conventional explanations stress the centrality of social class and social exclusion as motivating factors in many kinds of crime, most notably acquisitive property crime. If it can be shown that white-collar crime is frequent and routine, as Sutherland claimed, then such explanations are insufficient. Most of those involved in white-collar crime do not come from backgrounds characterised by low levels of education and high levels of deprivation and unemployment (see McCullagh 1996).

Problems of definition

However, it has been argued that while the extension of the term "white-collar crime" to include "crimes of the powerful" highlights the inadequacies of con-ventional explanations of crime it also loses something in analytical rigor. The crimes referred to are not necessarily committed by people who are powerful. One study in the United States (Wiesburd, Wheeler, Waring and Bode 1991), for example, found that the typical white-collar criminal was not a person whom we would normally think of as powerful or possessed of elite social status. They found that most of those prosecuted for fraud or embezzlement were in fact rather ordinary, middle class, middle income people. It has also been argued that some of the behaviours referred to by the term white-collar crime are not unequivocally criminal as strictly defined in terms of violation of the criminal law. Nelken (1994) points out that Sutherland himself was unable to publish the names of the companies, whose activities he described as criminal, because of his publisher's fear that these companies would sue for libel.

There have been a number of attempts to construct more suitable classifications for these kinds of offences but they tend to run foul of somewhat similar problems. Shapiro (1989), for example, has argued that white-collar crime should be included under the study of the maintenance and abuse of trust in society. The difficulties of personal oversight, the limitations of individual experience and the sheer complexity of modern societies mean that we have to trust many important organisations and the individuals in them to behave in a trustworthy manner. Our lives are often built on the anticipation that they will do so. Thus we anticipate that those who run, say, facilities for the provision of blood for medical purposes will follow exacting standards for the protection of blood products. When we find they do not, the fund of trust on which a society depends is depleted and an essential element of social cement is eroded. However, while this insight is useful in pointing to the abuse of trust in many forms of white-collar crime, it does not follow that the abuse of trust is unique to white-collar crime or that all forms of the abuse of trust are criminal.

Indeed, it could be argued that central to the difficulties in defining white-collar crime is the fact that the offences involved are different from ordinary crimes. According to Michael Clarke, corporate misbehaviour does not originate in "calculated deceit motivated by greed" as presumably ordinary crime does. It is, he argues, less damaging and results from duress, incompetence or negligence. "Public order is not", he argues (Clarke 1990:20), "violated in business offences as it is in conventional crime" and such offences have "a less threatening character".

Others dispute this. Steven Box (1983), for example, says that it is not accurate to classify these crimes as less threatening. While it may be true that tax evasion is not as threatening as physical assault, crimes such as pollution, the marketing of defective drugs, and the neglect of safety standards pose a very real danger and inflict very real injuries on many people. Research on hazards at work shows that most workers are at greater risk in the workplace than they are in the street (Hagan 1994:104). At the most prosaic level, the financial cost of white-collar crime is more substantial than that of conventional crime.

In addition, these theorists contend that "white-collar" crime is in essence the same as "ordinary crime" but its similarities are hidden from us by the way in which society deals with and responds to white-collar crime (Nelken 1994:360). The fact that white-collar crime is dealt with primarily by administrative methods of enforcement means that its criminality is not publicly dramatised and symbolised. Failure to characterise white-collar crime fully as crime means that the public never comes to appreciate and understand its prevalence and serious nature. There is a stark contrast between being a statistic in a health and safety report and being photographed coming down the steps of a courthouse in handcuffs. The main response of society to these kinds of offences is regulation without stigmatisation. In this way offenders escape the slur of disrepute that is embodied in criminal court procedures (Hagan 1994:1).

A Working Definition?

As we have seen there is a range of problems in defining and identifying white-collar crime. Some commentators claim that existing definitions are too wide and embrace a variety of behaviours that have few common characteristics. Others claim that the term frequently refers to behaviour that is neither illegal nor criminal. Finally there are those who argue that whatever about the law it is inappropriate to use a criminological framework in the understanding or the regulation of such behaviours.

It may however be possible to arrive at a working definition of the phenomenon. Part of the problem lies with the incoherence of Sutherland's original definition (see Nelken 1994: 361-366). He confused a number of different kinds of offences, most notably those where organisational resources were used to commit crime on behalf of the organisation and those where the crime is against the organisation. The difference between price-fixing from which the organisation benefits and embezzlement or fraud in which the organisation is the victim is a case in point.

This distinction has been built upon by Beirne and Messerschmidt (1991). They suggest that there are two distinct kinds of white-collar crime. One is "occupational crime", which refers to situations in which organisational resources and occupational position are used to commit crime. What is distinctive about it is that the gain is personal and accrues to the individual employee. The victim can be the corporation itself or the public that does business with it.

Beirne and Messerschmidt (1991) divide occupational crime into a number of distinct categories. One is employee theft or embezzlement. This is where employees fiddle their employers either through robbing them of cash, inventory or time. With some flexibility this kind of crime can encompass the range of fraud practised by citizens against the state either in the form of false claims for social welfare payments or tax evasion. Another category is occupational fraud. This is where individuals use their occupational status to defraud the public. The examples that Beirne and Messerschmidt (1991:180-183) use include fraud by physicians, primarily though unnecessary surgery, particularly coronary bypass and hysterectomy.

The other kind of white-collar crime is "corporate crime". This is where owners and employees use the resources of the organisation and of their occupational position to commit crime from which the benefit is to the corporation and through which organisational goals such as profit maximisation are furthered. If the object of occupational crime is personal gain the object of corporate crime is primarily corporate or organisational gain. This definition is intended to include corporate negligence or forms of violence, as for example where workers are knowingly exposed to dangerous working conditions or where the public is put at risk through the sale of dangerous products or by the flouting of pollution laws. It also covers corporate theft where the public is robbed through over-pricing of goods, through deceptive advertising, or through the kind of collusion between corporations that results in price-fixing.

The extent and frequency of white-collar crime

A key question about white-collar crime is its extent and frequency. These are essential elements in the consideration of its social significance. However a number of features of this kind of crime make it difficult to quantify these variables. For the most part such offences are not included in official statistics. The reasons for this include the fact that offending organisations and individuals are unlikely to draw their offences to the attention of the authorities, while corporations that are victims tend to be unwilling to report offences against them because of the consequences this would have for their public reputation. For example, banks are unlikely to go public on the extent of fraud against them, particularly when employees commit it. They are also reluctant to admit to fraud involving abuse of their automated banking systems because of the consequent loss of consumer confidence. The regulating agencies may also be reluctant to expose this kind of crime. Nelken (1994), for example, argues that the Bank of England is torn between its role as regulator of the banking system and an ingrained unwillingness to compromise the credibility of any of the major clearing banks. This is likely to produce an under-reporting of misbehaviour by the banks and against the banks.

The information that is available, such as that produced by specialised enforcement agencies – for example, those concerned with health and safety in work, with food standards and with pollution – is also problematic. It is difficult to interpret these data from a criminological perspective, as the number of violations recorded is often limited by the resources available to the organisations and by the policies of enforcement with which they operate. Such organisations tend to have limited resources. How they selectively deploy these limited resources may be a significant factor determining how many violations they uncover. It would be informative to know whether the violations they record are a product of random and unannounced inspections or of inspections carried out in response to complaints by the public or by other parties such as consumer groups, trade unions and activist organisations.

Such complaints may be comparatively rare, because by their nature victims of corporate crime may be hard to identify, particularly when the definition of victim is restricted to the identifiable, individual citizen. Thus within the terms of this kind of discourse it is not immediately obvious who is the victim of corporate tax evasion. It is also the case that victims are often unaware of their victimisation. For example, workers are sometimes unaware of their exposure to dangerous working conditions, consumers may be unaware of breaches in food safety standards, in the production of the food they eat, and companies may not be aware of collusive practices by competing companies.

There is also the additional complicating factor that, in contrast to more conventional crime, victims of corporate crime often have to fight to establish their victim status. This has been the case in a number of recent incidents of corporate pollution dramatised in Hollywood films like "Erin Brockovich" and "A Civil Action". It is also the case in situations of medical negligence and of the manufacture and sale of dangerous products. For example, the struggle of the victims of thalidomide, a drug sold by a company that was aware of its highly damaging side-effects, to establish their victimisation required immense commitment and entailed great personal costs. Such examples may be sufficient to deter other victims from even attempting to establish their victim status.

Why do they do it?

The issue of white-collar crime is further complicated when we turn to explanations for its occurrence. The diversity of the phenomena included under the term can defeat the attempts to construct a comprehensive explanation. For example, there are probably fundamental differences in motivation between crime on behalf of organisations and crime against organisations. There is also the added complication that many offenders are fairly well off to begin with and the motivations of these kinds of people can often be confusing to criminologists reared on the notion that criminality is an exclusive quality of the deprived. As a result a number of reviews conclude that "only banal generalisations are possible" (Braithwaite, 1985). Braithwaite's own conclusion, that both too much power and too little power cause crime, is a case in point.

Nonetheless, attempts to understand crime committed by organisations are an exception to this rule. These attempts have tried to combine an understanding of the structural opportunities that exist for such crime with an understanding of the motivations that may exist within organisations to avail of or ignore these opportunities (Shapiro 1989: 353). A typical example is the explanation put forward by Steven Box (1983). He argues that corporate crime is best considered as an innovative response by businessmen and those in large organisations to the strains of meeting cultural, social and economic prescriptions to maintain profits and organisational activities in difficult times.

According to Box, large corporations and organisations are goal-seeking entities. With corporations, for example, the goal is profit. However they face a series of obstacles to the achievement of these goals. These come from the pressures and tensions in the environment in which they operate. They include competitors who want to make more profits than they do and governments who want to regulate them in the public interest. They also include employees who form unions to demand higher wages and better working conditions, consumers whom the organisations needs to sell to but who want high-quality services and products in return, and the public which wants the environment protected.

This places organisations and corporations in an invidious position. They are under pressure to achieve particular goals. To achieve these they have to deal with the obstacles presented to them by the commercial and social environment in which they operate. In such circumstances the pressure to get around these obstacles is significant and produces many forms of corporate crime. So, for example, the pressures of competition can lead to industrial espionage to find out what competitors are up to, price-fixing to reduce the threat of a competitor with a lower price, and patent copying to reduce the time taken to invent and market new products. Pressure from governments can lead to the bribery of state officials and attempts to evade tax. Pressure from employees can produce unsafe working conditions and paying below minimum wages. Pressure from consumers can lead to false advertising and the marketing of dangerous products.

Box (1983) goes on to argue that, while the environment produces opportunities to engage in corporate crime, such crime is ultimately committed by people within organisations so the question remains, why do they do it? Box argues that a number of factors are important. One is that the risk of detection is low and, if detected, the risk of serious punishment is lower still. The legal system does not offer any serious impediments to the commission of corporate crime. Another is an organisational culture that promotes a series of "techniques of neutralisation". These are verbal justifications for particular actions that are seen as legitimate within the organisation and which free people from the moral bind of particular social norms and laws. Thus the notion that there is "no victim" or that "nobody is hurt by tax evasion" can serve as a justification for the activity and can soothe any negative and guilty feelings that an individual may have about breaking the law. Finally Box (1983) argues that the type of personality that is found in many senior office holders is one that can facilitate crime. They tend to be aggressive, assertive, and arrogant and as such are remarkable similar in temperament to those who commit ordinary crime.

What can be done about white-collar crime?

The complexities of the phenomenon also plague discussions about how such crimes can be regulated and controlled. One obstacle is the nature of modern organisations and corporations. These tend increasingly to be international in scope, while the legal systems that regulate them tend to be limited by national boundaries. This means that corporations can evade national laws by, for example, relocating dangerous manufacturing processes to countries where these practices are not illegal. This has been the case with industries using asbestos in the manufacture of brakepads for cars. Laws have been introduced in the United States to regulate such manufacturing processes. The response of the companies has been to relocate in Third World countries where there are no such limitations on their ability to pollute either workers or the environment (Beirne and Messerschmidt 1991).

There is also the issue of the nature of the law required to regulate corporations. It has been argued that such laws need to be particularly complex and sophisticated, reflecting the phenomenon they are intended to regulate. But it is in the nature of law that the more complex the law, the more likely it is to have loopholes. It is also true that the legal process in such cases favours those with the most resources. This enables well-resourced corporations to employ specialist lawyers to uncover loopholes and effectively escape whatever regulation the law was intended to create. Furthermore, complex corporate legislation tends to be difficult to enact and difficult to enforce.

However, the key issue in the regulation of this kind of crime lies in the question of the appropriateness of the criminal law and the effectiveness of the criminal sanction. For many theorists (see, for example, Clarke 1990:20) the criminal law is neither an appropriate nor an effective tool to use in corporate regulation. The criminal law is based on a notion of intention, *mens rea*. This means that to commit a crime those involved must act with the intention of causing harm. In most cases of corporate misbehaviour, according to Clarke, this kind of intention is either absent or extremely difficult to establish. There is little evidence of what is often referred to in legal terms as "an organising mind" behind such behaviour. Much of it is, he claims, the product of incompetence rather than felonious intention.

The response of critics is to acknowledge that criminal intention can be difficult to establish but the task is not insurmountable. John Braithwaite (1984), for example, has argued that organisations may present a public face of uncertain and imprecise systems of accountability to the outside world. But they have very clear systems of internal accountability. These tend to be mobilised in the distribution of rewards for organisational success or the distribution of sanctions for organisational failure.

It has also been suggested that the concept of intention with which the criminal law operates is a nineteenth-century proposition and one that is no longer appropriate to the complexities of the contemporary world. James Gobert (1994), for example, has argued that much regulatory law devalues the harm done by corporations. He argues that a "true" criminal backup is needed for serious corporate offences. To achieve this he suggests that we replace the concept of *mens rea* with that of *due diligence*. Under his model, a company would be criminally liable where "a crime is authorised, permitted or tolerated as a matter of company policy or *de facto* practice" (Gobert 1994: 728). It would be up to the corporation to show that it had taken the necessary steps to avoid the occurrence of harm. It would have to show that it acted with due diligence to prevent criminal activity.

This is not an entirely novel suggestion. It bears important similarities to another area of criminal activity that is also prone to under-reporting, where it is argued that intention is difficult to establish, and where women often have to fight to establish their status as victims. The Criminal Law (Rape) Amendment Act 1991 says that rape is unlawful sexual intercourse with a woman against her consent if a man knows she does not consent or does not take adequate steps to ensure that such consent is present. In other words, men need to act with due diligence.

There is also a range of questions around the appropriateness of the use of criminal sanctions. For example, at what level in the organisation should sanctions be applied? For some the risk is that individuals at a low level in the organisational or corporate world will be more easily identified and prosecuted and so scapegoated for misbehaviour for which they are not fully or entirely responsible. It is also the case, Nelken (1994: 381) argues, that "those effectively criminalised for business-related offences tend to be small business people" rather than executives from large and powerful business corporations.

It has also been asserted that the use of prison against white-collar offenders is unfair because it is a more painful experience for them than it is for other offenders. Benson and Cullen (1988) dispute this. They claim that such offenders have the social and personal resources to cope with prison life. In particular they have access to three coping strategies that are not always available to other prisoners. These are their denial of criminality of their actions, the frame of mind that encourages conformity with the demands of the institution and their sense of an imagined superiority to the other inmates.

Finally, there is the argument that the imposition of fines on organisations and corporation is futile because of the difficulties of finding a level of fines that would be sufficient to deter business from crime. In many cases the level of fines imposed is either small relative to the profits made by the business or else can be easily recouped by passing them on to consumers through higher prices and increased charges.

Indeed the overall thrust of many critics is that the decision not to use the criminal law or criminal sanctions against corporate misbehaviour does not stem from their ineffectiveness or from some sense that they might be inappropriate. It is the result of political choices about which misbehaviour to make criminal and about the kind of offenders for whom prison should be reserved. The enforcement of the law against "ordinary" crime is designed to maximise stigmatisation without any necessary guarantees in terms of effectiveness. With corporate crime the opposite is the case. The aim is compliance without stigmatisation.

2 WHITE-COLLAR CRIME IN IRELAND: APPLYING THE ANALYSIS[*]

In the preceding section we have outlined the range of issues that arise in the study of white-collar crime. In this section we address the issue of applying the analysis to Ireland. There is the undoubted perception in Irish society that white-collar crime is widespread, but this is difficult to substantiate empirically. Some

---

[*] This chapter borrows in a number of places from material in C. McCullagh (1996)

of these difficulties are intrinsic to the topic. Others are particular to the Irish situation. Underlying both is the under-developed nature of research in Ireland on crime in general, but in particular on white-collar crime.

The absence of research means that we cannot fully exploit the distinction between occupational and corporate crime. As a result it is possible to argue that white-collar crime is distributed more evenly across the social classes than, for example, a focus on crimes of the powerful might suggest. Yet a fruitful discussion of the phenomenon must be able to distinguish between, say, the participation of a tax official in fraud and the defrauding of the European Union by major corporations.

If we look at the kinds of "white-collar type" offences that are dealt with by the Gardai, they tend to be relatively minor offences such as small-scale prescription fraud, passing stolen cheques and defrauding the social welfare system. They are also small in number. According to the 1999 *Annual Report on Crime* they constituted 6% of all larcenies and 3% of the total amount of indictable crime. The majority (70%) involved passing forged or stolen cheques. Hence, if you go by official statistics, the marginalised working class have a monopoly on white-collar crime. But a full discussion of white-collar crime must be able to distinguish between serious cases involving those in significant positions of power and influence and relatively minor ones involving small amounts of, for example, expense fiddling. It is not possible to do this given the existing state of knowledge in Ireland and this is a major impediment to a comprehensive discussion of white-collar crime.

The extent of the problem

This absence of sustained research becomes an important problem when we attempt to calculate the extent of white-collar crime. There are however a number of disparate sources that combine to constitute a strong argument that this kind of crime is widespread.

The Report of the Committee of Inquiry into the Penal System (1985) put the combined cost of white-collar offences, such as tax evasion, the evasion of the payment of debts, the non-payment of workers' tax liability and their social welfare entitlements, abuses of the social welfare system and a wide range of other such evasions, at between £300 million and £1,000 million a year. This was between eight and twelve times the amount taken in conventional crime in 1984.

A study by accountants Stokes, Kennedy, Crowley (reported in the *Irish Times*, 5 February 1993) surveyed 301 companies but, because just over half of them were available for interview, its results are incomplete. Nonetheless, one hundred and twenty-eight of the firms interviewed said that they had uncovered fraud in the last three years. Two-thirds of these frauds involved amounts over £1,000. Just under 30% involved sums greater than £10,000 and 2% involved amounts over £1 million. Three-quarters of the total known frauds were not reported to the police.

The setting up of a new Garda Bureau for Fraud Investigation replaced a fraud squad that traditionally was understaffed and under-resourced. Its most recent report (Garda Síochána *Annual Report* 1999) indicates that there is some evidence of an increased public willingness to use its services. It noted two new trends in offences coming to the Bureau's attention. One was the number of complaints alleging either insider-dealing by people in corporate entities or organised insurance fraud. The other was what it described as "a significant number of senior officials within organisations coming to notice for allegedly committing large scale fraud over protracted periods" (Garda Síochána *Annual Report* 1999: 50).

Then there are the disclosures at various tribunals. They have revealed extensive schemes by the wealthy and powerful to evade tax. It is important to note that tax evasion is a criminal offence. This has been the situation since a Supreme Court ruling on 1945 (*Irish Reports* 1945: 183). According to the Collector General (*Cork Examiner*, 25 September 1990) it is not a victimless crime. "The victims", he is quoted as saying, "are the complying public". It also has what are, by Irish standards, severe penalties attached to it. Under the Finance Act 1983 the maximum sentence if convicted on indictment is five years in prison, a fine of £10,000, or both.

The Tribunal of Inquiry into the Meat Processing Industry (1994), more popularly known as the Beef Tribunal, directed attention to the extent of fraud against the European Union. These frauds involved the making of false claims by meat companies. They were claiming export relief for meat that never left their factories. The inquiry also revealed extensive evasion of income tax.

A particularly disturbing aspect of this was that the Department of Agriculture in some cases appears to have colluded with the deviant companies. According to a Supreme Court judgement, reported in the *Irish Times* (7 March 1997), the companies were given licences to export meat. They didn't do this but claimed to the European Union that they did. The Department was, according to Judge Blayney, aware that this was going on.

More recent reports indicate that the defrauding of the European Union continues to be a problem. The 1997 report of the Union's anti-theft unit, Uclaf, records Irish frauds of £7.03 million. These involved defrauding the cohesion fund and the agricultural guarantee fund. However as the unit refused to give details of specific cases it is impossible to show what kinds of white-collar crimes these can be classified as.

The Report of the Tribunal of Inquiry (Dunne's Payments) – known for short as the McCracken Tribunal – found that "Mr Ben Dunne (a prominent businessman) knowingly assisted Mr Michael Lowry (a politician) in evading tax" (1997: 21). It also drew attention to the existence of an elaborate scheme of offshore accounts set up by a major bank in Ireland. These accounts became known as the Ansbacher Accounts after the name of the bank in the Cayman Islands from which they were operated. According to the Tribunal Report (1997: 25), a sum of £38 million was involved. The money was placed on deposit in the Cayman Islands and then transferred back to Guinness Mahon Bank in Dublin. The Tribunal stated that while some of these accounts may have been for legitimate business purposes, the purpose of others was less sanitary. Its report (1997:47) claims, for example, that ex-Taoiseach Charles J. Haughey, received £1.3 million pounds as gifts from Ben Dunne and "allowed the money to be kept offshore in an attempt to ensure that the Revenue authorities would never know of the gifts". These accounts are currently under investigation by inspectors from the Department of Trade and Industry. Recent reports suggest that the number of such accounts, the amounts of evaded tax, and the extent of the breaches of exchange controls involved in operating these accounts may be far more extensive than had initially been assumed.

Then there are the series of other investigations into the behaviour of the banks. One was by RTE reporters Charlie Bird and George Lee (1998). This revealed the manner in which National Irish Bank had been "stealing money from customer accounts" through overcharging on fees on customer accounts (Lee and Bird 1998:ix). It had also been facilitating tax evasion by its wealthiest customers through the provision of illegal offshore investment schemes.

The provision of illegal off-shore investment schemes was not confined to National Irish Bank. An investigation by the Ombudsman into the issue of tax evasion, non-resident bank accounts and the behaviour of the banks, and it's subsequent expansion by the Dáil Committee on Public Accounts, revealed the extensive and fairly open promotion of tax evasion by the major banks. There was little evidence here of complex corporate crime. This was straightforward and relatively open. The work of the committee revealed that tax "was evaded by depositors through the opening of bogus non-resident accounts. Deposit-takers knowingly facilitated the practice". The evidence presented to the committee showed that bank officials organised "the opening and operation of bogus non-resident accounts for customers and indeed of establishing them for their own use". This "evasion was practised in a wider culture of more generalised tax evasion" (Committee of Public Accounts 1999, Chapter One, Section One).

The amounts involved were considerable. Allied Irish Banks, for example, paid £90.4 million to the Revenue Commissioners in settlement of their liability. Thirty-four and a half million was for tax arrears, the remainder a series of penalties and interest payments. The Agricultural Credit Corporation paid the revenue £17.9 million, £7.5 million of which was tax liabilities. Ulster Bank paid £4.2 million, £1.7 million was in unpaid DIRT, and the remainder was interest and penalties (*Irish Times*, 10 August 2000). The total amount collected by the Revenue Commissioners in unpaid taxes and penalties from five financial institutions reached £157 million by October 2000 (*Irish Times*, 4 October, 2000).

The revelations at the Moriarity and Flood tribunals have alerted some to the dangers of political corruption and confirmed the suspicions of others on the extent to which it has compromised the planning process. To date these investigations have not resulted in any criminal prosecutions and the extent to which they will in the future will for some be a measure of the willingness of the state to confront this kind of behaviour. The incidents that have resulted in court proceedings so far, such as the jailing of Liam Lawlor TD, have involved the behaviour of individuals before the tribunals.

The controversy over the mis-selling of insurance policies by major Irish companies draws attention to other kinds of dubious corporate behaviour (*Irish Times*, 7 January 1998). This involved the companies actively encouraging policyholders to substitute existing policies for what the companies knew were less favourable ones. Customers lost from the deal and the insurance companies gained considerably. Recent media reports suggested that the insurers may be fined for this (*Sunday Tribune*, 21 January 2001). Other dubious behaviour is also under investigation. This includes the European Union's investigation into allegations that the banks conspired to fix foreign exchange commission rates. There is also an investigation into whether the banks gave false information to the Revenue Commissioners about the extent of bogus non-resident accounts when they made secret tax settlements with the Revenue in the early 1990s (*Irish Times*, 3 November 1998).

Finally a number of court cases have given some limited insight into the extent of the disregard of health and safety legislation. In one case, a company, Zoe Developments, was prosecuted for an incident on a building site in which a worker was killed. The company was charged with thirteen breaches of health and safety legislation on that particular site. Evidence given in court revealed that the company had twelve previous convictions on other sites. According to the newspaper accounts of the trial, the judge described the company as " a criminal, and a recidivist criminal at that" (*Irish Times*, 11 August 1997).

These examples are not the product of systematic research but they are indicative that Ireland is no exception to the common findings of research on white-collar and corporate crime. There is every likelihood that in Ireland, as elsewhere, such crimes are frequent and widespread.

The inadequacies of the criminal law

Despite this evidence of corporate and white-collar misbehaviour and crime, there are a number of factors particular to the Irish situation that prevents its full extent being realised or publicised. The primary one is the nature of the existing criminal law. Much of it is inadequate to deal with the complexities of organisational and corporate crime. This was shown most acutely in relation to the case of the Blood Transfusion Service and the death of Bridgid McCole. She died as a result of receiving contaminated blood products produced by the Blood Transfusion Service (BTSB). According to the report of Justice Finlay (1998), 1,300 women are known to have contracted hepatitis and 200 haemophiliacs to have contracted HIV or hepatitis from contaminated blood products. The judge concluded that there was "negligence" by the Board and a "total failure" by the staff of the BTSB to maintain standards of donor selection. Bridgid McCole's family put pressure on the gardaí and on legal authorities to initiate a criminal prosecution for manslaughter against the Board. The Director of Public Prosecutions said that he was unable to initiate such prosecutions under the criminal law "as it stands at present" (*Irish Times*, 22 October 1997).

This is in marked contrast to the situation in Canada and France where similar negligence on the part of blood transfusion services resulted in criminal prosecutions. As Lara Marlowe (*Irish Times*, 10 March 1999) pointed out there were important similarities between the French and Irish situations. In both cases the relevant authorities responded to the problem in a slow and inadequate manner. In both cases the transfusion services used products that they knew to be tainted and in both cases officials and politicians denied responsibility. In France however the head of the Blood Transfusion Service during the relevant period served a prison sentence for the sale of contaminated blood products. The equivalent Irish office holder received what was perceived as generous severance pay. In addition in France two former government ministers were prosecuted for manslaughter. Though they were subsequently acquitted of the more serious charges, there was considerable disquiet at the manner in which the trial was conducted. In Ireland no such prosecutions have ever been initiated.

There are also problems with the law on corruption. According to John Bruton (*Irish Times*, 5 September 1997) the criminal offence of corruption is dealt with by British legislation of 1889 and 1916. The consequences are that it is difficult, if not impossible, to successfully prosecute politicians or the people who bribe them. This legislation does not require those who are aware of or who suspect corruption to report and if they act as whistle blowers they do not have immunity from prosecution. The law covers the bribery of politicians and public officials but does not criminalise other kinds of threat or inducement to influence their decisions. It is also unclear if it covers votes and decisions of the Dáil, as the definition of public bodies that it uses is those administered from money raised by rates. This legislation belongs to an era in which the notion of national politicians being tempted by bribes was inconceivable. Many would now question the continued credibility of such an assumption.

It has also been argued that existing health and safety legislation is inadequate to deal with the death rate in industrial accidents (*Irish Times*, 17 January 2001). In 1998, sixty-four people were killed in accidents in the work place and just under half of these (twenty-six) occurred in the construction sector. The Labour Party argued that the range of offences and the range of penalties under existing legislation do not reflect the seriousness of the situation. They proposed a Private Member's Bill in the Dáil that would provide for the offence of "corporate killing" in cases where management failure was the cause of death (*Irish Times*, 17 January 2001).

Finally the issue of outdated and inadequate legislation was addressed by Eamon Barnes who retired as Director of Public Prosecution in 1999. He gave a talk to law graduates (reported in the *Sunday Independent*, 24 July 1999). In the course of this, he said that "many obvious cases of fraud, theft and dishonesty go unpunished as there is no criminal offence to match the fraudulent activity".

Problems of enforcement

There is also a series of problems in situations where the criminal law to deal with corporate misbehaviour does exist. These relate to its enforcement. According to the National Crime Forum *Report* (1998: 111), there are notable differences in the treatment of white-collar crime. The *Report* noted an unwillingness to resort to the criminal law. According to the evidence available to the Forum, the criminal law is not routinely used, for example, in the enforcement of health and safety legislation. Here the relevant inspectors see themselves as "persuaders rather than police". There is "less likelihood that offenders in such matters will even be prosecuted". Offenders have to show a serious disregard for their warnings and a pattern of recidivism before the criminal law is invoked against them. The Crime Forum also felt that in other legislation such as that "prescribing reporting requirements for companies, there was a remarkable tardiness in applying the law".

This tardiness could also be found in the enforcement of tax law. According to Vincent Browne (*Irish Times*, 17 January 2001), the Revenue Commissioners knew for some time that there was ongoing major tax evasion involving the non-payment of DIRT tax by Allied Irish Banks. The evasion potentially deprived the Revenue of tens of millions of pounds, yet they did not act on it for a period of eight years. This is consistent with the accounts provided to the Beef Tribunal of delays in acting against the Goodman Company (see McCullagh 1996). Though the investigations section of the Revenue Commissioners became aware in December 1986 that serious criminal offences might be involved in irregularities in claims for European

Community subsidies on meat, which did not exist, it was two years before the fraud squad become involved. The Report of the Beef Tribunal (1994:402-403) concluded that these delays were not inordinate and there was "nothing sinister in them". Yet the Director of Public Prosecutions decided in May 1991 not to prosecute those involved in the fraud. In the course of a letter written on 16 May 1991 the senior legal assistant said that "[W]hatever hope there might have been of bringing home criminal responsibility for such activities was effectively eliminated by the inordinate delays in completing the investigations and in particular in referring the matter to the gardaí" (Report of the Beef Tribunal 1994: 398).

The problems with enforcement may be more deeply rooted than merely delays by the relevant regulators. It may well be a political problem. In the aftermath of the revelations on tax evasion by the banks, the Public Accounts Committee looked at what it considered was the failure of the Revenue Commissioners to prosecute tax evaders. They were interested in the factors that had created the culture and practice in which the Revenue Commissioners preferred to reach financial settlements with offenders rather than prosecuting them and opening corporate offenders to risk of imprisonment. This was particularly relevant, as members of the committee were concerned that the banks were able to pass on the costs of penalties in the form of increased charges onto their customers, particularly those who did not benefit from the evasion schemes. (see *Irish Times*, 23 September 2000).

Although the settlement reached between AIB and the Revenue Commissioners was the largest in the history of the state, the sum involved amounted to only five weeks bank profits (*Irish Times*, 4 October 2000). It was in this context that Jim Mitchell, chairman of the committee, suggested that jail sentences should be imposed on white-collar criminals as a lesson to the institutions for which they were responsible. Fines, he argued, meant nothing to institutions of this size. This claim is consistent with the range of research which indicates that state practices in this area may encourage rather than regulate and control corporate crime and misbehaviour (see, for example, Glasberg and Skidmore 1998).

A letter from the Director of Public Prosecutions (DPP) to the Public Accounts Committee said that between 1997 and June 2000 there had only been eight prosecutions for major tax fraud. It had been suggested that this was due to outdated legislation and in particular to difficulties in getting the kind of evidence that would satisfy legal requirements of proof. The DPP however argued that "while tax legislation is complex, it is probably no more detailed or complicated than other legislation dealing with other types of fraud and related offences". As a result the DPP was not convinced of the need to change this aspect of the law. Indeed, in evidence to the Committee, civil servants blamed the problem on the lack of political will and instanced situations in which attempts to tighten up tax laws were proposed and subsequently dropped by the government ministers involved.

The most dramatic illustration of the political unwillingness to deal with tax evasion is the tax amnesty declared in 1993. The Commission on Taxation (1985: 205) set up by the government made clear that "it is emphatically not the case that the criminal law has no role to play in tax enforcement". The level of staffing available to the Revenue Commissioners had increased in the early 1990s as a result of the reduction in the functions of the customs and excise service due to the open market within the European Union. This meant that conditions were perfect for a major campaign against tax evasion using the full weight of criminal procedures. The government's solution was to declare a tax amnesty in May 1993. Under its terms tax evaders could confess their criminal offences in private to the Revenue Commissioners, agree to pay a tax of 15% on their undeclared money and go in peace.

The problem of punishment

If white-collar offences overcome the range of obstacles that exist and succeed in getting into court to be criminally adjudicated what kinds of sanctions are imposed? The relevant evidence is sketchy and incomplete, but it does suggest that white-collar criminals may be treated differently to others. The only research on the topic is from the 1980s (Rottman and Tormey 1986). It looked at indictments for six offences before the Dublin criminal court between 1980 and 1984. The offences were obtaining goods by false pretences, fraudulent conversion, embezzlement, customs violations, and forgery and receiving offences. Though the authors of the study refer to these as the "classic Irish white-collar crime" (Rottman and Tormey 1986: 48), it is not clear as we have seen that these offences are necessarily committed by offenders from what might be termed white-collar backgrounds. It is also the case that in terms of our earlier clarification these might more suitably be designated as "occupational crime".

Nonetheless the authors concluded that there was a major difference between the way in which the courts sanctioned these offences and the ways in which they dealt with more "conventional" crimes. The conviction rate was lower with fifty-nine out of every hundred defendants found guilty compared to 68 out of every hundred individuals for "conventional" crimes. In addition only 20% of these convictions resulted in a prison sentence compared to 50% of convictions for "conventional" crimes. They concluded that for those offences, "the probability of conviction is low…[S]imilarly the prospect of imprisonment if convicted is low" (Rottman and Tormey 1986:52).

Conclusion

In this chapter we have suggested that in Ireland, as elsewhere, white-collar crime is a significant but under-appreciated and under-regulated problem. There is some evidence that this may be changing. This is indicated by public concerns over the revelations at various tribunals and by the potential offered by some recent changes in policing such as the Criminal Assets Bureau and the new improved Garda Fraud Squad. The Criminal Assets Bureau was intended to confiscate the assets of drug dealers and of those involved in organised crime. But its scope is not limited to organised crime and can extend to all assets that are the result of criminal activity. A European Union Task Force (*Irish Times*, 31 May 1999) singled out this power as particularly effective in preventing money laundering. The Bureau's conflict with the Flood Tribunal over the activities of retired Dublin planner George Redmond suggests that it may be willing to go beyond conventional crime.

However these initiatives will have to be accompanied by a number of other changes if the problem is to be adequately and decisively addressed. These include changes in the criminal law as it applies to corporate behaviour, changes in the willingness to invoke such law against offenders, and changes in the manner in which offenders are sanctioned. Failure to do so will sustain the perception that in Ireland there is a law for the rich and a law for the poor. To borrow a phrase from Reiman (1995), the feeling is that "the rich get rich and the poor get prison". The material that we have considered here would suggest that this belief is not without foundation.

However there is an additional problem. It is necessary to change the ways in which we respond to the misbehaviour of the powerful. But this must be done in a manner that does not contribute to and exacerbate the rampant penal expansionism. A taste of prison for rich and powerful offenders may have pleasing populist overtones, but if prison does not represent a solution for "ordinary" offenders, it is not a solution for corporate and other white-collar offenders either. Perhaps, as David Nelken (1994: 383-384) has suggested, the answer can be arrived at from the other end of the penal equation. Rather than extending the methods used to deal with ordinary criminals to business and corporate ones, maybe we could apply the methods through which we deal with business and corporate crime to our dealings with conventional crime. As Nelken suggests, these are designed to achieve regulation without stigmatisation. He argues that "it is usually necessary for an offender accused of ordinary crime to suffer the stigma of a conviction before consideration is given to compliance, whereas the opposite is true for business offenders" (Nelken 1994: 383). The process through which a "series of attempts at compliance as a prelude to prosecution" (Nelken 1994: 384) is utilised is not entirely absent from our treatment of ordinary crime. But its further extension into the response to ordinary crime would bring about more equality in our treatment of offenders from different backgrounds without at the same time surrendering to visceral demands for an increased prison population.

REFERENCES

Beirne, P. and Messerschmidt, J. (1991), *Criminology*, New York: Harcourt Brace Jovanich

Benson, M. L. and Cullen, F.T. (1988), "The Special Sensitivity of White Collar Offenders to Prison: A Critique and Research Agenda", *Journal of Criminal Justice*, Vol. 16, pp 207-215

Box, S. (1983), *Crime, Power and Mystification*, London: Tavistock

Braithwaite, J. (1984), *Corporate Crime in the Pharmaceutical Industry*, London: Routledge and Kegan Paul

Braithwaite, J. (1985), "White-Collar Crime", *Annual Review of Sociology*, Vol. 11, pp 1-25

Clarke, M. (1990), *Business Crime*, Oxford: Polity Press

Commission on Taxation 1985, *Fourth Report,* Dublin: Stationery Office

Committee of Public Accounts (1999), *Parliamentary Inquiry into DIRT: First Report* (the version used here is that available on the Internet at www.irlgov.ie/committees-99/c-publicaccounts/)

Garda Síochána (1999), *Annual Report on Crime*, Dublin: Stationery Office

Glasberg, D. S. and Skidmore, D. (1998), "The Dialectics of Corporate Crime: The Anatomy of the Savings and Loan Crisis and the case of Silverado Banking, Savings and Loan Association", *American Journal of Economics and Sociology*, Vol. 57, No. 4, pp 423-449

Gobert, J. (1994), "Corporate Criminality: New Crimes for the Times", *Criminal Law Review*, pp 722-734

Hagan, J. (1994), *Crime and Disrepute*, California: Pine Forge Press

Irish Reports (1946), *State versus Fawsitt*, Dublin: Incorporated Law Society of Ireland

Lee, G. and Bird, C. (1998), *Breaking the Bank*, Dublin: Blackwater Press

Mc Cullagh, C. (1996), *Crime in Ireland: A Sociological Introduction*, Cork: University Press

National Crime Forum (1998), *Report*, Dublin: Institute of Public Administration

Nelken, D. (1994), "White Collar Crime", in Maguire, M., Morgan, R. and Reiner, R. (eds.), *Oxford Handbook of Criminology*, Oxford: Claredon Press

Pearce, F. (1976), *Crimes of the Powerful,* London: Pluto

Reiman, J. H. (1995), *The rich get richer and the poor get prison : ideology, class, and criminal justice,* Boston: Allyn and Bacon

Shapiro, S. (1989), "Collaring the Crime, not the Criminal: Reconsidering 'White-Collar' Crime", *American Sociological Review*, Vol. 55, pp 346-365.

Tribunal of Inquiry into the Beef Processing Industry (1994), *Report*, Dublin: Stationery Office

Tribunal of Inquiry (Dunne's Payments) (1997), *Report*, Dublin: Stationery Office (the version quoted in the paper is that available on the Internet at www.homesteader.com/tribunal.htm)

Sutherland, E. (1949), *White Collar Crime*, New York: Holt, Rinehart and Winston

Rottman, D. and Tormey, P. (1986), "Respectable Crime: Occupational and Professional Crime in the Republic of Ireland", *Studies*, Vol. 75. No. 297, pp 43-55

Thrasher, F.M. (1927), *The Gang: A Study of 1,313 Gangs in Chicago,* Chicago: University of Chicago Press

Wiesburd, D., Wheeler, S., Waring, E. and Bode, N. (1991), *Crimes of the Middle Classes: White Collar Offenders in the Federal Courts*, New Haven: Yale University Press

10

"this otherwise delicate subject": Child Sexual Abuse in Early Twentieth-Century Ireland

Eoin O'Sullivan

INTRODUCTION

During the 1990s in Ireland, there was extensive publicity and bewilderment at the apparent dramatic increase in incidents of child sexual abuse[1], at the individuals convicted for such offences, and at the leniency of some of their sentences.[2] The term "Paedophile Priest", however unjust the appellation, became a subject of popular discourse,[3] and one abusing priest in particular, Fr Brendan

---

[1] Reports of child sexual abuse rose from 37 in 1983 to 2,441 in 1995. The Department of Health and Children has not issued more recent statistics

[2] For example, in the *Kilkenny Incest Case*, the perpetrator of the abuse, having pleaded guilty to charges of rape, incest and assault was sentenced to seven years penal servitude; the maximum sentence for incest with a female aged fifteen or more. Public outcry at his sentence led to the passing of the Criminal Law (Incest Proceedings) Act 1995 which increased the maximum sentence to life imprisonment. For further details see, O'Malley, T. (1996), *Sexual Offences: Law, Policy and Punishment*, Dublin: Roundhall/Sweet and Maxwell.

[3] Ferguson has argued that "the intense focus on the sexuality of priests constitutes a selective response in recent disclosures of sexual abuse which not only raise issues for the church, but serious questions about men, masculinity, the family, sexuality, and organisations in general. In constructing the debate in terms of clerical celibacy and the 'paedophile priest', attention is deflected from the fundamental issue that men from all social backgrounds commit such crimes of

---

Smyth, was indirectly responsible for the breakup of the Fianna Fáil-Labour Party coalition government, following allegations of the mis-handling of his extradition case by the office of the Attorney General.[4] The "X" case resulted in a constitutional referendum, the consequences of which are still being played out in Irish society.[5] Reported court cases on the "West of Ireland Farmer" (see endnote 1), the Kilkenny Incest case (see endnote 2), the swimming coaches, Derry O'Rourke[6] amongst others, and numerous allegations of sexual abuse of children in state funded reformatory and industrial schools[7] resulted in a sustained debate on child sexual abuse for apparently the first time in the history of the Irish state.

Sex crimes reported or known to the gardaí increased from 397 in 1990 to 968 in 1998 (the last year in which complete data is available).[8] However, many of these recorded offences relate to incidents that took place many years previously. Leon, for example, has shown that in the case of male sexual assault victimisation, of the 175 recorded cases in 1995, 61 had occurred over 10 years prior to the complaint being made.[9] On 1 June 2000 there were 354 sex offenders

---

violence and are policed by a range of organisations that are male dominated". Ferguson, H. (1995), "The Paedophile Priest: A Deconstruction", *Studies*, Vol. 84, No. 335, p. 250. See also the proceedings of conferences held by the National Conference of Priests in Ireland. NCPI (1999), *Child Sexual Abuse: The Irish Experience so Far and the Way Forward*, Dublin: NCPI; and NCPI (2000), *Child Abuse in Institutional Care: Learning from the Past and Hoping for the Future*, Dublin: NCPI. In a recent study it was argued that cleric sex offenders are similar to non-cleric sex offenders matched for age, education, and marital status. Langevin, R. and Curnoe, S. (2000), "A Study Of Clerics Who Commit Sexual Offenses: Are They Different From Other Sex Offenders?" *Child Abuse and Neglect,* Vol. 24, No. 4, pp. 535–545

4   See Moore, C. (1995), *Betrayal of Trust: The Father Brendan Smyth Affair and the Catholic Church*: Dublin: Marino Books. Smyth, a member of the Norbertine Order, who died of natural causes in the Curragh prison in August 1997, was sentenced to 12 years in jail having pleaded guilty to 74 charges of indecent and sexual assault committed over a period of 35 years. He had previously served three years in jail in Northern Ireland for 43 similar offences

5   The *X case* involved a fourteen year old girl who was statutorily raped by a middle-aged friend of her parents. With the support of her parents, it was arranged for her to have an abortion in England, but she was prohibited from doing so, in light of the constitutional ban on abortion in Ireland. See Holden, W. (1994) *Unlawful Carnal Knowledge: The True Story of the Irish 'X' Case,* London: Harper Collins

6   O'Rourke, a former Irish national swimming coach was convicted and sentenced to twelve years' imprisonment. For further detail, see First Interim Report of the Joint Committee on Tourism, Sport and Recreation (1998) *Protection of Children in Sport*, Dublin: Stationery Office

7   See for example, Raftery, M. and O'Sullivan, E. (1999), *Suffer the Little Children: The Inside Story of Ireland's Industrial Schools,* Dublin: New Island Books and Arnold, M. and Laskey, H. (1985), *Children of the Poor Clares: The Story of an Irish Orphanage*, Belfast: Appletree Press. For a detailed critique of thesis outlined in the former book, see Ferguson, H. (2000), "States of Fear, Child Abuse, and Irish Society", *Doctrine and Life,* Vol. 50, No. 1, pp. 20-31

8   For an analysis of trends in sexual crimes against children from 1973-1991, see O'Mahony, P. (1993), *Crime and Punishment in Ireland*, Dublin: Roundhall Press, pp. 46-47. More generally, on the "sexual revolution in Ireland" in the 1990s and its impact on the criminal justice system, see O'Mahony, P. (1996) *Criminal Chaos: Seven Crises in Irish Criminal Justice*, Round Hall Sweet and Maxwell, pp. 207-245

9   Leon, C. (1999), "Sexual Offences in Ireland, 1994-1997", *Irish Journal of Criminal Law*

(all males and 30 percent over the age of 50) in custody under sentence, compared to 98 in 1990.[10] Of course not all reported sex crimes and those sentenced for sexual offences, were sexual abusers of children,[11] but clearly a significant proportion were.[12] Murphy, in his overview of sexual offenders in Irish prisons in 1997, showed that 53 percent of sex offenders were serving sentences for offences against children, but were serving on average a shorter sentence than those convicted for sexual offences against adults.[13] If the 1997 proportion has remained constant, it would suggest that on the 1 June 2000 there were 188 prisoners serving sentences for sexual offences against children, or 21 percent of the total sentenced male prisoners for Group 1 type offences.

In response to these allegations, of and documented cases, of child sexual abuse, new guidelines and protocols have been established, by sporting organisations, the Catholic Church and the state to protect children from such abuse.[14] A commission (chaired by Justice Laffoy) was established to investigate abuse in industrial and reformatory schools following the broadcast of the *States of Fear* series on RTE.[15] A range of new legislation has been introduced to provide immunity from civil liability to any person who reports child abuse "reasonably and in good faith"; to increase the maximum sentences for those convicted of child sexual abuse from five years to fourteen years; and to provide a range of tracking requirements for certain sex offenders and new penalties for those involved in trafficking in and sexual exploitation of children.[16] Interestingly, the

---

[10] Irish Prison Service (2000), *Irish Prisons Service Report on Prisons and Places of Detention for the Years 1995-1998*, Dublin: Stationery Office. Despite the title of the report, it also includes a profile of committed prisoners on 1 June 2000. Regretably, no detailed annual report on the Irish prison system has been published since 1994. Sexual offences include the categories of rape, attempted rape, indecent assault, indecent exposure and other sexual offences. The category, "other sexual offences" would appear to refer to defilement of girls under seventeen

[11] For the only known study of the profile and sentencing patterns for sex offenders in Ireland, see O'Malley, T. (1996), *Sexual Offences: Law, Policy and Punishment*, Dublin: Roundhall Sweet and Maxwell, pp. 367-378

[12] The unsatisfactory nature of criminal justice statistics in Ireland has been frequently noted, but the quality and detail of the data appears to be disimproving rather than improving. It is hardly an exaggeration to state that more detailed information was available in 1900, than in 2000

[13] Murphy, P. (1998), "A Therapeutic Programme for Imprisoned Sex Offenders: Progress to date and Issues for the Future", *The Irish Journal of Psychology*, Vol. 19, No. 1, p. 191

[14] See *inter alia*, Report of the Irish Catholic Bishops' Advisory Committee on Child Sexual Abuse by Priests and Religious (1996), *Child Sexual Abuse: Framework for a Church Response,* Dublin: Veritas; Department of Health and Children (1999), *Children First: National Guidelines for the Protection and Welfare of Children*, Dublin: Stationery Office; Department of Education and Science (2001), *Child Protection – Guidelines and Procedures*, Dublin: Department of Education and Science

[15] The commission was established in May 1999 and given statutory remit under the *Commission to Inquire into Child Abuse Act, 2000*. The *Residential Institutions Redress Bill 2001* aims to provide financial awards to people who were abused while in residential care as children

[16] The Protection for Persons Reporting Child Abuse Act 1998; The Sex Offenders Act 2001 and the Child Trafficking and Pornography Act 1998

Committee of Inquiry into the Penal System which reported in 1985 had argued that "Much of the law dealing with this topic (sexual offences) is vague, uncertain and, in the opinion of some people, unfair. There is a case to be made for a comprehensive Sexual Offences Act which would deal with sexual offences, both heterosexual and homosexual, prostitution, brothel-keeping, incest, indecent exposure and kindred offences of a sexual or indecent nature".[17]

Thus, it would appear that in the 1990s, Irish society was made aware of the sexual abuse of children and responded quickly to protect children and to punish those guilty of abusing them.[18] As a recent statement from the Department of Justice, Equality and Law Reform put it, "the Government must, and will, do all it can to make sure that our children and other vulnerable persons will be protected as far as that is possible".[19] This situation is not unique to Ireland. Across many industrialised countries, a punitive socio-legal policy towards sex offenders against minors has emerged, driven by both the media and public demand, despite criminal statistics failing to confirm an escalation of sex crimes against minors.[20] However, an examination of Irish society during the first three decades after independence indicates that similar moral panics had occurred.

The conventional history of child sexual abuse suggests that the area was both discovered and constructed in the 1970s through the endeavours of various professionals and was influenced by the children's rights and women's movements of that period.[21] For example, a report sponsored by the Irish Council for Civil Liberties into child sexual abuse in Ireland argued that

> Discovery of child sexual abuse as a major problem is recent in Ireland, as it is internationally, and has developed rapidly. In 1983, the Irish Association of Social Workers hosted a pioneering workshop on child sexual abuse, from which a working party and the Incest Crisis Service developed. By 1985, the Rape Crisis Centres were identifying survivors of child sexual abuse as a major client group.[22]

---

[17] Committee of Inquiry into the Penal System (1985), *Report*, Dublin: Stationery Office, p. 53

[18] For a broad overview of children as victims of crime, see Morgan, J. and Zedner, L. (1992), *Child Victims: Crime, Impact, and Criminal Justice*, Oxford: Clarendon Paperbacks

[19] Department of Justice, Equality and Law Reform (2001), *Background Note on the Sex Offenders Act 2001*, Dublin: Department of Justice, Equality and Law Reform

[20] West, D. J. (2000), "Paedophilia: Plague or Panic?", *Journal of Forensic Psychiatry*, Vol. 11, No. 3, pp. 511-531

[21] Freud, of course famously proposed that the etiology of the hysteria he was treating in middle class Viennese women was to be found in childhood experiences of sexual abuse. However, his theory was rejected by his colleagues and he himself ultimately retracted this theory. See, Masson, J.M. (1984), *The Assault on Truth: Freud's Suppression of the Seduction Theory*, New York: Farrar, Straus & Giroux and Olafson, E., Corwin, D.L. and Summit, R.C. (1993), "Modern History of Child Sexual Abuse Awareness: Cycles of Discovery and Suppression", *Child Abuse and Neglect*, Vol. 17, No.1, pp. 7-24

[22] Irish Council for Civil Liberties (1988), *Report of the Child Sexual Abuse Working Party*, Dublin: ICCL, p. 12. See also McKeown, K. and Gilligan, R., (1991), "Child Sexual Abuse in the Eastern Health Board Region of Ireland in 1988: An Analysis of 512 Confirmed Cases", *The Economic and Social Review*, Vol. 22, No. 2, pp. 101-134 for a similar analysis

However, a closer examination of the various social and moral purity campaigns of the late nineteenth and early twentieth centuries, shows that a raft of legislation was enacted that aimed at the protection and regulation of children.[23] These cumulative legislative changes reconstructed our legal and social understanding of childhood and prohibited both certain sexual acts and the age at which sexual activity could legally commence.[24] Jackson has argued that, although the term child sexual abuse was not in vogue in the late nineteenth and early twentieth century, various euphemisms – such as "moral corruption, immorality, tampering, white slavery, juvenile prostitution, ruining" – were used to describe what we would today label child sexual abuse.[25] The Criminal Justice Amendment Act, 1885[26], described by Judith Walkowitz as "a particularly nasty and pernicious piece of omnibus legislation" in that it "gave police far greater summary jurisdiction over

---

[23] Key legislation included the various factory acts that regulated the number of hours children could work and fixed the age at which children could commence work; the various reformatory and industrial schools acts which created separate institutions for those children deemed guilty of committing offences and those who were viewed at risk of engaging in delinquency; the Punishment of Incest Act 1908 and school attendance legislation which made attendance at school compulsory for children under certain ages. See *inter alia*; Aries, P. (1962), *Centuries of Childhood*, London: Jonathan Cape; Dingwall, R., Eekelaar, J.M. and Murray, T. (1984), "Childhood as a Social Problem: A Survey of the History of Legal Regulation", *Journal of Law and Society*, Vol. 11, No. 2; May, M. (1973), "Innocence and Experience: The Evolution of the Concept of Juvenile Delinquency in the Mid-Nineteenth Century", *Victorian Studies*, Vol. XVII, No. 1; Platt, A. (1969), *The Child Savers - The Invention of Delinquency*, Chicago: University of Chicago Press; Pollock, L. (1983), *Forgotten Children: Parent-child Relations from 1500-1900*, Cambridge: Cambridge University Press; Nardinelli, C. (1980), "Child Labor and the Factory Acts", *Journal of Economic History*, Vol. 40, No. 4, pp. 739-755; Bailey, V. and Blackburn, S. (1979), "The Punishment of Incest Act of 1908: A Case study of Law Creation", *Criminal Law Review*, Vol. XI, pp. 708-718

[24] For further details, see Gorham, G. (1978), "The 'Maiden Tribute of Modern Babylon' re-examined. Child prostitution and the Idea of Childhood in late-Victorian England", *Victorian Studies*, Vol. 21, pp. 353-379

[25] Jackson, L.A. (2000), *Child Sexual Abuse in Victorian England*, London: Routledge, p. 2

[26] The 1885 Act's full title was (48 & 49 Victoria, Chapter 69) "An Act to make further provision for the Protection of Women and Girls, the suppression of brothels, and other purposes". In addition to the 1885 Act, other legislation that aimed at regulating female sexual activity and reproductive behavior included the 1861 Offenses Against the Person Act that contained clauses dealing with abortion, concealment of birth, and exposing children to danger in addition to rape, carnal knowledge, and procurement; the 1866 and 1869 Contagious Diseases Acts that imposed incarceration upon suspected prostitutes found to suffer venereal disease; and the 1872 Infant Life Preservation Act that regulated the baby-farming practices of working class mothers who could not care for their children because of employment outside the home. See for example Smart, C. (1992), "Disruptive bodies and unruly sex: the regulation of reproduction and sexuality in the nineteenth century", in Smart, C. (ed.), *Regulating Womanhood: Historical Essays on Marriage, Motherhood, and Sexuality*, London: Routledge; Arnot, M.L. (1994), "Infant Death, Child Care and the State: The Baby Farming Scandal and the First Infant Life Protection Legislation of 1872", *Continuity and Change*, Vol. 9, No. 2, pp. 271-311; Malcolm, E. (1999), "Troops Of Largely Diseased Women: VD, The Contagious Diseases Acts And Moral Policing In Late Nineteenth-Century Ireland", *Irish Economic and Social History*, Vol. 26, pp. 1-14

poor working-class women and children",[27] was the most significant indicator of this shift. This legislation raised the age of female consent to sixteen[28], from the earlier age of thirteen.[29] As a consequence, Smart argues, "it created and extended a particular, historically and culturally specific type of childhood to the age of sixteen".[30] However, we need to be mindful, that while a range of euphemisms did exist to describe child sexual abuse, an understanding of the physical and psychological consequences of such sexual activity was underdeveloped, and it was the morality of both the adult and the child that was the focus of concern. Interest in the sexuality of children was part of broader concern with redefining childhood associated with the latter half of the nineteenth century.

Although this chapter cannot hope to provide either a detailed or definitive history of child sexual abuse in Ireland,[31] it does aim to show the construction and framing of the concept of child sexual abuse by focusing on the debates that took place on the age of consent. The age at which sexual relations can commence is crucial to our understanding of child sexual abuse. For an adult to have sexual relations with a child may, from today's vantage point, be viewed as repugnant, but it was not always a criminal act. Until the middle of the nineteenth century, an adult could have consensual sexual relations with a thirteen year old girl, without any criminal penalty being attached. By 1935 such an act could result in a life sentence for the adult, regardless of the issue of consent or that the adult genuinely believed that the girl was over the age of consent. By focusing on these issues, we can see that debates on child sexuality and sexual relations between persons of differing ages are complex and subject to moral panics in the nineteenth and twentieth centuries.

AGE OF CONSENT DEBATES AND THE CRIMINAL LAW AMENDMENT ACT 1885

The origins of this legislation, although complex, are generally attributed to the

---

[27] Walkowitz, J.R. (1983), "Male Vice and Female Virtue: Feminism and the Politics of Prostitution in Nineteenth Century Britain", in Snitow, A. *et al.* (eds.), *Powers of Desire: The Politics of Sexuality,* New York: The Monthly Review Press and Walkowitz, J.R. (1992), *City of Dreadful Delight: Narratives of Sexual Danger in late-Victorian London,* London: Virago Press

[28] In addition, it strengthened existing legislation against prostitution and proscribed all homosexual relations

[29] For an analysis of the legislation on the age of consent prior to this Act, see Simpson, A.E. (1987), "Vulnerability and the Age of Female Consent: legal innovation and its effect on prosecutions for Rape in Eighteenth Century London", in Rousseau, G.S. and Portor, R. (eds.), *Sexual Underworlds of the Enlightenment,* Manchester: Manchester University Press, pp. 181-205

[30] Smart, C. (1999), "A History of Ambivalence and Conflict in the Discursive Construction of the 'Child Victim' of Sexual Abuse", *Social and Legal Studies,* Vol. 8, No. 3, p. 392

[31] For a fascinating account of medico-legal responses to allegations of child sexual abuse in mid-nineteenth century Dublin, see Lyons, J.B. (1997), "Sir William Wilde's Medico-Legal Observations", *Medical History,* Vol. 42, No. 1, pp. 437-453. On child sexual abuse in eighteenth-century Ireland, see Kelly, J. (1995), "A most Inhuman and Barbarous Piece of Villainy: An Exploration of the Crime of Rape in Eighteenth Century Ireland", *Eighteenth Century Ireland,* Vol. 10, pp. 78-107

investigative journalism of W.T. Stead. Indeed the legislation was generally known as the Stead Act. Believing that the existing legislation did not safeguard young girls from sexual exploitation, Stead published a series of articles in the *Pall Mall Gazette* which purported to uncover child prostitution and white slavery rings. At the center of his account, Stead reported how he had "purchased" an eleven-year-old girl from her mother to prove how easily vice could be obtained.[32] These articles, entitled "The Maiden Tribute of Modern Babylon",[33] sold over one and a half million copies and sparked a massive public outcry for more protective legislation.

Stead, and other observers, credited his articles with hastening the passage of the Criminal Law Amendment Act 1885. The Act was the latest in a twenty-five year series of legislation that raised the age of consent and delineated the penalties for sexual offences against women and minors. In 1861 the Offences against the Person Act was passed, confirming the age of consent at twelve, and making carnal knowledge of a girl under age ten a felony and of a girl between the ages of ten and twelve a misdemeanor. Additionally, indecent assault or attempted rape upon a girl under twelve was punished with up to two years imprisonment. The 1875 amendments to the Offences Against the Person Act 1861 further raised the age of consent to thirteen.

The Criminal Law Amendment Act 1885, as it finally passed on 14 August, repealed sections 49 and 52 of the 1861 Offenses Against the Person Act and the entire 1875 version. The new law raised the age of consent to sixteen and placed severe penalties upon those attempting "white slavery". Sexual assaults on girls under the age of thirteen were deemed felonious and assaults on girls between thirteen and sixteen or on imbecile women or girls were termed misdemeanors. The Act had sections that outlined the penalties for abducting and detaining in brothels girls under the age of eighteen.[34] The Act also provided for a term of imprisonment not exceeding two years, with or without hard labour, for any male person guilty of an act of gross indecency with another male person in public or in private, in effect criminalising homosexuality.[35] However, this legislation failed

---

[32] The child was Eliza Armstrong, a thirteen-year-old daughter of a chimney-sweep. As a result of his "purchase", Stead was charged with unlawfully kidnapping a minor, was found guilty and was imprisoned for three months in Holloway Gaol

[33] The title was inspired by an ancient Greek myth which described how the monstrous Minotaur was given seven boys and seven girls every nine years by the people of Athens

[34] For further details, see Stevenson, K. (2000), "Ingenuities of the female mind: Legal and Public Perceptions of Sexual Violence in Victorian Britain, 1850-1890", in D'Cruze, S. (ed.), *Everyday Violence in Britain, 1850-1950*, Harloe: Pearson Education, pp. 89-103 and Jackson, L.A. (2000), *Child Sexual Abuse in Victorian England*, London: Routledge

[35] The *Criminal Law (Sexual Offences) Act 1993* decriminalised homosexual acts between consenting adult males. It abolished the common law offence of buggery between persons but made it an offence to commit an act of buggery with persons of either sex under seventeen years of age or a mentally impaired person. The Act also replaced the offence of gross indecency with a new offence of gross indecency by a male with a male under seventeen years of age

to provide adequate protection against sexual abuse within families, in that where a girl had passed the age of sixteen, the law could not be applied retrospectively to punish ongoing incest. Following a concerted campaign, the Punishment of Incest Act 1908 was passed, which created the criminal offence of sexual relations between people who are related to each other.[36]

DEBATING SEX IN IRELAND: THE PROBLEM OF UNMARRIED MOTHERS AND IMMORALITY

The 1885 Act applied to Ireland, but is was not until the period immediately after independence[37] that a concerted debate on sexual abuse took place, couched as it was in various euphemisms, usually in the form of the "problem of the unmarried mother". The unmarried mother became an object of attention at this time, partly because it was perceived that the number of illegitimate births was increasing,[38] and also it was feared amongst Catholic writers that such women were subject to the attention of Protestant proselytisers.[39] It was a period that has become synonymous with the establishment of a narrow moral code, a "preoccupation

---

[36] For further details, see Bailey, V. and Blackburn, S. (1979), "The Punishment of Incest Act of 1908: A Case Study of Law Creation", *Criminal Law Review*, Vol. XI, pp. 708-718 and Bell, V. (1993) *Interrogating Incest: Feminism, Foucault and the Law,* London: Routledge

[37] For a summary of earlier debates, see Luddy, M. (1997), "Abandoned Women and Bad Characters: Prostitution in Nineteenth-Century Ireland", *Women's History Review*, Vol. 6, No.4, pp. 485-503

[38] The number of illegitimate births rose steadily during the 1920s and 1930s in Ireland, from 2.58 percent of total births in 1922 to 3.51 in 1934. However, it was widely belived that these percentages substantially underestimated the extent of such births. McAvoy has argued that "the accumulated evidence, even without taking into account forced marriage, miscarriage, abortion and infanticide, suggested that the problem of unmarried mothers was a growing one – and one often exported to England. McAvoy, S. (1999), "The Regulation of Sexuality in the Irish Free State, 1929-1935", in Jones, G. and Malcolm, E. (eds.), *Medicine, Disease and the State in Ireland, 1650-1940*, Cork: Cork University Press. On the issue of unmarried Irish mothers in England during this period, see Garrett, P.M. (2000), "The Abnormal Flight: the Migration and Repatriation of Irish Unmarried Mothers", *Social History*, Vol. 25, No.3, pp. 330-343

[39] The Rev. M.H. MacInerney, chairman of the rescue society known as St. Patrick's Guild was of the view that "Probably 600 or 700 'girls in trouble', mostly from the country, turn up in Dublin every year. There is not a single Catholic Rescue home to lend a hand to these unhappy girls, while proselytising agencies abound. Some 200, or perhaps not more than 170, of these poor creatures enter the Dublin workhouse; of the remaining 400 or 500, many drift into the souper homes or are preyed upon by harpies who pose as charitable workers. The more fortunate cases (perhaps a couple of hundred, all told) are cared for by four or five small rescue societies. These rescue societies have to work under heart-breaking difficulties and disadvantages. They can do little or nothing for the moral benefit of the unmarried mothers. At best they can only find some sort of lodgings for these poor creatures, find foster-mothers for the infants, and pay some portion of the fosterage fee. But very many of the foster-mothers are dirty, ignorant, drunken or mercenary; from which you can form an idea of what happens to the children when they happen to survive". MacInerny, M.H. (1925), "A Plea for Social Service", *The Irish Rosary*, Vol. 29, No. 3, pp. 169-170

with sex, (and) the virtual equation of immorality with sexual immorality"[40] among the Catholic hierarchy and an identification of the Irish state with a Catholic system of values.[41]

Unmarried mothers were perceived as doubly deviant, not only was she a threat to the social order, but her child could be infected with the deviant genes and perpetuate the threat to order. It was because of these fears and the failure of the workhouses to sufficiently imbue such women with responsibility, that separate institutions for "first-time offenders" developed. Workhouses with their mix of women who had "fallen" on more than one occasion where deemed unsuitable for the saving of women. With the establishment of new charitable institutions, the workhouses retained only those women deemed to be beyond salvation. As Spensky argues "only the mother of a first illegitimate child was considered as "deserving" of a treatment better than that of the workhouse where other lone mothers were received, because there she might be contaminated by tougher women, fail to repent and become a prostitute".[42] The children of both groups were also relabelled as "children in danger" (offspring of first-time offenders) and "dangerous children" (offspring of repeat offenders).

Considerable debate took place as to the most appropriate mechanism to meet the needs of "fallen girls" in the pages of the *Irish Ecclesiastical Record* in the early 1920s. Joseph A. Glynn, a prominent member of both the Society of St Vincent de Paul and the Catholic Protection and Rescue Society proposed that a large hostel/factory, capable of looking after upwards of 500 girls, be established in Dublin to meet their needs. This institution would be under the control of the bishops, but should be managed by a lay committee "owing to the difficulties of getting girls to enter a home controlled by nuns."[43] The Rev. M.H. McInerney argued against this proposal, suggesting instead the necessity for a large number of small rescue homes scattered throughout the county.[44] In a further contribution,

---

[40] Lee, J.J. (1989), *Ireland, 1912-1985: Politics and Society,* Cambridge: Cambride University Press, p. 645

[41] See in particular, Whyte, J.H. (1980), *Church and State in Modern Ireland, 1923-1979,* Dublin: Gill and Macmillan

[42] Spenskey, M. (1992), "Producers of Legitimacy: Homes for Unmarried Mothers in the 1950s", in Smart, C. (ed.), *Regulating Womanhood: Historical Essays on Marriage, Motherhood and Sexuality,* London: Routledge, p. 110

[43] Glynn, J.A. (1921), "The Unmarried Mother", *Irish Ecclesiastical Record*, Vol. xviii, p. 466. Interestingly, Devane in a subsequent article noted that "As to Homes, in *many* instances offenders have expressed to me in Court a desire to go, in *some* cases they have begged to be sent, to prison rather than a home. This seems a strange if not an unreasonable attitude to adopt, for which I cannot venture an explanation. (emphasis in original). Devane, R.S., "The Unmarried Mother: Some Legal Aspects of the Problem. Part 2", *Irish Ecclesiastical Record*, p. 185

[44] MacInerny, M.H. (1922), "A Postscript on the Souper Problem", *Irish Ecclesiastical Record*, Vol. xix, p. 254. In a subsequent article in the Irish Rosary, MacInerney argued that "here in Ireland we are too tolerant of abuses. We allow them to grow, and wax stronger, until they become so powerful

"Sagart" argued against the establishment of rescue homes as "the prominent existence of Rescue Homes, suggesting as they would a certain indulgent attitude towards moral lapses, would be calculated to lower the high ideals of our people, and is therefore, to be avoided, except in the very last extreme". He took the view that "the continuation of the system of individual treatment provided by a range of Catholic societies, due to its avoidance of scandal, its adaptability to various needs, and its enlisting of the force of personal sympathy, seems to be the right method of dealing with this complicated and delicate problem. There seems also, under God, every reason to trust that, if the system were developed prudently, it would be able to catch in its net practically all the girls who now flee to Proselytizing Homes, to unsafe Maternity Homes, to far-off Unions, or to England."[45]

The eventual system adopted, utilising the language of the criminal justice system, was to segregate between the "first offenders" and "recidivists". Such a policy was first recommended by the Poor Law Commission of 1906,[46] but not acted upon until the early 1920s. In 1922 the Sacred Heart Home in Bessboro, Co Cork, managed by the Sisters of the Sacred Heart of Jesus and Mary, was opened "for young mothers who have fallen for the first time and who are likely to be influenced towards a useful and respectable life".[47] Similar homes were established by the same Order in Roscrea in 1930 and Castlepollard in 1935. The Sisters of Charity of St. Vincent De Paul opened a similar institution on the Navan Road in 1918 and the Sisters of the Good Shepherd opened a home in Dunboyne, Co Meath, in 1955.[48] In addition, three special homes were provided by the poor law authorities in Tuam, Kilrush and Pelletstown.[49] Although not acted upon

---

that we are unable to strangle them. Many of you will have read the appalling revelations in the *Freeman* as to the immorality which is rampant in the underworld of Dublin. Those revelations show that a hoard of parasites – including groups of publicans, of lodging house keepers, of dressers, touts and usurers – batten on the White Slavery which exists in our midst and wax fat on the wages of sin. You will have read of the misconduct that takes place by night on suburban roads; and you will have heard of the thousand unfortunate night prowlers who infest the streets and lanes of this Catholic city." MacInerney, M. H. (1925), "A Plea for Social Service", *The Irish Rosary,* Vol. xxix, No. 3, p. 168

[45] 'Sagart' (1922), "How to Deal with the Unmarried Mother", *Irish Ecclesiastical Record*, Vol. xx, p. 150

[46] *Report of the Vice-Regal Commission on Poor Law Reform in Ireland* (1906), London: Stationery Office. For those recidivist women, the Commission recommended that they be committed by a Court of Justice to one of the labour houses to be established for vagrants and other persons of bad character, perhaps for as long as it was necessary to support any of their children at the public cost. See Eason, C. (1907), "The Report of the Viceregal Commission on the Irish Poor Law", *The Economic Journal*, Vol. 17, pp. 131-138

[47] *Annual Report of the Department of Local Government and Public Health* (1928), Dublin: Stationery Office, p. 113

[48] Flanagan, N. and Richardson, V. (1992), *Unmarried Mothers: A Social Profile,* Dublin: Department of Social Policy and Social Work/Social Science Research Centre, pp. 49-50

[49] Although these special institutions were financed by the local authority, they were in fact run by religious orders. Pelletstown was managed by the Daughters of Charity of St. Vincent de Paul, Kilrush was managed by the Sisters of Mercy and Tuam was managed by the Bon Secours Nuns

formally, the view of the Commission on the Relief of the Sick and Destitute
Poor, Including the Insane Poor in 1927 was

> that if an unmarried woman who applies for relief during pregnancy, or after giving
> birth to a child, is willing, when applying for assistance, to undertake to remain for
> a period not exceeding one year, there should be power to detain her for that period,
> in the case of a first admission. In the case of admission for the second time, there
> should be power to retain for a period of two years. On third or subsequent
> admissions the Board should have power to retain for such period as they think fit,
> having considered the recommendation of the Superior or Matron of the Home ...
> The term of detention we recommend is not an irreducible period and is not intended
> to be in any sense penal. It is primarily for the benefit of the woman and her child,
> and its duration will depend entirely on the individual necessities of the case.[50]

The development of the special homes not only removed unmarried mothers from
the unsavoury atmosphere of the county home, but also provided training that
lessened their chance of becoming pregnant for a second time. The view of the
Department of Local Government and Public Health was that

> On the whole the training in the special homes appears to have given satisfactory
> results. Very few girls who have been in these homes have been admitted during the
> year to county homes pregnant for a second time. Of those who have fallen again the
> majority spend only a short time in the special home either because of the death of
> the first child or through the interference of relatives.[51]

Particular concern was regularly expressed about the recidivist lone mothers, and
the causes of their repeated falls.

> These unfortunates regard their falls (for there are usually more than one) as
> unimportant. They have placed, perhaps, several illegitimate children in industrial
> schools or other places and are only waiting now until the latest child is old enough
> to be committed also ... the causes leading to these lapses from virtue are perfectly
> evident to all who trouble to observe life around them: no parental control, cheap
> romantic fiction, cinematograph performances showing vivid scenes often of low
> vices under an attractive semblance, all night dances in halls or dance places
> conducted without supervision, harmful and dangerous friendships, not to speak of
> other occasions too well known to need particular mention. In fact, the truth is that
> we have no cause for surprise if the young and inexperienced fall an easy prey to the
> terrible temptation with which their path is strewn.[52]

[50] Commission on the Relief of the Sick and Destitute Poor, Including the Insane Poor, (1927),
Report, Dublin: Stationary Office, p. 69
[51] Department of Local Government and Public Health (1936), *Report for 1934-35,* Dublin:
Stationery Office, p. 179
[52] Report of Miss Fitzgerald-Kenny, Lady Inspector of Boarded-Out Children, Department of Local
Government and Public Health, *Annual Report*, 1933-34, p. 326

The aforementioned Commission on the Relief of the Sick and Destitute Poor also addressed the issue of sexual offending in the context of illegitimate births. It noted that while the majority of lone mothers seeking relief were between the ages of 17 and 21, it did meet "exceptional cases where the ages were as low as 14 and 15". It reviewed the existing legislation on the age of consent and took the view that "the age of 16 is entirely too young for many girls to have full knowledge of and realise the consequence of an act that may be brought about by thoughtlessness and the seductive pleadings of the male partner in guilt" and argued that it should be "raised to 18, if not 19". In court proceedings involving age of consent cases, the commission argued that "juries should, if possible, be composed of an equal number of men and women jurors, and proceedings should not be open to the public or reported in the public press, although full transcript notes should be taken and preserved as court records".[53]

R.S. Devane and the Age of Consent

Among those who gave evidence to the Commission was the Rev R.S. (Dick) Devane SJ Devane had responded energetically to the series of articles in the *Irish Ecclesiastical Record*, referred to above, on the unmarried mother problem. He prefaced his contribution to the debate by stating that "It is to awaken interest among the clergy, the guardians of the people's morals, and to ensure that adequate protection shall be legally afforded to the growing girl, this otherwise delicate subject is here discussed".[54] Devane, showing considerable knowledge of the debates on age of consent and child sexual abuse taking place in Britain, argued that Ireland had fallen behind in protecting young girls from abuse. Summarizing the Irish legislation (primarily the Criminal Law Amendment Act 1885), he noted that the age of consent had been raised unconditionally to 16 in England and Northern Ireland. In the 1885 Act, to carnally know a girl under 13 was deemed a felony, whereas in the case of those aged 13-16, it was a misdemeanour. More significantly, in the case of those aged 13 to 16, it was a deemed a sufficient defence if the person accused had reasonable cause to believe the girl was of or above the age of 16 years. The proviso of reasonable cause to believe that the girl was of or above the age of 16 years was abolished in England and Northern Ireland with the passing of the Criminal Law Amendment Act 1922, except in the cases of young men under 24 charged for their first time under certain circumstances.[55] As Devane noted,

---

[53] Commission on the Relief of the Sick and Destitute Poor, Including the Insane Poor (1927), *Report,* Dublin: Stationary Office, pp. 72-73

[54] Devane, R.S. (1924), "The Unmarried Mother: Some Legal Aspects of the Problem", *Irish Ecclesiastical Record*, Vol. xxiii, p. 57

[55] For further details, see Home Office (1980), *Criminal Law Revision Committee – Working Paper on Sexual Offences,* London: HMSO

in Southern Ireland, this qualifying clause still exists, and its abolition and the raising of the "age of consent" is a matter of very grave importance, especially when one considers the independent and free and easy airs of the growing girl today, and the greater need for protection accordingly, not alone against others, but against her own silliness and stupidity – and perhaps even against the too frequent negligence of unnatural parents.[56]

Devane was also of the view that the age of consent should be raised to nineteen in Ireland, on the basis that "if precocious girls in industrial America are protected till eighteen, it would not be unreasonable to crave protection for the simple, innocent girls of an agricultural country like ours up to nineteen".[57]

In 1928 Devane made a further contribution to the debate by examining the report of the Commission on the Relief of the Sick and Destitute Poor. He happily endorsed their recommendations in regard to the age of consent and drew on the Departmental Committee on Sexual Offences Against Young Persons in 1925,[58] which he quoted at length to support his contention that the age of consent be raised. He noted that the Irish government had been approached to deal with this issue, but that no response had been forthcoming, before concluding with the rhetorical question "How many more children must be sacrificed before action is taken?"[59] Although it was to take a further two years, the government did respond to the issues raised by both the Commission and Devane.

COMMITTEE ON THE CRIMINAL LAW AMENDMENT ACTS (1880-85) AND JUVENILE PROSTITUTION

In June 1930, the government appointed a committee "to consider whether the following Statutes require amendment and, if so, in what respect, namely the Criminal Law Amendment Act 1880, and the Criminal Law Amendment Act 1885 as modified by later Statutes, and to consider whether any new legislation is

---

[56] Devane, R.S. (1924), "The Unmarried Mother: Some Legal Aspects of the Problem", Part 1, *Irish Ecclesiastical Record*, Vol. xxiii, p. 60

[57] Devane, R.S. (1924), The Unmarried Mother: Some Legal Aspects of the Problem", Part 1, *Irish Ecclesiastical Record*, Vol. xxiii, p. 67

[58] Departmental Committee on Sexual Offences Against Young Persons (1925), *Report*, Hansard, Cmd 2561 xv 905. The terms of reference for this Committee were "to collect information and to take evidence as to the prevalence of sexual offences against young persons and to report upon the subject, indicating any direction in which in their opinion the law or its administration might be improved". A similar Committeee was established in Scotland in 1924 "to enquire into the subject of sexual offences against children and young persons" which reported in 1926, Departmental Committee on Sexual Offences against Children and Young Persons in Scotland (1926), *Report*, Hansard, Cmd 2592. For an overview of the work of the committees, see Smart, C. (2000), "Reconsidering the Recent History of Child Sexual Abuse", 1910-1960, *Journal of Social Policy*, Vol. 29, Part 1, pp. 55-72

[59] Devance, R.S. (1928), "The Unmarried Mother and the Poor Law Commission", *The Irish Eccesiastical Record*, Fifth Series, Vol. xxxi, pp. 568

feasible to deal in a suitable manner with the problem of Juvenile Prostitution (that is prostitution under the age of 21)".[60] The committee was chaired by William Carrigan KC.[61] Devane gave evidence to the committee and published much of his evidence in *The Irish Eccesiastical Record.*[62] Devane summarised both the recommendations of the Commission on the Relief of the Sick and Destitute Poor and the Westminster established Departmental Committee on Sexual Offences Against Young Persons in support of his contention that the age of consent be raised. He concluded by claiming that

> an opportunity now offers which may not occur again for decades, for bringing the law relating to public morals into greater harmony with the spirit and ideas of our time and of our people. The moral looseness, so much in evidence among us since the Great War, is an outstanding reason for striving to maintain, and even to raise the standards of Public Morality by the passing of suitable legislation, thereby giving them fixity and prominence on the Statute book of the nation.[63]

Devane's submission was typical of the majority of submissions received by the committee, all decrying the apparent loosening of public morals over the previous decade. Perhaps the most significant submission received by the committee was from the garda commissioner at the time, Eoin O'Duffy. In his submission he argued that the existing legislation was made by Englishmen and was unsuitable for Irish conditions. Consistent with other submissions, O'Duffy believed that immorality had increased over the past decade, noting that "many of our people, even in rural areas, have changed within the past ten years, and the morally depraved who then would be exorcised from society are now regarded as rather clever and interesting".[64] To support his contention, he noted that "an alarming aspect is the number of cases with interference with girls under 15, and even under 13 and under 11, which come before the courts. These are in most cases heard of accidentally by the Garda, and are very rarely the result of a direct complaint. It is generally agreed that reported cases do not exceed 15 percent of those actually happening."[65]

---

[60] For further details see Keogh, D. (1994), *Twentieth-Century Ireland: Nation and State*, Dublin: Gill and Macmillan, pp. 71-73; and Kennedy, F. (2000), "The Suppression of the Carrigan Report: A Historical Perspective on Child Abuse", *Studies*, Vol. 89, No. 356, pp. 354-363

[61] Carrigan had earlier demonstrated his views of the issue of age of consent, in a court case where he commented the Irish people "were supposed to be a people of robust virtue; but if this case was heard in England it would not last five minutes, because the jury by direction would find the prisoner guilty…in this country, with all their boasting, they did not protect by law girls over 16". *Irish Independent*, 5 May, 1927

[62] Devane, R.S. (1931), The Legal Protection of Girls, *The Irish Eccesiastical Record,* Vol. 37, pp. 20-40

[63] Devane, R.S. (1931), The Legal Protection of Girls, *The Irish Eccesiastical Record,* Vol. 37, p. 40

[64] NA H247/41a, *Memorandum to the Committee on the Criminal Law Amendment Acts (1880-85) and Juvenile Prostitution*, p. 1

[65] NA H247/41a., p. 2

He went on to state, foreshadowing reactions to sentences handed down by the courts to persons convicted of child sexual abuse in the 1990s, that

> For the 15 percent of cases which do come to notice, legislation does not provide punishment sufficiently salutary to discourage the commission of an offence which, unless checked, will very fatally strike at the rudimentary fundamentals of society. Worse still, Judges have not been imposing the extreme penalties allowed. To impose a sentence of six months on, or to fine, a ruffian who destroys the innocence of a child under 13 is farcical.[66]

To support his case, O'Duffy gave illustrations of a number of cases which had come to the attention of the gardaí in 1930. These included: Mary O'Callaghan, aged six years and eleven months, who was indecently assaulted by William McCarthy, aged 37. McCarthy was given 6 months hard labour, as he pleaded guilty. Joseph C. Duffy, aged 27 years, committed sodomy with Patrick Twamley, aged 14 years, and committed acts of gross indecency with three other boys aged about 14. Duffy received 4 consecutive sentences of 12 months. Timothy Sweeney, aged 46 years, had unlawful knowledge of Norah Casey, aged 13 years. Sweeney received 3 years penal servitute. A Patrick Kelly, aged 42, had carnal knowledge of his daughter, aged sixteen and a half. He received 5 years penal servitute. T. Kelly aged 38, committed sodomy with his son, aged 10 years. He received 5 years penal servitute. Michael Canavan, aged 20 years, had unlawful carnal knowledge of Mary Quirke, aged 7 years. He received 21 months hard labour.[67]

O'Duffy recommended that the Criminal Justice Amendment Act 1885 required revision. Noting that there were 31 prosecutions for defilement of girls under 16 in Dublin City between 1924 and 1929, and that "offences on children between the ages of 9 and 16 are, unfortunately, increasing in the country" and "cases have occurred recently in which children between 4 and 5 have been interfered with",[68] the age at which such defilements should be classed as a felony should be raised from 13 to 16. In addition, any attempt to commit this offence should be classed as a felony. He also added that for any offences against girls under the age of 13, he strongly advised the "cat" be used and "not just a few strokes, but the most severe application the medical advisor will permit, having regard only to the physical condition and health of the offender".[69]

On the basis that many of these offences took place in the absence of parents or guardians, O'Duffy recommended that parents or guardians be penalised for this neglect. He further recommended that section 5 of the 1885 Act be amended to raise the age of consent to 18, that the provision that allowed a perpetrator the

---

[66] NA H247/41a, p. 2
[67] NA H247/41a, pp. 18-19
[68] NA H247/41a, p. 5
[69] NA H247/41a, p. 2

defence of believing the girl was above the age of consent be eliminated, that such offences be regarded as felonies and that the time limit for entering prosecutions be raised from 6 months to 12 months.[70]

Finally, all cases of sexual offences

> should be held in camera, or if the press is allowed to report such cases the name of the prosecutrix, or any particulars that would tend towards her identification, should be suppressed. We are aware that in many cases of carnal knowledge of young girls, of rape, and of indecent assault the person aggrieved, or the parents in the case of children, while anxious that the offender be brought to justice, suppress all information through fear of the consequences to the future of the girl which the publication of such prosecutions entail.[71]

The committee reported in August 1931, and made twenty-one recommendations, broadly endorsing the recommendations made by O'Duffy and others, including raising the age of consent to eighteen and extending the time period for commencing a prosecution. The report was submitted to the Cosgrave government, with an accompanying note from the Department of Justice advising against its publication. Following the general election of 1932, in which Fianna Fáil entered power for the first time, the newly appointed Minister for Justice, James Geoghegan, submitted a detailed memo to the Executive Council (cabinet) outlining why the report should not be published. The Department of Justice took the view that

> Commissions on matters of this kind are rarely helpful. In this country, decent people – the vast majority – feel that sexual offences should be punished vigorously. The desire is sincere, but vague. Commissioners are tempted to play up to this vague desire in order not to be outdone by the general public in the zeal for morality. Consequently, the reports of such commissions are liable to be too drastic, lacking judgement and unworkable in general, the report of this commission is no exception to the rule.[72]

The Department further argued that

> For the same reasons it would be far better if a Bill dealing with the matters reported on by the commission could be passed into law without public discussion in the Dáil. A judge or two, a lawyer or two, a well-balanced priest or two, an experienced police officer, meeting in private, all sharing the Catholic view on the moral gravity of sexual offences, could give the Government much helpful advice.[73]

---

[70] NA H247/41a, pp. 6-7
[71] NA H247/41a, p. 27
[72] NA H247/41a
[73] NA H247/41a

Following receipt of this memo, an all-party committee was established on a confidential basis, chaired by Geoghegan, the Minister for Justice, to explore how to proceed on the matter. Following the snap general election of 1933, in which Fianna Fáil were returned to power, the committee was re-established by P.J. Ruttledge, the new Minister for Justice, under the chairmanship of Geoghegan, now a backbench TD. This committee substantially diluted many of the recommendations made by the Carrigan Committee in particular, recommending that the age of consent be raised to seventeen, rather than the eighteen recommended by Carrigan and others.

THE CRIMINAL LAW AMENDMENT ACT, 1935

On 21 June 1934 Ruttledge introduced to the Dáil a "Bill entitled an Act to make further and better provision for the protection of young girls and the suppression of brothels and prostitution, and for those and other purposes to amend the law relating to sexual offences".[74] At the second stage of the Bill, Conor Maguire, the Attorney General, outlined the rationale for the Bill, claiming that "it has to be admitted that there has been an increase of offences against young girls in recent years in this country", which he attributed to "greatly enlarged opportunities for amusement and enjoyment, and the mingling of the sexes without that supervision which obtained in former days. It may also be said to be due in part to the relaxation of parental control".[75] Very little debate took place on the Bill within the Dáil as the Bill was "practically the report, with certain alterations, of the committee (the Geoghegan Committee) that has already sat"[76], thus rendering public debate unnecessary. The Bill was enacted as the Criminal Law Amendment Act 1935,[77] raised the age of consent to seventeen, made it a felony to have unlawful carnal knowledge with a girl under the age of fifteen and removed the defence that the perpetrator believed the girl to be of the age of consent. Unlike the legislation in England and Northern Ireland, no form of defence was available for males under twenty-four charged for the first time.

As table 1 shows, the number of sentences of imprisonment for defiling young girls rose rapidly as a result of the legislation. Between 1928 and 1935, sixty-one males were convicted and sentenced to imprisonment for defiling girls under thirteen, whereas between 1936 and 1940, one hundred were committed to prison.

---

[74] Dáil Debates, 1934, Vol. LIII, Col. 850
[75] Dáil Debates, 1934, Vol. LIII, Col. 1246
[76] Dáil Debates, 1934, Vol. LIII, Col. 1251
[77] For further details on the 1935 Act and the various changes made to it over the years, see O'Malley, T. (1996), *Sexual Offences: Law, Policy and Punishment*, Dublin: Roundhall/Sweet and Maxwell, pp. 93-105 and Department of Justice, Equality and Law Reform (1998), *The Law on Sexual Offences – A Discussion Paper*, Dublin: Stationery Office

Table 1: committals to prison, 1928-1950

	Defilement of girls under 13 (15 from 1935)	Defilement of girls under 16 (between 15 to 17 from 1935)
1928	9	5
1929	7	10
1930	7	9
1931	9	1
1932	9	6
1933	7	6
1934	8	10
1935	5	9
1936	14	30
1937	28	31
1938	26	26
1939	20	19
1940	12	14
1941	8	21
1942	16	11
1943	19	14
1945	23	41
1946	16	17
1947	19	29
1948	10	15
1949	9	16
1950	11	20

Source: Annual Reports on Prisons and Places of Detention. Various Years

Very little information is available on the characteristics of those committed to prison for the above sexual offences, their length of sentence etc. However, prisoner No. D.83222 in his autobiographical account of life in Irish prisons during the early 1940s wrote that "The sexual offenders are the most religious. These men are not hypocrites. Warders can observe a prisoner in his cell without the prisoner knowing he is being watched, and time and time again they have seen and heard sexual offenders on their knees, begging the Mother of God to save them from this revolting fiend which takes possession of them at times."[78] He also noted the abhorrence that the "ordinary decent criminals" had the for sex

---

[78] D83222 (1945), *I Did Penal Servitude*, Dublin: Metropolitan Publishing, p. 85

offenders and that in his view "Prison is the worst possible place for sexual offenders", that "a home, where they could receive the expert attention of a psychotherapist, not a jail, is the place for these men".[79]

It is more difficult to ascertain how many such offences were known to the gardaí during this period, as until 1947 only a summary of trends in crime were published in the Annual Statistical Abstracts. However, some detail is available. The *Irish Times* on 18 March 1936 carried the text of a speech given by Mr Justice Hanna at the annual dinner of the Companions of St Patrick held at the Metropole Restaurant in Dublin. In his speech, he argued that there was a severe lapse into immorality in Ireland, particularly in relation to the number of indecent assaults and sexual offences. In what seems analagous to today's Ireland, Justice Hanna stated that "It is clear that in the Free State the normal standard has been far exceeded in sexual offences, dishonesty in business, offences against public order and in juvenile crime".[80]

Table 2: sexual offences known to the gardaí 1927-1950

	Defilement of girls under 13 (15 from 1935)	Defilement of girls under 16 (between 15 to 17 from 1935)
1927	8	16
1928	16	17
1929	5	24
1930	8	10
1931	10	30
1932	10	24
1933	14	16
1934	17	25
1935	32	28
1947	26	46
1950	31	39

Source: JUS 8/451. Sexual crime and juvenile offences: memorandum in connection with Judge Hanna's speech, 1936 and An Garda Síochána Annual Reports. Various Years

In a response to Judge Hanna's claims, the Department of Justice prepared a memo dealing with, amongst others items, sexual crime in Ireland. The memo, using unpublished garda figures, argued that there was "no appreciable change in

---

[79] *Ibid.* p. 135
[80] *Irish Times*, 18 March, 1936

the figures for indecent assault on females, but unnatural offences and offences against girls show a definite tendency to increase. In regard to the last mentioned offence it must be borne in mind that the provisional figures for 1935 are based on the higher age limits, fifteen and seventeen, which are now in force as a result of a change in law. Unfortunately, the position in regard to this type of offence is worse than the table shows, because the offences against very young girls (under thirteen and, in the case of 1935, under fifteen) show a deplorable increase."[81] Detailed figures on these two offences are not available again until 1947, but show that the figure for 1935 was maintained.

"MARKED TENDENCIES TOWARDS SEXUAL IMMORALITY"

It was not only the Department of Justice that was expressing concern at the rise of immorality and sexual offences against young girls. The Department of Education, which had responsibility for regulating and financing reformatory and industrial schools (see endnote 3), were also exhibiting concern, albeit of a different nature.[82] In the early 1940s, the Archbishop of Dublin, John Charles McQuaid, wrote to the Department of Education seeking to establish a reformatory school to "receive girls under 17 who either (1) are convicted of legal sexual offences or (2) are placed in dangerous surroundings and have marked tendencies towards sexual immorality".[83] The Department noted that it was possible to place girls in either category in industrial schools, provided they were

---

[81] JUS 8/451, Sexual crime and juvenile offences: memorandum in connection with Judge Hanna's speech, 1936, p. 4

[82] Girls significantly outnumbered boys in Irish industrial schools, stayed longer, and were more likely to be received into care for fear of moral waywardness. For further details, see O'Sullivan (1997), "Restored to virtue, to society and to God, Juvenile Justice and the Regulation of the Poor", *Irish Criminal Law Journal*, Vol.7, No. 2, pp. 171-194 and Torode, R. and O'Sullivan, E. (1999), "The Impact of Dear Daughter", *Irish Journal of Feminist Studies*, Vol. 3, No. 2. pp. 85-97. On the regulation of girls within other jurisdictions, see Brenzel, B. (1983), *Daughters of the State: A Social Portrait of the First Reform School for Girls in North America, 1865-1905*, Cambridge: MIT Press; Cale, M. (1993), "Girls and the Perception of Sexual Danger in the Victorian Reformatory System*"*, *History*, Vol. 78, No. 253, pp. 201-217; Littlewood, B. and Mahood, L. (1991), "Prostitutes, Madgalenes and Wayward Girls: Dangerous Sexualities of Working Class Women in Victorian Scotland", *Gender and History*, Vol. 3, No. 2, pp. 160-175; Mahood, L. and Littlewood, B. (1994), The "'Vicious'" Girl and the 'Street-Corner' Boy: Sexuality and the Gendered Delinquent in the Scottish Child-Saving Movement, 1850-1940*"*, *Journal of the History of Sexuality*, Vol. 4, No. 4, pp. 549-578; Odem, M.E. (1995), *Delinquent Daughters: Protecting and Policing Adolescent Female Sexuality in the United States, 1885-1920*, University of North Carolina Press; and Schlossman, S.L. and Wallach, S. (1978), "The Crime of Precocious Sexuality: Female Juvenile Delinquency in the Progressive Era", *Harvard Educational Review*, Vol. 48, No. 1, pp. 65-94

[83] Department of Education/Special Education. File goo21a, Establishment of new reformatory, Kilmacud

under fifteen years of age. However, for those aged between fifteen and seventeen, committal to a reformatory school was only possible if the girl had been convicted for soliciting, keeping a brothel, procuring for a prostitute, or being a reputed prostitute and loitering in a public place for the purpose of prostitution. However, the number of girls convicted for those offences was small. Based on figures supplied by the Department of Justice, the Department of Education noted that over eighty girls were defiled annually. The Department of Education classified such girls into three categories: "(1) girls who live in surroundings which could not be considered as bad; (2) girls who live in surroundings which conduce to their downfall; and (3) girls who might be described as prostitutes". The Department was of the view that girls in categories (2) and (3) were in need of committal to a suitable institution, but rarely were so placed. Up to the early 1940s, the primary method of dealing with young girls, either convicted of a sexual offence, or deemed to be sexually aware, was to place them in the only girl's reformatory, St Joseph's in Limerick, run by the Sisters of the Good Shepherd. However, in a number of cases, the manager of the school, believing that such girls were not amenable to reformation, placed them in one of the Magdalene Homes run by the same congregation. A memo prepared by the medical inspector of reformatory and industrial schools, Dr Anna McCabe, gives a flavour of how such girls were treated.

> Two girls were committed under the Children Act 1908 to the reformatory school for girls in Limerick on 6 Dec 1941. The manager of the school agreed to accept them, believing that, because of their immature years, they might not have realised the gravity of their conduct and would be amenable to reform under her care. It has transpired, however, to quote the Manager's statement, that they are "only too well versed in immorality and are of such a type that, in justice to the other inmates in the school, mostly convicted of charges of larceny and petty theft, the manager considered their immediate removal from the school to be imperative. Arrangements have consequently been made to have the girls sent on licence to the care of Managers of penitentiary homes conducted by the same order as manages the reformatory school (Cork and Waterford). This method of dealing with cases of the kind, while effective as a means of keeping the girls away from their former surroundings and associates – the only alternative to which would be their unconditional discharge – has obvious defects from the point of view that in the penitentiaries to which they are being sent the girls must necessarily associate with adults whose presence there is also due to immorality and that the managers of the penitentiaries may not be in a position to give the attention which would be desirable to the general education of girls of immature years. This present procedure is simply a fortuitous arrangement made possible by the good will and charitable disposition of the members of the religious order concerned.[84]

---

[84] File goo21a, Establishment of new reformatory, Kilmacud 15/Oct/43, note to Secretary from Inspector

From the early 1940s, the Good Shepherd nuns started to refuse to accept any girl believed to be tainted with sexual immorality. Their main reason behind this decision was to force the Department of Education to provide them with funding for a second reformatory school, which would cater exclusively for such girls. However, when the Department of Education decided to establish such a school, it was the Sisters of Charity of Our Lady of Refuge[85] who were entrusted with the management. This new school was the St Anne's Reformatory School for Girls, which although established in the mid-1940s, was only legislated for in 1949, under the Children (Amendment) Act 1949. Despite the establishment of St Anne's, when the *Report on Industrial Schools and Reformatories* (The Kennedy Report) was published in 1970 it noted that girls, "considered by parents, relatives, social workers, welfare officers, clergy or gardaí to be in moral danger or uncontrollable are ... accepted in these convents for a period on a voluntary basis. From enquiries made, the Committee is satisfied that there are at least 70 girls between the ages of 13 and 19 years confined in this way who should properly be dealt with under the reformatory schools' system".[86]

CONCLUSION

Michel Foucault, in his history of sexuality, has suggested that "(t)he sex of children and adolescents has become, since the eighteenth century, an important area of contention around which innumerable institutional devices and discursive strategies have been deployed".[87] This chapter has attempted to show that, contrary to the popular assumption that the sexual abuse of children was unknown in Ireland until recently, a range of discourses were evident. Sr Stanislaus Kennedy, responding to allegations that she was aware of the sexual abuse of children in St Joseph's Industrial School in Kilkenny in the 1970s for example, stated that "the term 'sexual abuse' had not, as far as I know, even been coined – it was certainly never discussed even among childcare professionals".[88] Ferguson, similarly argued, in relation to the aforementioned 'West of Ireland Farmer' case, that "the McColgan children were subjected to sexual abuse at a time when our understanding of such crimes was less advanced than now" and that "the tragedy is that the case spanned a period when awareness of serious physical and sexual abuse was only beginning to develop".[89]

---

[85] The Sisters of the Good Shepherd were established in 1835 following organisational difficulties with the Sisters of Charity of Our Lady of Refuge

[86] *Report on Industrial Schools and Reformatories* (The Kennedy Report) (1970), Dublin: The Stationery Office, p. 39

[87] Foucault, M. (1978), *The History of Sexuality: Volume 1 An Introduction*, London: Penguin Books, pp. 30

[88] *Irish Times*, May 19, 1999

[89] Ferguson, H. (1998), McColgan Case – A Different Era, *Irish Times*, 26 January

While it may be accurate to state that the term "child sexual abuse" was not utilised, it is clear that a range of euphemisms for child sexual abuse was evident. More significantly, the debates on age of consent that took place in the late nineteenth and early twentieth centuries show that our understanding of child sexual abuse is socially and legally constructed, rather than an immutable reality waiting to be discovered. For example, in 1990, the Law Reform Commission recommended that the maximum age for feloniously having carnal knowledge with a girl, and consequently being liable to a maximum sentence of penal servitude for life, be dropped from fifteen to thirteen and that a defence of genuinely believing that the girl was of the age of consent could be taken into account by the court.[90] More recently, the discussion document on the law on sexual offences produced by the Department of Justice, Equality and Law Reform, while noting that there were some advantages to maintaining the existing position of no defence in the case of carnal knowledge of an underage girl stated that "with teenagers maturing earlier, genuine mistakes as to age can be made".[91]

Significantly, the debates focused almost exclusively on the sexuality of young females. Such females were constructed simultaneously as both victims and perpetrators. They had to be both protected from adult men and themselves, but adult men had also to be protected from them or in the words of Maguire CJ the legislation was geared "to protect young girls, not alone against lustful men, but against themselves".[92]

The notion that adult men might also wish to have sexual relations with young males appears to have been subsumed into more general debates on homosexuality, and thus rendered relatively invisible. The criminalisation of sexual acts between males, irrespective of age, until 1993 in Ireland appears to have resulted in an undifferentiated abhorrence towards such acts. However, not all were unaware of such acts between adults and children. In a circular issued by the provincial of the Christian Brothers in 1926, the use of a euphemism to describe sexual relations between Christian Brothers and their pupils is apparent.

> The child's spiritual endowments and the end to which he is destined naturally causes the thoughtful religious to "love him in God", while his natural charms tend to excite that "weak and sensual affection" that may prove to be ruinous to the child and to the teacher. Here is a DANGER SIGNAL that should never be lowered and should ever be heeded. The teacher who allows himself any softness in his intercourse with his pupil, who does not repress the tendency to "pets", who fondles the young or

---

[90] Law Reform Commission (1990), *Report on Child Sexual Abuse*, Dublin: Law Reform Commission

[91] Department of Justice, Equality and Law Reform (1998), *The Law on Sexual Offences – A Discussion Paper*, Dublin: Stationery Office, p. 67

[92] *Attorney General (Shaughnessy) v Ryan, (*1960) *Irish Reports*, p. 181

indulges in other weaknesses is not heeding the danger signal and may easily fall. Disastrous results for teacher and pupil have sometimes resulted from such heedlessness and effeminacy.[93] (emphasis in original)

As conceptions of childhood changed, a range of mechanisms and institutions were constructed to protect and reform children, in order to preserve their newly acquired status. Adult-child sexual contact became increasingly identified with moral harm in the Irish context and it was only from the 1980s, that other forms of harm, such as medical, physical or psychological, were coherently identified. Thus, it may be argued that, contrary to some accounts, the sexual abuse of children and the need to protect children from adults or, in the case of St Anne's Reformatory, from themselves, were discussed and debated in Ireland during the 1920s, 30s and 40s. As Carol Smart has suggested "it might be more appropriate to question the assumption that there really was a silence over sexual matters of this kind, or, if there was a silence, to ask who was doing the silencing".[94]

ENDNOTES

1 Described by the Irish Society for the Prevention of Cruelty to Children as "one of the worst-ever child abuse cases in the history of the state, the case involved the prolonged sexual and physical abuse of four of the six McColgan children by their father from the late 1970s to early 1990s. Following the conviction of the accused, Joseph McColgan, the McColgan children took a case against the North Western Health Board and a local GP, Dr Moran, seeking damages. Following a thirteen day hearing in the High Court, the North Western Health Board settled out of court for £1 million in January 1998. The Health Board promised to publish the findings of an independent inquiry into the McColgan case "within weeks". The report was eventually published in July 1998 and concluded that "There was a significant level of awareness of the issue of non-accidental injury and, subsequently, child sexual abuse at senior and middle management within the community care programme, and also within the hospital pediatric department. Notwithstanding this awareness, there is an understanding, on our part, that a genuine incredulity of sexual abuse existed initially and may have persisted at senior social work management level and with the family general practitioner". North Western Health Board (1998), *"West of Ireland Farmer Case": Report of Review Group*, Manorhamilton: NWHB, p 41. For a journalistic account of the case see McKay, S. (1998) *Sophia's Story*. Dublin: Gill and Macmillan

---

[93] Hennessy, P. J. Br. (1926), "Circular on Instruction in Christian Knowledge and Training in Christian Piety in Christian Brothers of Ireland (1934)", *Circular Letters of the Superior General of the Brothers of the Christian Schools of Ireland,* Dublin: Dollard Printing House, p. 347.

[94] Smart, C. (2000), "Reconsidering the Recent History of Child Sexual Abuse, 1910-1960", *Journal of Social Policy*, Vol. 29, Part 1, p. 56

2 This investigation concerned the sexual and physical abuse of a young woman by her father over many years. The notoriety surrounding the case arose out of media reports of the father's trial and sentencing for incest. It became known that the health and social services had had over one hundred contacts with the family in the thirteen years prior to the prosecution, during which time the abuse had continued. The television coverage of the case included an interview with the young woman, known by the pseudonym of "Mary", in which she criticised the social worker involved. In the wake of further widespread condemnation of the child care services, the Minister for Health announced a public inquiry, the first of its kind in Ireland. The inquiry team, under the chairpersonship of a judge, Catherine McGuinness, reported after three months. The report identified a number of deficiencies in both the child protection system, and in the professional activities of the various practitioners involved, particularly in relation to poor inter-agency co-operation, weaknesses in management and "lack of the necessary effective probing". McGuinness, C. (1993), *Report of The Kilkenny Incest Investigation*, Dublin: Stationery Office, p 88. See also Ferguson, H. (1993-4) "Child Abuse Inquiries and the Report of the Kilkenny Incest Investigation: A Critical Analysis", *Administration*, Vol. 41, No. 4, p 406.

3 The first reformatory school in Ireland was opened in Dublin in early 1859, and the first boy was admitted to the Glencree Reformatory on 14 April 1859. By 1870 there were ten reformatory schools certified throughout the country, five for girls and five for boys. The number of children committed to the reformatory schools rose from 140 in 1859 to 740 ten years later. Between 1870 and 1970, only one new reformatory was certified, and the number of reformatory schools declined, with many reformatories handing in their certificates and reclassifying themselves as industrial schools. Along with the need to provide more suitable places of detention for young offenders, there was a growing awareness of the need to provide residential care for the young homeless and destitute children of Ireland. After much debate the industrial school system was applied to Ireland in 1868, based on the models already in operation in England and Scotland. As with the reformatory schools, the number of industrial schools has varied over the past 150 years. The first industrial school was certified in 1869, and by 1875 fifty schools were in operation. By 1898 there was a total of seventy-one industrial schools in Ireland, seventeen industrial schools for Roman Catholic boys with certificates for 2,925 children, forty-four industrial schools for Roman Catholic girls with certificates for 3,975 children, four industrial schools for Protestant boys with certificates for 586 children, five industrial schools for Protestant girls with certificates for 409 children and one mixed industrial school for Roman

Catholic boys and girls with certificates for seventy-eight girls and twenty-five boys. The success of the industrial schools was such that the need for reformatories decreased in Ireland.

11

Drugs, Crime, and Prohibitionist Ideology[*]

Tim Murphy

INTRODUCTION

The majority of contributions to the ongoing public discussion of drug policy in Ireland continue to bear all the hallmarks of prohibitionist ideology: illegal drugs are represented as intrinsically and completely evil; the efficacy or otherwise of prohibition is not given any serious consideration (any increase in drug use or misuse is automatically ascribed to the evil power of the drugs themselves, the possibility that it could be an effect of drug policy is disregarded); the notion of a definite causal connection between drugs and crime is assumed rather than examined; and the question of drug law reform is not mentioned. This paper is concerned in particular with the manner in which "drugs" are held not only to be a social problem in and of themselves but also how they are portrayed as exacerbating another social phenomenon – the "crime problem". This approach in turn allows for the introduction and social acceptance of extremely severe and authoritarian criminal law measures to deal with illicit drugs.

The drugs-crime "connection thesis" follows from the pervasive but intellectually incoherent demonisation of those psychoactive drugs that are prohibited by law. This demonisation, and the attendant refusal to even contemplate the distinction between drug use and drug misuse, will be discussed

---

[*] Based on "Drugs, Drug Prohibition and Crime: a response to Peter Charleton", *Irish Criminal Law Journal* 6, 1 and 2, 1-18

in the first section of this paper. In the second section, the arguments of criminogenesis will be considered in detail and we will see that it is drug prohibition – rather than "drugs" – that is a major cause of crime. In the third section, we will consider some aspects of the question of drug law reform, particularly the misrepresentation of reform advocacy and the related non-oppositional stance of the political left on the issue.

THE DEMONISATION OF ILLICIT DRUGS

The American psychiatrist, Thomas Szasz, has observed that illicit drugs have replaced sex at the centre of "the grand morality play of human existence". Szasz writes: "No longer are men, women, and children tempted, corrupted, and ruined by the irresistibly sweet pleasures of sex, instead, they are tempted, corrupted, and ruined by the irresistibly sweet pleasures of drugs".[1] Certain drugs, in other words, are perceived primarily and exclusively as destructive and evil forces within contemporary societies. Reference to the perceived threat of evil destruction by illicit drugs is common among prohibitionist ideologues in Ireland. Grainne Kenny, a career prohibitionist, has written that cannabis users "do not have the right to destabilise democracy", and that drug law reform proposals amount to an advocacy of "chemical warfare on our most vulnerable citizens, the young and socially and emotionally deprived".[2] Peter Charleton, a lawyer active in the drugs area, while accepting that law enforcement "tends toward the seizure of only one tenth of available drugs", argues that this enforcement prevents drugs from otherwise "literally flood[ing] society and ... persist[ing] in its destruction". The continuance of the drug war, he suggests, "ensures ... that we are not engulfed by evil.[3]

This demonisation of illicit drugs is part of a more general process of the simplification of the complex policy issues raised by all drugs, including licit drugs. The multifarious and interdependent dimensions of drug policy questions require very careful consideration, and it is therefore necessary to explore them in a rational and calm manner, with reference to the full range of national and international research.

In ideal-typical terms, there are two distinct models of drug use within prohibitionist ideology. The "medical" model (historically associated with the drug policy of the United Kingdom) warns that various drugs are definitively dependence-producing and that such dependence ("addiction") constitutes a "disease"; it views drug addiction as primarily a public health issue and suggests

---

[1] Szasz, "The Morality of Drug Controls", in Hamowy (ed.), *Dealing With Drugs: Consequences of Government Control* (Lexington, 1987), at pp. 327-328

[2] "Why cannabis should not be legalised", *The Revenue Group Journal*, March 1998, p. 19, at p. 20

[3] Book review (1997) 15 *Irish Law Times* 88, at p. 89 [reviewing Murphy, *Rethinking the War on Drugs in Ireland* (Cork, 1996)]

that it should be dealt with by making certain of the substances in question inaccessible to citizens. The "moral-legal" model (the traditional drug policy of the United States), on the other hand, not only regards all illicit drugs as dangerous, it also condemns all illicit drug use as morally wrong; proponents of this model, while acknowledging the medical dimension of addiction, nonetheless invoke the punitive sanctions of the criminal justice system as the most appropriate response to drug-related activity.[4]

Although the drug policies of most states are now regularly justified on a combination of medical and moral grounds, the general trend of international drug policy during the course of the twentieth century has been away from the medical model and towards the moral-legal model.[5] In Ireland, pre-independence British policy (based on the medical model) has been revised in an *ad hoc* fashion, largely to suit the requirements of the transnational war on drugs initiated by the United States.

The basic legislative framework relating to the prohibition of certain drugs in Ireland is set out in the Misuse of Drugs Acts 1977 and 1984, and the Misuse of Drugs Regulations 1988. The "[smoking or otherwise using of] prepared opium" is made an offence under the 1977 Act (s.16). The key feature of that 1977 Act, however, is the creation of the category of "controlled drugs" – any substance, product or preparation that is specified in the Schedule to the Act (which may be ministerially altered) (s.2). Possession of controlled drugs generally, except under limited circumstances (eg in the case of a medical practitioner or pharmacist), is an offence. (Ss.3, 4). Other significant offences include the possession of controlled drugs for unlawful sale or supply (s.15) and the cultivation of the opium poppy or cannabis plant (s.17). It is also provided that the Minister for Health, for the purpose of preventing the misuse of controlled drugs, may make regulations regarding the manufacture, production, preparation, importation, exportation, supply, offering to supply, distribution, or transportation of controlled drugs, and also concerning the prescription of controlled drugs (s.5). The Misuse of Drugs Act 1984 introduced higher fines and harsher sentences for drug offences. Moreover, while it was central to the 1977 Act that drug offenders were a category apart from other criminals, and most drug offenders were therefore required to be remanded in custody pending probation and medical reports, the 1984 Act made this discretionary. Subsequent legislation, particularly, as we shall

---

[4] For a full account of these two models, see Van de Wijngaart, *Competing Perspectives on Drug Use: The Dutch Experience* (Amsterdam, 1991), p. 79

[5] See, generally, Butler, "Drug Problems and Drug Policies in Ireland: A Quarter of a Century Reviewed" (1991) 39 *Administration* 210; Duster, *The Legislation of Morality: Law, Drugs, and Moral Judgment* (New York, 1970); Musto, "The history of legislative control over opium, cocaine, and their derivatives", in Hamowy (ed.), *op. cit.*; and Fitzpatrick, *The Tyranny of Health: Doctors and the Regulation of Lifestyle* (London, 2001), especially pp. 96-117

see presently, the Criminal Justice (Drug Trafficking) Acts of 1996 and 1999, has continued the pattern of increased criminalisation.

More generally, as Hans T. van der Veen has observed, the underlying dynamics of this drug war must now be interpreted in light of structural changes in the global political economy. Those changes have produced new patterns of hierarchy and dominance in the international system, including a diminished separation between the domestic and the international frameworks for policy making and the management of affairs. In the case of drug policy, the internationalisation of both crime and law enforcement together constitute a phenomenon that is taking over the functions of the Cold War in legitimising the coercive use of state powers to foster internal order and discipline. As van der Veen has expressed it: "The two worlds of criminal entrepreneurs and coercive agencies of states are not separated by geographical boundaries; however, nor are they separated from the societies in which they function. As both increasingly attain transnational dimensions, they become more disposed to prevent themselves from being incorporated into society and, hence, from being subordinate to democratic control. At the same time, they increase their powers to penetrate the sovereignty of individuals and entire societies over the globe".[6]

There are major problems with the models on which this transnational drug war is founded. The disease theory of addiction that underpins the medical model gives a central position, in the drug-taking dynamic, to the drug itself. The rhetoric of prohibitionist "medical" ideology focuses, to the virtual exclusion of all other factors, on the particular drugs that are prohibited by law. In fact, in order to understand what impels someone to use an illicit drug and how that drug affects the user, three basic determinants must be considered. Norman Zinberg famously termed these determinants as "drug" (the pharmacological action of the substance itself), "set" (the attitude of the person at the time of use, including his personality structure), and "setting" (the influence of the physical and social setting within which the use occurs)".[7] The "drug-set-setting" analysis means that it is misleading to say that a drug, or drugs generally, "destroy people" or that they "kill". Most drugs *can* have these effects, but they are far from inevitable. The effect of a drug, when considered in either the short or long term, depends on environmental factors such as the psychological, social, cultural and economic context of the drug-taking. Moreover, when these factors are considered properly, it is apparent that drug addiction (whether one is considering legal or illegal drugs) "is not a property of drugs at all.... [It] is a property of the user".[8] Thus the disease theory

---

[6] See "The International Drug Complex", *Nexus*, April-May 2000 (pp. 23-28) and June-July 2000 (pp. 25-30), specifically at p. 30

[7] *Drug, Set, and Setting: The Basis for Controlled Intoxicant Use* (New Haven, 1984), p. 5

[8] Krivanek, *Addictions* (Sydney, 1982), p. 6. See also Peele, "A Moral Vision of Addiction: How People's Values Determine Whether They Become And Remain Addicts" (1987) 17 *Journal of Drug Issues* 187

of addiction has been rejected by virtually all of the leading authorities on the subject, including the World Health Organisation. Since 1981 the WHO has used the term "drug dependence" to refer to problematic drug use. This is defined as "a syndrome manifested by a behavioral pattern in which the use of a given psychoactive drug, or class of drugs, is given a much higher priority than other behaviors that once had a higher value."[9]

As for the moral-legal model, not only have punitive responses failed miserably to achieve any reduction in either drug demand or supply, the model is characterised by contradiction and inconsistency. For example, the global capitalist market functions to extend consumption and "[d]rug use, powerfully valued in terms of the hedonism that consumer cultures espouse, is no exception".[10] In this context Mugford draws attention to both the individualistic ethos of the enterprise culture and contemporary processes of consumption, in particular the broad ideological world of modern consumerism, built in part by advertising and its "images of excitement, achievement, sexuality, youth and pleasure". Far more radical interpretations of drug behaviour have also been suggested. Stephen Lyng has concluded that it is "a type of experiential anarchy in which the individual moves beyond the realm of established social patterns", and therefore that its pervasiveness represents "an important critical statement on the nature of modern social life".[11]

In addition, apart from criminal sanctions, the moral-legal model emphasises the role of preventive drug education in the "war" on drugs. But as Shane Butler has written: "[D]rug and alcohol education, even when it has not proved counterproductive, has failed to slow down or prevent initiation of alcohol consumption or illicit drug use by teenagers and young adults ... [P]reventive work ... cannot be entirely rational or characterised by logical consistency if national and international policies on these matters generally lack these characteristics". Butler also suggests that the lack of enthusiasm for evaluate educational preventive programmes "may be primarily symbolic rather than instrumental: in other words, one could surmise that adult society is less concerned with whether or not educational programmes achieve their specified aims and objectives than it is with the ritualistic and emphatic affirmation of its belief concerning the undesirability of drug use".[12]

---

[9] "Nomenclature and classification of drug and alcohol-related problems: A WHO Memorandum", *Bulletin of the World Health Organisation* (1981), quoted in Krivanek, *op. cit.*, p. 52

[10] Mugford, "Drug legalization and the 'Goldilocks' problem: Thinking about costs and control of drugs", in Krauss and Lazear, *Searching for Alternatives: Drug-Control Policy in the United States* (Stanford, 1991), p. 39

[11] "Edgework: A Social Psychological Analysis of Voluntary Risk-Taking" (1990), 95(4), *American Journal of Sociology* 851, at p 882

[12] Butler, "Alcohol and Drug Education in Ireland: Aims, Methods and Difficulties" (1994) 42 *Oideas* 125, at p. 137

The combined effect of these two models includes the failure to distinguish between recreational and circumstantial drug use, on the one hand, and dysfunctional and compulsive drug use on the other. Those who seek drug law reform consistently stress that emphasis should be shifted away from the prevention of all use to the prevention of dysfunctional use. Zinberg has commented on the consequences of prohibition for users as follows: "The development of social sanctions and rituals probably occurs more slowly in the secretive world of illicit drug use than with the use of a licit drug like alcohol. The furtiveness, the suspicion, the fears of legal reprisal, as well as the myths and misconceptions that surround illicit drug use, all make the exchange of information that leads to the development of social sanctions and controls more difficult".[13] In other words, the use of drugs is *more likely* to become misuse under the circumstances created by a war on drugs.

Most of the harm caused by opiate misuse, to give an example, is due primarily to the conditions of prohibition rather than to the opiates themselves. Counterintuitive though it may be, "as with marijuana, study after study has failed to find that the regular use of heroin, in conditions of relatively free availability, produces any substantial adverse effects on mental or physical health".[14] Heroin problems are mainly caused by "... the manner in which the drugs are administered and the accompanying lifestyle .... [The] physical complications frequently found among addicts ... are the result of unsterile injection practices, the sharing of syringes, the injection of drugs such as barbiturates which are not designed to be injected, and also infection caused by contaminants found in illicitly manufactured heroin".[15] This range of problems arises far more easily when drugs are prohibited than would be the case under a regulated, legal regime. This is in no way to deny that opiate misuse is unhealthy. Under any circumstances, long-term regular misuse of narcotic analgesics like heroin leads to constipation, reduced sexual drive, disruption of menstrual periods, and poor eating habits.[16] However, whether misuse occurs is essentially a behavioural and social issue, not a "killer drug" issue. Moreover, it is only under prohibition that certain additional dangers are present, dangers that more readily transform drug use – where no problematic behavioural pattern exists – into misuse.

Another common misconception involved in drug demonisation is the notion that certain drugs can act as a "gateway" to others. For example, Peter Charleton has written that softer drugs, "almost invariably, in my experience, act as a dress

[13] Zinberg, "The use and misuse of intoxicants: Factors in the development of controlled use", in Hamowy (ed.), *op. cit.*, at p. 266

[14] Duke and Gross, *America's Longest War: Rethinking Our Tragic Crusade Against Drugs* (New York, 1993), p. 62

[15] Stimson and Oppenheimer, *Heroin Addiction: Treatment and Control in Britain* (London, 1982), p. 16

[16] Henry, *The British Medical Association Guide to Medicine and Drugs* (2nd ed., London, 1991), p. 423

rehearsal to the use of Cocaine and Heroin".[17] A more accurate reflection of the reality of drug progression is provided by Jara Krivanek. Referring to empirical studies on this subject, she writes:

> ... what the general public and some professionals often overlook is the fact that involvement with one drug does not necessarily mean progression to the next one. Virtually all marijuana users had earlier tried alcohol or cigarettes, usually both; but only a percentage of alcohol and cigarette users [about 45 per cent] go on to use marijuana. A tiny fraction of these, some 3 per cent, then go on to try heroin.[18]

Again, the critical factor in progression is not the drug: it is the environmental considerations now generally conceptualised as set and setting.

The drug-set-setting analysis has been acknowledged by Irish policy makers.[19] In the first report of the Ministerial Task Force on Drugs it was noted that the submissions which it had received had consistently "identified the same under-lying causes of problem drug use as had already been identified by the Group, ie social disadvantage/exclusion, characterised in high levels of unemployment, poor housing conditions, low educational attainment, lack of recreational facilities, etc". As Shane Butler[20] noted of this report, "for the first time ever, Irish policy makers have publicly and unequivocally accepted that a causal link exists between poverty and serious drug problems, and that demand reduction measures should be selectively aimed at those neighbourhoods or communities where a high prevalence of drug problems coincides with generalised social exclusion or disadvantage". However, that consideration has not resulted in any substantial departure from the demonisation of illicit drugs, or any deviation from the general policy of criminal prohibition.[21] As Butler points out: "While the *First Report of the Ministerial Task Force* was concerned with demand-reduction measures, it is important to bear in mind that the Government was simultaneously involved with several new legislative initiatives aimed at the prevention of drug trafficking and the confiscation of illegal drug assets. There was, in other words, no abandonment or diminution of the commitment to *supply* side policies, and it is this retention of the basic philosophy of the war on drugs which largely explains why the [report],

---

[17] Charleton, "Drugs and Crime – Making the Connection: A Discussion Paper" (1995) 5 *Irish Criminal Law Journal* 220, at p. 220

[18] Krivanek, *op. cit.*, p. 8 (emphasis in original)

[19] See, generally and specifically at p. 33, *First Report of the Ministerial Task Force on Measures to Reduce the Demand for Drugs* (Dublin, 1996), which discussed policy regarding heroin and other opiates, and the *Second Report of the Ministerial Task Force on Measures to Reduce the Demand for Drugs* (Dublin, 1997), which discussed policy regarding non-opiates

[20] "Review Essay: The War on Drugs: Reports from the Irish Front", *The Economic and Social Review*, Vol. 28, No. 2, April 1997, pp. 157-175, at p. 164 [reviewing Murphy, *op. cit.* and *First Report of the Ministerial Task Force on Measures to Reduce the Demand for Drugs*]

[21] Butler, "Review Essay: The War on Drugs: Reports from the Irish Front", at p. 164

despite containing some important new policy approaches, cannot be seen as initiating a radically new era in Irish drug policy making."

DRUGS AND CRIME

The demonisation of illicit drugs in prohibitionist ideology incorporates the notion that their negative influence extends to criminogenesis. Charleton, referring to this alleged "connection with crime" in the Irish context, has written:

> 80% of serious street level crime is caused by drug addiction .... The era of a high level of crime is with us .... The nature of the particular increases [in crime levels] points to the addict as the cause. From 1973 over a period of 18 years robbery has increased in levels of commission by more than four times and burglary by almost six times. The cause of this is drug abuse.[22]

"Drug abuse", Charleton elaborates, "is criminogenic in two ways". The first way is that it "is illegal to use Ecstasy, Cannabis, Cocaine, Heroin, LSD and amphetamines". The second way in which Charleton suggests drug abuse is criminogenic has in fact two distinct aspects. Firstly, he refers to the actions of "entire communities" in Dublin's inner city: "[F]or a time they publicly challenged the legal order by causing the eviction of abusers from their neighbourhood". Secondly, he reiterates the view that "[d]rug abuse has caused a vast upsurge in violent and invasive theft".[23]

Charleton's assertion that it is illegal to use various prohibited drugs is incorrect: with the exception of heroin, it is not a statutory offence in Ireland to *use* any of these drugs. Given that the main forms of offences used to charge drug offenders are possession of drugs, importation of drugs, and possession of drugs for the purposes of supply, this legislative exclusion of drug use would not appear to be of much practical significance. However, on closer examination, it is in fact hugely significant. In Sweden, for example, the use of illegal drugs is prohibited and the consequence has been an ongoing attack on the human right to bodily integrity in that jurisdiction. The law which introduced the criminal offence of illegal drug use in Sweden was passed in 1988. As one commentator has remarked, "it was felt that the passing of such a law ... would have an important psychological, or symbolic effect", even though, at that time, the punishment was limited to a fine.[24] Later, in 1993, the consumption of drugs was made an imprisonable offence. Now, the practical operation of the law, far from being psychological or symbolic, involves an intensified police surveillance of behaviour,

---

[22] Charleton, "Drugs and Crime – Making the Connection: A Discussion Paper", at p. 221
[23] *Ibid.*
[24] Gould, "Sweden's Syringe Exchange Debate: Moral Panic in a Rational Society" (1994) 23 *Journal of Social Policy* 195, at p. 215 (n. 2)

in particular looking for signs of illegal intoxication. Blood and urine samples are taken from suspects by police. One senior Swedish police official has explained the rationale underlying this law as follows: "We are disturbing [the users], standing in the way of their activities, threatening them with compulsory treatment and making life difficult for them. The more difficult it is, the more the other way of living stands out as a better alternative, that is a drug free life."[25] It has been remarked by observers that the 1988 and 1993 "use laws" have accomplished nothing in that they are having no effect on drug availability or use.[26]

Contrary to Charleton's assertion in this regard, Irish law – like the law of several other European states[27] – does not go to the authoritarian extremes of Swedish law. The general Irish legislative exclusion of drug use from the list of drug offences reflects the fact that, previously, drug use in Ireland was considered as a medical or health issue, and those who misused drugs were regarded as patients rather than criminals. Despite the domestic (and international) trend towards more "criminalisation" rather than more "medicalisation", this has not generally extended to making drug use a statutory offence. In this sense, as Jacques Derrida has put it, the principle "dictating respect for private life and a right to freely dispose of one's person" is still, in Ireland as well as elsewhere, "at least formally and hypocritically respected".[28]

Beyond this question of drug use in itself, the main point made in this context is of course that drug-related activity – possession, importation, etc – is criminogenic. For example, Charleton and McDermott observe: "When it comes to drug addiction we are dealing with criminogenic substances which relate to people's failings and weaknesses, the inter-relationship of groups within society and the horrible effects that it has on self-inflicted victims and those who, in turn, become the victims of those victims".[29] Yet this view of criminogenesis is a mere statement of the obvious: of course drug-related activity is criminogenic if it is a criminal offence to possess, import, etc, the drugs in question. Murder, to give another example, is criminogenic; the reason for this is that murder is a criminal offence. Indeed, all criminal offences are in this sense "criminogenic". As Ethan Nadelmann has pointed out in the context of United States drug law: "In the absence of drug-prohibition laws, these activities would obviously cease to be crimes".[30]

---

[25] Quoted in Lenke and Olsson, "Sweden: Zero Tolerance Wins the Argument?", in Dorn, Jepsen and Savona (eds.), *European Drug Policies and Enforcement* (London, 1996), p. 111

[26] See Yates, "The Situation in Sweden" (1996) 7 *International Journal of Drug Policy* 88, and Lenke, "The Development of Drug Abuse in Sweden", *Oberoende*, 1/2, 1998

[27] See The Netherlands Ministry of Foreign Affairs, Ministry of Health, Welfare and Sport, Ministry of Justice, and Ministry of the Interior, *Drugs Policy in the Netherlands: Continuity and Change* (Directorate of the Ministry of Health, Welfare and Sport, 1995), p. 6

[28] "The Rhetoric of Drugs", in Weber (ed.), *Points ... (Interviews with Jacques Derrida, 1974-1994)* (Stanford, 1995), p. 228, at p. 232

[29] "Drugs: The Judicial Response (Part II)", *The Bar Review*, June 1998, p. 370, at p. 374

[30] Nadelmann, "The Case for Legalization" (1988) 92 *The Public Interest* 3, at p. 17

The view that "drug abuse" *causes* crime, particularly property crime, is another view that is commonly assumed in debates on crime in Ireland. Charleton remarks that it has caused a "vast upsurge in violent and invasive theft". Nonetheless, the real cause of crime in this context is not "drugs": once again, it is drug prohibition. Drug prohibition is criminogenic through the inflationary effect it has on drug prices. Otherwise cheap drugs are made expensive by the war on drugs and various forms of property crime are a direct consequence of this. This type of crime is in fact one of the social costs of drug prohibition. Other major social costs are the cost of drug-law enforcement, including policing, judicial system, and incarceration costs; the tendency towards the encroachment of civil liberties which inevitably accompanies drug criminalisation; and the alienation from the rule of law which many otherwise law-abiding citizens experience because of drug prohibition.

In the final analysis, this drugs-related crime is thus not caused by "drug abuse" or "drug addiction", but rather by the demand for drugs in situations where the state has legislated to drive the market underground.[31] As Nadelmann has commented on this type of "criminogenesis": "[If drugs were] significantly cheaper – which would be the case if they were legalized – the number of crimes committed by drug addicts to pay for their habits would, in all likelihood, decline dramatically. Even if a legal-drug policy included the imposition of relatively high consumption taxes in order to discourage consumption, drug prices would probably still be lower than they are today."[32]

A similar argument rebuts the suggestion put forward by Charleton that "drug abuse" in some way causes inner city "evictions"; again, the communities' "public challenges" to the legal order stemmed from the problems associated with drugs under a prohibitionist regime. The high levels of drug misuse and property crime associated with drug prohibition, when coupled with conditions of social and economic deprivation, give rise to understandable anger and frustration.

It is also often suggested that "drugs" cause the criminal activity associated with drug gangs and, in particular, the infamous "drug barons". But yet again it is drug prohibition that brings about this crime. Prohibition creates (or, at the very least, facilitates) a criminal class, that is, those who operate the illicit drug market. Further, as we are all too well aware in Ireland, illegal markets breed violence: they do so "not only because they attract criminally-minded individuals, but also because participants in the market have no resort to legal institutions to resolve their disputes".[33] The way in which to "eliminate the drug barons", as Niall Stokes

---

[31] For this argument in an Irish context, see McCullagh, *Crime in Ireland: A Sociological Introduction* (Cork, 1996), p. 221

[32] Nadelmann, *op. cit.*, at p. 17

[33] *Ibid.*, at p. 18

has written in the context of heroin misuse in Ireland, is to eliminate the reason for their existence: "It seems blindingly obvious ... that the best way to beat the drug barons is to take their market away from them. This can be done in two ways: by education and rehabilitation; and by supplying heroin – not methadone – cheaply, to registered addicts. And if, to do this, it is necessary to legalise heroin and create a legitimate trade in the drug under state supervision, then that is the route to go."[34]

In terms of a final idea occasionally put forward by the prohibitionist lobby – that the use of prohibited drugs often leads directly to aggressive and violent (and often criminal) *behaviour* – the evidence is simply not there to support this view, particularly not as a straightforward causal relationship. As Jeffrey Fagan writes in a discussion relating to all forms of intoxication, which also highlights further the influence of set and setting:

> How aggressive behaviour is influenced by the ingestion of various substances is not well understood. There are fundamental differences between substances in their association with aggression; various intoxicants affect both mind and body differently. Research on the nexus of aggression and substance use has consistently found a complex relation, mediated by personality and expectancy factors, situational factors, and sociocultural factors that channel the arousal effects of substances into behaviour types which may or may not involve interpersonal aggression. The effects of intoxicants also differ according to the amounts consumed per unit of body weight, tolerances, and genetic or biological predispositions. Accordingly there is only limited evidence that consumption of alcohol, cocaine, heroin, or other substances is a direct, pharmacologically based cause of crime.[35]

The above range of arguments against the simplistic drugs-crime "connection thesis" are not novel. For example, the many problems with the "connection thesis" were neatly summarised by David Richards in 1981: "It is said that drug users support their habits by theft and robbery, that drug use releases violence, induces illegal trafficking in drugs, and enlarges the scope of organized crime operations. None of these considerations in fact justifies the criminalization of drug use; indeed, criminalization itself fosters these evils. It forces drug users into illegal conduct to obtain money for drugs and brings them into contact with the criminal underground, the covertness of which breeds incidental crime ... Arguments of criminogenesis are generally circular and question-begging."[36] Perhaps the crucial issue here is to note that they are arguments that have not been met. When there is reference to a "public debate" about "drugs and crime" in

---

[34] Stokes, "The Message", *Hot Press*, 29 May, 1996

[35] Fagan, "Intoxication and Aggression", in Tonry and Wilson (eds.), *Drugs and Crime (Crime and Justice: A Review of Research – Volume 13)* (Chicago, 1990), p. 243

[36] "Drug Use and the Rights of the Person: A Moral Argument for the Decriminalization of Certain Forms of Drug Use" (1981) 33 *Rutgers Law Review* 607, at p. 646

Ireland, it is invariably a debate where one group – those favouring the status quo – simply refuse to engage with important arguments.

Instead, prohibitionist rhetoric constitutes a form of scare-mongering based on ignorance of the most salient aspects of the "drugs and crime" dynamic. Such ignorance is extremely dangerous and harmful. The perceptions of "drug abuse" that it generates are presented as part of the justification for the "zero-tolerance" rhetoric and authoritarian manoeuvres of the prohibitionist war on drugs. As Randy Barnett has stated in the context of United States drug legislation, "because of the lack of a complaining witness, the criminalization of victimless conduct will inevitably require the techniques of a police state".[37]

The Irish Criminal Justice (Drug Trafficking) Acts of 1996 and 1999 are typical measures in this regard. Serious questions have been raised about the former piece of legislation, particularly the powers of detention granted and the implications for the right to silence.[38] It has been argued, for example, that the 1996 Act "has real potential to produce injustice, and indeed miscarriages of justice, rather than effectively addressing ... drug trafficking".[39] The 1999 Act has similar potential. This legislation creates a new offence, with directions as to minimum periods of imprisonment, relating to the possession of drugs with a value of £10,000 or more for the purpose of sale or supply.[40] The Act provides that evidence of the "market value" of the drugs concerned may be given only by a police officer or an officer of customs and excise.[41] This is in fact the situation as it pertains at present in respect of all manner of drug prosecutions, but the 1999 Act, by creating a new offence of this nature, gives added significance to that situation. In short, the official system of "market valuation" notoriously over-prices the street value of drugs.[42] Unless the official valuation system is reformed in accordance with the basic requirements of justice, conviction and imprisonment under this legislation for possession of drugs such as cannabis and cocaine with a street value of *less* than £10,000 is a likely prospect. Such a reform, of course, would do nothing to diminish the serious deficiencies and questionable morality of laws of this kind.

---

[37] "Bad Trip: Drug Prohibition and the Weakness of Public Policy" (1994) 103 *Yale Law Journal* 2593, at p. 2622

[38] See Keane, "Detention Without Charge and the Criminal Justice (Drug Trafficking) Act 1996: Shifting the focus of the Irish criminal process from trial court to garda station" (1997) 7 *Irish Criminal Law Journal* 1-21, and Ryan, "The Criminal Justice (Drug Trafficking) Act 1996: Decline and Fall of the Right to Silence?" (1997) 7 *Irish Criminal Law Journal* 22-37

[39] Ryan, *op. cit.*, at p. 22

[40] Section 4, Criminal Justice (Drug Trafficking) Act 1999

[41] *Ibid.*

[42] Questions concerning other issues – including purity of drugs seized, regional variations in prices of drugs and the general fairness of this valuation procedure – have also been raised. See speech by Frank Buttimer to Criminal Law Committee Seminar, Law Society of Ireland, 2 October 1999

DRUG LAW REFORM – THE HARM REDUCTION OPTION

In practical terms, the future of Irish drug policy is inevitably linked to international, particularly European, drug policy. This does not, however, preclude gradual domestic changes. Forms of drug decriminalisation, as distinct from drug legalisation, exist in various European jurisdictions, including the Netherlands, Italy, Spain and Germany. Drug decriminalisation refers to a legal regime where possession of prohibited drugs for personal use, and sometimes even possession of relatively small quantities for sale, is tolerated, but where large-scale distribution is not. The punitive sanctions of the criminal law are still central to the state response to the availability of illicit drugs.[43] On the other hand, legalisation refers to a form of regulation where the construction of the criminal law in relation to currently prohibited drugs would be radically altered. Punitive criminal sanctions would no longer apply generally to the drug trade, although the law, including the criminal law, would continue to play a role in drug policy. Just as with presently legal drugs, drug legalisation would include clear restrictions and conditions of various kinds, relating, for example, to age, and to time, place, and manner of sale, as well as criminal sanctions for violations of these limitations; different restrictions and conditions would apply to different drugs, depending on a variety of factors, including, for example, the toxicity of a standard quantity of the drug and the levels of risk in cases where the drug is misused. In Ireland, there has been some discussion of the options of decriminalisation and legalisation but, once again, prohibitionist ideology has had a distortive effect.

The arguments for the liberalisation of drug laws are typically represented in prohibitionist ideology as belonging to one of two types. Either they are said to be based on a form of libertarian philosophy – the idea that individuals should be free to do as they please, including harm themselves, without interference from the state – or on a neoliberal advocacy of economic efficiency in the allocation of state resources – the idea that drug law liberalisation is a sensible policy based on cost/benefit analyses. It is on the basis that those who advocate drug law reform are advancing one or both of these types of arguments that they are regarded by many as championing the cause of the leisured middle classes, whose rate of recreational drug use has accelerated in recent decades. They are, therefore, viewed as exhibiting a callous disregard for those individuals, families and communities whose lives have been torn apart by drugs and who are predominantly from the economically disadvantaged sectors of society. For example, during the discussions on the subjects of decriminalisation and legalisation at the

---

[43] For the inconsistencies inherent in such a system, see Murphy and O'Shea, "Dutch drugs policy, Ecstasy and the 1997 Utrecht CVO Report" (1998) 8 *Irish Criminal Law Journal* 141-164, at pp. 146-7

1998 Irish National Crime Forum, Vincent Toher of the Dublin Inner City Drugs Task Force said that "the dangerous subtext with decriminalisation is to say that perhaps these communities can't be saved, and perhaps they're not worth saving".[44] Another example is provided by Mary Holland's report on the same discussions in *The Observer.* After detailing the views of a small number of former addicts who spoke to the Forum, Holland wrote that "against [that] background, the arguments about legalisation seemed remote, even offensive".[45]

Moreover, as a consequence of these representations, the institutionalised and non-institutionalised left – the political groupings that one would expect to provide oppositional or alternative perspectives on the issue – generally accede to and support the official prohibitionist consensus. Socialist analyses of drug policy tend to focus on the correlation between certain types of treated drug misuse and class-related disadvantage and to perceive drugs as an additional "oppressor" within capitalist societies. Psychoactive drugs are generally regarded as impeding the development of proper consciousness on the part of the oppressed classes in society and also as directly inflicting hardship – in the sense of medical and other harm – on those classes. It is in this sense that the famous epigram to the effect that religion is the opium of the people can be said to reflect socialist attitudes towards drugs as much as towards religion. While alcohol and habitually-consumed pharmaceutical drugs have by no means been excluded from the general "anti-drug" perspective on the left[46], the particular wrath of socialists (like that of liberals, conservatives, etc) has been reserved for presently prohibited drugs. There are of course exceptions to the general leftist position. [47]

The key problem in this regard is the assumption that *all* arguments for drug law reform derive from one or other, or both, of the two ideological sources mentioned above.[48] However, the strongest argument for reform in this area is that it would be the most effective means of reducing drug-related harm across all sectors of society. The open, legal regulation of drug use would bring about con-sequences such as greater scope for proper drug education, safer drug use, and the removal of prohibition-related problems like drug-associated property crime. Drug policy based on the principle of harm reduction would be guided mainly by a perspective on drug use where the government's role would be to prevent people from unthinkingly starting to use drugs without knowing enough about them or

---

[44] Quoted in Cleary, "Pros and cons for legalising cannabis", *The Irish Times*, 21 March, 1998

[45] "Help us, don't punish us, say young drug addicts", *The Observer*, 22 March, 1998

[46] See, for example, Smith, "Dry Spells Ahead", *Marxism Today*, August 1988

[47] See, for example, Ahmed and Browne, "Mowlam: Rethink on drugs due", *The Observer*, 5 November, 2000

[48] Of course such types of argument do exist. For an example of the former, libertarian type of argument, see Barnett, *op. cit.* For an example of the other, economic type, see Taubman, "Externalities and Decriminalization of Drugs", in Krauss and Lazear (eds.), *op. cit.*

under the influence of other people, and to make medical and social assistance available to drug users with problems.

While it is evident that the decriminalisation or legalisation of presently prohibited drugs offers the best option in terms of the reduction of the harm that drug-taking can undeniably entail, it has rarely been suggested that this should happen other than gradually. As one commentator has noted: "In containing drug problems it is important to recognize that the criminal status of drug use is a major factor in causing problems for addicts and the community in general. However ... the transition from the present situation to a more measured response to drugs should be a gentle one. It would seem unwise to make too many (new) drugs publicly available in a short time, because time is required for society to 'domesticate' new drugs for general usage and to adapt to a new way of thinking."[49]

From the point of view of the left, it is not suggested that the argument for drug law reform is an argument that can or should be "hived off" from other concerns. The proposal that socialism should reorient itself in order to be identified with the international campaign for the end of drug prohibition arises from understandings of drug use that place it in its proper psychosocial and socio-cultural context. The importance of the drug-set-setting analysis, when examined in the light of the other arguments presented in this paper, indicates that while the problems associated with drugs can be significantly reduced by ending prohibition and embracing harm reduction, other social reform and restructuring is required for drug problems to be tackled in the most effective way possible. Socio-economic restructuring *is* essential if present drug misuse related to poverty, unemployment and educational disadvantage is to be properly addressed. The crucial point about drug law reform *in and of itself* is that it has the potential to reduce drug-related harm among members of all socio-economic classes; substantial amounts of resources could be transferred away from authoritarian state activity and spent instead on treating those who learn or otherwise develop patterns of dysfunctional use, and non-problematic drug use, as through previous centuries, would not be an activity that invited state coercion. This may not accord precisely with traditionalist interpretations of socialism, which tend to be exclusively or largely class-oriented. Yet such interpretations are hardly tenable any longer.[50] On the other hand, the dimensions of drug policy questions are too multifarious, interdependent and complex for them to be mere questions of "identity" or "recognition". Moreover, the issues involved appear to transcend the conception of socialism as the achievement of more equality between persons

---

[49] Van de Wijngaart, *op. cit.* p. 118; see also Fromberg, "Prohibition as a Necessary Stage in the Acculturation of Foreign Drugs", in Heather, Wodak, Nadelmann and O'Hare (eds.), *op. cit.*

[50] See, for example, Fraser, "From Redistribution to Recognition? Dilemmas of justice in a 'Post-Socialist' Age" (1995) 212, *New Left Review*

than inequality.[51] At any rate, it is beyond our purposes to engage fully with the contemporary debates around the meaning of "socialism". Suffice to say that the harm reduction option discussed here is founded on a reduced role for the criminal law in the area of drug policy, and to observe that, whatever the precise meaning of socialism, it surely cannot involve a failed scheme that routinely fines, incarcarates and imprisons individuals and that contributes to the worst types of drug problems.

In the Netherlands, for example, while it is acknowledged that drugs can have harmful effects, the medical and moral models of drug use are rejected and the drugs themselves are not demonised or blamed in isolation. Instead, the *health interests* of citizens are prioritised to the extent that even the criminal law is oriented towards that end. As a 1995 Dutch policy document stated:

> Following the recommendations of the Working Party on Narcotics (1972), the government of the day saw no reason to base its policy on the idea that any use of the drugs concerned in itself represented an unacceptable risk to society. Whether or not such a risk existed would depend partly on the circumstances in which the drugs were used and the extent of their use. It was in the light of these factors that the prevention and control of the risks of drug use to society and individuals were made the primary objective of policy.
>
> This drugs policy has never been amended ...
>
> The Dutch view is that "the interests which have to be protected by the criminal law are primarily health interests.[52]

The results of this responsible and pragmatic Dutch philosophy of harm reduction have been well-documented. As Paul O'Mahony has observed, "the best scientific evaluations of the Dutch approach indicate that it is a definite, if limited, success".[53] Yet in the Irish policy debate it is more common to hear statements such as that Dutch policies have caused explosions in the crime rate, and that, "far from freeing up the judicial system ... they are grinding it to a halt".[54] While informed observers will rightly ignore incorrect statements of this kind,[55] they fit well with the incoherent drug demonisation and the flawed drugs-crime "connection thesis" of prohibitionist rhetoric.

---

[51] For this conception, see Bobbio, *Destra e Sinistra* (*Left and Right*) (Rome, 1984)

[52] The Netherlands Ministry of Foreign Affairs *et al, op. cit.*, pp. 5-6

[53] O'Mahony, *Criminal Chaos: Seven Crises in Irish Criminal Justice* (Dublin, 1996), p. 82; see also, The Netherlands Ministry of Foreign Affairs *et al, op. cit.*; van de Wijngaart, *op. cit.*; and Murphy and O'Shea, *op. cit.*

[54] Kenny, *op. cit.*, at p. 20

[55] See The Netherlands Ministry of Foreign Affairs *et al, op. cit.* See also, R. Stevenson, *Winning the War on Drugs: To Legalise or Not?* (London, 1994)

CONCLUSION

In one sense, the problem with Irish drug policy is very simple: it continues to be far removed from any ethos of energetic, critical or rational overall examination. It is therefore not surprising that the *precise* basis of Irish drug policy remains unacceptably elusive. Consider the following:

> Irish drug policy is almost three decades old, and not once during this period have the underlying assumptions been systematically evaluated and a broad, coherent foundation for policy making established. As a result, each new occurrence in drug development and each new use pattern have been viewed as unfamiliar, with the unfamiliarity breeding a sense of crisis, and the crisis precipitating *ad hoc* policy responses.

In fact, two words in the original quotation have been changed: it should begin "American drug policy is seven decades old ...",[56] yet it is even more applicable to the Irish situation. As an issue of public policy, drugs have never been the subject of a comprehensive analysis in the Irish state. Instead, our drug policy to date has merely comprised a series of revisions of pre-Independence British policy, tailored to suit the "self-evident" assumptions of American-led trans-national prohibitionism. Irish drug policy reviews have been restricted to an analysis of how best to implement prohibitionist policies; they should have the authority to investigate all forms and all aspects of drug use and misuse and to explore all policy options. Such a review would, of course, have to address and answer the basic question: why is the reduction (or, indeed, minimisation) of drug-related harm not the central aim of Irish drug policy?

---

[56] *United States National Commission on Marihuana and Drug Abuse, First Report, Marihuana: A Signal of Misunderstanding* (1972), p. 19, quoted in Jonas, "Solving the Drug Problem: A Public Health Approach to the Reduction of the Use and Abuse of Both Legal and Illegal Recreational Drugs" (1990) 18 *Hofstra Law Review* 751, at p. 757

SECTION 3

SOCIETY AND CRIME

12

Introduction

Paul O'Mahony

CLASSICISM VERSUS POSITIVISM IN CRIMINOLOGY

It is customary to define the early development of criminology in terms of the division between the classical and positivist schools of thought. The classical school is associated with Cesare Beccaria, and was inspired by the publication in 1764 of his highly influential treatise, *On Crimes and Punishment*. Beccaria was a man of the Enlightenment concerned to reform the barbaric "bloody code", then prevailing throughout Europe and meting out extremely brutal and often arbitrary and disproportionate punishment for wrong-doing. His focus was on the philosophical, legal and procedural principles that should undergird criminal justice.

Chief among these principles were: that people should be treated equally before the law and punished only in accordance with the law; that punishment should be based on the act rather than the class of person who commits the act; that punishment should be based on a pleasure/pain reckoning so that the pain of punishment will always outweigh the pleasure to be gained from the crime; and, perhaps most importantly, that punishment should be commensurate with the seriousness of the offence and, though a prompt and effective deterrent, should be kept to the minimum. Like current criminal law, the classical perspective assumes that the human actor is a rational agent endowed with free will. Man is capable of weighing the good and bad consequences of his actions both for himself and others and, in the light of this knowledge, is capable of freely choosing to commit crime or not. Most importantly, since man acts on the basis of his rational, self-regarding, cost/benefit analysis of the situation, he can be swayed to avoid crime, if he sees that it carries a high risk of appropriately severe punishment.

The positivist school, on the other hand, was influenced by evolutionary theory and the development of empirical scientific methods and statistics. Positivists hold that human behaviour is determined not by the excercise of free will but by biological and environmental factors beyond the individual's control. This dichotomy between free will and scientific determinism is at the core of the opposition between classicism and positivism. Lombroso (1911) is frequently credited with being the most important pioneer of the positivist approach in criminology. Lombroso misguidedly believed it was possible to identify born criminals from physical features that were thought to be indicative of a more primitive stage of evolutionary development, such as huge jaws and strong canine teeth. While the influence of Beccaria can still be traced in the Irish criminal legal system and Constitution, the early positivist theories of criminality and their inherent "biology as destiny" assumptions were quickly rejected and replaced by theories emphasising the impact of the social environment. In recent decades, however, there has been a resurgence of interest in biological and genetic factors and their putative role in the development of aggression and criminality (eg Eysenck 1977; Mednick 1980; Quay 1993).

SOCIOLOGICAL DOMINANCE OF CRIMINOLOGY

Modern criminology, especially in its search for theoretical explanations of crime, has long been dominated by sociological modes of thought. The twentieth century witnessed a ferment of sociological thinking about the nature and roots of crime with diverse theories rapidly coming into and falling out of fashion. These theories focused on, among other concepts, the function of crime and criminals within the wider social and political economy (Durkheim 1902); the interplay of dominant cultures and deviant subcultures (Cohen 1955; Cloward and Ohlin 1960; Matza 1969); the processes of social labelling and stigmatisation (Lemert 1951; Becker 1963; Goffman 1963); anomie, disorganisation and strain, especially that linked to industrialisation, urbanisation, materialistic consumerism and the weakening of bonds within extended families and local communities (Merton 1969); and conflict, social control and power relations, especially relations between economic and social elites and the marginalised groups in society that they perceive as dangerous or disruptive (Turk 1969; Quinney 1974; Walton and Young 1998). Downes and Rock (1995) have described "the inevitable half-life of sociological fashions: there is an ingrained impatience with the old which condemns every set of new ideas to a limited vitality".

Despite this transience, the evident relevance and enriching diversity of the sociological theoretical debate on criminal deviance cannot be denied. Criminological theories within the broad sociological tradition provide a wealth of insights into the social worlds and the socially conditioned personal motivations of those who commit crime and proceed to establish criminal careers. Most importantly, these theories stress the links between criminal behaviour and the socio-political and cultural context. Sociological theories demonstrate how, as Downes and Rock (1995) suggest, "deviant subcultures represent limited answers to the difficulties of living in a hostile and discouraging world". In this way, sociological theories act as a useful counterbalance to the individual-centred bias of the criminal justice system itself. While the criminal justice system is mainly concerned with allocating blame to individual, presumably rational, self-determining, human actors, sociological theories stimulate, legitimate and necessitate an interrogation of the role of society, political structures and the economy in the production of crime and criminals.

Albert Cohen (1955), a subcultural theorist, argues that subcultures evolve in order to solve problems posed for groups of people by the social structure. He sees the emergence of delinquent gangs amongst teenagers who have failed at school as their means of acquiring status and hitting back at the school and the broader social system which have branded them as failures. Cohen describes six distinctive features of delinquent gangs: 1) their non-utilitarian focus; 2) their malicious, destructive outlook; 3) their concern to attack and invert respectable values; 4) their short-term hedonism; 5) their versatility; and 6) their emphasis on gang autonomy and on loyalty as the primary virtue.

Cohen's theory not only helps explain what might otherwise appear to be the inexplicable negativity and self-destructiveness of certain types of gang, but does so by relating the group dynamics of such gangs and the individual psychology of their members to social structures, societal value systems and institutional practices. It is this commitment to the notion of crime as a social product, as a reaction to a pre-existing political and socio-economic order of values, and as an outcome of a system of social relations, that distinguishes sociological from the kind of biological and psychological explanations of crime that tend to emphasise motivational forces circumscribed by the individual.

Merton (1969), an anomie theorist, as another example, links crime to the fact that society engenders in its members specific goals, which reflect a set of culturally approved desires and aspirations for material and social success. Yet, society denies certain disadvantaged groups access to the legitimate means for acheiving highly desired goals. Socially constructed barriers produce strain and frustration in group members, who react by inventing their own alternative, often illegitimate, methods for getting ahead and finding success.

More recently, Turk (1969) and other conflict theorists have argued that laws do not exist for the good of all members of society but represent the interests of elite groups, who wield enough power to get the laws enacted. Law, in this view, is a means of maintaining the status quo – particularly in regard to the distribution of property, wealth, power and access to opportunity – and controlling those who might be a threat to the interests of the powerful groups in society.

Perhaps even more radical are the claims of labelling theory (Lemert 1951; Becker 1963). This theory proposes that society actively creates criminals. In essence, the argument is that the criminal justice system labels people involved in minor and probably transitory deviance as criminals and thus permanently stigmatises and defines them. The labelling process sets in motion a self-fulfilling prophesy whereby the stigmatised are socially excluded and subject to many pressures to live up to negative expectations of them. The stigmatised person's own acceptance of and identification with the label "criminal" reinforces the process and greatly increases the likelihood of further criminal behaviour.

THE NEED FOR A HOLISTIC MULTIFACTORIAL MODEL OF CRIMINAL BEHAVIOUR

Sociological theorists vary greatly in the extent to which they acknowledge the role of biology and psychology in the genesis of crime. Mostly they ignore the issue, preferring instead to highlight the role of social structural factors such as class and social processes like differential association (Sutherland and Cressey 1978) and labelling. However, there is an implicit recognition of the importance, if not the primacy, of psychological processes in a great deal of sociological theorising. As Feldman (1993) argues, "we detract nothing from the sociological pioneers of modern criminology in pointing out that some of what they did is more properly construed as psychology".

In the final analysis, an holistic, multifactorial model of criminal behaviour must be adopted. It is clearly erroneous to rely on categorical, either/or thinking that pits the social, psychological and biological levels of analysis against each other, as if they were mutually incompatible forms of explanation. Behaviour is determined both by the social environment, by the inherited biology of the individual and by psychological motives, which have their roots in inborn temperamental and cognitive capacities, but which are continuously shaped by unique personal experience and learning gained in the social environment.

Motives, including criminal motives, though they are clearly located in and owned by the individual, are not generated purely within the individual and are not solely a reflection of the individual. On the contrary motives are generated in the interactions between the individual and the outer world, including the socio-cultural world of ideas, values and hierarchies. Motives are fundamentally conditioned by norms, belief systems, attitudes, and values, which are themselves rooted in the social context. Motives are determined by the whole network of relationships and opportunities for action defined uniquely for each individual by his social world. There is an unbreakable circle of reciprocal interactions (Bandura 1977) – the motivated person determines his own behaviour; the behaviour reshapes the person; the environment, including the unique biology of the individual, conditions both the motivations of the person and his behaviour;

and the person and his behaviour affect the environment.

THE CENTRAL IMPORTANCE OF SOCIALISATION

Socialisation is, arguably, the key to a comprehensive understanding of the genesis of crime. As Garland (1990) has stated: "It is only the mainstream processes of socialization (internalized morality and a sense of duty, the informal inducements and rewards of conformity, the practical and cultural networks of mutual expectation and interdependence etc) that are able to promote proper conduct on a consistent and regular basis". The obverse of this is that most, if not all, offending behaviour can be attributed to failures in socialisation. The socialisation process, which inculcates a set of sensibilities and values in the individual, occurs mainly within the family but also in the local community and in school and peer groups.

Socialisation is central, first because it is directly productive of significant psychological and behavioural differences in the capacity to self-regulate and in the propensity to respect the rights of others; and second because, as an explanatory construct, it bridges the gaps between the biological, psychological and social levels of analysis. The concept of socialisation unambiguously points to the role of familial, social and cultural factors in the development of the individual conscience. Socialisation is a name for a complex, highly variable and contingent programme of training that has at its core the transmission, from the social collective to the individual, of cultural beliefs, values and specific codes of behaviour. But socialisation refers to a formative process inevitably mediated by individual psychology and biology.

Socialisation takes a different pattern for each individual, partly because of the uniqueness of each person's biogenetic endowment, that is their inborn competences and traits, but partly because of differing social reactions within families and other groups to both similar and different individuals. So, for example, individual biogenetic differences between brothers help account for differing propensities for crime. This can be because inborn differences are linked to personality traits that carry a risk of criminal involvement, such as aggressiveness or impulsiveness, or are linked to other personal attributes, such as optimism, intelligence, resilience, good looks and a pleasing demeanour, that promote positive or negative social reactions and, very crucially, impact on success or failure at school. In any given case, these biologically based but socially processed differences may be more influential than aspects of the social environment that can be categorised as purely sociological, such as poverty and social class. So, there are numerous examples of brothers raised in almost identical, extremely deprived circumstances, where one brother turns to crime but the other totally avoids it.

Sociological theories are hard-pressed to explain, without reference to biology and psychology, the immense differences in the propensity for crime between women and men. Biological and genetic differences between the sexes are crucial and are built upon and imbued with cultural meaning by the socialisation process, that is by the differing societal reactions to women and men. However, as Feldman (1977) contends, in reference to biological propensities for crime, "the division of the world into the criminal and the law-abiding is largely a comforting delusion. Predisposing individual differences are relevant, but the environmental control of the acquisition, performance and maintenance of criminal behaviour is powerful and pervasive". Both the underlying biological and psychological differences and their social construction in specific contexts and cases and the concrete opportunities available to the individual in his or her social world are essential to any explanatory account of the far lesser involvement in crime of women compared to men.

THE ROOTS OF JUVENILE DELINQUENCY AND CRIMINALITY

Large scale, longitudinal research projects (eg West and Farrington 1977; McCord 1978; Huizinga et al 1996) have in recent years begun to unravel the complex tangle of potential causes of crime. These studies have been particularly effective in identifying key aspects of socialisation within the family that are correlated with future delinquency. They have established that parental neglect or rejection, lack of discipline or inconsistent discipline in the childhood home, exposure to the criminal behaviour of adult role models, parental advocacy of anti-social attitudes and values, peer pressure, low intelligence and school failure, large family size, material want and boredom, can all play an important role in promoting juvenile delinquency and should be regarded as significant risk factors for a future criminal career.

The late teenage years are the peak years for criminal offending and nearly half of all officially recognised crime is committed by teenagers. The international literature (eg Short and Nye 1957; Christie et al 1965) indicates that many teenagers from all sorts of backgrounds experiment with minor delinquent behaviour, including crimes of dishonesty, aggression and vandalism. But, most significantly, research (Wolfgang et al 1972) has shown that the group who go on to have a serious criminal career are a small minority and not by any means representative of teenagers as a whole or even of teenagers of the deprived lower social classes. As the Cambridge Delinquency Study (West and Farrington 1977) has convincingly shown, certain types of susceptible, inherently troublesome children from a small number of particularly dysfunctional and multiply-disadvantaged families account for a very large proportion of relatively serious teenage crime.

These findings reinforce the view that the socialisation process, most especially in the home, is the core mechanism in the production of crime-prone individuals. Low intelligence, impulsiveness and attention deficit disorder at the biogenetic end of the spectrum, and poverty and social exclusion at the socio-cultural end, are critically important but can sometimes be overcome if children are socialised successfully, that is if they are cared for in a loving, positive, enabling family environment, provided with effective models of conduct, and insulated from negative outside influences. Conversely, chaotic, abusive and emotionally cold family life and insufficient guidance, that is to say negative or inadequate family socialisation, can lead to anti-social, aggressive, or crime-prone children even in the best of material circumstances or when the children lack predisposing, biogenetic characteristics.

However, Irish research (O'Mahony 1985, 1997) has been unequivocal in identifying poverty, paternal unemployment, poor housing, low social status, school failure, family disruption and large family size as characteristics of both young and adult offenders, confirming the picture that negative or inadequate socialisation is far more prevalent in adverse social conditions. Furthermore, this research suggests that persistent serious offending may be associated with quite small, circumscribed communities of especially disadvantaged families to an even greater extent than in Britain. The key insight is that social deprivation, while not always a direct cause of criminality, is, because of the strains it places on particularly vulnerable and ill-equipped families, strongly associated with negative or inadequate socialisation, which are direct causes of offending behaviour.

The Inter-Departmental Group, in its report *Urban Crime and Disorder* (1992), identified the crucial, socio-economic factors – eg poverty and lack of educational and employment opportunities – that make an important contribution to juvenile crime. The Group concluded that these factors can and must be tackled, if the rising trend in juvenile crime and urban disorder is to be halted and reversed. The Group noted that these broadly defined socio-economic dis-advantages are compounded by other very prevalent, family-based, personalised ills, such as "alcoholism in the home, juvenile alcohol and drug abuse, poor parenting, including child abuse and neglect, lack of self-esteem, boredom and truancy".

The Group is undoubtedly correct in its general diagnosis. For example, certain areas of Dublin with highly concentrated and multiple forms of social deprivation have been especially vulnerable to the opiate drugs epidemic of the last two decades. The negative synergy of the culture of poverty and substance abuse has had a distinct and immensely powerful influence in promoting delinquency and crime. Furthermore, in its prescriptions for preventative action, the Group correctly balances the need to focus on families and their extremely significant contribution to the quality of socialisation with the need to recognise that social deprivation and disadvantage independently promote conditions that tend to constitute a very poor environment for the socialisation of children. This is important because, when emphasising the centrality of socialisation, it is essential to avoid blaming parents, who themselves are often the hapless products of the cycle of disadvantage. It is also essential to recognise that many loving parents with pro-social values and excellent parenting skills struggle against the odds in crime and drug ridden neighbourhoods to raise their children to be law-abiding citizens. Unfortunately, the powerful influence of the neighbourhood environment and the peer group often overwhelms their best efforts.

There are, then, important individual-based, largely biogenetic factors, related to physique, temperament, personality, and academic ability, that play a pivotal role in the genesis of delinquency and especially serious repeat offending. But there is no doubt that the socialisation process, occurring mainly within the family, peer group, school and local neighbourhood, plays a vital role. Broader social, political and economic factors, such as a neighbourhood permeated by a hard drugs culture or the highly inequitable distribution of wealth, property, power and opportunity in society, impact directly by creating needs and opportunities that can lead to crime and indirectly, but decisively, by their influence on socialisation.

THE ROLE OF SOCIETY IN THE GENESIS OF CRIME

The links between society and crime are innumerable and highly complex. Society after all defines crime and decides how severely it will be punished and how rigorously and fairly the criminal law will be enforced. But, while irreducible socio-cultural factors also play a major role as causes of crime, they invariably do so as strands in an inextricable web of interacting causal factors at the biological, psychological and socio-cultural levels. A comprehensive picture of crime must take account of the interplay of causal factors at all levels, but often, depending on the nature of the question being examined, social factors will have a justified primacy in explanatory accounts. For example, investigation of possible class bias in criminal justice decision making is inevitably mainly concerned with social hierarchies and power relations.

Fluctuations in the amount and type of crime experienced by society over time or between geographical areas and social classes are other issues that require a primary focus on changing and differing social conditions, even if, in the final analysis, the key process may well be the influence of these social changes and differences on the socialisation of individual children.

Accordingly, the sharp rise in crime in Ireland in recent decades is very frequently explained in terms of social changes. The main candidate causes are: rapid urbanisation and the decay of communal solidarity and the formerly dominant Catholic moral value system; industrialisation and the growth of a market-driven, consumerist, materialist, individualist ethos; and globalisation in terms of travel, commerce and communication and especially in terms of the omnipresent Anglo-American entertainment monoculture, which transmits vast amounts of sometimes liberating information alongside powerful new models for interpersonal behaviour. A demographic argument is also popular. This explains Ireland's previously very low crime rate by reference to past large-scale emigration of the most crime-prone group, young males. Again this is chiefly a social explanation, linking low crime to stagnant economic conditions and the stability and conservatism of an Ireland deprived of many of its most energetic and potentially troublesome young people.

There are always, however, tensions lurking beneath the surface of discussions on the impact of social factors on crime; tensions that are connected to the fact that the criminal justice system finds it necessary and proper to blame individuals for criminal behaviour, regardless of heredity, family upbringing and wider social conditions. These difficulties indicate that unresolved theoretical differences between the classical and positivist approaches, particularly the free will/determinism issue, still haunt criminal justice. For example, one Irish report on the penal system (ICJP and ICC 1985) warns against "a sentimental, demeaning and ultimately subversive tendency to deny justification for punishment by diminishing the individual offender's responsibility and therefore his guilt to vanishing point, on the grounds of environmental, psychological or other factors. Human dignity is compatible with being punished, since punishment entails recognition of the autonomy and responsibility of the offender, who is held able to answer for himself and his offence". The law allows for a limited number of exculpatory conditions, that is mistake, accident, provocation, duress, immaturity through youth or mental incapacity, and insanity. These few conditions are held to impair, in different ways, the ability to intend and choose. Otherwise, in almost all cases, the law simply assumes that people are criminally responsible for their offences and, in this way, it individualises the crime problem and largely excludes consideration of both biogenetic and environmental influences.

Deterministic, scientific accounts of behaviour, on the other hand, explain criminal behaviour in terms of the biological, psychological and social factors that operate upon the individual and may, therefore, seem to explain it away. But scientific explanation of criminal acts does not have to be seen as clashing with or undermining the attribution of criminal responsibility. It is possible to retain the core of the classicist notion of free will without denying the scientific doctrine of causal determinism. The legal presumption of criminal responsibility, after all, is a byproduct of society's need to prescribe how people should behave, regardless of the various other causal influences on them; it refers to the discourse of *what ought to be,* not the discourse of *what is.* This active prescriptive process involves the production of a whole new set of socially generated, causal pressures that work on the individual in tandem with biological, psychological and other social factors. The process is founded on but at the same time helps create the domain of values, which is necessary to any human system of co-operative, social living.

But the legal presumption of criminal responsibility is not an unwelcome, disputed imposition; on the contrary, it simply reflects our personal experience of command over our own lives. Human agency is unique because intelligence allows us to self-reflect, set goals and plan for the future, thereby creating not just a sense but a genuine realm of autonomy. Values, principles, and the notion of personal responsibility are not objective and are not scientifically derivable, but they are nonetheless real and play a critical role in the direction of human conduct. Normal people are those whom we assume to be, and who intuitively believe themselves to be, capable of intending and choosing their own actions. We hold normal people criminally responsible as part of our way of constructing a social order of values, rights and obligations in an indifferent, material world where they do not naturally exist.

Despite the complexity of the issue of personal responsibility and the pervasive bias towards individualising crime issues, it is obvious that there are features of our society, of the way in which society is organised and manages itself, that tend to lead some of its members more than others into criminal activity. It makes eminent sense to attempt to identify those features through research and analysis and to actively address those of them that are amenable to social action. The whole criminal justice enterprise can be regarded as a form of social policy focused chiefly on past anti-social acts, but aimed at preventing future similar acts through the deterrent effects of law enforcement and criminal sanctioning. A broad vision of crime prevention must embrace all the many different kinds of social policy and social engineering that can have a crime reductive or preventive impact. Many social enterprises, even if their primary focus is not on crime prevention – for example, reducing the excessive use of alcohol by the young, improving access to education and employment for the socially excluded, enabling positive socialisation by parents, and creating a more equitable society – are at least as important as legislation, law enforcement and punishment to the struggle to create a crime free society.

REFERENCES

Bandura, A. 1977, *Social Learning Theory,* Englewood Cliffs NJ: Prentice Hall

Beccaria, C. 1764, *On Crimes and Punishment,* in English 1963, Indianapolis: Bobbs-Merrill

Becker, 1963, *Outsiders,* New York: Free Press

Christie, N., Andenaes, J. and Skirbekk, S. 1965, "A Study of Self-reported Crime", *Scandinavian Studies in Criminology* 1

Cloward, R. and Ohlin, R. 1960, *Delinquency and Opportunity,* New York: Free Press

Cohen, A. K. 1955, *Delinquent Boys: The Culture of the Gang,* Glencoe Illinois: Free Press

Downes, D. and Rock, P. 1995, *Understanding Deviance,* Oxford: Clarendon Press

Durkheim, E. 1902, "The Evolution of Punishment", in *Durkheim and the Law,* Lukes, S. and Scull, A. (eds), Oxford: Oxford University Press

Eysenck, H. 1977, *Crime and Personality,* London: Routledge and Kegan Paul

Feldman, P. 1977, *Criminal Behaviour,* London: Wiley

Feldman, P. 1993, *The Psychology of Crime,* Cambridge: Cambridge University Press

Garland, D. 1990, *Punishment and Modern Society,* Oxford: Clarendon Press

Goffman, E. 1963, *Stigma,* Englewood Cliffs NJ: Prentice Hall

Huizinga, D., Loeber, R. and Thornberry, T. 1996, *The Prevention of Serious Delinquency and Violence; Implications from the Programme of Research on the Causes and Correlates of Delinquency,* Washington DC: Department of Justice

ICJP and ICC, Irish Commission for Justice and Peace and Irish Council of Churches 1985, *Punishment and Imprisonment,* Dublin: Dominican Publications

Interdepartmental Group 1992, *Urban Crime and Disorder,* Dublin: Stationery Office

Lemert, M. 1951, *Social Pathology,* New York: McGaw-Hill

Lombroso, C. 1911, *Crime: Its Causes and Remedies,* Boston: Little, Brown

Matza, D. 1969, *Becoming Deviant,* New York: Prentice Hall

McCord, J. 1978, "A Thirty Year Follow-up of Treatment Effects", *American Psychologist* 33, 284-289

Mednick, S. 1980, "A Biosocial Theory of the learning of Law-abiding Behaviour", *Criminology Review Yearbook*

Merton, R. 1969, "Social Structure and Anomie", in Cressey, D. and Ward, D. (eds.), *Delinquency, Crime and Social Process,* New York: Harper and Row

O'Mahony, P., Cullen, R. and O'Hora, H. 1985, "Some Family Characteristics of Irish Juvenile Offenders", *Economic and Social Review* (17,1)

O'Mahony, P. 1997, *Mountjoy Prisoners: A Sociological and Criminological Profile,* Dublin: Stationery Office

Quay, H. 1993, "The psychobiology of undersocialised aggressive conduct disorder: a theoretical perspective", *Development and Psychopathology* 5 ,165-180

Quinney, R. 1974, *Critique of Legal Order: Crime Control in Capitalist Society,* Boston: Little, Brown

Short, J. and Nye, F. 1957, "Reported behaviour as a criterion of deviant behaviour", *Social Problems* 5

Sutherland, E. and Cressey, D. 1978, *Criminology,* Philadephia: Lippincott

Turk, A. 1969, *Criminality and the Legal Order,* Chicago: Rand McNally

West, D. and Farrington, D. 1977, *The Delinquent Way of Life,* London: Heinemann

Wolfgang, M., Figlio, R. and Sellin, T. 1972, *Delinquency in a Birth Cohort,* Chicago: University of Chicago Press

Walton, P. and Young, J. 1998, *The New Criminology Revisited,* London: MacMillan

13

Prisons, Politicians and Democracy[*]

Philip Pettit

Fergal O'Connor has always been outstanding among Irish political theorists for his capacity to relate abstract theory to concrete issues. To those of us who were lucky enough to be able to learn from him – in my case as a colleague at University College Dublin – the first lesson he represented was the need to justify theoretical ideas by the perspective that they gave us on day-to-day questions. I am conscious of not having learned that lesson well enough but it is never too late to make amends. And so in the spirit of his example, I start with lowly but pressing problems in penal practice and try to reveal a connection with issues in high democratic theory.

THE PRISON PROBLEM

One of the most extraordinary features of today's democracies is that, regardless of other differences in their aspirations and achievements, they more or less uniformly rely on imprisonment as the principal response to crime. I say that this is extraordinary because it has long been a matter of common sense observation, and it is now a well-established finding of criminology, that prisons do not serve well the cause of combating crime. Not much knowledge is required to see that prisons are brutalising and stigmatising institutions that deepen the alienation of offenders from the general society. And not much reflection is needed to see that they are likely to serve as recruiting and organising networks for those of dedicated criminal intent.

---

[*] In *Questioning Ireland*, J. Dunne, A. Ingram and F. Litton (eds.), Dublin: Institute of Public Administration, 2000

Why have prisons proved such a resilient feature of the democratic landscape? How have they managed to survive the growing evidence about their counter-productivity and the efforts of those professional and associational groups who have subjected them to a barrage of criticism? Criminologists, prisoners' rights groups, civil liberties associations, even victims' movements have subjected prison to withering criticism. And all to no avail. The resort to incarceration remains a steady and indeed a strengthening feature of many western democracies.

In searching for an explanation it may prove useful to move away from prisons, and even away from contemporary democracies. The Irish-Australian historian, Oliver MacDonagh (1958), is well known for his explanation of the emergence of the nineteenth-century administrative state. And that explanation, I want to suggest, offers a very plausible model of why imprisonment has proved so resilient.

The MacDonagh thesis is an attempt to explain the cascade of administrative reforms that emerged and stabilised in Victorian Britain: reforms in the mines and factories, in the employment of children, in the conditions on emigrant ships, and in a variety of other areas. The thesis is that those reforms materialised under the impetus of one and the same mechanism. The mechanism involved, first, the discovery of a scandal; second, the development of public outrage about the scandal; and third, a requirement on politicians to do something in order to respond to the scandal. We can call it the scandal machine.

According to MacDonagh, this scandal machine served in the first instance to introduce reforms in a given area and then, later, to reinforce and increase the effect of the reforms. As he describes the typical story, the machine initially had the effect of getting government to make an inquiry and to set up regulatory constraints; some years afterwards, when the scandal was found to have survived those constraints, it goaded government into establishing a regular inspectorate; and then a few years later, after the revelation of continuing scandal, it forced government to set up a proper bureaucracy to oversee the area in question.

The MacDonagh thesis is that we can explain the growth of the nineteenth-century administrative state by the cumulative effects of this simple but powerful mechanism. That state was not the intentional product of a Benthamite project of reform; it did not come of a utilitarian spirit sweeping through the halls of Westminster. It was the precipitate rather of a pattern that no one planned and that few understood. The growing administrative state was forced upon British democracy by systemic pressures, not by philosophical ideology or political will.

It is easy to reconstruct the elements that made the scandal machine so powerful. Nineteenth-century Britain was a more or less literate culture in which the press offered a ready outlet for the revelation of scandal; it was a more or less humanistic culture – the response to the Irish famine notwithstanding – in which scandal easily ignited outrage; and it was an increasingly democratic culture in which politicians had to prove themselves responsive to the feelings of the people. It was the combination of those forces, and not the vision or the leadership of any individual or group, that gave rise to the different aspects of the new governmental regime.

When we read MacDonagh's account of the rise of the administrative state it is easy to think of the mechanism at work as a sort of benign, invisible hand. Or at least that is easy for those amongst us who see the administrative developments that he charts as positive and progressive measures. But the scandal machine is not inherently benign in its effects, or so I now want to suggest. It can operate as often in the manner of an invisible foot as an invisible hand.

Consider the manner in which social work agencies are constrained by the scandal machine in their decisions as to whether certain children should be taken into care. If an agency decides that the children are better left with their parents or guardians then it runs a serious risk. Should anything bad happen, the newspapers and the television can be relied upon to reveal the scandal, to generate popular outrage and to call government down upon the head of the agency responsible. If the agency takes the children into care however, then short of large numbers being involved it can be more or less certain of escaping such bad effects. And this is so even if the reasons for taking the children into care are not professionally compelling: even if the option of taking the children away from their homes is a matter of just playing bureaucratically safe.

It does not take much imagination to see how in this type of case the scandal machine may operate like an invisible foot, not an invisible hand. The machine can easily ensure, at least in the absence of other safeguards, that social work agencies work for ill, not for good, in dealing with children at risk. It can have the result that children who would be much better left in their homes, perhaps under some sort of monitoring arrangement, are actually taken into institutional care.

We have seen what the scandal machine is and we have noticed that it may operate for good or for bad, depending on the circumstances in question. It is time, with these observations in mind, to return to the case of prisons. What I want to suggest is that the MacDonagh model provides a good explanation of what may be happening in this area. It does not need a lot of thought to see that the scandal machine operates with particular momentum in matters of criminal justice and that it can readily account for the resilience of the resort to imprisonment.

We can see how the scandal machine operates at the heart of penal practice if we ask ourselves what would be likely to happen in the event of a government reducing the maximum sentences available for given crimes, introducing new opportunities for early release, and arranging for a greater use of alternatives to imprisonment: say, a greater use of fines and community service orders. It is as sure as night follows day that at some point after the inauguration of such reforms an offender who would otherwise be in prison will commit some more or less sickening sort of crime. And it is equally sure that when such a thing happens it will constitute a matter of scandal, a cause of public outrage and a ground for calling on politicians to roll back the reforms which they had begun to institute.

There is no difficulty in seeing why such a crime would be a matter of scandal and outrage. We live in a society where the press and television have a vested interest in presenting people with the sensational and the shocking and in drumming up moralistic sentiment about the horrors involved. It is a well-tested Fleet Street formula that people like savouring the scandalous and having their outrage pumped and primed; it is common wisdom indeed that they are willing to pay for the pleasure.

Because there is no difficulty in seeing why the crime envisaged would be a matter of scandal and outrage, so there is no difficulty in understanding why it would force politicians, in all likelihood, to backtrack on the reforms they had initiated. When politicians are called upon to respond to the occurrence of a sickening crime, then there is only one plausible response they can make. They have got to show themselves as concerned and as angry as the most outraged in the community. And they have got to do that in the newspaper headline or the thirty-second sound bite. Let them fail to be sufficiently expressive of concern and anger and they will easily be upstaged by more vociferous opponents.

How can politicians be expressive in the required way? How other than by calling for a return to hard and harsh punishment? We will show these vandals, these vermin, what ordinary, decent folk think of such behaviour; the metaphors and the cadences will be familiar to every ear. We will crack down like government has never cracked down before on this sort of affront; the melancholy message is drearily predictable.

The reason why politicians are bound to be driven to this retributive, punitive response is that the forum in which they operate lends itself to no other language. The theatre of public responsibility and political will requires nothing less than an operatic display of fellow feeling and fellow outrage. Never mind if the words get lost. The audience isn't interested in what you are actually going to do; it wants to see and know that you care. Your job is to give the outrage voice and, in giving it voice, to orchestrate a chorus of demands for a return to the world where society is tough on crime.

If this line of thought is right then the criminal justice area is governed by the logic of the scandal machine and is subject to the control of an invisible foot. It is guaranteed never to move away from the pattern of counter-productive imprisonment that currently dominates our response to crime. Montesquieu (1989, 203) spoke over two hundred years ago of the danger that society would be subject, in its criminal laws, to what he called "the tyranny of the avengers". The scandal machine looks like a mechanism that ensures, unfortunately, that this sort of tyranny we will always have with us.

THE DEPOLITICISING SOLUTION

But perhaps I should rephrase that message. The tyranny of the avengers looks like something we will always have with us, at least so long as decisions about imprisonment are made by democratically elected politicians under the pressure of public, theatrical demands. For just as democratic responsiveness played a part in ensuring that the scandal machine produced those positive reforms described by MacDonagh, so it plays a crucial part in ensuring that that machine produces the resilient pattern of imprisonment with which we have learned, at no small cost, to live.

The observation is important because it points us towards the only sort of feasible change that might save us from the tyranny of avengers. The change I have in mind can be described in a single word: depoliticise. If decisions about sentencing and penal policy were depoliticised, if they were entrusted to a network of expert and impartial committees that monitored the aggregate effects of every initiative taken, then – then and only then – there might be some chance of rationalising the way in which we run our criminal justice system.

Without going into the details of the change envisaged, it is clear why we might look to it with a degree of confidence. Think about how central banks have come to depoliticise various financial decisions in most contemporary democracies and think of the way in which this enables politicians to resist popular pressures to introduce what might very well be irresponsible policies. They can say that the issue is not one in their province. And they can say that it is an issue on which it would be improper for them, or for any amateur or outsider, to criticise the decision-making body. Thus they can protect themselves from media assault by passing the buck elsewhere and they can ensure that there is somewhere else to pass the buck – there are people willing to accept appointment to central bank boards – by arguing that those who are appointed for their expertise and impartiality are not fair targets of popular criticism.

The depoliticisation move is known in discussions of constitutional democracy as a gagging initiative: an initiative in which the politicians silence themselves, or have silence thrust upon them (Holmes 1988). I think that the failure to resist the pressure of the scandal machine in the criminal justice system, the failure to rectify manifestly irrational aspects of our criminal justice practice, shows that the only way to make ground in this area may be to gag the politicians and to transfer the decisions to non-political bodies. If war is too important to be left to the generals, criminal justice is too important to be left to the politicians.

I realise that I have not presented an adequate argument for depoliticising criminal justice decisions. In order to make a proper case for such a reform I would need to marshal the empirical evidence of current failure, I would need to canvass the problems with alternative possibilities of reform, I would need to detail the proposal I have in mind and I would need to establish its attractions by showing how well analogues work in other areas. Also I would need to plan an implementation procedure that would allow for bringing the strategy into play in stages, with evidence of the success of each stage being necessary for progressing to the next stage.

I hope I may be forgiven for assuming in the absence of a proper argument that the depoliticisation option would be better than the status quo. That assumption is not outlandish, if only because the status quo is so barbaric. For anyone familiar with the brutal practice of prisons on the one hand and the evidence of their counter-productivity on the other, the status quo in criminal justice must begin to look about as morally compelling as a system of slave-holding (Braithwaite and Pettit 1990).

DEPOLITICISATION AND DEMOCRATIC THEORY

One reason I may be forgiven for not arguing properly in favour of depoliticising criminal justice is that my interest in the proposal, for present purposes, derives from an interest in the theory of democracy. Assume, if not that it is certainly better to depoliticise criminal justice, at least that this is likely to be so. Assume, if you prefer that whether or not criminal justice should be depoliticised certainly depoliticisation is an attractive option in other areas of government: say, in the area of central-bank decisions. Any such assumption will serve to generate the question to which I now want to turn.

That question bears on how the theory of democracy can look with any favour on a depoliticising proposal. Under most accounts of democracy, the attraction of the arrangement is that it puts public decisions – say, decisions on matters relating to public goods – where they properly belong: in the hands of the people or in the hands of the people's representatives. The orthodox democratic theories suggest that good public decisions are decisions that express the popular will or, if not the actual popular will, at least an informed counterpart of that will: for example, the sort of will that might be expected to emerge among popularly chosen representatives who systematically debate the issues involved. In a democracy the people are politically sovereign, it is said, albeit they may cede legal sovereignty to their representatives (Dicey 1960). And under most assumptions that means that the polity works well, and the point of democracy is achieved, just so far as things are organised so that the sovereign's will is ... well, sovereign.

The problem with any depoliticisation arrangement is that on these will-based or voluntarist theories of democracy, it is not clear how such an arrangement could be justified. Depoliticisation involves taking decisions away from the people and away from the people's representatives. In particular, it involves taking away legislative and administrative decisions of the kind that belong with the people under established views of democracy: it is generally conceded that

judicial decisions are reasonably left in unelected hands. And that suggests that if
we endorse depoliticisation in any area of policy, then we are not true democrats
but rather elitists of some kind. We wish to authorise not the people or the
people's chosen spokespersons but rather, as it will be said, a corps of faceless,
rational bureaucrats.

The challenge here is worth dwelling upon, even savouring. I remember
attending a discussion among academics from different fields in Canberra about
five years ago. The meeting was focused on some general political issues and a
particularly forthright historian posed a problem for the gathering. He was a
democrat, he said, or at least had always considered himself to be such. And yet
he could not accept that decisions on a variety of matters – he mentioned capital
punishment as one example – should be left in the hands of the people; he didn't
even think that they should be left with representatives who considered
themselves bound by the opinions of their constituents. The people, in his view,
were just not up to making decisions of the sort envisaged. Was he inconsistent,
he wanted to know. Did he have to make a choice between populism and
democracy, on the one hand, or elitism and rationality on the other?

The issue before us is just the same. Can we endorse depoliticisation, in
particular depoliticisation in the area of criminal justice, while claiming to be
faithful to the ideal of democracy? I want to argue now that we can. It is true that
voluntarist theories of democracy would represent depoliticisation as essentially
inimical to democratic ideals. But voluntarist theories of democracy, so I want to
suggest, are not the only game in town. There is an alternative vision of democracy
– a critical or contestatory theory I call it (Pettit 1997) – and under this approach
depoliticisation can often be just the sort of thing that democracy requires.

THE CONTESTATORY THEORY OF DEMOCRACY

Where democracy exists then by almost all accounts the people as a whole enjoy
a sort of collective autonomy that parallels the personal autonomy for which
individual agents aspire. But there are two versions of the ideal of personal
autonomy and they suggest, by analogy, two quite different versions of the
democratic ideal.

The usual account of personal autonomy is voluntarist in character, like the
usual account of democratic autonomy. What it suggests is that persons are
autonomous just to the extent that they have taken charge of their own beliefs,
their own desires and, consequently, their own decisions. They have tried, so far
as possible, to suspend the formative influence of childhood and conditioning and
they have sought to endorse only such beliefs and only such desires as they have
found personally compelling. They have appropriated the intentional states that
guide their behaviour, making them truly their own. They have achieved the sort

of construction of the self for which existentialists yearned. They have become autonomous in the etymological sense of making the self its own nomos or law. "Wo Es war", in Freud's expression of the idea, "soll Ich werden". Where there was just an impersonal process leading up to the formation of belief and desire – where there was It – there shall be a self in control: there shall be I.

While the voluntarist or existentialist ideal of personal autonomy has certain heady charms, it should be clear that it does not have any lasting appeal. It is entirely infeasible, since there is no one amongst us who is capable of the radical re-examination and reconstruction for which it calls. How can we probe into the origins of our every opinion and preference in order to decide whether it is the product of pathology or whether we can own it as the authentic property of the self? And even if it were feasible, we would still have reason to be unmoved by this voluntarist ideal. It gives expression to an atomistic longing to be isolated from community, particularly the intimate presence which community assumes in parents and teachers and other sources of authority and influence. It represents, as Sartre freely admitted, a desire for godhead: a desire to be thought thinking itself, in Aristotle's phrase; a desire to be one's own creator. It is a shallow, characteristically adolescent ideal, not something vindicated in adult experience.

But it would be a great mistake if disenchantment with the voluntarist ideal of autonomy led us to give up on the notion of autonomy as such. For there is clearly another version that the ideal may assume: a critical or reflective version rather than a voluntarist one. Under this picture of autonomy the history of a person's beliefs and desires – the fact that they originate in childhood and conditioning, for example – is neither here nor there. The important thing is not where the beliefs and desires came from but whether they are maintained in such a manner that the person is capable of critically reflecting on them and capable, should reflection so prescribe, of changing them in certain ways. The crucial achievement is counterfactual or modal, not historical; it consists in the ability, in the event of criticism revealing problems, to stand back and amend.

There are two dimensions, of course, to this critical ideal of autonomy. People will score high in autonomy so far as they are exposed to critical reflection, first of all, and so far as they have the capacity, second, to allow the results of criticism to impact on what they believe and desire. Exposure to critical reflection arises mainly from exchange with others, however; you can fail to achieve it only by sealing yourself into a solipsistic or monocultural shell. And so the more salient aspect of autonomy is the critical or responsive dimension. To be autonomous is to be attached to your ideas and values, not in the pathological manner that would make it impossible for you ever to rethink them, but in the rational way that leaves you open to the possibility of change. It is to be unhindered, at least in the main, by such traditional pathologies as those that we describe as compulsiveness, weakness of will, prejudice, bias and dogmatism.

Because there is a voluntarist and a critical version of personal autonomy, so there are two versions of democratic autonomy. We are accustomed to think of a community as autonomous and democratic to the extent that the will of the people rules: whatever is law is a matter of general consent, if only virtual or tacit or implied consent. But I suggest that we should think of a community as autonomous, not just to the extent that the people have chosen and endorsed everything that happens, but also to the extent that the people have a dual capacity in relation to whatever happens and whatever becomes law. They can challenge whatever happens – this parallels the possibility of critical reflection – and where the challenge is vindicated they can enforce a change: this parallels the possibility of critical reflection being effective.

The democratic ideal in question does not care essentially about where public decisions come from, any more than the critical version of personal autonomy cares about where a person's ideas and values originate. What is of primary concern from the point of view of this ideal is whether the people retain the ability to contest those decisions and to contest them with some chance of having an effect. The key feature of democracy consists, not in the fact of general consent and popular will – if there could ever lie a fact about such matters – but in the capacity for people in every section of the community to raise a potentially effective challenge to any decisions that they judge to be inappropriate.

We can return now to the depoliticisation proposal and the problem that it raises for a voluntarist theory of democracy. For it should be obvious that if we go along with a contestatory component in our theory of democracy then we can take a very different view of such a proposal. Under the contestatory approach the important thing in the organisation of democracy will be to ensure in any given area of policy that there are channels whereby contestation can be raised and given a proper hearing: given a hearing in which the decision made can be reasonably expected to answer to our shared sense of the relevant considerations or, at least, to our shared sense of reasonable decision-making procedures. There is no reason in principle why the best way to establish this contestatory possibility may not involve a measure of depoliticisation.

There is every reason indeed to think that the only way to ensure the possibility of effective contestation in the area of criminal justice is precisely to depoliticise. Our argument in the first section, sketchy though it is, shows that there is little hope of politicians being able to hear and respond to the challenges of criminology and commonsense to the barbarism and inefficiency of current penal practice. Politicians are forced to hear those challenges in a forum where rituals of public outrage are also allowed and it is absolutely clear that in such a theatrical forum the challenges stand no chance of being taken seriously. The only hope of arranging for a proper hearing is to let the challenges be considered and assessed in a depoliticised environment: in precisely the sort of environment that might emerge under the proposal that we sketched.

The fact that we go along with the depoliticisation proposal then does not mean that we have to renounce democracy and accept that we are elitists. For while the proposal takes away power from the politicians, there is a real sense – a contestatory sense – in which it gives power to the people. Democracy and depoliticisation are not inherent opposites. They conflict with one another only under a voluntarist image of democracy, not under the image that we have sketched in this section.

REPUBLICANISM AND THE CONTESTATORY THEORY

But I would like to add a few words in order to emphasise that the contestatory theory of democracy is not a novelty – not an invention of my own – and not something disconnected from received values. The theory belongs with the long, republican tradition of thinking about politics (Pocock 1975, Skinner 1978, 1983, 1984). And that tradition has a powerful attraction in the contemporary scene.

The republican tradition is associated with Cicero at the time of the Roman republic; with a number of writers, pre-eminently Machiavelli – "the divine Machiavel" of the Discourses – in the Renaissance Italian republics; with James Harrington, Algernon Sydney and a host of lesser figures in and after the period of the English civil war and commonwealth; and with the many theorists of republic or commonwealth in eighteenth century England and America and France. These theorists – the so-called commonwealth men (Robbins 1959) – were greatly influenced by John Locke and later the Baron de Montesquieu; indeed they claimed Locke and Montesquieu, with good reason, as their own. They are well represented in documents like Cato's Letters (Trenchard and Gordon 1971) and, on the American side of the Atlantic, the Federalist Papers (Madison, Hamilton and Jay 1987).

The key notion in the republican tradition, as I have argued in a number of other places (Pettit 1993, 1997), is the distinctive view of liberty or freedom that republicans maintained. Under this view, freedom does not consist in non-interference, as liberal theorists generally say, nor indeed in the power of participating in popular decision-making with which liberals like to contrast such freedom (Constant 1988). Republican freedom belongs neither with the negative image of liberty nor with the positive (Berlin 1958). It requires an absence of something, as does the liberal or negative ideal, but not the absence of interference. What it requires, rather, is the absence of what I call domination.

One person dominates another, on my account, to the extent that they have the ability to interfere on an arbitrary basis in that person's choices; they have the ability to interfere in those choices without having to be guided by the victim's interests or ideas. One person dominates another through standing over them, even if stand is all they do: even if they never strike. One person dominates another through having the other person under their thumb, even if they never press that thumb: even if they always stay their hand. Domination exists wherever there is subjection and vulnerability.

The republican ideal of freedom as non-domination delegitimates asymmetries of power such as those that have characteristically been associated with the relationship of employer to employee, man to wife, lender to debtor, bureaucrat to welfare client, and so on; in such relationships, after all, the stronger often has the capacity to interfere more or less arbitrarily with the weaker, even if that capacity is not likely to be exercised: even if liberals, therefore, would not be concerned about it. That is to say that the republican ideal is socially radical. But the ideal will appeal as an ideal for state activity only so far as we can be sure that in setting up the state we do not set up the sort of Hobbesian Leviathan that would represent the greatest dominator of all: that would dominate us more effectively than any dominators it might seek to inhibit. Can we do anything, then, to guard against the state being a mastering or dominating presence? The state will interfere with everyone to the extent that it employs coercive law: that is why liberals are so wary of it. But can we do anything to make sure that it is at least a non-mastering interferer: to make sure that its interference is forced to track people's interests and ideas?

The answer is that while there is a variety of things we can do – republican proposals range from the rule of law to limited tenure in office to the separation of powers – the most crucial requirement is that we institute a contestatory form of democracy. That the government is democratic in the voluntarist sense is not going to ensure that it does not dominate people: the majority can be a more effective tyrant than any one individual. But that it is democratic in the contestatory sense will ensure an absence of political domination. It will mean that people in the society are in a position to contest any public decision – contest it with a reasonable chance of effectiveness – on the grounds that it is inimical to their interests and ideas: that it deals with them in a manner which any citizens in their position would be bound to reject. If people have such a power of contestation – and I am speaking of an ideal – then and only then will they be assured against domination by the state.

I hope that this connection with the republican tradition may add weight to the case for conceiving democracy in the contestatory image and, ultimately, to the proposal for depoliticising criminal justice practice. It should show that that image and that proposal belong with a long and well-tested tradition of thought, even if the tradition has had a bad run in the last century or so. Consider John Locke's (1965) argument that if government has the aspect of a legal contract – this connects with the voluntarist tradition – it also has the aspect of a legal trust. That argument led Locke to hold that the people have a right to challenge and resist a person in public office if the trust is not well discharged: if the person assumes a power, according to Tom Paine's (1989, 168) formulation, "in the exercise of which, himself, and not the *res-publica*, is the object" (cf Sydney 1996, 199-200). When we defend the contestatory conception of democracy we do no more than resurrect this republican way of thinking and give it a proper place in democratic theory.

REFERENCES

Berlin, Isaiah 1958, *Two Concepts of Liberty*, Oxford: Oxford University Press

Braithwaite, John and Pettit, Philip 1990, *Not Just Deserts: A Republican Theory of Criminal Justice,* Oxford: Oxford University Press

Constant, Benjamin 1988, *Constant: Political Writings*, B. Fontana (ed.), Cambridge: Cambridge University Press

Dicey, A.V. 1960, *An Introduction to the Law of the Constitution*, E.C.S.Wade (ed.), (10th edn) London: Macmillan

Holmes, Stephen 1988, "Gag rules or the politics of omission", in J. Elster and R. Slagstad (eds), *Constitutionalism and Democracy*, Cambridge: Cambridge University Press

Locke, John 1965, *Two Treatises of Government*, Peter Laslett (ed.), New York: Mentor

MacDonagh, Oliver 1958, "The 19th century revolution in government: a reappraisal", *Historical Journal*, Vol. 1, 1958

Madison, James, Alexander Hamilton and Jay, John 1987, *The Federalist Papers*, Isaac Kramnik (ed.), Harmondsworth: Penguin

Montesquieu, Charles de Secondat 1989, *The Spirit of the Laws*, (tran. and ed.) A.M. Cohler, B.C. Miller and H.S. Stone, Cambridge: Cambridge University Press

Paine, Tom 1989, *Political Writings*, Bruce Kuklick (ed.), Cambridge: Cambridge University Press

Pettit, Philip 1993, *The Common Mind: An Essay on Psychology, Society and Politics*, New York: Oxford University Press. Paperback edition, with new postcript, 1996

Pettit, Philip 1997, *Republicanism: A Theory of Freedom and Government,* Oxford: Oxford University Press

Pocock, J.G.A. 1975, *The Machiavellian Moment: Florentine Political Theory and the Atlantic Republican Tradition*, Princeton: Princeton University Press

Robbins, Caroline 1959, *The Eighteenth Century Commonwealthman*, Cambridge, Ma: Harvard University Press

Skinner, Quentin 1978, *The Foundations of Modern Political Thought*, 2 vols. Cambridge: Cambridge University Press

Skinner, Quentin 1983, "Machiavelli on the Maintenance of Liberty", *Politics,* 18: 3-15

Skinner, Quentin 1984, "The Idea of Negative Liberty", in R. Rorty, J.B. Schneewind and Q. Skinner (eds), *Philosophy in History*, Cambridge: Cambridge University Press 1984

Sydney, Algernon 1996, *Court Maxims*, H.W. Blom, E.H. Muller and Ronald Janse (eds), Cambridge: Cambridge University Press

Trenchard, John and Thomas, Gordon 1971, *Cato's Letters* (6th edn 1755), New York: Da Capo

14

The Portrayal of Crime in the Media – Does it Matter?*

Michael O'Connell

INTRODUCTION

The purpose of this chapter is to examine the potential consequences of media coverage of crime. However, the effects examined are those not directly behavioural such as in the area of offending. Rather the focus is on the way in which the media may shape and determine (or perhaps distort) the attitudes, knowledge, and views of the public. That the media actually determine opinion around crime is certainly not accepted by all researchers in the field (see the discussion for further elaboration of this position). Among those who do accept it, there are a number of distinct positions. For example it has been suggested that there is a conservative fear of the erosion of public decency, a mirror-image radical position in which moral panics foment public hysteria, the notion of the media as site of ideological struggle and finally, the media-as-jester (see Reiner 1997). The hybrid position of this chapter argues that the media do not directly set out to distort public opinion, but by *entertaining* people with crime, rather than *informing* the public about it, certain consequences follow. In other words, a steady stream of salacious and lurid crime stories sells newspapers but ultimately distorts the public understanding of crime as a serious social problem. As Williams and Dickinson (1993; 33) argue, "the salience given to certain types of crimes, notably those involving sex or violence, creates a distorted picture of reality which is reflected in

---

* Some of the material in this chapter was previously published in the *European Journal of Communication* 14, 1998, 191-213

the beliefs of news consumers". This appeared to be a plausible explanation of much of the discourse about crime in Ireland in the 1980s and 90s and I conducted a series of studies, with co-researchers, into this question which I have attempted to summarise in this paper.

THE ATYPICALITY OF CRIME NEWS

Somebody once pointed out that a lot of social science is the science of the bleedin' obvious. The readers may be perfectly aware that crime news is far from representational of what is happening in society. On the other hand, they may not be aware of this and while much of common sense about the world is valid, some is not. Therefore an attempt at confirmation and measurement of the unrepresentativeness of media stories was made (published in greater detail in O'Connell 1999). Thus the research style used is in the tradition of quantitative content analysis where description is preferred over interpretation. A good example of a more exciting but perhaps more intuitive approach can be found in Kidd-Hewitt and Osborne (1995).

In order to assess the portrayal of crime in the Irish media (or at least in its press), a largely quantitative content analysis of the crime stories appearing in four Irish newspapers over a two month period was carried out. The four news-papers were *The Irish Times*, *The Irish Press*, *The Star* and *The Evening Herald*. These were selected to be representative of both the "quality" press (*The Irish Times*) as well as the tabloid press (*The Star*), and included a newspaper from both main newspaper stables dominant at the time, the Press newspaper group (*The Irish Press*) as well as the *Independent* newspaper group (*The Evening Herald*, the capital's leading evening paper). The analysis period was from the beginning of December 1993 to the end of January 1994. This two month period was chosen because it was immediately prior to a survey sweep investigating public views of crime in Dublin (see details below of O'Connell and Whelan 1996). The total number of articles selected for analysis was 2,191, an average of just less than forty-three articles for each day and about eleven crime articles per newspaper per day. The data were collected by a team of trained coders following a standardised coding schema to gather information such as the type of offence covered, the type of story, characteristics of the offender and victim, number of words in the story, location of story in the newspaper and so on.

The analysis of this fairly large sample of crime news suggested that there were at least four obvious biases at work. The first was in the selection of crime stories which dealt disproportionately with extreme and violent offences. The most common Irish crime story appearing related to the offence of murder at 12.3% of all cases. Yet in the official garda statistics for 1993, murder made up only 0.004% of recorded crimes. Table 1 below compares the offence frequency between the sampling data and the garda statistics for the ten most commonly media-reported crimes.

Table 1: a comparison of offence frequency between the sampling newspaper data and the garda crime figures for 1993

Offence	% from sample	% from garda figs.	Ratio of sample to garda figs.
Murder	12.3	0.004	3075.00
Manslaughter	4.6	0.003	1533.00
Abduction	3.0	0.005	600.00
Malicious wounding	6.0	0.010	600.00
Child sex abuse	3.1	0.006	517.00
Arson	4.2	0.011	382.00
Possession of dangerous weapons	2.5	0.007	357.00
Armed robbery	15.8	0.090	176.00
Assaults	8.4	0.079	106.00
Rape	6.7	0.077	87.00

Of course, offences from outside Ireland were also covered (37.9% of all reports dealt with foreign crimes). But coverage of foreign crimes was, if anything, even more skewed, towards the extreme seriousness pole. Murder for example made up 29.4% of all non-Irish crime stories. In summary, there was ample evidence of a disproportionate number of extreme criminal offences in the Irish press. This pattern is so strong that the following claim can be made: typical crimes in the Irish press appear rarely in the official crime statistics and typical crimes in the official figures appear rarely in the Irish press account of crime.

Secondly, not only was there a bias towards more extreme stories appearing in the press, these stories were also given more coverage within the newspaper. Using "wordage" or number of words written as the key measure, it was noted that much more lengthy stories appeared for offences like murder, rape, child sexual abuse and manslaughter than say for larcenies, minor drug offences or minor frauds. This distortion inflated the effect already confirmed for offence frequency.

Thirdly, characteristics of victims and offenders played a part in selection for coverage. The data provided at least tentative evidence for a vulnerability hypothesis – that is more physically vulnerable victims were preferred (in terms of length of article) over less vulnerable ones while less vulnerable offenders were preferred over more vulnerable ones. Using age and sex as markers for vulnerability (females and the young and old coded as more physically vulnerable than males and those aged between sixteen and fifty-five), this pattern was confirmed for age and even more strongly for sex. In order to control for offence variation, just one offence, murder, (about which most words had been written) was selected for further analysis. There were 156 stories where the sex of offender and victim in a murder case was known. Figure 1 below displays the mean number of words written for male and female victims and offenders. As can be seen, the greatest contrast between physical vulnerability of victim and offender is preferred (female victim and male offender) while stories with male victims and female offenders are downplayed. While recent high profile cases in Ireland may suggest great levels of interest in a small subset of cases where the murderer is female, perhaps where her image has been strongly sexualised, the data suggest that this is not the norm.

Figure 1: effect of victim and offender sex on newsworthiness (wordage) of articles relating to murder

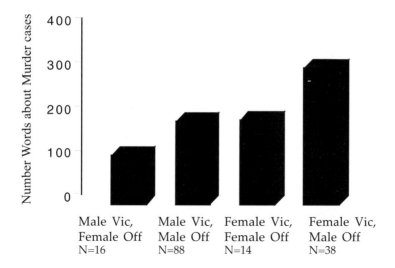

The final bias uncovered by the analysis was the pessimism of overview stories. Overview stories (14.8%) were those which dealt not with any one incident of an offence but provided commentary on either multiple incidents of an offence (eg "Child snatch cases rocket says unit") or of crime trends in general ("Quinn pledges to fight crime"). The stories were overwhelmingly negative in that they tended to deal with "explosions" in particular offences, warned people in certain areas or jobs to be alert to new types of crimes, mentioned needed or upcoming "crackdowns" or "blitzes" on crime, demanded changes in the law or spoke about "cushy" prison conditions. Overall the image of crime in overview articles was a generally negative and pessimistic one, with strong themes of moral mini-panics in the warning or catastrophic tones used in describing trends and the wider picture. In summary, it is argued that the four biases noted above are the main ways in which a misrepresentative picture of crime appears in the press.

The patterns emerging from this analysis are similar to distortions found by researchers internationally. Cirino (1972) found that 13% of US national television news was crime news while, in a later analysis, Graber (1980) estimated it to be roughly the same at about 12.5%. Graber also found that crime news in the newspapers tends to be read consistently by a greater percentage of subscribers than other types of news. Violent crime is also seen as more newsworthy by editors. Bortner (1984) found that crime news tends to focus largely on violent personal street crimes like murder, rape and assault, while ignoring more common crime such as theft and burglary. Graber (1980) reported that homicide constituted 0.2% of the crime known to police in the US but accounted for 26.2% of crime news whereas non-violent crime accounted for 47% of known crime but only 4% of crime news stories. A later study by Liske and Baccaglini (1990) found that while homicide had stayed stable at 0.2% of Index crimes, it then accounted for 30% of news stories.

Other studies carried out on the same topic in the US, the UK and France (see Dussuyer 1979; Gordon and Heath 1981; Mawby and Brown 1984; Surette 1984, 1998; Gabor and Weimann 1987) all support Robert's claim that "news media coverage of crime and punishment reflects a view of the criminal justice system that is biased towards serious and sensational crime" (1992; 117). The European findings do not differ from those in the US. Van Dijk (1978) reported that crime stories involving violence were ten times more frequent than actual offences involving violence. Ditton and Duffy's (1983) analysis of the Scottish press showed that about 45% of all reported crimes involved violent or sexual crimes. Williams and Dickinson (1993) studied the British press and found that although the "tabloid" press gave more space and prominence to crimes involving sex or violence than did the "broadsheets", nevertheless the picture of crime in both was skewed towards the extreme.

THE PUBLIC PERCEPTION OF CRIME

There is always a risk that one may overestimate the power of the media or underestimate the shrewdness of its users. Perhaps the distortions of the media do not feed into the views of the public. It is necessary to assess public opinion towards crime. As Quinney has noted, "reaction to all that is associated with crime rests initially upon knowledge about crime"(1975; 176). With virtually no exception, all research into the knowledge the public holds about crime suggests that both the prevalence and seriousness of crime is overestimated. The 1984 British Crime Survey (BCS) found that "respondents made alarmingly high estimates of crime rates – far in excess of actual risks" (Williams and Dickinson 1993; 34). Roberts has provided an excellent review of the studies in this area and concluded that "the public has inaccurate, overly negative views of crime statistics" (1992; 109). In Canada, roughly 5% of crimes involve violence yet when asked to estimate this percentage, 75% of the public arrived at a figure of 30% or over (Doob and Roberts 1983). Indermaur's (1987) study also showed that although the murder rate had remained constant over time, the public estimated a strong increase. Flanagan and Maguire (1990) showed that while crime rates have fluctuated over the past fifty years, a majority of the public at any given time tended to estimate an increase on the previous year. The offences that are perceived to be increasing the fastest are those involving extreme violence (Environics Research Group 1989). The public also tends to believe that the crime rate will increase in the near future (Useem et al 1990). These misperceptions are shared by the public of any industrialised nation that has been surveyed on the topic (Roberts 1992).

In an Irish context, the crime problem appears to be an issue of great concern. Opinion polls demonstrate high levels of fear and pessimism surrounding crime. An *Irish Times*/MRBI poll reported that "Most people fear crime is getting worse and are unhappy with what's being done", (*The Irish Times*, 3 February, 1997). The criminologist, McCullagh (1996), has claimed that levels of concern about crime in Ireland are "as high as comparable figures for major American cities" (1996: 11). In November 1996, an overwhelming majority, through a referendum, backed a draconian change of the bail law in Ireland, permitting the denial of bail to individuals accused of certain offences, on various extended grounds. Another Irish criminologist noted that the change in bail law "was part of a wider agenda to erode civil liberties, which has already seen the introduction of seven-day detention and a significant curtailment of the right to silence ... such is the extent of the present hardline consensus that these incursions on individual rights have been adopted with hardly a murmur of dissent" (O'Mahony, 19 November 1996, *Irish Times*).

In a piece of research designed to assess the nature of Irish opinion about crime, O'Connell and Whelan (1996) carried out a postal survey of 1,000 Dubliners, selected by systematic random sample from the electoral register. There was a response rate of 64.8% (using Dillman's TDM, see Dillman 1978). The respondents were asked to assess the seriousness of ten offence scenarios (see Appendix A), the prevalence of those offences compared to five years previously (see Appendix B) as well as provide information about their own experience of victimisation in the three years prior to the survey and some demographic details.

The sample estimated that all ten offences were on the increase. Furthermore, when comparing the five offences (eg violent assaults) assessed as more serious by the sample with those five seen as less serious (eg frauds), the public estimated that the former or most serious were increasing in prevalence most rapidly. Official statistics, while flawed, are generally likely to provide some objective measure of change in frequency over time. Comparisons between the garda or official estimates of change over the five year period and the public estimates were independent of one another. In other words, assuming the official statistics capture to some degree the change over time of objective rates of particular offences, then it is clear that the public estimate is not based on these objective changes since there is no correspondence in the rate of change estimated by the public compared to the gardaí.

So if public opinion is not determined by actual crime rates, what does influence it ? Crime victimisation was considered as a possible key variable but the analysis revealed no difference in prevalence estimate between those suffering any offence, any property offence, or any offence against the person in the previous thirty-six months. A multivariate analysis suggested that age, sex and newspaper readership did make a significant difference. To sum up, the analysis showed that the public had a negative view of the crime situation and believed all offences to be on the increase with the most serious ones increasing most quickly. This pattern did not match the levels of crime and their changes in the official statistics. Previous victimisation did not explain the variation in mean prevalence estimate but a multi-variate analysis showed that sex, age and newspaper readership were significant predictors of respondents' prevalence score.

DIFFERENCES BETWEEN AUDIENCES

It was noted above that readerships of different newspapers have differing "prevalence" estimates of crime. That may not be surprising since people who read different newspapers probably differ in many respects – social class, educational level, political orientation and so on. What was interesting in this finding though was that newspaper readership was significant while other potential variables such as those mentioned above and also recent history of victimisation were not in predicting respondents' prevalence estimate. Comparing newspaper readerships, those respondents who regularly read Independent Group newspapers (*The Irish Independent* and *The Evening Herald*) had the highest or most pessimistic view of crime prevalence. This echoed an argument made by two prominent journalists more than a decade earlier who had accused the Independent Group editorial executives of adopting a policy designed to change the presentation of the issue of crime from one of "a manageable problem into a crisis ... The level of crime against readers would itself be exaggerated and the threat would be generalised to all" (Kerrigan and Shaw 1985; 10). Thus, this provides some "soft" evidence that press portrayal determines public opinion. It is assumed here that prevalence estimate provides a proxy measure for pessimism about crime or what

Gerbner et al (1980) have called "mean world attitudes" to crime. Table 2 provides more comprehensive detail of the prevalence scores of O'Connell and Whelan's (1996) sample of respondents by newspaper readership. Higher prevalence scores indicate perception that crime is increasing more quickly.

Table 2: a one-way analysis of variance comparing recoded newspaper readership groups (4) with mean prevalence estimate for 10 offences (N= 564)

Newspaper group	Count	Mean crime prevalence estimate	F ratio	F prob
Independent	262	8.81	4.31	<0.01
Tabloid/Others	48	8.70		
Press	98	8.44		
Times	156	8.38		
Total	564	8.62		

DIFFERENCES BETWEEN NEWSPAPERS IN CRIME PORTRAYAL

From the previous section, differences between the readerships of Irish newspapers were noted. If the hypothesis that the media are at least partly responsible in determining the public misperception of crime is correct, then it seemed reasonable to assume that there should be certain observable differences in the way these newspapers presented crime stories which corresponded with their readers' different levels of pessimism about crime. It should be noted that the argument is not that some mainstream media distort the news while others do not. Rather the position being argued is that minor but noticeable differences in editorial views between newspapers about the degree to which crime news should be exploited are responsible for the small but significant differences in the perspectives of the readers.

In the content analysis summarised at the beginning of the chapter, the four papers sampled were representative of the four recoded newspaper groups listed in Table 2, ie *The Evening Herald* is the evening paper of the Independent Group, *The Star* was the most frequent tabloid newspaper read by the sample, *The Irish Press* was the daily of the Irish Press Group and *The Irish Times* made up the final category. The number of crime stories in each of these newspapers in the sampling period was counted and divided by the total number of stories in the newspaper in order to generate a measure of proportion of crime news per newspaper. Table 3 shows that if newspapers are ranked according to crime proportion of news, they emerge exactly as they did by readership estimates. In other words, this measure, proportion of crime articles to total articles correspond to crime prevalence perceived by respective newspaper readerships.

Table 3: the average number of all news articles, crime articles, proportion of crime news and prevalence estimate rank for the four newspapers sampled

Newspaper (average per day)	Irish Times	Irish Press	Star	Evening Herald
Average no. crime articles	9.98	9.47	10.74	12.76
Average no. all articles	172.4	128.5	116.4	119.7
Proportion crime news	0.0579	0.737	0.0923	0.1066
Prevalence estimate rank (from O'Connell and Whelan 1996)	4th	3rd	2nd	1st

On the assumption that more sensationalist crime articles would use large attention-grabbing headlines, a ratio measure was constructed using area of headline in cm^2 of each article and entire article area. The formula, for each article, was [area of headline in cm^2] / [area of entire article in cm^2]. It was hypothesised that the *Star* and the *Evening Herald* would devote proportionally greater space to headlines for articles about more serious offences, in a sense to lure the readers to those articles. It must be remembered that more serious offences tend to have more newspaper space devoted to them so one might anticipate that the headlines of more serious articles will take up less area proportionally of the entire article, unless the headlines are deliberately designed to be bigger for more serious offences. Figure 2 presents the mean proportion of space devoted in each newspaper to the headline to either offences against the person or other offences (generally offences against property).

The barchart indicates that for more serious offences (those against the person), the proportion of area devoted to the headline was smaller in the *Irish Times* and in the *Irish Press* than for less serious offences. However, the opposite pattern occurred in the case of the *Star* and the *Herald*. There is evidence therefore of an attempt by the newspapers whose readerships have more pessimistic views on crime to make more serious crimes relatively more sensational. The relative space given to headlines for just two prominent offences was also examined; murder (very serious) and burglary (moderate seriousness). The results are presented in Figure 3 below.

Figure 2: Ratio of headline area (to article size) by crime category across newspapers

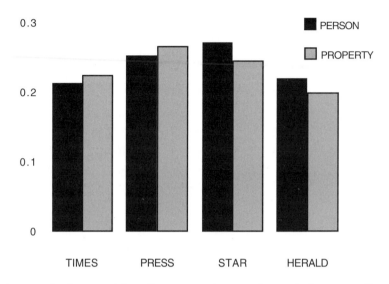

Figure 3: Ratio of headline area (to article size) by two offences across newspapers

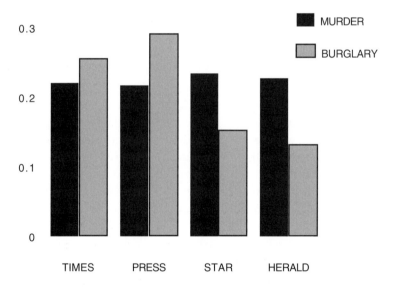

The difference between newspapers was stronger here and clearly showed that the *Star* and *Evening Herald* gave proportionally much more space to the headlines of high serious offences than did the *Irish Times* or *Irish Press*. This provides evidence that there is a match between the greater sensationalist view of crime held by the readerships of the former newspapers and the editorial/presentational style of those newspapers. The interaction effect between the newspaper and offence (murder and burglary) on the dependent variable, proportion of space devoted to headline, is significant; P-value in a two-way interaction = 0.016.

The differential skew towards crimes against the person was also demonstrated when the mean wordage used for crimes against the person versus other crime stories was compared across the four newspapers. While crimes against the person were given significantly more coverage or were more newsworthy in all newspapers than other crime stories, they were especially so for the *Star* and *Evening Herald*. The ratio in word length between the two types of crime category (crimes against the person: other crimes) for the *Irish Times* was 1.42 (n=397), for the *Irish Press* was 1.62 (n=386), for the *Star* was 1.74 (n=473) and for the *Evening Herald* was 1.96 (n=608). Again the same matched pattern emerged between the degree of pessimism of readership displayed in the earlier survey findings and the measure of relative newsworthiness.

The newspapers were also compared on the variable offence location. Table 4 presents the frequency of offences reported in the four newspapers which were either committed within the Republic of Ireland or outside. The *Evening Herald* differed substantially (and significantly, Chi-square prob. < 0.0001) from the other newspapers. Although it was reporting a substantial number of foreign crime news (second only to the *Star*), its percentage and raw number of home crime stories are far greater than the other newspapers.

Table 4: frequency and percentage of offence locations reported across four newspapers

Newspaper	Ireland	Foreign	Total
Irish Times	232 (60.3%)	153 (39.7%)	385 (100%)
Irish Press	227 (60.2%)	150 (39.8%)	377 (100%)
Star	275 (58.3%)	197 (41.7%)	472 (100%)
Evening Herald	429 (70.4%)	180 (29.6%)	609 (100%)

A significant difference also emerged with regard to the status of the offence within the criminal justice system being reported. The proportion of *Evening Herald* stories dealing with the later stages of an offence being handled by the criminal justice system (ie where the trial was ongoing or was completed as opposed to where the case was still pre-trial) was substantially lower than in the other three newspapers, as Table 5 shows.

Table 5: percentage of crime-related articles dealing with Irish-located offences either prior to or during/after trial by newspaper

Newspaper	Pre-trial	During or post-trial
Irish Times (n=229)	58.1	41.9
Irish Press (n = 224)	60.7	39.3
Star (n=272)	56.3	43.7
Evening Herald (n=428)	67.5	32.5

Heath's (1984) work, cited above, is relevant here. She has argued, from survey analysis data, that two factors of crime-reporting implicated in generating greater fear of crime are the proximity and controllability of the offences. Because the *Evening Herald* reports more local offences and also proportionally less of those which have achieved closure through the criminal justice system (ie gone to trial), then this may be indirect evidence supporting the hypothesis that the *Evening Herald* generates more fear through the type of offences which is reported in its crime news.

In summary therefore, it is reasonable to conclude that substantial quantitative differences between the newspapers emerged in a direction corresponding to the degree of pessimism about crime demonstrated by the readerships of the respective newspaper groups.

COMPARING THE VIEWS OF JOURNALISTS

In a study published in 1998, O'Connell et al pursued the comparison between the four newspapers but in a different direction than the analysis above. The crime reporter on each of these papers was approached in order to discuss the selection and reporting of crime news in the paper. The *Irish Press* group however went into liquidation a few months before the interviews took place (September 1995) and therefore only three reporters were ultimately interviewed. Through semi-structured interviews, the researchers examined whether a correspondence existed between the news values or journalistic outlook of the reporters and the pessimism of their respective readerships. In other words, differences rather than similarities in outlook were sought and the degree to which any differences between journalists' outlooks and their readerships' misperceptions matched was examined. Below are some selected quotes from the journalists in the course of a semi-structured interview and an interpretation of those remarks. The comments of the reporter are displayed in italics and the author's interpretation in plain text.

Star *reporter*

(Of the four newspapers contrasted above, the *Star* had the second highest crime prevalence estimate).

The reporter rejected the idea that newspapers distort the public view of crime or generate unreasonable fears about it. Not only were people able to divorce themselves from the media account of crime but they could employ it to gain a vicarious sense of comfort – somebody else was suffering, not themselves.

> It's argued that newspapers overemphasise crime, that they create a false impression in the public mind that there's a hell of a lot of crime out there ... This is a bit of an old wives' tale ... I think like watching TV, people are able to divorce themselves ... they want to look at crime in a vicarious way, at other peoples' troubles and take a delight in the tribulations that certain people are going through, and console themselves "well, at least that isn't me"... A lot of the time people are very well adjusted, thank you very much, and they know the newspaper is full of bad news. And they're not freaked out by the amount of crime ... it's almost a pat on the back in some ways... like it or not, people are patting themselves on the back saying "thank God, I don't live in a place where there are itinerant slashhook murderers".

He argued that informal information about local crime was a much more powerful influence on peoples' fears. If any form of the media was responsible for the distortion of the public image, then it was TV and the cinema industry.

> You'd be far more likely to be impressed for instance if your neighbour where you live says "hey be careful, there was a brick thrown through my window last night". That's going to freak you out a lot more than reading about taxi men being threatened with blood filled syringes. Crime stories are not real for people. Certainly, there will be some people who are on the edge, who will be fearful but those people are predisposed to be fearful. I mean they will be the elderly. TV is far more powerful than the printed word.

He insisted that newspapers had to be interesting, and not direct representations of reality. He argued that people "innately" had a sense that crime news was not real or representational.

> You've got to make newspapers interesting for people, they can't be statistical digests ... People innately know what is news. If you were told there was a handbag snatched in Dublin last night, you'd shrug your shoulders and say so what? So it's a specious argument to say that newspapers should also be reflecting the mundane-ity of crime. The very rarity means it's in the paper, people innately know that ... People know what the real rate of risk is.

He argued that all newspapers are very similar whatever editors and journalists might argue. Each newspaper followed the prejudices of its readers and whatever differences emerged did so because the newspaper producers thought that their readers wanted something different.

> All newspapers reflect the prejudices of their readers, even those that pretend not to, even those that cloak their content in careful verbiage and so on. Everybody. I mean if you look from the *Irish Times* down to the middle market, to us and across the board to the *Daily Telegraph* and so on, the *Mail* and the *Sun* and so on, they all use crime as a mainstay of their diet.

To summarise, his position was that newspapers do not paint a representative picture of crime but that the public is relatively sophisticated. This sophistication gives it an awareness that news is the exception rather than the rule. By acknowledging this, a vicarious sense of comfort in the troubles of others can be drawn from crime news.

Irish Times *reporter*

(Of the four newspaper categories, its readership had the lowest crime prevalence estimate).

The reporter was reluctant to take a clear side on whether the media determined or was shaped by public opinion. While cautious about his own ability to predict how readers might deal with crime news, he argued ultimately, as the *Star* reporter did, that a newspaper could not reflect the mundane reality about crime.

> To go back to your point about whether the public realises that the news it sees is exceptional, I think probably it does because mundane things simply don't go into newspapers, nor do boring sentences such as "although Mr. Keating was murdered yesterday, there were only twenty murders a year in Ireland and this hasn't risen since 1961", something like that. I mean if we reported on everything equally we wouldn't have a paper, we'd have some kind of diaries.

However running along side this view of an essentially sophisticated readership, he also appeared to regard readers as very vulnerable to newspaper influence. He regarded scepticism and journalistic integrity as the methods by which the public was protected from simplistic distortions.

> Reporters including myself would suffer a certain amount of frustration if we never got to explain how many crimes are committed by people of certain categories and why they're out and so on ... I was down in Templemore recently and something like ninety police were graduating and one newspaper said seventy new gardaí are being assigned to Dublin to fight the crime wave. Now, that article gave the impression that crime was dramatically increasing and they were scraping together as many cops as they could to send in to Dublin but the facts were that because these guards are trained in garda stations for fifteen months out of their two years' training, those

seventy cops had been in place in Dublin for more than a year. So when I wrote my article on the subject I led with something else and I was careful not to give the impression that there was a crime wave.

The concern for public opinion and giving the wrong impression are clear here and extended even into the political outlook of the readers on crime policy where he argued that he had a role in changing certain misguided views on the criminal justice system.

Now I'm still very surprised by people I meet who are well-educated ... people who think, who would have a very negative view about things like putting government money into building better prisons with more facilities for rehabilitation. I would say there is a case in my job for presenting clearly the arguments for rehabilitation.

He made by far the strongest claim to a different approach to crime reporting.

Where it might make a difference would be in the sort of features or analyses you present about crime because we would be seen as a newspaper which supports the notion of a liberal democracy, the expression of ideas, minority interests and so forth and we would tend to try and explain the complexities behind things like the so-called crime wave, rather than merely list crime and tell the public that they're under, you know, increasing attack.

He repeatedly argued that the crucial difference between the presentation of crime in the *Irish Times* and in other newspapers was the determination of the reporters and editors to regularly complement the daily flow of apparently discrete criminal offences with analysis of the trends of crime.

We do feel an obligation to report changing social trends and explain everything in its context. I think we're failing if we do not get off the sort of treadmill of day-to-day stories every now and then to write a feature or an analysis on why the crimes we're reporting about are taking place.

To summarise his position, he appeared to argue on some occasions that an unrepresentative picture of crime in the press was natural and that the public did not expect mundane reality to be faithfully and slavishly recorded. On the other hand, this appeared to run counter to his concern not to add to fears about the 'crime wave' by ambiguous or false reporting as well as his belief that he could influence public opinion about crime through his newspaper.

Evening Herald *reporter*

(Of the four newspaper categories, its readership had the highest crime prevalence estimate).

The reporter had a position on the representativeness of crime in the media which was quite distinct from the other reporters. Unlike them, he argued that there genuinely was a crisis in Ireland but particularly in Dublin because of the crime wave. Crime had reached unprecedented levels.

> Crime has taken over the city and a lot of readers would be middle-aged people who would have known Dublin when it was relatively crime-free and now we have a city which is targeted by the gangs, they can do almost whatever they like.
>
> The most recent figures show that for the first time ever in the history of the state, the level of serious crime has surpassed the 100,000 figure so there's no doubt about it, crime is on the increase[1]. Serious crime is on the increase, I heard the DPP saying recently that the level of gratuitous violence has shocked him. The former chief justice, Thomas Finlay, said likewise that the level of violent crime has really surpassed all his expectations, he never thought he'd see the day when there was so much violent crime in this country. You have the situation where elderly people, handicapped people, all those sort of vulnerable people are chosen by addicts and robbed and mugged and what not.

Given his view that crime was out of control, he believed that if anything, the newspaper coverage of crime could only underestimate its prevalence and that many crimes would remain unreported.

> There are a lot of crimes against the elderly, you can't overstate them because they happen nearly every week, we might only get a few of them. I think we report a lot less crimes against the elderly than actually happen. And I don't think we frighten the elderly whatever we do because I think there isn't a person who doesn't have friends or acquaintances who haven't been victims of crime. I think that creates a sort of sense of fear and a sense of alertness that is there already without us adding to it or aggravating it.

He regarded the extensive coverage of crime given by the media as positive and argued that it could spur the gardaí into action as well as keeping the public in a state of vigilance against the criminals.

> If you take the mid-eighties, when there was a large number of, a lot of travelling criminals hitting the elderly in parts of the midlands and the west and south west. I think it was the daily newspapers which highlighted that trend and eventually forced the guards to do something about it.

His position can be summarised as follows: crime is out of control. It is the duty of crime reporters to cover this crisis extensively and inform the public. Rather than producing unnecessary levels of fear, the high level of reporting keeps an

---

[1] This was an inaccurate assertion. Serious crime (presumably he was referring to recorded indictable offences) surpassed the 100,000 level in 1983. Since then, in the garda annual report, only the 1994 indictable crime figures surpassed the 100,000 mark but were still below the 1983 figures. The year 1983 also leads the figures for offences against the person, see O'Mahony (1993) and McCullagh (1996)

already fearful public vigilant and forces the gardaí to act decisively against the offenders.

Overall the small divergences between journalists were interesting; the explicit rejection of media determining public opinion by the *Star* journalist, its tacit acceptance by the *Irish Times* reporter, the ultra-pessimism towards crime held by the *Evening Herald* reporter. It appeared that crime journalists, while undoubtedly holding the same general principles on what makes good crime news, expressed and qualified those principles in different ways.

Discussion

The widely-held criminological assumption that "the salience given to certain types of crimes, notably those involving sex or violence, creates a distorted picture of reality which is reflected in the beliefs of news consumers" (Williams and Dickinson 1993: 33) was noted above. Similarly, an Irish criminologist has argued that "media coverage gives a higher level of coverage to crime than it warrants and tends to emphasise crimes of violence rather than the more common crimes against property. As a result levels of fear of crime are higher than they should be" (McCullagh 1996: 10). The problem with these claims is that they make a very strong general assumption about the relationship between the audience and the media. More specifically, a top-down model of the relationship is implied as against a bottom-up one. "Top-down" and "bottom-up" in this sense refer to the polar ends of the continuum of approaches made to studying the media (Katz 1980). The top-down end of the continuum characterises the media as omnipotent, "operating totally (on every ear and eye, directly (without interference) and immediately (evoking collective reactions)" (Katz 1980: 121). The bottom-up extreme places power in the hands of the media user, who selects between different forms of the media in order to gratify individual needs.

Criminological assumptions about the public perception of crime as an outcome of media representations clearly can be considered top-down in approach, ie public opinion about crime is shaped by the media. While the author favours this interpretation, bottom-up criticisms must be examined. The ethnomethodological tradition in particular has argued that the audience cannot be seen simply as passive consumers of media bias. Instead it is argued that people bring their own values and knowledge to the process of message interpretation which makes the outcome of media-audience interaction unpredictable. Anderson and Sharrock (1979) for example argue that people are not as naive as the top-down model assumes – the public understands that newspapers do not present a grimly factual account of the world around them. Crime stories, along with other news items, are selected for coverage not because they are representative of the "real world" but because they are "attention grabbing, eyebrow raising, indignation arousing, titillating, tension generating, interest holding etc" (1979: 370). In other words, they argue that people are not "cultural dummies", they understand that news is about the exceptional and unusual rather than the routine and usual. The public expects crime news to be about murders, not speeding violations. Therefore Anderson and Sharrock suggest that while media analysts may be able to show that there is a newspaper bias towards violent and sexual crime, they are wrong to assume that this must inevitably skew the readers' perceptions. As competent social actors, people are not unaware of media bias. Nor are they media-dependent – they have informal sources of information about the "reality" of the crime problem, eg the experiences of themselves, their friends and neighbours.

The position argued in this chapter is that the top-down assumptions made by criminologists are valid and that media portrayal is a major determinant of a distorted public perception of crime. Cognitive psychologists have demonstrated that people use certain kinds of heuristics or short-cuts in processing information. A key heuristic is that of "availability" and Nisbett and Ross (1980) have shown that more available or reported events come easier to mind. Estimates of the frequency of an event are determined by this mental availability. Lichtenstein et al (1978) analysed a sample of US newspapers and showed that while deaths by murder are less frequent than those by suicide, murders tend to be given about fifteen times more coverage in the press. They then asked a sample of people to estimate causes of death and found that numbers of murders were overestimated while numbers of deaths by suicide were underestimated. It seems reasonable to assume that the availability heuristic operates with regard to crime perception, eg if the press focuses disproportionately on violent crimes while rarely reporting, say, white-collar fraud, then the public is likely to overestimate the frequency of violent crime and underestimate the frequency of white-collar fraud.

Nor is there clear evidence that the public employs its awareness of media bias to adjust perceptions of the seriousness of the crime problem. Parisi et al (1979) have shown that people are inclined to believe that the crime situation is at least as serious as its portrayal in the media. Empirical evidence also undermines the argument that people obtain a wider picture of crime by combining formal and informal sources of knowledge. Knowles (1982) found that almost 95% of a sample of US residents reported that the news media were their most important sources of information about crime. Last and Jackson (1989) also confirmed that the vast majority of their respondents claimed to use the mass media to inform themselves about crime and studies by Graber (1979), Dominick (1978) and Greenberg (1969) have reached similar conclusions.

In summary, this paper has presented evidence suggesting that the press portrayal of crime in Ireland is biased in a number of measurable ways. It is argued that this explains why public perception of crime in Ireland is discordant with the relatively low crime rates prevailing in the country. One of the key determinants of public perception of crime prevalence was found to be newspaper readership (over other explanatory measures like objective changes in the crime rates, the experience of victimisation or social class and education). Differences between newspapers in terms of the proportion of crime news presented and the method of portrayal as well as corresponding differences between the crime reporters of these newspapers provide confirmatory evidence for a top-down position in understanding the impact of crime news upon public opinion.

REFERENCES

Anderson, D.C. and Sharrock, W.W. (1979), "Biasing the news: Technical issues in Media Studies", *Sociology,* 13: 367-385

Bortner, M.A. (1984), "Media images and public attitudes towards crime and justice", in R. Surette (ed.), *Justice and the Media*, Springfield: Thomas

Cirino, R. (1972), *Don't Blame the People*, New York: Vintage Books

Dillman, D. A. (1978), *Mail and Telephone Surveys: The Total Design Method*, New York: Wiley

Ditton, J. and Duffy, J. (1983), "Bias in newspaper reporting of crime news", *British Journal of Criminology*, 23: 762-763

Dominick, J. (1978), "Crime and law enforcement in the mass media", in C. Winick (ed.), *Deviance and Mass Media*, Calif.: Sage

Doob, A. and Roberts, J. (1983), *An Analysis of the Public's View of Sentencing*, Ottawa: Department of Justice

Dussuyer, I. (1979), *Crime News: A Study of 40 Ontario Newspapers*, Toronto: University of Toronto, Centre of Criminology

Environics Research Group (1989), *The Focus Canada Report: 1989*, Toronto: Environics Research Group Limited

Flanagan, T.J. and Maguire, K. (eds.) (1990), *Sourcebook of Criminal Justice Statistics-1989*, Washington, DC: US Department of Justice, Bureau of Justice Statistics

Gabor, T. and Weimann, G. (1987), "La couverture du crime par la presse: Un portrait fidele ou deformé?", *Criminologie*, 20: 79-98

Gerbner, G., Gross, L., Morgan, M. and Signorelli, N. (1980), "The mainstreaming of America: Violence profile no. 11", *Journal of Communication*, 30: 10-29

Gordon, M. and Heath, L. (1981), "The news business: Crime and fear", in D.A. Lewis (ed.), *Reactions to Crime,* Calif.: Sage

Graber, D. (1980), *Crime News and the Public*, New York: Praeger

Graber, D. (1979), "Evaluating crime-fighting policies", in R. Baker and F. Meyer (eds.), *Evaluating Alternative Law-Enforcement Policies*, Lexington: Lexington Books

Greenberg, B. (1969), "The content and context of violence in the media", in R.

Baker and S. Ball (eds.), *Violence and the Media*, Washington DC: US Government Printing Office

Heath, L. (1984), "Impact of newspaper crime reports on fear of crime: Multimethodological investigation", *Journal of Personality and Social Psychology*, 47: 263-276

Indermaur, D. (1987), "Public perception of sentencing in Perth, Western Australia", *Australian and New Zealand Journal of Criminology*, 20: 163-183

Irish Times/Market Research Bureau of Ireland (1997). Most people fear crime is getting worse and are unhappy with what's being done. *Irish Times*, 3 February

Katz, E. (1980), "On conceptualizing media effects", *Studies in Communication*, 1: 119-141

Kerrigan, G. and Shaw, H. (1985), "Crime hysteria", *Magill*, 18 April

Kidd-Hewitt, D. and Osborne, R. (eds.) (1995), *Crime and the Media*, London: Pluto Press

Knowles, J. (1982), *Ohio Citizen Attitudes Concerning Crime and and Criminal Justice*, 3rd ed., Columbus: Governor's Office of Criminal Justice Services

Last, P. and Jackson, S. (1989), *The Bristol Fear and Risk of Crime Project (A Preliminary Report on Fear of Crime)*, Bristol: Avon and Somerset Constabulary

Lichtenstein, S., Slovic, P., Fischoff, B., Layman, M. and Combs, B. (1978), "Judged frequency in lethal events", *Journal of Experimental Psychology: Human Learning and Memory*, 4: 551-578

Liske, A. and Baccaglini, W. (1990), "Feeling safe by comparison: Crime in the newspapers", *Social Problems*, 37: 360-374

Mawby, R. and Brown, J. (1984), "Newspaper images of the victim: A British study", *Victimology: An International Journal*, 9: 82-94

McCullagh, C. (1996), *Crime in Ireland: A Sociological Introduction,* Cork: Cork University Press

Nisbett, R. and Ross, L. (1980), *Human Inference: Strategies and Shortcomings of Social Judgement*, New Jersey: Prentice Hall

O'Connell, M.F. (1999), "Is Irish public opinion towards crime distorted by media bias?", *European Journal of Communication*, 14: 191-212

O'Connell, M.F., Invernizzi, F. and Fuller, R. (1998), "Newspaper readership and the perception of crime: Teting an assumed relationship through a triangulation of methods", *Legal and Criminological Psychology*, 3: 29-57

O'Connell, M.F. and Whelan, A.T. (1996), "The public perception of crime prevalence, newspaper readership and "mean world" attitudes", *Legal and Criminological Psychology*, 1: 179-195

O'Mahony, P. (1996), Bail is too complex for a referendum. *Irish Times*, 19 November

O' Mahony, P. (1993), *Crime and Punishment in Ireland*, Dublin: Round Hall Press

Parisi, N., Gottfredson, M., Hindelang, M. and Flanagan, T. (eds.) (1979), *Sourcebook of Criminal Justice Statistics-1978*, Washington, US Department of Justice, Bureau of Justice Statistics

Quinney, R. (1975), "Public conception of crime", in R.L. Henshel and R.A. Silverman (eds.), *Perception in Criminology*, Toronto: Methuen

Reiner, R. (1997), "Media made criminality: The representation of crime in the Mass Media", in M. Maguire, R. Morgan and R. Reiner (eds.), *The Oxford Handbook of Criminology* (2nd. ed.), Oxford: Clarendon Press

Roberts, J. (1992), "Public opinion, crime and criminal justice", in M. Tonry (ed.), *Crime and justice: An Annual Review of Research*, vol. 16, Chicago: University of Chicago Press

Surette, R. (1998), *Media, Crime and Criminal Justice – Images and Realities* (2nd. ed.), London: Wadsworth

Surette, R. (1984), *Justice and the Media,* Springfield: Thomas

Useem, B., Knowlton, J., Burgess, L., Lewis-Klein, A. and Curry-White, B. (1990), *Public Opinion on and Perspectives of Drugs and Crime in Missouri*, Louisville: University of Louisville, Urban Institute

van Dijk, J. (1978), *The Extent of Public Information and the Nature of Public Attitudes towards Crime*, The Hague: Ministry of Justice, Research and Documentation Centre

Williams, P. and Dickinson, J. (1993), "Fear of crime: read all about it?", *British Journal of Criminology*, 33: 33-56

APPENDIX A

Here is a number of situations in which different offences might be committed. What we would like you to do is to rate the seriousness of these offences. Below each offence, there is a scale from 1 to 11. Please circle a number along the scale which reflects how serious you think that offence is. If you think it is not at all serious, then mark 1; if you think it is extremely serious then mark 11; if you think it is of medium seriousness, then mark 6, and so on.

(a)   The offender attacks a victim with a knife and the victim dies.

Not serious- 1 ... 2 ... 3 ... 4 ... 5 ... 6 ... 7 ... 8 ... 9 ... 10 ... 11 Extremely serious

(b)   The offender breaks into a person's house and steals property worth £30.

(c)   The offender dishonestly obtains social welfare benefits to the value of £30.

(d)   The offender sells cannabis to an adult.

(e) The offender assaults a garda officer with his fists. The garda officer is injured and sent to hospital.

(f) The offender, a fourteen year old boy, has sexual intercourse with a fourteen year old girl with her consent.

(g) The offender sets up a bogus company and through it, fraudulently obtains £3,000 from a big manufacturer.

(h) The offender, using physical force, robs a victim of £75. The victim is injured but is not sent to hospital.

(i) The offender sets up a bogus mail-order company and through it fraudulently obtains £1,500 from a number of private individuals.

(j) The offender, a policeman, who discovers a burglary in a shop, steals £30 worth of goods from the store.

APPENDIX B

We would also like to know your views about whether crimes like those described in the previous page are becoming more or less common today. Please compare the situation at present with the levels of crime that you recall from five years ago. Please circle a number along the scale which reflects how common you think that type of offence is. If you think it is much less common than five years ago, then mark 1; if you think it is much more common now then mark 11; if you think the situation has not changed, then mark 6; and so on.

Much less common now   Same as five years ago   Much more common now

(a) Murders.

(less common) 1 ... 2 ... 3 ... 4 ... 5 ... 6 ... 7 ... 8 ... 9 ... 10 ... 11 (more common)

(b) Burglary

(c) Social welfare fraud

(d) Cannabis dealing

(e) Assaults on gardaí

(f) Under-age sex

(g) Fraud on businesses

(h) Violent muggings

(i) Fraud on individual members of the public

(j) Garda corruption

15

Justice for Young Offenders in a Caring Society[1]

Mr Justice Robert Barr

There are two recent developments in the jurisprudence of criminal law in Ireland which indicate an important sea change in the quest for justice in that area. The first is a recognition of the effect of harm done to those who are victims of crime and their status in the context of criminal investigation and prosecution. The second is a reawakening of interest in rehabilitation as being in many cases the most effective way of reforming the wrongdoer and turning him or her away from crime – thus saving other innocent people from being victimised in the future. Both of these advances are interlinked. The recognition of harm suffered by victims of crime has emphasised the crucial importance of rehabilitating the criminal in the interest not only of the offender but also of the public at large in limiting exposure to criminal injury.

There has been radical revision of the entire courts structure in Ireland which is about to come into operation this year. I had the honour of serving on the working group which let to its creation. At the request of the Minister for Justice, Equality and Law Reform one of the areas which we examined in depth was the concept of special drugs courts similar to those pioneered in the USA in the last decade where selected offenders who volunteer for participation are put through an intensive course of rehabilitation and treatment under judicial supervision. It is designed to break the pattern of drug related crime in their lives and establish for them a proper place in society. The American experience has been most

---

[1] *Irish Criminal Law Journal* 9, 1999, 1-7

encouraging. Their drugs courts have success ratios in excess of 75 per cent and the consequent reduction in drug related crime is substantial. In the light of our research and recommendations, the government has decided to establish similar drugs courts in Ireland and a committee of experts is currently devising a structure for pilot courts to initiate the scheme. One aspect of our research has touched upon what I perceive to be the greatest injustice in contemporary Irish life – our failure as a caring society to take sufficient steps to rescue from crime those who are born to it and have the misfortune to exist without reasonable support in the marginalised economically and socially deprived fringes of our society.

Crime statistics in Ireland are inadequate to establish precise details as to the number of children and young offenders having the degree of social and economic deprivation which I postulate. However, our drug court research and consultation with senior members of the probation and welfare service, the Garda Síochána, specialist social workers and judicial colleagues with long experience of crime involving juvenile and young offenders, establishes a clear picture of the harsh realities in this area. There has also been, particularly in the past decade, research by sociologists and criminologists into various aspects of crime and the young offender which has been of outstanding value in analysing the gravity and urgency of this problem.[2] The philosopher, P. Riordan (1994), has cogently summarised his criticism of the contemporary situation in Ireland:

> As long as crime continues to be co-related with social and economic deprivation, we must seriously doubt the justice of the pre-existing order until such time as an articulate understanding of the common good is translated into effective programmes to incorporate the marginalised and alienated into the balance of benefits and burdens which constitutes Irish society, our penal policy will continue to be dominated by the objective of protecting those who are included in the social fabric from those who are effectively excluded.

Dr Paul O'Mahony (1997), in a recent analysis based on a survey of 108 prisoners selected at random in Mountjoy Prison referred, inter alia, to the following statistics which graphically underline how our penal system is weighed heavily against the marginalised poor. Of those examined 37 per cent had lost a parent before the age of fifteen; 15 per cent had a parent imprisoned; 45 per cent had no substantive work or educational qualifications; 29 per cent were illiterate; 66 per cent were heroin users; 30 per cent had made a suicide attempt and 29 percent had hepatitis or were HIV positive. Furthermore, statistics establish that in Dublin 73.3 per cent of those charged with crime in the District Court are from the most economically deprived areas of the city (Bacik et al 1997).

---

[2] See References

The broad spectrum of research into crime and the young establishes the following facts. Drug addiction is the root cause of crime involving the young, particularly in urban areas. It is reliably estimated that in Dublin at present there are about 13,000 known opiate addicts. Many of them require several "fixes" a day for which the going rate on the street is £10 to £18 each. In short an expenditure of £250 or more per week is commonly required to fuel addiction. In practical terms much of the expenditure must be funded from crime – muggings, robbery and burglary being the most common sources. A distressing aspect of contemporary life in our capital city is that many elderly and vulnerable citizens are preyed upon and live in terror of drug addicts. The latter in turn are also liable to domination by dealers who in return for free "fixes" use them as "pushers" or couriers of their drugs.

Heroin addiction is seriously debilitating and leads to many medical and social complications including, all too often, early death of the sufferer. Most addicts are in the age group 16-26 years and are mainly from economically deprived sectors of the community, though addiction of the young occurs at all levels of society.

In broad terms there are two categories of young drug offenders. The first, though probably having an economically deprived background, have the benefit of significant social stability and support in the home. The drug court rehabilitation scheme is particularly appropriate for rescuing such offenders. The treatment under the aegis of the court will involve the parents and other close family, including instruction on how they might best support and monitor the offender on an ongoing basis after his or her rehabilitation process has been successfully completed. This is a crucial safeguard against re-offending.

The second category of young criminals may not suffer from drug addiction, though drugs will be a factor in most cases, and may have gravitated into a life of crime essentially through social and economic deprivation. I have in mind youngsters born into the most marginalised segments of our society who have drawn very short straws in life, ie children from utterly deprived often dysfunctional homes who have not known love, care or support in any meaningful sense. These are children who from an early age may have been running wild or living rough in an uncaring world with companions, some older than themselves, who lead them into a way of life where criminal behaviour is the norm. It seems to me that these are the members of our society who need support most of all. They desperately require to be rescued from the web of crime in which they have become enmeshed with terrible inevitability. I believe that the reason why we have not focused sufficiently on socially and economically deprived young offenders is that, clouded by their criminal behaviour which may be vicious and apparently incorrigible and the harm they do to others, we have failed to recognise an obvious truth – that they themselves are grievously damaged victims of social injustice. We are not vindicating their fundamental right to be cherished equally in our society. Most males in this category will remain drug addicted and involved in related offences. Some will gravitate into major crime. The probability is that a majority will return again and again to prison and will never succeed in unshackling themselves from a life of crime.

There are no official statistics on incidents of re-offending by those who have had custodial detention and who come from seriously deprived backgrounds, but an opinion expressed by a senior probation officer is that on average the incidence of re-offending is as high as 75 per cent. Dr O'Mahony's Mountjoy Prison survey indicates that 95 per cent of those interviewed (almost all of whom were in their early to late twenties) had previous convictions; 31 per cent had received their first conviction before they were fourteen and 64 per cent by age seventeen; 77 per cent had served sentences in St Patrick's Institution for Young Offenders and 13 per cent had spent time in state reform or industrial schools for children. Of those who had served an earlier custodial sentence 7 per cent had first been in custody before the age of fifteen and 57 per cent before the age of eighteen. These figures underline the apparent failure of penal custody as a viable means for achieving reformation of young offenders.

Research and experience has established beyond serious controversy that custodial prison sentences, though probably inevitable as punishment for major crime, rarely achieve rehabilitation of the criminal and are often counter-productive. There are various factors which contribute to that situation, eg prison overcrowding, lack of sufficient educational and work training programmes and lack of adequate post-prison support and acceptable work prospects after prison – particularly for the very marginalised. However, it seems to me that over and above these shortcomings the real difficulty is that prison carries with it a stigma that reinforces a sense of alienation and low self-esteem which is characteristic of many young offenders and hinders their prospect of rehabilitation in prison. Most are at least subconsciously aware that their chaotic way of life, particularly drug addiction, leads only to misery and a failure to achieve worthwhile meaningful existence. As Dr O'Mahony and others have pointed out an inability to sustain even basic human relationships is commonplace among young deprived prisoners.

I believe that rehabilitation of juvenile and young offenders from the marginalised outer fringes of our society is most likely to be achieved on a voluntary basis. At first sight that might seem to be a contradiction in terms. How can a scheme of rehabilitation based on voluntary incarceration hope to work when the offender may have an established background of vicious uncaring criminal behaviour? In my view the concept is not as bizarre as it may seem. What I have in mind is that juveniles or young offenders from the grievously deprived sector of society, who senior probation officers believe may respond to a judicially orchestrated rescue operation, shall be referred to the rehabilitation court for acceptance in cases where the evidence against the accused is well-established and he or she indicates an intention to plead guilty. The trial judge will explain to the accused that he or she is being offered an opportunity for voluntary rehabilitation which will entail in-house drugs treatment (if necessary), counselling, education and job training for twelve months followed by further training and work experience organised by FAS (if required), hostel accommodation and the ultimate provision of reasonable long-term employment. It will be explained that what he or she is being given is a real opportunity to break out from misery and to establish a worthwhile place in the community.

The essence of the carrot is that no stigma attaches to voluntary custody and top quality detoxification is on offer. The stick is that the beneficiary will be warned that the proposed regime is rigorous, then he or she will be subjected to monthly monitoring by the judge in court and that failure to comply with its terms and to co-operate with the regime can cause the subject to be withdrawn from the scheme whereupon he or she will be sentenced to the term of imprisonment which is appropriate to the crime or crimes for which the volunteer is before the court. The selected offenders are likely to regard the proposed scheme of rehabilitation as being substantially more attractive than a term of imprisonment and in my view the probability is that they will not lightly throw away the apparent advantages which it offers. Once he or she is on board it is a matter for highly skilled personnel to stimulate a growth in self-esteem and a realisation of the advantages which are on offer. If there are misgivings about whether this concept is workable, the outstanding achievements of the group of homes for marginalised boys operated by the Lillie Road Centre offers much encouragement.

The proposed pilot drugs court, which will be based entirely on the concept of voluntary rehabilitation, provides an ideal opportunity for launching the rescue operation which I advocate. I hope that the new court will not be confined to drug offenders who because of family background and the probable availability of meaningful support in the home will require a comparatively low level of rehabilitation facilities and in-house continuous treatment (if any) only for actual detoxification. Those who are greviously deprived and have no realistic home support should be included also. They will require in-house maintenance for all aspects of the rehabilitation package for a minimum period of one year and perhaps longer. I believe that the pilot court should have available to it, in addition to the residential facilities required by the general rescue scheme, a suitable residential premises for not more than eight to ten such offenders. (I understand that the Lillie Road Centre's experience is that viable voluntary units should not exceed this number of inmates).

A permanent staff of six specially trained personnel would be required per unit, including specialists in detoxification and counselling, a probation officer, teachers in general education and job training instructors. Service in such units may not appeal to many and the selection of skilled, dedicated staff who have a real enthusiasm for the scheme is crucial to its success. Other essential requirements include ongoing psychological assessment and a chaplain to infuse the project with the charisma of Christ. The cost of rehabilitating grievously deprived offenders is likely to be substantially higher than for those who do not require to live in, and the success ratio may be lower than for the easier group who have the benefit of home support. However, the inescapable fact remains that justice requires that from the beginning such additional resources should be made available for rehabilitation of some grossly deprived offenders. It is imperative that drugs court rehabilitation shall be seen to be open to all regardless of social advantage or degree of deprivation if there are reasonable grounds for the belief that the volunteers may co-operate in their rehabilitation.

Where the proposed one year in-house treatment is successful a further problem arises in the case of those with seriously deprived social backgrounds and lack of viable family support. If they then return to the same milieu of chaotic deprivation from which they emerged when volunteering for court orientated rehabilitation, the probability is that they will be unable to withstand peer pressures to revert to drugs and crime. In that event the advantage of rehabilitation will be thrown away. Such persons will require a back-up service in the nature of hostel accommodation and probably continuing job training leading to an offer of permanent worthwhile employment. I believe that there is a role for the private sector in funding the final phase in the rehabilitation process. I apprehend that there are socially enlightened individuals and corporate bodies who would be ready and willing to play a crucial part in that regard if satisfied that the special court for young offenders is achieving real rehabilitation of the grievously deprived. I believe that they would regard participation as a major contribution willingly given towards the common good of society.

Finally, although the scheme of judicial rehabilitation of grievously deprived young offenders which I advocate will require substantial resources and state funding, there is a silver lining for the financial planners. The average annual cost of a prison place in Ireland is in excess of £46,000. It is reasonable to assume that a young offender from a grievously deprived background who is involved in drugs and related crime and has a criminal history since early youth is likely to spend at least five to ten years in jail in the course of life. For every such person who is rehabilitated through the proposed scheme the state is likely to save upwards of £250,000. In addition, numerous potential victims will avoid misery and the loss of cash and property worth many thousands of pounds.

I have done no more than to provide an impression of the judicial rehabilitation scheme I have in mind. There are other problems, including a restructuring of statute law, which need to be worked out but none would seem to present serious difficulty. I look forward to real movement in the pursuit of justice for grievously deprived young offenders and the vindication of their constitutional right to fair treatment which is so long overdue.

REFERENCES

Bacik, I. et al (1997), "Crime and Poverty in Dublin", 7 ICLJ 104-133

Fahy Bates, B. (1999), *Aspects of Childhood Deviancy – A Study of Young Offenders in Open Centres in the Republic of Ireland*, published by author

Davis, L. (1998), "A Brief Outline of the Juvenile Justice System in Ireland", 3(9) *The Bar Review* 427-430

Hanly, C. (1997), "Childhood Offenders: The Changing Response of Irish Law", 19 DULJ (NS) 113-138

Keogh, E. (1997), *Illicit Drug Use and Related Criminal Activity in the Dublin Metropolitan Area*, Garda Research Unit

O'Malley, T. (1994), *The Irish Juvenile System in Human Rights: A European Perspective*, Round Hall Press, pp 303-325

O'Mahony, P (1997)., "Punishing Poverty and Personal Adversity", 7 ICLJ 152-170

O'Mahony P. (1985), "Some Family Characteristics of Irish Juvenile Offenders", 17 *The Economic and Social Review* 29-37

O'Mahony, P. (1997), *Mountjoy Prison: A Sociological and Criminological Profile,* Dublin: Stationery Office

O'Sullivan, E. (1997), "Juvenile Justice and the Regulation of the Poor", 7 ICLJ 171-194

Ring, M.E. (1991), "Custodial Treatment of Young Offenders", 1(1) ICLJ 59-67

Reports

INTO (1995) *Youthful Offending: A Report* (Dublin)

Probation and Welfare Service Annual Report (1994), Dublin: Stationery Office

Annual Report on Prisons and Places of Detention (1994), Dublin: Stationery Office.

Law Reform Commission, Consultation Paper and Report on Sentencing, LRC, (Dublin: LRC 1993 and 1996)

16

The Impact of the Northern "Troubles" on Criminal Justice in the Irish Republic

Aogán Mulcahy

INTRODUCTION

Amidst ongoing debate about the links between crime and locale, one important question is the impact that violent upheaval in one jurisdiction may have on neighbouring jurisdictions, particularly at a time when many commentators express the view that globalisation has led to the demise of the nation state as a focal point for social organisation and regulation. My aim in this chapter is to examine this issue in relation to the Northern Ireland conflict and its impact on crime and criminal justice in the Irish Republic. It is beyond my scope here to offer a definitive assessment on such a broad topic – although this surely is a project worth undertaking – and so my comments remain speculative. This reflects the broad nature of the subject matter, but also highlights the absence – until recently, at least – of a sustained tradition of criminological research in the Irish Republic. Moreover, within that existing literature, there has been little sustained effort to assess the conflict's impact on crime and crime-related issues. In the following pages, I discuss the Northern conflict's impact on the Republic in terms of several aspects of crime. First, I consider how the Troubles have affected the level and nature of crime in the Republic. Then I examine its impact on the criminal justice system generally, looking in turn at the Republic's legislative framework, the Garda Síochána, and the prison system. Before moving on these issues, however, it is worth considering the reason for the lacuna in Irish criminological research.

CRIMINOLOGY, AND THE LACK OF IT, IN IRELAND

The enormous absolute and relative costs of the troubles established the UK as the most violent western liberal democracy during the years of conflict. Within British criminology, however, the conflict has in large part been "ignored" (Brewer et al 1997, p 4). Although one important exception to this is the attention it received from a number of critical criminologists and others (discussed below), this general omission is highlighted in the *Oxford Handbook of Criminology* (Maguire et al 1997). There, Downes and Morgan note the human and financial costs of the conflict and observe that "[t]he costs in terms of negative effects on public trust in British institutions have been incalculable" (1997, p 127). Despite this self-evident significance, the conflict merits little more than a few isolated mentions throughout the 32 chapters and 1,250 pages of text.

The same criticism is generally true of criminology in the Irish Republic, partly reflecting the general absence of an Irish criminological research tradition. Rolston and Tomlinson's description of criminology as "Ireland's absentee discipline" (1982, p 25) was particularly apt. Prior to the 1980s, the amount of criminological work done in and on Ireland was miniscule. Since then, several notable, if relatively recent, developments have begun to reverse this situation, most visibly through the establishment of criminology institutes and centres in several universities throughout Ireland. Brewer et al (1997) nevertheless subtitle their book on crime in Ireland, *Here be Dragons*, in reference to the "unknown" quality attached to crime and related issues in Ireland.

Several factors relate to how this situation developed. First, the historically low levels of crime in Ireland may have ensured that issues of crime and justice were a low priority for government, and consequently there has been a striking absence of government-funded criminological research (and indeed, social science research generally). The Department of Justice, for instance, first established a research budget as recently as 1997. Second, the social sciences in Irish academic institutions have until recently been fairly marginal within those institutions. Third, the sociology that has been conducted has generally been preoccupied with issues of social policy (Clancy et al 1995). It is noteworthy that while the development of criminology in Britain had its origins predominantly in the spheres of law and psychology, the rapid expansion of the discipline coincided with the development of interactionist and Marxist/critical perspectives in the 1960s, a development that was largely absent in Ireland. In addition to these various factors, however, it seems undeniable that the Northern Ireland conflict has had a "chill factor", inhibiting the development of Irish criminology (Rolston and Tomlinson 1982; Tomlinson, Varley and McCullagh, 1988). Critiques of law and state might have appeared too contentious for many scholars who were not anxious to become embroiled in broader political debates. It is also likely that the Catholic Church's heavy involvement in "youth justice" in Ireland shielded those institutions from the oversight and critique to which they otherwise might have been subject.

Whatever the precise reasons for criminology's underdevelopment in Ireland, that particular corner has now been turned (this book representing one dimension of the process). But while there is now a distinctive "Irish" criminological literature, it too has paid scant attention to the conflict's impact. In the major overviews of crime and criminal justice in Ireland – such as O'Mahony's (1993) *Crime and Punishment in Ireland* and McCullagh's *Crime in Ireland* (1996) – Northern Ireland barely rates a mention. In Brewer et al (1997) *Crime in Ireland 1945-95*, considerable mention is given to the impact that the conflict had on the prevalence and management of "ordinary" crime in Northern Ireland, but there is no systematic analysis of such issues in relation to the Republic. In fact, apart from the work of Brewer et al, the most sustained external attempt to measure the conflict's impact on crime and justice issues has been in relation to its impact in Britain.

CONTENTIOUS AND CONTAGIOUS: NORTHERN IRELAND AND ITS IMPACT ON CRIMINAL JUSTICE IN BRITAIN

Within the British context, developments in the administration of justice in Northern Ireland were frequently cited by critical criminologists and others as evidence of the growing power of the "authoritarian state" and its impact on criminal justice issues (Bunyan 1977; Hall and Scraton 1981; Sim, Scraton and Gordon 1987). The theme of this approach was that Northern Ireland's contentious present was Britain's predictable future: the policies and practices evident in Northern Ireland (such as heavily-armed police, non-jury courts, etc) would, sooner or later, visit Britain's shores and, indeed, Europe generally (Tomlinson 1993). While Hogan and Walker (1989, p 171) suggest that "imitation" of developments in Northern Ireland "has not always been pernicious", the concern expressed here drew on a metaphor of contagion, reflecting what Hillyard (1987) described as the "normalisation of special powers". So, rather than remain confined to dealing with political violence and thus peripheral to the rest of the criminal justice system, the emergency legislation and other measures enacted in response to the conflict were increasingly being viewed – and used – as part of the "ordinary" legal landscape. Its "temporary" description belied its marked longevity, while its "emergency" character was at odds with its gradual "normalisation" (Hillyard 1993, 1987; Ní Aoláin 2000).

Thus the Prevention of Terrorism (Temporary Provisions) Act (PTA), introduced in 1974 following the Birmingham pub bombings in which the IRA killed nineteen people, gradually became a near-permanent legal fixture. Although the British Home Secretary, when introducing it to parliament, described its provisions as "draconian" and "unprecedented in peacetime", it continues to be renewed, while also being amended and extended on several occasions (in 1984 the scope of the act was extended from Northern Irish matters solely, to cover "international terrorism" generally). In addition to the longevity of this "temporary" emergency legislation, the provisions for arrest and interrogation in the PTA and the Emergency Provisions Act appeared increasingly to be used for purposes other than that for which they were (arguably) intended. A large majority of people questioned under emergency legislation were not charged, the implication being that arrest and interrogation was used as part of a broader framework for gathering intelligence rather than as a means to gather information relating to a specific criminal allegation. From the Act's inception to 1982, only 2 percent of those detained under its provisions were charged (Geraghty 1998, p 96), while of the 7,052 people questioned under the act between 1974 and 1991, 86 percent were released without charge (Hillyard 1993, p 5).

In addition to legislation and special powers generally, policing also emerged as a major concern. "Policing by consent" remains *the* rhetorical trope of policing in Britain, but it was a paramilitarised mode of policing that developed in colonial Ireland, and subsequently in Northern Ireland. As the conflict unfolded in the late 1960s and early 1970s, during which the RUC was severely criticised, the force underwent an extensive process of professionalism in an effort to improve relations with the Catholic community in particular, and to increase the force's effectiveness generally. This process was characterised on the one hand by a discourse of consent and service (Mulcahy and Ellison 2001), and on the other by an enormous increase in the force's technological capacity to deal with para-military organisations and large-scale public disturbances (Ellison and Smyth 2000). As the RUC enhanced these latter capabilities, the "militarisation" (Hillyard 1997) underpinning them became increasingly evident.

Some forms of militarisation remained restricted to Northern Ireland. This was most evident in relation to the use of "Plastic Baton Rounds" (PBRs, and their precursors, "Plastic Bullets"). While the firing of PBRs in Northern Ireland was a routine occurrence during the conflict, with its usage characterised by a distinct lack of oversight (Committee on the Administration of Justice 1996), senior police officers balked at using them on British soil (even during riots in 1985 in which a police officer was hacked to death) in case this irreversibly damaged the pacific image of the English "bobby". In relation to other aspects of policing, however, there was greater willingness to put to use the "lessons from Ireland" (Hillyard 1985). This critique alleged that Northern Ireland was serving as a testing ground for measures to contain the industrial unrest and inner-city riots in Britain during the 1970s and 1980s, as well as political dissent generally (Ackroyd et al 1980; BSRSS 1985; Bunyan 1980; Manwaring-White 1983). While Northern Ireland may not have constituted a formal experimental site for criminal justice initiatives (Hogan and Walker 1989), senior British police officers visited Northern Ireland "to discuss riot control and learn from their 'success'" (Reiner 2000, p 68) and it seems likely that some of the practical experience gained there in areas such as crowd control was put to use in the 1984/5 miners' strike in Britain. Similarly the increasing move in Britain towards "intelligence-led policing" resonates with the covert surveillance techniques that were (and remain) to the fore of policing in Northern Ireland (Geraghty 1998; Hillyard 1997). As a consequence of this broad trend, Hillyard (1985) argued that the "lessons from Ireland" were profoundly depressing ones, with grave implications for civil liberties and the character of the criminal justice system in Britain. How, then, would these issues unfold in the Irish Republic?

THE NORTHERN CONFLICT AND CRIME IN THE IRISH REPUBLIC

The Northern conflict has impacted on crime in the Republic in a variety of interrelated ways. There are clear difficulties with calculating the financial cost of the conflict, but several estimates have been made. The New Ireland Forum (1984, pp 15-6) estimated that the direct cost of the conflict between 1969 and 1982 was IR£1,100 million, while further indirect costs – in terms of lost output to the economy – amounted to IR£1,200 million (in 1982 prices) for the same period. Tomlinson (1995, p 10) estimated that the total cost of the conflict between 1969 and 1994 was £23.5 billion sterling, with 10.5 % of these costs (£2,467.5 million pounds sterling) being incurred in the Republic.

Measuring paramilitary involvement in crime is, however, particularly difficult. Much paramilitary crime is "hidden" and goes unreported, including intimidation (of witnesses and others), extortion rackets, smuggling activity, VAT fraud, and so on. Other crime involves members of paramilitary organisations engaging in crime for purely personal benefits. Amongst republican paramilitary organisations, the INLA in particular has been persistently and convincingly linked with various forms of "apolitical" crime (Holland and McDonald 1994). In fact, one of the key features of the conflict's impact is the very complexity of it. The National Crime Forum (1998) outlined what it viewed as some of these intricacies:

> The emergence of political subversives has meant that more guns have become available to ordinary criminals and there has been a big increase in the number of armed robberies. Disaffected political figures flirting with the regular underworld

have made their terrorist skills and their superior weapons available on occasion. The interaction between political subversives and regular criminals has been complex and complicated, each group enlisting co-operation from and providing support to the other only when it suited it and never without a reserve of some suspicion. From the policing point of view the gardaí were faced with a complex situation where crimes were bring committed by people motivated by very different objectives. The prioritised preoccupation of the gardaí with political subversives during the late seventies and throughout the eighties created conditions where organised crime could thrive and where a drug culture, with all its attendant problems for the criminal justice system, could take root without focused opposition (p 14).

Some of the complexities involving paramilitaries and ordinary criminals are evident in the case of Martin Cahill, one of the most infamous criminals in recent Irish history. Cahill's criminal career included an attempt to undermine a prosecution he was facing by killing a government forensic scientist. Cahill apparently decided to use a car-bomb having seen its effectiveness in Northern Ireland and also because this might implicate paramilitaries in the forensic scientist's murder. On another occasion, Cahill attempted to sell a famous collection of paintings he had stolen to the UVF. On yet another occasion, after Cahill successfully robbed a jewellery business that the IRA had decided was too risky to rob, the IRA demanded half the proceeds. Cahill refused. He was shot dead by the IRA in 1994, shortly before it declared its ceasefire (Williams 1998). When we consider that some of Cahill's accomplices had paramilitary connections, the complexities of the relationship between political violence and "apolitical" ordinary crime are highlighted still further.

MEASURING THE "SPILLOVER" OF CRIME

Even while discussing the conflict's impact, and despite the vagaries of crime rates, it should be noted that most commentators attribute one of the lowest crime rates in Europe to Ireland. Rottman argues that up until the mid-1960s crime levels in Ireland were "almost imperceptible" (1980, p 145). Thereafter crime levels increased dramatically, nearly doubling between 1965 and 1970, and continuing to rise steeply and steadily in subsequent years until it peaked in 1983, when 102,387 indictable offences were recorded. In a little under twenty years, levels of recorded crime had increased sixfold. Since the early 1980s the crime rate has fluctuated, declining in the late 1980s, reaching a new peak in 1995, and declining again in recent years. Victimisation studies offer a more nuanced (though hardly conclusive) picture of crime in Ireland than that provided by official figures, and their findings suggest that for some crimes, victimisation rates in Ireland are closer than previously thought to comparable figures for other countries (Breen and Rottman 1985; O'Connell and Whelan 1994; Central

Statistics Office 1999; see also Mayhew and White 1997). Nevertheless, levels of crime in Ireland consistently appear amongst the lowest in Europe and the industrialised world in general (Brewer et al 1997).

Given the intensity of the conflict, particularly in the early 1970s, some commentators claimed that violence was literally spreading southwards. In the *Report on Crime for 1975* (p ii), the Garda Commissioner wrote: "Violent criminal activity designed to intimidate for political purposes in the border areas has undoubtedly influenced crime trends throughout the whole country. This is particularly noticeable since 1969". This broad claim, however, is undermined by several important qualifications.

First, despite Ireland's dramatic rise in crime levels from the mid-1960s onwards, most European countries experienced a similar rapid rise in crime rates to that in Ireland. The onset of this and the precise trajectory of the crime increase are clearly related to the specific circumstances in any given society, but the broad trend seems clear: during the 1960s, 1970s and 1980s, rapid increases in the crime rate were evident in most industrialised societies. This suggests that in addition to purely local factors, other broader processes were also at work. Such claims were frequently made by garda commissioners in the early 1970s, who linked the rise in Irish rates with processes of urbanisation and industrialisation, higher levels of prosperity, as well as changes in family structures and in the public's general attitudes towards authority and hitherto widely-respected institutions (see *Report on Crime* 1970-75). Certainly, the rapid rise in crime rates coincided with widespread social changes in Ireland that Rottman described as "a transformation not by stages but in one rapid step" (1980, p.116). Rapid urbanisation, internal migration, a rise in general prosperity levels coupled with a widening gap between rich and poor, all had a profound impact on the nature of Irish society, and especially on attitudes to, opportunities for, and responses to crime (Brewer et al 1997). Second, while the crime rate did increase in the Republic during the years of the conflict, the "watershed" year identified by Rottman, 1964, predates the outbreak of widespread violence in Northern Ireland. Third, while there may have been an "overspill" of criminal activity from Northern Ireland, this is most likely limited to specific forms of crime rather than crime in general. This is not to underestimate the direct impact of the conflict on crime in Ireland, particularly violent crime, but rather to invite a more qualified assessment of its impact.

As crime rates increased unchecked until the 1980s, issues surrounding crime and the efficacy of crime control policies assumed unparalleled significance within Irish political discourse (Breen and Rottman 1985). Although rural crime has on occasion generated widespread public concern, particularly violent crime involving elderly victims (McCullagh 1999), it was urban crime that provoked the greatest reaction, particularly the high concentration of crime in Dublin. This concern echoed with the alleged emergence of a new era of violent crime in

Ireland, fuelled in part by events in Northern Ireland. Armed robberies were one indicator of this, rising from twelve in 1969 to 228 in 1979. Much of this increase was directly attributable to paramilitaries seeking funds to purchase weaponry and finance other expenditures. Murder rates (excluding cases of manslaughter) also increased rapidly, although from a strikingly low base rate. On only six separate years between 1945 and 1969 (inclusive) did the number of murders in Ireland reach double figures and the average was 7.8 murders per year between 1960 and 1969. From the 1970s onwards, the murder rate increased considerably, generally reaching twenty or more murders per year until the early 1990s. Sutton (1998) estimates that in the Irish Republic between 1969 and 1998, 107 people were killed in incidents directly related to the conflict, representing approximately 3 per cent of the total number of fatalities in the conflict. Nearly one-third of these deaths occurred in 1974 when loyalists bombed Dublin and Monaghan. On no other year during the conflict did the number of conflict-related fatalities in the Republic reach double figures. Moreover, most of these incidents were concentrated around the border area (Poole 1997). Significantly, the largest increases in the number of murders occurred in 1995 when forty-three murders were recorded, and while the number of murders has declined somewhat since then (running at 38 per year for 1997-99) this remains far above the figures recorded during the height of the conflict. Thus, while the conflict explains some of the increase in the number of murders in Ireland, a large proportion of this was the result of other factors, and appears to be linked with the general rise in crime levels in Ireland.

Violent crime is one indicator of paramilitary activity, but the vast bulk of crime in Ireland is property crime and the rise in the incidence of these crimes accounts for the majority of the changes in the Irish crime rates. While the murder rate trebled (from eight to twenty-three) between 1961 and 1991, the burglary rate increased by a factor of fifteen, from 2,000 burglaries in 1961, to almost 31,000 in 1991 (McCullagh 1996). The reclassification of offences in 1975 makes the analysis of long-term trends difficult, but the general trend remains clear. Between 1976 and 1995 violent crime ("offences against the person", reported as Group I offences) accounted for an average of 2.5 per cent of all indictable offences recorded in Ireland (and it never reached above the 1978 rate of 3.7 per cent of offences). The incidence of violent crime has risen, but it generally has done so at a far lower rate than property crime which continues to account for the over-whelming majority of crime in Ireland (Brewer at al 1997).

While the 1980s witnessed growing concern about violent crime in general, much public attention focused on the rise of drug-related crime. Again, this concern was largely directed towards events in Dublin, which witnessed a rapid rise in drug-related offences during the early 1980s as heroin use greatly increased. This was accompanied by vocal public criticism of gardaí response to the problem, and several local organisations were formed to counter drug crime, resulting in various clashes not only with individuals allegedly involved in drug dealing, but also with the gardaí (Bennett 1988; Reynolds 1998; Williams 1998). One retired civil servant "admitted that the Department of Justice and gardaí were shaken by the scale of the problem in the early 1980s, especially in Dublin." Senior gardaí even asserted that "drugs have been the biggest single influence on the crime profile during their time of service" and that "drugs had a profound impact, bigger than terrorism, on the crime profile in the Republic of Ireland..." (Brewer et al 1997, pp 46-7). One of the reasons why drug use had such an immediate and profound impact on the crime profile in Ireland is the less-than-adequate response it received from official agencies. Some of this may be related to the pressures of the conflict, insofar as the security threat absorbed resources that would otherwise have been invested in crime prevention measures. But the poor official response seems more likely due to a general inertia and disinterest towards drug use and the impact of heroin use on marginalised communities (discussed below in relation to policing).

Overall some unknown – although probably small – proportion of the overall increase in crime figures in Ireland was directly related to the Northern conflict, but the vast majority of it was not. Even though the direct impact of the conflict was most evident in relation to violent crime, this was largely confined to specific crimes committed by or at the behest of paramilitaries (eg armed robbery, rather than assault generally) which comprise only a small proportion of offences against the person. The conflict may have exercised a greater impact in indirect ways, in terms of facilitating opportunities for crime in a number of ways (including greater availability of weapons, as well as diverting government energies away from the development of cohesive crime prevention measures) but such an influence is difficult to quantify. Indeed, the most visible consequences of the conflict are on the criminal justice system rather than levels of crime, in terms of policing, prisons, and the Republic's legislative framework.

THE LEGISLATIVE FRAMEWORK: EMERGENCY MEASURES AND SPECIAL COURTS

The conflict has very visibly affected the operation of the criminal law in the Republic. According to the Department of Justice (1997), the conflict has ensured that "[s]trategies to combat subversive crime involve a distinct approach in terms of legislative provisions, Garda intelligence and evidence gathering, court arrangements and custodial policy" (para 5.24). In terms of legislative provisions, a body of "emergency" legislation provided state officials with expanded powers, while a "special criminal court" was also established to hear cases originally linked to political violence, although in practice it also tried cases unrelated to paramilitary activity. One of the features of emergency measures in the Irish Republic is the general lack of review to which these powers are subject (Hogan and Walker 1989); nevertheless their influence·on the Irish legal landscape has been substantial.

Emergency Measures

In 1939 the Irish government formally declared a "state of emergency" that ran until 1976. A series of events – the kidnapping of a prominent Dutch business-man, a major train robbery, the bombing of the Special Criminal Court as part of an escape attempt, and the assassination of the British Ambassador and a civil servant – prompted the government to enact the Emergency Powers Act 1976 (EPA). This gave police the power to hold suspects without charge for up to seven days. The original state of emergency was ended, and a new state of emergency related to the Northern conflict was immediately declared. This latter state of emergency was formally ended in February 1995, some months after the 1994 paramilitary ceasefires.

The EPA complemented the extant Offences Against the State Act 1939 (OASA), and together these measures gave the government and security forces enormous license to counter any perceived threats to state security. During the early-mid-1970s, the OASA was used as the basis for a substantial number of prosecutions (seventy-eight in 1973), but during the late 1970s the number of OASA prosecutions dwindled dramatically, and throughout the 1980s and 1990s the Act was rarely used to prosecute offences on more than one occasion in any given year (see Garda Commissioner's *Report on Crime*, various years). Despite its decline as a basis for prosecutions, it was routinely used to detain suspects for questioning. Between June 1972 and 1989, more than 27,000 individuals were arrested under Section 30 of the Act (O'Leary and McGarry 1996, p 47). Its provision enabling a suspect to be held for questioning for up to forty-eight hours without arrest ensured its popularity among police officers. Following the Omagh bombing in which twenty-nine people were killed, the Act was further amended in 1998 in ways that curtailed the right to silence and expanded garda powers of detention for purposes of interrogation (O'Donnell 1999, p 188).

The Special Criminal Court

In the event that the "ordinary courts were inadequate to secure justice and public peace and order", the Offences Against the State Act 1939 allowed for a Special Criminal Court (SCC) to be established. The SCC was first established in 1939 in response to fears that IRA activity in Britain could jeopardise Ireland's neutrality during the Second World War. Initially composed entirely of army officers, the SCC sat until 1946 after which it ceased to operate. It sat again briefly in 1961-2, again in response to an IRA campaign, but following the IRA's ceasefire in 1962 the proclamation setting up the court was revoked (Farrell 1997, p 2). As the violence in Northern Ireland escalated in the early 1970s, the government stated that the ordinary courts were inadequate to deal with these events, and a new government proclamation again established the SCC, with judges rather than army officers trying the cases.

The SCC was established as a jury-less court, with cases typically being heard before three judges. Although the rationale for the SCC was jury-intimidation in the case of paramilitary-related crime – similar to the rationale behind the establishment of the single judge Diplock courts in Northern Ireland – no specific examples of intimidation were actually cited. It tried "scheduled offences" – offences linked with paramilitary activity – but the Director of Public Prosecutions also had the power to direct that any other offence could be tried in the SCC if the ordinary courts were deemed inadequate to try that offence. Following an amendment to OASA in 1972, the sworn testimony of a garda chief superintendent that an accused was a member of an unlawful organisation was sufficient to constitute proof of membership. While this had to be corroborated by other evidence if the defendant denied membership of an unlawful organisation, "the level of corroboration required was not very high" (Farrell 1997, p 3).

The court has been subject to several serious criticisms. First, it has been accused of adopting a less than vigilant approach to allegations of police ill-treatment of suspects during interrogation (for example, in the case of Paul Ward where the court accepted that he had been ill-treated but still convicted him). Second, the court has been criticised for the fact that it also hears cases unrelated to paramilitary activity, including a case in 1997 that involved charges of possession and supply of cannabis. On another occasion, some of those charged with the murder of Josie Dwyer (killed by anti-drugs activists) were tried in the ordinary courts while others charged with the same offence were sent to the SCC. However, while the DPP has the power to refer cases to the SCC, there is no obligation to explain the rationale for doing so in a particular case. The legislative framework arising from the threat to state security generally, has provided enormous powers to the authorities, but one of their striking features is the extent to which they have been used in capacities beyond their original remit. Such a development confirms the tendency for emergency legislation gradually to influence the entire legal landscape (Hillyard 1987).

THE IMPACT ON POLICING

The framework of policing in Ireland is intrinsically linked with broader issues of state security. As the Commissioner stated: "The *primary* role of An Garda Síochána is to ensure the security of the state" (*Annual Report* for 1997, p 2; emphasis added). This is an important deviation from traditional descriptions of the gardaí role that specifically emphasised "civic" policing and a "community" orientation (Allen 1999; Brady 2000). Although the Department of Justice (1997) claimed that "the battle against subversive or terrorist type activity has always been accorded the highest priority – and very significant commitment of resources" (para 5.25), it is difficult to disentangle the impact of the conflict from that of other factors. In the years following the outbreak of conflict, the size of the force expanded rapidly. In 1969, it was about 6,500 strong, while by 1981 it had increased to 10,000 members, and by 1984 to 11,200 (McNiffe 1997), although much of this was due to the fact that for years garda numbers had been allowed to fall below its establishment figure (Allen 1999). While numbers declined somewhat thereafter, it is significant that the recent moves to expand garda numbers to 12,000 occurred following the 1994 paramilitary ceasefires, and reflect Fianna Fáil's crime control policies rather than any direct threat to state security. Its commitment to expand the force to a record level was a key plank of its election manifesto.

Exact figures for the deployment of garda resources towards security duties are not available, but of the approximately 1,200 officers stationed in the border region, most are inevitably involved in security duties, even if only to a minor extent or on an occasional basis. The Special Branch based in Dublin focuses on state security, while detectives stationed around the country may also be involved in security matters (such as surveillance), with the exact numbers varying according to the specific requirements at hand.

The rapid escalation in violence during the 1970s required immediate action from the gardaí. Republican paramilitaries were "pretty good at what they were at so it was incumbent on us to improve our skills". Special units such as the Special Task Forces were formed which sought to curb the armed robberies that had increased so dramatically in number during the 1970s. Other developments related to cross-border co-operation in security matters. While one RUC chief constable's opinion was that, in this regard, garda "capacity and contribution was small" (cited in O'Halpin 1999, p 333), the 1985 Anglo-Irish Agreement nevertheless put such co-operation on a firmer institutional footing. The conflict also brought immediate consequences in terms of officers' safety. Of the fourteen officers killed since 1970, twelve were the victims of republican paramilitaries. McNiffe (1997) attributes four of these deaths to the INLA, six to the IRA, and the remaining two to unspecified republicans (a further two officers were killed in a car crash while providing an escort for a cash shipment). The significance of these conflict-related deaths is apparent in the fact that prior to the conflict 1942 was the last occasion on which a garda was murdered on duty. Despite this, the effort directed against paramilitary activity was not without its benefits in terms of organisational development. According to one senior garda officer:

> It gave all our people an experience in serious crime incidents that in normal circumstances, in a country of this size, you wouldn't have … It hampered the force's

ability to deal with crime generally but it gave us an awful lot of experience. If you take ballistics, we're one of the world's foremost authorities on it; and improvised weaponry, our officers are lecturing all over the world about it. The force was changing anyway, but it probably accelerated our development to a very high degree, expediting the whole thing. (Interview No. 1)

One of the key issues arising here is the conflict's impact on the deployment of criminal justice resources in the Republic. Even during the early 1970s the Garda Commissioner complained of the "heavy demands on manpower" that the conflict generated, "[a]t a time when police resources are under severe pressure" (*Report on Crime* for 1973, p i). In the 1974 *Annual Report*, the Commissioner again noted the difficulties in deploying resources towards crime prevention "when so many members of the force have to be employed on duties of a security nature" (*Report on Crime* for 1974, p i). This situation prevailed throughout the conflict, and in 1997 the Department of Justice (para 5.25) stated that "the impact of subversive activity ... has been enormous and has significantly reduced the capacity of the system to deal with other forms of crime".

While this argument might at face value appear persuasive, it raises the question of whether the conflict might be used as a scapegoat for broader deficiencies within the criminal justice system. It is, after all, largely a matter of conjecture whether the absence of a conflict would have seen far greater resources directed towards crime prevention. During the early years of the conflict, while the force was in the process of major expansion, many officers were transferred temporarily to border regions to supplement the numbers there, but these officers were typically drawn from low-crime rural divisions. One senior garda officer was adamant that "the cities were never drained [of police] to supplement the border" (Interview No. 1), and so it seems unlikely that the rise in crime in Dublin and other urban centres can be explained in terms of a shortage of police due to the conflict. Much of the crime rise in Dublin during the late 1970s and early 1980s is probably linked with the rapid development of a serious drugs problem in specific areas at that time. Certainly it was during this period that powerful criminal gangs came to the fore. But, as discussed earlier, crime was rising quickly anyway, and illegal drugs formed just one component of this. What seems most striking about the response of the gardaí and other criminal justice agencies to drugs, is not that it was diluted by the pressing demands of state security, but that it was so minimal in the first place. Thus one garda officer (Interview No. 1) noted that while drugs were available throughout the 1970s, drug use "wasn't *seen* as a major problem in the country. It was left to the gardaí, seen as a garda problem. "Multi-agency" was not a word you heard in the 1970s. So the '70s was largely a decade of inaction." Such inaction in relation to "soft drugs" (which comprised the vast majority of drugs available in Ireland during the 1970s) is not necessarily a matter of major concern, but the fact that such inaction continued into the 1980s when heroin began to exert such a massive influence speaks volumes about the lack of police engagement with community concerns and especially the low priority accorded to meeting the needs of marginalised groups. On that basis, the primary factor associated with the lack of an effective governmental response to serious drug abuse in Dublin was not so much the imperative of state security as indifference and inertia.

While the rise in crime during the 1970s and 1980s generated a range of challenges for crime control policy, the conflict brought a different set of pressures to bear on criminal justice agencies. One of the most serious consequences of the Troubles for the gardaí was that it implicated officers in scandals arising from allegations of systematic ill-treatment of suspects, typically paramilitary suspects. According to Farrell, "the government allowed a group to emerge in the gardaí, popularly known as the Heavy Gang, who specialised in the use of brutality to secure confessions" (1993, pp 122-3). Related to this, several high-profile cases collapsed due to "the courts not being satisfied that alleged confessions in garda custody were voluntary" (Walsh 1999, p 262). An Amnesty International mission to Ireland in 1977 also expressed concern about police treatment of suspects in custody. The government established an official inquiry into interrogation procedures (Ó Briain 1978), but further allegations of serious misconduct continued to dog the force. Some of these allegations raised questions of whether the conflict had fundamentally changed the orientation of policing in the Republic (Walsh 1999). In addition to concerns that gardaí were ill-treating paramilitary suspects, other allegations surfaced of collusion between some gardaí and republican paramilitaries. Concern about police powers was also evident in relation to the sheer scale of Operation Mallard in 1987, during which 50,000 houses were searched for paramilitary weapons (O'Halpin 1999; Walsh 1999). It is important to note, however, that much of this criticism involves behaviour unrelated to the conflict, and reflects political patronage and the long-standing physical force tradition in Irish policing, as much as any threat to state security (Brady 2000; Dunne and Kerrigan 1984; Farrell 2000; Inglis 2001; Joyce and Murtagh 1983; O'Mahony 1996). For instance, the Council of Europe's (1999, 1995) reports by the Committee on the Prevention of Torture highlight persistent allegations of ill-treatment of suspects in garda custody. It noted that the "such allegations regarding the use of excessive force by police officers highlights the need for the Irish authorities to remain particularly vigilant in this area" (1999, para 14).

While the conflict in Northern Ireland is one reason why the gardaí might be criticised and the behaviour of its officers called into question, the nature of the conflict is also a compelling reason why such criticism is so infrequently made, in official circles at least. As Walsh (1999) notes, elected politicians, particularly the Minister for Justice, demonstrate enormous reticence in their willingness to criticise the gardaí and this is probably due in large part to government reliance on the force's security role. Walsh (1999, pp 400-1) quotes one former Minister for Justice speaking during a Dáil debate who berated those who would subject the force to inappropriate criticism in relation to a kidnapping:

> There is nothing between us and the dark night of terrorism but that Force. While people in this House and people in the media may have freedom to criticise, the Government of the day should not criticise the Garda Síochána. We all know that there are mistakes in the operation but it is obscene that the Government and the Minister responsible should be the first to lead the charge in the criticism of the Garda Síochána.

Given the seriousness of these scandals, and political reticence to criticise the gardaí in public, it is unclear what the consequences of such events have been. O'Halpin states that the "force's public stock fell" because of allegations surrounding the "heavy gang" (1999, p 328), but one senior officer felt that the guards had come through such allegations relatively unscathed:

> The public were very, very supportive, totally supportive right throughout the troubles, even in the border counties where they would have been inconvenienced more than anywhere else ... I don't think that any of that ["heavy gang" allegations] had any long-term impact on our public standing. I don't think any of those powers have been abused. I think that people would have difficulties in pointing to any specific instance ... I don't think we should make any excuses about exercising the powers available to us. It is necessary to still have them – look at various groups now who are not on ceasefire ... (Interview No. 1)

Walsh argues that the gardaí were able to weather the storm because "public support for the gardaí was so widespread and strong, compared with that for sub-versives, that the government was able to defuse the situation by the appointment of an inquiry into the treatment of persons in garda custody" (Walsh 1999, p 262), which ultimately was largely ignored. The high levels of public confidence in the gardaí (Hardiman and Whelan 1998) may indeed have insulated it from the most potentially destabilising consequences of such scandals, but a focus on "overall" levels of confidence masks important differences in the attitudes and experiences of different sectors of society. Amongst marginalised populations, typically those at the "receiving end" of policing, levels of support are noticeably lower. One 1987 public opinion survey found that fifty-seven of respondents agreed that the statement that "the Garda Síochána sometimes exceed their powers by abusing suspects physically or mentally" (Bohan and Yorke 1987, p 80). It seems inevitable that such public perceptions are related to scandals arising from the conflict.

THE IMPACT ON THE PRISON SYSTEM

The conflict's impact on the prison system has mainly related to issues arising from paramilitary prisoners held in custody. Prior to the outbreak of the troubles, a handful of IRA prisoners were held in Mountjoy and in the Curragh. As the escalating conflict ensured that more paramilitaries were imprisoned, these were initially housed in Mountjoy. Following a major riot in 1972 and the escape of three prisoners by helicopter in 1973, Portlaoise prison was designated the main centre for paramilitary prisoners. In addition, Limerick housed female paramilitary prisoners, while male paramilitary prisoners were held there from 1981 onwards. A handful of loyalist prisoners were held in Mountjoy. The presence of large numbers of paramilitary prisoners was a major security concern for the prison authorities. As one senior Prison Service official put it: "they were disciplined, dangerous, and you knew they might be thinking about escape, and of course they had support on the outside" (Interview No. 2). Other commentators noted that they presented "an array of daunting problems: difficult to house, awkward to handle, not simple to occupy, not cheap to guard" (Osborough 1985, p 187). As a consequence, Portlaoise was characterised by high levels of security, and it became "more of a fortress" (Interview No. 2). The staff/prisoner ratio in Portlaoise increased from 100:114 in 1973 to 100:63 in 1985 (Whitaker Report 1985). Additional security was provided by the gardaí and the army.

The number of paramilitary inmates fluctuated from year to year, reaching a maximum of approximately 200 during the late 1970s and early 1980s, and subsequently declining to perhaps 120 for a number of years, and to approximately 80 in the early 1990s (O'Mahony 1993). In recent years, most paramilitary prisoners whose organisations were on ceasefire were released as a confidence-building measure, or specifically under the provisions of the 1998 Good Friday Agreement. At present, several dozen members of the Real IRA (opposed to the peace process) are held in Portlaoise, while a handful of other paramilitaries are held at Castlerea. Exact figures for the total number of paramilitary prisoners detained in the Republic since the conflict began are not available, but one individual involved in prisoner welfare estimated it could be as high as 4,000 individuals (Interview No. 3).

The sheer scale of the conflict had not been anticipated by the prison authorities and personnel shortages required a huge recruitment drive to increase staffing levels. Moreover, the prisoners' demands for some form of political prisoner status, similar to the "special category status" regime for paramilitary prisoners in Northern Ireland, was a constant source of protest and tension. In the early 1970s, this extended to public protests outside the prison in support of the prisoners' claims. As one prison source noted: "They didn't want to be viewed as criminals." They continually sought recognition as politically-motivated prisoners, "and informally that was the regime that operated" (Interview No. 2). Prisoners had considerable day-to-day autonomy over their activities, and were housed according to paramilitary affiliation. While there was some contact between officers and paramilitary inmates, most of the communication from prisoners to the prison authorities was channelled through the officer commanding, the senior paramilitary officer. In addition to politically motivated prisoners, Portlaoise also housed a number of ordinary prisoners – trustees known as the "Working Party" – responsible for day-to-day maintenance of the prison and who received "extra remission and relatively liberal conditions as compensation" (Whitaker Report 1985, p 261). Paramilitary prisoners did not work, and in fact were involved in negotiating the provision of Open University courses to the prison. One prison officer noted that paramilitary prisoners were "very group-oriented", and that as a body of prisoners they were strikingly disciplined and organised. However, because the different paramilitary groups were held separately, the prison service had to duplicate many of its services to ensure, for instance, that the various organisations used the exercise yard at different times, on a "time-share" basis as it were.

Security, however, remained the major consideration from the prison authorities' point of view: security was "top of the agenda, security of the state, security of the prison, you were always upgrading security" (Interview No. 2). Tighter security arrangements were instituted following escapes, including greater restrictions during visits. Prisoner protests over strip-searching, curtailments on free association, as well as demands for improved conditions generally were the focal point for conflict between prison officers and inmates (Interview No. 3). There were persistent allegations of staff brutality towards inmates, and one prison officer was killed in Dublin in 1983 by paramilitaries, a governor of Portlaoise had bombs placed underneath his car, and several other prison officers received death threats.

The Irish government's decision to allocate Portlaoise prison to paramilitary prisoners inevitably exacerbated the situation of chronic overcrowding that characterised the Irish prison system (O'Donnell 1998; O'Mahony, 2000). But the striking feature of the Irish prison system is that while the numbers of paramilitary prisoners stabilised, the remainder of the system was characterised by ongoing and massive expansion. This was explicitly linked with the advent of a serious drug problem in Ireland. Representatives of the prison service stressed that the impact of the conflict was "not as important as the impact of drugs overall," which had a "far, far greater impact" on the prison system. Once "drugs and the demand for drugs had come in, you had all that petty crime to fund drug use. The impact of subversives never expanded beyond Portlaoise. The numbers of subversive prisoners adjusted up and down … but it never really had an effect beyond Portlaoise" (Interview No. 2). While there were only four major penal institutions in operation in Ireland when Portlaoise was designated for paramilitary prisoners, by 1995 this had risen to more than a dozen institutions.

The increase in crime generally also impacted on the Portlaoise regime. The advent of "big-time, serious, dangerous" criminals, particularly in the form of armed and organised gangs, meant that some "ordinaries" were transferred to Portlaoise, primarily because of the security threat posed by such prisoners. Prison sources viewed this as a permanent feature of the system: "There is a future for Portlaoise, whether there are subversives or not." In that sense, the contemporary significance of Portlaoise is that its security features can be utilised in response to the increase in non-subversive crime, particularly serious organised crime.

LAW AND ORDER, AND THE LESSONS OF CONFLICT

It is one of the massive ironies of modern Ireland that the expansion of the criminal justice system to unprecedented levels – in terms of the prison building programme, recruitment to the gardaí, and powerful legislation targeting drug offenders and organised crime – occurred in the (apparent) aftermath of the conflict rather than during it. Hillyard even suggests that, historically, "the key law and order strategy" of successive Irish governments "was to do nothing" (2000, p 6). Rather, the most discernible shift in law and order discourse was associated with the enormous economic growth during the 1990s and Fianna Fáil's increasing commitment to punitive crime control measures (O'Donnell 1999; O'Donnell and O'Sullivan 2001).

Insofar as the conflict has had a direct impact on the contours of crime and criminal justice in the Irish Republic, it appears to have been largely confined within specific parameters. The conflict may have contributed to a gradual brutalisation of Irish society in some ways, particularly in terms of authoritarianism within government and criminal justice agencies, but its discernible influence on crime levels in Ireland has been surprisingly low. Quite simply, the Republic has never been convulsed by the conflict. Much of this is due to the character of the conflict, through its specific conceptions of "legitimate targets" and its largely localised violence. For whatever reason, though, the spillover has been minimal. This is in no way to disregard the conflict's impact: it has seen levels of crime rise, people killed, state powers expanded dramatically, and prisons filled. While it has shaped various aspects of the criminal justice system in decisive ways and absorbed a massive level of resources, its impact has been dwarfed by the sheer scale of other changes. The most striking shifts in criminal justice in Ireland since the 1970s are due to the rapid increase in ordinary crime rather than to the Troubles. Indeed, it is possible that increased European integration, rather than any developments in Northern Ireland, will generate the greatest momentum in the "drive towards the bottom" (Kapteyn 1996), if each country – in an effort to reduce extra-European immigration, deter asylum-seekers, and minimise the scope of being used as a European toe-hold for international crime – seeks to out-do each other by introducing increasingly punitive measures (see also Tomlinson 1993).

If the "normalisation of special powers" in Northern Ireland is a development that has been mirrored somewhat in the Irish Republic, the question remains as to whether the Republic will prove as receptive on other matters. To what extent, for instance, can the Republic learn from innovative developments in Northern Ireland, in terms of restorative justice and police reform generally? Comparison of the RUC and the Garda Síochána reveals a disturbing lack of oversight and accountability surrounding policing in the Republic. The Garda Commissioner has recently stated that he is not opposed to independent investigation of complaints against the police, and the Irish Labour Party has recently called for many of the Patten Report recommendations to be implemented in the Irish Republic, and also for a Police Complaints Ombudsperson to be established (Cusack 2000). Irish politicians have a long tradition of ignoring the innovations recommended in a variety of reports into the penal system and policing (such as the 1978 Ó Briain Report and the 1985 Whitaker Report; see O'Donnell 1999). Having been left *relatively* untouched by the conflict, will the Irish Republic prove equally immune to the positive lessons of conflict resolution?

REFERENCES

Ackroyd, C., Margolis, K., Rosenhead, J. and Shallice, T. (1980), *The Technology of Political Control*, London: Pluto

Allen, Gregory (1999), *The Garda Síochána*, Dublin: Gill and Macmillan

Bennett, Don (1988), "Are They Always Right? Investigation and Proof in a Citizen Anti-Heroin Movement", in M. Tomlinson et al (eds.), *Whose Law and Order?,* Belfast: Sociological Association of Ireland

Bohan, Peter and Yorke, David (1987), "Law Enforcement Marketing: Perceptions of a Police Force", *Irish Marketing Review* 2: 72-86

Brady, Conor (2000), *Guardians of the Peace*, London: Prendeville

Breen, Richard and Rottman, David (1985), *Crime Victimisation in the Republic of Ireland*, Dublin: Economic and Social Research Institute (Report No. 121)

Brewer, John, Bill Lockhart and Paula Rodgers (1997), *Crime in Ireland 1945-95: 'Here be Dragons'*, Oxford: Clarendon

British Society for Social Responsibility in Science [BSSRS] (1985), *TechnoCop: New Police Technologies*, London: Free Association Books

Bunyan, Tony (1977), *The History and Practice of the Political Police in Britain*, London: Quartet

Central Statistics Office (1999), *Quarterly National Household Survey: Crime and Victimisation, September-November 1998*, Dublin: Central Statistics Office

Clancy, Pat et al (1995), *Irish Society: Sociological Perspectives*, Dublin: Institute of Public Administration

Committee of Inquiry into the Penal System (1985), *Report of the Committee of Inquiry into the Penal System* (Whitaker Report), Dublin: Stationery Office

Committee on the Administration of Justice (1996), *The Misrule of Law*, Belfast: CAJ

Council of Europe (1999), *Report to the Irish Government on the visit to Ireland carried out by the European Committee for the Prevention of Torture and Inhuman or Degrading Treatment or Punishment (CPT) from 31 August to 9 September 1998* <http://www.cpt.coe.int/en/reports/inf9915en.htm>

— (1995), *Report to the Irish Government on the visit to Ireland carried out by the European Committee for the Prevention of Torture and Inhuman or Degrading Treatment or Punishment (CPT) from 26 September to 5 October 1993* <http://www.cpt.coe.int/en/reports/inf9514en.htm>

Cusack, Jim (2000), "New Body Proposed to Monitor the Garda", *Irish Times,* 24 November

Department of Justice (1997), *Tacking Crime: A Discussion Document*, Dublin: Stationery Office

Downes, David, and Rod Morgan (1997), "Dumping the 'Hostages of Fortune'? The Politics of Law and Order in Post-War Britain", in Mike Maguire, Rod Morgan and Robert Reiner (eds.), *The Oxford Handbook of Criminology*, 2nd edition, Oxford: Oxford University Press

Dunne, Derek and Gene Kerrigan (1984), *Round Up the Usual Suspects*, Dublin: Magill

Farrell, Michael (2000), "The Role of the Police in a Democratic Society", Paper presented to "Policing and Human Rights" Conference, Dublin Castle, 3rd November

— (1997), *The Special Criminal Court – The Facts*, Dublin: Irish Council for Civil Liberties <http://www.iccl.criminalj/scc/briefing97.html>

— (1993), "Anti-Terrorism and Ireland: The Experience of the Irish Republic", in Tony Bunyan (ed.), *Statewatching the New Europe*, London: Statewatch

Geraghty, Tony (1998), *The Irish War*, London: HarperCollins

Hall, Stuart and Phil Scraton (1981), "Law, Class and Control", in Mike Fitzgerald, Gregor McLellan and Jennie Pawson (eds.), *Crime and Society*, London: Routledge/Open University Press

Hardiman, Niamh and Christopher Whelan (1998), "Changing Values", in William Crotty and David Schmitt (eds.), *Ireland and the Politics of Change*, London: Longman

Hillyard, Paddy (2000), "Politics in Transition: Some Reflections on Law and Order Policies in London, Dublin and Belfast", Paper presented at the Social Policy Association of Ireland annual conference, University College Dublin, October

— (1997), "Policing Divided Societies: Trends and Prospects in Northern Ireland and Britain", in Peter Francis, Pamela Davies and Victor Jupp (eds.), *Policing Futures*, Basingstoke: Macmillan

— (1993), *Suspect Community*, London: Pluto

— (1987), "The Normalisation of Special Powers: From Northern Ireland to Britain", in Phil Scraton (ed.), *Law, Order and the Authoritarian State*, Milton Keynes: Open University Press

— (1985), "Lessons from Ireland", in Bob Fine and Robert Millar (eds.), *Policing the Miners' Strike*, London: Lawrence and Wishart

Hogan, Gerarld and Clive Walker (1989), *Political Violence and the Law in Ireland*, Manchester: Manchester University Press

Holland, Jack and Henry McDonald (1994), *INLA: Deadly Divisions*, Dublin: Torc

Inglis, Tom (2001), "Policing the Irish State", Unpublished paper, Department of Sociology, University College Dublin

Kapteyn, Paul (1996), *The Stateless Market*, London: Routledge

Maguire, Mike, Rod Morgan and Robert Reiner (eds.) (1997), *The Oxford Handbook of Criminology*, 2nd edition, Oxford: Oxford University Press

Manwaring-White, Sarah (1983), *The Policing Revolution*, Brighton: Harvester

Mayhew, Pat and Philip White (1997), *The 1996 International Crime Victimisation Survey (Research Findings No.57)*, London: HMSO

McCullagh, Ciaran (1999), "Rural Crime in the Republic of Ireland", in G. Dingwall and S. Moody (eds.), *Crime and Conflict in the Countryside*, Cardiff: University of Wales Press

— (1996), *Crime in Ireland*, Cork: Cork University Press

McNiffe, Liam (1997), *A History of the Garda Síochána*, Dublin: Wolfhound

Mulcahy, Aogán and Graham Ellison (2001), "The Language of Policing and the Struggle for Legitimacy in Northern Ireland", *Policing and Society* 11/2 (April): In Press

National Crime Forum (1998), *Report of the National Crime Forum*, Dublin: Institute of Public Administration

New Ireland Forum (1985), *Report of the New Ireland Forum*, Dublin: Stationery Office

Ní Aoláin, Fionnuala (2000), *The Politics of Force*, Belfast: Blackstaff

Ó Briain Report (1978), *Report of the Committee to Recommend Certain Safeguards for Persons in Custody and for Members of An Garda Síochána*, Dublin: Stationery Office

O'Connell, A. and A. Whelan (1994), "Crime Victimisation in Ireland", *Irish Criminal Law Journal* 4: 85-112

O'Donnell, Ian (1999), "Criminal Justice Review 1998", *Administration*, 47/2 (Summer): 175-211

— (1998), "Challenging the Punitive Obsession", *Irish Criminal Law Journal* 8: 51-66

— and Eoin O'Sullivan (2001), *Crime Control in Ireland*, Cork: Cork University Press

O'Halpin, Eunan (1999), *Defending Ireland*, Oxford: Oxford University Press

O'Mahony, Paul (2000), *Prison Policy in Ireland*, Cork: Cork University Press

— (1996), *Criminal Chaos*, Dublin: Round Hall/Sweet and Maxwell.

— (1993), *Crime and Punishment in Ireland*, Dublin: Round Hall/Sweet and Maxwell

Osborough, W. N. (1985), "An Outline History of the Penal System in Ireland", pp 181-90 in *Report of the Committee of Inquiry into the Penal System*, Dublin: Stationery Office

Poole, Michael A. (1997), "Political Violence: The Overspill from Northern Ireland", pp 153-77 in Alan O'Day (ed.), *Political Violence in Northern Ireland*, London: Praeger

Reynolds, Paul (1998), *King Scum*, Dublin: Gill and Macmillan

Rolston, Bill and Mike Tomlinson (1982), "Spectators at the 'carnival of reaction'?", in Mary Kelly et al (eds.), *Power, Conflict and Inequality*, Dublin: Turoe Press

Rottman, David (1980), *Crime in the Republic of Ireland*, Dublin: Economic and Social Research Institute (Report No. 102)

Sim, Joe, Phil Scraton and Paul Gordon (1987), "Introduction: Crime, the State and Critical Analysis", in Phil Scraton (ed.), *Law, Order and the Authoritarian State*, Milton Keynes: Open University Press

Sutton, Malcolm (1998), '*Bear in mind these dead...*': *An Index of Deaths from the Conflict in Ireland, 1969-1998* <http://cain.ulst.ac.uk/sutton/index.html>

Tomlinson, Mike (1995), "Can Britain Leave Ireland?" *Race and Class,* 37/1: 1-22

— (1993), "Policing the New Europe: The Northern Ireland Factor", in Tony Bunyan (ed.), *Statewatching the New Europe*, London: Statewatch

—, Tony Varley and Ciaran McCullagh (1988b), "Introduction", in Mike Tomlinson et al (eds.), *Whose Law and Order?,* Belfast: Sociological Association of Ireland

Walsh, Dermot (1999), *The Irish Police*, Dublin: Round Hall/Sweet and Maxwell

Williams, Paul (1998), *The General*, revised edition, Dublin: O'Brien Press

Interviews

Interview No. 1 – Senior Garda Officer (2001)

Interview No. 2 – Two Senior Officials in the Prison Service (2001)

17

The Third Pillar of the European Union

The emerging structure of EU police and judicial co-operation in criminal matters, and its impact on Irish criminal justice and civil liberties

Eugene Regan and Paul O'Mahony

INTRODUCTION

The member states of the European Union have created a European-wide internal market without borders but have maintained their individual national criminal law systems. Thus criminal law and its enforcement remains the preserve of the member states of the European Union[1] while criminal activity increasingly takes place across national borders.

Cross-border crime, where elements of the crime are committed in different member states, poses serious problems for national police and judicial authorities acting in isolation. The detection, investigation and prosecution of crime of a cross-border nature necessarily involves co-operation between member states and their police authorities.

Recent years have seen considerable growth in organised crime and drug-related crime across Europe. It is widely believed that criminal gangs have been better able than most people and organisations to exploit the freedom of movement

---

[1]   Articles 29-42, Treaty of the European Union (TEU)

and the internal market, which have been major achievements of the process of European integration. There is thus an urgent need to improve co-operation between police and criminal justice and judicial systems on such issues as extradition and intelligence and evidence gathering and sharing. So, while international conventions have been important and useful in this area, there is also a powerful impetus within the EU towards streamlined and more effective arrangements for extradition and co-operation in criminal matters between the member states.

Criminals have been additionally aided in the extension and globalisation of their activities by the immense advances in computer and communications technology. The need for law enforcement agencies to collaborate and develop high technology systems that will measure up to the ever more complex demands of combating crime is obvious.

The rising trend in cross-border crime has led in recent years to an increase in co-operation between member states and their police authorities within the context of the European Union. The Amsterdam Treaty provided a new framework for co-operation by member states in the area of police and judicial co-operation in criminal matters[2] and the Tampere European Council has established a programme of measures designed to combat cross-border crime in the Union.

This chapter examines the background to the current programme of the European Union in the area of police and judicial co-operation in criminal matters and how measures adopted at the level of the Union may influence national criminal law, policing and the criminal justice system in general and how they may affect civil liberties in Ireland.

THE TREATY OF THE EUROPEAN COMMUNITY[3] AND CRIMINAL LAW

While member states retain responsibility for criminal law and policing this is not to say that the European Community has not had an effect on the criminal laws of member states. There is a binding obligation[4] on member states to take all appropriate measures to fulfil the obligations arising out of the Treaties or resulting from action taken by the institutions of the Community and to abstain from any measure which could jeopardise the attainment of the objectives of the Treaty such as the freed movement of goods, people, services and capital.

---

[2] Article 33 TEU

[3] The Treaty of the European Community (TEC) concerns the traditional area of Community policies (eg internal market, competition, agriculture, structural funds) which fall under Pillar 1. The Treaty of the European Union (TEU), while laying down a series of objectives of the Union and the fundamental principles on which it is based is concerned essentially with two policy areas, Common Foreign and Security Policy (CFSP) and Police and Judicial Co-operation in Criminal matters, which constitute Pillar 2 and Pillar 3 respectively

[4] Article 5 of the Treaty of the European Communities (TEC)

The European Court of Justice has clarified the relationship between national and community criminal law in stating that "in principal, criminal legislation and the rules of criminal procedure are matters for which the members states are still responsible but that community law also sets certain limits in that area as regards the control measures which it permits the member states to maintain in connection with the free movement of goods and persons."[5]

In addition, general principles of law as laid down in the Treaties or as enunciated by the European Court of Justice must be reflected in national criminal laws. "National legislative provisions may not discriminate against persons to whom community law gives the right to equal treatment or restrict the fundamental freedoms guaranteed by community law."[6]

While the Community has no competence in the area of national criminal legislation, which falls outside the scope of community law, the borderline between community law and national criminal law is by no means clear-cut and there is a range of community legislation dealing with combating of criminal activity in a number of areas including the sale of counterfeit goods, smuggling of antiques, insider dealing, drug prevention, and fraud against the community budget.

TREVI AND SCHENGEN

In 1976 the Trevi Group was established by the Council of Justice and Interior Ministers of the EEC. This Group was mainly concerned with co-operation between member states in combating terrorism, the illegal drug trade and organised crime. Various working groups were established including a working party on co-operation in the field of law. The Maastricht Treaty endeavoured to streamline, within a European Union framework, the intergovernmental co-operation which had taken place since the 1970s among member states in all matters related to justice and home affairs, including police and judicial co-operation. Thus the following policy areas were placed in the Third Pillar of the Treaty of the European Union and categorised as areas of common interest to all member states: asylum policy, border control, immigration policy, combating drug addiction, combating fraud, judicial co-operation in civil matters, judicial co-operation in criminal matters, customs co-operation and police co-operation.

Co-operation between member states outside the Community framework had been taking place both in relation to the free movement of persons and to police and judicial co-operation in criminal matters for many years. Such co-operation intensified in the early 1980s. The most notable achievement of such inter-

---

[5] Case 203/80, Criminal proceedings against Guerrino Casati [1980] ECR 2595
[6] Case 186/87, *Ian William Cowan v Tresor Public* [1989] ECR 195

governmental co-operation, outside the community framework, was the agreement signed by France, Germany and the Benelux countries in Schengen in Luxembourg on 14 June 1985 culminating in the Schengen Implementing Convention on 19 June 1990. The principle objective of this Convention was to eliminate checks on the movement of persons at internal borders within the Schengen area and transfer such checks to the area's external frontier. In order to achieve this objective "flanking" measures in areas such as asylum, visa and immigration policy, police co-operation and the exchange of information were provided for. Notwithstanding the creation of the Third Pillar by the Maastricht Treaty the Schengen agreement did not become part of the European Union or Community law at that time.

THE AMSTERDAM TREATY

Transfer of Third Pillar matters to Pillar 1

The Amsterdam Treaty provided that all of the policy areas considered as matters of common interest in the Third Pillar of the Maastricht Treaty, with the exception of the provisions on police and judicial co-operation in criminal matters, be transferred to Pillar 1 covered by the EC Treaty. The Treaty of Amsterdam also provided that within five years of its entry into force the Council shall adopt measures aimed at ensuring the free movement of persons and the necessary flanking measures in the area of asylum, immigration and border control.

Incorporation of Schengen

In addition, the Treaty of Amsterdam provided for the incorporation of Schengen within the framework of the European Union/Community. The Schengen Convention established provisions on the free movement of persons and flanking measures to protect security within the Schengen area. In incorporating Schengen it was agreed that Community procedures (Pillar 1) should apply to the free movement provisions of Schengen but that the "intergovernmental type procedure" (Pillar 3) would apply to flanking security measures.

In the light of the incorporation of Schengen within the European Union Framework and the allocation of the provisions of police and judicial co-operation in criminal matters within the Schengen Convention to the new Third Pillar it follows that for a full understanding of the measures likely to be adopted in the area of police and judicial co-operation in criminal matters it is essential not only to take account of provisions of the Treaty of Amsterdam but also the detailed provisions of the Schengen Convention which cover such areas as police co-operation, mutual assistance, application of the *non bis in idem* principle, extradition, transfer of the execution of criminal judgements, narcotic drugs, the protection of personal data and the establishment of an information system.

The incorporation of Schengen into the EC and EU Treaties means that all forms of co-operation between police and judicial authorities in member states now takes place within the context of the European Union. Accordingly, any initiative by member states in the area of police and judicial co-operation in criminal matters must in future be developed in a European Union context involving all of the European institutions in accordance with the provisions of the new Third Pillar.

Police and judicial co-operation in criminal matters is the only area of co-operation between EU member states which remains in the Third Pillar following the Treaty of Amsterdam. Indeed apart from common foreign and security policy in the Second Pillar it is the only policy area in which co-operation among member states is regarded as essentially intergovernmental in nature.

Police and judicial co-operation in criminal matters

The provisions of the Amsterdam Treaty on police and judicial co-operation in criminal matters[7] provided that the Union's objective shall be to provide citizens with a high level of safety within an area of freedom, security and justice by developing common action among the member states in the field of police and judicial co-operation and criminal matters and by preventing and combating racism and xenophobia. This objective is to be achieved through three essential mechanisms:

(i) closer co-operation between police forces and other authorities in member states directly and through Europol

(ii) closer co-operation between judicial and other competent authorities of the member states and

(iii) approximation, where necessary, of rules on criminal matters in the member states.

ENLARGEMENT

Copenhagen Principles

The pending enlargement of the Community to Eastern Europe, involving former Soviet satellite states with a dubious record regarding respect for human rights, the rule of law and democratic government, gave rise to the need for a more explicit definition of the principles upon which the EU/Community was founded. In particular it was considered essential to lay down the certain criteria to which acceding member states must adhere as a pre-condition of entry to the Union.

---

[7] Articles 29-45 TEU

Accordingly, what are called the Copenhagen Principles were adopted which set down requirements for membership including the stability of institutions, the need to guarantee democracy, the rule of law, human rights and respect for and protection of minorities.[8]

Fundamental principles of the Union

The Copenhagen Principles were given a Treaty base in the Amsterdam Treaty which provided that: "The Union is founded on the principles of liberty, democracy, respect for human rights and fundamental freedoms, and the rule of law which are common to the member states". [9] The Amsterdam Treaty also made provision for the first time for the imposition of sanctions against member states that do not respect these principles. Concern to eliminate war and human rights abuses, dreadfully epitomised by World War II and the horror of the Holocaust, was the primary inspiration for the creation of the Community and has continued to be one of its major guiding objectives. According to Barrett[10], "increased integration in internal security matters and the creation of a European legal space can be argued to be the logical consequence of the ideals which motivated the foundation of the European Communities". This implies that a profound respect for fundamental rights underpins all the activities of the Union.

An area of freedom, security and justice

The Amsterdam Treaty amended the Treaty of the European Union (TEU)[11] and the Treaty of the European Communities (TEC)[12], provided for the development of the Union as an area of freedom, security and justice. The concept of an area of "Freedom, Security and Justice" gives recognition to the inter-relationship and inter-dependence of these concepts which help to define the European Union. This new objective of the Union underlines the role of the European Union as guarantor of the fundamental rights of its citizens.

The objective of developing the European Union as an area of freedom, security and justice is to be achieved by a range of policies which fall essentially into two main categories: policies related to the free movement of persons, which fall under the EC Treaty or Pillar 1; and policies on police and judicial co-operation in criminal matters, which fall under the Treaty of the European Union or Pillar 3.

---

[8] Conclusions of the Copenhagen European Council 1993
[9] Article 6 of the Treaty of the European Union (TEU) ·
[10] Barrett G. (1997), "Co-operation in Justice and Home Affairs In The European Union – An Overview And Critique", in *Justice Co-Operation in the European Union,* Dublin: IEA at 6
[11] Article 2 TEU
[12] Article 61 EC Treaty

Charter of fundamental rights

A further elaboration of the principles to which the Union and member states must adhere is found in the new Charter of Fundamental Rights adopted at the Nice European Council in December 2000. In addition to the problems posed by enlargement the establishment of this Charter is motivated by a genuine desire to ensure that the European Union acts and is seen to act in the interests of all citizens of the Union. The preamble to the Charter states that: *Taking inspiration from its cultural, humanist and religious heritage, the Union is founded on the indivisible, universal principles of human dignity, freedom, equality and solidarity; it is based on the principles of democracy and the rule of law. It places the individual at the heart of its activities, by establishing the citizenship of the Union and by creating an area of freedom, security and justice.*[13]

Policing in an enlarged EU

The problem of enlargement looms ominously over efforts of member states to pursue common action in the area of crime prevention in the European Union within the framework of the new Third Pillar. In the present Union there is already a confusing array of disparities and incompatibilities between legal systems, especially between the civil law and common law countries. What is contemplated is enlargement of the Union to include countries from the former Eastern Bloc with histories of totalitarian government and associated judicial and police systems. Enlargement inevitably entails a further major challenge for the new Third Pillar programme in criminal law matters.

"Police state" traditions are ruled out by the Copenhagen Principles and the provisions of the Amsterdam Treaty[14], and while European Union funds are being provided to Eastern European countries to facilitate a radical overhauling of their judicial and policing systems, much remains to be done to secure the establishment in these countries of the kind of civil liberties regimes expected of a member state of the Union.

Acquis in Justice and Home Affairs

The pending enlargement of the Union gave rise to the need to define the Acquis of the European Union in the field of Justice and Home Affairs, including the Acquis in police and judicial co-operation in criminal matters. States joining the European Union must adopt the Acquis in EU/ EC law, or body of law in being at the time of joining, as part of the conditions of membership. However, while the Acquis in most fields of Union activity could be readily identified this was not

---

[13] Charter of Fundamental Rights (fundamental.rights@consilium.eu.int)
[14] Article 6 and 7, Treaty of the European Union

the position in the case of Justice and Home Affairs. This was due in large part to the fact that only a very limited number of measures were adopted in Justice and Home Affairs within the framework of the European Union. Many of the Conventions drawn up at European Union level had not entered into force, with the notable exception of the Europol Convention which entered into force on 1 October 1998 allowing Europol to commence operations on 1 July 1999. In drawing up the Acquis in Justice and Home Affairs and in particular in the area of police and judicial co-operation in criminal matters the Union had to have recourse to Conventions adopted under the auspices of the United Nations, the Council of Europe and the OECD. The Acquis of the European Union in the field of Justice and Home Affairs was drawn up on 30 March 1998 in the context of the new enlargement of the Union.[15]

The Acquis in Justice and Home Affairs also includes a series of Joint Positions, Joint Actions, Council Resolutions and Recommendations. The most important Joint Actions include the Action Plan on Drugs and an Action Plan to Combat Organised Crime, both of which have been recently updated.[16] These provide a framework for comprehensive co-operation among member states in combating crime in these areas.

TRANSPARENCY, DEMOCRATIC ACCOUNTABILITY AND JUDICIAL CONTROL

There have been a number of key factors which have influenced the Amsterdam Treaty provisions on the new Third Pillar – in particular, the need to facilitate the free movement of people within the Union, the increasing realisation that crime and effective law enforcement in the European Union is one of the primary concerns of European citizens and the need for greater co-operation by police and law enforcement authorities to combat an increase in organised and serious cross border crime in Europe. At the same time the new Third Pillar provisions have also been shaped by a need for greater transparency, democratic accountability and judicial control of policies adopted in the area of police and judicial co-operation in criminal matters

Co-operation among member states under the new Third Pillar, as with Pillar 2, is still classified as intergovernmental in nature, yet there were a number of fundamental changes (outlined below) introduced by the Amsterdam Treaty which suggest that that designation is no longer entirely appropriate in the case of the new Third Pillar.

---

[15] Reference Council 6474/3/98

[16] European Union Drugs Strategy 2000-2004 and *The Prevention and Control of Organised Crime: A European Union Strategy for the Beginning of the New Millennium* (2000/C 124/01 OJ 3/5/2000)

The European Commission

The European Commission will now have a right of initiative, together with member states, in coming forward with proposals in the area of police and judicial co-operation in criminal matters, a right specifically excluded by the Maastricht Treaty. While the unanimity rule places the Commission in a less pivotal role than would normally apply were decisions to be made by qualified majority, nevertheless the introduction of a right of initiative opens up new possibilities for the Commission to play a leading role in introducing policies and monitoring their implementation in the area of police and judicial co-operation in criminal matters.

The European Parliament

The European Parliament must be consulted by the Council before adopting any measures other than a common position defining the approach of the Union. In the absence of an opinion of the Parliament within a specified time limit the Council may act. The Amsterdam Treaty also provided that the Presidency and the Commission shall regularly inform the European Parliament of discussions in Third Pillar matters. The European Parliament may also refer questions to the Council and make recommendations. The provision for the holding of an annual debate on progress in the new Third Pillar will allow for greater transparency and democratic accountability at European level in respect of measures taken in this area.

The European Court of Justice

The European Court of Justice will have jurisdiction to give preliminary rulings on various decisions adopted pursuant to the provisions on police and judicial co-operation and criminal matters. While the jurisdiction of the Court is circumscribed the extension of its jurisdiction in the area is a major innovation.

Legal binding measures

The legal instruments of the new Third Pillar, are now binding on member states. The Treaty of Amsterdam, however, made it explicit that the new Third Pillar instruments, framework decisions and decisions, shall be binding on member states, albeit without direct effect.

Thus the right of initiative of the Commission, the right of the Parliament to be consulted, the new jurisdiction of the European Court of Justice and the binding nature of decisions in new Third Pillar matters suggests that co-operation in police and judicial co-operation in criminal matters in the new Third Pillar can no longer be classified as purely intergovernmental in nature.

Furthermore, the fact that the creation of an area of freedom, security and justice is designed to deal with matters of direct concern to European citizens will no doubt provide the leverage for the European Commission and Parliament to become more centrally involved in developments in the area of police and judicial co-operation in criminal matters. This in turn will ensure more openness, transparency and understanding of the policies and measures likely to be adopted in the area of police and judicial co-operation in criminal matters.

However, while the Amsterdam Treaty represents a major step forward in creating greater transparency, democratic accountability and judicial control in the manner in which measures are adopted in the area of police and judicial co-operation in criminal matters much remains to be done as evidenced by the statement of the President of the European Commission Romano Prodi to the effect that: *we currently have a paradoxical situation in which even the deliberations of the fifteen Justice Ministers on such sensitive issues as penal law and police co-operation escape the scrutiny of Parliament and the Court of Justice. This cannot go on.*[17]

THE CORPUS JURIS

In 1995 the European Commission initiated a research project on identifying the legal framework within which the financial interests of the Community could best be protected. The end product of this research work was the publication in 1997 of the Corpus Juris which established a new European criminal code for the detection, investigation and prosecution of offences affecting the financial interest of the European Community. The Corpus Juris calls for a genuine harmonisation of criminal law and procedures for dealing with fraud against the financial interests of the Community, the application of this code to the whole of the Union and the establishment of a European public prosecutor's office. The authors argued that traditional forms of co-operation in dealing with such fraud have proved ineffectual.

The publication of the Corpus Juris gave rise to a public debate on criminal law and procedure in the European Union. The European Parliament in a Resolution[18] in 1999 welcomed the Corpus Juris and specifically approved the establishment of an independent European Public Prosecutor. In addition, the Parliament suggested that the Corpus Juris could serve as a model for future developments in the area of criminal law and its enforcement in the European Union. However, aspects of the Corpus Juris did come in for criticism, such as provisions for detention without trial and trial by judge only. These initial reactions gave rise to a follow-up study which examined the necessity, legitimacy

---

[17] Speech by President Romano Prodi at the Plenary Session of the European Parliament, Strasbourg, 3 October, 2000

[18] Resolution on criminal procedures in the European Union (Corpus Juris) A4-0091/99 (13 April, 1999)

and feasibility of the Corpus Juris and a revised version of the Corpus Juris was published in 2000. While having the status of a research study at this point in time the Corpus Juris has helped to highlight the fundamental problems involved in the harmonisation of criminal law and procedure in the European Union and in pointing the way to potential solutions to those problems.

This is an alternative approach to dealing with the problem of divergent criminal legal systems in the European Union. The Corpus Juris is radical in that it cuts through the tangled web of conflicting traditions in criminal justice procedure and sets up a new model which embodies the most important principles from both common and civil law traditions. It brings clarity to bear on highly complex and divergent systems within the European Union and puts in their place a single efficient and transparent system which places the issue of civil liberties centre stage. The Corpus Juris envisages the position of a judge of freedoms whose primary task is to protect the fundamental rights of the accused and witnesses. The judge of freedoms, it is suggested, will check and authorise, normally in advance, measures taken utilising the powers of the European Public Prosecutor. The judge of freedoms will work to ensure that all such measures are lawful and regular and that they respect the principles of necessity and proportionality.

The Corpus Juris is no longer merely a research project but forms the basis of the Commission's recent proposal for a Treaty amendment, in the context of the Intergovernmental Conference concluded in December 2000, which would provide for the appointment of a European Public Prosecutor in accordance with the Corpus Juris.[19]

BUILDING ON THE AMSTERDAM TREATY

The Amsterdam Treaty provided for police co-operation in such areas as operational co-operation, data collection, training and common evaluation of investigative techniques. (Article 30(1)). The Treaty also provided for co-operation through Europol (Article 30(2)) which may be involved in operational actions or may initiate investigations. In the area of judicial co-operation in criminal matters, the Treaty of Amsterdam provided for co-operation between judicial authorities in facilitating extradition, ensuring compatibility of rules, preventing conflicts of jurisdiction and progressively establishing minimum rules relating to the constituent elements of criminal acts.

---

[19] Communication from the Commission – Additional Commission contribution to the Intergovernmental Conference on institutional reforms – The criminal protection of the Community's financial interests: A European Prosecutor, Brussels 29/09/2000 Com(2000) 608 final

The Vienna Action Plan

The Vienna Action Plan of the Council and the Commission on how best to implement the provisions of the Treaty of Amsterdam on developing an area of freedom, security and justice, of which police and judicial co-operation in criminal matters is an essential component, was adopted by the Justice and Home Affairs Council of 3 December 1998. This Plan, which details the priorities for the next two to five years in the area of police and judicial co-operation in criminal matters, states that: *The agreed aim of the Treaty is not to create a European security area in the sense of a common territory where uniform detection and investigation procedures will be applicable to all law enforcement agencies in Europe in the handling of security matters...* The Action Plan goes on to state that: *The Treaty merely, provides an institutional framework to develop common action among the member states in the indissociable fields of police and judicial co-operation in criminal matters.*

In approving this Action Plan in Vienna on 11 and 12 December 1998 the European Council called *for particular attention to be paid to the creation of a European judicial area, in accordance with the Treaty of Amsterdam, endowed with the necessary instruments for effective judicial and police co-operation, in particular within the Schengen area, to the further development of the role of Europol as an operational tool for the member states to fight organised crime...* In the area of judicial co-operation in criminal matters the Action Plan represents, to a certain extent, exhortations to member states to implement what has already been agreed at the level of the Council of Justice and Home Affairs ministers such as the Convention on Mutual Assistance in Criminal Matters and Conventions on Extradition.

The main emphasis in the area of police co-operation is placed on developing the capacity of Europol to assist and co-ordinate police efforts within the Union in combating crime including illegal immigration, terrorism and organised crime.

Tampere European Council

The special meeting of the European Council held on 15 and 16 October 1999 in Tampere, Finland, was specifically designed to give further guidance to the actions of the Union in creating an area of freedom, security and justice in the Union and in particular the Unionwide fight against crime.

The European Council suggested that the project of creating an area of freedom, security and justice in the EU should be based on three fundamental principles; compatibility and convergence of legal systems, mutual recognition of judgments and the establishment of a scoreboard on implementation by member states. The European Council at Tampere granted a new mandate to the European Commission in the area of justice and home affairs including that of introducing a Scoreboard for monitoring implementation of policies by member states.

In the area of police co-operation Tampere called for the establishment of a European Police Chiefs operational task force, a European Police College and Eurojust – composed of national prosecutors, magistrates and police officers.

The co-ordination or approximation of national criminal laws is to be focused initially on specific areas of criminal activity of a transnational nature such as financial crime, drugs, trafficking in human beings, high-tech crime and environmental crime. The approximation of criminal law and procedures in respect of tracing, freezing and confiscating of funds is a priority and Europol's mandate has been extended to this area.

Beyond Tampere

Since Tampere developments in the area of police and judicial co-operation in criminal matters have moved with a new urgency. The Council of Justice and Home Affairs adopted a new comprehensive Action Plan to Combat Organised Crime.[20] The Commission's Scoreboard[21] setting out the policies to be implemented and deadlines for their adoption has been approved and is to be updated every six months under each Council Presidency. The United Kingdom's application to participate in the Schengen Acquis has been agreed. Accession negotiations have commenced with the Eastern European applicant countries on the Chapter on Justice and Home Affairs. The Council has adopted a framework decision aimed at improving the criminal law protection of the Euro currency. The Council has adopted the Convention on Mutual Assistance in Criminal Matters which supplements existing arrangements in the 1959 Council of Europe Convention, the Benelux Treaty and Schengen Acquis as integrated in the European Union by the Amsterdam Treaty. The Heads of State and Government in its meeting at Feira, Portugal, has adopted a Report on the integration of Justice and Home Affairs matters, including that of police and judicial co-operation in criminal matters, into the area of EU external policy.

There is little doubt that this work will ultimately have demonstrable and far-reaching effects on the policing and criminal law systems of member states.

Impact of new Third Pillar in Ireland

Acquis in Justice and Home Affairs

Ireland has adopted or is in the course of adopting legislation which will implement in full the Acquis in Justice and Home Affairs. Accordingly, much

---

[20] *The Prevention and Control of Organised Crime: A European Union Strategy for the Beginning of the New Millennium* (2000/C 124/01 OJ 3/5/2000)

[21] Scoreboard to review progress on the creation of an area of freedom, security and justice in the European Union (Com(2000) 167 final/2 Brussels 13/4/2000)

recent criminal law legislation has been influenced by measures adopted in the context of the European Union. Ireland's implementation of the Acquis in police and judicial co-operation in criminal matters is summarised in Table 1.

Table 1: Implementation of Acquis in JHA – police and judicial co-operation in criminal matters in Ireland[22]

Europol Act 1997 The Establishment of a European Police Office ('Europol Convention) 26 July 1995
Child Trafficking and Pornography Act 1998 Joint Action concerning action to combat trafficking in human beings and sexual exploitation of children, 24 February 1997
Criminal Assets Bureau Act 1996
Transfer of Sentenced Person Act Council of Europe Convention on the Transfer of Sentenced Persons, 25 May 1987
Criminal Justice Act 1994 (Part V11) European Convention on Mutual Assistance in Criminal Matters 1959 Convention on Laundering, Search, Seizure and Confiscation of the Proceeds of Crime UN Convention against Illicit Traffic in Narcotic Drugs and Phystropic Substances (Vienna) 1988
Extradition (European Convention of the Suppression of Terrorism) Act 1987 European Convention on the Suppression of Terrorism 1977
The Criminal Justice (Fraud Offences) Bill 2000 Convention on the Protection of the European Communities Financial Interests, 26 July 1995
Prevention of Corruption (Amendment) Bill 2000 The Convention drawn up on the basis of Article K 3(2)© of the Treaty on European Union on the Fight against Corruption involving Officials of the European Communities or Officials of member states of the European Union, done at Brussels, 26 May 1997 The Convention on Bribery of Foreign Public Officials in International Business Transactions, drawn up under the auspices of the Organisation for Economic Co-operation and Development and adopted at Paris, 21 November 1997, and The Criminal Law Convention on Corruption, under the auspices of the Council of Europe and done at Strasbourg, 27 January 1999

---

[22] *The New Third Pillar Co-operation Against Crime in the European Union,* edited by Eugene Regan, published by the Institute of European Affairs, Dublin, 2000, p. 14

Schengen

Given the importance to Ireland and the United Kingdom of co-operation with other member states in the fight against organised and serious crime in the European Union, the major advances made under Schengen, most notably in developing the Schengen Information System, and the similarity between many of the new Third Pillar and Schengen Acquis provisions, it is not surprising that both governments indicated a willingness at an early stage to participate in the *law enforcement and criminal judicial co-operation derived from the Schengen provisions.*[23]

The United Kingdom submitted a formal application on 20 May 1999 to participate in those measures of the Schengen Acquis that relate to law enforcement and criminal judicial co-operation, including the Schengen Information System, by exercising the provision of Article 4 of the Schengen protocol. The UK's application to participate in the Schengen Acquis was finally agreed by the Justice and Home Affairs Council on 29 May 2000. While Ireland also intends to participate in the Schengen Acquis in relation to police and judicial co-operation in criminal matters it is not known at the time of writing what is the current status of Ireland's application.

Judicial co-operation

Traditionally there have been three main forms of judicial co-operation: extradition, mutual assistance and transfer of sentenced persons.

Extradition generally does not arise unless there is an express treaty obligation to extradite.[24] Where a treaty is not required countries will only extradite on the basis of reciprocity. The two main difficulties with extradition are the requirement of dual criminality (the offence in the state seeking extradition must correspond with the offence in the country from which extradition is sought) and the reluctance of civil law countries to extradite their nationals.

The current system of *mutual assistance* originated with the European Convention for Mutual Assistance of 1959. The Council of Europe Money Laundering Convention and the United Nations Drug Trafficking Convention[25] also provide for mutual assistance. The 1994 Criminal Justice Act (section 46 to 56) which incorporates the three Conventions into Irish law came into effect on 15 November 1996 and provides for the taking of evidence for use abroad, the

---

[23] Declaration of British and Irish Delegations at the Council of Justice and Home Affairs held on 12 March, 1999

[24] Eg *Holmes v Jennison* 14 Pet. 540 (1840) and *R v Governor of Brixon Prison, ex parte Soblen* [1963] 2 QB 283

[25] United Nations Convention against the Illicit Traffic in Narcotic Drugs and Psychotropic Substances, 1988, and the Council of Europe Convention on Laundering, Search, Seizure and Confiscation of the Proceeds from Crime, 1990

service of foreign documents and the enforcement of foreign confiscation orders. There is no system in place, however, whereby an accused may obtain evidence from another state to assist in his defence and in practice it is difficult for an accused to challenge how evidence was collected in another state.

The new Convention on Mutual Assistance adopted in June 2000 extends the scope and character of mutual assistance in a number of important respects.

i) In creating an obligation to provide assistance for the interception of communications but assistance need only be given in the circumstances in which such interception would be permitted to a national authority under domestic law.

ii) In permitting the taking of evidence by video and telephone links.

iii) In providing for creation of joint investigative teams by the police forces of participating member states and for controlled deliveries of suspect assignments and covert operations, although member states may enter reservations in respect of operations that would amount to entrapment.

iv) In permitting the use of information or evidence obtained pursuant to a request for any other purpose for which assistance could have been sought, even where the requested state does not consent.

v) In providing for the transfer of sentenced persons for the purposes of investigating offences even where the person does not consent, although member states may enter a reservation in regard to the issue of consent.

The Draft Convention on Mutual Assistance and Co-operation between Customs Administrations (Naples II) is intended to permit "hot pursuit" across borders and the continuance of surveillance of suspects when they have entered the territory of other member states. It also aims to permit customs authorities to conduct covert investigations in the territory of other member states, to carry out controlled suspect deliveries, and to set up joint investigation teams.

The Council of Europe Convention on the *Transfer of Sentenced Persons* was adopted in 1983 and became operative between member states of the European Communities in 1987. The Transfer of Sentenced Persons Act 1996, incorporating the said Convention into Irish law, permits states in given circum-stances to send and receive sentenced persons who have applied to serve their time in their country of nationality.

The Treaty of Amsterdam provided for speedier and more effective procedures in the areas of extradition and mutual assistance by developing greater compatibility in rules and by agreeing common definitions of offences. However, the Tampere European Council has concluded that mutual recognition will in future form the cornerstone of judicial co-operation in the Union. Many Conventions already adopted or in draft form are based on the principle of mutual recognition such as the Convention on the Enforcement of Foreign Criminal

Sentences, the Council of Europe Convention on the International Validity of Criminal Judgements, the Draft Convention on the enforcement of Driving Disqualifications and the Draft Agreement for the Mutual Enforcement of Financial Penalties for Traffic Offences.

Mutual recognition of judicial decisions and judgments in criminal matters involves acceptance by member states of the validity of different judicial systems, substantive laws and rules of evidence, which form the basis of the decisions and judgments taken in other jurisdictions. Mutual recognition allows for diversity in legal systems but some harmonisation of member states' criminal laws and procedures is required to ensure mutual trust and confidence in each other's legal system. In other words "common minimum standards"[26] will be adopted to the extent that they prove necessary to facilitate the application of the principle of mutual recognition. The Tampere Conclusions envisage this principle applying to pre-trial orders, admissibility of evidence and enforcement of judgments. Subsequently, the Council identified decisions concerning the freezing of assets as a priority in this regard. Work is progressing rapidly on the development of the concept of mutual recognition and a programme of measures for its implementation is to be adopted by the Commission and the Council as early as December 2000.

Europol and policing

The Tampere Conclusions provide that "Europol has a key role in supporting Union-wide crime prevention, analyses and investigation".[27] Europol has a central role in promoting co-operation of police authorities in combating crime in the European Union. The establishment of joint teams to conduct criminal investigations in one or more member states, with Europol acting in a support capacity, is considered essential to derive maximum benefit from police co-operation between member states. The newly approved Convention on Mutual Assistance in Criminal Matters will most likely provide the legal basis for the operation of such teams.[28] Ultimately, Europol may itself create joint investigative teams in certain areas of crime and prompt member states to initiate specific investigations. The establishment of a European Police Chiefs Operational Task Force to exchange experience, best practices and information and contribute to the planning of operative actions must be done in co-operation with Europol. Furthermore, Europol is guaranteed the necessary support and resources to carry out its tasks by the European Council

---

[26] Conclusion No. 37 of the Tampere European Council
[27] Conclusion No. 45 of the Tampere European Council
[28] Article 13 of the Convention on mutual legal assistance in criminal matters, 2000

The Irish police force participates in all of the exchange of information and training programmes managed by the European Commission designed to further co-operation between police authorities throughout the European Union. In accordance with the provisions of the Europol Convention, Ireland has established a National Unit which will carry out specific tasks vis-a-vis Europol, such as planning information and intelligence, responding to Europol's requests for information for storage in the computerised system.

Article 30.2.2(a) expands the activities of Europol from that of a liaison and information exchange agency into the area of active operations and enables Europol "to facilitate and support the preparation, and to encourage the co-ordination and carrying out of specific investigative actions by the competent authorities of the member states, including operational actions of joint teams comprising representatives of Europol in a support capacity".

While current plans for an operative Europol and the number and type of crimes, with which it is competent to deal, are to some extent limited, there is obvious potential for the development of Europol into an FBI-type force. Equally, there is likely to be pressure to extend Eurodac (the new EU finger-printing system for asylum-seekers) so that it encompasses the fingerprints of convicted criminals from all the countries of the EU. The successful operation of Eurodac would encourage such expansion and act as a model for future developments, such as an EU DNA database. The Deputy Director of Europol, Willy Bruggeman,[29] has said that Europol does not aim to have a large central database but rather seeks to have accessible, compatible national databases. Europol will rely on the national authorities to indicate when, in accordance with its national laws, intelligence can be shared. However, given the variety and complexity of national laws in this regard and the priority given to information sharing among police authorities, the lack of independent monitoring of information sharing is a cause for concern.

Furthermore, Europol is to have a small central database to support its analytical function. This database will hold information not just on convicted criminals but also on suspects, contacts, witnesses, associates and even victims. The Irish Data Protection Commissioner, Fergus Glavey,[30] points out that much of the Europol Convention is devoted to spelling out what can and cannot be stored in the Europol database.

Article 23 requires the provision of a National Supervisory Authority in each member state and Article 24 provides for a Joint Supervisory Body with an internal committee "designated to hear appeals from decisions by Europol in

---

[29] Bruggeman W., from a speech to an IEA seminar "Future Scenarios for the Third Pillar", 14 June, 1999

[30] Glavey, Fergus, "Accountability, Data Protection and Third Pillar Arrangements", in *The New Third Pillar Co-operation Against Crime in the European Union*, edited by Eugene Regan, published by the Institute of European Affairs, Dublin, 2000

respect of an individual's right of access as provided for in Article 19 and right to the correction and deletion of data provided for in Article 20". The internal committee will have a representative from each Member State. These provisions are clearly essential and a valuable means of remedying situations involving wrongfully obtained information. However, in the context of secret national databases and a secret and comprehensive analytical Europol database, it is hard to see how these provisions will have a significant role in preventing infringements of the individual citizen's right to privacy.

FUNDAMENTAL RIGHTS AND CIVIL LIBERTIES

The Treaty of Amsterdam has transformed the Third Pillar of the Maastricht Treaty by transferring immigration, border controls, visas and judicial co-operation in civil matters into the Community sphere and confining the new Third Pillar to police and judicial co-operation in criminal matters. The new Third Pillar is now focused on areas which directly affect civil liberties.

The internal market and freedom of movement are major goals of the Union and have inevitably raised difficulties about immigration and the status of third country nationals and asylum seekers. A major rationale for the introduction of the Third Pillar was the urgent necessity to safeguard freedom of movement and the internal market by establishing new legal and information-sharing procedures for dealing with immigrants, asylum seekers and even business and tourist visitors to the EU. In this context it is clear that the status of all residents of member states and the treatment by the Union of third country nationals is a matter of legitimate concern to civil libertarians. The possible emergence of different classes of citizenship, with differing attached civil liberties, is a matter of particular concern. Until recently, Ireland has not had significant immigration nor has it had to face the problem of asylum seekers. In the last few years this situation has changed dramatically and the treatment of refugees has now become a live social and political issue with substantive civil liberties implications. There are many problems of great relevance to Ireland that, clearly, will only be resolved at the EU level.

While the need for Unionwide co-operative action to combat crime is obvious, it is equally obvious that the means and methods of co-operative action in criminal law and its enforcement in the European Union must be subject to the highest standards of civil liberties, if European Union citizens are not to feel that integration diminishes rather than enhances their fundamental rights. The issue is one of finding the correct balance between the powers of the criminal justice system – now being given an additional EU dimension and writ large on a far more complex multiplicitous European stage – and the rights of the individual citizen.

This is a particular problem for the common law countries, Ireland and the UK, which may well come under pressure to adjust their systems to align with the criminal law and procedures of the majority civil law member states of the EU. Accordingly, it may be in Ireland's interest to work actively with the UK on these issues.

The EU Third Pillar agenda not only faces the problem of significant differences in member states in the area of criminal procedural traditions – for example in the role and importance of the jury, in the operationalisation of the presumption of innocence and in judicicial involvement in investigation – but also in the even more fundamental matter of the definition of what constitutes criminal activity. This is most vividly illustrated in the area of drug crime. Hedy D'Ancona's recent report[31] for the European Parliament's Civil Liberties Committee points to difficulties in reconciling very different ideologies about drugs. Within the EU, policies in this area vary from blatantly repressive, prohibitionist, zero tolerance approaches to relatively tolerant, decriminalisation and harm reduction approaches.

Furthermore, there has been considerable disquiet about decision-making and policy-making procedures in the Third Pillar which were regarded not only as cumbersome and inefficient, but most crucially from the civil libertarian perspective, to be lacking in democratic participation and oversight by judicial review.

From the civil libertarian point of view, a key aspect of the democratic deficit in the Third Pillar area is the lack of information and understanding amongst the ordinary citizens of Ireland and the rest of the Union about the Third Pillar agenda and the ongoing changes. If the Third Pillar agenda advances, it will become an urgent necessity that the public be well informed about the process and its rationale. People will need to be assured of the overall benefits of any changes especially those which may affect their domestic regime of civil liberties.

Civil liberties in Ireland[32]

In Ireland, the Constitution is the bedrock of civil liberties. The Irish Constitution specifies some of the basic rights of citizens and empowers an independent judiciary to interpret and vindicate the rights of citizens as laid down by the Constitution. The basic rights specified in the Constitution include the right to life, person, good name and property,[33] to equality before the law,[34] to personal liberty,[35] to the inviolability of one's home,[36] to be tried on any criminal charge

---

[31] D'Ancona H. (1998), Report to the European Parliament Civil Liberties Committee
[32] Civil liberties as defined for the purposes of this chapter are confined to the rights of citizens affected by the operation of the state's criminal justice system
[33] Article 40.3.2
[34] Article 40.1
[35] Article 40.4.1
[36] Article 40.5

only in accordance with the law,[37] to trial by jury[38] and not to be subject to retrospective criminal legislation.[39] In vindicating the rights of citizens the Irish judiciary, exercising its prerogative to interpret the Constitution, has extended the framework of constitutional safeguards, relying on the "unenumerated rights" contained in Article 40.3.1 of the Constitution and has extended the scope of the citizen's constitutional rights in many positive ways, establishing a generally satisfactory regime of constitutionally based individual rights in criminal justice. However, this process of positive, judge-made law has co-existed with a judicial acquiescence in the use of the Emergency Powers Act and the Offences Against the State Act that may dilute civil liberties in this country.

The current regime of civil liberties, especially as it applies to criminal procedure and the endeavour to protect the individual's basic right not to be convicted incorrectly, is a highly complex and delicately balanced mosaic. At the heart of the regime are the principles that a suspect is presumed innocent until proven guilty beyond a reasonable doubt and that the burden of proof lies with the prosecution. A complex set of procedural rules, governing the key component actions in the criminal justice process, such as arrest, search, detention, the collection and use of evidence, interrogation and the running of trials, has evolved and constitutes, inter alia, what is considered to be a workable and principled balance between the powers and rights of the state and the accused.

This complex legal framework is not entirely fixed or beyond criticism. Ireland does not have an optimal, proven and finally settled regime of civil liberties. The operating of prisons is still governed by the 1947 rules,[40] which allow for corporal punishment, starvation diets and other vestiges of an earlier era and new rules proposed in 1994[41] were severely criticised as falling short of the minimum standards set by the European Prison Rules.[42] The debate continues in regard to such issues as the right to silence, the right to bail and the exclusionary rule, whereby unconstitutionally obtained evidence can be ruled inadmissible. The police have sought and gained greater powers of search and detention. Legislation restricting bail and allowing preventative detention has been introduced. Legislation to restrict the right to silence is also being introduced. Civil libertarians have attempted, to a large extent unsuccessfully, to resist such changes. Recent trends in legislation and the continued use of Special Powers and the

---

[37] Article 38.1
[38] Article 38.5
[39] Article 15.5
[40] Rules for the Government of Prisons Statutory Instrument 320 of 1947
[41] Department of Justice, *The Management of Offenders: A Five Year Plan* (1994), Dublin: Stationery Office
[42] Irish Commission for Justice and Peace (1994), *Human rights in prison,* Dublin: Irish Bishops' Commission for Justice and Peace, and O'Mahony P. (1995), "On Human Rights in Prison", *The Furrow* (46:3) 144-152

acceptance in Irish criminal courts of uncorroborated retracted confessions[43] is a cause of great concern. One cannot, therefore, be confident that an Irish government would resist pressure for changes either at a domestic or European Union level that might irrevocably compromise the Irish civil liberties regime.

The ECHR

In examining possible future changes and challenges to Irish civil liberties arising from the new Third Pillar it is relevant that the European Union leans very heavily on the European Convention on Human Rights (ECHR) for the expression and definition of fundamental rights, including those associated with the criminal justice system which may be classified as civil liberties. The ECHR played a significant role in the limited public debate in Ireland in the 1996 bail referendum. The ECHR states clearly that it is permissible under the Convention to refuse bail to an accused on the grounds that this might prevent a future offence. This ECHR position contradicted that of the Irish Supreme Court and thus constituted a lower standard of civil liberties than did the Irish Constitution prior to that referendum.

The ECHR is thus to some extent a minimum standards document that reflects an attempted compromise between very different legal systems. The ECHR has, nevertheless, played an immensely important role in creating a European culture of human rights and represents a widely accepted set of basic principles of fundamental rights and is obviously the key instrument in the evolving European Union consensus on these issues. This is underlined by the fact that all member states of the EU have adopted or are about to adopt the ECHR as part of their domestic law.

The current situation in Ireland is that the government proposes that the ECHR be incorporated into Irish law at a sub-constitutional level through an interpretative model of incorporation, which "means, in effect, that every statute should, subject to the constitutional obligation of the court to give effect to its clear meaning, be interpreted and applied as far as the Constitution permits in accordance with the Convention".[44] It should be said that Gerard Hogan SC, an eminent constitutional lawyer, is of the view that "incorporation is unlikely to make any profound difference in strict legal terms given the existing provisions of our fundamental rights guarantees in the Constitution".[45]

The principal articles of the ECHR relevant to the present discussion are Articles 3 (prohibiting torture, inhuman or degrading treatment or punishment), 4

---

[43] O'Mahony P. (1997), "The Garda Síochána and the Ethics of Police Interrogation", *Irish Criminal Law Journal* (4:1) 129-140

[44] Opening Address by Attorney General Michael McDowell SC to Law Society of Ireland Conference on the Incorporation of the ECHR into Irish law, 14 October, 2000

[45] The Incorporation of the ECHR into Irish Domestic Law, Law Society Conference, 14 October, 2000

(prohibiting the holding of persons in servitude or slavery), 5 (dealing with the conditions under which detention is lawful and allowing the review of the legality of detention), 6 (concerning the presumption of innocence and the right to a fair trial) and 8 (concerning respect for private and family life, home and correspondence). The European Prison Rules (1987) also have a significant role as guidelines, although they have no formal or legal status. From the civil libertarian perspective, the provisions for derogation, under Article 15(1), do create problems For example, in *Brogan v UK* (1984), the UK was found to be in breach of Article 5(3), which requires a suspect to be brought promptly before a judge. However, the UK derogated from the Convention on this issue. Similarly, in the Court's very first case, *Lawless v Ireland* (1961), internment without trial was held not to be in breach, because Ireland had derogated from the terms of the Convention, as, under Article 15(1), is allowable in a time of national emergency

A significant recent development is the extension of the operations of the Council of Europe into the area of monitoring mechanisms, designed to improve the protection and enforcement of human and fundamental rights. In Ireland, this process is most obvious with respect to the role of the Committee for the Prevention of Torture (CPT), which has now visited Ireland twice to examine conditions of detention. The CPT is a very useful instrument, insofar as it creates public debate, raises consciousness of key, but often neglected, issues and facilitates the setting of high standards in everyday criminal justice practice.

Mutual assistance

The new Convention on Mutual Assistance raises a series of civil liberties concerns. In the first place, the Convention will facilitate a wide degree of co-operation in the interception of telecommunications that will largely ignore the different rules in different member states regarding permitting law enforcement agencies to intercept telecommunications.

Important safeguards have been written into the Convention with respect to interception – that irrelevant material should be deleted either before or after transfer of the intercept, that the subject of the interception should be notified of the interception, and that the evidence in intercepted, recorded and transcribed correspondence should not be used for any purposes other than that forming the basis of the request for assistance. These safeguards are in line with the Council of Europe's Recommendation R(85)10 and seek to ensure that interception "is resorted to only where it is absolutely necessary, as it implies a far-reaching invasion into the privacy of the subscriber, who enjoys protection under Article 8 of the ECHR". However, these safeguards as laid down in the Convention are to be discretionary, not mandatory.

Secondly, the whole area of covert investigation and surveillance and seizure and search on behalf of another jurisdiction is rife with possibilities for infringements of civil liberties and it would appear that monitoring provisions in the Convention in this regard are inadequate. The Convention allows for the control of suspect deliveries, for example illicit drugs, which raises possible problems of entrapment and reliance on informants who are not under police control.

Thirdly, there is no provision for "allocating legal responsibility for any damage to and/or interference with the rights of the individual caused by measures taken as a result of mutual assistance activities".[46]

Europol

Europol, including the Europol Drugs Union, Eurodac (the fingerprint recording system for asylum seekers), and the Schengen Information System (currently evolving into EIS) are initiatives with direct and immediate implications for civil liberties. The latter two information systems were instruments initially designed for migration and asylum controls but which can also be employed for crime-control purposes.

The key civil liberties issues, arising from Europol and the other current initiatives in the Third Pillar area in respect of information sharing, are related to the need to construct effective checks and balances on surveillance, intelligence gathering, and information storage and exchange.

Two central issues are the quality of data gathered and the legality of the means of intelligence gathering. There must be some disquiet about the possibility that information received by one member state from another might be the result of the exertion of undue force, perhaps even torture, or the use of methods of evidence-gathering that would be illegal or unconstitutional in the receiving state. Europol represents a centralised, highly structured system for the sharing of information and may well operate in a way that enhances the legality of information gathering. On the other hand, the primary focus of Europol is undoubtedly on the value of information for fighting crime and not on its provenance. By and large, the legality of information will be taken for granted – that is on trust – and there would appear to be few effective safeguards against the use of wrongfully obtained information. Because much of the information gathered by police authorities may arise from mere suspicion, the issue of the quality of shared information is of primary importance.

In general, it appears that, at the level of Europol, it is likely that there will be a presumption of the legality and validity of the information received with few if any means for Europol to confirm the trustworthiness and provenance of the information received. While Europol will operate in a manner consonant with the data protection legislation in each of the member states, this provides little

---

[46] House of Lords (1998) Paper 72, Select Committee on the European Communities, "Mutual Assistance in Criminal Matters": Minutes of Evidence, at 20

consolation, because computerised investigative information about crime or suspected crime is generally exempt from such control. Personal data concerning activities of the state in areas of criminal law were excluded from the EC Data Protection Directive. den Boer[47] argues that there is a need for clear and accessible mechanisms to monitor activities in this area and to curtail and remedy abuses of information by the new systems being established at the level of the Union.

CONCLUSIONS

The need for greater co-operation at the level of the European Union in combating Unionwide crime has been acknowledged at the highest political level. The European Union Heads of State and Government have stated that *people have the right to expect the European Union to address the threat to their freedom and legal rights posed by serious crime. To counter these threats a common effort is needed to prevent and fight crime and criminal organisations throughout the European Union. The joint mobilisation of police and judicial resources is needed to guarantee that there is no hiding place for criminals or the proceeds of crime within the European Union.*[48] Thus the prevention, detection and prosecution of organised and serious crime at the level of the Union are now at the top of the EU's political agenda. This is so notwithstanding the fact that the Amsterdam Treaty reserved to member states responsibility for the maintenance of law and order and the safeguarding of internal security. It is recognition of the increasing importance of cross-border crime within the European Union and of the inability of a single Member State acting on its own to combat such criminal activity effectively.

While there is a reluctance by member states to countenance a ceding of sovereignty in the area of criminal law and policing the reality is that the cross-border nature and sophistication of organised and serious crime within the European Union is such that greater co-operation, involving as it does some pooling of sovereignty among member states, is essential if individual member states are to retain effective control over such criminal activity affecting their jurisdiction.

The Third Pillar measures on police co-operation and mutual assistance in criminal matters are clearly advancing quite rapidly and already cover areas of complexity, both legally and technically, which the general population might find surprising and mystifying. The intergovernmental nature of these measures means that they involve no real attempt at harmonisation of laws and procedures; rather, difficulties arising from differences in the systems are short circuited by mechanisms that place the onus of accountability for the legality and fairness of

---

[47] den Boer 1997, "Wearing it inside out: European Police Co-operation between Internal and External Security", in *European Foreign Affairs Review* 2.4
[48] Conclusion No. 6 of the Tampere European Council

procedures on one or other of the co-operating countries. These countries are then bound to act only in accordance with their own laws and under the general provisions of the ECHR. The primary emphasis of the measures is on securing viable and effective mechanisms of co-operation rather than on ensuring the protection of fundamental rights as a precondition for such co-operative activity.

den Boer[49] has stated that "Sweden and Finland's accession to the EU has brought with it a civil policing culture which literally seems miles away from the semi-military policing cultures in Southern Europe. In Southern Europe, the repressive approach to crime problems prevails and there is a high level of tolerance vis-à-vis information networking and grey information exchange and institutional links between police and prosecution services".

The Irish tradition of policing is similar to that of the Nordic countries – though not as strong in terms of accountability – and it is very much the tradition of an unarmed police force, enforcing the law within the context of popular consent. In Ireland, in addition, the judicial role is totally separate from and independent of the prosecution role. In the context of co-operation between police agencies from both traditions, there must be some concern that civil policing traditions might be diluted or contaminated by militaristic approaches or approaches that do not fully respect the independence of the judiciary from the prosecution process. Equally, it is a matter of concern that new structures and procedures within Europol should not be moulded in a fashion that compromises essential civil policing traditions or common law principles such as the presumption of innocence.

Given the many complex and challenging difficulties thrown up by the Third Pillar, there is a clear need at both the national and EU level for a more proactive approach to the protection of civil liberties. To some extent this has been recognised with the call by the European Council for the consolidation in a Charter of the fundamental rights applicable in the Union. The protection of fundamental rights is seen as a founding principle of the Union and an indispensable prerequisite for its legitimacy. Establishing a Charter is seen as a means of making the importance of respect for fundamental rights more visible to the Union's citizens. The Charter should contain the fundamental rights and freedoms (human rights) as well as basic procedural rights guaranteed by the ECHR and others derived from the constitutional traditions common to the member states (civil liberties as defined in this chapter). The Charter should also include fundamental rights that pertain only to Union citizens and economic and social rights as established by the European Social Charter and the Community Charter of the Fundamental Social Rights of Workers.

---

[49] den Boer 1997, "Wearing it inside out: European Police Co-operation between Internal and External Security", in *European Foreign Affairs Review* 2.4

This is clearly a positive step that will provide an opportunity to address and perhaps resolve some of the critical differences between the civil liberties traditions of the member states and extend upon the foundation of the rather minimalist principles of the ECHR. There would be an added positive dimension to the concept of EU citizenship and obvious practical advantages for EU citizens if fundamental rights were enshrined as an integral part of EU law.

However praiseworthy, this Charter of Rights must be a supranational rather than an intergovernmental instrument and will be of limited value if it merely sets out aspirational general principles rather than legally binding obligations on member states. Only in this way will it have a positive and permanent impact on the civil liberties regimes of member states. Furthermore, the effective implementation of the Charter will necessarily involve the European Court of Justice having jurisdiction to vindicate the citizens' fundamental rights whenever these have been violated by EU institutions or member states.

At a less elevated but more practical level a strong argument can be made in favour of the immediate establishment of some form of Independent Monitoring Agency on Civil Liberties at EU level, charged with monitoring the actual impact of the new forms of co-operation in police and criminal law matters provided for under the new Third Pillar. This agency, which should be independent of all member state and EU institutions, could inform the individual citizens of their rights, process specific complaints and inform citizens of the remedies available. Such an agency could also assess the impact on civil liberties of all new measures adopted under the Third Pillar and publish the results of its analysis. It could undertake specific investigations of alleged malpractice and order remedies where appropriate. As a disseminator of information and a repository of complaints such an agency could usefully inform the policy makers in adopting more refined and effective systems which guarantee fundamental rights in the European Union.

The way forward is to build powerful, independent mechanisms for the protection of civil liberties into the institutional structure. The need for organised monitoring structures applies equally at the local Irish level. It is clearly desirable that the government would fund an independent body, charged with the task of examination of the impact on Irish civil liberties of all the Third Pillar initiatives. A joint committee with the British with a view to monitoring and helping manage the evolution of both common law jurisdictions, in the context of increasing pressure to adapt to civil law methods, would also be invaluable. It is likely that, in the absence of such systems for the protection of fundamental rights and for the gathering, analysis and dissemination of information on the effects of Third Pillar developments on civil liberties, the ordinary citizen will increasingly feel himself or herself to be the impotent subject of a Kafkaesque system of unintelligible complexity and insidiously sinister powers.

SECTION 4

THE COURTS

18

Introduction

Paul O'Mahony

The courts play an essential role in the criminal justice system, trying and processing cases and dispensing justice and sanctions in accordance with the law. Most observers would probably profess general satisfaction at the evident professionalism, independence, integrity and, perhaps most important of all, freedom from corruption of the Irish judiciary. However, in recent years the reputation of the judiciary has not been entirely unblemished and the most significant case in which judges came under suspicion, the Sheedy case, finally led to the resignation of a High Court judge, a Supreme Court judge and a senior court official.

The controversy focused on the procedurally irregular, early release by the courts, in late 1998, of a well-connected, middle-class person, who had been sentenced to four years imprisonment for manslaughter while drunk-driving. A relative of the convicted man had approached a Supreme Court judge on the street and discussed the case. The judge, as a consequence of this conversation, made an intervention which facilitated the review of the case and Sheedy's subsequent early release. There were other irregularities in the manner in which the case was handled in the Circuit Court. All of this led to allegations of favouritism, class bias and political influence in the supposedly independent and impartial judicial process.

As a response to the Sheedy case and other instances of alleged judicial misconduct and to the general pressure for greater accountability and transparency in all sectors of the public service, proposals have been made for a disciplinary council to investigate complaints against judges. A committee of the judiciary has proposed a council that will examine alleged cases of misconduct and will be empowered to issue a private or public reprimand or, in the most serious cases, a recommendation that the judge be impeached and removed from office by the Oireachtas. While the judiciary itself proposes that this body should be entirely composed of judges, the Minister for Justice, Equality and Law Reform has argued that, while a majority of judges on the regulatory council would be appropriate as a mechanism for maintaining judicial independence, there should be substantial lay representation.

There has also been public concern about another area of discretionary power in the criminal process, that is the power of the Director of Public Prosecutions to pursue or not to pursue particular prosecutions. While the need to maintain the independence of this office is generally recognised, the new public demand for transparency and accountability has ensured that the director's office will at least provide an aggregated, outline account of the reasoning behind decisions not to prosecute in an annual report to the minister.

The Irish judiciary is an appointed body of men and, increasingly, women, who all have a background in professional law. There is no lay magistracy as in England and Wales and there is no form of election to the judiciary as in parts of the US. Judges are appointed by the government, but, since 1995, this is done on the advice of a Judicial Appointments Board, which is chaired by the Chief Justice and has representatives from the judiciary, the legal professions and the lay public. This new procedure, which entails newspaper advertisements for all judicial positions, including membership of the Supreme Court, was prompted by the new-found concern in Irish society for transparency and accountability.

Previously, judicial appointments were highly politicised. As one commentator, drawing attention to the dangers of the old system, put it, "alliance with a particular political party can almost certainly bring political favour, possibly resulting in a judicial appointment" (Houlihan 1986). The current system of appointment is not immune to political favouritism, but it introduces a strong component of peer review and extends the scope of scrutiny over the process. Generally, it can be said that the judiciary, although overwhelmingly middle-class and often from a legal family background, has tended to include a strong representation of minorities. For example, the Supreme Court presently includes Protestant members and until recently included a Jewish member, though the country is, nominally at least, 95% Catholic.

In addition to concerns about the impartiality of the appointment system and, occasionally, about the probity of the manner in which judges exercise their powers, there is very serious public disquiet about the efficiency and efficacy of the courts system, about the consistency and appropriateness of judicial sentencing and about the actual impact of criminal sanctions on the reduction of crime. It is widely believed that aspects of current criminal law, especially those dealing with criminal procedure, are antiquated, inadequate, and not appropriate to modern circumstances. Common law and statute law in the area are the result of the accretion over centuries of a complex, unwieldy set of legal rules and procedures. There have been numerous court cases in recent years where the police, prosecution, defendants and their legal counsels, victims and even the judiciary themselves appear frustrated at the vagaries, complexities and limits of the current criminal legal structure.

The dominant public and political attitude today depicts the legal system as weighted in favour of defendants (or, in popular discourse, criminals) rather than crime victims or society at large. This attitude, which would probably not withstand a robust critical analysis, has nonetheless translated into pressure on the established tradition of legal procedures and principles designed to provide due process and protect civil liberties, particularly the civil liberties of criminal defendants. For example, in recent legislation there has been considerable encroachment of various kinds on the underlying core principle of the presumption of innocence.

The most obvious example of the public and political zeal for hardline legal reform is the bail referendum of November 1996, in which an amendment to the Constitution was passed by a three-to-one majority allowing for preventative detention of suspects awaiting trial. In other words, it allowed the refusal of bail on the grounds of reasonable suspicion that the suspect would commit an offence if freed on bail. But there have been other examples, such as in the case of drugs dealers the introduction of seven day detention without charge and the curtailment, in certain circumstances, of the right to silence. The Criminal Justice (Drug Trafficking) Act 1996 provides that failure by a person, being questioned or charged under this Act, to mention a fact, which they subsequently choose to rely on at trial, can be treated by the court as corroboration of other evidence. Furthermore, Minister for Justice John O'Donoghue has announced that he intends a radical reform of criminal justice procedures and has already abolished the preliminary hearing at the District Court level, an important safeguard against trivial or expedient prosecutions by the police.

Suggesting that Ireland may already have unfair and unbalanced laws and procedures governing detention and interrogation, the Court of Human Rights in Strasbourg, in a ruling in the case of *Heaney and McGuiness v Ireland* of November 2000, concluded that the restrictions on the right to silence, under Section 52 of the Offences Against the State Act 1939, were in breach of Article 14 of the European Convention on Human Rights, which pertains to the right to silence and the privilege against self-incrimination. This Section compels persons detained for questioning under the Act to give an account of their movements on pain of committing a criminal offence punishable by six months imprisonment.

There is another indication of recent international disapproval of Irish criminal procedures and, especially, of the use of emergency powers. On 4 May 2001, the

UN Human Rights Committee issued a ruling, under the UN Covenant on Civil and Political Rights, that the Irish State had failed to demonstrate that the decision to try Joseph Kavanagh before the Special Criminal Court was based on reasonable and objective grounds. Only one of the seven charges against Kavanagh, who was convicted and sentenced to twelve years in 1997 for kidnapping the chief executive of National Irish Bank, was a scheduled offence under the Offences Against the State Act. The UN Human Rights Committee found that Kavanagh's right to equality before the law and to equal protection of the law had been violated. In particular, the Irish practice of sending cases to the Special Criminal Court on the basis of a certificate from the Director of Public Prosecutions but without any explanation was condemned as a violation of the accused's right to a jury trial.

Also indicative of a general critical attitude to the criminal legal system are the occasional popular and media outcries about sentences handed down by the courts in individual cases – often involving sex crimes. These furores over "hard cases" have occasionally contributed directly to the introduction of new legis-lation, as, for example, when maximum sentence lengths for certain types of offending have been increased, including the introduction of life sentences for some drug offences and for rape. Similarly, the state was granted through legis-lation the power to appeal a sentence on the basis that it was too lenient, following an outcry over the imposition of only a suspended sentence of imprisonment for rape in the Lavinia Kerwick case (O'Malley 1994).

While in many respects the new attitude of active political shaping of the criminal law and criminal procedures is to be welcomed as a sign of increased democratic control and, perhaps, of socio-political maturity, there are grounds for anxiety that ad hoc changes arising out of a populist political agenda and an emotionally charged, often confused public debate will in the long term not be in the best interests of the system or of justice. For example, Caroline Fennell (1993), a legal expert, has stated that "'Public opinion' has been central to the changes that have been wrought. Spurred on by perceived crises or events in the media, Irish legislators have rushed to assuage fears and temper particular concerns by changing laws to accommodate 'different' views". Similarly, the National Crime Forum (1998) has warned that "erosion of the rights of defendants should be approached with extreme caution, especially in view of the danger that pressure to tilt the balance against the accused may be driven by a media-fuelled public concern".

The pace of change in criminal law and criminal procedure in Ireland in recent years has been very rapid and promises to continue or even accelerate. Unfortunately, there has not been nearly enough cool reflection on and informed analysis of this process of change. There is a general lack of coherence in the area and this is not being properly addressed but is rather intensifying. For instance, the former Director of Public Prosecutions, Eamonn Barnes, has recently made an impassioned and sophisticated plea that the Irish system should adopt some of the approaches of the Continental, inquisitorial judicial process. However, his interesting proposals remain largely unexamined and ignored.

It is also the case that while significant changes, for example to the bail laws, have been rather hurriedly adopted, there has been insufficient attention paid to the underlying practical problems that beset the system. For example, one District Court judge customarily looks up the defendants who come before him on a computerised list of people against whom there are outstanding bench warrants (for failure to appear at another court hearing). The prosecuting garda is often found to be unaware of the many outstanding bench warrants that come to light (O'Mahony 1996b). This clearly exposes an inadequate and inefficient system, evidently lacking an information database and network sufficient to the needs of both the garda and the courts.

It appears that the courts system often lacks the means and the will to pursue cases properly. For example, in March 2001 the Comptroller and Auditor-General's office (*Irish Times* 2001) produced a report indicating that more than a third of all on-the-spot motoring fines in 1998 went unpaid and almost half of these unpaid fines were cancelled or allowed, lapse with a loss of £1.6 million to the exchequer. The report concluded that "most of the offences which go unpunished do so because of weaknesses in the administration and management of fine cases by the Garda Síochána or the Courts Service". Similarly, the system of estreatment of forfeited bail money has for some time been in a total shambles and in some areas has barely operated at all (O'Mahony 1996a). The worry is that while largely cosmetic legislative changes to the system receive much publicity and form the basis for political claims that effective action is being taken, the infrastructural, practical problems that severely inhibit the system will continue unabated.

There are numerous other serious, practical problems with the courts system, ranging from a lack of adequate court buildings and holding cells etc, to failure to develop modern information systems, to poor management and administrative structures, to lack of financial accountability, and to inordinate delays in hearing trials. Recently, average delays in criminal trials have varied from about six to nine months in the District Courts up to almost two years in the Central Criminal Court. At another level, there is concern about the efficiency of and level of resources available to the legal aid system. A core issue is the effectiveness of relatively poorly paid and hard-pressed free legal aid defence lawyers. There is concern that, by comparison with those dependent on legal aid, the wealthy are able to mount highly professional and well-prepared defences and thereby unacceptable inequalities are introduced into the system.

However, there has been some real progress in the general area of the reform of the court system. On the one hand, a substantial number of additional judges have been appointed and a pilot drugs court with the power to sentence non-violent drug-abusing offenders to drug rehabilitation treatment has been established. On the other hand, the Denham Committee on the Courts (1996-98) has produced an incisive and comprehensive critical analysis of the problems of the system. Most significantly, in reponse to the Denham Committee's analysis, a properly resourced Independent Courts Service has been established and is beginning to address the practical and management problems. A rational and credible framework for remedying some of the problems is now in place and considerable progress has been made in improving courts accommodation, making the court process more user-friendly for the ordinary citizen and improving the court experience for victims and witnesses.

One major outstanding problem, however, is the current lack of information on sentencing, the key activity of the judiciary in the criminal courts. While a Judicial Studies Institute has been established in order to provide judges with a forum for education and discussion of sentencing and other issues, there is a highly detrimental vacuum of statistical information and research analysis on the vital function of sentencing. It is hard to see how judges can operate effectively in a system that does not provide them with detailed systematic feedback on their operations and most especially on their sentencing decisions. Indeed, the judiciary itself is aware of this highly unsatisfactory situation and has supported the Law Reform Commission's recommendation for a Sentencing Board that would compile and analyse information on sentencing. The Denham Committee has also recommended that sentencing research should be one of the core functions of the Courts Service, and the National Crime Forum, in its report (1998) states that "perhaps a sentencing review unit within the judiciary might provide a mechanism to help produce the required degree of consistency and transparency".

Information on sentencing is not just essential to the effective functioning of the judiciary, it is also a basic requirement for a full understanding of the criminal justice process, of what it entails and what it achieves. It is clearly important to have as much information as possible on sentencing since it is at the heart of the penal process. There is also the not unimportant matter of the evaluation of the performance of the judiciary in sentencing matters, with regard to consistency, appropriateness, rationality, impartiality etc.

There is a clear need to put the process of producing official criminal justice statistics and analysis on a proper footing. Rottman (1984) has succinctly described three essential criteria for information on criminal justice that the state has yet to fulfil: "1) that it provides the public with an accurate indication of the problem and of what is being done about it; 2) that it allows for accountability and evaluation of what the police, courts, prison service, and Department of Justice have done; 3) that it allows for rational planning.

The judiciary is independent, but in a democracy it is right and fitting that the people should have access to valid and comprehensive information on how judges sentence so that they can draw their own informed conclusions and, if necessary, voice criticism. This task would, of course, require studies that go well beyond the simple compilation of actual sentences. It would be necessary to correlate sentences with the characteristics of individual cases with regard to more subjective matters such as perceived culpability, the seriousness of the offence, the relevance of mitigating circumstances, and the express purposes of the sentence.

At present people attempting to understand the court system and how it is changing are still labouring with the same utterly inadequate level of data described by Rottman in 1984 – "A few tables in the Statistical Abstract indicate the caseloads and the outcome of cases commenced in a particular year. But such information is totally insufficient for even the most elementary description of what the courts are doing and what decisions they are reaching." Trends in sentencing are very important. For example, at present it is impossible to ascertain with any confidence the degree to which increasing prison numbers are related to increasing use of prison sentences by judges or to increasing use of longer prison sentences or to increasing use of remands in custody following the referendum on bail.

Figure 1: trial outcomes Dublin District Courts, 4, 5, and 6 November 1995

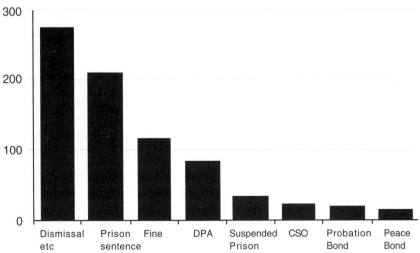

DPA = Dismissal under the Probation of Offenders Act 1907; CSO = Community Service Order
Source: O'Mahony 1996b

As Figure 1 indicates, the sentencing situation is complex. This Figure describes the breakdown of outcomes of one month's cases in the Dublin District Courts. There are many alternative sanctions to custody and it is vitally important for us to understand how, to what extent, in what circumstances, and to what effect they are used. Given that the main purposes of sentencing are deterrence, re-habilitation, public denunciation and punishment, it is surely essential to gather data on the differential success of the various types of sentence. Equally it is important to study the whole question of pleas, ie the role of guilty pleas, plea-bargaining (which exists only in an unrecognised, tacit form in the Irish courts), and contested trials. The prevalence of and reasons for dismissals and acquittals are also of great interest.

This dearth of hard data and analysis on sentencing is all the more serious because of the compelling evidence that the Irish judiciary is out of line with judicial practice in the rest of the EU in its use of imprisonment. Although the number of prisoners in Ireland at any one time per capita of general population is comparatively moderate, when one focuses on the numbers sent to prison (the imprisonment rate) rather than on the numbers held in prison at any one time (the detention rate), the use of incarceration by the Irish courts is found to be extremely high. Looking at committals under conviction only, we find that the Irish imprisonment rate in 1992 was 174 per 100,000 of the general population. This compared with only 34 per 100,000 in France, 24 in Italy, 12 in Portugal, and 90 in the Netherlands (Council of Europe 1993). These are remarkable differences and demonstrate a very heavy use of imprisonment by the Irish courts.

The importance of this finding is underlined by the fact that the crime rate is considerably lower in Ireland than in most of the European countries that use imprisonment far less. Indeed the Irish crime rate is less than a third of the EU average. A dramatic contrast that conveys the distinctiveness of the Irish reliance on prison is that, for every 1,000 crimes recorded by the police, just fourteen people are sent to prison in England and Wales, whereas sixty-eight are sent to prison in Ireland. This means that Irish judges imprison many offenders for relatively petty crimes. Accordingly, about 75% of people are convicted to prison for non-violent offences; many petty offenders are imprisoned on their first offence (O'Mahony 2000); and in recent years around one-third of committals to prison are for failure to pay a fine (Annual Reports on Prisons). Fine-defaulting prisoners tend to spend only a short period in prison, but have committed offences which were originally considered by the court not to merit imprisonment. It is important to note that the Irish reliance on imprisonment and especially on short terms of imprisonment for minor offenders cannot be credited with a significant contribution to the relatively low Irish crime rate, because all the evidence suggests that the recidivism rate for Irish prisoners is one of the highest in the developed world (O'Mahony 2000).

This lack of balance in sentencing cannot be attributed solely to the punitive attitude of judges. The judiciary is constrained by the capacity of the system in respect of community-based sanctions. Indeed, the sentence review system initiated by judges in recent years is evidence of a judicial concern to keep sentence length down. The review system was also partly a response to the "revolving door" syndrome of early release due to overcrowding – an expedient that could be construed as undermining the integrity of the sentencing decision. This review system, which has been more or less abolished by a Supreme Court judgement (*The People v Finn*) in November 2000, involved the recall of an offender to court, usually after two or three years of a long sentence, with the possibility that the judge might suspend the remainder of the sentence if the offender was shown to have made use of the rehabilitative opportunities within prison.

Judges are forced to operate within the practical constraints of the system and the fact is the state has failed drastically to provide an adequate system of alternatives to prison. It has failed to introduce sensible measures, such as attachment of earnings, which would keep fine-defaulters out of prison; it has failed to introduce constructive, innovative approaches such as restorative justice conciliation and restitution; and it has failed to ensure a proper level of resources for the current system of alternative sanctions to custody, such as probation supervision and community service. While considerable investment has been made in the prison system, the Probation and Welfare system has for many years been allowed to stagnate. Less than 200 probation officers, with huge caseloads, presently struggle to maintain the system of community-based sanctions in a country that has more than fifteen times that many prison officers.

While, therefore, there is a huge and urgent need for empirical research on sentencing and the operation of the courts and their ancillary services, there is also a strong case that the whole body of criminal law and criminal procedure is deserving of close examination and possibly wholesale reform. In this regard, the Law Reform Commisssion already plays a leading advisory role and has produced many valuable reports (1987 etc). However, there is a need for a more focused debate and a much more concerted research effort, involving experts from legal science, jurisprudence, political science, administration and criminology, as well as indepth consultation with the general public.

REFERENCES

Annual Reports on Prisons, Department of Justice, Dublin: Stationery Office

Council of Europe 1993, *Penological Information Bulletin* No. 18, Strasbourg: Council of Europe

Denham Commission on the Courts 1996-1998, *First to Sixth Reports of a Working Group on a Courts Commission,* Dublin: Stationery Office

Fennell, C. 1993, *Crime and Crisis in Ireland: Justice by Illusion,* Cork: Cork University

Houlihan, M. 1986, "The Relevance of the Courts" in *Anti-social Behaviour,* Limerick: Mid-West Regional Development Authority

Irish Times 2001, 31 March, *Report on the Auditor-General's Report on Fines*

Law Reform Commission 1987, *Consultation Paper on Rape,* Dublin: Stationery Office

Law Reform Commission 1990, *Report on Child Sexual Abuse,* Dublin: Stationery Office

Law Reform Commission 1993, *Consultation Paper on Sentencing,* Dublin: Stationery Office

Law Reform Commission 1994, *An Examination of the Law of Bail,* Dublin: Stationery Office

Law Reform Commission 1994, *Report on non-fatal offences against the person,* Dublin: Stationery Office

Law Reform Commission 1995, *Consultation Paper on Intoxication as a Defence to a Criminal Offence,* Dublin: Stationery Office

National Crime Forum 1998, *Report,* Dublin: Stationery Office

O'Mahony, P. 1996a, *Criminal Chaos: Seven Crises in Irish Criminal Justice,* Dublin: Round Hall Sweet and Maxwell

O'Mahony, P. 1996b, *An investigation of the operation of the bail system in the Republic of Ireland,* Dublin: Department of Justice

O'Mahony, P. 2000, *Prison Policy in Ireland; Social Justice versus Criminal Justice,* Cork: Cork University Press

O'Malley, T. 1994, "The First Prosecution Appeal against Sentence", *Irish Criminal Law Journal* 4, 192

Rottman, D. 1984, *The Criminal Justice System: Policy and Performance,* Dublin: NESC

19

The Courts Service

P.J. Fitzpatrick

INTRODUCTION

The Irish Courts Service was established in November 1999. Before describing the new service and prior to examining the challenges that lie ahead it is important to reflect on the reasons for the changes, ie the reasons for the establishment of the new Courts Service.

A vacuum was left when the Irish State was established in the 1920s. No department such as that of the Lord Chancellor in England and Wales was established in Ireland. It is understandable in a historical perspective that a newly independent democratic country did not wish to establish a Lord Chancellor's department. Our Constitution is built on the concept of the separation of powers. Instead the scheme implemented was that the Department of Justice managed the courts and their funding apart from judicial salaries. The Department of Justice is the administrative underpinning of the minister who, as a member of the cabinet, is part of the executive branch of government. Thus, a department underpinning the executive was also to manage the courts, the judicial branch of government.

The establishment of an independent Courts Service is an historic move representing unfinished business from the establishment of the state. The state itself moved towards a Constitution closer to that in countries such as the United States of America than that of the United Kingdom. In light of this constitutional framework a Working Group on a Courts Commission studied the administrative infrastructure of the courts in other jurisdictions prior to making recommendations.

The Irish Courts Service as proposed by the Group and now enacted into law represents progress towards a modern structure. It is a uniquely Irish structure which bears some similarities to systems in other countries, and yet at its core it is a wholly Irish organisation pursuant to the Irish Constitution and created to meet the needs of the Irish community. It is a system designed to enable efficient and effective management so that justice may be delivered with greater speed and efficiency to the people. The modernisation of the courts system is taking place at two levels: the creation of a new structure, the Courts Service, and the introduction of modern management techniques throughout the system, as well as the implementation of a major information technology programme.

The Service is responsible for the management and administration of all court services in the state. The Service has no functions relating to the administration of justice. The legislation establishing the Service specifically protects the independence and autonomy of judges in discharging their judicial functions. Judges are not employees of the service. Of course judges and the Service work very closely with each other. There is a high level of interdependence between judges and the Service and one of the functions of the Service is to provide support services for judges.

REPORTS OF THE WORKING GROUP ON A COURTS COMMISSION

The Working Group on a Courts Commission was established in 1996, chaired by Mrs Justice Susan Denham, Judge of the Supreme Court, with the following terms of reference.

1   To review, (a) the operation of the courts system, having regard to the level and quality of service provided to the public, staffing, information technology, etc; (b) the financing of the courts system, including the current relationship between the courts, the Department of Justice and the Oireachtas in this regard; (c) any other aspect of the operation of the courts system which the Group considers appropriate.

2   In the light of the foregoing review, to consider the matter of the establishment of a Commission on the Management of the Courts as an independent and permanent body with financial and management autonomy (as envisaged in the December 1994 document entitled "A Government of Renewal").

3   To have investigative, advisory and recommendation functions and to make a report (and any interim reports and recommendations as they see fit) to the Minister for Justice on the foregoing matters.

The first report of the Working Group (1996) examined the management and financing of the courts. The report noted that the Irish courts system as established in 1924 remained largely unaltered. Yet there had been an enormous increase in civil and criminal litigation with some courts having to cope, on a regular basis, with cases of a length and complexity virtually unknown in earlier times. The administrative infrastructure of the courts had not evolved sufficiently to meet these challenges and there existed an unacceptable delay in the determination of cases. At best this caused an unnecessary stress and anxiety to litigants and, at worst, caused grave injustice.

The overworked and poorly organised court staff, provided administrative support to overburdened judges who were routinely required to work long hours outside of court sitting times. There was a lack of adequate back-up and support services to judges who, together with the staff, operated in inadequate court buildings.

There were many contributing factors to these problems, not least of which were the absence of clear management structures and no clear lines of account-ability and responsibility. No clear reporting structures existed, with a lack of regular channels of communications between the various constituencies which made up the courts' administration. Beyond this, adequate performance measure-ments, the setting of objectives and minimum planning beyond day-to-day procedures, did not take precedence. There was also poor understanding of and non-implementation or innovation in the use of information technology.

The Working Group noted that there was minimum training and development of staff, and little identification of needs, adequate job descriptions or performance standards for staff to follow. This all operated within the framework of a lack of professional management to support any of the above requirements. Structures for responding to initiatives for change were cumbersome and there was evidence of apparent remoteness of the administration system from the judiciary.

A feature of the administrative structures was the fragmentation of administrative systems between each of the courts jurisdictions and an inadequate organisational relationship between the Department of Justice, Equality and Law Reform and courts staff resulting in a basic lack of empowerment or decision making.

The report also concluded that there were a lack of structures to enable responsiveness to the views of court users, lack of financial information on the courts available in an understandable format, and a lack of meaningful statistical information on court activity. On top of this there were no annual reports or a strategic plan for the courts system. Regarding the relationship with the public and court users, the report identified the lack of provision of dignified and adequate courthouses; it noted there was no information service to the public; and reported that the delay in processing litigation in parts of the Court system was at an unacceptable, even a critical, level.

The Working Group was of the view that the problems could not be remedied by the appointment of additional judges, however welcome that was, but what was urgently required was a radical reappraisal of the administrative structures of the courts system. The Working Group considered that access to justice was a fundamental right of citizens and that there was an obligation on the state to provide an efficient and effective courts system through which justice could be dispensed and that system must be accessible to all citizens without undue delay and without incurring unnecessary cost through inefficient or poor management of resources.

The primary recommendation of the Group in its first report was that there should be established by law as a matter of urgency an independent and permanent body to manage a unified court system. The Working Group recommended what the main functions of the Service ought to be and these were subsequently included in the legislation establishing the Service.

The Group recommended that because the functions of the proposed Service did not include the administration of justice (having regard to the constitutional requirement to delineate the powers of the legislative, executive and judicial arms of government) it would be appropriate for judges to work with others on issues such as budgets, accommodation and other administrative matters.

The second report of the Working Group (1996) dealt with case management and court management. The Group continued to find many of the problems which had been detailed in the first report. The Group in its second report recommended the following.

- That the necessary steps be taken to enable appointments to the Presidency of Benches to be for seven years non-renewable.
- That there be greater flexibility in the use of resources to the President of each Bench so that he may request a judge to work on a specific issue, for example the coordination of the Family Courts, the Listing of Cases, the organisation of resources.
- That the Rules Making Committees be enabled to be active vehicles for introducing improvements in the Courts System.
- That ex-officio members be entitled to delegate membership of the Committee to another and that the necessary legislative amendments be carried out.
- That when the proposed Courts Service is established the Chief Executive Officer or his nominees together with a senior member of the staff of the relevant jurisdiction nominated by the Chief Executive Officer be members of each of the Rules Making Committees and the necessary legislative steps be taken.
- That the resources of the proposed Courts Service be available to the Rules Making Committees.
- That each Rules Making Committee make an annual report to the Courts Service for inclusion in the annual published report.

The Group also examined judicial case management and recommended and set out an ongoing consultation process to facilitate continuing debate on this issue.

The third report (1996) concentrated on two specific areas: a) the legal framework for the proposed Service; and (b) broad management approaches to the changing structure.

The fourth report of the Group (1997) was in response to a request from the Minister for Justice that the Group prepare a report on the specific subject of the post of Chief Executive of the Courts Service.

The Group also produced a report (1997) on presentations made to the Conference on Case Management organised by the Group in May 1997.

The fifth report of the Working Group (1998) related to the establishment of Drug Courts and the Working Group also prepared a Paper on Information and the Courts (1997).

The sixth and final report of the Group (1998) addressed issues within the areas of: Information and the Courts; Family Courts; Court Vacations; and Judicial Conduct and Ethics

THE COURTS SERVICE ACT – 1998

The government accepted the recommendation that an independent agency be established to manage the courts. The Courts Service Act 1998 established the Service, determined the membership and functions of the board, the functions of the Service and the functions of the chief executive officer. The 1998 Act also provided for the establishment of a transitional board. The functions of the transitional board were to make arrangements for the establishment of the Service, and to appoint a chief executive officer (designate).

The transitional board was established in May 1998. A chief executive (designate) was appointed and took up duty in January 1999. A work programme for the establishment of the Service and for the transfer of functions from the Department of Justice, Equality and Law Reform was prepared. A target date of November 1999 was set for the establishment of the Service. The work programme was completed on schedule and the Service was established on target on 9 November 1999 just four years following the setting up of the Working Group and three years following the publication of its first report recommending a separate agency.

THE COURTS SERVICE

The functions of the Courts Service are set out in section 5 of the 1998 Courts Service Act and are

- to manage the courts
- to provide support services for the judges
- to provide information on the courts system to the public
- to provide, manage and maintain court buildings
- to provide facilities for users of the courts.

The Courts Service is accountable to the Minister for Justice, Equality and Law Reform and, through the minister, to the government. It is also accountable to the Dáil Public Accounts Committee. The chief executive officer is the accounting officer and will appear before this and other Dáil committees when requested. The Service must also provide an annual written report to the minister of its activities during the previous twelve months. The Service will account to the public by the publication of strategic plans and annual reports.

The Board

The board of the Courts Service consists of a chairperson and sixteen members. The chairperson is the Chief Justice or another judge of the Supreme Court nominated by him/her. The composition of the board is

- the Chief Justice or a Supreme Court judge nominated by him/her
- a judge of the Supreme Court elected by the ordinary judges of that court
- the presidents of the High Court, the Circuit Court and the District Court or judges of these courts nominated by the respective presidents
- a judge of the High Court, the Circuit Court and the District Court elected by the judges of the respective courts
- a judge nominated by the Chief Justice in respect of expertise in a specific area of court business
- a practising barrister, nominated by the chairman for the time being of the Council of the Bar of Ireland
- a practising solicitor, nominated by the president for the time being of the Law Society of Ireland
- an elected staff member
- an officer of the Minister for Justice, Equality and Law Reform
- a nominee of the minister representing consumer interests
- a nominee of the Irish Congress of Trade Unions
- a further nominee of the minister of a person with relevant knowledge and experience in commerce, finance or administration
- the chief executive officer

The functions of the board are to consider and determine policy for the Service and to oversee the implementation of that policy by the chief executive officer. In carrying out its functions the board must have regard to the resources of the

Service and the need to secure the most beneficial, effective and efficient use of such resources, and any policy or objective of the government or a minister of the government insofar as it may affect or relate to a function of the Service. The board has the authority to appoint committees and to date has established three committees: a Finance and Audit Committee; a Family Law Court Development Committee; and a District Court Committee.

The chief executive officer is the accounting officer for the Service and is responsible for the management, control of staff, administration and business of the Service. He/she is responsible to the board for the performance of his/her functions and for the implementation of the policies and programmes approved by the board. The chief executive officer may arrange to have some of his/her functions delegated to others.

The senior management structure is comprised of the chief executive officer and six directors: a Director of Operations for the Supreme and High Courts, a Director of Operations for the Circuit and District Courts, a Director of Human Resource, a Director of Finance, a Director of Corporate Services and a Director of Estates and Buildings.

Funding for the Service is provided by the state. In the year 2001 the total funding is £66.69m. The Service employs just in excess of 1,000 staff in 70 offices in Dublin and throughout the state.

EXTERNAL ENVIRONMENT

The environment in which the courts and court officers operate has changed enormously during the course of the last two decades. There is an increased emphasis on accountability in the public service generally and the rapid pace of technological change has major implications for the way court offices manage their business. For all of these reasons the Service must be proactive and founded on forward planning.

The Courts Service is very conscious that it operates in a dynamic environment. This environment has altered dramatically and is currently undergoing shifts which are unprecedented and which require a vibrant and responsive organisation to keep pace. These changes have contributed to the establishment of the Service and a critical role for the Service will be to seek to anticipate changes in the environment and to be proactive. The actual and anticipated changes and developing trends are in the political, social, economic and technological spheres. Those impacting on the Courts Service include

- an increasing emphasis on accountability right across the public service
- continuing rapid developments in the information technology area and their capacity to impact on the operations of the courts, most recently reflected in the government's e-commerce initiative

- greater complexity in legislation and the consequent requirement for the courts to be in a position to respond speedily
- an increasing awareness of rights and greater recourse to litigation
- an increase in legislation which impacts on the business of the courts
- increasing public expectation regarding the quality and timeliness of services provided
- strong willingness on the part of the legislature to tackle crime and delays in the administration of justice
- recent moves towards alternative means of dispute resolution
- increasing numbers of support and interest groups
- international developments and links with other jurisdictions
- increasing impact of European Union initiatives, including the introduction of the Euro
- changing trends in social relationships and family models
- current difficulties in recruiting and retaining staff throughout the public service.

An effective Service is critical to an effective system for the administration of justice by the judiciary. The Working Group on a Courts Commission (1996) stated "an efficient management system is of the utmost importance to the courts and the state ... The service which is provided by the court system is the means by which the public obtain justice. An inefficient service impedes justice. In addition, the Courts Service is of importance to the commerce and business community. Commerce is at a disadvantage if the system is inefficient and ineffective."

EARLY INITIATIVES

The transition and transfer of functions to the Service was implemented smoothly with no disruption to services. Prior to establishment day agreement was reached with the unions representing staff on a whole range of issues critical to a smooth transition and these included

- design and implementation of senior management structures with clear lines of accountability
- unified staff structures
- new arrangements for filling promotional posts (ie competitive interview and abolition of seniority system).

Strategic planning

The Service has prepared its first three year strategic plan which was published in November 2000. This plan contains our mission statement, the values and principles that will underpin the implementation of the plan and our high-level goals and objectives for the next three years. Annual business planning has commenced in all directorates and offices and is the means by which the strategies contained in the strategic plan will be implemented throughout the organisation. Business processes are being reviewed in all offices and court rules are being examined to identify the changes necessary to facilitate computerisation and other business process improvements. A performance management system is also being introduced.

Information technology

We have prepared and published a five-year Information Technology Strategy (February 2001) which will cost in excess of £50m (at current prices). Considerable progress has already been made in implementing new computerised systems. A new criminal case management tracking system has been implemented in the Dublin and Limerick District Courts. Local and wide area networks have been installed in Dublin and will be installed in all offices in the state this year. Implementation of a major courts accounting and funds management system(s) will commence shortly. A new financial management system will also be implemented this year. A major civil case management and tracking system is being planned at present. Our five-year Information Technology Strategy includes the introduction of a whole range of e-services including e-filing, e-submissions, e-payment, etc. The implementation of the plan will enable the Service to deliver the government's policy to put in place arrangements to enable citizens to conduct their business with the state electronically.

Information

Providing information on the courts system is a key mandate for the Service. An information office has been established and includes a statistics unit. A number of information booklets have been prepared, published and widely distributed. A website (www.courts.ie) has been developed and contains much information about the courts system, the Courts Service and all our publications. The legal diary is published on the website each evening for the following day(s). A Courts Service newsletter is now published five times per year and is widely circulated to staff, judges and practitioners. Our first annual report has been published and a new media relations service has been put in place.

Court buildings

There are at present almost 230 buildings where courts sit, seventy of these are rented, almost eighty are used exclusively by the courts and the remainder are jointly occupied. Many of the court buildings around the country are in the ownership of the local authorities and the Courts Service has commenced the transfer of ownership of sixty of these buildings to the Service. One of the biggest and most expensive tasks facing the Service is the provision of modern day acceptable buildings and facilities for all court users. Most venues require substantial upgrading and/or replacement. An interim five-year building plan was completed in mid-2000 with an implementation cost of £119.5m. By the middle of 2001 a seven-year building plan will be completed. This will include all venues to be upgraded/refurbished over the next seven years. Since establishment building projects have been completed in nine locations. Construction is under-way in a further six locations. Planning of major progammes are well advanced in a further thirteen locations. Early planning has commenced in a further sixteen locations. Plans have been finalised for a major Family Law Centre in Dublin. Plans are well advanced for a major reorganisation/upgrading programme in the Four Courts. A consultation protocol has been put in place to ensure that all users are consulted about plans for all new projects.

Judicial support unit

A judicial support unit has been established to provide administrative support and assistance to the judiciary, the Judicial Studies Institute and the Judicial Appointments Advisory Board.

Projects

A pilot Drug Court has been established for a period of eighteen months in the Dublin Metropolitan District Court which provides for the imposition of a drug treatment programme as an alternative to a custodial sentence for persons convicted of non-violent drug offences.

A pilot project to provide information on activity and judgments, while pro-tecting the identities of the parties and with their consent, will shortly commence in the Dublin Family Law Courts.

A major training programme for all staff has been developed by our human resources directorate and funding for staff training has been substantially increased. Court rules are being examined to identify the changes required to facilitate computerisation and other business process improvements.

The foregoing is but a sample of the many issues being addressed by the new Service. Of course there are many others, all of which would be impossible to detail in this chapter. I have sought to convey an overview of the modernisation programmes in which the Service is involved.

REFERENCES

Working Group on a Courts Commission 1996, First Report, *Management and Financing the Courts*, Pn2691, Dublin: Stationery Office

Working Group on a Courts Commission 1996, Second Report, *Case Management and Court Management*, Dublin: Stationery Office

Working Group on a Courts Commission 1996, Third Report, *Towards the Courts Service*, Commission Pn3274, Dublin: Stationery Office

Working Group on a Courts Commission 1997, Fourth Report, *The Chief Executive of the Courts Service*, Commission Pn3766, Dublin: Stationery Office

Working Group on a Courts Commission 1997, A Working Paper, *Conference on Case Management*

Working Group on a Courts Commission 1997, A Working Paper, *A working paper on Information and the Courts*

Working Group on a Courts Commission 1998, Fifth Report, *Drugs Court*, Pn 5186, Dublin: Stationery Office

Working Group on a Courts Commission 1998, Sixth Report, *Conclusion*, Pn 6533, Dublin: Stationery Office

20

The Practice of Sentencing in the Irish Courts

Ivana Bacik

INTRODUCTION

The starting point for any consideration of sentencing practice in the Irish courts must be a comment on the lack of raw data. In short, very little is known about the reality of sentencing practice in Ireland. It is this lack of basic data that hinders most seriously the development of any real knowledge about sentencing practice. In this chapter, it is proposed to present a review of what literature is available on the actual practice of sentencing, and to attempt an analysis of sentencing practice based on the limited empirical data.

PRINCIPLES OF SENTENCING

Because statistics on sentencing practice are not readily accessible, it is difficult to determine what criteria or principles in fact guide judges in this jurisdiction in their determination of sentence. No source for guidance in sentencing exists for judges in this jurisdiction. By contrast, in many other jurisdictions sentencing guidance is provided either by means of a statutory sentencing scheme, or through guideline judgments given by superior courts.

The Law Reform Commission recommended in 1996 that a sentencing policy, based on the "just deserts" model, should be developed by the legislature, and enshrined in non-statutory guidelines.[1] The severity of the sentence would be

---

[1] *Law Reform Commission Consultation Paper on Sentencing*, Dublin: Government Publications, 1993, and *LRC Report on Sentencing*, Dublin: Government Publications, 1996 (LRC 53-1996)

determined in proportion to the seriousness of the crime, which itself would be measured according to two factors; the degree of harm caused or risked by the offender, and his or her level of culpability. This model was, however, criticised by a minority of the Commission, who favoured a more rehabilitative approach.

In his seminal work on Irish sentencing law and policy, O'Malley recommended both limited statutory intervention, similar to the English Powers of the Criminal Courts Act 1973, and appellate court guidance, to be provided by the Court of Criminal Appeal through grouping together similar cases and creating benchmark judgments. However, he also suggested that "descriptive guidance" for judges in sentencing should be facilitated through developing a "sentencing information system".[2]

Such a system would provide judges with case histories or case summaries out of which key terms could be highlighted, so that a judge could see how other judges were sentencing in similar cases. A start has been made in this regard, through the introduction of seminars on sentencing for Circuit Court judges, an initiative being run by the president of the Circuit Court which commenced in 1999. These seminars may in time produce more formal sentencing manuals for judges, which in turn will lead to greater consistency among judges in their sentencing practice.

Similarly, since the early 1990s more attention has been given to the provision of information to district judges about sentencing practice. Newly appointed district judges now attend an induction course and sit with another judge, who acts as a mentor, for some weeks before sitting alone. A handbook is circulated to all new district judges, and two meetings of district judges are held each year, at which sentencing matters, among other issues, are discussed. A residential conference for the judges is also held every year, at which specific topics such as drugs offences are discussed in depth.

This new approach to judicial training goes some way to creating O'Malley's model of "descriptive guidance" and, if it becomes more formally structured, may well enable the development of an effective sentencing policy.

SENTENCING OPTIONS

Leaving aside the absence of a stated policy to guide judges in sentencing, a range of sentencing options exists. The penalty of the immediate custodial sentence is available, known as imprisonment in the case of adult offenders, or detention in respect of juvenile offenders. The alternative custodial option of penal servitude was abolished by the Criminal Law Act 1997, although in recent decades it was for most practical purposes identical to imprisonment. Judges may also impose

---

[2] O'Malley, T., *Sentencing Law and Practice*, Dublin: Round Hall Ltd, 2000, pp. 451-2

suspended custodial sentences. There is no statutory basis for the suspended sentence, but judges have traditionally assumed the power to suspend sentences, and the practice of suspension has been given the imprimatur of the Supreme Court in a number of cases.[3] Similarly, the practice arose whereby judges would frequently insert a review date into a sentence, in order to give offenders a prospect of rehabilitation. An offender given a review date understood that if he or she conformed to prison rules, or took advantage of treatment for drug addiction, for example, the remainder of the sentence would be suspended upon the review date.

Like the suspended sentence, the practice of inserting review dates was never put on any statutory footing. But unlike the suspended sentence, the review practice has now been expressly disapproved of by the Supreme Court. The Court ruled in November 2000 that the review practice amounted to a breach of the doctrine of separation of powers, holding that: "it is clearly for the Oireachtas to decide whether to retain the present system unaltered, to retain it on a clearer and more transparent basis, to devolve the function wholly or partly to a parole board or some other entity, or indeed to confer it on the courts".[4] As yet there is no indication as to what action, if any, the Oireachtas will take in response to this judgment.

Finally, since the implementation of the Criminal Justice (Community Service) Act 1983, judges may now impose Community Service Orders as an alternative to custodial sentences. This non-custodial option in sentencing has recently been the subject of a major empirical study, considered below. Apart from these options, a convicted offender may also or alternatively be fined, ordered to pay compensation to the injured party, or to undergo supervision by the Probation Service for a specified period of time. Finally, the sentencing judge may grant a dismissal or discharge, without proceeding to a conviction, under section 1(1) or 1(2) of the Probation of Offenders Act 1907.

Sentencing powers differ depending on the level of the court in which the case is heard. The District Court has power to hear summary offences, and indictable offences under certain conditions. Its sentencing powers are limited to the imposition of a maximum prison term of twelve months (rising to twenty-four months in respect of two or more offences). The powers of the Circuit, Central and Special Criminal Courts are limited only by the statutory maxima imposed in respect of particular offences.

Proposals are presently in place for the development of a further alternative to custody in sentencing, through the establishment of Drug Courts. Now established on a pilot basis, these courts present an exciting alternative to the present options

---

[3] See for example *Re McIlhagga,* unreported, Supreme Court, 29 July, 1971, and O'Malley, *op. cit.,* at pp. 288–92

[4] *People (DPP) v Finn,* Supreme Court, unreported, 24 November, 2000, at p. 43

available to judges in sentencing those offenders convicted of drugs offences or those whose crimes are related to their drug addiction.[5] Those offenders deemed suitable for the Drug Court process, are required after assessment to participate in a tailor-made treatment programme, involving the services of FAS, the Department of Education and Science, and the Probation and Welfare Service. The aim of the Drug Court project is to provide a scheme for rehabilitation for certain offenders, under the auspices and control of the court, although without excluding the use of punishment should the circumstances so warrant. However, the concept of drugs courts can be problematic, in that such courts entail of necessity a co-ordination between the workings of the health and justice sectors. Butler has argued that fundamental cultural differences exist between these two sectors in Ireland, and that these must be acknowledged and addressed before such courts can work effectively.[6]

MANDATORY AND MINIMUM SENTENCES

Although the Irish approach to sentencing is based upon the common law model which emphasises the need for judicial discretion, there is one area in which the sentencing judge has no discretion; that of the mandatory sentence. Where mandatory sentences are prescribed for particular offences, the stated penalty automatically attaches once the defendant is convicted. Perhaps the best-known mandatory sentence is that of life imprisonment for murder;[7] but mandatory sentences also attach to a number of summary offences. The Road Traffic Act 1961, for example, provides for fifteen offences (including driving while intoxicated and dangerous driving) in respect of which a court must make a "consequential disqualification order".

Most recently, the legislature has introduced a minimum ten-year sentence for certain drug trafficking offences. This carries the proviso that it will not apply where there are "exceptional and specific circumstances", which would make the sentence "unjust in all the circumstances".[8] The judge, in deciding if such circumstances apply, may have regard to a number of factors, including whether a guilty plea was entered and at what stage it was entered. O'Malley has described this provision as introducing a scheme of "presumptive" rather than "mandatory" sentencing.[9]

---

[5] See the *First Report of the Drug Court Planning Committee Pilot Project*, Dublin: Government Publications, 1999

[6] Butler, S., "A Tale of Two Sectors: A Critical Analysis of the Proposal to Establish Drugs Courts in the Republic of Ireland", in Springer, A. and Uhl, A. (eds.), *Illicit Drugs: Patterns of Use – Patterns of Response*, Innsbruck, Austria: Studien Verlag, 2000

[7] Criminal Justice Act 1990, section 2; section 3 of the same Act provides for a mandatory minimum sentence of forty years' imprisonment to be imposed in cases of specific types of murder (eg murder of a garda or prison officer in the course of duty)

[8] Criminal Justice Act 1999

[9] O'Malley, *op. cit.,* p. 102

APPEALS AGAINST SENTENCE

In a system where the superior courts have not handed down any guideline judgments, and there is no statutory sentencing scheme, appeals against sentence constitute the only effective check on the initial sentencing decision.

Those convicted before the District Court may appeal against conviction and/or sentence to the Circuit Criminal Court, which can increase or reduce the sentence imposed by the District Court, once it remains within the limits of the sentencing jurisdiction of the District Court. Those convicted before the Circuit, Central or Special Criminal Court take their appeals to the Court of Criminal Appeal (CCA), which is due to be abolished when the relevant provisions of the Courts and Court Officers Act 1995 take effect. This will mean that all appeals against sentence or conviction from the Circuit, Central and Special Criminal Courts will lie to the Supreme Court, which is likely to apply the same principles as the CCA. Foremost among the CCA principles in hearing appeals is the principle that it will not disturb the sentence imposed by the trial judge, unless it was "wrong in principle".

Under section 2 of the Criminal Justice Act 1993,[10] the Director of Public Prosecutions (DPP) may apply to the Court of Criminal Appeal to review a sentence which he considers to be unduly lenient. The court may substitute any sentence that the sentencing court could lawfully have imposed. *Byrne* was the first case referred under this Act, in which the CCA stated the principles that should govern such appeals, in particular the guiding principle that "nothing but a substantial departure from what would be regarded as the appropriate sentence" should justify the court's intervention.[11]

THE ROLE OF THE EXECUTIVE

Mandatory sentences aside, the exclusivity of the judicial role in the selection of sentence is implicit in Article 34 of the Constitution, and has been confirmed by the Supreme Court.[12] However, once a prisoner has been sentenced to imprisonment and finally disposed of by the courts, the actual time that he or she serves in prison is a matter for the Executive. The Irish Prison Service, which has charge of managing the prison system, remains a division of the Department of Justice, Equality and Law Reform. The Service has responsibility for the processing of all decisions relating to the management of prisoners' sentences. It is envisaged that, with the passing of a Prison Service Bill, this will become a

---

[10] (as amended by section 4 of the Courts and Court Officers Act 1995)

[11] [1995] 1 ILRM 279. For a more detailed review of the principles governing the hearing of appeals taken by the DPP under this section, see Liston, J., "Cases and Commentary", 10 *Irish Criminal Law Journal* 2000

[12] *Deaton v Attorney General and the Revenue Commissioners* [1963] IR 170

separate independent statutory agency. The establishment of such an independent agency to run the prisons was recommended by the Whitaker Committee, and more recently by an expert group set up to examine options for change.[13]

At present, a prisoner is subject to the 1947 Prison Rules.[14] New draft rules drawn up by the Department of Justice in 1994 have yet to be implemented.[15] Under Rule 38, all inmates have a statutory right to remission of one quarter of their sentence. In addition, prisoners may be allowed out on Temporary Release at the discretion of the prison authorities.[16] The establishment of a statutory parole board to advise the minister on release dates for long-term prisoners was recommended by the expert group. This board would replace the existing Sentence Review Group, a non-statutory body that reports to the minister for Justice with recommendations on the treatment of long-sentence offenders.

Until the Irish Prison Service becomes a separate independent agency, and until new prison rules and a new statutory parole board is created, it is clear that the Executive role in the running of prisons may be subject to much criticism. As O'Mahony writes, "The arbitrary manner of early release and the fact that it is at the discretion of the Executive, represented by a handful of Department of Justice officials, is a travesty of justice ... It is hard to imagine any policy better designed to subvert the intentions of sentencing and to undermine the authority of the judiciary."[17] In practice, the intervention of the Executive through the granting of early or temporary release may ensure that the actual sentence served is very different from the notional sentence handed down by the judge.

However, in one aspect of sentencing at least, the role of the Executive has been greatly diminished since 1995. In that year, on an application by a District Judge, the High Court considered the power of the Minister for Justice to remit fines and commute sentences imposed by the courts. The evidence showed that approximately 5,000 petitions for remission or commutation were received annually by the minister. Of these, it appeared that over 55 per cent were granted some reduction of the penalty originally imposed. In his judgment, Geoghegan J held that this petition procedure appeared to operate as a "parallel or alternative system of justice to that provided for by Article 34 [of the Constitution]".[18] Since this judgment, the government is now seriously restricted in its capacity to remit

---

[13] *Towards an Independent Prisons Agency*, Report of Expert Group, Dublin: Government Publications, 1997

[14] *Rules for the Government of Prisons 1947*, S.I. No. 320 of 1947

[15] *The Management of Offenders – A Five Year Plan*, Dublin: Department of Justice, 1994

[16] For more detailed consideration of the rules governing temporary release and remission, see McDermott, P.A., *Prison Law*, Dublin: Round Hall Ltd, 2000, pp. 397-420. See also Criminal Justice (Temporary Release of Prisoners) Bill 2001

[17] O'Mahony, P., *Criminal Chaos*, Dublin: Round Hall Sweet & Maxwell, 1996, p. 92 *et seq*, for a discussion of the need for an independent prisons board

[18] *Brennan v Minister for Justice* [1995] 1 IR 612

judicial penalties, although O'Malley suggests that it would have been preferable if this change had been made instead by way of constitutional amendment.[19]

SOURCES OF DATA ON SENTENCING IN IRELAND

Establishing what options are available to a sentencing judge is relatively straightforward. Ascertaining the way in which judges apply these options generally is much less easy, due to the difficulty with accessing data. Part of the problem lies in delays in the publication of data, and in the multiple sources for such data. First, the Annual Reports on Prisons and Places of Detention are usually published some years in arrears. The most recent such report available (in October 2001) is for 1994, although some more up-to-date statistics are available on the website of the Irish Prisons Service, on www.irishprisons.ie/statistics.asp. Since 1983, the reports have included statistical tables classifying committals in the year under review by reference to offence, gender, age, length of sentence and previous committals. Such data are useful for the deduction of broad sentencing patterns, but have to be treated with caution, particularly as they deal with numbers of committals rather than of offenders.

A different report, the *Annual Statistics on Prisons and Places of Detention for 1994* (published in May 1998), provides an interesting analysis of trends in committal rates between 1991 and 1994.[20] The introduction to this useful statistical report expresses the hope that from 1998 onwards, similar reports would be provided within a few months of the end of the year under scrutiny. However, to date no further such statistical reports have been produced.

The Annual Report of the Probation and Welfare Service provides some general information on the numbers placed by the courts on the various programmes operated by the service. Its usefulness is greatly reduced by its use of broad offence classifications such as "sexual offences". Again, these reports are published some years in arrears, the most recent available being for 1996. The statistical abstracts from the Central Statistics Office provide some general information on the workload of the District Court, although this is obviously of limited value for research on sentencing for serious offences. There does not appear to be any publicly-available source of information on the use of suspended sentences, since a person given a fully-suspended sentence will not come within the jurisdiction of either the prison service (unless the sentence is activated) or the probation service.

The Garda Síochána Annual Reports are published most frequently, with the 1999 report the most recent available as of October 2001. However, these reports only provide information on crime rates and detection rates generally, that is

---

[19] O'Malley, *op. cit.,* p. 96
[20] *Prisons and Places of Detention: Annual Statistics for 1994*, Dublin: Government Publications, 1998

number of crimes recorded, the number of crimes in respect of which prosecutions were commenced, the number of prosecutions which resulted in a conviction. The reports do not record statistics on disposal of offences.

IRISH EMPIRICAL STUDIES ON SENTENCING PRACTICE

On the basis of the information available through these various sources, several empirical studies have been carried out with the aim of gaining some insight into sentencing practice. The Whitaker Report provided a review of those studies published before 1985, beginning with the Needham study of the Galway District Court.

THE NEEDHAM STUDY

Needham selected a 5% random sample of the 17,464 offences disposed of in the Galway District Court during the period 1978-81.[21] Of the total number of 291 indictable cases in his study, 80% pleaded guilty or were convicted. Of that group, 11.2% were given sentences of imprisonment, 13.3% were given suspended sentences, 34.8 per cent were fined, 17.2% were given the benefit of the Probation of Offenders Act 1907, 5.6% had their cases adjourned generally and Probation Orders were issued for 6%. For 8.6% of defendants, the offence was taken into consideration with other charges of which he or she was convicted. The remaining 3% were sent forward on a signed plea of guilty for sentence in the Circuit Criminal Court.

THE WHITAKER COMMITTEE NATIONAL DISTRICT COURT STUDY

Needham's study related exclusively to the Galway area. However, the Whitaker Committee commissioned a special national survey to obtain more information on sentencing in all the criminal courts. During the survey period of four weeks commencing 18 June, 1984, 3,123 persons were processed in the District Courts nationally. Verdicts were reached in respect of 89.1% of this total figure (2,783 persons). Overall, 75% of defendants were found guilty and 11% not guilty. The national survey found that sentences of imprisonment were imposed on 20.4% of those found guilty. The most common type of sentence, however, was the fine, which was imposed on 46.9% of defendants. Suspended sentences were used rarely, amounting only to 2% of sentences. Orders under the Probation of Offenders Act 1907 were made in respect of 18% of all dispositions.

---

[21] Needham, M., *The District Court – An Empirical Study of Criminal Jurisdiction*, thesis submitted for LLM degree, University College Galway, 1983

According to the national survey, the degree to which prison sentences were imposed differed dramatically depending on the type of offence for which the defendant had been convicted. Only 4.1% of those convicted of drunken or dangerous driving were imprisoned, compared to 37.3% of those convicted of burglary offences, and 36.4% of those convicted of "unauthorised taking" of cars. In cases of assault, 22.5% of those convicted were imprisoned, rising to 28.9% where they were convicted of the more specific offence of assault on a garda.

THE ROTTMAN AND TORMEY SURVEY

Rottman and Tormey, contributors to the Whitaker Report, had reviewed the outcomes experienced by 840 defendants in their 1984 study of the criminal practice of the Dublin Circuit Court. They found that case dispositions were overwhelmingly by a plea of guilty; 61% of all defendants so pleaded, but in relation to the 21.8% who went to trial on a plea of not guilty, acquittals vastly exceeded convictions. Only 28.4% of trials led to a verdict of guilty. The charges against 12.9% of defendants never went to trial because the prosecution entered *nolle prosequis* on all charges.

Among the 68% of all defendants who are ultimately convicted, the most frequent sentence imposed was that of imprisonment. Almost one half of those convicted (49%) received a prison sentence, with a further 38% receiving a suspended prison sentence. This contrasts with the Whitaker study finding that only 2% of those convicted in the District Courts nationally received suspended sentences. The third most frequent sanction was the Probation of Offenders Act 1907. Again, by contrast with the District Court, only 4% of convicted offenders in the Circuit Court received a fine as their sole penalty.

Taking the conviction rate of 68% and the imprisonment rate on conviction of 49%, Rottman and Tormey found that one-third of defendants returned for trial before the Dublin Circuit Criminal Court were committed to prison, with the average sentence being just over two years (27.4 months). Most sentences fell within a band of one to five years, with two years the most frequently imposed prison sentence (32% of all sentences). Only 4% of sentences exceeded five years.

Defendants who pleaded guilty tended to receive shorter sentences, on average, than did those who were convicted at trial. In addition, most Circuit Court cases were found to turn on pleas of guilty to all, some or reduced charges, based on plea compromises. The presence of such compromises was seen to be evident in the pattern with which charges were dropped and sentences imposed in the Circuit Criminal Court. Defendants typically faced multiple charges and rarely entered pleas of guilty to all charges.

WHITAKER REPORT CONCLUSIONS

The Committee reviewed the imprisonment statistics from all of the criminal courts, concluding that in the District Courts, roughly one in five of those convicted receive prison sentences, compared to one in two in the Circuit Criminal Court. Similarly, just over half of those convicted (56.3%) receive prison sentences in the Central Criminal Court, and 48.1% in the Special Criminal Court. Fines are the most common penalty in the District Court, representing 46.9% of outcomes for convicted offenders, but fines constitute only 4.4% of outcomes in the Circuit Court, and 2.1% and 1.3% in the Central and Special Criminal Courts respectively.

The Committee reviewed the changes likely to affect the size of the prison population following its report. It suggested that, in particular, the passing of the Criminal Justice Act 1984, especially the provision introducting majority verdicts in jury trials, was likely to increase the conviction rates in the courts, thereby leading to an increase in the numbers of those committed to prison. Other factors which it considered would change the number of committals included the introduction of Community Service Orders as alternatives to custodial sentences which should decrease committals, but on the other hand punitive public attidudes and increased sentencing powers for the District Court were both likely to encourage more and longer sentences of imprisonment. Public opinion could lead to the increased use of imprisonment especially in respect of certain types of offence, such as unauthorised taking of vehicles or drugs offences.

Since the Whitaker Committee concluded its groundbreaking study of the Irish penal system, it is unfortunate that no similar study has since been conducted. Thus, we simply do not know – although we might surmise – that the subsequent increase in the use of imprisonment was due to changes brought about by the Criminal Justice Act 1984. We certainly know that there has been a dramatic increase in the numbers of those in prison; but other factors such as a decrease in reliance upon temporary release may make those trends less remarkable. It is clear that a follow-up to the Whitaker Report, based upon well-resourced and detailed empirical study, is long overdue.

One other significant empirical work published before the Whitaker Report was concluded also deserves mention. In a study focusing on the impact of gender on the sentencing decision, Lyons and Hunt conducted a survey of District Court and garda larceny records for the Dublin Metropolitan Area, covering the first half of 1979.[22] They chose the offence of larceny as being most objectively quantifiable, since details about the items stolen and their monetary value are usually available;

---

[22] Lyons, A. and Hunt, P., "The Effects of Gender on Sentencing: A Case Study of the Dublin Metropolitan Area District Court", in M. Tomlinson, T. Varley and C. McCullagh (eds.), *Whose Law and Order*, Belfast: Sociological Assocation of Ireland, 1983

and also because it was the crime most often committed by both women and men, making up 60% of all recorded offences in 1979. They examined the records relating to 108 women and 120 men, finding that, when other variables were excluded, women were still treated more leniently in 70% of cases. They concluded that District Court judges were placing more weight on factors such as marital status, family background and parenthood in the sentencing of women.

POST-WHITAKER REPORT

Studies on sentencing conducted since 1985 have tended to focus on particular aspects of sentencing practice, either on specific courts, specific offences, types of penalty or types of offender; so it remains difficult to obtain a general overview of sentencing nationally.

STUDIES ON DISTRICT COURT SENTENCING PRACTICE

Quite a number of studies have focused on the sentencing practice of the District Court. One such study, by Bacik et al, covering both court appearance and sentencing statistics, sought to examine links between economic deprivation and crime.[23] A random sample of 2,000 cases heard in the Dublin District Court (Bridewell Courts) in the years 1988 and 1994 was analysed. The cases were encoded according to various aspects of the case and the offender. Information taken for each case included the sex, date of birth and home address of each defendant, as well as the offence/s he or she was charged with and the outcome of the case. A material deprivation index was used to measure the level of deprivation in the 189 district electoral divisions chosen to represent the study area.

The results of the study were divided into two sections. First, looking only at court appearance, key characteristics of the population of the sample were compared with the general population and the degree of mismatch between both groups was noted. Age, sex and level of community deprivation were found to be the key factors predicting the likelihood of court appearance. In other words, it was found that defendants appearing before the Dublin District Courts are overwhelmingly young, male and from areas with high levels of community deprivation. Of the sample in this study, 88.9% were male, with a median age of 23. Indeed, while males between the ages of 15 and 34 years made up 14.5% of those persons aged between 15 and 64 in the study area, they made up 49.4% of defendants in the study. Further, while those from the most deprived areas made

---

[23] Bacik, I., Kelly, A., O'Connell, M. and Sinclair, H., "Crime and Poverty in Dublin: An Analysis of the Association between Community Deprivation, District Court Appearance and Sentence Severity", in I. Bacik and M. O'Connell (eds.), *Crime and Poverty in Ireland*. Dublin: Round Hall Sweet & Maxwell, 1998

up only 35.5% of the study area population, they made up 73.3% of those appearing before the District Courts.

The second section of the study was devoted to an analysis of the outcomes of the sample of cases. A multi-variate statistical analysis based on ordinal measures was used to investigate whether certain characteristics of the offender such as sex, age, social class and residence contributed to variation in the sentences given down. The authors found an apparently significant variation in sentencing to exist; 29% of those defendants from the most deprived areas were found to receive custodial sentences, compared to 19% of those from the least deprived areas. It was also found that defendants from more deprived areas are 49% more likely to receive a custodial sentence than those from less deprived areas, once other variables are taken into account.

The findings of this study indicate that the deprivation level of a particular community may be a factor leading to the increased likelihood of a court appearance for those, particularly the young men, from that community. The study also indicates that the community deprivation level may be a factor leading to the increased likelihood of a custodial sentence for those defendants from that community.

In the course of conducting an investigation of the operation of the bail system, O'Mahony also examined the sentencing practice of the Dublin District Courts.[24] He analysed the workload of District Courts 4, 5 and 6 (now 44, 45 and 46) for the month of November 1995. During this month, the three courts dealt with a total of 6,627 different cases involving an estimated 2,850 different people. In respect of the sample of 810 to which his study related, 34% were acquitted or had their charges struck out or dismissed. While 5% were returned for trial to the Circuit Criminal Court, 14% received fines, and 21% received some other non-custodial sentence (such as a suspended sentence, community service order or probation supervision). The remainder, amounting to just over a quarter of this group (26%), received sentences of imprisonment.

STUDIES ON DISTRICT JUDGES' ATTITUDES IN SENTENCING

Some research has also been done on the attitudes of district judges to sentencing. As part of a broader study on judicial attitudes to imprisonment, Vaughan conducted a survey of District Court judges, by way of questionnaires and interviews.[25] He concluded that few of the judges believed in the capacity of prison to reform the individual, but rather that they saw custody as having a wider

---

[24] O'Mahony, P., *An Investigation of the Operation of the Bail System*, unpublished report for the Minister for Justice, 1996
[25] Vaughan, B., *The Judiciary and the Penal System*, Dublin: Irish Penal Reform Trust, forthcoming

effect, through its deterrence of potential offending and its role in protecting society from the acts of offenders.

Thus, from the judges' point of view, the most beneficial effects of custody were brought about through principles of deterrence and incapacitation. Vaughan also found that many of the judges in his sample felt the need for training and greater access to information on sentencing practice of their colleagues, although they differed in their view as to whether disparity in sentencing actually exists.

More recently, Riordan conducted research into the practice of the Dublin District Courts when dealing with drug related offenders, in order to establish whether the nucleus of a Drug Court already exists.[26] Riordan analysed cases dealt with in Courts 44, 45 and 46, which deal with the vast majority of drug related criminal cases in the Dublin Metropolitan area, limiting his research to those cases in which social enquiry reports on drug related issues were ordered by the Court. As part of his study, he convened a focus group of district judges, in order to ascertain the attitudes among judges to sentencing in drug related cases. He found that the practices of the Dublin District Courts in dealing with drug related offenders is different to that utilised where drugs are not an issue; judges clearly favour adjourned supervision as a way of monitoring drug related offenders. As to motivation in sentencing, some judges expressed a preference for rehabilitation as a sentencing model, but others were more sceptical about the potential for rehabilitation of offenders.

TYPES OF OFFENCE: SENTENCING IN SEXUAL OFFENCES

In 1996, as part of a text on sexual offences, O'Malley presented a basic empirical study of sentencing in rape cases.[27] He collected news items from the *Irish Times* on sentencing for rape over an eight-year period, together with transcripts from CCA judgments between 1992 and 1994. He took a random selection of ninety cases in 1995. His study identifies certain patterns in rape sentencing; two-thirds of the offenders were given prison sentences ranging from five to ten years, and half were sentenced to terms ranging from seven to ten years.

Thus, he says it is reasonably safe to assume that somewhere within the five-to-ten year bracket, probably somewhere in the seven-to-ten year bracket, lies a benchmark sentence for rape. In the Z case, the Court of Criminal Appeal took note of sentences imposed in fifty unlawful carnal knowledge cases heard between 1987 and 1993.[28] The court noted that "in only three cases are there

---

[26] Riordan, D., *Diversion to Treatment: A Study of Drug-Related Cases in the Dublin Metropolitan District Court*, thesis submitted to the University of Dublin, Trinity College, in part fulfilment of the requirements for the MSc in Drug and Alcohol Policy, June, 2000

[27] O'Malley, T., *Sexual Offences Law Policy and Punishment*, Dublin: Round Hall Sweet & Maxwell, 1996, at pp. 367-376

[28] *Court of Criminal Appeal,* 14 March, 1995

sentences at the level of seven years' penal servitude". The court therefore felt justified in adopting seven years as the starting point to which it could apply mitigating factors, or if necessary apply aggravating factors to depart upwards. Previously, however, the Supreme Court had expressly declined an invitation to offer a guideline judgment for sentencing in respect of rape.[29]

TYPES OF PENALTY: COMMUNITY SERVICE ORDERS

In 1999, Walsh and Sexton published the first comprehensive study assessing the use by the judiciary of the community service order.[30] The CSO is a relatively new sentencing option introduced by legislation in 1984. It is a court order requiring the offender to do a specified number of hours of unpaid work in the community. It can only be imposed as an alternative to a sentence of imprisonment or detention.[31]

The study covered a national sample of a total number of 1,093 offenders, those in respect of whom a CSO had been made between 1 July, 1996, and 30 June, 1997. From various sources, the authors made findings about the profile of relevant offenders, types of offence and application of CSOs. They concluded that the standard recipient of a CSO is a young, single male, unemployed with poor educational qualifications and vocational skills, living in his parents' home. Just over half the recipients have a previous criminal record, and a significant proportion are likely to have served a prison sentence or CSO in the past.

The most frequent types of offence in respect of which CSOs are ordered are larceny (22%), less serious assault (15%) and driving offences (15%). A considerable variation in the spread of offences was found to exist across the District Court areas, however. In one area, for example, all but one of the CSOs in the sample had been imposed for driving offences.

The authors suggested that CSOs are being used in some cases where a custodial sentence might not otherwise have been imposed. Indeed, they found a prevalent attitude among judicial and other practitioners that the legislation was too restrictive, in confining the CSO as a substitute for a prison term. Most other European jurisdictions permit CSOs to be used in conjunction with certain other punishments and, to a limited extent, as a substitute for non-custodial sanctions. By comparison, the Irish legislation is less flexible, permitting CSOs to be used only as a stand-alone substitute for a custodial sentence.

The 1983 Act stipulates that a CSO cannot be imposed for less than forty hours nor more than 240 hours. But the authors found considerable variation in the average length of CSOs imposed across different court areas. The national

---

[29] *People (DPP) v Tiernan* [1988] IR 250
[30] Walsh, D. and Sexton, P., *An Empirical Study of Community Service Orders in Ireland*, Dublin: Government Publications, 1999
[31] Under the Criminal Justice (Community Service) Act 1983

average length of a CSO is 141 hours, but averages across court areas range from a high of 216 hours in one area to a low of seventy-six hours in another.

Whenever a judge imposes a CSO, he or she must also specify an alternative prison term, to be served if the offender fails to carry out the CSO. The average length of the alternative prison term imposed was found to be 5.1 months, but again the authors found surprising variations, concluding that "The relationship between the number of CSO hours and length of alternative prison term varies substantially and randomly across court areas".[32]

The findings of the first national CSO study make for interesting reading, but some disturbing conclusions may be drawn. The most obvious is the extent of disparity in the application of what should be a very straightforward sentencing option, for which detailed legislative provision has been made. Clearly, there is a problem in the lack of flexibility within the legislation, but even so, it is beyond doubt that greater communication should be carried out among sentencers to enable more consistency in the application of the CSO.

TYPES OF OFFENDER: SENTENCING OF YOUNG OFFENDERS

As with most other aspects of Irish sentencing practice, there is little literature available on the sentencing of juveniles (those under eighteen). All of the options available to judges in sentencing adults also apply in relation to juvenile offenders.[33] However, in place of imprisonment, young offenders are instead sentenced to detention in young offenders' institutions.

In 1970, Shanley published work on the use of the formal caution within the JLO (Juvenile Liaison Officer) scheme,[34] while some years later O'Mahony et al conducted a research project on the family characteristics of young offenders detained in one detention centre, Shanganagh Castle, between 1979 and 1983.[35]

O'Donovan carried out research into juvenile offenders on behalf of the Probation and Welfare Service in the late 1980s,[36] and at around the same time Farrelly's study of the juvenile justice system provided a qualitative analysis of the types of criminal activities engaged in by young people from Dublin's north inner city.[37] However, until 1999 these studies represented the only empirical literature

---

[32] Walsh and Sexton, *op. cit.*, at p. 98

[33] For a discussion of the dispositional options available to the courts in dealing with young offenders, see Ring, M.E., "Custodial Treatment of Young Offenders" (1991) 1 *Irish Criminal Law Journal* 59-67 and Vaughan, B., "Breaking out of Jail: Generating Non-Custodial Penalties for Juveniles" (2000) 3 *Irish Criminal Law Journal* 14-18

[34] Shanley, P., "The Formal Cautioning of Juvenile Offenders" (Winter 1970) *The Irish Jurist* 262-279

[35] O'Mahony, P. *et al*, "Some Family Characteristics of Irish Juvenile Offenders" (1985) 17(1) *The Economic and Social Review* 29-38

[36] O'Donovan, D., *Report*, Dublin: Probation and Welfare Service, undated (1987)

[37] Farrelly, J., *Crime, Custody and Community*, Dublin: Voluntary and Statutory Bodies, 1989

touching on the sentencing of young offenders. In that year, two studies were published; a report by the Probation and Welfare Service, and an internal report commissioned by the government, both of which are considered briefly below.[38]

In his study, O'Donovan obtained data on the outcome of 12,628 of the total of 12,660 cases that came before the Dublin Metropolitan Children's Court in 1985. He found that 4,083 of his sample involved summary offences, and that the vast bulk of these, 83.7% were disposed of by way of supervision by the Probation Service, dismissal under the Probation Act (DPOA), or struck out. Only four cases were dealt with by way of community service order, 10.3% by way of fine, and the remaining 5.8% were sentenced to detention, either in St Patrick's Institution or in other detention centres. In relation to the 8,545 indictable offences in the sample, again the vast majority (89.5%) were disposed of through supervision, strike out or DPOA. A total of 327 were returned for trial to the Circuit Criminal Court, community service orders were imposed upon only six offenders, and fines ordered in respect of 136. The remainder, 426 or 4.9%, were sentenced to detention.

Overall, O'Donovan found that while fines were more widely used in summary cases, they still only represented one tenth of disposals there. Taking both categories together, he found the incarceration rate to be 5.2%; higher than the finding for 1982, where out of a total of 15,663 cases, only 498 were disposed of through custodial or residential care, giving an overall incarceration rate of only 3%.

In 1999, the Probation and Welfare Service published its report on young offenders in penal custody, a study in which a total of 150 sentenced young offenders, aged between sixteen and twenty-two years, were interviewed in March 1998.[39] While the purpose of the study was to ascertain the nature of the respondents' experience with the Probation and Welfare Service, the data produced by the researchers is of more general interest in throwing some light on the sentencing of young offenders.

For example, in their review of respondents' experience of community sanctions, the authors found that one in three of all those surveyed had not had an opportunity for supervision by the Probation and Welfare Service prior to their first custodial sentence. Although over three-quarters of the respondents (78%) had been referred to the Service for a pre-sanction report before their first custodial sentence, not all of these were given the opportunity to avail of supervision at the same time. Moreover, the research appears to support the view that having served at least one custodial sentence, the offender's chances of receiving an opportunity for supervision by the Service in the community may decline significantly thereafter. While 66% of all respondents had received an

---

[38] Geiran, V. *et al*, *Report on Young Offenders in Penal Custody*, Dublin: Probation and Welfare Service, 1999; and McLoughlin, E., Maunsell, C. and O'Connell, M., *Children in the Irish Juvenile Justice System*, Dublin: Government Publications, forthcoming

[39] Geiran *et al, op. cit.*

opportunity for supervision by the Service before their first custodial sentence, this had dropped to 28.8% who received a similar opportunity after their first and before their current sentence.

Over half (50.6%) of all respondents were serving sentences for property-related or "other" offences (such as fraud etc). Of the remainder, 28% had been sentenced primarily for offences against the person, 15.3% for unauthorised taking of a vehicle, and 6% for possession of drugs for the purpose of supply. In relation to previous sentences, seventy-seven respondents (51.3%) were serving their first sentence in detention, and a total of 116 (77.3%) were serving either their first or second custodial sentence. Two of the respondents had served the maximum number of sentences any respondent received, that is eight previous periods in custody. In short, just over half the respondents had been sentenced on account of property and other miscellaneous offences of a relatively minor nature. Three-quarters of them were serving a first or second custodial sentence.

In the conclusion to this report, the authors observed that their research sample represented, by definition, a group of offenders with whom community-based sanctions from the courts have proved least successful. However, this observation might be treated with some caution, since the study found, significantly, that one in three young offenders do not actually receive an opportunity for supervision by the Probation and Welfare Service before their first custodial sentence is imposed. This finding deserves particular emphasis, especially given the authors' conclusion that those offenders who are at particularly high risk of re-offending and of receiving escalating custodial sentences seem to benefit most where they are identified at an early age. Such offenders must be afforded access to community-based interventions targeted at specific problems, areas and risk factors for crime, defined by the authors as including anti-social attitudes, substance abuse, poor self-control or family problems, if the negative spiral leading to further incarceration is to be interrupted.

The most recent study relating to the treatment of young offenders is that produced in 1999 for the Juvenile Justice Review Group, under the auspices of the Department of Justice, Equality and Law Reform.[40] This study provided an analysis of cases involving children who appeared before the District Courts in Dublin, Limerick and Galway City in the months of October 1997, April 1998 and October 1998. The total number of 2,455 charge sheets in the study represented 568 individual offenders, with 538 in the Dublin area. The study found that two-thirds of the children appearing before the Children's Court in Dublin were from a relatively small area of Dublin, characterised by high levels of deprivation. One out of ten children appearing before the Dublin court whose cases had been

---

[40] McLoughlin, E., Maunsell, C. and O'Connell, M., *Children in the Irish Juvenile Justice System*, *op. cit.*

disposed of in the designated months of the study received a custodial sanction. In a second strand to the study, the researchers found, however, that when they measured case outcome according to charge sheets rather than individual offenders, custodial sanctions represented the most frequently used penalty for male offenders. By contrast, probation was the model most often used in cases involving female offenders (who represented 8.4% of the total sample).

The researchers also drew interesting conclusions in relation to sentence length; for example finding that an association exists between age and sentence length, with younger offenders receiving harsher sentences. In a third strand of the research, an in-depth profile was conducted of a sample of eighty-four children who had been convicted and in respect of whom probation reports had been prepared. Detailed findings were made in relation to the children's family circumstances. Mean family size for young offenders, for example, was 4.6 children, by comparison to the national average of 2.05 children. Close to 30% of the sample had experienced the absence of one parent for long periods of their lives, and evidence of parental substance abuse was also recorded in almost 30% of the sample. In 38% of the sample, a member of the child's family was reported as also having been involved in criminal offending. The mean age at which the children were recorded as having committed their first criminal act was calculated as being 14.2 years, and the vast majority of children had been engaged in criminal activity prior to the current offence.

This important study represents a significant contribution to the body of empirical literature on sentencing in Ireland. However, the findings as to the typical background and circumstances of child offenders depressingly mirror those in other studies relating to adult prisoners, who also tend to be from backgrounds characterised by high levels of deprivation and low levels of employment, and who usually have a prior history of offending.[41]

UP-TO-DATE FIGURES ON SENTENCING IN IRELAND

Finally, some indication of present sentencing practice may be obtained from a brief review of existing sources of data. According to the Annual Report on Prisons and Places of Detention for 1992, the average daily prison population in 1992 was 2,185. This represented a 2% increase over the 1991 figure of 2,141, continuing an upward trend since 1981. The daily average in custody in institutions holding juveniles (St Patrick's and Shanganagh Castle) was 191 in 1992, an increase of 8.5% over the 1991 figure of 176, and a reversal of a downward trend since 1988.

---

[41] See O'Mahony, P., *Crime and Punishment in Ireland*. Dublin: Round Hall Ltd, 1993, Chapters 4 and 5; and O'Mahony, P., *Mountjoy Prisoners: A Sociological and Criminological Profile*, Dublin: Government Publications, 1997

The number of adults committed to prison on conviction was 4,756, what the Report described as a "significant increase" of 37% over the 1991 figure of 3,472. The figures for committals to St Patrick's Institution in 1992 also showed increases, since the number committed to serve periods of detention rose from 963 in 1991 to 1,101 in 1992, an increase of 14%.

The commentary provided in the 1992 report states that it was not possible to be definitive about the reasons for such a large increase in committals. The report noted, however, that the Garda Síochána crime figures did not warrant the increase, since only a 1% increase in recorded crime was shown from 1991 to 1992. The report concluded that:

> Other possible reasons include the increased use of custodial sentences for minor offences. The fact that the majority of the increase of 1,422 (adults and juveniles) in committals on conviction is made up of the increase in those sentenced to less than three months – 903 (63% increase) – would support this theory. Comparative courts statistics are unfortunately not available.[42]

In 1994, the total number of prison committals under sentence was over 5,700, which exceeded the total combined number (4,283) of probation, community service orders and deferred supervision orders in the same year.[43] The Annual Statistics on Prisons and Places of Detention for 1994 note a consistent increase in both short sentences (up to one year) and longer sentences between 1991 and 1994.[44] While a 20% increase in shorter sentences was significant, far more significant was the increase of 44.3% in the number of sentences imposed in the five-to-ten year category between those years.

Most committals were still for sentences of less than one year (75% in 1994), and indeed 53% of all sentences were for less than six months. The average sentence imposed was approximately eleven months. The report provides useful tables detailing trends in numbers sentenced to imprisonment, showing a steady rise from 3,200 adult persons sent to prison under sentence in 1990, to 5,758 in 1994. Breakdowns of the figures under headings of age, gender, type of offence and length of sentence are also given.

According to the most recent statistical abstracts available from the final source of information, the Central Statistics Office,[45] the total number of summary and indictable offences processed through the District Courts in the year 1994/95 was 502,025, and in 1995/96 it was 458,725. Confusingly, these statistics are kept according to year ending 31 July, whereas the garda and prison figures are kept

---

[42] *Annual Report on Prisons and Places of Detention for the year 1992*, Dublin: Government Publications, 1992, p. 83

[43] O'Malley, T., *Sentencing Law and Practice, op. cit.,* p. 48

[44] *Prisons and Places of Detention: Annual Statistics for 1994, op. cit.*

[45] *Central Statistics Office Statistical Abstracts*, 1998-99, Dublin: Government Publications

on a calendar year basis. Of these totals, in the 1995-1996 year, 89% of the total represented summary offences, and these were dealt with by the District Court in the following way. In respect of 2.6% of the total number of summary offences, a sentence of imprisonment or detention was imposed. A further 34% were dealt with by way of fines; 63% were dealt with "otherwise – probation etc" and a mere 5% were dealt with by way of community service order.

Of the total of 43,234 indictable offences also disposed of by the District Court in 1994/95, a much higher proportion resulted in the imposition of a prison sentence. Imprisonment or detention was ordered in respect of 24%; community service orders imposed in 4%, and fines in respect of 7% of these offences.

Finally, the limited statistics offered on the website of the Irish Prisons Service provide further convincing evidence of the consistent increase in imprisonment over the past few years. The website provides a "snapshot" of the prison population on the second Wednesday in December in each year for the last five years. This snapshot approach shows that while the prison population for December 1996 amounted to 2,277 persons, the population in December 1999 had reached 2,671 persons and by December 2000 the number of persons in prison stood at 2,948. This represents a significant increase in the number of persons imprisoned; a rise of 29.5% in our prison population, over a period of only five years.

CONSISTENT OVER-USE OF IMPRISONMENT

It is clear therefore from any analysis of sentencing statistics and empirical studies on sentencing conducted over the years, that the use of imprisonment as a sanction is increasing at a remarkably consistent rate, despite the absence of any stated sentencing policy. Whatever rationale for sentencing may be adopted, those groups and experts who have reviewed the Irish penal system over the years have all recommended less use of imprisonment, yet committal rates have continued to rise in recent years.

In 1985, the Whitaker Committee recommended that prison should be a punishment of last resort;[46] this view was shared by the Law Reform Commission, and in 1994 by the Department of Justice itself.[47] Most recently, the *Report of the National Crime Forum* recognised that "imprisonment is not an effective strategy for reducing crime", emphasising that community-based sanctions should be used whenever practicable.[48]

---

[46] *Report of Committee of Inquiry into the Penal System, op. cit.* The Committee also recommended that there should be no more than 1,500 prison places available

[47] *The Management of Offenders – A Five Year Plan*, Dublin: Department of Justice, 1994

[48] *Report of the National Crime Forum, op. cit.*, at p. 139

Yet since 1985, the number of persons in prison has increased steadily, despite the fact that the crime rate, while it has fluctuated, has never risen significantly above the figure of 102,387 indictable crimes recorded in 1983 and indeed has been declining steadily since 1996.[49] In 1988, McCullagh opined robustly that "the judiciary are increasingly unwilling to use the range of non-custodial sentences and are opting instead to send more offenders to prison and to send them for longer periods of time".[50] He described this as the "increased punitiveness of the judiciary", identifying a trend towards longer sentences, which he suggests began arguably in the late 1970s. In short, McCullagh suggested that the "unhampered operation of judicial discretion has produced a penal crisis", and that the judiciary should be subject to some external control in making sentencing decisions.[51]

In his recent critical overview of prison policy in Ireland, O'Mahony similarly presents a bleak picture of sentencing practice.[52] He comments that the bare figures available indicate that there is no straightforward, necessary connection between the amount of crime committed or at least recorded in the Garda Síochána annual reports, and the number of people being sent to prison. For example, in both the mid-'80s and the mid-'90s, immediately following periods of peak levels of recorded crime, but at a time when recorded crime was actually declining, there were marked upswings in the numbers of people being committed to prison by the courts.

Between 1980 and 1985, there was a 50% increase in the numbers sent to prison, and this new higher rate of imprisonment was maintained in the late-'80s, despite the stabilisation and indeed decreases in crime rates. Between the years 1990 and 1995, the new, higher rate of imprisonment of the 1980s was further built upon, and almost 2,000 more people were sent to prison per annum in 1995 than in 1990. Between 1996 and 2000, there was a further increase of 29.5% in the numbers in prison on any given day.

But unfortunately, as O'Mahony writes, "There are no available, detailed studies providing analysis of these important trends".[53] Nor indeed are data avail-

---

[49] Brewer, J., Lockhart, B. and Rodgers, P., *Crime in Ireland 1945-95: Here Be Dragons*, Oxford: Clarendon Press, 1997, see pp. 16-27. In 1995 a new peak of 102,484 indictable crimes was recorded in the Republic of Ireland, but this number has since fallen to below 1983 levels. The number recorded in 1996 was 100,785, falling to 90,875 in 1997, and an even lower total of 85,627 indictable offences in 1998. This fall was continued in 1999 with a total of only 81,274 indictable offences recorded. For an analysis of the declining crime rate, see O'Sullivan, E. and O'Donnell, I., "Why is Crime Decreasing" (2001) 1 *Irish Criminal Law Journal* 2-4 and see O'Donnell, I. and O'Sullivan, E., *Crime Control in Ireland: the politics of intolerance*, Cork University Press, 2001

[50] McCullagh, C., "A Crisis in the Penal System?", in M. Tomlinson, T. Varley and C. McCullagh (eds.), *Whose Law and Order*, Belfast: Sociological Association of Ireland, 1988, at p. 164

[51] McCullagh, C., *Crime, Punishment and Unemployment* (unpublished work, 1988)

[52] O'Mahony, P., *Prison Policy in Ireland*, Cork: Cork University Press, 2000

[53] O'Mahony, *ibid.*, p. 28

able on such vital matters as the relationship between the use of imprisonment and the levels of recorded crime, the patterns and seriousness of offending, or the specific use made by the courts of alternative sanctions.

CONCLUSION

In conclusion, in the absence of comprehensive sentencing data, and in the absence of any stated sentencing guidelines or policy, it is impossible to establish the reality of sentencing practice in our courts. What empirical work exists does go to show that, although inconsistencies appear to exist, some consistency can unfortunately be discerned in the increased use of imprisonment by the courts, despite decreasing crime rates. However, in order to develop a clearer picture of sentencing practice, a proper statistical framework is required. The planned introduction of computerisation of District Court records is long overdue, but at least represents a step in the right direction. In researching the 1998 Bridewell Courts study, it was necessary to plough through stacks of files, containing often indecipherable handwritten records, scrawled down by busy District Court registrars and then locked away in a dusty basement. It will now become easier to access those records, at least, with all the valuable information they possess.

Equally, however, it is necessary that more detailed national statistics on crime are both kept up-to-date and made accessible to researchers. The routine collection and publication of data on sentencing, in particular, would be hugely beneficial in terms both of enabling greater public awareness as to actual sentencing practice, and also of facilitating the judiciary by providing guidance as to sentencing consistency.

Routine collection of data, once introduced, could then be complemented by more specific studies on particular aspects of the penal system, such as the Walsh and Sexton CSO study. Such studies are invaluable in providing a focus on difficult questions such as the effect of various sentences on different types of offender, the characteristics of different types of offender, and also very practical matters such as the relationship between the sentences originally imposed and those actually served.

It is clear, overall, that a new approach to penal policy is required, based on an emphasis on the provision of information on sentencing, not least to the judiciary so that it no longer has to make sentencing decisions in a vacuum. More resources must also be provided to ensure that alternatives to custody are available.

Only when more information is available, and accessible to greater numbers of practitioners, policy-makers and judges, in particular, can a coherent sentencing policy be developed. Such a policy should aim to ensure that judicial discretion is exercised in a more structured way, with an emphasis on rehabilitative strategies, more widespread use of community-based sanctions, and substantially less use of imprisonment. Clear guidelines should be provided for judges as to alternative sanctions, and the potential for rehabilitation of individual offenders should be emphasised more strongly.

The empirical studies conducted to date provide a tantalising glimpse into aspects of sentencing practice in this jurisdiction. But, in order to put the practice into its proper perspective, a comprehensive overview must be available. This cannot be done until sentencing statistics become more accessible.

21

Punishment and the Popular Mind:
How Much is Enough?[1]

Hugh O'Flaherty

In this paper, I propose to examine aspects of the criminal justice system. The primary focus will be on punishment and sentencing. In setting the scene, the interrelationship between the media and the criminal justice system will be examined. Thereafter, the underlying rationales of punishment will be analysed and some of the factors considered by the Irish courts when sentencing will be outlined.

OVERVIEW OF THE COURT STRUCTURE

At the outset, it is perhaps appropriate to give an overview of the relevant courts in the context of the criminal justice system. Responsibility for minor offences that are triable summarily, eg parking offences, speeding and minor larcenies, is assumed by the District Court. Its power is limited to ordering fines of up to £1,500[2] and/or up to two consecutive terms of twelve months imprisonment for two or more offences dealt with simultaneously. More serious offences are dealt with by the Circuit Court which has original jurisdiction in relation to all

---

[1] This paper was delivered on 23 May, 1995, at the First World-wide Common Law Judiciary Conference at Washington DC and subsequently published in O'Flaherty, H., 1999, *Justice, Liberty and the Courts,* Dublin: Round Hall Sweet and Maxwell

[2] Under the Road Traffic Acts the District Court can order a fine of up to three times the annual tax for the offence of driving an untaxed vehicle. In the case of heavy goods vehicles this can amount to substantially more than £1,500

indictable crimes except murder and rape. Article 34.3 of the Irish Constitution invests the High Court with full original jurisdiction in, and power to determine, all matters and questions whether of law or fact, civil or criminal. When the court is exercising its criminal jurisdiction it is known as the Central Criminal Court. The Court of Criminal Appeal is entrusted with the task of hearing appeals from the Central Criminal Court, the Circuit Court and the Special Criminal Court. It consists of three judges – one Supreme Court judge and two High Court judges – and sits from time to time when convened by the Chief Justice.[3]

THE MEDIA AND THE CRIMINAL JUSTICE SYSTEM

In recent years the best-seller lists in Ireland have been dominated by books such as *King Scum, Gangland* and *The General,* a book which purports to tell the true story of Dublin crime boss Martin Cahill, murdered in 1995. The popularity of such books is a reminder of the general public's perennial fascination with things criminal – a fascination which the media has continually exploited, from the stirring tales of Sherlock Holmes to sensationalist biographies of serial killers, through to the seemingly endless stream of magazines with such titles as *Tales of Crime, Unsolved Mysteries* and the like. Martin Cahill himself understood the power of the media to influence public opinion and used visual humour – most famously, the wearing of Mickey Mouse underwear on the occasion of court appearances – to promote himself as a popular outlaw-type figure, rather than the vicious gang boss he in fact was.

Aside from the mythologising of individual criminals, journalists also play a significant role in reflecting, and in shaping, public perceptions of the criminal justice system. Shock-horror tales of brutality and violence fill the pages of our daily newspapers, often accompanied by reports of politicians and other social commentators telling us that the current "wave" of crime has reached "epidemic"proportions. The favoured topic in Ireland in recent times has been sexual crime – particularly cases of rape or of child sexual abuse. While the increase in sexual crime is indeed very alarming, the tendency of the media to sensationalise and highlight offences of this type heightens public fear and outrage and enormous pressure is brought to bear on the various agencies involved in law and order to "do something about it" – or, at least, to be seen to be doing something about it. Politicians, placed in office by popular election, are constantly aware of the Damocles' sword of public opinion hanging over their heads and this awareness can have a strong influence on penal legislation in

---

[3] Section 4 of the Courts and Court Officers Act 1995 provides for the abolition of the Court of Criminal Appeal by ministerial order in consultation with the Chief Justice and the President of the High Court and the vesting of its jurisdiction in the Supreme Court

'sensitive' areas such as rape or drug-related crime.

The glare of public hostility can also fall on the judiciary in their role of sentencing convicted criminals. This is especially likely to happen where the case involved has already been the subject of much publicity. In July 1992, a Mr C. pleaded guilty to the rape of a young woman. At the time of the offence he was eighteen years of age, she was nineteen and they had been going out together for some months. Once questioned about the incident, he admitted his guilt, accepted that his conduct had caused serious harm and pleaded guilty when the case came to trial. Flood J, a judge of the High Court, adjourned sentence for twelve months and, when the case came up for final disposition, sentenced the offender to nine years' imprisonment suspended, subject to certain conditions, for a period of six years.[4] The judgment which accompanied this decision drew much praise from many members of the academic and practising legal professions for its thoroughness and is widely regarded as the first Irish judgment to address in an extended manner the issues which face a judge in attempting to decide what a "fair" sentence should be. The public reaction, however, was less than complimentary. The victim, in the aftermath of the original trial, had made a brave decision to identify herself and speak to journalists about the trauma of her experience and her distress at the decision to adjourn sentence. Consequently, media treatment of the suspended sentence was set in the context of extraordinary levels of public empathy towards the rape victim and highlighted her reaction to the judgment in emotive headlines:

A VICTIM'S SOBS ECHO AS THE JUDGE READS ON (*The Irish Times*, 15 July 1993)

I FELT I HAD BEEN RAPED IN COURT FOR THE THIRD TIME (*The Irish Times*, 15 July 1993)

FOR VICTIM AND FOR WOMEN, THE TRIAL STILL GOES ON (*The Irish Independent*, 15 July 1993)

For weeks afterwards letters poured into newspapers from people outraged that a convicted rapist had seemingly been "let off" and questions were asked as to how "in touch" the judges were with the feelings of Irish people in relation to the seriousness of rape as an offence. The pattern of media spotlight followed by public outcry was repeated in March 1995 when the Court of Criminal Appeal gave judgment in the case of *The People (DPP) v Z.*[5] The unusual background to the case ensured that the judgment would have a high public profile. In March 1992, the Irish Supreme Court had given judgment in *AG v X and ors.*[6] – the case involving the right of a fourteen year old school girl to travel to England to have an abortion. Abortion had for long been illegal in Ireland and an amendment to the Constitution in 1983 was thought by most people to have copperfastened this

---

[4] *The People (Director of Public Prosecutions) v W.C.* [1994] 1 ILRM 321

[5] Unreported, Court of Criminal Appeal, 14 March 1995

[6] [1992] IR 1

position. However, in a judgment which appeared to surprise both the proponents of the Eighth Amendment and those who opposed it, the court held that a right to an abortion did in fact exist where it was established as matter of probability that there was a real and substantial risk to the life of the mother if the pregnancy was not terminated.

The plight of the unfortunate school girl at the centre of the X case had dominated national life for some weeks prior to the decision. When it became known that her pregnancy was as the result of an alleged rape by a married man who had been a close friend of the girl's family, popular sympathy was running at fever pitch. The man in question subsequently pleaded guilty to charges of unlawful carnal knowledge and indecent assault and was sentenced to a total of fourteen years imprisonment. His appeal against the severity of the sentence formed the ratio of the Z case mentioned above. Taking into account the range of sentences imposed in other cases of unlawful carnal knowledge, as well as various personal circumstances of the accused, the Court of Criminal Appeal decided to reduce the man's sentence to two terms of four years to be served concurrently. Once again, the judiciary found themselves at the centre of a storm of emotive criticism from politicians, women's organisations and ordinary members of society.

PRESENT DAY THINKING ON PUNISHMENT

These controversies are indicative of a change in Western attitudes towards the question of punishment. An era of idealism, in which criminal behaviour was seen largely as a psycho-social rather than a moral problem, has now given way to a harsher aesthetic with a greater emphasis on "giving offenders what they deserve" and on protecting society from wrongdoers. In America, a significant aspect of that trend consists of restrictions on judicial discretion; whether by introducing presumptive sentencing guidelines (as in Minnesota) or by more drastic measures such as the "three strikes you're out" legislation passed in California, and now numerous other states, which mandates a twenty-five-years-to-life sentence for a third felony conviction. Of course, this pendulum-swing between "offender-oriented" and "offence-oriented" sentencing policies is nothing new: penal history in the last two centuries has followed a cycle of scientific enthusiasm for the "treatment" of prisoners leading inevitably to a retributive backlash as such treatments failed to "cure the disease" of crime or were proved to be based on false premises. In the eighteenth century, there were physiognomists like J.K. Lavater who related the antisocial tendencies of the criminal to the irregularities of his outward features. In the first quarter of the nineteenth century *phrenology* was all the rage and various doctors claimed to be able to distinguish "the criminal" by the shape of his or her skull. The publication of Darwin's *Origin of the Species* in 1859 (and a later work, *The Descent of Man*) paved the way for a feverish interest in *eugenics* – social engineering through selective racial breeding. Darwin himself encouraged the idea that "the criminal" could in fact be a racial throwback to primitive man – "reversions to a savage state, from which we are not removed by very many generations" and the logic of this thought was developed by eugenists such as L.O. Pike, who asserted that:

> Like consumption or other hereditary disease, the criminal disposition would in the end cease to be inherited if all who were tainted with it were compelled to live and die childless[7].

Such ideas were borne aloft on the spirit of the age, sustained by a general craving for a scientific treatment of the problems of social life before, almost inevitably, being shot down for lack of hard evidence. With the dawn of the twentieth century, however, the twin disciplines of psychology and sociology gave rise to new hopes of reform for "criminally minded" individuals. As David Garland observes in his excellent work, *Punishment and Modern Society*:[8]

> For much of the present century, the term "rehabilitation" was a key element of official ideology and institutional rhetoric. This all-inclusive sign provided a sense of purpose and justification for penal practice and made punishment appear meaningful for its various audiences.

However, in more recent years the pendulum has once again swung the other way. Disillusionment began with the lack of any substantial data which might point towards the success of reform programmes but criticisms have also been advanced at a theoretical level. Compulsory reform programmes and the placing of wide discretionary powers in the hands of probation officers and treatment professionals have been attacked as infringing the fundamental right of individual offenders to a fair and definite sentence. Beneath such issues, however, lies an implicit challenge of far greater moment: for the first time in nearly two centuries, questions are being asked as to whether present penal structures can have any socially beneficial effect at all.

ASPECTS OF IRISH SENTENCING LAW

Although there are informally accepted tariffs of appropriate sentences known to judges and practitioners, it is probably true to say that in Irish sentencing law and practice there is less disposition towards guideline judgments than in other

---

[7] *A History of Crime* (1876)
[8] David Garland, *Punishment and Modern Society* (Clarendon Press, 1990)

common law jurisdictions and a great deal is left to intuition and accumulated judicial experience. Most judges endeavour to stay abreast of appellate decisions and relevant literature. Many also make it their practice to visit the principal prisons to which offenders will be sent. Attendance at seminars organised by the American and Canadian Bar Associations has also proved beneficial and informative. Nevertheless, inspite of these and other steps, most judges are forced generally to fall back on what they hope to be a reasonably informed concept of the "going rate" for particular offences. The outcomes are obviously important since sentence appeals are relatively lengthy and convoluted processes. The Irish appellate courts in general only make minor or piecemeal alterations to sentences and vary them when the trial judge demonstrably erred in principle. In practice, therefore, only a minority of sentencing judgments are in fact appealed which increases the importance of trying to minimise error and maintain consistency, considerations which sheer volume of work sometimes militates against.

RELEVANT CONSIDERATIONS WHEN SENTENCING

What then, in practice, are the factors that primarily influence sentencing? The traditional and conflicting objectives of sentencing, namely retribution, deterrence, incapacitation and rehabilitation have to be balanced in each case. Obviously, the principal aspects to be assessed in any individual case will be the seriousness of the offence, the background and record of the accused person and the course taken by the accused in so far as the sentencing issue may have arisen from a jury verdict of guilty or an early plea of guilty before the trial (which may be viewed as a cold-blooded reflection that the prosecution witnesses had attended and the jury were in a position to deal with the case). A sentencing judge will also consider the consequences of the crime, the incidence of the particular type of crime in question and may have regard to aspects of public policy applicable to particular types of cases. For instance it will obviously cut less ice than usual for defence counsel to plead that his client is a person of hitherto excellent character if the case is one that concerns the importation of large amounts of heroin through Irish sea or airport terminals, or if the accused has been detected handling the proceeds of a large armed bank robbery: the very reason that the accused has been recruited in these spheres is because of his ostensible respectability and there is clearly a need to deter others from succumbing to similar temptations. A court will also look to the general domestic and/or employment background of an accused and the attitudes of a spouse, parent or siblings since these may provide an indication as to the likelihood of the accused re-offending. Regard may also be had to whether or not the accused has any particular aptitudes or talent of a sporting or artistic bent since these may enhance the prospects of returning to an orderly and structured life in the community.

Consideration will also be given to the degree to which the accused has co-operated with the authorities. This will involve questions as to whether or not there was a prompt confession, whether stolen proceeds or a firearm used in the particular crime were recovered, whether there appears to be real remorse on the part of the accused (for virtually every accused contrives remorse) and whether the co-operation of the accused shown materially assisted the prosecution in detecting others more centrally involved in the crime under investigation. Regarding the latter factor reticence in this regard cannot be deemed to be an aggravatory aspect in sentencing but it does not prevent a court from regarding as a further favourable factor an unusual degree of co-operation over and above the more traditional preamble to confessions ("I and two fellows I don't want to name committed x … on a robbery last night.")

Other factors include considerations pertaining to offenders who come from particularly dysfunctional or deprived backgrounds, the particular arduousness of a prison regime for certain types of offenders on ethnic or nationality grounds, and whether or not the offender genuinely suffers from a serious health condition such as AIDS or serious suicidal ideation. It has been informally, but not unreliably, estimated that approximately 80% of Dublin's indictable crime is drug-related. Thus, in appropriate cases, a court will naturally look at the feasibility of an offender successfully addressing his addiction and the possibility of a suitable supervised regime at some stage in the sentencing equation. One likewise cannot ignore factors such as the capacity of the prison system or the fact that in certain types of cases, particularly those of a sexual nature, it may be merely reinforcing recidivism to pronounce a finite sentence which the offender may serve with a sense of denial and martyrdom only to resume his offending activities with impunity upon due release. In such cases, where there is acknowledgement of wrongdoing, there is surely much to be gained from structuring sentences so that an offender is committed to participate on programmes within the community during the latter stages of a sentence which may significantly lessen the prospects of his conduct giving rise to future victims or, at the very least, will result in further incarceration should he re-offend or depart from any conditions imposed by the court.

The foregoing does not remotely purport to be a definitive checklist. It merely seeks to indicate some of the factors that have to be evaluated and addressed in each case. The devices of partial suspension of sentences and of subsequent review of sentences imposed by the same sentencing court have their drawbacks in so far as they extend the duration of sentence hearings and, on occasions, necessarily introduce a somewhat undesirable want of certainty or finality. Indeed, the latter device is obviously very much in the twilight zone of a court's exercise of jurisdiction and must be sparingly used if at all[9]. However, prison governors and others have commented that its occasional utilisation can powerfully influence the motivation and behaviour of serious offenders in custody. Sometimes, particularly for serious first time offenders, a decision imposing an actual or a wholly-suspended three year sentence is too stark or simplistic and although what might be termed *a la carte* sentencing is open to criticism, on occasion it adequately fulfils the conflicting considerations inherent in sentencing.

In certain emotive types of criminal cases, such as sexual offences against children, violence against the elderly and certain serious types of white collar fraud, it is true to say that the atmosphere in Ireland in recent years has become appreciably more fevered. Whilst our national and local media may not quite have attained the techniques of communication espoused by the *National Enquirer* they have comparatively little to learn in that regard. A headline of the ilk of "Wimp judge frees sex killer" obviously sells more papers than a dispassionate and factual account of the proceedings and this may arguably be said to have significantly influenced the quality and objectivity of reporting of a significant minority of controversial cases. It is all the more necessary, therefore, that courts – whilst not shirking from imposing stern sentences in appropriate serious cases – sentence on the basis of calm, reasoned and objective consideration.

The four traditional headings under which punishment has been justified are Rehabilitation, Deterrence, Incapacitation, and Retribution. Perhaps at this juncture it would be useful to assess their status in current Western legal culture.

Rehabilitation

Rehabilitative programmes reached their zenith world-wide in the 1960s and 1970s. Until 1975, all fifty American states, as well as the District of Columbia and the federal jurisdiction, had indeterminate sentencing systems. The judge determined the nature of the sentence and, if imprisonment was ordered, stated the maximum or minimum sentence, or both. A parole board then decided when the offender would be released. In England, the Criminal Justice Act 1967 set up a similar parole board. Although no such body was ever established in Ireland, what little judicial pronouncements there have been on the purposes that govern sentencing practice have cited reform as a primary aim – usually along with deterrence (of which, more later). Walsh J in *The People (AC) v O'Driscoll*[10] declared that:

---

[9] Indeed the review practice was expressly disapproved of by the Supreme Court in its ruling, *People (DPP) v Finn* (unreported, 24 November 2000, at p. 43). The Supreme Court held that the review practice amounted to a breach of the doctrine of separation of powers, stating that: 'it is clearly for the Oireachtas to decide whether to retain the present system unaltered, to retain it on a clearer and more transparent basis, to devolve the function wholly or partly to a parole board or some other entity, or indeed to confer it on the courts'

[10] (1972) 1 Frewen 352

... the objects of passing sentence are not merely to deter the particular criminal from committing a crime again but to induce him as far as possible to turn from a criminal to an honest life ...[11]

His sentiments were echoed by Gannon J in *The State (Stanbridge) v Mahon*,[12] who added a slight element of retribution to the mix:

... The first consideration in determining the sentence is the public interest, which is served not merely by punishing the offender and showing a deterrent to others but also by affording a compelling inducement and an opportunity to the offender to reform.[13]

Both statements were quoted with approval in the *W.C.* case. There, Flood J defined the sentencing issue as a question of "... whether the public good requires what on the circumstances of his case would be a largely symbolic exercise of imposing a custodial sentence, or alternatively, to permit Dr. Mooney and the probation service to continue the already implemented task of seeking to rehabilitate this young man".[14] Thus, the prospect of reform was clearly chosen over any ideas of general deterrence.

However, as I have mentioned already, notions of rehabilitation have undergone trenchant academic criticism in recent years throughout the Western legal world. Research seems to show that treatment hitherto used in the administration of criminal justice has not generally had any significant effect on recidivism. The Irish Law Reform Commission in its 1996 *Report on Sentencing*[15] has added its voice to the growing numbers advocating a change of emphasis in the penal system away from notions of rehabilitation.

Deterrence

As with rehabilitation, deterrence has lost its lustre in the eyes of many criminologists and penal scholars. It is accepted that imprisonment does engender some level of general deterrence, but as English expert Andrew Ashworth observes:

... it is a perilous journey from this proposition, that judicial sentencing exerts an underlying deterrent influence on social behaviour, to the proposition that by increasing and decreasing their sentencing levels within tolerable limits, the courts can bring about substantial changes in rates of offending. Only in rare and unusual circumstances is this likely to happen: most of the evidence goes the other way.[16]

---

[11] *Ibid.*, at 359
[12] [1979] IR 214
[13] *Ibid.*, at 218
[14] *The People (Director of Public Prosecutions) v W.C.* [1994] 1 ILRM 321
[15] Law Reform Commission Report on Sentencing (LRC 53-1996)
[16] Andrew Ashworth, *Sentencing and Criminal Justice*, (Butterworths, 1995); see also Ian O'Donnell, 'Challenging the Punitive Obsession' (1998) 8 ICLJ 51

Sentencing commissions in Australia and Canada, after exhaustive reviews of available research, concluded that the evidence presented was woefully inadequate to provide a good estimate of the magnitude of any deterrent effect that may exist. Research has established that it is *certainty*, rather than *severity* of punishment, that has a deterrent effect. Those about to commit a crime will not generally consider the consequences at all; if they do, they will be more concerned with the likelihood of being apprehended, tried and convicted than with the possible harshness of any sentence they might receive.

Deterrence is often mentioned in the context of the state "sending a message" to those who might be inclined to break the law and encouraging them not to do so. The problem with this is that it fails to take into account the context in which the "message" is being received. Statistics in countries across the world show strong links between recidivism and an accumulation of social and personal problems – alcohol abuse, long-term unemployment, poor education, dysfunctional families etc. In such disadvantaged circumstances, the deterrent effect of penal sanctions is greatly reduced. What this means is that, broadly speaking, general preventive measures only serve as a deterrent to those who are not criminally active; they encourage habitual avoidance of criminal acts among those who already habitually obey the laws of the land. Therefore, where a deterrent policy is being pursued, one class of persons (the criminally active) is being punished in order to remind another class of persons (the non-criminally active) that crime does not pay. On what moral basis is this justifiable?

Incapacitation

This justification for punishment lies in the capacity of imprisonment to remove an identified offender from society at large thereby preventing him from committing further crimes for a period of time. Incapacitation may be termed the most "pragmatic" reason for punishment: it is obviously achievable and holds out no great hopes of affecting the psychological make-up or moral code of the offender – unlike deterrent or rehabilitative philosophies. However, it can prove extremely costly. Estimates from the California Department of Corrections in 1995 indicated that the state would need to build fifteen prisons over the next five years to hold the extra inmates imprisoned under the "three strikes" legislation, at a price tag of 4.5 billion dollars. The prison population in California was expected to grow by more than 70% as a result of this law. In Ireland, even without such harsh laws, we are struggling to keep pace with a growing prison population. In this regard, it is worth noting that the Law Reform Commission has advocated that imprisonment should only be as a sentence of last resort.[17]

---

[17] *Ibid.*

There is another objection to incapacitation as a primary sentencing aim that is of particular relevance to Ireland and the United States in the light of the constitutional guarantees of due process and fundamental fairness. Most incapacitate policies are based on attempts to predict which offenders are more likely to re-offend. In reality, such identification is extremely difficult: researchers in England and America found that between 50 and 66 per cent of those expected to re-offend did not in fact do so when left at large. To allow a sentencing policy based on such a huge margin of error would surely offend against the right to liberty as enshrined in the US and Irish Constitutions.

Retribution

At one level, retributive philosophy is quite simple: I have committed an offence and therefore I deserve to be punished. It is saved from mere revenge by the principle of *just deserts* – which once meant "an eye for an eye", but now usually means no more than that the punishment should be proportionate to the crime. However, at a deeper level, important questions remain, not least of which is, why do I deserve to be punished? The "rightness" of a retributive approach may have seemed clear in earlier, more homogeneous societies such as Old Testament Israel with unanimously held beliefs and a clearly defined moral code; but can a non-utilitarian, purely moral justification for punishment stand up in modern society where there is far less homogeneity? The real problem with retribution in modern complex societies is its circularity: we agree that punishment is to be reserved for those offences serious enough to deserve it – these we call crimes; yet ultimately, in the absence of agreed moral absolutes, the existence of such punishment is our only foolproof indicator of whether a given act is a crime or not.

OVERALL ASSESSMENT OF SENTENCING RATIONALES

It can be seen from the above analysis that none of the major rationales for punishment is without flaws, although quite a powerful argument can be advanced for a policy of retribution when tempered by the principles of proportionality and parsimony (the idea that punishment should not impinge upon the personal rights of the offender beyond the amount necessary to exact retribution for the offence). This is the policy that has been recommended by the Irish Law Reform Commission[18] and also by sentencing commissions in Canada, Australia and England. However, there remains the question of public interest: the state punishes ostensibly on behalf of the people and, as we have seen, the public has an interest in seeing that its version of "justice" is being done. This is not to say

---

[18] See the Law Reform Commission, *Report on Sentencing, op. cit.*, fn. 12

that the formulators of sentencing policy should bow to public pressure fuelled by media saturation, nor even to suggest that there exists an accurate picture of what the popular mind on punishment actually is; the man or woman in the street may not be able to give you any more than a jumble of half-formed moral principles, inchoate sentiment and popular media slogans in answer to the problem. Yet I think it safe to assume that elements of all four major rationales will be present. In which case, could we be justified in excluding some or most of these from sentencing policy?

Of course, if rehabilitation, deterrence, incapacitation and retribution are all to be included in some form, a hierarchy of importance must be created. This is the approach suggested by Galligan:

> ... many penal measures are meant to serve a variety of goals so that it would be odd to have to characterise each solely in terms of its punitive element; it would also be hard to abandon those which are humanitarian and reformative in spirit ... [alternatively] there is no reason in principle why penal policies cannot be ranked in order of importance, nor is there any reason for not having fairly clear criteria for their application.[19]

SENTENCING POLICY – A MATTER FOR THE JUDICIARY OR THE LEGISLATURE?

Once an underlying approach to sentencing has been agreed, it then remains to decide how best to implement it. Here, we enter the nebulous area of the separation of powers. To what degree should the legislature restrict judicial discretion in sentencing? In Ireland, Article 34.1 of the Constitution ensures the independence of the judicial function from interference by the other organs of state by providing that justice is to be administered in courts – and, in criminal cases, only in courts. The selection of the sentence to be imposed in individual circumstances has been held to constitute an intrinsically judicial function and, accordingly, a function which may only be exercised by judges in courts. However, Article 34.1 cannot be read as guaranteeing the courts *absolute* discretion in the administration of justice. For instance, the legislature is entitled in the course of penal legislation to prescribe the *range* of penalties which may be imposed. Thus, while it would be unconstitutional for the legislature to interfere with the court's sentencing decision in an individual case, it would not offend the separation of powers doctrine for the legislature to prescribe the penalty for a class of offence or for all offences. Neither is it necessarily unconstitutional for the Oireachtas to prescribe mandatory sentences; indeed, prior to the mid-1880s, mandatory sentences were the norm and courts had no

---

[19] D.J. Galligan, *Guidelines and Just Deserts: a Critique of Recent Trends in Sentencing Reform* [1981] *Crim LR* 295

discretion at all. Given these wide powers of the legislature to set the boundaries within which judicial discretion is exercised, it would seem unlikely that the separation of powers doctrine would prohibit the introduction of sentencing guidelines by the Oireachtas or the dictating of overall sentencing policy to the courts. After all, similar provisions in the United States Constitution have not prevented various states from introducing rigorous presumptive guidelines.

The question then arises as to whether the legislature or the judiciary would be better suited to forming a coherent sentencing policy. It may be argued that the courts are in the best position to formulate sentencing policy because they deal with sentencing cases every day. However, years of relatively unfettered discretion for Irish judges has not resulted in an identifiable uniform approach to sentencing. In the Irish court system, where the principle of co-ordinate jurisdiction means that judges of the same court are largely free to disregard each other's sentencing decisions, it is at the appellate stage that sentencing policy is judicially shaped; in particular, in the Court of Criminal Appeal and the Supreme Court. Yet the ability of these courts to formulate policy is constrained by the structure within which they operate. Appeals against sentence are infrequent in Ireland and, in any event, there is a danger that any general statements on sentencing practice made in such cases could be held as *obiter dicta* by a lower court or distinguished on the facts. In its *Report on Sentencing* the Law Reform Commission recommended that non-statutory guidelines aimed at formulating a coherent sentencing policy should be introduced.[20] Statutory guidelines were adopted in Finland in 1976, in Sweden in 1989 and in England upon the enactment of the Criminal Justice Bill 1991.

CONCLUSION

The last two decades have been a period of turbulence for penal systems across the world. Hitherto accepted rationales for punishment have been found wanting and yet it is hard to see what should take their place. Public concern over rising crime feeds media hype and this in turn brings new pressure to bear upon judges who are attempting to do justice in individual cases. To succeed, it is vital that the various organs of state work together to create a coherent sentencing framework within which judicial discretion may be exercised. In Ireland, at least, much work remains to be done.

---

[20] Law Reform Commission, *Report on Sentencing, op. cit.*, fn. 12

22

The Central Criminal Court:
A View from the Bench[*]

Mr Justice Paul Carney

To confirm that my recollection was accurate in relation to the nature of sexual crime when I came to the Bar, I asked the registrar of the Central Criminal Court to retrieve for me all Bills of Indictment in sexual cases for 1966, telling him that he could stop at ten. He came back to me telling me that he had to stop at two, for that's all there were. In those days, the majority of sexual cases would have remained dispersed throughout the country in the various Circuit Courts, but it nevertheless comes as a shock that the Central Criminal Court should be concerned with only two sexual cases in the year, fairly minor ones at that. Those were the leisurely days when the Central Criminal Court, according to my recollection, had to dispose of about one murder case a term, always the responsibility of the junior judge, every word of the evidence being published in the newspapers both at deposition and trial stage.

In those days, all indictable crime could reach the Central Criminal Court as of right. Certain cases, principally murders, were returned to the Central Criminal Court directly following return for trial by the District Court. Section 6 of the Courts Act 1964 allowed any indictable crime not directly returnable to the Central Criminal Court to be transferred there at the instance of either the prosecution or the defence.

The twin-tracks of direct return and transfer gave effect in the criminal area to the provision in Article 34.3.1 of the Constitution that the High Court has a full

[*] Originally presented at the University of Capetown, South Africa, September 1999

original jurisdiction in and power to determine all matters and questions whether of law or fact, civil or criminal.

Professor David Gwynn Morgan, in his paper on constitutional interpretation delivered to the Irish Historical Society at UCD on 15 September 1987, said that it was an open secret that many persons were invoking the right to transfer simply because of the delay in trials before the Central Criminal Court which flowed from the number of persons who were insisting on trial before that court. My own recollection is that what was found most provocative was that persons charged with the stealing of a bar of chocolate elected for trial on indictment in the first instance and then had their trials transferred to the Central Criminal Court.

To deal with this problem, the Oireachtas, in my view, over-reacted to the problem in its enactment of Section 31 of the Courts Act 1981. As Henchy J said giving the mandatory single judgment of the Supreme Court in *Tormey v Ireland* (1985) IR p 289 at p 293:

> Section 6 of the Act of 1964 was the sole vehicle of transfer until it was repealed by the Courts Act 1981. The present right of transfer is contained in Section 31 of the latter Act. The effect of the provisions of Section 31 and the repeal of Section 6 of the Act of 1964 is to abolish completely the right of transfer to the Central Criminal Court.

Following the passage of the Courts Act 1981, the right of both the prosecution and defence to transfer trials to the Central Criminal Court was abolished and it exercised by direct return from the District Court jurisdiction over the following crimes: (a) treason; (b) piracy; (c) genocide; (d) murder and murder related offences; and (e) certain offences under the Offences Against the State Acts.

Rape and aggravated sexual assault were added at a later date as a result of successful lobbying by those who lobby government in respect of sexual crime. There has never, since the foundation of the state, been a prosecution for treason, piracy or genocide. Nor has the Central Criminal Court yet to my knowledge had to concern itself with a crime under the Offences Against the State Acts, though I understand that one may be on its way. The effect of this is that whatever its theoretical jurisdiction, the Central Criminal Court is, as a matter of reality, confined to the trial of murder and rape.

People have been murdering and raping each other from time immemorial and, accordingly, the law in relation to these crimes is well settled. They are the easiest and most unchallenging cases to try. These are the cases which fall to be tried by the judges of the High Court, the highest judges of first instance in the Central Criminal Court, the criminal division of the High Court.

Far more difficult cases are those concerning money laundering, fraud, particularly where there is a trans-national dimension, cases relating to the importation and trafficking in drugs and whatever cases may result in trial on indictment from the McCracken, Flood, Moriarty and Lindsay Tribunals and the

Laffoy Commission. Such cases cannot be prosecuted at a higher level than the Circuit Court, a court described, to the chagrin of its members, as an inferior court by reason of the local and limited nature of its jurisdiction. The High Court, being established under the Constitution, is described as one of the superior courts.

It seems to me an absurdity that a billion pound fraud cannot be tried in the highest criminal court of first instance, not because it is above the jurisdiction of that court but because it is beneath it. The billion pound fraud cannot rise higher than trial in the Circuit Court and, depending on the place of arrest, perhaps be triable in a remote part of the country. It does not seem to me to be any answer to say that the Circuit Court can impose the same penalties, applies the same law and follows the same procedures. It is a court of local and limited jurisdiction and while not limited in terms of sentence, is limited on the civil side to a jurisdiction of £30,000 and is accustomed to dealing with matters of that order of magnitude.

The High Court has the daily experience of dealing with matters of company law, insolvency, fraud, conflict of laws, European Law and trans-national matters generally. It was on the Chancery side of the High Court that the first inroads were successfully made against fraud by Costello J (as he then was). Not much has happened since in the fraud area in the Circuit Criminal Court because not much is being sent to that court for trial.

The present distribution of criminal business between the courts was challenged unsuccessfully on constitutional grounds in *Tormey v Ireland* (1985) IR p 289. The Supreme Court held that the constitutional imperative that the High Court have full original jurisdiction in all matters and questions pertaining to crime was satisfied by the High Court having a supervisory jurisdiction by way of judicial review.

This approach might not satisfy the European Union which not, as yet, having criminal courts of its own requires that its budget be protected under the domestic law of each member state. The financial control division of the Commission (DG20) is acutely conscious that those engaged in fraud "forum shop" throughout the community, that is they seek the most congenial and safest environment for their fraud, and it might not be happy with the level at which the billion pound fraud against the community budget falls to be prosecuted in Ireland. If it were unhappy, it could take proceedings against Ireland under Article 5 of the Treaty of Rome before the European Court of Justice in Luxembourg.

Currently, the Central Criminal Court is handling nearly 160 Bills of Indictment a year consisting of murders and rapes. In 1998, there were twenty-nine murders and 129 rapes. The numbers of murders are relatively constant but the rapes increase at an exponential rate. Police research indicates that this is not likely to change in the foreseeable future.

Contested trials take longer than they used to. Were each of the 158 Bills of Indictment now coming before the court annually to be contested, the High Court would have time for little else. Fortunately, there is a high level of pleas of guilty and a special sentencing discount for those accused who organise their affairs so as not to occupy a trial date has proved successful. Sentencing in the sexual area is an emotive issue. The courts, while endeavouring to be consistent one case with another and taking into account the individual circumstances of each case, each victim and each accused person, must in reality:

1   strike a balance between the demands of a vengeful society and what is acceptable to the accused person so as to bring forward the optimum number of pleas of guilty

2   maintain a balance between the sentence imposed for sexual crime and the effective sentence extracted by the executive for the crime of murder so that it does not become worth the rapist's while to kill his victim as a matter of routine to avoid apprehension.

The level of sentences being currently imposed for sexual crime has significantly dropped since the days of *DPP v Tiernan* (1988) IR p 250. Those sentences themselves were an exponential increase on the three years for rape levels of the 1960s because of increased incidence and viciousness. Were the Tiernan levels in operation today, the probabilities are that pleas of guilty would not be forthcoming and the disposal rate would grind to a halt.

The nature of sexual crime has changed out of all recognition over the last twenty to thirty years. It used to take the form simply of the unlawful insertion of the male penis into the female vagina in circumstances which would now be described as date rape, eg the Bull Wall rape of the late 1960s where some hitherto respectable youths manufactured such a lethal cocktail of drinks that they lost control of themselves and forced sexual intercourse on their girlfriends. Few cases are as straightforward anymore. Most cases nowadays will involve a com-bination of oral, anal and vaginal rape accompanied by great violence. Those three forms of forced intercourse now generally go together. Some cases will additionally involve the use of an implement for vaginal or anal penetration. There is generally no contraceptive protection employed but if there is, it may be a supermarket plastic bag or a bank coin bag. What I have come to call classical rape is now so rare that I comment on the absence of the usual aggravating features when it occurs.

The majority of sexual attacks by strangers involve a credible threat to kill, leading the victim to believe that she is as a matter of virtual certainty about to die. Parliament has recently re-enacted the threat to kill provisions of the Offences Against the Person Act 1861, providing a penalty of ten years imprisonment. In only one case that has come before me has this statutory provision been invoked. I cannot for my part understand how the prosecuting authority can feel free to ignore the recently expressed wishes of Parliament.

There is a high rate of acquittals in contested rape cases, the reasons for which one can only speculate about. It could be that in some of these cases juries would accept the threat to kill dimension of the prosecutrix's claim. We will not know until the prosecuting authority places the matter before juries for their determination.

The high rate of acquittals in contested cases is related to and may in part be accounted for by the high rate of pleas of guilty. It may be that those who have no room to manoeuvre by virtue of the evidence being overwhelming have pleaded guilty leaving the cases "with a fight in them" to be contested. It is noticeable, however, that in certain categories of cases there is a marked reluctance to convict. There have been a surprising number of cases coming forward where the prosecutrix went to rest in an upstairs bedroom during a late night party. She claims to have woken up to find another guest at the party, known or unknown to her, inside her having sexual congress with her without her consent. While there has been one conviction in such a case, it seems to be a category of case in which there has usually been a reluctance to convict. This appears to be the experience also in England where there is a move for the creation of a new offence to make it acceptable to juries to convict again in cases of the type popularly categorised as date rape. The English jury is not apparently prepared to convict in such cases under the description of rape simpliciter.

Juries in Ireland also display a marked reluctance to convict in cases where the girl has met a stranger in a disco and goes with him in the early hours of the morning into his car or into his flat. In these situations, the most horrific sexual attacks have been described in evidence but there has been frequently a hostile reaction to the prosecutrix from the jury. Are they saying, "she deserved what she got for going into a stranger's car or flat in the middle of the night"? We don't know. What we do know is that these juries are, on average, pretty evenly sexually mixed and a study of the jury's demeanour in the jury box would suggest that the female members of juries are the prosecutrix's severest critics.

In some of these cases, the members of the jury have undoubtedly got it right but in others they may have acquitted where the complaint was genuine. In such cases the victim will only believe that the jury disbelieved her though that may not be the case at all. An infinite variety of reasons other than disbelief may have led to an acquittal. Because of the secrecy of the jury room we will never find out the reason. As was said by Haugh J. in delivering the judgment of the Court of Criminal Appeal in *The People (Attorney General) v Longe* (1967) IR 369 (at p 377): "In our opinion the principle is well established that the nature of the deliberation of a jury in a criminal case should not be revealed or inquired into".

I believe that the genuine complainant whose rapist is acquitted suffers more on that account than from whatever happened to her on the night of the rape. I have no way of knowing whether prosecutrixes are pressurised into continuing with complaints they are reluctant to pursue. Such pressure could come from parents, boyfriends, policemen, prosecutors, Rape Crises Centre and Victim Support counsellors. I have no way of knowing whether such pressure exists but

I would be very concerned if it does, particularly in relation to those cases which can be profiled as unlikely to result in a conviction.

I have adverted to the increasing violence, perversion and aggravating features which now attend most cases coming before the court. I can, at any given time, identify the case which shocks me the most but I do so now in the certain knowledge that within a couple of months that case will have been displaced by another. The case currently holding the blue riband is one in which a husband over eleven years daily beat and raped his wife in every fashion, but over and above that allegedly sent her out "on the game" to acquire strangers' sperm on her body for him to lick off. Our society has become desensitised by the violence of these cases and they provoke little reaction any more other than the routine question to me, "how do you put up with it day after day".

What is now provoking reaction is what the cases currently coming in show about contemporary morality and sexual practices of boys and girls in the thirteen to seventeen year age group. They are acquiring strong drink without the knowledge of their parents and engaging in oral sex with total strangers. The cases reveal that girls of thirteen upwards will not just give oral sex but actively seek it. The boys, to cultivate their images as studs may have to take oral sex from four different thirteen to seventeen year olds, who may be strangers to them, on the same evening. This is considered safe sex and is socially acceptable to the young. Proceeding to vaginal sex is regarded as unsafe and is considered bad form. It is when this happens either through drink or arousal, that the matter comes to the attention of the court.

Rape is the most emotive of crimes and has been the subject of the most intense and successful political lobbying. Prior to 1980, rape was a crime with some special rules (the corroboration warning and the admissibility of the recent complaint) but otherwise triable in all respects as any other crime.

Some lobbyists, I am sure, would secretly like the law to move to the position where conviction follows automatically from accusation. Sexually mixed juries are seeing to it that that does not happen. I believe that it would be interesting to bring together in one text all the changes which have been procured in the law relating to sexual offences over the last twenty years by political lobbying.

The Courts Act 1981, as already noted, drove sexual crime out of the High Court and dispersed it to the various Circuit Courts around the country where it would have gone unnoticed on a national basis. Lobbying very quickly brought serious sexual crime back to the High Court on an exclusive basis. The influence of the Rape Crises Centres will be appreciated when it is noted that the Director of the Dublin Rape Crises Centre is on the board of both the Courts Service and the Judicial Appointments Board. I do not say this in any pejorative way, but merely state it as a material fact.

The Criminal Law (Rape) Act 1981 introduced a statutory definition of rape and extended the offence to capture the situation where a man's lack of knowledge that the woman was not consenting was due to recklessness on his part. This was the last time sexual crime was to be defined in Irish Law in "sexual", that is gender-biased, terms. Sexual crimes created or defined since are equally capable of being committed by a woman upon a man as the other way around. The 1981 Act then introduced a restriction on evidence being adduced or questions being asked in cross examination in relation to previous sexual experience of the alleged victim with any person other than the accused except with leave of the trial judge who may only give leave if satisfied that in effect conviction or acquittal will turn on whether or not the permission is given. A Private Member's Bill, introduced by Liz McManus TD, in her final days as Democratic Left justice spokesperson, provided for legal representation to be made available to the alleged victim on the application for leave. The proposal has been adopted by the present Minister for Justice, Equality and Law Reform and there is in place a commitment that such legislation will be enacted.

The government has held the line, however, on giving representation to the victim from the commencement of the investigation through trial and beyond. Pressure to achieve this objective or as much as can piecemeal be achieved will no doubt continue with even greater intensity the more is achieved.

Anonymity of the accused is provided for until after conviction. Anonymity of the victim is provided for but may be set aside if that be necessary to induce persons to come forward as witnesses. I am not aware of such a course ever having been followed. There is also provision for a public interest removal of the victim's anonymity and again I am not aware of this provision ever having been invoked.

In 1990, the law of sexual offences went unisex. Indecent assaults on males and females were consolidated as sexual assaults and new offences were henceforth created on the basis that each sex could commit them upon one sex or the other. Aggravated sexual assault was created as a sexual assault that involves serious violence or is such as to cause injury, humiliation or degradation of a grave nature to the person assaulted.

The new crime of rape under Section 4 was created as meaning a sexual assault that includes the penetration of the anus or mouth by the penis or penetration of the vagina by any object held or manipulated by another person. The enactment of this Section reflects, in my view, a growing up and an abandonment of prissiness by the Oireachtas. A decade earlier, the problem was sought to be dealt with by increasing the penalty for indecent assault from two years to ten years without spelling out the problem that was being addressed. This Section came about as a result of pressure from the victims, requiring that what happened to them be called rape and not a bland term like indecent assault, which could equally be a legal description of a playful slap on the bottom.

Section 5 of the 1990 Act extended the crime of rape to marital rape. The number of prosecutions as a result has been small. Section 6 abolished any defence on the ground of age. This is now bringing into the dock an increasing number of youths who were aged from thirteen at the date of the alleged offence. Section 7 abolished the rule of law whereby a corroboration warning was mandatory in sexual cases.

The 1990 Act provides for the bringing in of alternative verdicts if the evidence does not support the offence charged but would sustain another or lesser offence. This provision was no doubt drafted in an effort to close off all possible avenues of escape for a guilty person but it does not have regard to the mechanics of the court process. The Director of Public Prosecutions is free to include in an indictment all counts which he has evidence to support. He can even include counts which represent fall-back positions. For a judge, however, to have to charge a jury in terms of Section 8 of the 1990 Act is in effect inviting them to bring in a compromise verdict of conviction on a lesser offence. The Section, in my view, tempts injustice.

Sexual cases are heard in private with the verdict and sentence being pronounced in public. The press are entitled to attend and while the statue does not give them an express right to report, this is implied subject to the anonymity restrictions. The judge has a discretion in relation to whom he or she allows to remain in court. The work of the court is reported by an agency service which operates to a high standard. The tabloid newspapers, I cannot but notice, put on the agency copy the by-line of a staff member who has never been next or near the court. The agency copy, of its nature, only gives a flavour of the case or sentence, due to space restrictions. It is a matter of regret to me that serious journalists, legislators and social commentators generally never spend any time observing the work of the court but continue to shoot from the hip in often ill-informed comment. Such persons would be given permission to attend, certainly by me, notwithstanding the exclusion of the public provisions of the statutes. Those who have lobbied so successfully in relation to imposing rules and constraints on the court will in general not have observed first hand how it operates.

A section in a 1999 criminal justice statute which has not yet been commenced by the minister provides that the courts are, in appropriate cases, to be entitled to impose maximum sentences notwithstanding a plea of guilty. In my court that would generally mean a life sentence. When this provision is commenced, why should any accused person be advised to plead guilty? He would be accepting unlimited exposure. No matter how overwhelming the evidence, he may as well take his chance on the unexpected acquittal which does happen. The thinking behind the section is either: the accused will plead guilty in any event or the result of the trial is preordained.

Verdicts are preordained only in show trials, which we do not have, and accused persons are advised by an independent bar of the highest quality and independence. This section is sending out a signal which may be regretted.

The foregoing represent some random thoughts from my time as senior judge of the Central Criminal Court in Ireland. Do I see any improvement on the horizon? I regret to say, the answer is no.

23

The Victim and the Criminal Justice Process

Lillian McGovern

WHAT IS THE STATUS OF THE VICTIM OF CRIME IN THE CRIMINAL JUSTICE SYSTEM AND HOW DOES THE VICTIM PERCEIVE THE CURRENT SYSTEM?

From the victim's perspective the criminal justice system as it currently operates in Ireland almost entirely excludes the victim from an active role in the process of responding to the convicted offender. Punishment is a key component of this process and normally the system does not provide the victim with any meaningful role or sense of active participation in state-managed punishment. It may be useful to very briefly outline the historical background to this current position, whereby the victim finds himself or herself virtually excluded from the resolution phase of the criminal justice process.

In Irish law up to the early part of the nineteenth century the responsibility for prosecuting an offender lay with the individual, that is the person injured by the offence. The victim gathered the evidence, paid the lawyer and, of course, paid the costs if the case failed to be proved. An inherent problem in such a system was the imbalance of power that it created. A powerful and wealthy offender could intimidate an impecunious victim, thus avoiding any court hearing. Had there been an awareness of the concept of victims' rights at that stage of our history, there would probably have been a more speedy acknowledgement that the onerous task of prosecution then forced upon the victim was unjust and that more of the burden should be shouldered by the state.

Over the years the imbalance in the criminal justice process, relating to inequalities in wealth and social influence, began to be redressed with the introduction of police services. The police eventually assumed the responsibility for gathering evidence and prosecuting cases. The final step in that process was the Prosecution of Offences Act 1974 which set up the independent office of the Director of Public Prosecutions, who prosecutes all serious cases in the name of the state. However, by accepting this responsibility for prosecution, the state introduced a new form of imbalance of power. The offender in turn became a vulnerable party, pitted as he or she was against the almost unlimited power and might of the state.

In order to address this new imbalance and protect the alleged offender, a whole corpus of law has evolved, to enable the offender to put his/her case clearly and to protect him/her from unfair prosecution and punishment. Legal advice and representation has been made available to offenders and strict legal rules have been developed to govern the manner in which evidence can be presented. The underlying philosophy of the current system can be encapsulated in the maxim that it is better that nine guilty persons go free than that one innocent person be convicted.

It is also clear that the relationship between the offender and the state has come to dominate the process of criminal justice prosecution and punishment. The victim has come to be regarded as a person with a responsibility first to assist the police by reporting the crime and second to provide evidence for the prosecution. In other words the victim's presence in the process is required solely to act as witness for the state. Historically, the victim, in the course of gaining relief from the unwanted and unfair personal responsibility for prosecution, has been pushed to the sidelines and become largely irrelevant in the eyes of the professionals who operate the system. It is within this historical context that the victims' movement began.

The needs and rights of victims of crime have attracted increasing political and professional interest since the early 1970s. Then, there was a vague feeling that more could be done to improve the victim's lot. A range of small interest groups was formed to achieve reform. Many developments in Europe affecting victims of crime echo previous events in North America, despite the differences between legal systems. Indeed, the various European legal systems differ considerably from each other in their philosophy and organisation, but have nevertheless all shown in recent years an increased interest in the role of the victim.

Against this general background of increasing awareness of the needs of victims, the first victim support service was established in Bristol in the UK in 1975. With the support of the police, probation and social services, similar "schemes" were established over the following years with the eventual creation of a British national body in 1979. By 1996 Victim Support UK was offering assistance to more than a million victims of crime each year and schemes were operating in all parts of the country. Parallel national schemes were also set up in Scotland and Northern Ireland and were fairly soon followed by the establishment of similar organisations in France and the Netherlands.

Victim Support was established in Ireland by Derek Nally in 1985. Starting with a small number of branches and virtually no funding, the organisation, through its volunteers, offered the necessary practical help and emotional support to victims of crime. Relying heavily on government support the organisation has grown and developed since 1985.

People's reactions to being victimised are individual and unpredictable. While there are some discernible patterns, it can never be assumed that a particular offence will have predictable consequences for individual victims. People respond to crime in diverse and sometimes surprising ways. Feelings of fear, shame, resentment, anger against the offender and the criminal justice system, humiliation and a variety of other emotions are all very common. For some, a need to protect themselves from further offences or even a total feeling of disempowerment and an inability to cope are also common. For others, there may be total withdrawal or even refusal to believe that the crime has occurred. Physical symptoms include inability to sleep or concentrate, being jumpy and easily startled. In some cases victims' self-esteem and social lives may suffer.

One reason why criminal acts can be particularly difficult to come to terms with, compared for example with equally harmful accidents, is that they have been perpetrated deliberately by a human agent. The experience of becoming a victim of crime is fundamentally different from that of being a victim of an accident or illness, because the crisis has been brought about intentionally by another person. Crime victimisation, therefore, is an experience that can fundamentally alter a person's view of the world, especially their view of the trustworthiness of others.

With over 500 trained and screened volunteers working through a network of over forty branches, the service provided by Victim Support to victims of crime is unique. Trained volunteers provide a confidential, non-judgemental "listening" ear to those affected by crime. The service both accepts self-referrals by victims of crime and works with the Garda Síochána, who on a regular basis forward details of victims of crime to the local co-ordinator of Victim Support. A volunteer visitor is allocated to a case within a few days and the volunteer makes an approach to the victim either by telephone or by visiting.

The service is firmly founded on a community-based approach, with members of local communities reaching out to those affected by crime in their own area. As well as offering emotional support visitors provide practical advice and help on matters such as security, insurance and crime prevention. Those victims who require further assistance may be visited more than once, but the majority of referrals are dealt with after one or two contacts. It is important to appreciate that volunteer visitors are not trained as counsellors. In cases where victims clearly need the assistance of a counsellor, they are referred on to appropriate specialist agencies. In 1999 Victim Support helped and assisted over 8,000 victims of crime with over 48% of victims presenting as a result of burglary.

Automatic referral from the Garda Síochána has been the basis of Victim Support's referral policy over many years. The system of referral was negotiated with the Garda and the Department of Justice in such a way as to ensure that certain categories of crime victim would be offered equal access to the services of Victim Support. With the introduction of the European Standards of Data Protection (EU 1995) and impending human rights legislation that will make the European Convention on Human Rights part of domestic law, it is possible that automatic referral from the Garda Síochána to Victim Support will no longer be available. This will present new and uncertain challenges for the victim movement since experience of organisations in other countries that have undergone similar changes shows huge decreases in the number of victims supported. A requirement to provide services in a new fashion, such as through the establishment of outreach services, seems imminent. This will certainly have the consequence that a much smaller number of cases will result in a much higher level of work. Internal cultural changes in Ireland and the increased awareness of the need to assure transparency and accountability and to respect basic rights such as the right to privacy will continue to impact on the way social services agencies, such as Victim Support, and the Garda Síochána carry out their business.

As a growing and developing organisation, Victim Support has initiated many new services for victims since 1985. These services were established based on identified need and modeled on examples of best practice from both the UK and beyond. The Court Victim/Witness Service, for example, provides support and assistance to those attending court. Trained volunteers provide support and information about the court process to witnesses, victims and their families, before, during and after the trial. However, these volunteers do not play any active role in the court process.

In response to the increasing rate of murder in Ireland, Victim Support developed a support service to families and friends of those who have lost someone in violent circumstances. Assistance is provided on all the urgent practical matters which follow a sudden death. Specially trained volunteers can provide information to the relatives of victims on the complex criminal justice system, can help them with dealings with media, and can accompany them to police stations or coroner's court. Very often a volunteer works closely with the family for a prolonged period of time.

Other services developed over the last number of years include the establishment of a specialist service to tourists who have been victimised while on holiday in Ireland. This service is seen as a "best practice" model in Europe and beyond. In 1998, a twenty-four hour national freephone helpline was established. This helpline is a particularly vital point of contact for people who do not wish to report a crime, offering as it does a fast and confidential means of exploring what help may be available locally.

In identifying future needs Victim Support, in conjunction with other agencies, is currently initiating specialist educational programmes for schools. Victim Support already runs programmes for those involved in the criminal justice system, aimed at raising their awareness of the effects of crime on victims and their families. In addition, the organisation is currently investigating the need for support services in the area of bullying, both in the workplace and in schools. The emerging multi-cultural nature of Irish society has also created the need for specific training in issues such as racism and xenophobia.

As a large national organisation with an established relationship with the Department of Justice, Equality and Law Reform and other government departments, Victim Support has some political influence. Measures of success in this area can be seen in many areas of the criminal justice system. Volunteers involved in the Court Victim/Witness Service noted that victims and their families frequently had unwelcome and distressing encounters with the accused when they went to court to give evidence. They also found that court officials often failed to provide basic information about the criminal process and about the progress of a case of the kind that victim/witnesses commonly needed. Very often families found it impossible to find a seat in a crowded courtroom. In response to the needs described and highlighted by Victim Support, the newly established Courts Services Board has guaranteed the provision of a "Victim Support" room in every courthouse in Ireland, new systems for the provision of vital information and special seating arrangements within the courtroom for victims and their families.

As an experienced advocate of victims' rights and needs, Victim Support recognised the huge deficiencies in the information provided to victims and their families. Victims need to be kept fully informed with a continuous update on the status of their case. This need was clearly identified in the recent Economic and Social Research Institute survey (Watson 1999) on the nature and circumstances of crime. Findings showed that fewer than two victims in five were satisfied with the follow-up information provided by the gardaí on their case. Similarly, only one quarter of the individual victims were satisfied with the outcome of their case.

THE CHARTER OF VICTIMS' RIGHTS

The publication of the Charter of Victims' Rights in the Criminal Justice System (Department of Justice, Equality and Law Reform 1999) by the government was a significant development in addressing the need for clear and concise information for victims and their families. Each of the key agencies in the criminal justice system lay out what victims and their families can expect from the system and, more importantly, what redress they have if their expectations are not met. Each agency has named a liaison person as a contact point, if required. It is a significant development that Victim Support, as a voluntary organisation, is included as a key player in the Charter of Victims' Rights. However, the crucial question is, as with any Charter, how realisable are the fine ideals expressed?

Although the Victims' Charter is available on demand from Victim Support, all garda stations, and the Department of Justice, Equality and Law Reform, its existence and purpose are not widely known outside these agencies. The layout and the content is clear and understandable but acknowledges its own inherent limitations as a tool for instantiating the rights of victims by placing considerable emphasis on how to make complaints about criminal justice agencies and on where to obtain further information.

Instead of using copies of the Victims' Charter itself, the gardaí have taken the section dealing with their duties and republished it separately as the Garda Victims' Charter. This is what will be provided to a victim in a garda station. This has the unfortunate result that victims receive only one small section of information rather than receiving the full and complete version of the Charter.

While each of the agencies named and listed has given firm undertakings to keep victims and their families informed of each state of the process, eg dates of appeals, pre-release hearings, temporary or early release dates, it appears in follow-up dialogue with the relevant agencies that systems do not yet exist which can facilitate and ensure this process. Each victim needs about six different types of information which are relevant at various stages in the case. Most of that information is held separately by the various agencies, so what is required are properly co-ordinated systems of information exchange, whereby accurate and up-to-date data can be transmitted quickly to the victim. Those systems simply do not exist in Ireland as yet.

Other areas of concern for Victim Support around the Victims' Charter relate to areas of substantive policy. Victim Support is a strong advocate of the victim having an input into the parole process but the Charter does not envisage such an approach. On the other hand, Victim Support is opposed to the manner in which the Charter provides an opportunity for the Probation and Welfare Service to have an input into the completion of the Victim Impact Statement. The irony of placing such a responsibility upon the Probation Service, whose primary responsibility remains the supervision of offenders, has not been lost on Victim Support and the organisation will continue to monitor the effectiveness of the Victims' Charter especially in regard to difficulties arising from this dual and potentially contradictory role placed on the Probation and Welfare Service. In general, Victim Support will monitor the effectiveness of the Charter and highlight issues as they arise.

THE VICTIM IMPACT STATEMENT

Victim Support was largely instrumental in achieving the introduction of the Victim Impact Statement into criminal proceedings. Based on best practice in New Zealand, the 1993 Criminal Justice Act provided for the introduction of this "snap-shot" statement by the victim. The statement is intended to describe the personal impact of the crime – on the victim's life physically, emotionally, psychologically, financially or in any other way.

Subsection 1 of Section 5 of the Act provides that "in determining the sentence to be imposed on a person for an offence to which this section applies, a court should take into account and may, where necessary, receive evidence or submissions concerning, any effect (whether long term or otherwise) of the offence on the person in respect of whom the offence was committed".

Subsection 3 of the Section says "where a court is determining the sentence to be imposed on a person for an offence to which this section applies, the court shall, upon application by the person in respect of whom such offence was committed, hear the evidence of the person in respect of whom the offence was committed, as to the effect of the offence on such person being requested to do so".

The significance of this provision by the Oireachtas cannot be overstated. In effect, the Victim Impact Statement, which is given to the judge after the offender has pleaded or is found guilty, for the first time gives the victim recognition and a real sense of participation in the proceedings. In addition, it can sometimes save the victim the added trauma of giving evidence in open court and, in the case of a sexual case, can spare the victim further harrowing cross-examination.

Commenting on the use of the Victim Impact Statement at a conference held in Dublin Castle in December 1997 Judge Michael Moriarty stated: "I think that it is fair to say that incorporation of Section 5 of the 1993 Criminal Justice Act did significantly reflect a culture change that had belatedly dawned upon Irish lawyers and judges and other professionals involved in the court system, that the position of the victim simply had to be faced up to realistically".

However, within the victim movement and, more specifically, within Victim Support there are differing views on the role and significance of the Victim Impact Statement. While Victim Support Ireland sees its completion as vital in ensuring a more meaningful role for the victim in the criminal justice procedure, partners Victim Support UK considers that victims should not be given the additional responsibility or burden of having a role in sentencing.

In a recent development the UK Home Office has drafted a Victim Personal Statement Scheme. This scheme is being introduced as part of a range of measures intended to improve the position of victims of crime within the criminal justice system and enable them, if they wish, to have a higher level of involvement in the criminal justice process.

This scheme will allow the victim to make a statement once the crime has been reported. This statement then becomes part of the overall case files and can be updated at each stage during the process. The statement is available to all agencies involved and is disclosable. Other important details can also be held on this statement such as whether the victim would like to receive further information about the progress of the case, concerns about bail or details about vulnerability as a victim. This information can be updated at any stage during the entire process.

This move towards a more holistic approach to the long-term needs of victims has been widely welcomed by all involved in the criminal justice system in the UK and especially by Victim Support UK which views this development as significant in capturing all relevant information on behalf of the victim and ensuring that victims' needs and rights are taken into account throughout the process.

COMPENSATION FOR VICTIMS

A non-statutory "Scheme of Compensation for Personal Injuries Criminally Inflicted" was introduced in the Republic of Ireland following the Dublin and Monaghan bombings. This scheme was amended in 1986 to exclude awards in respect of pain and suffering. Following the review of the Northern Ireland scheme and the report of the Victims' Commissioner, John Wilson, in 1999, as well as developments within this area in the European context, it was decided to carry out a review of the scheme by the Department of Justice, Equality and Law Reform.

The scheme is funded by the state Exchequer and is administered by the Criminal Injuries Compensation Tribunal, which is made up of seven members who are practising barristers or solicitors. The Tribunal also administers the payment of compensation to members of the Garda Síochána on the basis of the Garda Síochána Compensation Act 1941 and to prison officers on the basis of the 1990 Scheme of Compensation for Personal Injuries Criminally Inflicted on Prison Officers.

At present the victim/applicant has the onus of proving entitlement to compensation and so must send all necessary supporting evidence with the completed application form. Staff of the Tribunal then investigate the application. Applicants can choose to be legally represented but the Tribunal will not cover the cost of this. Advice on how the scheme works is included in the Tribunal's annual report.

Compensation is currently payable for personal injury or death which is directly attributable to a crime of violence, or received because of, or in the course of, the victim coming to the assistance of a member of the gardaí, or received because of or in the course of attempting to save a human life.

Compensation is not payable where injuries were sustained as a result of a traffic accident, where the offender and victim were living together as members of the same household or as recognition for pain and suffering following the crime.

Both the UN 1985 Declaration on the Basic Principles of Justice for Victims of Crime and the Abuse of Power as well as the European Convention on the Compensation of Victims of Violent Crimes (Council of Europe 1983) propose that states should endeavour to provide financial compensation to victims who have sustained significant bodily injury or impairment of physical or mental health as a result of serious crime, where no compensation is available from the offender. Forty-three states have signed and ratified the European Convention. To-date Ireland has not yet done this.

The purpose of state compensation is to recognise on behalf of society the experience which victims of crime have suffered and to help the victim to recover and to live as normal a life as possible in the circumstances. As such, awards should be made for psychological as well as physical injury. There should be parity of awards for similar degrees of pain and suffering whether due to physical or mental injuries. In fatal cases, there should be provision for those who were financially dependent on the victim and, further, the scheme needs to make provision for interim payments in such circumstances. Most importantly any compensation should be seen as part of an overall, integrated support service for victims of crime and not isolated from other means of addressing victims' social, psychological and economic situation, such as provision of emotional support or housing.

Victim Support continues to lobby for improvements to the compensation scheme in Ireland, in line with the existing scheme in the UK and proposed scheme in Northern Ireland. An overall review of this scheme is currently being undertaken by the Department of Justice, Equality and Law Reform.

THE INTERNATIONAL PERSPECTIVE AND ITS INFLUENCE ON IRELAND

Victim Support does not work in isolation but rather is part of a much larger victim movement both in a European and worldwide context.

The European Forum for Victim Services was established in 1990 by all the national organisations in Europe working for victims of crime. The Forum, now made up of fourteen member organisations, exists to promote the development of effective services for victims of crime throughout Europe, to promote fair and equal compensation for all citizens across Europe regardless of the nationality of the victim concerned, to promote the rights of victims of crime in the criminal justice system, and to exchange experiences and information and share best practice and knowledge between member organisations.

In 1999 the Forum published its Statement of Victims' Rights to Standards of Service, which sets out the minimum standards which should apply in any organisation providing support services to victims of crime. This statement follows the Statement of Victims' Rights in the Process of Criminal Justice (1997) and the Statement of Social Rights of Crime (1998) which sets out the basic principles and rights victims should expect to receive in respect of healthcare, home security, employment, privacy, income, education, compensation and support services.

The work of the Forum is currently concentrating on developing best practice in training and support for staff and volunteers as well as taking an advocacy role in supporting new member organisations from Eastern European countries to develop appropriate services within their own jurisdictions. This work is carried out within the diverse context of the widely differing criminal justice systems of European states but also within the context of the ongoing development by the EU of a set of minimum standards which will apply right across the continent. In addition, as with all voluntary sector work, core funding is an ongoing problem with the Forum currently seeking ongoing, guaranteed funding from the EU Commission to progress its work-plan.

The World Society of Victimology is a not for profit non-governmental organisation with consultative status, category 11, with the Economic and Social Council of the United Nations and the Council of Europe. Based in Germany, its members are brought together from around the world by the mutual concern for victims. Membership includes victim assistance practitioners, researchers, social workers, physicians, lawyers, university professors and students. The World Society of Victimology aims to promote research on victims and victims' assistance as well as advancing the co-operation of international and local agencies and groups concerned with the problems of victims.

The World Society of Victimology hosts an international symposium on victim issues every three years and produces the *Victimologist*, a regular newsletter. The World Society of Victimology works with intergovernmental organisations as an active promoter of research about victims, assistance to victims and respect for victims' rights. It pioneered a UN Charter of victims' rights, which resulted in a General Assembly Resolution – the *Declaration on the basic Principles of Justice for Victims of Crime and Abuse of Power.*

WHAT'S LEFT TO BE DONE

As the victims' movement grows in the new millennium and as the criminal justice system continues to evolve there will continue to be an important role for organisations that will highlight the needs of victims in the overall process.

The long-awaited Children Act 2001 will almost certainly lead the way for the introduction of a restorative justice model at least in the area of youth offending. The Garda Síochána, in a number of pilot programmes, have already begun to look at family conferencing as a way of diverting young offenders from further crime. The Probation and Welfare Service is also undertaking the initiation of a victim-offender mediation programme. Both of these initiatives will have immediate implications for the welfare and status of the victim.

The value of restorative justice to the victim of crime is relatively straightforward and understandable in that it provides an opportunity for explanation, reassurance and resolution of the offence. Basically victims want to know

Why me?
Will it happen again?
Does the offender know the impact that the crime has had?
What will the offender do to make amends for the harm done?

For any model of restorative justice to be successful it is essential that the expectations and needs of each victim are considered. This precondition does not necessarily entail a very serious impediment to progress, for most often a victim simply requires an explanation and apology from the young offender. However, primary guiding principles underlying the mediation process or conferencing must be that the victim takes part entirely of his or her own free will and is provided with adequate support, and that expectations on all sides are realistic and achievable.

However, The National Crime Forum noted in its report (1999) that while the restorative justice approach had much to offer, especially in dealing with crimes committed by the young, greater use of non-custodial sanctions would involve not just changes in the law but a profound change in public attitudes.

Perhaps one of the most significant developments in this area since the advent of the new millennium is the commitment to enact a Human Rights Act, which will incorporate the European Convention on Human Rights (ECHR) into Irish law. The Council of Europe adopted this Convention in 1950 to protect Europe from the type of atrocities experienced during the Second World War. The Human Rights Act will have a significant effect on the criminal justice system and therefore will have an impact on victims and witnesses and will mean that people will be able to rely on the rights and freedoms set out in the ECHR in courts in this country rather than having to take their case to Europe.

Possible changes under the human rights legislation with indirect effect on victims and witnesses include the possible need for victims/witnesses to be cross-examined as to why a defendant should be refused bail or the likelihood of having to appear at bail reviews.

Defendants, in the course of ensuring that their right to a fair trial has not been breached, are likely to raise challenges under the Act. For example, they could raise concerns relating to hearsay evidence, inferences from silence, unlawfully obtained evidence or disclosure of evidence. This will involve additional time required at trials and will almost certainly result in victims and witnesses experiencing delays.

The rights of victims and witnesses, however, will be further protected under this legislation. There is a now positive obligation on the state relative to the violation of one individual's rights by another. This means that people will have the right to adequate legislation to protect them from crime by way of the deterrent effect of making criminal acts illegal and by way of providing recourse through the courts, if a criminal act is committed.

The Act also means that public authorities such as the Garda Síochána, Health Boards etc have to do all they can to avert the risk to life of an identifiable group or individual. This can be taken as a duty to provide appropriate protection. Under the Act the authorities must do all that can reasonably be expected of them to avoid a "real and immediate" risk to life. This obligation is particularly relevant in cases of domestic violence or harassment where there is a known threat to a named individual.

The Act also provides for redress if a public authority fails to provide such protection. In the past this has not been available, because a pubic authority could not be sued for negligence because public policy confers immunity on public bodies.

It is also important to note that there is no right to compensation from the state in the Convention for injuries inflicted by another individual. Therefore any changes made to the current criminal injuries compensation scheme will not be bound by this legislation.

While action to affirm victims' rights and to improve their lot has begun on many fronts, mainly instigated by political and ideological considerations, research has been lagging behind and is, in many instances, totally lacking. One cannot help but wonder why it is that when the area of victim services is flourishing, research on the effects of victimisation and on the impact of victim assistance is so hard to come by. In Ireland, all research carried out in this field has been based on recorded crime only, ie only crime which has been officially reported to an Garda Síochána. Therefore, it has been very difficult to gauge the actual levels of crime in Ireland let alone measure the actual impact of those crimes upon the victim. In the absence of independently acquired scientific data, such as exists in other jurisdictions, one is forced to use best guess estimates.

A study undertaken by the Economic and Social Research Institute entitled *Victims of Recorded Crime in Ireland* (Watson 1999) looked at the nature and circumstances of crime, the victim's reaction to it and the long-term psychological effects. It also examined the victims' evaluation of the service received from the gardaí and their views on how it could be improved. The study was seen as complementary to a previous study carried out by the Central Statistics Office (CSO 1999) through its Quarterly Household Survey.

The results of the ESRI survey showed that the impact of crime on the individual is often perceived as inconvenient rather than traumatic. One incident in six involves some element of violence or threat with only 3% of the crimes against individuals leading to permanent or recurring physical problems for the victim. Predictably, the figure was higher for victims of assault as such, standing at one-fifth with permanent or recurring damage.

The research also concluded that most victims do not experience lasting psychological distress as a result of crime. However, at the time of the interview, over two-fifths of the victims of violent crime still experienced distress.

The risk of victimisation was also assessed. Victims tend not be the most vulnerable members of society. Compared to the general adult population, the risk of being a victim was greater for males than females, higher for adults in the middle years than for older adults and for those in the higher social classes than those in the manual social classes. However, as might be expected, women and the elderly experienced greater distress than men and younger adults when they were victimised.

Implications of the survey include that there are a number of areas where services to crime victims need improvement, for example there is a clear need to provide follow-up information to victims on the progress and outcome of the case, to support victims during the court procedure, and to help victims, especially victims of violent crime, cope with the emotional trauma associated with the incident. These findings have major implications for the victim movement, in particular Victim Support. It must remain a priority for Victim Support to raise public awareness of its existence and services and to find new ways of reaching out to those victims who require assistance.

The production of more detailed statistics on unreported as well as reported crime is essential to the achievement of a more complete understanding of crime and its effects on victims in Ireland. This kind of expanded victimisation study could be undertaken at a relatively small cost. The additional detail could include: a distinction between crimes against individuals, households and organisations; a count of all reported non-indictable incidents, including those where no pro-ceedings are taken; and, generally, greater transparency regarding the counting and classification of incidents.

So what real progress has taken place over the last number of years in addressing the needs of victims of crime? Largely as a result of media reporting there has been an increase in public awareness of the plight of the victim in the criminal justice system. The Celtic Tiger has resulted in a significant increase in funding for victim services over the last number of years. However, there con-tinues to be many fronts on which progress needs to be made and too many crime victims still "fall through the cracks" in the system.

A well defined, fully implemented inter-agency approach which specifically addresses the needs of crime victims is required to ensure that victims of crime receive the information and services they need and deserve. Greater co-operation and meaningful systems for exchanging information between each of the justice agencies would surely facilitate a more effective and workable justice system. Surely, goals for the criminal justice system can be drawn up that are in everyone's interest, the interest of the police, of prosecutors, victims and the community as a whole. These goals might be to solve crimes, prosecute cases, remove dangerous individuals from the community, and in all ways treat victims so as to foster their co-operation with the system and trust in the system.

REFERENCES

Council of Europe (1950), *European Convention on Human Rights and Fundamental Freedoms,* Council of Europe: Strasbourg

Central Statistics Office (1999), *Quarterly National Household Survey: Crime and Victimisation,* Dublin: Stationery Office

Department of Justice, Equality and Law Reform (1999), *Charter of Victims' Rights in the Criminal Justice System,* Dublin: Stationery Office

European Forum for Victim Services (1999), *Statement of Victims' Rights to Standards of Service*

European Forum for Victim Services (1998), *Statement of Social Rights of Crime*

European Forum for Victim Services (1997), *Statement of Victims' Rights in the Process of Criminal Justice*

European Union (1995), Directive 1995/46 European Standards on Data Protection EU: Brussels

Council of Europe (1983), *European Convention on the Compensation of Victims of Violent Crimes,* Council of Europe: Strasbourg

Moriarty, Judge Michael (1997), Address to Conference, "Working Together – An Integrated Approach to Victims of Crime", held in Dublin Castle in December 1997

National Crime Forum Report (1999), Dublin: Stationery Office

Report of the Victims' Commissioner (1999), "*A Place and a Name*", Dublin: Stationery Office

UN 1985 Declaration on the Basic Principles of Justice for Victims of Crime and the Abuse of Power, Geneva: UN

Watson, D. 1999, *Victims of Recorded Crime in Ireland,* Dublin: Oak Tree Press

24

A Tale of Two Sectors:
a Critical Analysis of the Proposal
to Establish Drug Courts in the
Republic of Ireland*

Shane Butler

1 INTRODUCTION

1.1 The proposal to set up drug courts in Ireland

In line with most other countries, Ireland has tended over the past thirty years or so to describe its public policy on illicit drugs as one which seeks to combine tough criminal justice sanctions with a humane therapeutic response. This has proven to be a difficult balance to achieve both philosophically and practically, and frequently it has involved the use of rhetoric which categorises offenders somewhat stereotypically into "innocent" victims and "evil" drug dealers. For example, in his introductory address to the Working Party on Drug Abuse, Ireland's first official committee to study drug use and related problems, the Minister for Health of the day distinguished between addicts, who "should be regarded as sick people in need of medical care to be treated with sympathy and understanding and be helped in every way possible to overcome their dependency on drugs", and drug dealers, who

---
* In *Illicit Drugs: Patterns of Use, Patterns of Response*, Springer, A. and Uhl, A. (eds.), Austria: Studien Verlag, 2000

"deserve no sympathy and should be punished to the full extent permitted by the law" *(Report of the Working Party on Drug Abuse* 1971, p 59).

Despite the difficulties which have consistently characterised healthcare/ criminal justice collaboration in relation to drug use and related problems, and which will be looked at in some detail later in this paper, the decision to explore the establishment of dedicated drug courts in Ireland in the mid-1990s was the first major public policy initiative to address this issue explicitly. There are a number of factors and events which explain why the drug courts initiative should have arisen at this time. The sense of moral panic surrounding drug use, which had waxed and waned over the years in Ireland, reached an unprecedented high in 1996 with the murder of Veronica Guerin, a well-known journalist, apparently by criminals involved in drug dealing; the sense of public revulsion which followed this murder accelerated and strengthened legal developments, including the creation of increased police powers, which were intended to deal severely with drug offenders. At the same time, research conducted by O'Mahony (1997) confirmed the admittedly complex link between drug use and crime, with 66% of a sample of prisoners surveyed in Mountjoy, Ireland's largest prison, reporting that they were heroin users, while research by the Garda Síochána (the Irish police force) revealed that of 7,757 individuals charged with indictable offences in the Dublin Metropolitan Area over the course of a year, 3,365 (43%) were identified as hard drug users (Keogh 1997).

The increased volume of drug-related work being processed by the courts, the probation service and the prison system had not been matched, however, by structural or institutional innovations within these systems, and a sense of frustration began to emerge amongst criminal justice professionals at what appeared to be the inability of the system to respond rationally or effectively to drug-related crime. Irish public sector management, which had been largely unchanged since the establishment of the state in 1922, was reviewed during this period and major reforms were recommended under the rubric of the *Strategic Management Initiative* (SMI), all with a view to introducing modern management systems into the public sector. A major element in the SMI was its recognition of the fact that the attainment of important public policy objectives is frequently dependent upon the co-operation of two or more sectors of government, and drug problems were identified early on in this process as constituting such a "cross-cutting issue" (Boyle 1999). It was not surprising therefore that the question of clarifying and rationalising the respective roles of health and justice in the management of drug-using offenders should be raised at this time, and in late-1998 the Minister for Justice, Equality and Law Reform requested the Working Group on a Courts Commission (a committee which had already made significant strides in reforming the administration of courts in Ireland) to investigate and report on the establishment of a drug courts system in Ireland. The working group tackled this task with what by bureaucratic standards seemed almost indecent haste, reporting in February 1998 (Working Group on a Court Commission, *Fifth Report: Drug Courts* 1998) with a positive recommendation for the introduction of this concept to Ireland.

1.2 The origins of the drug courts concept in the USA

Comparative drug policy research, particularly that which contrasts British and American policy, has tended to emphasise the degree to which American policy throughout the twentieth century has favoured criminal justice over health service interventions (Trebach 1982; Strang and Gossop 1994). The rhetoric of American drug policy has consistently portrayed illicit drug use as though it were the ultimate evil, to which no public policy response could be too harsh, and since the Nixon presidency of the late-1960s there have been periodic declarations and re-declarations of a "war on drugs". Towards the end of the Reagan administration, in 1988, American policy became even tougher with the introduction of the concept of "zero tolerance", which involved the extension of heavy criminal justice sanctions from commercial drug dealers to ordinary users, even casual users; understandably, this led to even higher numbers of drug users being processed through the criminal justice system and ending up in prison.

It would be erroneous to suppose, however, that in giving primacy to the criminal justice sector American policy makers totally ignored or excluded the therapeutic dimension. On the contrary, there is a long tradition in the USA of diverting drug-using offenders into treatment systems prior to adjudication, just as there is a tradition of coercing convicted offenders into various forms of residential or non-residential treatment (Inciardi, McBride and Rivers 1996). Outcome studies of treatment systems for convicted drug offenders were generally disappointing, however, and Martinson's review of these systems in the early-1970s – which, broadly speaking, concluded that "nothing works" – appears to have been particularly offensive to American sensibilities (Martinson 1974).

It is against this background that the development of dedicated drug courts from 1989 onwards must be understood. The courts, as a result of the zero tolerance philosophy, were more burdened with recidivist drug-using offenders than ever, while their collaboration with the healthcare or treatment sector seemed confused and ineffective. While numerous variants of the drug courts concept were to emerge during the early-1990s, there were some underlying beliefs and fundamental characteristics which were common to all of these new systems and which should be enumerated here:

> it was recognised, drawing on the concept of "differentiated case management", that since not all cases coming before the courts were the same they should not all be processed in precisely the same way, and on this basis it was argued that it might be more rational and efficient to create special courts which would deal exclusively with drug-using offenders

- it was reaffirmed that the threat of criminal justice sanctions might be used as leverage to motivate offenders to make good use of treatment services and facilities, but that this might be best facilitated by a process which was non-adversarial, consisting of judges, prosecutors, defenders and treatment providers collaborating towards this end
- it was proposed to assign a new role to judges in these drug courts, a role which involved the judge in a therapeutic function rather than in the more traditional punitive capacity and which consisted of intense and continuous monitoring of the defendant's attendance at and performance within the treatment system.

1.3 Intersectoral collaboration in the public management of drug problems

From a theoretical perspective this analysis of drug court concepts and practices, both in their country of origin and in Ireland, is primarily informed by the sociological writings of Joseph Gusfield (Gusfield 1996), who has devoted a lifetime to the study of the social construction of alcohol problems in the USA. In summary, Gusfield's work has focused on the way in which different societal institutions have at different times succeeded in claiming "ownership" of this social problem. What Gusfield means by this is that at certain times a particular institution, such as the medical profession, the legal profession or a church, may succeed in having its own cultural definition of a phenomenon accepted as being valid either scientifically or morally, so that the institution is then seen as having a legitimate claim to play a dominant role in the societal management of that problematic phenomenon. He also points out, however, that despite the appearance of solidity and consensus which may practically and philosophically surround such claims to ownership of a specific public or social problem, the meanings are frequently contested and there may be, quite close to the surface, political or economic conflict between two or more institutions concerning the ownership of the problem.

Public sector management may simply view drug courts as pragmatic initiatives to achieve better collaboration between the two sectors which are mainly involved, all with a view to achieving a common goal. Applying Gusfield's ideas, however, one is alerted to the possibility that the two sectors may have quite fundamentally different and conflicting cultural perspectives on what constitutes "drug abuse" and also that the notion of a common goal may be illusory.

1.4 The aims of this paper

The aims of this paper, therefore, are to look critically at the proposal to create drug courts in Ireland, bearing in mind the possibility that this initiative may not simply be a matter of public sector strategy or administrative commonsense, but that it may be complicated by differing philosophical or ideological positions as well as by conflicts over status or access to scarce public resources.

2 DRUG TREATMENT SYSTEMS IN IRELAND

2.1 The evolution of drug treatment systems in Ireland from the Mid-1960s

The enactment of the Dangerous Drugs Act 1934, the first anti-drugs legislation since the achievement of self-government in 1922, appears to have been prompted solely by Ireland's accession to the Geneva Convention of 1931, and it was not until the mid-1960s that the Irish authorities became convinced of the necessity to develop policy in this area. The Working Party on Drug Abuse, which has already been mentioned, conducted its business between 1968 and 1971 and made wide-ranging recommendations for legislative change and other policy developments in this field. Statistics on the extent of drug use and related problems, which at this time were primarily derived from the reports of the Garda Síochána, suggested that drug use was largely confined to the Dublin area and consisted in the main of soft drug use; opiate use and intravenous use were practically unknown (*Report of the Working Party on Drug Abuse* 1971, pp 10-15). However, the structure of treatment services for problem drug users in Dublin was decided quickly and pragmatically, without reference to the Working Group, when at the initiative of the Department of Health a centralised treatment facility was set up at Jervis St Hospital in Dublin's city centre in 1969. This facility, which soon was designated the National Drug Advisory and Treatment Centre, reflected developments in Britain at this time, when drug dependency units (DDUs or "clinics") were being established in the wake of the Second Brain Committee, and when the role of the general medical practitioner was being seen as relatively unimportant if not actually counterproductive. Voluntary treatment services for problem drug users were slow to emerge in Dublin, and it was not until 1973 that the first (and, for the next decade, the only) such service was established: this was the Coolemine Therapeutic Community, an American-style "concept house", which applied a confrontational approach to behaviour change within a residential setting and which saw total abstinence as the only valid goal of treatment.

There are perhaps just two main points to be made about Irish drug treatment services in the light of this early history. In terms of treatment models, it became established that services for drug users should be centralised and delivered by specialist care-givers and therapists, with no credence being given to the idea that such services could be normalised by being delivered by primary care-givers in localised or community-based settings. Furthermore, the treatment models which became the norm in Ireland also tended axiomatically to the view that total abstinence was the only acceptable goal of therapeutic interventions. The second point to be made about Irish drug treatment services refers to the policy-making process rather than to content or substantive issues involved here, and what emerged from this early period was a tradition of making decisions without public debate or discussion of alternative treatment models; it was as though the decisions to be made about treatment and rehabilitation were based on such a clear consensus that no public debate was necessary. No formally constituted drugs policy advisory body was set up and the task of evaluating treatment services appeared to rest somewhat ambiguously with the Department of Health (Butler 1991).

Although "drug abuse" was discussed politically and by the media during these early years in the customary language of moral panic, the enactment of new legislation was a relaxed and relatively leisurely affair. The resulting statute, the Misuse of Drugs Act 1977, was enacted nine years after the Working Party had been set up to advise on this matter, and the Commencement Order which brought the new legislation into effect was not made until 1979.

Section 28 of the Misuse of Drugs Act 1977 deals specifically with the provision of treatment options, as an alternative to incarceration, for convicted drug-using offenders. The policy intent of this section seems quite clear: the legislators wished to have such offenders (although offenders who were deemed to be commercial dealers were dealt with in a less favourable way) medically assessed prior to conviction and, where it seemed appropriate, to have prison sentences suspended subject to conditions laid down by the courts. Much of the content of this section of the legislation may be seen as being broadly similar to what the Irish criminal courts had been doing generally, in terms of suspending sentence where the probation or the healthcare system monitored and reported upon the progress of offenders within therapeutic or rehabilitative services. However, Section 22 authorised the Minister for Health to designate an appropriate institution as "a designated custodial treatment centre", and the courts were empowered to detain convicted offenders in this centre as opposed to ordering their detention in conventional prisons.

Following the introduction of the Misuse of Drugs Act 1977, the courts continued to collaborate with the healthcare system in the management of convicted drug-using offenders, but this collaboration was largely based on traditional lines with the Probation and Welfare Service playing a mediating role. However, the designated custodial treatment system never became an operational reality. Following the enactment of the legislation, there was no continuing political commitment to the implementation of this specific aspect of the new law and, in the absence of such political commitment, neither the healthcare nor the criminal justice sector displayed any interest in developing this intersectoral initiative.

2.2 The opiate epidemic, HIV and harm reduction

Quite dramatically, during 1979 and 1980, the drug scene in Dublin changed and intravenous heroin use became prevalent in a number of deprived inner-city areas and in some of the outer suburbs (Butler 1991). Policy responses to this style of problem drug use were slow to emerge and initially it seemed as though political and administrative systems were in total denial of this new reality, which was so at odds with how Irish people wished to view themselves and their country. However, what had originally been described colloquially as an "opiate epidemic" was eventually accepted as an ongoing reality, and policy measures to cope with it were gradually devised. The existing treatment system, which was inflexibly centralised and insistent on abstinence as the only legitimate thera-peutic goal, became even more problematic from 1983-84 onwards when the role of needle-sharing amongst intravenous drug users in the transmission of HIV was clearly identified. Equally problematic was the perception previously alluded to that debate on drug treatment issues was unnecessary, and the absence of formal policy-making structures.

Compared with other countries (Klingemann and Hunt 1998), Irish health policy makers faced a similar range of problems in deciding upon the style of treatment service provision for problem drug users, but understandably it was public health issues – originally just HIV/AIDS issues but later hepatitis C issues – which dominated for much of this period. As was the case elsewhere, the dilemma for Irish policy makers was whether they should continue to insist that, since "drug abuse" was such a self-evident social evil, treatment must have abstinence as its sole aim, or whether they should opt for more pragmatically-based treatment systems, such as methadone maintenance and needle and syringe exchange. In summary, what happened in Ireland was that between 1985 and the end of the century drug treatment policy and practice changed towards harm reduction, which included not merely the introduction of specific strategies such as methadone maintenance but also a decentralisation of services and the creation of outreach services. These changes were made within the Irish healthcare system in an incremental and covert style, largely without either public debate or official announcement; this served to avoid public controversy, but it also appears to have resulted in a somewhat confused situation where other sectors of government – including the criminal justice sector – were unclear as to what was happening on the treatment and rehabilitation side. By way of contrast, the introduction of harm reduction services within neighbouring Britain could be seen as reverting ideologically to the traditional "British system", but in any event these changes were debated in a relatively public style and were justified by the much-quoted conclusion of the Advisory Council on the Misuse of Drugs that: "The spread of HIV is a greater danger to individual and public health than drug misuse" (Advisory Council on the Misuse of Drugs 1988, p 75).

By 1997, therefore, when the Working Group on a Courts Commission was asked to consider the possibility of introducing the drug courts concept to Ireland, the Irish healthcare sector had shifted radically towards the use of harm reduction models, although this shift had occurred so gradually and so quietly that the criminal justice sector may not have understood its full extent or been philosophically in tune with it. While it could be argued that this covert style of policy making was functional in that it allowed for the introduction of liberal-seeming drug treatment policy into a relatively conservative political culture, it could not in management terms be seen as entirely helpful or as exemplary of intersectoral collaboration.

3 THE DRUG COURTS PROPOSAL IN IRELAND

The report of the Working Group on a Courts Commission

As mentioned above, the report (which will be referred to hereafter simply as *Drug Courts*) recommending the setting up of drug courts in Ireland was completed in early 1998. The Working Group which drew up the report was chaired by a Supreme Court judge, as well as having five other judges among its members, and was almost entirely representative of the criminal justice sector, with no representation from the Irish healthcare sector. In preparing its report, the Working Group had drawn heavily on the American experience and this had included a visit to Ireland by drug court experts from the USA for the purposes of a special conference on this topic. This influence from the American drug courts system does not seem to have been balanced by an equal degree of contact with the Irish treatment services, and reading the report in the context of the changes which have occurred in these services in recent years, it would seem that the Working Group was relatively unfamiliar with them. Instead, the philosophy implicit in *Drug Courts* and at times the explicit rhetoric of the report is that of the American "war on drugs". Nowhere is this more apparent than in the report's melodramatic opening sentences which declare that: "Drug abuse is a cancer in our society. It destroys individuals, families and communities" (*Drug Courts,* p 11).

The report does admittedly refer to policy developments in countries other than the USA, and looks in particular at Germany, Sweden, Australia, and England and Wales. In its summary of developments in England and Wales, which deals with legislative proposals to create "Drug Treatment and Testing Orders", the report quotes from a policy document to the effect that: "The success of any new legislation will depend on the availability of treatment and the resolution of cultural differences between the criminal justice system and treatment providers, underpinned by strong interagency arrangements" (cited in *Drug Courts,* p 27). However, the Working Group does not seem to have taken this principle seriously in its own analysis of the Irish scene, in the sense that it makes no explicit effort to identify cultural differences which might impede collaboration between the two sectors in the creation of drug courts in Ireland.

Chapter 5 of *Drug Courts* describes the complex network of statutory and voluntary drug treatment services which currently exists in Ireland, referring to it as "The Supporting Infrastructure", a phrase which could be read as implying that treatment systems have a subordinate relationship to the criminal justice sector, which might not be the most tactful way to initiate new collaborative relationships between the two sectors. What is also striking in this chapter, however, is that it does not advert explicitly to the dominance of harm reduction philosophy and strategies in the Irish healthcare sector or discuss the implications of this for the criminal justice sector. In fact, it is only in its recommendations section (Chapter 7) that the Working Group has a short paragraph on methadone maintenance which says that "while total abstinence is the optimal object of a drugs treatment programme the alternative system of methadone maintenance should not be excluded" (*Drug Courts,* p 64). Ironically, the report, which is dated February 1998, was only published and made widely available in September 1998, just before the introduction of a new "methadone protocol" which was intended to regulate and normalise methadone prescribing by Irish general medical practitioners. It is made clear in Appendix D, which is the text of an overview of American drug courts prepared for the conference held on this topic in Dublin in early 1998, that maintenance prescribing of methadone is not seen as an acceptable treatment modality by most drug courts in the USA (*Drug Courts,* p 87).

Another item in the report which suggests that it reflects a traditional criminal justice perspective on illicit drug use, rather than the perspective of healthcare workers, is its insistence on making categorical distinctions between "addicts" and "dealers". It is argued of drug courts that: "These are courts for drug addicts, not drug dealers" (*Drug Courts*, p 15), a contention which is repeated later in the report. This distinction is the same as that made by the Minister for Health thirty years earlier when Irish drug policy was in its infancy, but it is not one which healthcare professionals (or indeed practising lawyers) find persuasive. Illicit drugs tend to be relatively expensive and for many users there are limited means of raising the money necessary to sustain their habit; one of these means is to do some small-scale drug dealing themselves so that many – if not most – users are also dealers. Within the criminal justice system offenders are categorised as "addicts" or "dealers" on the basis of the market value of drugs found in their possession, and the Working Group refers to the proposal (since implemented) to have mandatory prison sentences for offenders convicted of having possession of drugs with a market value in excess of £10, 000. The Working Group does not favour this development, commenting that: "Mandatory sentencing is the antithesis of the philosophy behind the Drug Court process" (*Drug Courts,* p 40), yet it seems clear that its strict enforcement would exclude from treatment and incarcerate many users who could not realistically be described as large-scale commercial dealers. Healthcare workers who have ongoing therapeutic relationships with drug users, particularly within harm reduction services, tend to accept philosophically that, however undesirable it may be, drug-dealing is part of the total lifestyle of their clients; *Drug Courts* does not appear to acknowledge this, but retains the traditional stereotypical distinction between users and dealers.

Finally, it is striking that in its review of treatment services ("the supporting infrastructure") the Working Group does not advert to the potential for conflict with the healthcare sector, which has built up its own services and facilities slowly and expensively and might view the drug courts proposal as a hijacking of healthcare resources for criminal justice purposes. It is clear that diverting offenders into treatment rather than prison will save money for the criminal justice system – it is noted that the cost of building a prison place in Ireland is approximately £100, 000 per inmate and that the cost of maintaining a person in prison is approximately £ 46, 000 per annum (*Drug Courts,* p 53) – but it is not clear whether there will be a transfer of resources from the criminal justice to the healthcare sector as a kind of dowry to facilitate this process.

4 DISCUSSION AND CONCLUSION

4.1 Drug problems as cross-cutting issues within Irish public sector management

It was suggested earlier in this paper that in the language of modern public sector management drug-related problems may be seen as "cross-cutting issues"; what this means is that their management transcends any one sector of government and calls for the collaboration of a number of governmental sectors. Two of the most important sectors in this area are health and justice, the two which have been looked at here in relation to the proposal to set up dedicated drug courts in Ireland, but many other sectors – such as education, housing or employment – also may be seen as having a part to play in the management of drug issues. It has been argued here that it is superficial and ultimately illusory to see the establishment of drug courts as nothing other than a practical management tool to co-ordinate the workings of two sectors; instead, it is argued, that fundamental cultural differences have arisen between health and justice and that policy developments must acknowledge and deal with these differences.

It is made clear in *Drug Courts* that this is a preliminary document and that another committee will have to take charge of the implementation of the proposed new courts. However, the Working Group, which was so impressive in terms of the speed with which it tackled the task set by the Minister for Justice, might have been better advised to co-opt representatives of the healthcare system and to recognise and engage with the ambiguity which characterises harm reduction, although to do this would undoubtedly have delayed the process of reporting.

4.2 The ownership of drug problems

To return to Gusfield's theoretical work which was referred to above, it would seem that despite the clarity and strength of the rhetoric with which drug problems are sometimes discussed and indeed denounced, there is no longer – if indeed there ever was – a cultural consensus on this subject. Ownership of drug problems has always been shared, primarily between health and justice, but with the gradual emergence of harm reduction within the healthcare sector in Ireland, as elsewhere, the process of sharing has become more fraught. What appears to have complicated the shared ownership of drug problems in Ireland is the surreptitious introduction of harm reduction into a healthcare system which had previously been abstinence-based. Some countries debated this issue and decided *for* harm reduction, while other countries debated it and decided *against* it; in Ireland there was virtually no public debate and the introduction was such a covert and incremental process that other sectors – in particular the justice sector – were slow to realise the extent and significance of this change. The meaning of illicit drug use, which was traditionally clear and unambiguous, has become increasingly contested. To some at least within the criminal justice system it remains a "social cancer", while to many within healthcare its meaning has become more subtle and ambiguous. Perhaps what this study of the Irish drug court proposals suggests is that policy developments which are essentially concerned with shared ownership cannot make progress without at least some acknowledgement of these contested meanings.

REFERENCES

Advisory Council on the Misuse of Drugs (1988), *AIDS and Drug Misuse (Part 1),* London: Her Majesty's Stationery Office

Boyle, R. (1999), *The Management of Cross-Cutting Issues,* Dublin: Institute of Public Administration

Butler, S. (1991), "Drug Problems and Drug Policies in Ireland: A Quarter of a Century Reviewed", *Administration*, 39: 210- 233

Gusfield, J. (1996), *Contested Meanings: The Construction of Alcohol Problems,* London: The University of Wisconsin Press

Inciardi, J., McBride, D., Rivers, J. (1996), *Drug Control and the Courts,* London: Sage

Keogh, E. (1997), *Illicit Drug Use and Related Criminal Activity in the Dublin Metropolitan Area,* Dublin: An Garda Síochána

Klingemann, H., Hunt, G. (eds.) (1998), *Drug Treatment Systems in an International Perspective: Drugs, Demons and Delinquents,* London: Sage

Martinson, R. (1974), "What works? Questions and answers about prison reform", *The Public Interest*, 35: 22-54

O'Mahony, P. (1997), *Mountjoy Prisoners: A sociological and criminological profile,* Dublin: Stationery Office

Report of the Working Party on Drug Abuse, (1971), Dublin: Stationey Office

Strang, J., Gossop, M. (eds.) (1994), *Heroin Addiction and Drug Policy: The British System,* Oxford: Oxford University Press

Trebach, A. (1982), *The Heroin Solution,* London: Yale University Press

Working Group on a Courts Commission (1998), *Fifth Report: Drug Courts,* Dublin: Stationery Office

SECTION 5

POLICING

25

Introduction

Paul O'Mahony

At the close of 1999, the strength of the Garda Síochána was 11,458 (Garda Annual Report 1999), including 9,092 gardaí, 1,876 sergeants, 263 inspectors and 227 higher ranks. There is ongoing recruitment following a government commitment to bring the overall garda strength to 12,000 by 2001. There has been a 47% increase in the size of the Garda Síochána since 1973, when there were 7,794 members. The current size of the force means there is a ratio of one policeman to approximately every 325 citizens. In international terms, this is a quite favourable ratio and can be compared with the situation in Denmark where the ratio is about one policeman to every 500 citizens and England where it is about one to every 400.

In addition in 1999, the Garda Síochána employed 1,744 civilian ancillary staff. However, this is a very small civilian support staff by comparison with other jurisdictions – for example, in Britain, civilian staff working for police forces are equivalent to about 40% of the numbers of policemen (Reiner 1994). The majority of the civilian staff are either cleaners, general operatives or traffic wardens and only about 800 are in administrative and clerical posts. But there are currently, according to the Garda Annual Report (1999), "firm proposals on a comprehensive programme of civilianisation". The National Crime Forum (1998) has recommended a more vigorous approach to civilianisation, stating that "starting with the premise that only overtly professional policing duties and not any of the ancillary administrative, technical support or other paperwork would continue to be performed by gardaí, would lead to more substantial freeing of professional garda resources for more central tasks".

Recent years have been a time of rapid development for the Garda Síochána. There have been many positive developments both at the level of organisational structure and in the introduction of new technologies, training methods, and operational systems. The training college at Templemore has been put on a new, professional footing as a third level institution and a Garda Research Unit attached to the college has been set up. There has also been major investment in a new information technology system, called PULSE (Police Using Leading Systems Effectively), which will provide two-way access to central records at all garda stations in Dublin and all divisional and district headquarters throughout the country. PULSE will facilitate police intelligence on crime and criminals, but is also designed to computerise many routine police systems such as warrants, summonses, management of bail and barring orders, recording of court outcomes, driving licence production, and even letters to crime victims.

Other initiatives in the area of new technology include: a new radio communications system; the expansion of CCTV systems in urban areas; a computerised data base for fingerprints with a much improved, automated system for fingerprint identification; the provision of a number of unmarked camera and computer equipped cars to tackle speeding offences; and a new air support unit with both a fixed wing aircraft and a helicopter, which became operational in 1997. Indicative of the diversity of modern policing approaches, are the Garda Dog Unit, involving eighteen gardaí and nineteen dogs, trained in drug and explosive detection and crowd control, and the Mounted Unit, involving nine gardaí and nine horses, which was set up in 1998 and is now based in stables at Aras An Uachtarain, from which it patrols the city centre and major sporting events in Dublin.

In 1993, the then Garda Commissioner, Patrick Culligan, published the Corporate Strategy Policy Document 1993-97. This was a thoughtful and informed document that emphasised the major impact on modern police activities and functions of social and economic change. This document signalled a commitment amongst the upper echelons of the force to a new "managerial science" approach to policing in Ireland. This mirrors developments in Britain and elsewhere, whereby, according to Reiner (1994), "police leaders have tried to reorientate the culture of policing around an explicit mission of service and ethos of consumerism".

A Steering Group (1997) also considered, under the government's Strategic Management Initiative, issues related to the management, effectiveness and efficiency of the Garda Síochána. There have been many recent organisational changes in response to the recommendations of the Steering Group. The commissioner is to become the accounting officer for the Garda Síochána, thus granting the force, which incurred a gross expenditure of over £600 million in 1999, more autonomy in the financial area. Management has been regionalised, and there are now six regional divisions, each headed by an assistant commissioner.

On the other hand, a number of centralised bureaux and units have been established in order to build and more effectively deploy the expertise to handle specialised areas of crime. This includes the Anti-racketeering Unit, which has focused on the use of illegal hormones in the agricultural community, the Garda National Drugs Unit, the National Crime Bureau, the National Crime Prevention Unit and the Garda Bureau of Fraud Investigation. The latter, which was initiated in 1995, has had a significant impact in the areas of commercial fraud, computer crime, cheque and credit fraud and money laundering and illustrates the ongoing globalisation of certain areas of police activity. In 1999, the assessment unit of the Bureau reviewed 458 complaints, 316 of which had an international dimension and originated with Interpol or under the Convention for Mutual Assistance in Criminal Matters.

Perhaps the most noteworthy recent development in terms of new structures has been the Criminal Assets Bureau, which was set up in October 1996. This bureau is a significant innovation not only because it identifies and then proceeds, through the courts, to freeze or confiscate the criminally derived assets of offenders, most especially drugs dealers, but also because it involves a multi-agency approach. It is staffed by gardaí and officers from the Department of Social Welfare and the Revenue Commissioners (both taxation and Customs and Excise wings). This bureau has already had some notable successes and within two years of its establishment had confiscated over £10 million worth of assets. The bureau is credited with the disruption of major criminal gangs and the flight from Ireland of a number of leading criminal figures. It has also branched out into the investigation of corruption amongst public officials. There has been some civil libertarian criticism of the financial approach to targeting criminals. This is because it operates within a civil law framework, which permits the state to shift the burden of proof onto the defendant with respect to, for example, the source of income or proof of payment of appropriate taxes.

Coinciding with this restructuring and modernisation, for the first time in eight years, the total number of recorded indictable crimes fell in 1996 and, in the following three years, there were further successively steeper falls in crime. Indictable crime figures declined from 102,484 in 1995, the highest figure since the foundation of the state, to 81,274 in 1999 – a drop of almost 21% in four years. The Garda Commissioner, Patrick Byrne (Garda Annual Report 1999), has claimed that "undoubtedly the various initiatives, strategies and enhanced resourcing, reinforced by the excellent community assistance and legislative changes, have been pivotal in achieving the desired objective". Improved garda effectiveness may have been a factor, but as Morgan and Newburn (1997) suggest "though the police should be encouraged to make the most effective use of the resources available to them, neither they nor the public should be misled about the causes of crime, and thus the solutions to crime. There is little evidence that anything the police do has much more than a very marginal impact on crime levels." After all, official research in Britain (Home Office 1995) indicates that as little as 7% of all indictable crime is cleared up, that is attributed to an identified culprit, by the police.

There have been several other major developments in the period since 1995 that help account for the reduction in recorded crime. There has been major economic growth with consequent increased affluence and an enormous drop in unemployment rates, including that of the long-term unemployed. The wider availability of reasonably paid work may well have reduced the number of people becoming involved in crime. Economic buoyancy and the social partnership movement (Government of Ireland 1996) have also lead to very substantial investment in educational and training projects aimed at the social inclusion of marginalised groups and disadvantaged youth and this too may have had a crime reductive impact. The greatly enlarged methadone maintenance programme, since 1996, has helped stabilise the lives of many heroin addicts, who were previously involved in crime to feed their habit (Keogh 1997). There has also been a large increase in incarceration in the period, with the prison population expanding from around 2,000 to over 3,000. This increase is likely to have reduced crime, if only through its incapacitative effect.

The gardaí are proud of recent improvements achieved in the detection rate for indictable crime. The detection rate improved in each of the nine years up to 1998 – to then stand at 44%. The detection rate declined marginally in 1999, to 42%, but this remains a very considerable gain over the average figure for the 1980s, which was in the low thirties. Gardaí sources claim (Garda Annual Report 1999) that "the improvement in the detection rate represents a very strong performance by An Garda Síochána". Given the deficiencies and ambiguities of official statistics, including widespread under-reporting by the public and changing definitions, and given the fact that secured convictions, not to mention prevention and deterrence, rather than detections are more relevant measures of successful police performance, this claim must be regarded as somewhat overstated.

Despite the apparent improvements in crime rates and garda effectiveness, the recent history of the Garda Síochána has not been a record of unalloyed success. There have been a number of serious problems, not necessarily related to the prevalence of crime, which have tarnished the reputation of the force amongst the general public. A prime example is the acrimonious split in the Garda Representative Association, which in 1996 led the then Minister for Justice, Nora Owen, to propose to introduce legislation aimed at reinstating a single representative body for the ordinary gardaí. Speaking on this issue, she stated that this "division is eating away like a disease at the image and the fine reputation of the Garda Síochána ... I cannot allow a dispute like this to gnaw away at the morale and confidence of the gardaí." This long-running dispute amongst the rank and file gardaí, originating in disagreement over pay issues, spawned an unprecedented level of dissension amongst the gardaí themselves and resulted at one point in the existence of three bitterly opposed groups claiming to represent elements of the gardaí.

By 1998, the gardaí were reunited but they then began pressing for increased pay in an unprecedentedly bold and cynical campaign. The Garda Síochána are forbidden by law to strike; but, in 1998, they instituted a new form of protest, in which many thousands of them telephoned in, on a specific day, to say they were sick and could not attend for work. This form of protest became known popularly as "the blue flu". The government soon settled the pay claims of the gardaí, but not before further damage was done to the public reputation of the force.

There have been quite a number of other public relations disasters for the Garda Síochána, which raise questions either about their competence or about their attitudes and ethos. In 1996, a prosecution against a murder suspect, Frederick Flannery, collapsed when the judge dismissed the case and ordered that it could never again be brought against the suspect because of unethical conduct by the gardaí managing the case. The judge castigated what he called "appalling Garda behaviour", designed to "subvert the course of justice in the trial". Other ongoing, scandalous cases include an alleged conspiracy to falsify evidence by a number of gardaí in County Donegal and claims by the arresting gardaí in the case of triple murderer, Brendan O'Donnell, that their evidence about the arrest was distorted in reports written by higher ranking garda officers. These cases are not readily dismissed as instances of the "bad apple" theory – the view that every large organisation must have the occasional miscreant – because they inevitably raise the more disquieting spectre of endemic, systematic garda malpractice in the handling of evidence. Little has been done by the Garda Síochána to assure the public that these kinds of problems, which have recently surfaced with some regularity, are not typical of garda practice and that adequate internal mechanisms are in place to prevent their reoccurrence.

The shooting dead in 2000 by the Emergency Response Unit of the disturbed young man John Carthy, who was armed with and several times discharged a shotgun, was also highly controversial because it brought into question the garda commitment to the minimal use of lethal force. There are continuing serious doubts, arising from this case, about the quality of training for such crisis situations and about garda capacity to differentiate levels of risk and manage seige negotiations in a flexible, safe and sensitive manner.

A vitally important area in which the Garda Síochána are open to severe criticism is their handling of civil liberties and basic human rights. In particular, there appear to be problems surrounding methods of interrogation (see O'Mahony later in this section) and the holding and handling of suspects. Ironically, garda difficulties in this area are highlighted by the fact that in recent years the Garda

Síochána have been vocal in lobbying for increased powers and have been quite successful in this quest, gaining increased powers of detention and curtailment of the right to silence with respect to drug dealers.

The international body, the Committee for the Prevention of Torture and Inhuman or Degrading Treatment or Punishment (CPT 1995), published a report on a 1993 investigatory visit to Ireland, in which they raised serious questions about detention in Garda custody. The CPT was led, "in the light of all the information at its disposal", to the extremely uncomfortable conclusion that "persons held in certain police establishments in Ireland – and more particularly in Dublin – run a not inconsiderable risk of being physically ill-treated". The CPT went on to emphasise the important role of police culture and attitudes in this area and stated that "the best possible guarantee against ill-treatment is for its use to be unequivocally rejected by police officers".

The CPT made a second visit to Ireland in 1998 and in their report (CPT 1999) stated that they had "continued to receive allegations of physical and psychological ill-treatment of persons held in police custody in Dublin and elsewhere in the country" and that in the course of their second visit "a significant number of those interviewed alleged that they had been physically ill-treated by police officers". Two interviewees, who were medically examined, had injuries compatible with their allegations.

In this context of alleged garda incompetence and malpractice, the issue of the accountability of the Garda Síochána is obviously of central importance and there is currently much dissatisfaction around this area. In reference to the Garda Complaints Board, the chief mechanism for processing citizens' complaints, the National Crime Forum (1998) stated that "many members of the public do not make a distinction between investigation by the Board using garda personnel and investigation by the gardaí, leading to the perception that the gardaí are investigating complaints against themselves". The CPT (1995) also examined the Garda Complaints Board and were disquieted by the rarity of disciplinary action against gardaí accused of mistreating arrestees. They saw fit to comment that the presence of serving police officers on the Complaints Board is capable of "damaging public confidence in the capacity of the complaints system to deal objectively with complaints about police conduct". They believed that the present system was unlikely to be considered impartial by either complainants or police officers. A fully effective system "must be, and be seen to be, independent and impartial". A fully independent Board is obviously required and, as the National Crime Forum suggested, recourse to an Ombudsman might be worth considering.

Finding credible mechanisms for accountability with respect to individual citizen complaints about possible abuses of authority is obviously crucial, but there is also a need in Irish policing to redress what is perceived as a profound lack of democratic accountability. The Minister for Justice, of course, plays a democratically based plenipotentiary role with respect to policing policy, but there is no police authority as in Britain and Northern Ireland. Besides, a police authority may not be an adequate solution, for, according to Reiner (1994), the police authority in Britain has only as much influence "as the Chief Constable and the Home Secretary deem it wise to accord it".

The police wield significant powers and exercise a wide degree of discretion in both individual case decision-making and general policing policy. By their use of discretion, by what and whom they choose to ignore as well as by what and whom they make their primary focus, the police help define what is crime and who is criminal. Reiner (1994) has argued that "the essential concept of policing relates to the idea of security through surveillance and the threat of sanctioning" and that routine policing is targeted at "the social residuum at the base of the social hierarchy". There is considerable potential for stereotyping, stigmatising, discrimination and other forms of systematic bias in policing. These kinds of police bias may have negative effects on whole communities, especially their young, male, unemployed members.

In certain especially disadvantaged areas, there are mutually hostile and suspicious attitudes between the police and large sectors of the population. The growing cultural and ethnic pluralism of Ireland also presents new and difficult challenges. Above all, the community action against drugs movement in the mid-nineties has vividly demonstrated how whole communities can feel alienated from the police. Protest by these activists involved street marches, evictions of drug dealers and some illegal vigilante attacks. There was also a great deal of orderly, well-organised self-policing, that is surveillance of the community by the community, aimed at keeping drugs and drug dealers out of local areas. These actions, which for a time threatened to usurp police authority in some of Dublin's poorest districts, amounted to a popular demonstration of a deep-felt sense that drug-ridden communities were being ill-served by the Garda Síochána.

It can be argued that mechanisms for democratic oversight, consultation and input to policing policy are sorely lacking in Ireland. This is a particularly serious matter for the marginalised, multiply deprived and often drug-ridden communities that are the subject of much police attention. However, within broader society, the closure of rural garda stations, the increasing reliance on technology, the growth of private policing by security firms in shopping malls and other private areas where the public do business, and the move away from foot patrols to motorised policing, among other changes, have already strained the traditional sense of solidarity between the police and the general public.

The paradigm of community policing is often regarded as the panacea for modern police forces keen to retain or win back the consent, support and respect of the community. Skolnick and Bayley (1988) sum up community policing as entailing community-based crime prevention, a shift of a large proportion of police from emergency response to crime prevention work, increased public account-ability and consultation and decentralisation of command. The mass protest movement in many of the drug-ridden localities of Dublin drew attention force-fully to the need for new forms of police/community liaison. This has prompted the gardaí to embark on a major new programme of consultation with local community representatives, especially in the context of Local Drugs Task Forces. It remains to be seen if this approach will pay worthwhile dividends in terms of improved police relations with marginalised communities.

There have been other significant developments in the area of community policing. The Garda Síochána have set up the National Crime Prevention Unit and have initiated and supported many Neighbourhood Watch and Community Alert schemes. The gathering strength of the victim support movement has also meant that the Garda Síochána are now more aware of the plight of victims and exhibit more sensitivity in their dealings with them. Perhaps the most radical initiative in the community policing area, however, has been the force's greatly increased involvement in youth diversion and training programmes. There are now more than fifty of these proactive, crime preventative schemes (Bowden and Higgins 2000).

The Children Act 2001 raises the age of criminal responsibility from seven to twelve and stresses diversion from the criminal justice system for young offenders over twelve. It will thus strongly encourage garda involvement in early intervention and prevention. The Garda Juvenile Diversion Scheme, a system for formally or informally cautioning incipient young offenders and thereby diverting them from the courts, has, until recently, been the most significant garda preventive initiative. The scheme has grown greatly in recent years – in 1980, there were 1,366 informal and formal cautions of young people; in 1990, 3,180; and in 1996, 10,539. Figures have declined somewhat since then, but this may well be a reflection of recent decreasing crime rates. The gardaí claim great success for this scheme, stating that since its inception, 89% of all those cautioned have reached the age of eighteen without being prosecuted for a criminal offence. The Juvenile Diversion Scheme has been put on a statutory basis by the Children Act. The scheme has certainly made an important contribution as a preventive measure and will continue to play a major role under the new Children Act alongside the newer preventative garda projects. However, there is a clear need for evaluation of the scheme's effectiveness with particularly troublesome young people, who qualify as at serious risk of a persistent criminal career.

All these initiatives indicate considerable progress on an agenda of "community policing" and proactive crime prevention. They may presage a redefinition of the role of the police in modern Irish society and a fundamental change in citizens' expectations of the police. Alderson (1979), a former English Chief Constable, has written about the need for "a new social contract for police" which will reflect the multi-faceted nature of modern policing. However, it is likely that the active crime-fighting role will continue to dominate both priorities and perceptions. In this regard, popular images and stereotypes of the police as potent crime investigators, law enforcers and protectors of life and property often work to the detriment of the police, encumbering them with unrealistic expectations of their own and the public's making. It is worth recalling that, according to one British study (Home Office 1993), "in a typical day, only 18% of calls to the police are about crime, and only about 40% of the police officer's time is spent dealing directly with crime". The police have many valued functions, which need to be recognised, ranging from managing traffic flow, controlling crowds and monitoring elections to assisting the old and incapacitated in times of crisis and issuing licences and permits (Bayley 1979).

The current era of extraordinarily rapid and profound social and technological change presents many conflicting challenges to the Garda Síochána. In some respects the new police "social contract" demands a return to more traditional methods. For example, community policing involves the deployment of police to specific local areas with a high level of continuity in order to build trust, communication and special local knowledge. At the same time improved transport and communication and the EU single market have internationalised crime and necessitated more sophisticated and internationally co-ordinated police responses. While it is essential for the police to embrace powerful new technologies, they need to adapt them so that they do not increase the social and psychological distance between the police and the community of people, whom they are meant to serve. The police must also forge effective new working relationships with all kinds of social agencies, which have an interest in crime reduction and prevention, and enter into a new form of partnership with the general public and local communities. In this immensely complex context, police respect for civil liberties and effective systems to assure police accountability will be more important than ever.

REFERENCES

Alderson, J. 1979, *Policing Freedom,* London: Macdonald and Evans

Bayley, D. 1979, "Police Functions, Structure and Control in Western Europe and North America: Comparative and Historical Studies", in *Crime and Justice; An Annual Review of Research* (Tonry, M. and Morris, N. eds), Chicago: University of Chicago Press

Bowden, M. and Higgins, L. 2000, *The Impact and Effectiveness of the Garda Special Projects*, Dublin: Department of Justice, Equality and Law Reform

Committee for the Prevention of Torture and Inhuman or Degrading Treatment or Punishment, December 1995, *Report on Irish places of detention,* Strasbourg: Council of Europe

Committee for the Prevention of Torture and Inhuman or Degrading Treatment or Punishment 1999, *Second Report on Irish places of detention,* Strasbourg: Council of Europe

Garda Síochána 1993, Corporate Strategy Policy Document 1993-97, Dublin Garda HQ

Garda Annual Report 1999, Dublin: Stationery Office

Government of Ireland 1996, "Partnership 2000 for Inclusion, Employment and Competitiveness", Dublin: Stationery Office

Home Office 1995, *Digest 3 Information on the Criminal Justice System in England and Wales,* London: HMSO

Home Office 1993, *Police Reform: A Police Service for the 21st Century,* London: HMSO

Keogh, E. 1997, *Illicit Drug Use and Related Criminal Activity in the Dublin Metropolitan Area,* Dublin: Garda Headquarters

Morgan, R. and Newburn, T. 1997, *The Future of Policing,* Oxford: Clarendon Press

National Crime Forum 1998, *Report*, Dublin: Stationery Office

Reiner R 1994, "Policing and the police", in *Oxford Handbook of Criminology,* (Maguire M., Morgan R. and Reiner R. eds), Oxford: Clarendon Press

Skolnick, J. and Bayley, J. 1988, "Theme and Variation in Community Policing" in *Crime and Justice; An Annual Review of Research,* (Tonry, M. and Morris, N. eds) Chicago: University of Chicago Press

Steering Group on the Efficiency and Effectiveness of the Garda Síochána 1997, *Report*, Dublin: Stationery Office

26

Challenges Facing
An Garda Síochána

Commissioner Pat Byrne

All managers, whether they operate in a business, a government agency, a church, a charitable foundation, or a university, must, in varying degrees, take into account the elements and forces of their external environment. While they may be able to do little or nothing to change these forces, they have no alternative but to respond to them. They must identify, evaluate, and react to the forces outside the enterprise that may affect its operation.[1]

INTRODUCTION

All bodies, whether in the commercial field, public or state service or voluntary organisations, must regularly appraise their practices and procedures. A police service is no different. An Garda Síochána does, and must continue to, appraise and reappraise its methods of operation.

A police service must be constantly evolving, in keeping with the ever-changing society. Often the police service reacts to change and on other occasions it leads or initiates change. This process is a vital component not only in policing, but also in the public service generally.

An Garda Síochána exists to serve the citizens of this state. Its mission statement covers all three layers of society – the personal protection of the

---

[1] Harold Koontz and Heinz Weihrich (1988), *Management,* 9th ed., McGraw Hill International Editions (p. 600)

individual, the community partnership and the security of the state itself. The Commissioner of An Garda Síochána is charged with responsibility for providing an effective and efficient policing service for this country, within the prevailing budgetary and legislative constraints.

The *raison d'être* of An Garda Síochána is not easily defined. Traditionally, An Garda Síochána has endeavoured to provide all things, to all men, at all times. It has over time engaged its personnel, time and money in areas which, by modern standards, are not considered to be core or primary functions of a police service. While some of these areas have been removed from the garda portfolio, some remain and there may well be a debate on what precisely society wants An Garda Síochána to do.

The distinction is sometimes drawn between efficiency and effectiveness. An attractive, though somewhat simplistic definition of the two terms is – *efficiency is doing the thing right; effectiveness is doing the right thing.* We in An Garda Síochána need to regularly examine our operations and functions and ask ourselves repeatedly if we are doing the rights things or doing these things right. An assessment of actual and potential challenges will inform the development of suitable remedies.

We have examined and will continue to examine police services in other jurisdictions, identifying strategies and processes that may be of benefit to An Garda Síochána. While this is in itself a useful exercise, there are no "off the shelf" solutions to our policing requirements. They must be appropriate to the unique culture, values and expectations of Irish society.

An Garda Síochána has, in recent years, endeavoured to establish what the public wants and expects of it. Through the publication of a corporate strategy[2] the organisation has clearly outlined what it considers to be its primary objectives and functions. Through the publication of annual policing plans[3] it has brought these corporate aims to a micro level, concentrating on the point of delivery. The evaluation of these plans provides a form of feedback, both for the organisation itself and the citizens it exists to serve, on the performance of the organisation, a measurement of achievements against expectations/targets.

From an internal perspective, An Garda Síochána has engaged fully in the Strategic Management Initiative[4], along with the remainder of the public service. Large organisations are slow to change and organisational cultures are often difficult to influence. However, the Strategic Management Initiative is progressing and is endeavouring to provide a clearer focus for the organisation and adopt a

---

[2] *An Garda Síochána Corporate Strategy 2000-2004*, An Garda Síochána, 2000
[3] *An Garda Síochána Annual Policing Plan 2000,* An Garda Síochána, 2000
[4] *Report of the Steering Group on the Efficiency and Effectiveness of the Garda Síochána*, June 1997, Government of Ireland, 1997

series of strategic processes and structures which will allow for the provision of the required service, when and where it is required within a cost effective framework.

This paper is not intended as a definitive thesis. Limits of time and space do not permit. Rather, it is intended as a brief look at some of the key and most pressing challenges facing the organisation over the coming years. These will be dealt with under the following headings:

- Internationalisation of crime
- Drug related organisations
- Alcohol related crime
- Traffic
- Human resources
- Terrorist crime
- Maintaining the support of the community
- Managing a national information technology system
- European and international influences
- General policing.

INTERNATIONALISATION OF CRIME

We all now live in a "global village". Voice and text data can be transmitted instantaneously to almost any part of the globe. International travel has become a part of everyday life for many. It is little wonder that national boundaries no longer delimit criminal activity. Crime is now organised internationally. Criminal associations and syndicates have tentacles extending across the globe.

Organised criminal activity is dynamic by nature. It need not be confined to rigid structures. It has shown itself to have the capacity to be entrepreneurial, business-like and highly flexible in responding to changing market forces and situations. Criminal groups appear to be becoming increasingly involved in the licit as well as the illicit market, using non-criminal business specialists and structures to assist them in their criminal activities.

Just over ten years ago the Soviet Communist system in Eastern Europe collapsed, and with it the economies of many of the former eastern block countries. In the intervening years organised criminal associations from these countries have been expanding their operations into Western Europe, where they have become involved in the illicit drugs trade, prostitution, pornography, illegal trafficking in human beings, and money laundering activities.

As a result of the increased sophistication of many organised criminal groups, they are able to utilise legal loopholes and differences between EU member states, exploiting the anomalies in the various systems. They can take advantage of the free movement of money, goods, personnel and services across the European Union and beyond. There are approximately 120 separate police forces in the fifteen EU member states.

The manner in which many criminal groups operate has altered considerably. While such groups have been in existence for a long time, it is now the case that they have become highly sophisticated and operate in much the same way as multinational companies, with networks which extend to different countries. Computer component theft is an area that lends itself well to internationalisation. A million pounds worth of memory chips will easily fit into the boot of a car. A single chip may be worth more than an ounce of cocaine. Many of these components, because of their size and mass production, lack unique identifying serial numbers. These characteristics, and the fact that, unlike illegal drugs, possession of these items is not prohibited per se, makes computer components immensely attractive and internationally tradable. These criminal enterprises are undermining legitimate business through money laundering and their activities.

Information technology and in particular the Internet recognise no international frontiers. This makes the medium a prime vehicle for international crimes such as child pornography, hacking, credit card fraud, fraudulent investments, etc.

This international threat calls for a dynamic and co-ordinated response by all law enforcement agencies, a response that not only takes into account national strategies but also seeks to become an integrated and multidisciplinary strategy at an international level. Addressing the ever-changing face of organised crime requires that this response and strategy remain flexible.

DRUG RELATED ORGANISATIONS

The vast majority of illicit drugs used in Ireland originate outside the state. Heroin comes mainly from Southern Asia; cocaine from South America; and cannabis from North Africa. By its very nature, trafficking in illicit drugs is an international operation. Drug trafficking, distribution and sale benefit substantially from organisation, both local and international.

Major international drug trafficking groups have evolved in Ireland over recent years and these have developed their own contacts internationally to the extent that they are now involved in purchasing drugs at source. They have also developed major international associations.

An Garda Síochána prosecutes between 5,000 and 7,000 drug offenders annually. Many of the major drugs players previously operating in this country have fled in recent years because of the level of attention they received from our enforcement agencies. Similarly, many drug trafficking organisations have been dismantled due to the combined efforts of An Garda Síochána, the Criminal Assets Bureau, the Customs Service and the Navy.

This fracturing of the illicit drugs scene in Ireland presents its own difficulties. Traffickers continue to operate from abroad, with less police attention. Less well-known individuals step in to the national scene to replace those who have fled abroad.

By virtue of its geographical location, Ireland is playing an increasingly pivotal role in the worldwide movement of drugs. Large-scale seizures over recent years have confirmed Ireland as a recognised gateway to Europe for illicit drugs. Our 3,000 miles or so of often rugged and sparsely populated coastline makes ideal territory for those who wish to import without detection.

In co-operation with police forces elsewhere we continue to pursue individuals and organisations resident at home and abroad involved in the drugs trade. Through active inter-agency co-operation and a flexibility of approach, exemplified by the establishment of the Criminal Assets Bureau, significant progress can continue to be made in this important fight against organised drugs related activity.

ALCOHOL RELATED CRIME

Recently there has been increased public focus on public order issues. A number of factors have contributed to this. Among these are – our relatively young population, a diminution of parental control, and increased affluence among our young people. Allied to all this is our historical dependence on licensed premises as focal points for social activity – our so-called "pub culture". As a result, we have more young people consuming large quantities of alcohol, sometimes combined with drugs. As a consequence, some become boisterous and lose their natural inhibitions. This sometimes leads to situations of disorder and even violence. On the whole, the problem tends to be predominantly an urban one.

Common factors in public order problems throughout the country include – groups of young people congregating on public streets and in open spaces, consuming intoxicating liquor and/or drugs, behaving in a disorderly fashion. Many of the youths involved are under eighteen years of age. This activity may be associated with social or other events and creates a public nuisance and engenders apprehension and occasionally fear, particularly among the elderly.

The cultural acceptance of drinking permeates all sectors of Irish society. A sizeable proportion of our young people see alcohol consumption and, to some extent, drug misuse as being integral to social interaction. Alcohol is a common factor or ingredient in most public order situations. In recognition of this, An Garda Síochána has targeted the enforcement of liquor licensing legislation as a key component in our strategy for facing the challenge posed for it. In particular, matters such as underage drinking, on-street alcohol consumption, public intoxication, and drug abuse on licensed premises are the focus of special attention. The following are some of the key measures:

- the establishment of Operation Oíche, targeting public order related offences
- the extension and development of Closed Circuit Television Systems
- Garda Youth Crime Prevention/Diversion Projects
- Garda Age Card System
- Garda Juvenile Diversion Scheme
- Garda Síochána Schools Programme
- Special Public Order Units.

Enforcement cannot be the whole answer to alcohol misuse. Parents in particular have a very large responsibility for ensuring their children socialise in a safe environment, and that they show proper example by the responsible use of alcohol.

The extended pub opening hours, introduced during 2000, clearly place additional demands on Garda resources. What impact they are having on the actual level of assaults is not yet clear, but the matter is being closely monitored.

Looking to the future, I have recently established the Garda Youth Policy Advisory Group to advise me as to the causes of public disorder and street violence associated with alcohol misuse by young people, and on possible solutions to deal with these issues. A wide spectrum of interests, including the voluntary and statutory, extending across the public and private sectors, are represented. It is expected that future strategies, aimed at treating the problem in a holistic fashion, will be developed arising from the Group's deliberations.

TRAFFIC

While travel technology has in general terms improved our lives hugely and we can now travel distances in a few hours which took weeks, months and even years previously, the use of this technology also has a very negative impact on thousands of lives in Ireland every year. Each year approximately 450 people lose their lives on our roads. Several thousand are injured, many never recover fully. It can now take longer to travel short distances in our cities by car than on foot. It is not unusual for people to spend three or more hours every day travelling to and from work. Life and time are precious commodities. Once lost, neither can ever be recovered.

An Garda Síochána has two distinct roles in relation to road traffic: Traffic Management and Traffic Law Enforcement.

- Traffic Management involves everything to do with traffic movement along our roads. It means ensuring that measures necessary to allow traffic to flow as freely and safely as possible are in place, and it requires continuous liaison and co-operation with other organisations such as local authorities, etc.

- Traffic Law Enforcement involves providing a legal deterrent to people contravening the relevant legislation. This is primarily done using the threat of detection and punishment – creating an atmosphere where potential law breakers do not break the law for fear of detection and the legal and other consequences of this.

The Irish economy is continuing to grow at an unprecedented and unforecasted rate. What has been achieved during the past five years or so has far exceeded what any forecaster or planner could have dreamt of. Vehicle registrations have grown from 86,924 in 1995 to 174,229 in 1999. By the end of the year 2000, provisional figures show, some 230,000 new cars were registered. The total number of vehicles on our roads has grown from just over one and a quarter million in 1995 to well over one and a half million at present. Over the next five years we are expected to have some two million vehicles registered. It is likely that economic development will continue to be concentrated in the greater Dublin area. Availability of accommodation will continue to be a problem. More and more people will be forced to move to rural towns and villages. Long distance daily commuting will continue to increase. Due to economic prosperity and increasing social and work pressures the use of performance enhancing and recreational drugs will increase. The national road network will be improved with the development of four Strategic Road Corridors. These will carry the bulk of long distance traffic.

Despite the huge growth in road traffic volumes in recent years, we, with our partners, have been successful in preventing a corresponding rise in road casualties. In fact since 1997 we have seen a 12% reduction in the number of road traffic fatalities. An Garda Síochána throughout the country has achieved this through the co-operation of all the agencies with responsibility for road safety and on the back of strong enforcement measures.

The Road to Safety – the Government Strategy for Road Safety, 1998-2002[5] provides the framework for the achievement of a 20% reduction in the number of road traffic casualties during its period of operation. Following from *Operation Lifesaver* it identifies speeding, drink driving, and seatbelt wearing as key target areas in order to reduce road casualties. Over the coming months and years, as enforcement levels reduce the effects of these contributors the challenge will be to fine-tune our operations in order to focus more closely on other factors. Future strategies will be based on detailed research and analysis of real-time information allowing us to respond in a timely and finely targeted fashion to key result areas.

Increased traffic volumes, new policing structures and strategies, increasing regulation, etc will all have the effect of increasing the levels of enforcement

---

[5] *The Road to Safety – Government Strategy for Road Safety 1998-2002* (1998), Department of the Environment and Local Government

required and also the levels achievable. We must look at extending the range of areas covered by the Fine-on-the-Spot system. Allied to the Fine-on-the-Spot system is the proposal by government to introduce a "Drivers' Points System". We must have effective and efficient systems in place to support an expanded Fine-on-the-Spot system and points system. In anticipation of these developments work has already begun by our IT and traffic personnel on the development of a processing system capable of efficiently handling the workload.

Little over ten years ago personal computers were few and far between. The Internet did not exist. Who could have foreseen then what has occurred in the inter vening years? In the area of traffic policing, technological developments have the potential to revolutionise how we go about our work. Developments in digital technology in particular show huge potential. It is the ability to automatically capture high quality images and transmit them to remote locations using either existing fiber optic infrastructures or microwaves, for automated processing, which is exciting police management worldwide. We must maximise the potential usage of such emerging technologies.

HUMAN RESOURCES

As an equal opportunity employer, An Garda Síochána is firmly committed to the equal treatment of all personnel and to the elimination of all forms of dis-crimination. Specialist appointments have been made to consider equality issues and to implement policies. The garda commitment reflects the principles of the Employment Equality Act 1998, to ensure that no discrimination within the context of the proscribed discriminatory grounds exists. An Garda Síochána will continue to embrace strategies and work practices that acknowledge and embrace the necessity for the equal treatment of all.

Industrial relations are at the heart of service delivery and fair and equitable internal policies and practices help to ensure that external service delivery accords with the same principles. The morale of a workforce is an important element of positive service. Proper performance indicators, incentives and rewards are a fundamental element of productivity and performance. While adhering to the consultative process, due consideration will be given to putting in place mechanisms that encourage and acknowledge good service.

While recognising the need for highly trained and focused police officers – managerial, operational and administrative – the contribution of non-garda support staff needs to be recognised and developed. A suitable career and pay structure for civilian support staff needs to be developed to appropriately embrace the tremendous contribution that they make within the garda organisation.

TERRORIST CRIME

We have been fortunate to have witnessed profound changes in the state security situation over recent years. The Northern Ireland peace process has brought about a cease-fire by many of those previously involved in violence.

Some dissident republican groups, however, continue with their activities. In addition to sporadic acts of violence, these groups are also involved in other nefarious activities with the primary purpose of raising funds for the purchase of arms and explosives, and generally to support their terrorist activities. Most notably they are involved in smuggling and counterfeiting operations along the border.

As the peace process continues to bring about changes in the political and governmental landscape of Northern Ireland, increasing levels of disillusionment among sections of the unionist/loyalist communities opposed to change can be anticipated. Support for dissident loyalist groups and their activities is likely to grow. It is expected that, over the short to medium terms at least, these groups will become increasingly active and pose an intensified and substantial threat to the security of the state.

For many years the United States of America primarily, but also Canada, have been rich sources of funds for republican and loyalist organisations. Funds are the life-blood of terrorist activity and without these funds the duration and intensity of the campaigns of violence in Northern Ireland could not have been sustained. With the development of the peace process, these sources have diminished but are still important. The blocking of these sources is vital to the long-term success of the peace process.

Though the indigenous terrorist environment has stabilised considerably over recent years, international terrorism is a growing phenomenon. Factors such as the spread of the Islamic fundamentalist movement, ethnic strife such as the Basque and Kurdish movements, the effects of increasing globalisation and anti-US sentiment, and the growth of environmental or eco-terrorism, have contributed to this situation.

The expansion of the European Union to the East and the lessening or removal of restrictions on free movement within the zone have meant that Ireland is now more open and susceptible to international terrorist attacks.

Near to home An Garda Síochána needs to continue developing close links with the Northern Ireland police service. With increased normalisation of policing along the border area close co-operation will be central to countering terrorist activity. On a global scale, also, we need to continue to develop our working relationships with other police and security services and to foster useful sources of intelligence.

MAINTAINING THE SUPPORT OF THE COMMUNITY

"Policing by Consent" has been a fundamental tenet of how An Garda Síochána has provided the policing service in Ireland since its establishment over seventy-five years ago. Without the very high level of community support that it has enjoyed down through the years, the organisation could not have been as successful as it has.

Irish Society is going through a period of unprecedented change. Our growth rate has ensured this. In the course of one decade our economy has been transformed from one of the poorest in Western Europe to one of the richest. From having a quarter of a million of our population unemployed, full employment is now a reality. We used to export our young people to our richer neighbours. Over the next five years we will need to achieve net immigration of 200,000 people in order to meet our economy's growing workforce needs. No-one would wish to turn the clock back, but the progress we have made was not achieved without major social costs.

We now have more double income households, housing shortages, longer commuting distances, more vehicles, longer working hours, a more hetero-geneous society. In general people have less time outside of work during which to involve themselves in voluntary or community activities. This places greater demands on the statutory bodies to fill the voids created. As a society we need to ensure that some of the fruits of our economic success are focused on fulfilling some of these vital roles. An Garda Síochána must tailor its service delivery to meet the changing needs of our customers, in the form of more flexible work practices, the use of technology, etc.

Some two hundred years ago Edmund Burke[6] wrote:

> Because half a dozen grasshoppers under a fern make the field ring with their importunate clink, while thousands of great cattle, reposed beneath the shadow of the oak, chew the cud and are silent, pray do not imagine that those who make the noise are the only inhabitants of the field, that they are many in number, or that, after all, they are anything other than little, shrivelling, meagre, hopping, though loud and troublesome, insects of the hour.

An Garda Síochána must ensure that we heed Burke's advice and that we continue to listen carefully for the quieter sounds.

The community itself must be seen as an equal part of the equation. Without participation and the support of the community any police service will falter. An Garda Síochána has endeavoured to engage the community in a partnership approach and through initiatives like the Garda National Quality Bureau and Customer Panels at various levels, the service recipient – the customer – is being

---

[6] as cited in Charles Handy (1997), *The Hungry Spirit,* Hutchinson (p. 103)

consulted and afforded an input into the type and level of policing in their respective areas. This service notion, and more importantly the delivery of a quality service, is an area that An Garda Síochána must, and will, continue to progress and expand.

An Garda Síochána is committed to continually boosting the level of police service provided. Our mission statement[7] reflects this commitment: *To achieve the highest attainable level of Personal Protection, Community Commitment and State Security.* The primary step in achieving our mission is to ensure that the downward trend in crime continues, thereby reducing the exposure of people to criminal behaviour in the first instance. Thereafter, we need to concentrate on continually improving detection rates to ensure that the guilty are brought to justice. The expeditious detection and processing of offenders is central to that aim.

Until recent years Irish society was relatively homogeneous. The vast majority of the population was born and grew up in this country. We learned about our laws and society's norms from our parents, teachers and community in general. As a nation we have never found it necessary to involve ourselves in the provision of formal instruction on these topics. It is hardly reasonable to expect that new immigrants will be intuitively aware of the laws and rules of our society. When we change jobs we undergo induction courses. When we begin playing a new game we are given a list of rules. Yet, when people from different cultural backgrounds come to live among us we expect them to integrate seamlessly. The consequences for all from such an approach are clear. Other countries have developed systems of induction for immigrants. We must do likewise.

Public support must not be taken for granted. An Garda Síochána must continue to work ever more closely with members of the community in helping to build a society in which we can all take pride and that will hopefully form a model that others will wish to follow.

MANAGING A NATIONAL INFORMATION TECHNOLOGY SYSTEM

The primary challenge which technology presents to any organisation is the ability to recognise its worth and to harness it to best effect. The acquisition and proper use of information technology is an important success factor for organisations.

An Garda Síochána is in the throes of introducing a national information technology system, PULSE – Police Using Leading Systems Effectively. This is the single largest project ever undertaken by the organisation, costing many tens of millions of pounds and extending over a number of years.

The development of PULSE had a number of imperatives. Previously we had

---

[7] *Annual Report of An Garda Síochána* 1993, An Garda Síochána

a number of "stand-alone" systems that did not communicate with each other and were not Year 2000 compliant. These held information on such matters as crime, criminal records, vehicles, and firearms. With PULSE we have a single system capable of handling all of our information needs into the future. Organisational success is dependent on timely and high-quality information being available to its managers to inform the decision-making process. PULSE is designed to fulfil both needs.

Some challenges still remain. The system must be further developed and extended to other areas that can benefit from computerisation. These include Summonses and Charges, Prisoner Log, Property Matching, Bail, and Messaging. These are planned for introduction during the coming year. Similar to the earlier stages of the project, matters such as

- training
- system integrity and security
- compliance with the data protection requirements
- the establishment of a communications programme to ensure the organisation is fully aware of the changes in work practices, roles and responsibilities
- timely and accurate data entry and matching information to existing data on PULSE
- managing the people issues associated with the changes
- continued organisation involvement in the design, development and implementation of future releases of PULSE.

will need to be afforded particular attention in order to ensure that the benefits accruing to An Garda Síochána from the vast resources and effort invested in the project are maximised.

EUROPEAN AND INTERNATIONAL ISSUES

Ireland has now been a full participant in the process of European integration for a generation. We have benefitted enormously from membership of the European Union, and have at the same time contributed constructively to the Union's development, not least in our contribution in the Justice and Home Affairs area. Irish people see the European Union, not simply as an organisation to which Ireland belongs, but as an integral part of our future. We see ourselves, increasingly, as Europeans. So, also do members of An Garda Síochána.

As a nation we have benefitted greatly from the transfer of EU funds, which have helped create the fastest growing economy in the Union. There have been other transfers – of skills, of excellence and of best practice. To this end An Garda Síochána has developed relationships with police forces in every EU member state, primarily through EU funded programmes under the EU Justice and Home Affairs area such as OISIN[8].

Gardaí have participated in the exchange of best practice over a wide area of policing, from organised crime, terrorism, drug trafficking, money laundering to policing a developing multi-ethnic society. Through these programmes we have learned about failed policies and best practice. But, the exchange is not just one way. An Garda Síochána is now recognised as a world centre of excellence in at least four areas of policing: Police Training; Community Policing; Anti-Terrorist Police Training and in Asset Tracing, Restraint and Seizure.

An Garda Síochána intends to fulfil its obligations on law enforcement issues and initiatives on an EU wide basis. For example the Treaty of Amsterdam[9] has opened up new possibilities for further police co-operation within the European Union for the creation of an area of freedom, security and justice in the Union.

A reflection of the importance that An Garda Síochána places on international policing issues and its increasing commitment to international police co-operation is the current posting of liaison officers in The Hague, Madrid, London and Paris.

Within the European Union there are three main trends in policing a new Europe.

1   The process of policing systems towards integration on both horizontal and vertical levels. This involves enhanced co-operation and a move towards harmonisation of some aspects of criminal law through conventions, council decisions and protocols.

2   There is a process of increasing the notion of a common border, resulting in Schengen.

3   There is a general enhancement of law and order issues, where the citizens of Europe through their governments wish to live in an area of freedom, security and justice, bearing in mind of course human rights.

An Garda Síochána is helping to shape the future of EU law enforcement through it's involvement, along with the Department of Justice, Equality and Law Reform, in the various EU Working Groups set up to increase further co-operation between law enforcement agencies and combat criminal activity across the EU. One example of this was the publication recently of a document with thirty-nine recommendations on fighting organised crime, entitled: *The Prevention and*

---

[8] On 20 December, 1996, the Council of Ministers of the European Union adopted the OISIN Programme (Joint Action 97/12 JHA, Official Journal of the European Communities L7, 10.1. 1997, page 5), a framework to develop and enhance co-operation between police, customs and other law enforcement authorities of member states and to provide such authorities with greater insight into working methods of their counterparts in other member states

[9] Treaty of Amsterdam 1996, Art. 29-42, Police Judicial Co-operation in Criminal Matters

Control of Organised Crime: – A European Union Strategy for the Beginning of the New Millennium.[10]

The Commission[11] set out a "scoreboard" outlining policies to be implemented and deadlines for their adoption with member states as forerunner countries in relation to specific issues. I have requested that Ireland be a forerunner with respect to two of the recommendations at the EU level concerned with developing strategies to harmonise the EU response to crime. These are (i) Drug Trafficking and (ii) the Seizure of Assets.

An Garda Síochána intends to meet the challenges of international policing by working hand in hand with

- other European law enforcement agencies bilaterally on a case to case basis
- the EU Commission and Third Pillar Working Groups, such as the Multi-Disciplinary Group on Organised Crime, the Police Co-operation Working Group and the Drug Trafficking Group, among others. These working groups determine the future policy and direction in the EU Justice and Home Affairs area
- Europol. The Treaty of Amsterdam and the Tampere conclusions call for the strengthening of Europol. Members of An Garda Síochána actively participate in all activities of Europol, including the allocation of permanent Garda Liaison Officers at Europol Headquarters in The Hague
- the Schengen Agreement. The UK has formally applied to join the Schengen Agreement and An Garda Síochána is currently preparing for Ireland to follow the UK's example of applying to join the Schengen Agreement. The key benefit to An Garda Síochána will be full access to the Schengen Information Systems. Travel between the UK, Ireland and mainland Europe will be more open and this will present further challenges for An Garda Síochána, at points of entry into the state
- Interpol. An Garda Síochána will continue to co-operate with and participate in Interpol which facilitates co-operation with the other 176 members of Interpol. An Garda Síochána is frequently asked to assist in international investigations
- the Organisation for Security and Co-operation in Europe (OSCE[12]) is a security organisation of fifty-five participating states. In its region it is the

---

[10] *The Prevention and Control of Organised Crime – A European Union Strategy for the Beginning of the New Millennium.* Adopted pursuant to Title VI of the Treaty on European Union published in *Official Journal of the European Communities –* C124, Volume 43, 3 May, 2000

[11] A Scoreboard to review progress on the creation of an area of Freedom, Security and Justice in the European Union (Com 2000, 167 final/2 Brussels 13/4/2000)

[12] Organisation for Security and Co-operation in Europe – *www.osce.org*

primary instrument for early warning, conflict prevention, crisis management and post-conflict rehabilitation. Its approach to security is comprehensive and co-operative. It deals with a wide range of security issues, including arms control, preventive diplomacy, confidence- and security-building measures, human rights, election monitoring and economic and environmental security. Increasingly An Garda Síochána is being asked to participate in a growing number of missions, a participation which is regularly reviewed

- UN missions. The role of An Garda Síochána is well documented. Gardaí are seen internationally as highly skilled and effective police officers
- the UN in formulating conventions to combat the spread of criminal activity, for example the proposed UN Convention on Organised Crime
- the Council of Europe. The Council is currently preparing a convention to combat the use of cybercrime. Through the Department of Justice, Equality and Law Reform, An Garda Síochána is contributing to the formulation of this convention, which is seen by the gardaí as particularly important considering the amount of technological companies based in Ireland. The Council also prepared the Convention on Human Rights, which Ireland is due to sign shortly. There is no conflict between human rights and policing because both human rights and police powers are protected by law. An Garda Síochána believe that protection of and respect for human rights are essential elements of good policing.

The Garda Síochána *Corporate Strategy*[13] clearly outlines our responsibilities in our policy on the global village, as indicated in the following excerpts:

> An Garda Síochána will work with European and World Policing organisations and agencies such as Europol and Interpol to help curb drug trafficking. In Ireland, the scale of drugs supply will require a concerted and multi-agency approach more particularly on the demand reduction side. The integration of the national effort to curb drugs misuse requires review to improve existing effective policies.
>
> The gardaí will work with the EU Commission and the Council of Europe in briefing and benchmarking on new and current European policing issues including the protection of human rights.

An Garda Síochána fully endorses the Tampere Conclusions[14], which noted that

> People have the right to expect the Union to address the threat to their freedom and legal rights posed by serious crime. To counter these threats a common effort is needed to prevent and fight crime and criminal organisations throughout the Union.

---

[13] *An Garda Síochána Corporate Strategy 2000-2004,* An Garda Síochána, 2000
[14] Conclusions of the Special European Council meeting at Tampere, Finland, on 15 and 16 October, 1999, in relation to police and judicial co-operation in criminal matters

The joint mobilisation of police and judicial resources is needed to guarantee there is no hiding place for criminals or the proceeds of crime within the Union (conclusion No. 6).

CONCLUSION

Although the future can seldom be predicted with accuracy and unforeseen circumstances may interfere with the best-laid plans, unless there is planning, actions tend to be aimless and left to chance. It is necessary for garda management to continuously peer into the future and decipher perceived trends or developments likely to impact on our sphere of responsibility. It is appropriate that, at a time when we stand astride the second and third millenniums, we should look forward to some of the policing challenges facing An Garda Síochána and how we may best manage them.

The future will be demanding. The environment in which we operate is changing apace. Tried and tested solutions to challenges of the past will not ensure a successful future. New challenges demand new solutions. In the new global village police services must learn together and from each other, and must co-operate as never before.

27

The Garda Síochána: a Legal and Constitutional Perspective

Dermot Walsh

THE ESTABLISHMENT OF THE GARDA SÍOCHÁNA

Prior to the establishment of the Garda Síochána, Ireland outside of Dublin was policed by the Royal Irish Constabulary (RIC), while Dublin was policed by the Dublin Metropolitan Police (DMP). Although both were composed of constables whose status derived from the common law, the former bore all of the hallmarks of a gendarmerie.[1] Not only was it a national police force under close central government control but it was also organised, trained and equipped along military lines. In addition to providing a police service it played a vital role in the suppression of political dissent, violent opposition to the State and public disorder. The DMP on the other hand was modeled more closely on the London Metropolitan Police. While the RIC was disbanded in 1922 on the establishment of the state the DMP survived until 1925 when it was merged with the Garda Síochána.

One of the most pressing tasks facing the founders of the new Irish state in 1922 was the replacement of the discredited and demoralised RIC.[2] To this end a

---

[1] See T. Bowden, *Beyond the Limits of the Law,* Harmondsworth: Penguin, 1978; S. Palmer, *Police and Protest in England and Ireland 1780-1850,* Cambridge: Cambridge University Press, 1988

[2] For detailed accounts of the history surrounding the establishment of the Garda Síochána, see C. Brady, *Guardians of the Peace,* Dublin: Gill and Macmillan, 1974; L. McNiffe, *A History of the Garda Síochána,* Dublin: Wolfhound Press, 1997; G. Allen, *Policing Independent Ireland 1922-1982,* Dublin: Gill and Macmillan, 1999

committee was set up in February 1922 under the chairmanship of Michael Staines (subsequently the first Commissioner of the Garda Síochána). The committee's report made important recommendations on the image and political neutrality of the new force. Apart from that, however, it did not seek any fundamental change in direction with respect to legal status and structures.[3]

The government proceeded to recruit to the new force based on the model recommended by the Staines Committee. Progress was interrupted by a mutiny among a section of the recruits stationed at Kildare in the summer of 1922. The subsequent commission of enquiry into the mutiny made important recommendations which resulted, among other things, in the Garda Síochána being established as an unarmed, civilian police service. Although only a few months old at the time the force was technically disbanded and reformed with selective enrolment. Michael Staines resigned his position as commissioner and was replaced by Eoin O'Duffy.

The Garda Síochána (as it was originally designated) was not put on a statutory footing until more than one year later by the Garda Síochána (Temporary Provisions) Act 1923. This Act was designed to remain in force for one year. In due course it was replaced by the Garda Síochána Act 1924. This, in turn, was heavily amended and supplemented by the Police Forces Amalgamation Act 1925 to make provision for the amalgamation of the Garda Síochána and the DMP to form the Garda Síochána we know today. Although they have been amended and supplemented on several occasions since, the 1924 and 1925 Acts can be described as laying the basic statutory foundation for the Garda Síochána. The primary purpose of this chapter is to offer a broad survey of the legal and constitutional status of the force, which has been created by these provisions.

LEGAL PERSONALITY

Body of individuals

One of the most distinctive features of the Garda Síochána is the fact that it does not have a legal personality separate and distinct from that of its individual members.[4] Indeed, the Police Forces Amalgamation Act 1925 does not deal directly with the legal status of the force at all. It stipulates that the force shall consist of "... such officers and men as the [government] shall from time to time determine ..."[5] Generally, the officers are appointed, and can be dismissed, by the government while the other members are appointed, and can be dismissed, by the

---

[3] D. Walsh, *The Irish Police: A Legal and Constitutional Perspective*, Dublin: Round Hall Sweet & Maxwell, 1998

[4] D. Walsh, *op.cit.* at Ch. 2

[5] Police Forces Amalgamation Act 1925, s. 5(2)

garda commissioner. The Act also stipulates that the garda commissioner has the power of general direction and control over the force, subject to regulations on general management matters issued from time to time by the Minister for Justice, Equality and Law Reform.[6] Nowhere, however, does the legislation suggest that either the garda commissioner or the minister constitutes the legal personnification of the Garda Síochána or the embodiment of police power.

Common Law Peace Officer

The fact that the force lacks a legal personality separate and distinct from that of its individual members suggests that even today, more than two hundred years after organised police forces were first established in this country, the legal concept of police is still dominated by the ancient common law peace officer.[7] This perception is reinforced by the fact that the legislation establishing the Garda Síochána does not entrust the full complement of police powers and duties to a centralised figure such as the garda commissioner or the minister who could then delegate police tasks to members of the force. Instead the legislation seems to have adopted by default the arrangements which have informed organised policing in Ireland since 1786 and which are quintessentially English in origin.

Under these arrangements it is the individual member of the force, as distinct from the garda commissioner or minister, who is the primary legal actor.[8] The full complement of police powers and duties are invested by law in the office held by each individual member. Many of these powers and duties emanate from the common law and inhere in each member of the force by virtue of his or her status as a peace officer. Such fundamental police duties as preventing and detecting crime, maintaining public order and keeping the peace are not entrusted statutorily on each member of the force. There is no need. They already inhere in each member by virtue of his or her status as a common law peace officer. The same applies to such basic powers as the use of force in keeping the peace and restoring public order. Of course many police powers today derive from a statutory source. Significantly, the legislation creating such powers confers them directly on each member of the force, as distinct from the garda commissioner or Minister for Justice, Equality and Law Reform.

Independence of members

The retention of the individual peace officer as the primary legal actor in an organised police force has important constitutional implications for the exercise of police powers.[9] Since police powers and duties vest in each member of the

---

[6] Police Forces Amalgamation Act 1925, s. 8(2)
[7] D Walsh, *op.cit.* at Ch. 3
[8] *Ibid.*
[9] *Ibid.*

force by virtue of the office which he or she holds, it follows that they can be exercised only on the responsibility of the individual member concerned. When engaged in the investigation and detection of a crime, it is a matter for the individual member to decide whether, for example, to effect an arrest. Of course, he or she may be requested to effect an arrest by a senior officer. Ultimately, however, the decision to act must be his or hers alone. The request from a senior officer cannot in itself provide a complete legal basis for the member's actions. Even if the objective preconditions for the exercise of his or her power of arrest are present, it will still be a matter for the discretion of the individual member whether or not to effect the arrest. If he or she exercises that discretion in favour of arrest purely on the basis that he or she had been instructed to do so, the member will have failed to exercise a genuine discretion and the arrest will be unlawful. It follows that no executive authority, not even the garda commissioner or the minister, can lawfully direct how a member of the Garda Síochána should exercise his or her police powers or discharge his her law enforcement duties in any individual case. The individual member is independent in such matters.

This independence of a member of the Garda Síochána can be explained partly by the fact that he or she is exercising powers which are conferred statutorily on him or her. Ultimately, however, the member's independence arises from his or her status as an office-holder. When enforcing the law in his or her capacity as a peace officer he or she is exercising an original authority attaching to that common law office.

The unusual status of members of the Garda Síochána suggests that the force may have difficulty functioning as a coherent and organised component of the public administration of the state. Certainly, there is no other hierarchical body of public servants in which each member shares a common office and, irrespective of the position held in that hierarchy, is independent in the exercise of the powers and duties attaching to the office. In practice, however, the individual members of the Garda Síochána have been welded into a disciplined and cohesive organ-isation largely through the exercise of the commissioner's power of general direction and control and the minister's power to makes regulations on the general management of the force. Each of these will be dealt with in turn.

MINISTERIAL REGULATIONS

The regulatory power

For the most part the primary legislation establishing the Garda Síochána does not deal in any detail with the managerial and administrative structures which are essential to ensure that the large body of office-holders can function as a cohesive, disciplined and accountable unit. Apart from basic provisions on the appointment and removal of officers and the general powers and responsibilities of the garda commissioner the primary legislation prefers to leave these vital matters to ministerial regulations.[10]

Section 14 of the Police Forces Amalgamation Act 1925 confers the minister with a general power to make regulations on the internal management of the force. This is supplemented by a number of more specific piecemeal provisions enabling the minister to make regulations on the important issue of rates of pay and allowances to the several ranks and grades within the force,[11] and the grant and payment of pensions, allowances and gratuities to members of the force, their widows, children and dependants. Section 14 is much more wide-ranging in scope. It reads as follows.

> The Minister may from time to time, subject to the approval of the Government, make regulations in relation to all or any of the matters following that is to say:
> (a) the admission, appointment, and enrolment of members of the amalgamated force
> (b) the promotion, retirement, degradation, dismissal, and punishment of members of the amalgamated force
> (c) the duties of the several ranks of the amalgamated force
> (d) the maintenance, training, discipline, and efficiency of the amalgamated force
> (e) the formation of representative bodies of members of the amalgamated force
> any other matter or thing relating to the internal management of the amalgamated force.

Admission, appointment and promotion

This section 14 power has been used very effectively to establish the Garda Síochána as a centralised, hierarchical and disciplined police force. The standards and procedure for admission, appointment and enrolment to the force are all governed by regulations.[12] The admission and appointments regulations set basic standards on age, character, education, physique and health.[13] An applicant who satisfies these standards and who completes a traineeship programme successfully is eligible for appointment to the rank of garda. Ultimately the power of appointment rests with the commissioner. Promotion within the force is also governed by

---

[10] See D Walsh, *op.cit.,* Chs. 2 and 4 for detailed discussion of these powers and the regulations made pursuant to them

[11] It also makes provision for the continuance in force, subject to any variation by an order made under this section, of the Garda Síochána Pay Order 1924, the Dublin Metropolitan Police Pay Order 1924 (suitably modified), the Dublin Metropolitan Police Allowance Order 1920 (suitably modified) and the Garda Síochána Allowances Order 1924

[12] See D. Walsh, Ch. 2

[13] The current regulations are Garda Síochána (Admissions and Appointments) Regulations 1988, as amended by Garda Síochána (Admissions and Appointments) Regulations 1997

detailed regulations which set out the standards and procedures applicable for promotion to each rank up to and including the rank of assistant commissioner.[14]

Discipline

The regulations on discipline set out a code of disciplinary offences coupled with a detailed procedure to be followed in the investigation, determination and punishment of any disciplinary infractions by members of the force.[15] Undoubtedly, these regulations play a key role in enabling the Garda Síochána to function as a cohesive unit. They provide the essential vehicle for transmitting the central authority of the garda commissioner down through the ranks. Disciplinary offences such as insubordinate conduct or failing or neglecting promptly to carry out any lawful order are very useful in ensuring that individual members and teams within the force operate in accordance with the directions and policies of the commissioner and senior officers. The weight of the commissioner's formal disciplinary authority under the regulations is also augmented by his capacity to dispense informal "rewards" and "sanctions" such as those associated with being assigned to particular duties or posted to certain parts of the country.

Ranks

The hierarchical rank structure of the force is also governed by secondary legislation,[16] although this has not always been the case.[17] From 1923 until 1972 the officers and members of the force have been organised into hierarchical ranks prescribed by primary legislation. Since 1972 the power to fix the rank structure and the official complement in each rank has been vested in the government. While the numbers in each rank have changed regularly since the force was first established, the actual designation of the ranks has remained constant. In hierarchical order from the top down, they are: commissioner, deputy commissioner, assistant commissioner, surgeon, chief superintendent, superintendent, inspector, station sergeant, sergeant and garda. While the legislation makes at least partial provision for the senior ranks, it is silent on the responsibilities of the ranks from chief superintendent right down to garda.

Section 14 of the 1925 Act confers upon the Minister for Justice, Equality and Law Reform the power to make regulations on the duties of the several ranks. In practice, it would appear that this power has never been exercised. By default,

---

[14] Garda Síochána (Promotion) Regulations 1987

[15] Garda Síochána (Discipline) Regulations 1989. For detailed analysis, see D. Walsh *op.cit.* at Chs. 7 and 8

[16] Secondary legislation in this context refers to measures (eg regulations) which have been issued by the minister pursuant to a power conferred upon him by an Act of Parliament. The latter constitutes primary legislation

[17] See D. Walsh, Ch. 2

therefore, it is the commissioner who determines the duties attaching to each rank through the exercise of his power of general direction and control of the force.

Representative bodies

Section 14 of the 1925 Act also confers on the minister the power to make regulations on the formation of representative bodies for the force.[18] Further details are provided by section 13 of the 1924 Act[19] which stipulates that the associations will be linked to the rank structures of the force.[20] These measures reflect a tight central government control on the freedom of members of the Garda Síochána to organise in industrial relations matters. Indeed, there is a statutory prohibition on a member of the Garda Síochána joining a trade union or other such association apart from those established by the minister under section 14. This represents an attempt to strike a balance between the basic freedom of members of An Garda Síochána to organise in order to seek improvements in their terms and conditions of employment and the vital need to ensure continuity in the provision of policing services in times of political, industrial and social unrest. Closely associated with the latter concern is the concomitant need to ensure that the enforcement of the law is, and is seen to be, impartial when dealing with political, industrial and social conflict.[21]

The first ministerial regulations establishing representative associations were issued in 1923 under the Garda Síochána (Temporary Provisions) Act 1923.[22] Today there are four associations: the Garda Representative Assocation (GRA); the Association of Garda Sergeants and Inspectors (AGSI); the Association of Superintendents and the Association of Chief Superintendents. Throughout the 1980s and for most of the 1990s there was considerable internal friction within the GRA and the AGSI, particularly between detective and non-detective personnel and also between Dublin members of the force and those in the rest of the country. In 1994 this resulted in a sizeable number of Dublin based members withdrawing from the GRA and the unauthorised establishment of a Garda Federation. For a time it looked as though the impasse would have to be dealt with by new legislation which would give the minister even stronger powers of control over the formation and structure of garda representative bodies. Ultimately a general election and a change of government intervened. Subsequent negotiations proved successful in resolving the problem. The unauthorised Garda Federation was disbanded and the proposed legislation was dropped.

---

[18] *Ibid.*
[19] As substituted by Garda Síochána Act 1977, s. 1
[20] Detectives do not constitute a separate rank for this purpose; *Aughey v Ireland* [1986] ILRM 206
[21] An attempt to challenge the constitutionality of the legislation restricting the freedom of members of the Garda Síochána to form or join trade unions was challenged unsuccessfully in both the High Court and the Supreme Court in *Aughey v Ireland* [1986] ILRM 201 and [1989] ILRM 87
[22] See L. McNiffe at pp. 142-156 for details of these regulations and an overview of the activities of the representative bodies over the first thirty years

Conciliation and arbitration scheme

Closely associated with the subject of representative bodies is the Garda Síochána conciliation and arbitration scheme.[23] Unlike the representative bodies, however, the conciliation and arbitration scheme is non-statutory. The current scheme is based on two Circulars adopted in 1977 and a memorandum of understanding between the minister and the garda representative bodies.[24] It was established primarily for the purpose of providing machinery through which pay claims and conditions of service can be negotiated between the minister and the commissioner on the one hand, and the representative bodies on the other hand. It also provides a forum through which to secure the fullest co-operation between the state, as employer, and the members, as employees, for the better discharge of the functions of the Garda Síochána.

The machinery consists of a Conciliation Council and an Arbitration Board. The former is composed of six representatives each from the employers and the staff. Not more than four members of the employers' side must be civil servants representing the minister, and not more than two must be members of the force representing the commissioner. On the staff side all six must be members of the Garda Síochána. The chairperson of the Council must be a serving civil servant nominated by the Minister for Justice, Equality and Law Reform and the Minister for the Public Service. The composition of the Arbitration Board is identical to that of the Council, although the personnel will be different.

A wide range of internal management matters can be discussed within the Council. These include: claims relating to pay and allowances; hours of duty; standards of accommodation; principles governing the allocation of living accommodation, superannuation, leave, recruitment, promotion, discipline, transfers; and suggestions for promoting the efficiency of the force. Other matters can be discussed if the minister or ministers, as the case may be, agree that they are appropriate for discussion. The Arbitration Board is competent to arbitrate on claims for adjustment of rates of pay and allowances, periods of annual leave or sick leave, total weekly hours of work and overtime, where the claim has been discussed and has been the subject of recorded disagreement at the Council.

Compensation scheme

It is also worth noting that members of the Garda Síochána benefit from a statutory compensation scheme for death or personal injuries inflicted upon them in the performance of their duties.[25] Although the relevant provisions are laid

---

[23] See D. Walsh, *op.cit.,* Ch. 2

[24] "A Scheme to Provide Conciliation and Arbitration Machinery for Members of the Garda Síochána and the Ranks of Chief Superintendent, Superintendent, Inspector, Station Sergeant, Sergeant and Guard", as amended

[25] See D. Walsh, *op.cit.* at Ch. 2

down in primary as distinct from secondary legislation,[26] nevertheless the Minister for Justice, Equality and Law Reform plays a central role in the operation of the scheme. Broadly speaking, if a member suffers criminal injuries in the performance of his or her duties, he or she can apply to the minister for authorisation to apply to the High Court for compensation. If the injury is non-minor in character the minister must grant authorisation, otherwise he has a discretion in the matter. In the High Court the claim is heard by a single judge who will award compensation and fix the amount to be paid by the Minister for Finance where the judge is satisfied that the requirements of the legislation have been satisfied.[27]

Deployment

Although the Minister for Justice, Equality and Law Reform has no operational control over the deployment of members of the Garda Síochána, he does have a significant input into the physical distribution of the force throughout the country.[28] Since the minister controls the budget for the force, it is he and not the comissioner who decides where a garda station will be built and where a station will be closed. Moreover, the Garda Síochána Act 1924 specifically confers on the minister the power to direct the manner in which the force shall be distributed and stationed throughout the country. For the most part, however, it would appear that the minister leaves it to the garda commissioner to decide on the complement of gardaí attached to any particular station.[29] Nevertheless, there can be no doubt that the Minister also influences the deployment of extra gardaí to certain parts of the country, particularly the border, in response to major threats.

COMMISSIONER'S DIRECTION AND CONTROL OF THE FORCE

Statutory power

The commissioner plays a vital role in welding the individual members of the Garda Síochána into an organised and disciplined police force. Although each member retains his or her discretion in the exercise of the law enforcement powers and duties attaching to his or her office, the commissioner exerts a decisive influence on the contents of policing policies and practices. Within the parameters of the legislative provisions and ministerial regulations the commissioner, pursuant to his statutory power of general direction and control of the force, can

---

[26] Garda Síochána (Compensation) Act 1941 as amended by the Garda Síochána (Compensation)(Amendment) Act 1945
[27] For further details, see Walsh at pp. 41-44
[28] See D. Walsh, *op.cit.* at Ch. 4
[29] Walsh, at pp. 85-86

dictate operational priorities, operational practices, the establishment of specialist units, internal management structures and practices, the delegation of authority down through the ranks, the allocation of duties to individual members, ranks and units, the distribution of personnel throughout the state, training, promotion and so on.[30] The commissioner's authority in these matters is enhanced by his status as disciplinary authority for the force.

Specialist units

The most visible manifestation of the commissioner's directive control of the force is the existence of specialist units. Some of these are very large and effectively permanent; the primary examples being the detective branch and the traffic branch. Smaller and more specialised units include: the national drugs unit, the murder squad, the bureau of fraud investigation, the fingerprint section, the ballistics section and the sub-aqua unit. Others are created on an ad hoc basis and last for a relatively short period of time before being disbanded or reformed. With one significant exception all of these branches and units are created under the authority of the commissioner pursuant to his power of general direction and control. They have no independent statutory base and, as such, can be disbanded or reformed from time to time at the administrative discretion of the commissioner. They all constitute integral parts of the Garda Síochána and are subject to the general regulations and commissioner authority applicable to the rest of the force. Allocation of duties and personnel to these units and branches is solely a matter for the commissioner.

The one significant exception is the Europol National Unit.[31] It is established as a distinct unit within the Garda Síochána in fulfilment of Ireland's obligations under the Europol Convention. Unlike the other garda units, however, it has its own statutory base in the Europol Act 1997. The Minister for Justice, Equality and Law Reform, following discussions with the garda commissioner, is obliged to designate by order a Europol National Unit within the Garda Síochána. While the head of the unit must be a member of the Garda Síochána of at least chief superintendent rank, not all members of the unit need be members of the Garda Síochána.

Another specialist body worth mentioning because of its very close links with the Garda Síochána is the Criminal Assets Bureau.[32] This is a unique development in Irish policing in so far as it brings together in a single crime-fighting agency the Garda Síochána, the Revenue Commissioners and the Department of Social, Community and Family Affairs. A distinctive feature of the Bureau is the fact that

---

[30] See D. Walsh, *op.cit.* at Chs. 3 and 4
[31] *Ibid.* at Ch. 13
[32] See P. McCutcheon and D. Walsh, *The Confiscation of Criminal Assets: Law and Procedure*, Dublin: Round Hall Sweet & Maxwell, 1999

it is primarily concerned with securing the confiscation of the assets of suspected criminals through a specially designed civil process, as opposed to securing convictions against criminals through the normal criminal process. Technically, it is not an integral part of the Garda Síochána. However, its chief officer must be a member of the Garda Síochána of chief superintendent rank. He or she is appointed by and is answerable to the garda commissioner.

General policies and standing orders

The commissioner's operational control of the force is exercised both personally and directly and by delegation through senior officers. Standing policies and practices are set out in the Garda Síochána Code and other such internal documents and communications which are amended from time to time.[33] The contents of these range over a very wide spectrum including: the exercise of arrest powers, the treatment of suspects in garda stations, the searching of suspects, the operation of the juvenile liaison scheme, the handling of prosecutions, road traffic matters, the enforcement of licensing laws, the gathering of criminal intelligence, and so on. The commissioner also sets specific operational priorities from time to time by issuing directives to the force generally, by the provision of additional resources to specialist teams and units and by the creation of new teams and units.

Management structure

The implementation of the commissioner's operational policies and practices on the ground depends heavily on the efforts of senior management at headquarters and throughout the country. Not only do they provide the vital conduit for the implementation of the commissioner's policies, but they also play a significant role in shaping operational policing policies and practices. At headquarters, the commissioner's primary supports are the deputy commissioner, strategic and resource management, and the deputy commissioner, operations. The former has responsibility for three branches, each headed by an assistant commissioner.[34] The country as a whole is divided up into six regions for operational purposes, each headed up by an assistant commissioner.[35] Each region is subdivided into divisions (23 in total), each of which is normally headed up by a chief super-intendent or superintendent. Each division is further sub-divided into districts. The head of a region, division or district, as the case may be, is responsible for the effective policing of his or her area and for the application of the policies and practices laid down by the commissioner and senior management.

---

[33] See D. Walsh, *op.cit.* at Ch. 6

[34] "A" Branch covers finance, services and community relations; "B" Branch covers human resource management and research; and "C" Branch covers crime, security and traffic

[35] Dublin Metropolitan Area, Southern Region, South Eastern Region, Western Region, Northern Region, Eastern Region

COMMISSIONER'S AUTONOMY

The theory

The legislation establishing the Garda Síochána does not directly address the relationship between the commissioner and the executive in operational policing matters. Similarly, the legislation allocating police to the remit of the Department of Justice, Equality and Law Reform does not provide an unequivocal statement of the division of responsibility between the minister and the commissioner. Since the legislation confers the power of general direction and control over the force on the commissioner alone, and does not specifically subordinate the commissioner to the minister or any other executive authority in his exercise of that power, it would seem reasonable to assume that the commissioner is autonomous in operational policing matters.[36] Support for this interpretation is forthcoming from English case law on the status of the commissioner of the London Metropolitan Police. It does not follow, however, that the commissioner's independence in legal theory is always translated into practice. While the government may not have the power to issue binding instructions to the commissioner on operational policies generally or the exercise of police powers or duties in individual cases, it does have the means to exert a significant influence, at least indirectly, on the contents of operational policies, practices and priorities.[37] Interference in individual cases, even of an indirect nature, would be highly improper.

The practice

Control over financial resources, together with powers of appointment and dismissal, give the government the leverage which ensures that the commissioner will pay close attention to the government's views on operational policies, practices and priorities.

The Garda Síochána is financed primarily from the Central Exchequer in accordance with the terms of the separate garda Vote sanctioned by the Dáil. This in itself places the government in a pivotal position to promote or block planned developments which will impact on garda operational matters. However, government control is strengthened immeasurably by the fact that the accounting officer for the Garda Vote is the secretary in the Department of Justice, Equality and Law Reform, instead of the commissioner. Splitting financial responsibility from managerial responsibility in this manner not only flies in the face of established practice in public administration but it also impinges upon the commissioner's autonomy in the general direction and control of the force. If, for example, he wants to buy specially reinforced vehicles to combat joy-riding he

---

[36] See D. Walsh, *op.cit.* at Ch. 4
[37] *Ibid.* at Ch. 5

will know that this might be queried by the accounting officer on the ground that his estimate provided only for the purchase of conventional vehicles. Similarly, if he was considering expenditure on equipment, not specially provided for in his estimates, to capitalise on an upsurge in interest in the community relations programme, one of the factors he will have to take into account is the attitude of the accounting officer.

The current practice is to avoid the sort of detailed interference which seems to have prevailed in times past. Nevertheless, the status of the secretary as accounting officer means that the commissioner is subordinated to the department to an extent which far exceeds that applicable to the heads of most other major public bodies which have a statutory existence independent of their parent departments.

The government's powers of appointment and removal with respect to members of the Garda Síochána are extensive. All officer appointments and dismissals from the office of commissioner right down to (and including) the rank of superintendent vest in the government. While the government must afford a fair hearing to any such officer before removing him or her from office, it would appear that they have less security of tenure than members holding non-commissioned ranks. Certainly, the commissioner (and presumably deputy and assistant commissioners) can be dismissed from office simply if the government loses confidence in him. Unquestionably, this must apply indirect pressure on the commissioner to accommodate the government of the day in its requests with respect to operational policies, priorities and practices. Ultimately, a commissioner who has the support and confidence of the government of the day will find it easier to achieve his objectives for the force than one who is frequently at odds with the government. New initiatives, for example, may require the creation of new officer positions and the choice of personnel to be appointed to those positions. In such matters the commissioner is dependant on the goodwill of the government of the day. Earning and retaining that goodwill often requires a sensitivity to government concerns in policing matters.

GARDA FUNCTIONS

Definition

A distinctive, but by no means unique, feature of the legislation establishing the Garda Síochána is the absence of a clear statutory prescription of the functions of the force. Apart from the stipulation that it shall be a "force of police",[38] there is

---

[38] Garda Síochána Act 1924, s.1(1). In the Police Forces Amalgamation Act 1925 it is referred to as a police force; s. 5(1)

no attempt to define what matters should be within its remit and what matters should be outside. The Dáil and Seanad debates on the Bill preceding the legislation reveal a clear presumption that the force was being established to discharge the traditional police responsibilities of preventing and detecting crime, keeping the peace and maintaining public order.[39] At no stage is there any suggestion or realisation that the force could also be deployed for other purposes, such as the preservation of a certain political, moral, economic or social order in the state. To some extent this might be attributed to the absence of Fianna Fáil representatives from the debates as they, at that time, should have been alive to the danger of a national police force being used as a political tool in the hands of the government of the day. It can also be explained, however, purely on the grounds of historical continuity. The DMP had been established as a "force of police" with no statutory definition of its role. The same applied to the RIC. Not surprisingly, an identical formula was in use for contemporary forces in Britain. Indeed, this peculiar approach can be traced right back to 1785 and English hostility to the very concept of an organised police force.

It does not follow that the Garda Síochána's role cannot be defined. In fact a detailed picture of its role can be constructed from the description of a "force of police" and from the status of a member of the Garda Síochána as a "peace officer".[40] By describing the Garda Síochána as a force of police the legislature clearly intended it to discharge the traditional law enforcement functions associated with its counterparts and predecessors throughout Ireland and Britain. The term "police" had been used in Britain and Ireland since the mid-eighteenth century to designate a body of men organised to discharge "police" functions which hitherto had been associated with constables and other local executive and judicial officials, namely crime prevention and detection, the maintenance of the peace and the preservation of public order.[41]

Crime and public order

The crime prevention, crime detection and public order maintenance functions of the gardaí are clearly reflected in the contents of the common law and statutory powers which vest in a member of the force, and in the policies and priorities laid down for the force as a whole by the garda commissioner in the exercise of his power of general direction and control. Each individual member of the force is conferred by law with a very broad range of powers of arrest, detention, entry, search and seizure which, depending on the contents of the individual power, can

---

[39] The legislation referred to here is the Garda Síochána (Temporary Provisions) Act 1923
[40] See D. Walsh, *op.cit.* at Ch. 5
[41] See contents of the declaration taken by each member on being appointed to his or her office; Police Forces Amalgamation Act 1925, s. 11 and Schedule 4

be used to take a criminal suspect into custody, to gather evidence against a suspect, to keep the peace and to maintain public order. These are supplemented by powers of stop, search and question which, again depending on the contents of the individual power, can be used for the purpose of crime prevention, crime detection and the maintenance of the peace and public order. As a broad generalisation, a member can use force which is reasonable in the circumstances to effect an arrest etc and to restore the peace.

This emphasis on crime and public order is also reflected in the internal management, structures and training, as well as in the commissioner's instructions to members of the force. The maintenance of a large permanent detective branch, for example, confirms the importance of crime detection. The maintenance of a large and permanent traffic branch, regular foot and mobile patrols and a permanent garda presence throughout the country, the juvenile liaison scheme etc all emphasise crime prevention and public order maintenance. The provision of equipment such as batons, riot shields, helmets, visors and firearms, coupled with training in their use, indicate a concern with public order maintenance. Similarly large sections of the Garda Síochána Code are devoted directly or indirectly to law enforcement and public order maintenance matters. In addition, there are separate manuals on crime reporting and recording and criminal investigation techniques, among others.

Law enforcement

The garda function has never been confined to crime and public order. In common with their ancestors in the office of constable prior to the introduction of organised police forces in these islands, they have been expected to provide a much broader law enforcement service. In particular, this encompasses the enforcement of public regulations aimed at the improvement of living and working conditions in society generally. More often than not compliance with the regulations is backed up by the criminal sanction, thereby blurring the distinction between this aspect of the police function and the traditional crime and public order aspects. Many of the garda powers under the general heading of road traffic would come under this heading, as do a wide range of powers associated with social and economic regulation. The latter include powers to stop, question, search, arrest and detain persons in order to maintain certain standards of social behaviour on the streets, as well as powers of inspection and search on private property to maintain certain standards in trade, industry and commerce. It is also worth noting that the Garda Síochána traditionally have assisted in the administrative implementation of many of the regulatory powers aimed at improving living and working conditions and the efficient administration of the state.

State security

State security has been an important function of the Garda Síochána since its establishment. Indeed, the force combines its role as a civil police service with that of the state security service. This is reflected in the presence of specialist units such as the Special Detective Unit and the Intelligence Section. Equally, each member of the force is conferred with a number of specific powers of stop, search, question, arrest, detention, entry, search and seizure which were introduced, at least originally, to combat the threat of internal and external subversion. Most, but not all, of these powers are to be found in the offences against the state legislation.

Accident and emergency

Finally, it is important to acknowledge the important accident and emergency service provided by the Garda Síochána. Each member of the force is under a common law duty to protect life.[42] This duty sometimes expresses itself in the arrest of criminally violent persons who are posing a threat to the life or safety of others. It is by no means confined, however, to action in the context of crime control and public order. Members of the force will come across, or be called out to, situations where life is in danger as a result of accidental fires, flooding, storms, the activities of mentally unstable persons and so on. Unlike ordinary citizens, a member of the Garda Síochána is under a common law duty to take action to protect life in these situations. It is hardly surprising, therefore, that the government also relies on the Garda Síochána to perform a central role in coping with major accidents and emergencies. Divisional, district and station offices, for example, must have copies of the hazardous substances emergency plan and the major accident plan. Indeed, it is the responsibility of the gardaí in the Dublin metropolitan area, and in each division, to prepare a major accident plan. Responsibility for putting it into effect rests with the senior fire officer in consultation with the senior garda officer. When the decision is taken to put it into effect, however, the gardaí are expected to play a primary role in its implementation, and afterwards to take responsibility for identifying the dead and preserving evidence for subsequent inquests.

Others

This brief survey of the garda function can be criticised for being incomplete. That in itself, however, is a reflection of the fact that the garda function has never been definitively prescribed. In practice the garda acts, and is expected to act, in a much wider range of situations than any other branch of the civil administration of the state. Not only does it cover functions, such as crime control and public

---

[42] *R v Dytham* [1979] QB 722

order which are exclusive to it, but it is also expected to discharge functions which might be more appropriately assigned to other government departments and public bodies. In many respects the Garda Síochána can be described as the general factotum of central government and, perhaps, of society. While this may confer certain advantages on the government it is not necessarily in the best interests of the force itself or of the policing service which it provides. The ill-defined nature of the garda role can undermine the capacity of the force to deliver an efficient police service and it can pose practical problems for the accountability of the force.

ACCOUNTABILITY

Accountability to the public remains one of the great unsolved challenges of policing not just in Ireland but probably also in most common law jurisdictions. In Ireland, much of the problem stems from a blurring of the exact status of individual members of the force, the status of the force as a whole and the respective responsibilities of the garda commissioner and the Minister for Justice, Equality and Law Reform. The three primary mechanisms through which members of the Garda Síochána, can be can publicly called to account are: the law, the complaints procedure and the Oireachtas.

The law

Each member of the Garda Síochána is answerable to the law for the exercise of his or her powers and the discharge of his or her duties in exactly the same manner as any other citizen.[43] There are no special exemptions or concessions for the member who acts beyond the law in apprehending an offender or investigating an offence. Accordingly, if he or she uses more force than is necessary when effecting an arrest, or unlawfully breaks into a dwelling when searching for contraband goods, he or she will be liable to be prosecuted for an appropriate offence against the person or property, as the case may be. He or she may also be sued for compensation. While there is no difference in principle in such matters between a member of the Garda Síochána and an ordinary citizen there are certain practical factors which can conspire to ensure that the law is less effective in punishing or providing a remedy against the former than the latter. These can be treated separately for the purposes of criminal law and civil law.

The criminal law

Where a citizen lodges a criminal complaint against a member of the Garda Síochána, almost invariably that complaint will be investigated by fellow

---

[43] See D. Walsh, *op.cit.* at Ch. 10

members of the force.[44] It does not follow, of course, that the investigation will be any the less rigorous than it would have been had the complaint been against a citizen. Nevertheless, there will always be a suspicion that the investigation is not as thorough as it should be, especially where the complaint consists of something that the member has allegedly done in the course of a criminal investigation against the very same individual who has lodged the complaint. It is also worth noting that the conduct of the investigation is likely to be different in some significant respects than would be the case for an investigation into a citizen suspect. Generally, the garda suspect will not suffer the psychological trauma of being arrested and taken into custody, away from his familiar surroundings and into the hostile and alien environment of a garda interrogation room. For the most part the garda suspect will be called in for questioning by his superiors during his normal working day at a date and a time which is convenient for him. Typically he will have sufficient advance notice to secure the services of his solicitor and/or a member of his representative body. He will be fully familiar with his surroundings and the investigation techniques being used. Indeed, the whole procedure is more akin to that of an employer interviewing an employee about some incident which has taken place at work. It is hardly surprising, therefore, that few criminal charges are preferred against gardaí relative to the number of complaints lodged against them.[45]

Particularly difficult cases to investigate are those in which gardaí collectively have resorted to investigative and/or interrogation practices which go beyond the limits of the law. It is easy to imagine a group of detectives resorting to heavy-handed interrogation practices when questioning terrorist or organised crime suspects, particularly if the investigation relates to the death of or serious injury to fellow members of the force. So long as the suspect is not seriously injured it would be a brave member who would break ranks with his colleagues to co-operate fully and frankly with an internal investigation into what happened in the interrogation room. More often than not such investigations are met with a "wall of silence" which is virtually impossible to penetrate. This is reflected in the fact that no gardaí have ever been prosecuted for assaulting terrorist suspects during interrogation despite the serious concerns which have been expressed about the use of physical force in the interrogation room since at least the mid-1970s.

Even where an investigation does produce *prima facie* evidence of criminal wrongdoing against a member, there are other factors which can militate against a successful prosecution. The decision on whether to prosecute is taken by the Director of Public Prosecutions (DPP). While he applies exactly the same criteria

---

[44] *Ibid.* at Ch. 11

[45] In 1997, out of 169 garda complaints referred to the DPP, three prosecutions resulted (with no convictions)

in the case of a complaint against a member of the Garda Síochána as he does in the case of an ordinary citizen, there are circumstances which can at least convey the appearance of greater leniency towards gardaí. Inevitably, there is a close working relationship between the DPP and the Garda Síochána in the investigation and prosecution of criminal offences generally. It is hardly surprising, therefore, that a citizen complainant may suspect bias in a case where the DPP decides, for perfectly legitimate reasons, not to prefer criminal charges against a member of the force on foot of the citizen's complaint. Since the DPP does not give reasons for his prosecutorial decisions, this suspicion may be fuelled by the fact that the complainant will rarely be in a position to appreciate the soundness of the DPP's decision not to prosecute in his or her individual case. It must also be said, of course, that there may be circumstances where the DPP would decide for public policy reasons not to prefer charges against a member of the Garda Síochána in circumstances where charges would be preferred if the individual concerned was an ordinary member of the public.

A civil claim

In principle a civil claim for damages would appear to offer better prospects than the criminal prosecution for calling individual gardaí to account for improper conduct.[46] Not only can it reach situations where a member has intentionally used unlawful force against the person or property of the citizen, but it can also provide a remedy for negligent police action which has caused loss or injury to the citizen. Moreover, the problem of bias which may affect the investigation and decision-making in the criminal process cannot be a feature here because the conduct of the case is entirely in the hands of the aggrieved citizen. The remedy through the civil action is personal to the complainant in contrast to the criminal prosecution which is conducted on behalf of the state. In that sense it offers a more direct and individual form of police accountability than the criminal prosecution. Indeed, the complainant almost has the best of both worlds under the civil action because the state will normally accept liability where a member of the Garda Síochána is successfully sued in a civil action for things done in the course of his or her duty. This ensures that the successful litigant will actually receive the amount awarded to him in compensation.

The attractions of the civil action as a police accountability mechanism are being realised in practice. The number of actions and the amounts being paid out in damages are increasing annually. This, of course, could simply be the result of a sustained deterioration in police standards. A more likely explanation, however, is an increased willingness among members of the public to call individual members of the force to account through an action in damages. A similar trend is

---

[46] See D. Walsh, *op.cit.* at Ch.10

evident in Northern Ireland and in police forces throughout Great Britain. It does not follow, however, that the civil action for damages holds the solution to the complex challenge of police accountability. It too suffers from a number of limitations.

The most obvious weakness is that the civil action cannot reach all forms of improper or inadequate policing which result in injury, loss or distress to members of the public. For the most part it is confined to serious assaults, loss of liberty, damage to property and personal injury resulting from careless driving or negligent conduct. In practice, of course, those aspects of policing which irritate most people are relatively minor such as members of the force acting in a high-handed manner, using more force than is reasonably necessary to restrain petty offenders, failing to respond to calls for assistance, serious delay in responding to calls for assistance and negligently failing to identify or apprehend the perpetrator of a criminal offence. Even where such actions do technically qualify as actionable wrongs they are rarely serious enough to warrant court action. Unless there are prospects of at least a four figure sum being awarded in compensation it will usually not be worth the emotional distress, inconvenience and financial risk involved in taking an action against a member of the Garda Síochána. Almost inevitably the private litigant will be completely dependant on legal aid or the services of lawyers who are prepared to work on a no win-no fee basis. The member of the force, on the other hand, will have the financial and moral support of his representative body, and ultimately the State, behind him. It is not exactly an equal contest.

It is also worth mentioning judicial review as a possible means of calling the garda commissioner to account for law enforcement policies or practices which are considered discriminatory or oppressive by an individual or body of citizens. In practice, however, the courts are extremely reluctant to second-guess the commissioner in the law enforcement policies, priorities, strategies or decisions which he deems necessary in the exercise of his power of general direction and control of the force. As yet there has been no reported case in which a citizen has successfully challenged a law enforcement policy decision taken by or under the authority of the commissioner.

Citizens' complaints procedure

The citizens' complaints procedure was introduced in 1986, ostensibly to overcome many of the shortcomings in the existing procedures for dealing with citizens' complaints against the police.[47] At that time complaints which did not result in a criminal prosecution were handled purely through the standard internal police discipline procedure which is totally lacking in any form of independent checks or balances. Needless to say there was considerable public dissatisfaction

---

[47] For detailed analysis, see D. Walsh, *op.cit.* at Ch. 9

with a procedure in which complaints against the Garda Síochána were received, investigated, adjudicated and disposed of purely within the force itself. Accordingly the Garda Síochána Complaints Act 1986 introduced a separate procedure to deal with citizens' complaints. Not only is this procedure distinct from the internal disciplinary procedure but it incorporates significant independent elements.

The central feature of the citizens' complaints procedure is the Garda Síochána Complaints Board. It consists of a chairman and eight ordinary members appointed by the government from time to time as the occasion requires. The chairman must be a practising barrister or solicitor of at least ten years standing, while the ordinary members must include at least three practising barristers or solicitors of at least ten years standing and the garda commissioner or his nominee. The term of office of each member is for a period of five years which is renewable. In addition to the chairman and the ordinary members the 1986 Act makes specific provision for the office of chief executive to which attaches a number of important powers and duties.

The Board's role in the handling of complaints commences once a complaint is lodged. Unless the complainant states in writing that he does not want his or her complaint to be considered by the Board it will be referred automatically to the Board. The chief executive will then subject it to a preliminary admissibility test. A complaint will be admissible under the procedure only if: the complainant is a member of the public; the complainant was either directly affected by, or witnessed, the conduct alleged; the alleged conduct constitutes a criminal offence or an offence under the disciplinary code; the conduct is alleged to have occurred within six months of the date of the complaint; neither the commissioner nor the Minister for Justice, Equality and Law Reform has appointed someone to hold an inquiry into the alleged conduct before the complaint was lodged; the member concerned has not been dismissed or reduced in rank; and the complaint is neither frivolous nor vexatious. If the complaint survives this admissibility test it will be investigated by a member of the Garda Síochána not below the rank of superintendent or, if the circumstances so warrant it, inspector. The investigating officer is appointed by the commissioner, although he or she will actually carry out the investigation under the supervision of the Board. His investigation report is submitted in the first instance to the chief executive of the Board who, in turn, will transmit the report together with his comments and recommendation to the Board.

If, after considering this material, the Board decides either that the complaint was inadmissible or that no breach of discipline is disclosed it will inform the parties accordingly and that will be an end of the matter. If it feels that a breach of discipline of a minor nature is disclosed it can refer the matter to the commissioner to be dealt with informally by way of advice, admonition or warning. If, however, the Board feels that a breach of discipline which is not of a minor matter is disclosed it must refer the matter to a tribunal and notify the commissioner accordingly. The tribunal will consist of three persons. Two of them must be non-garda members of the Board who have not been involved in the investigation of the case at an earlier stage. The third member must be a member of the Garda Síochána other than the member who sits on the Board. He or she is nominated by the commissioner, must be of chief superintendent rank or above and must not have been involved at an earlier stage in the handling of the case. The tribunal will sit in private to hear the case against the member concerned presented by the chief executive. It will decide whether the member is in breach of discipline and, if he or she is found to be in breach, what disciplinary action if any action should be taken. The member can appeal to a Garda Síochána Appeals Board consisting of a chairman (a judge of the Circuit Court) and two ordinary members, one of whom must be a practising barrister or solicitor of at least ten years standing. The other cannot be a current or former member of the Garda Síochána.

From this brief outline it is evident that the complaints procedure is long and convoluted. Indeed, it can be even more complex and slow where, as is often the case, the complaint gets caught up in associated civil and/or criminal proceedings. Admittedly, there is also provision for the informal resolution of complaints, but this is not invoked as often as one might expect.[48]

Although the citizens complaints procedure has been operating now for over twelve years it has not quite managed to earn the confidence of either the public or the rank and file of the Garda Síochána. Even the Complaints Board itself is increasingly unhappy about the capacity of the procedure to deliver effective accountability. In its review spanning the six-year period from 1993 to 1998 it repeats earlier calls for reforms and makes further suggestions on how the procedure could be strengthened.[49] The rank and file of the Garda Síochána have always been suspicious of the procedure. They perceive it essentially as an unfair and unnecessary bureaucratic burden which is wide open to abuse by criminal and subversive elements. The high number of complaints which are rejected as being frivolous or vexatious is often cited as proof of this analysis.[50] The general public, by contrast, are more likely to view it as inherently biased in favour of gardaí and incapable of providing redress for even the most blatant examples of garda abuse. Such perceptions are supported by the extraordinarily low level of success for citizens complaints which have been processed through the machinery. Indeed, the statistics paint a very worrying picture about the capacity of the complaints procedure to deliver effective police accountability. Typically, the number of

---

[48] In 1997 out of a total of 1,163 complaints which were processed only 26 were resolved informally. The equivalent figures for 1996 and 1995 respectively are: 1,292 and 17; and 1,140 and 35

[49] *Third Report of the Garda Síochána Complaints Board in Relation to the Operation of the Garda Síochána (Complaints) Act 1986,* Dublin: Government Publications Pn. 6559, 1998

[50] Forty-two percent of the complaints received in 1997 were rejected as being frivolous or vexatious. The equivalent figures for 1996 and 1995 respectively are 55% and 41%

complaints which actually make it through to a tribunal hearing are negligible while less than 2% are referred to the commissioner to be dealt with as minor breaches, with approximately the same number being resolved informally. By way of contrast, almost 60% are rejected as inadmissible, almost 20% are withdrawn, with about the same number being dismissed.

Dissatisfaction with the handling of complaints against the police is by no means confined to Ireland. Many other jurisdictions which rely on or which have experimented with the complaint board model have had similar experiences. Some jurisdictions have discarded the use of the board model in favour of an ombudsman model. It is submitted that there would be considerable merit in exploring the possibility of replacing our current board based procedure with the ombudsman procedure which has been introduced recently in Northern Ireland. Indeed, it is worth noting in this context that the Northern Ireland system is the result of a comprehensive and incisive investigation and report on the subject by Dr Maurice Hayes, a member of Seanad Éireann.

Accountability through the Oireachtas

For administrative and political purposes the Department of Justice, Equality and Law Reform is responsible for the police. It follows that the Minister for Justice, Equality and Law Reform answers to the Dáil for the Garda Síochána. He also introduces and defends the Garda Vote and legislative bills on matters affecting the police.[51]

The minister is regularly questioned in the Dáil about police matters ranging from the size of the garda complement at a particular station to the garda policy on the enforcement of the drug laws to the standard of police service in a particular locality. While this provides a very valuable and necessary opportunity for democratic scrutiny of the police, it does not deliver the degree of accountability which one is entitled to expect in a liberal democracy. One of the most striking features of the minister's response to questions on the garda is the frequency with which he will decline to accept responsibility for the matter raised. In particular, if the question concerns operational matters or the allocation of resources by the Garda Síochána the minister will be careful to preface his remarks by saying that it is a matter for the garda authorities to decide such matters. The most he can do is convey information from the force to the House. In this, of course, the minister is perfectly correct. By analogy with an English chief constable, the garda commissioner is the authority in whom responsibility for law enforcement is vested at common law. Moreover, the general direction and control of the Garda Síochána is statutorily vested in him alone. The minister has no power to direct

---

[51] For detailed analysis of the operation of police accountability to the Dáil see D. Walsh, *op.cit.* at Ch. 12

the commissioner on what law enforcement policies or strategies he should adopt or how he should allocate his resources.

Efforts to render the minister more directly and fully answerable in policing matters are typically resisted by appeals to the overriding need to protect law enforcement against the appearance or substance of party political control. The price being paid for this sacred cow of police independence, however, is a major black hole in the democratic accountability of the police. The public are denied a forum through which the commissioner and/or his senior officers can be called to account publicly and directly for the quality of police service in particular localities, the strategies being pursued against particular types of crime, the policies and practices being pursued generally or in the treatment of particular groups or interests and so on. Accountability over such matters is vital to persuade the whole public that the police service is responsive to their needs, is giving value for money and ultimately can be trusted with the immense powers and resources that are put at its disposal. Admittedly, such accountability needs must not be satisfied at the expense of turning the Garda Síochána into a political football. Perhaps some progress can be made in squaring the circle by exploring the establishment of a network of police community liaison groups throughout the country, greater decentralisation of police power and organisation and a statutory obligation on the commissioner and local police commanders to take into account the views of the relevant liaison groups when formulating and revising policing policies and strategies. Any such arrangement would also have to be supported by greater transparency on the part of the Garda Síochána with respect to such policies and strategies.

Up until very recently it might have been thought that Dáil committees could be developed into an effective mechanism of democratic police accountability. It may be, however, that the John Carthy affair will expose the fundamental weaknesses in the current committee system as a tool of police accountability. At the time of writing the attempts by the Joint Committee of the Oireachtas on Justice, Equality, Defence and Women's Rights to investigate the disputed circumstances in which John Carthy was shot dead by members of the Emergency Response Unit appear to have been stymied by the refusal of members of the Unit to give evidence before the committee. The threat of a judicial challenge by the police to the procedures being followed by the committee is looming. This whole episode highlights the difficulties which have yet to be overcome in devising mechanisms which can deliver effective accountability for police law enforcement operations which have given rise to public concern.

CONCLUSION

The Garda Síochána is surely unique in the public administration of the state by virtue of the peculiar legal status of its individual members and the constitutional status of the force as a whole. Key aspects of its distinctive features can be traced back to the origins of organised police forces in these islands in the latter half of the eighteenth century and even to methods of policing which can be traced back to Anglo-Saxon times in Britain. As might be expected, there have been major changes in the size, internal management and professionalism of the Garda Síochána, as well as in the powers and duties of individual members, since it was established almost eighty years ago. Further changes can be expected as progress is made in the implementation of recommendations of the Steering Group on the Review of the Garda Síochána[52] and in response to developments at European Union and international levels.

Apart from the establishment of the Garda Síochána Complaints Board there have been no major innovations in policing structures or accountability processes since the establishment of the force. Arguably, this failure to develop policing structures, concepts and accountability in line with changes in society is contributing to a loosening of the very close identity between the Garda Síochána and the public which has been a marked feature of this state at least up until the 1990s. The basic principles and processes of police governance and accountability which were designed to suit the needs of a bygone age are proving inadequate to serve the needs of an increasingly affluent, sophisticated, urbanised, technologised, mobile, multi-cultural, and impersonalised society. Similarly, they are proving inadequate to deal with the huge growth in police powers and technology which has been a distinctive feature of policing in this jurisdiction throughout the 1990s and into the twenty-first century.

The failure to develop new methods of police governance and accountability in this jurisdiction is highlighted by comparative developments over the past decade in both Northern Ireland and Britain. The implementation of the report of the Patten commission on policing in Northern Ireland will serve to emphasise how far Ireland has fallen behind in these matters and the urgency with which they need to be addressed.

---

[52] See *Report of the Steering Group on the Efficiency and the Effectiveness of the Garda Síochána*, Dublin: Government Stationery Office, 1997

28

Recent Developments
in Forensic Science

James Donovan

INTRODUCTION

The term "Forensic Science" applies to the use of science in crime investigation and presentation of the results of scientific analysis in court to facilitate the attainment of the best decision. The sciences involved are chemistry, biology, molecular biology, physics, analytical science and botany. Forensic science interacts with other professions in a variety of arenas, such as medicine in Forensic Pathology, dentistry in Forensic Odontology and engineering in Forensic Engineering. Nowadays, Forensic Accounting is emerging in the examination of company accounts to discover if fraud was perpetrated.

The application of chemistry, biology and physics are mainly undertaken by scientists and technical staff in a forensic science laboratory. However, some aspects of forensic science work, such as fingerprint detection and identification and document examination, are done by specially trained members of An Garda Síochána.

A forensic laboratory spends a large portion of its time in straightforward chemical analysis, such as in analysis of controlled drugs to verify their composition for criminal charging and court evidential purposes, in the analysis of material to see if it can be classified as an explosive and in the analysis of blood, urine and human organs to detect intoxicants, drugs and poison that may have caused death. Another portion of a laboratory's work is related to linking suspects or crime victims to scenes of crime and this also uses a lot of analytical work. The significance of such results must be interpreted for the court as occurs, for example, when blue cotton fibres are found at the scene of a murder and the suspect was known to be wearing the same coloured blue jeans at the time of the crime but interpretation might show that such evidence is of almost no probative value because that particular type of jeans is very common. By contrast, if blood found on the suspect matches that of the victim by DNA profiling with, say, statistics of 1 in 1000 million against any one other than the victim generating the blood, then that evidence will be interpreted as extremely strong.

SCENES OF CRIME

The scene of any crime has always been of considerable importance from the point of view of collecting evidence and attempting to recreate what had happened. However, modern technologies which can produce a lot of information from very small particles of matter have made procedures at a scene very important. It would now be unusual not to have a serious crime scene "roped off" by tape bearing the logo of An Garda Síochána and it would also be unusual for people to enter a crime scene not covered in a disposable white boiler suit with overshoes in order to ensure that trace evidence was not brought into or taken out of the scene accidentally or carried to other scenes.

Some traditional types of evidence have been given a new lease of life in recent years by the new technologies. The most obvious of these is the detection of fingerprints and their comparison. The use of fingerprints as a means of detecting criminal suspects goes back to the early 1930s in Ireland and the traditional method of dusting with aluminium powder is well known. However technological advances have been instrumental in detecting prints that previously could not have been observed by the powder. The most immediately relevant are the portable monochromatic light sources which cause the latent prints at scenes to be detected and consequently to be further examined. Laser lights are also used and research is being currently undertaken to detect useful prints on dead bodies as occasionally after murder the killer will relocate bodies. Metal deposition as undertaken in a vacuum chamber and fuming with super glue under specific humidity and temperature conditions allow the detection of previously unavailable prints on very widespread items such as plastic bags.

However, the greatest advance in fingerprinting technology occurred when computer memory became large enough to deal with the multiple detail in every fingerprint and it was shown that computers could hold all ten fingerprints of a large number of persons and speedily and reliably compare these with latent prints found at a scene. This advanced computer system is working very well at Garda HQ and allows fingerprints to be compared overnight. The search involves a far greater number of prints than was possible under the manual system of "bundles" where only the prints of criminals in a local area could be searched.

Another type of physical evidence which has re-established itself are impressions of sole prints left at the scene. The best known are those left in soil or mud and are indentations. Modern techniques provide a number of casting materials which give much better definition of fine details of the indentations. Sole prints left on bank counters, chair seats, glass and cloth are nowadays "lifted" by various techniques and compared with a suspect's shoe and again like a fingerprint the sole prints can be scanned into a computer and software known as SICAR can indicate the type of shoe or trainer which made the mark and Gardaí can be helped to look for a suspect with that make of footwear. It is also possible to be definitive from the comparison of damage etc to the sole of a trainer or shoe to the extent of stating with considerable confidence that a particular trainer or shoe made a particular impression.

PAINT

The most obvious forensic example of every contact leaving a trace is in the case of a "hit and run" incident. Where a pedestrian is struck by a vehicle the force of impact melts the top layer of paint into the clothing. This paint is pressed deep into the weave of the cloth and using microscopy the paint fragments can be retrieved and by analysis the make, model, year of manufacture and of course colour of the car can be determined. This information will considerably aid garda investigations. When a suspect car is seized, the paint fragments found in the clothing of the injured party are compared to the paint of the car, first by comparison microscopy. Then the bonding medium is analysed by Fourier Transform Infrared Spectroscopy (FTIR). This latter technique is powerful in its ability to analyse very small quantities of organic material while its associated computerised databases allow the identification of the material almost immediately. The FTIR spectrometer is attached to a high powered microscope which means that once you can see a particle of anything under the lens then the spectrograph of it can be obtained to give an identification.

Paints found in households are particularly useful as evidence when transferred onto, say, jemmy bars used to lever open windows or doors during house breakings. Beside the issue of matching the size and type of a suspect instrument to the marks created on the door or window, paint residues on the instrument can be of great evidential value. For example, on a jemmy bar there will generally be found a number of smears of paint of the outer layers of the paint of the forced door or window. The use of microscopy to compare colours and the techniques of FTIR and Scanning Electron Microscope with x-ray analysis (SEM-XRF) are powerful and effective techniques for linking items like paint back to a source.

GLASS

Glass has a particularly important role to play in forensic investigations, since glass is frequently broken in the course of crime and fragments are usually widely available to investigators. The most obvious occurrence is the breaking of window panes in criminal damage or breaking and entry offences. Since glass is not a solid substance, being a super cooled liquid, there is release of energy when it is broken and more than 20% of particles of glass will fly back onto the person breaking the glass. In the hair and garments of the person who breaks glass there will almost always be found small particles of glass.

The best parameter of glass analysis is Refractive Index (RI) measurement. To measure the RI of a glass particle the technique of the Mettler Hot Stage on microscope is used. The apparatus is attached to data handling facilities and a VDU. The Becke Line method is utilised to observe the edge of a glass particle "disappear" into the oil in which it is placed. The specific temperature of disappearance is noted and gives the value of RI. A figure correct to five places of decimals is obtained and by reference to a data base the frequency of occurrence of glass with that particular RI value can be determined. This detailed information is useful because it helps the court to assess the significance of glass-related evidence. Obviously the fact that glass particles were found on a suspects hair and garments is highly relevant, particularly if the particles match a pane broken at the crime scene and the pane was made of a relatively rare type of glass.

Another use of glass occurs in hit and run accidents where head lamp glass can be left at the scene. Head lamp glass will have a design pattern and letters and numerals unique to the model of car and by reference to a data base the model and make of car from which it came can be determined, thus helping an investigation.

FIREARM RESIDUES

When the trigger of a firearm is activated the hammer strikes the base of the cartridge and the blow detonates a very small amount of a shock sensitive chemical; the resulting flash detonates the main charge of explosive in the round of ammunition. The resulting large quantity of gas expels the bullet. Dust from the explosion emerges from around the breech and muzzle.

The relevant matters of evidence in firearms are the cartridge which, if left at the scene, could have hammer marks and breeches marks unique to that firearm. With a database of cartridge cases already test fired, a gun can be indicated and on seizure can be positively identified.

In a rifled weapon the bullet as it progresses up the barrel is given a spin by grooves cut in the barrel to make it go straighter and faster. These grooves impress lines onto the metal body of the bullet and the distances between each striation form an unique "fingerprint" for that weapon, which is impressed on each bullet as it passes through. Thus the collection of spent cartridge cases from the scene and bullets, particularly bullets in human tissue, is very important as these can be definitively linked back to a weapon. The small amount of shock sensitive chemical in the base of the round of ammunition explodes when the base is struck by the hammer. The debris from the explosion is expelled around and about the firing mechanism and, along with gases, forwards through the muzzle. This debris consists of particles of metal of lead, antimony and barium. Because of their extremely small size these particles do not obey Newtonian physics and on emerging from the gun cool into spherical shapes. The particles will settle on the hands of the person who fires the gun and will stay there for about three hours. The particles will also be deposited on the upper clothing of the shooter and there will last for about twenty hours of wear. A sawn off shot gun carried inside an anorak will also leave traces of the residue on the adjacent cloth.

By swabbing hands or clothing some of the round particles of lead, antimony and barium are removed and these can be visualised in a Scanning Electron Microscope (SEM) by bombarding the particles with an electron beam. Any so treated will generate x-rays which can be detected by an x-ray detector and put through a computerised system which measures the energy levels of the x-rays generated. Since each metal will have its own particular energy level the metals in the particles can be identified. Nowadays a SEM can be automated so that eight swabs can be examined and the shape and composition of each particle can be determined by the machine and those of relevance checked subsequently. Since firearms use is normally connected to serious crime, the finding of firearm residues is of considerable relevance in murder, armed robbery, threatening behaviour and sometimes in rape.

FIRE

Fire when uncontrolled in any environment does an awesome amount of damage with huge costs involved. Any fire burning in less than an excess of oxygen – and this condition applies to most fires – generates the highly toxic gas, carbon mon-oxide. The very hot gases generated in a fire can cause death. The first question in fire investigation is to determine if it was arson or accidental. Obviously determining if a break-in had occurred at the premises is very relevant. Also important is to determine if there was more than one seat of fire as more than one seat can, but does not always, indicate arson.

Forensic laboratory involvement in the investigation of a fire can include analysis of material recovered from the fire scene to identify flammability. The examination of debris from the bits of a suspected incendiary device is also fairly common. The usual function of the laboratory is to examine debris collected by gardaí at the scene for the presence of some fire accelerant such as petrol, paraffin oil or diesel. Normally capillary column gas chromatography with flame ion-isation detector are used to get the required spectrum for the fire accelerant used. The method is based on taking the fire debris in a nylon bag and heating it. A sample of vapour inside the bag and above the debris is taken and injected into the gas chromatograph-mass spectrometer. A spectrum will be obtained if a hydrocarbon liquid is present.

A gas chromatograph-mass spectrometer or, alternatively, the technique of Nuclear Magnetic Resonance is used to verify the identity of various oils in a sample.

EXPLOSIVES AND EXPLOSIONS

The determination of an explosive substance available in bulk is a relatively straightforward matter whether it be the old fashioned mixture of ammonium nitrate and diesel oil or the modern military explosive, SEMTEX, which is a mixture of RDX (cyclotrimethylenetrinitramine) and PETN (pentaerythritol tetranitrate). Methods used in the determination range from Thin Layer Chromatography to Gas Chromatography, to GC/MS (gas chromatography/mass spectrometry) to MS/MS (tandem (two) mass spectrometer) .

Trace explosives on hands and objects are somewhat more difficult in the first place because there are often problems in locating and swabbing free the traces. Because of the principle of "every contact leaves a trace" the person who moulds an explosive substance into a bomb casing will get traces of that explosive under their fingernails and onto the skin. However, the traces are readily lost by washing of the hands and, in the case of nitrobenzene and nitroglycerine, by absorption through the skin and metabolism of the substance under the skin.

After an explosion, finding the traces of the components of the explosive used is important since it can indicate what group was likely to have caused the explosion. Finding pieces of the detonating mechanism is also very important because this device could be very individualistic, pointing clearly to a particular manufacturer. The debris from a bomb site should be sifted through very carefully for the bomb fragments. Any absorbent material close by such as the foam rubber in car seats or human tissue will collect and retain flying pieces of bomb. If the injured human person survives but it is not possible to get at the fragment within the tissue, it is known that such particles can still be expelled by the body up to eighteen months after and can even then be very useful to an investigation.

DRUGS OF ABUSE

Forensic laboratories have recently tended to become largely drugs laboratories because of the enormous increase in the volume of drug substances seized by the police and the need to determine if they are controlled substances under the law of the land. The annual percentage increase has tended to vary from 5% to 50%. Well over half of substances seized turn out to be cannabis resin, also known as hash. To verify that a substance is cannabis resin the hairs unique to the plant must be identified and an unusual colour test and a very distinctive Thin Layer Chromatogram must be run.

The herb material itself, cannabis (also known as marijuana), is not as popular as cannabis resin. For all the different resin and plant materials very advanced techniques can be used to identify the individual cannabinoid substances present.

In Ireland, once any trace of a controlled substance is detected then proceedings are taken before the court, which has the responsibility of deciding if the amount of drugs seized is sufficient only for a person's own immediate use or constitutes enough to supply to others.

The most serious drug from the point of view of health consequences and general criminality is heroin. Heroin has also been the most important drug in the process whereby drug dealers have in recent years amassed immense personal wealth. There have been many attempts to try to discover this drug in transit, as for example in airports by very sophisticated gas chromatograph-mass spectrometer and X-ray equipment. However, this endeavour has been without much success. The use of sniffer dogs, who detect the chemicals used to convert the morphine in the opium into heroin, is the most consistently successful approach to detection of contraband heroin but initial success has induced many heroin transporters to wrap the drug in different substances to fool the dog's nose.

Ireland proposed the procedure of "drug profiling" during its last presidency of the EU in the mid-1990s. This procedure allows samples of heroin seized across Europe to be compared. This comparison is based on the fact that the process of producing heroin from the opium poppy head is long and complex, resulting in a unique and thus distinctive and identifiable final composition of the heroin batch. The process begins when the opium poppy head is scarified as it grows in the field. A resinous material oozes out and is allowed dry. This material is opium and is removed and taken to a clandestine laboratory where it is treated by a variety of chemicals. The morphine in the opium is thus converted to heroin.

Each drug batch will have a distinctive profile which can be identified and matched and compared. Mixed with the heroin there will usually be found monoacetyl morphine, morphine, and other opiates; a number of alkaloids from the poppy such as thebane and noscapine; chemicals used to convert morphine to heroin; drugs added to the heroin (which nowadays tend to be caffeine and paracetamol); and, finally, sugars which are added to bulk up the heroin powder. Another factor is the variable concentration of heroin, which usually ranges from 30% to 60% of the total batch of powder but can range from 5% to 90%. Consequently, so-called heroin powder is a potentially hazardous mixture of a variable quantity of heroin with a wide variety of chemicals. One would not readily inject individually the drugs in this dangerous cocktail and, furthermore, the many drug interactions between all of the different substances make the average street deal of heroin an extremely unpredictable and potentially lethal mix.

Cocaine and amphetamine are also popular drugs and due to increasing prosperity cocaine in particular is very sought after in certain circles. The advent of gas chromatography/mass spectrometry combined with an automated analyser have allowed laboratories to keep up with the huge volume and increasing diversity of drugs being seized by police.

A major change in the drug scene in the last ten years, besides the general increase in the volume of drugs used and seized, was the appearance of the Ecstasy-type drugs. All are based on amphetamine with the most common being methylene-dioxy-methyl-amphetamine, MDMA. However, their most novel feature is the ability to enter the brain and increase the amount of the neurotransmitter, serotonin. This has a strong stimulant effect on the central nervous system but, as the drug leaves the body, the amount of serotonin dips below normal and induces various levels of depression besides physical tiredness.

This drug is sold as a tablet and of relevance besides colour and size is the design impressed on the tablet – car signs like Mitsubishi, Mercedes, Peugeot are popular. Europol in the Hague circularises the designs seized in an EU county to all EU countries. However, some tablets sold as Ecstasy do not contain any amphetamine related drug, that is they are "fake" in the sense of falsely labelled. One of the popular psychoactive substitutes used in such fakes is Ketamine which is a local anasthetic for large animals and induces hallucinations in humans.

Drugs of Ecstasy and fakes are made in clandestine laboratories and there will be a variable quantity of the drug in each tablet and many different chemicals from the manufacturing process which would have been cleared away in properly ordered and quality-controlled pharmaceutical preparation. Thus each tablet is an unknown mixture of potent and possibly dangerous chemicals.

FORENSIC TOXICOLOGY

Forensic toxicology involves the detection of drugs and poison in human organs. The most common drug of abuse in humans is ethyl alcohol, which is both a powerful mood changer and strongly addictive. The testing for alcohol is most common in the context of suspected drunken driving. Tests rely on measurement of blood or urine by gas chromatography. Nowadays a breath analyser based on Infra Red analysis is becoming common in garda stations. Alcohol has a strongly disinhibitory effect and the measurement of blood alcohol levels can be relevant to many crimes including murder and rape as well as domestic violence.

Alcohol also figures as a cause of death on its own if the blood/alcohol level exceeds 500 milligrams per cent. Such extreme levels of alcohol consumption can occur when, for example, people take on a wager that they can rapidly drink a whole bottle of spirits. Alcohol also interacts to potentiate the effect of many drugs and poisons. Classically a mixture of barbiturates and alcohol has been a common cause accidental death and a frequent method of suicide.

While the most important function of toxicology is to determine if someone has been murdered by poisoning, this is a most unusual occurrence and the determination of how someone took their own life is the normal work. The advent of the technology of solid phase extraction has improved the separation of drugs from human tissue considerably. The different families of drugs must be separately extracted because they are bound in different ways. For example, the phenothiazine antidepressants are tightly bound to the red blood cells and must be removed by heat and acid.

BODILY FLUIDS

The surface covering a body is extremely delicate and breaks readily, generally releasing blood in the form of spurts, drops and smears onto objects. Consequently, in criminal activity involving violence, there is a strong possibility that blood will be generated and will be deposited on an assailant, on an object used in the assault and in other ways. Crimes with violence where blood can be involved include murders, rape, assault, house breakings, unlawful taking of vehicles and hit and run accidents.

Since one of the purposes of crime scene examination is the understanding of what happened, the distribution of blood spatters is of considerable relevance particularly when linked with DNA analysis to indicate where and in what patterns identified and attributed samples of blood were found. For example, finding the blood along with an eye brow hair of a deceased victim, who has been kicked in the face, on the toecap of the boot of a suspect is very strong evidence against the suspect.

In sexually motivated murder and sex offences another body fluid, semen, can be deposited at the scene. Both blood and semen are particularly valuable from the point of view of DNA profiling and, if samples are properly taken, they can indicate that a fluid came from a particular individual with what amounts to near absolute certainty. DNA profiling has been an enormous advance in crime detection and will continue to improve in effectiveness with respect to speed of analysis and improved capacity to work with very small samples.

A DNA database is available to law enforcement authorities in some countries and has been of considerable use. In these countries samples are routinely taken for DNA profiling from persons convicted of crime, usually relatively minor crime, on the basis that those who commit serious crime often already have a criminal history. In the UK about half a million persons are on the DNA database. The DNA profile is obtained from buccal cell swabs, that is from swabs from the inside of the cheeks of the mouth. Every week about 8,000 crime stains are run through the computerised database and generally about 1,000 of them are matched with an identified DNA profile of a known criminal. In Ireland currently it is not possible legally to have such a database.

Of course, one of the most relevant and useful functions of DNA profiling in a major investigation is to eliminate someone as a suspect for a crime and this is particularly useful in cases of murder and rape.

HAIRS AND FIBRES

Based on the principle of exchange when two people struggle together, fibres from their clothing will be cross transferred. Thus, examining the clothing of each party will allow detection of the fibres of the other. If the fibres are the same by colour and composition then the transfer can be said to be very significant. Comparison and analysis is done by comparison microscopy, that is use of thin layer chromatography to compare dye extracted from the fibres and a micro-spectrophotometer to "draw" a graph of the shade of colour of the dye. A match on these parameters is very definite.

Head hairs occur very often in a range of offences and comparison microscopy is always used, but if colouring or chemical treatments have been undertaken on the hair then the evidential value is greater.

Transfer of pubic hair sometimes occurs in sexual assaults and when identified as such and its colour does not match the victim but matches the suspect or vice versa then the evidence is highly relevant.

It is expected that in due course DNA will be extractable from hair and this will make hair of considerable evidential value because it would be definitively linked to the "owner". At the moment a lot of tissue about the hair root is required to get any sort of DNA profile and frequently this is not available.

COURT

The essence of forensic scientific evidence is that it is understandable to a lay audience, that it is amenable to examination by defence scientists, that it is suitable for delivery in public court under oath and that it is capable of withstanding cross examination. The ability to communicate science is particularly important to forensic scientists.

When working on a case a forensic scientist needs to maintain notes in a suficiently organised way that will be understood by the fellow scientist who will consider the file before despatch of the report as part of the legal question and answer process. Notes may also be required to be produced in court or for examination by a defence scientist. When writing the report enough comment or explanation has to be given to ensure the hard scientific facts are understood. It is too late to try to add explanatory comment in the witness box as the defence can object to the scientist adding anything not in the statement, even if the comment favours the defence.

In the witness box a scientist is in alien terriority and lawyers know the procedure intimately so it is a stressful place in that it is the nature of scientists to explain and to try and help others understand, but the common law adversarial system does not allow for that. Generally forensic scientists would prefer the European system where there is a better opportunity of explaining. When presenting evidence in court, besides the problem of communicating with members of the legal profession there is sometimes the problem of communicating clearly and comprehensibly with a jury of unknown educational background. Communicating accurately can pose challenges when the target audience includes people with little scientific background or knowledge and next to no familiarity with technical issues such as fibre and hair comparisons, paint comparisons, and DNA profiling.

Nowadays, there is an increasing tendancy to use statistics and probabilities. Obviously probabilities are very relevant in DNA profiling and in the interpretation and presentation of other evidence. But generally the application of statistics is more relevant to the scientist's preparation of his own statement because of the extra difficulty of getting a jury to accurately understand the application of statistics. It is an area in which there are pitfalls, particularly in that evidence can be interpreted as more significant than it is, so that the forensic scientist's statements which interpret the underlying statistics and probabilities of a situation for a jury must be carefully considered and expressed.

29

Policing Ireland:
Past Present and Future

Johnny Connolly

INTRODUCTION

Police accountability has been described as "one of the thorniest conundrums of statecraft" because it involves a commitment to "watching the watchers".[1] Police accountability is about ensuring that the police are subject to oversight in the exercise of their extensive legal powers and it is also about ensuring that policing policy is subject to public influence and direction. Walker[2] makes a useful distinction between internal and external forms of accountability. The former exists within police forces and relates to the relationship between officers working in a hierarchical structure. The latter involves the relationship between the police and external agencies or interests such as government and the public. Walsh[3], in his recent study *The Irish Police-A Legal and Constitutional Perspective*, provides a comprehensive account of the legal mechanisms and structures that have evolved as a means of holding the Garda Síochána to account. A survey of these measures suggests however that they have failed to fulfil this function.[4]

---

[1] Reiner, R. and Spencer, S. (1993), *Accountable Policing: Effectiveness, Empowerment and Equity,* London: Institute of Public Policy Research, pp. 1-23

[2] Walker, N. (1998), "Police Accountability", *Encyclopedia of Applied Ethics,* Volume 3, p. 542

[3] Walsh, D. (1998), *The Irish Police, A Legal and Constitutional Analysis,* Round Hall Sweet & Maxwell

[4] Connolly, J. (1999), "The Irish Police: The Pursuit of Accountability", *Irish Criminal Law Journal,* Vol. 9, pp. 110-126, Round Hall Sweet & Maxwell

The absence of adequate accountability measures has recently been highlighted by two controversial cases. The killing of a young man, John Carthy, in controversial circumstances by members of the Garda Síochána Emergency Response Unit (ERU) has provoked an unprecedented public outcry. Secondly, irregularities in the investigation of the death of a man in County Donegal in 1996 have emerged into the public domain, opening, in the process, a virtual "can of worms".[5] Ongoing revelations about this controversy have implicated members of the force in the forced extraction of confessions, extortion, the harassment of suspects, the intimidation of lawyers and a politician, and the electronic interference with defence lawyers' telephones. It has also been alleged that members of the force were involved in "planting" illegal drugs in a local nightclub so as to obtain a conviction against its owner and in falsifying Irish Republican Army explosives finds so as to obtain promotion.

In response to the John Carthy shooting, a coroner's inquest was held. This however had no investigative role and did not have the competence to attribute responsibility or culpability to anyone. Recently, following on from the public disquiet about the incident, and with great reluctance on the part of the Garda Síochána, an internal garda report on the incident was brought into the public domain. This report, which was totally uncritical of the garda operation, was also unnecessarily hurtful and insensitive to the Carthy family. The report contained references to the deceased man's drinking and gambling habits, difficulties he was allegedly experiencing in personal relationships and contained derogatory comments about his sporting abilities. It also repeated suggestions that his sister had been intoxicated on the day of the shooting, suggestions she has consistently denied. A bizarre addition to this tragedy was the invitation by the garda commissioner to the FBI to conduct an investigation into the garda operation. The FBI, discredited internationally following its handling of the siege at Waco Texas, in which almost eighty people died, ultimately criticised the Garda Síochána for not shooting Carthy promptly enough. Apparent inconsistencies between the forensic evidence tendered at the Coroner's Inquest by the state pathologist and the statements of members of the ERU has ensured that ongoing calls from the Carthy family for an independent judicial inquiry into the shooting are being received sympathetically by the media and the general public. The more recent establishment of an Oireachtas, or Parliamentary, inquiry into the incident has done nothing to dampen these demands and, if anything, it has intensified them. The Oireachtas inquiry, which, at the time of writing, has been suspended pending the resolution of a legal dispute about evidential matters, has been criticised from a number of quarters. Indeed, the two largest garda representative bodies, urging

5 Allen, L. and Mara, S. "Clear and Present Danger", *Magill: Ireland's Current Affairs Monthly*, September, 2000

that the issue be taken "out of the political arena", have added their voices to the calls for an independent judicial inquiry into the whole affair[6].

The Donegal case has led to at least two internal garda inquiries. In the process of the Carty inquiry, the largest in the history of the force, over one thousand garda members and civilians have been interviewed. Although one garda member has been suspended and five others transferred, only one prosecution has resulted from the inquiry to date. In March 2001 a man, described in the media as a "small time criminal", was charged with making a false report to the Garda Síochána[7]. The Donegal case has also led to the striking out of over one hundred and fifty garda charges against a local businessman and his family by the courts due to judicial concerns about the circumstances surrounding them, and the intervention of the Law Society on behalf of the solicitors concerned regarding the integrity of their telephones. In a related incident, another businessman, nightclub owner Frank Shortt, had a conviction for knowingly permitting drugs to be sold on his premises overturned by the Court of Criminal Appeal. Mr Shortt however, whose nightclub has subsequently been burned down, has served a three year jail sentence as a result of that conviction and was also forced to pay a fine of £10,000. Mr Shortt had also made allegations against a number of garda members in Donegal. Furthermore, one garda member, in resisting corruption charges, is reported to have threatened to release information in his possession which, it is suggested, could "plunge the gardaí into the biggest crisis in the force's history". Pending compensation claims in relation to the Donegal fiasco could cost the state millions of pounds in compensation. The damage caused by these incidents to the credibility and authority of the Garda Síochána is, however, inestimable.

These controversies have come to public prominence moreover at a time when the crime control capacity of the state and the Garda Síochána is increasingly being questioned. The permanence of high crime rates and increased public fears of crime, particularly violent crime, have combined to call into question the role and function of the Garda Síochána in contemporary Irish society. In this chapter it is suggested that in Ireland we are encountering what has been described as a post-modern policing reality whereby one of the foundational myths upon which modern society is based is eroding.[8] This myth, according to Garland,[9] is that "the sovereign state is capable of providing security, law and order and crime control within its territorial boundaries".

Just as many of the institutions which have come to define the character of Irish society since independence, the Catholic Church, the judiciary, and the

---

[6] *Irish Times*, 23 April, 2001
[7] *Sunday Business Post*, 18 March, 2001
[8] Reiner, R. (1992), "Policing a Postmodern Society", *Modern Law Review*, Vol. 55, No. 6, pp. 771-81
[9] Garland, D. (1996), "The Limits of the Sovereign State: Strategies of Crime Control in Contemporary Society", *British Journal of Criminology*, Vol. 36, No. 4

political system have come under intense and unprecedented scrutiny, so the historical claim of the Garda Síochána to "possess moral authority as servants of the people"[10] is increasingly being questioned. How the Garda Síochána and the Irish government manages and responds to this crisis of accountability at this time will have a significant impact on the future of Irish policing. Before we focus attention on this response, it is useful to consider the basis upon which the Garda Síochána has come to assume the authoritative and largely unquestioned position it has enjoyed heretofore.

POLICING AND THE POLICE

Police studies and research tend to occur within a general presumptive framework about policing.[11] There is no doubt as to who the police *are*, a state agency dressed in blue, and what *they* do we accept as *the police function.*[12] Furthermore, we believe that without this "thin blue line" our society will descend into chaos. This "police fetishism" rests on a widely held assumption that the police are a prerequisite of social order.

Policing, as a process of social control is "arguably a universal requirement of any social order".[13] Criminological studies however have revealed that *the Police* have only a limited impact on crime rates.[14] It is partly due to the limitations of state policing that policing remains, as Marenin[15] has argued, "a field of contest among the state, private interest groups ... and communities over the division of authority and responsibilities for constructing and protecting secure routines of daily life".

This "contest" has become increasingly visible in recent times in the Republic of Ireland. Firstly we have witnessed a rapid growth in forms of private policing.[16] Private security officers outnumber garda numbers by approximately three thousand members.[17] Private policing, as it occurs in Ireland, typically involves security guards at shopping malls, public houses, dance clubs or other private

[10] The first Commissioner of the Garda Síochána, Michael Staines (1885-1955), declared that the "Garda Síochána will succeed, not by force of arms or numbers, but by their moral authority as servants of the people"

[11] Cain, M. (1979), "Trends in the Sociology of Policework", *International Journal of Sociology of Law,* Vol. 7, No. 2, pp. 143-67

[12] Reiner, R. (1997), "Policing and the Police", in Mike Maguire, Rod Morgan and Robert Reiner (eds.), *The Oxford Handbook of Criminology* (2nd ed.)

[13] Reiner *op. cit.*, 1997, p. 1004

[14] Clarke, R. and Hough, M. (1984), *Crime and Police Effectiveness,* London: Home Office Research Unit; Bayley, D. (1994), *Police for the Future,* New York: Oxford University Press

[15] Marenin, O. (1996), "Changing Police: Policing Change", in Marenin, O. (ed.), *Policing Change, Changing Police: International Perspectives,* Garland, New York and London, p. 309

[16] Johnson, L. (1992), *The Rebirth of Private Policing,* Routledge

[17] McCullagh, C. (1996), *Crime in Ireland: A Sociological Introduction,* Cork University Press; Irish Government Publications (1997), *Report of the Consultative Group on the Private Security Industry,* Dublin: Stationery Office

enterprises. Although private security firms exercise an increasing amount of control over the rights and free movement of citizens, particularly when they control access to the spaces in which much public life increasingly occurs such as large multi-functional shopping and entertainment malls, for the Garda Síochána this form of policing does not necessarily imply a threat to its role. Private policing is generally consistent with the smooth functioning of a market economy, therefore, despite its social control implications, it is something that government seeks to regulate rather than remove.

An entirely different government and police response, however, can be identified in relation to the emergence of recent community self-policing initiatives. This more contentious form of policing has recently emerged in deprived Dublin communities to combat the local heroin trade. This phenomenon of community self-policing previously occurred in the 1980s when heroin first appeared in Dublin.[18] The recent re-emergence of such initiatives has occurred due to an intensification of the heroin problem, resulting in severe loss of life in specific localities and the widely held perception in such areas that the government and the Garda Síochána were either indifferent to the crisis or unable to cope.[19] This community-based anti-drugs policing initiative typically involved the holding of public meetings in community halls during which alleged drug dealers were called to account by local residents, the establishment of all-night vigils to frustrate open street level drug dealing and the organisation of marches on the homes of alleged drug dealers. Such was the success of this initiative in the short term, with regards to ending the open-drug dealing that had been occurring in some locations, that one newspaper report suggested that the Garda Síochána was effectively being displaced in such areas. The Garda Síochána was described as "trailing along behind drug marches ... watching people police themselves".[20]

This phenomenon has often led to conflict between the Garda Síochána and the "anti-drugs activists", the former often accusing the latter of engaging in illegal practices of intimidation and of being a "front" for political subversives such as the Irish Republican Army. Such claims by the Garda Síochána, which are given further credence in the media, have been used to justify a disproportionate state response where extraordinary legal measures such as seven day police detention powers and juryless courts, originally enacted in response to the crisis in

---

[18] Flynn, S. and Yeates, P. (1985), *Smack, The Criminal Drugs Racket in Ireland*; Bennett, D. (1988), "Are they Always Right? Investigation and Proof in a Citizen Anti-Heroin Movement", in Mike Tomlinson, Tony Varley and Ciaran McCullagh (eds.), *Whose Law and Order,* Belfast: Sociological Association of Ireland, pp. 21-40, McCullagh (1996) *op. cit.*

[19] Connolly, J. (1997), *Beyond the Politics of Law and Order – Towards Community policing in Ireland,* Belfast: Centre For Research and Documentation; Connolly (1998), "From Colonial Policing to Community Policing", *Irish Criminal Law Journal,* Vol. 8, No. 2, pp. 165-96

[20] *Irish Times*, 22 October, 1997

Northern Ireland, have been employed against anti-drugs activists.[21] Allegations of police harassment of anti-drugs activists were also reported.[22]

The conflict between the Garda Síochána and community anti-drugs groups is generally presented by the Garda Síochána, and mainstream political and media commentators, in terms of the need to uphold the rule of law and prevent negative forms of "vigilantism".[23]

At a deeper level however, this conflict reveals a more profound concern felt by the Garda Síochána and the Irish state, with preserving the garda claim to a monopoly over the power to police. The power to police, particularly the power to exercise legitimate violence in the name of policing, has become over the passage of time one of the defining features of the modern state. The assumption by citizens of the policing role therefore raises questions as to the legitimacy of the state policing process and, through it, the state itself .

In one respect, through such initiatives, we are witnessing the unravelling of a state policing ideology developed in England in the eighteenth century and then exported to Ireland. The formulation of this ideology has been associated particularly with two brothers, Henry and John Fielding.[24] The basis upon which public policing rests is premised on two primary contentions.

Firstly, it was argued that crime was increasingly sophisticated and that this required a similarly sophisticated response. A professional police force of crime control experts was needed. Hence the creation of the so-called "bow street runners" in the 1750s. The Fielding brothers, through their prolific publication of pamphlets on crime and disorder, stressed the difficulty of the job, thus endeavouring to demonstrate that it required professionals with expertise allied with adequate financial, technical and legal support. Secondly it was argued that state officials could more easily be rendered accountable in the administration of these finances and in the exercise of these enhanced powers. One of the consequences of this

---

[21] See for example *Irish Times,* "IRA linked to Dublin Drug Attacks" 31/05/96; "Republicans linked to rise of the vigilantes" 31/05/96; "Sinn Fein sees a political bonus in drugs issue" 01/10/96

[22] See *Irish Times,* "Questions of policing raised by arrests in inner city" 17/06/ 96; *The Sunday Tribune,* "Tensions Rise on drugs policing" 19/01/97; "Abuse alleged against gardaí", "Women accuse gardaí of intimidation" 14/07/96

[23] It is not being suggested here that anti-drugs groups do not involve people who support the Irish republican movement, the working-class basis of Sinn Féin as a political party suggests that this is probably likely. It is that the Garda Síochána, media commentators and other political interests groups allocate a disproportionate influence over the anti-drugs activity to such groups as part of an attempt to de-legitimise the activity as a whole. This ignores the more diffuse basis of its support and minimises the popular democratic and self-regulatory mechanisms that exist within such spontaneous movements. It is also not being suggested that intimidation and illegality do not occur. In 1996 a local drug user and alleged drug dealer, Josie Dwyer, was killed in Dublin's inner city by anti-drugs activists. Also, anecdotal evidence suggests that people have been wrongly accused and targeted by anti-drugs activists

[24] Rawlings, P. (1995), "The Idea of Policing: a History", in *Policing and Society,* Vol. 5, pp. 129-49

period was that the role of the public in the policing process was clearly circum-scribed. Public involvement was essentially limited to supplying information.

The attempt to assume centralised control by the state over the policing process was met with a great deal of resistance among the English ruling classes in the eighteenth century. Such an idea hinted of foreign tyranny. As Emsley [25] writes, "In England the idea of an uniformed body of policemen patrolling the streets to prevent crime and disorder was anathema. Such a force smacked of the absolutism of continental states. The fact that these models were French, in itself, was suffi-cient to make most eighteenth century English gentlemen conceive a police force as something inimical to English liberty".

Eventually however, the merits of the New Police, particularly its usefulness to the task of controlling the rural and urban poor became obvious. To overcome opposition, a distinctive organisational style and image was created. This, as Reiner[26] suggests, "emphasised the idea of the police as an essentially civilian body, minimally armed, relying primarily on the same legal powers to deal with crime as all citizens shared, strictly subject to the rule of law, insulated from governmental control, and drawn from a representative range of working-class backgrounds to facilitate popular identification". This more localised English police system was then presented as resting on the consent of the English public, thus reflecting the inherent democratic credentials and thus civilisation of the English. As one writer put it, "Our English Police system ... rests on foundations designed with the full approval of the people, we know not how many hundreds of years before the Norman conquest".[27] Early resistance to centralised control over policing in England has contributed to the maintenance of a more localised policing system there today. There are at present forty-five separate police forces in England.

The Fielding brothers had advanced the idea of total law enforcement through a technical, apolitical process operated by experts in which popular involvement was narrowly confined. This ideology suited conditions of relative political stability, where there was a degree of consensus amongst the population as to the legitimacy of the state. Such political consensus could never be assumed by the authorities in Ireland however. In Ireland, the exercise of state policing power would be determined by the ability of the British state to acquire legitimacy for its laws among the population. Its failure to obtain such legitimacy among large sections of the population would ensure that policing was seldom apolitical.[28] This situation existed throughout the empire.[29]

---

[25] Emsley, C. (1991), *The English Police: A Political and Social History,* Hemel Hempstead: Wheatsheaf, p. 217

[26] Reiner (1997), *op. cit.,* p. 752

[27] Lee, M. (1901), *A History of Police in England,* London: Methuen

[28] Macmillan, G. (1993), *State Society and Authority in Ireland: The Foundations of the Modern Irish State,* Gill & Macmillan; Ellison, G. and Smyth, J. (2000), *The Crowned Harp*

[29] Brogden, M. (1987), "The Emergence of the police – The Colonial Dimension", *Brit. Jour. Crim.,* Vol. 27, No. 1

Thus the policing system inspired by the Fielding brothers was for domestic consumption only. A far more centralised and militarised version would be exported to the colonies, the testing ground for this experiment being Ireland. The principal task which would ultimately confront the founders of the Irish state which emerged in the wake of revolution and civil war in the early nineteen twenties would centre upon their ability to reconcile the ideology inherent in the idea of a professional police, premised upon the notion of policing by public consent, with a highly centralised force entailing rule from the top and established as such, primarily because no such consensus existed.

POLICING IRELAND – A COLONIAL LEGACY

Recent and more critical analyses have challenged the basic assumptions upon which much Anglo-American police historiography is based.[30] They have emphasised the extent to which professional police forces have developed as part of an apparatus of social control, the overall purpose of which is to maintain the privileged position of dominant groups. In particular, some writers have pointed out how the imperial dimension of British police history has been largely ignored.[31]

Irish police historiography, with few exceptions,[32] has also tended to downplay the significance of the colonial dimension, minimising in particular the oppressive character of the Royal Irish Constabulary, and its central political function in asserting British state authority throughout Ireland. In doing so police historians in Ireland have adopted what Brogden[33] describes as "the tunnel vision of students of British policing (which) has frustrated an adequate account of police origins and functions." This failure to appreciate the importance of the colonial dimension of Irish policing history renders any analysis of contemporary Irish policing incomplete. The policing model upon which the Garda Síochána rests today is largely unchanged from that which was imposed in Ireland in the eighteenth century. It is submitted that many of the current problems associated with contemporary policing are rooted in the preservation of an anachronistic policing model.

The Garda Síochána and the Royal Ulster Constabulary were both modelled on the Royal Irish Constabulary (RIC). The RIC was disbanded in March 1922 as part of the Anglo-Irish Treaty which followed the Irish war of independence from 1919

---

[30] Reiner (1997), *op. cit.*

[31] Brogden *op. cit.*; Palmer, S. (1988), *Police and protest in England and Ireland,* Cambridge: Cambridge University Press; Brogden, M. and Shearing, C. (1993), *Policing for a New South Africa,* Routledge

[32] For more critical accounts see Brady, C. (1974), *Guardians of the Peace,* Gill & Macmillan; Connolly (1997) *op. cit.*; Ellison and Smyth *op. cit.*

[33] Brogdan (1987), *op. cit.,* p. 4

to 1921.[34] The RIC was primarily a force of occupation upon which was conferred ordinary policing duties. It represented Dublin Castle, the centre of British authority, throughout rural Ireland. It had a hand in virtually every aspect of rural life. Its role included looking after school attendance regulations, implementing the weights and measures Acts, collecting and maintaining agricultural statistics, enforcing licensing laws, overseeing evictions, intelligence gathering and the monitoring of political suspects. Central to the process of imperial expansion is cultural transformation and the RIC were also to perform a role in this respect. It policed popular practices such as pattern days, fairs, wakes, and it consolidated the use of English as the publicly used language. As Brady[35] colourfully asserts, "They were the eyes and ears of the Castle, and where necessary they were its strong right hand. They were, in short, the single, strong and utterly reliable service which had enabled Britain to hold Ireland in a condition of relative tranquillity in the previous hundred years". The RIC was an armed force and, by 1914 it was housed in 1,129 barracks and eighty-three temporary huts throughout the country. The RIC was responsible for policing the entire country except for Dublin, which retained its own police force, the Dublin Metropolitan Police until 1925 when it was amalgamated with the Civic Guard to form An Garda Síochána.

Although by 1914 eighty-one per cent of the rank and file of the RIC were Roman Catholic, primarily the sons of small farmers, the loyalty of the force was ensured by means of a highly centralised command structure and through ensuring that the officer grades were preserved for those whose loyalty to the administration was unquestioned. This latter characteristic, typical of colonial police forces, ensured that up to the disbandment of the force in 1922, Protestants still occupied a disproportionately high number of officer positions.[36] Ireland was heavily policed with the number of police officers per head of population three times that of England and Wales.

Although individual policemen were popular at times of relative calm, at times of social, political or economic strife the political role of the RIC, which reflected its primary loyalty to the crown, would ensure a rapid deterioration in its relations with the general population. This occurred during the "Famine" years between 1845 and 1850, during the Young Ireland rebellion of 1848 and the Fenian rebellion of 1867 when, in the words of Brady,[37] the force earned an

---

[34] For a comprehensive analysis of ealy developments in policing during this period see Brady *op. cit.*; McNiffe (1997), *A History of the Garda* Síochána; Allen, G. (1999), *The Garda Síochána: Policing Independent Ireland 1922-1982,* Gill & MacMillan. For an account of the political context in which the Garda Síochána emerged see O'Halpin (1999), *Defending Ireland. The Irish State and its Enemies Since 1922,* Oxford

[35] Brady *op. cit.,* p. 2

[36] The political and economic privileges afforded Protestants within the Irish colony would generally ensure their loyalty to the state

[37] Brady *op. cit.,* p. 11

"undying hatred and rancour among the rural population". This was further exacerbated during the land war of the 1880s. The fate of the RIC was sealed however as a result of the role they were called upon to perform during the independence struggle of 1919 to 1921. The victory of Sinn Fein in the 1918 British general election led to the appointment of a Provisional Irish Government who, refusing to take their seats in the Westminister parliament, established an Irish Parliament, Dáil Éireann. The British government refused to recognise the legitimacy of this Parliament and the Anglo-Irish war began. In January 1919 two RIC constables were killed in an ambush by the Irish Republicans Army (IRA).[38] This event, often regarded as the first rebel offensive of the Anglo-Irish war, forebode the severe police casualties that were to ensue throughout the conflict.

The political strategy adopted by the British Government in pursuing their campaign against the IRA would ensure that the police would bear the brunt of the casualties. As McNiffe[39] points out, the refusal of the British administration to accept the IRA contention that they were fighting a war led to the reinforcement of the police rather than the army. Inevitably the RIC would be a principal target of the insurgency movement. One of the first steps in the independence campaign was the call by the Provisional government for a boycott of the RIC. The augmentation of the RIC by the notorious "Black and Tans" in the spring of 1920 would ultimately seal their fate as far as the general population was concerned. Between January 1919 and July 1921 425 RIC men were killed and a further 725 were wounded. During 1920, the most brutal year of the conflict, hundreds resigned from the force. The RIC was forced to withdraw from large areas of the rural countryside and at least half of the barracks it had occupied up until then.

Meanwhile Sinn Fein would encourage the population to take their grievances to the Dáil courts which had been established as an alternative to the British system of law enforcement and which by 1920 were functioning relatively successfully in twenty-eight counties.[40] Many of the decisions of these courts would be carried out by the republican police, members of the IRA who had assumed police duties.

The historical failure of the British state to acquire widespread legitimacy amongst the Irish population had always ensured the continuation of a dual policing and judicial power.[41] One of the first critical tests to be confronted by the emerging Irish State would be whether it could overcome this historical legacy

---

[38] The term IRA was not generally used to describe the republican forces until 1920

[39] McNiffe *op. cit.*

[40] Kotsonouris, M. (1993), *Retreat From Revolution: The Dáil Courts 1920-1924*

[41] Connolly (1997), *op. cit.*; Bell, C. (1997), "Alternative Justice in Ireland", in N. Dawson, D. Greer and P. Ingram (eds.), *One Hundred and Fifty Years of Irish Law,* Belfast: SLS Legal Publications; Auld *et al* (1997), *Designing a System of Restorative Community Justice in Northern Ireland,* Belfast: published by the authors

and establish a system of justice and policing to which the general population could give allegiance.

RE-INVENTING THE ROYAL IRISH CONSTABULARY

The emergence of An Garda Síochána

The period 1922 to 1925 is crucial to an understanding of contemporary policing in Ireland. The current statutory basis for the Garda Síochána is to be found in the Garda Síochána Act 1924 and the Police Forces Amalgamation Act 1925. Furthermore, the organisational structure and legal status of the Garda Síochána remained remarkably similar to the RIC. Also, the ideological premise upon which the Garda Síochána would seek to claim its authority in the future would be formulated during this period. This would be encapsulated in the declaration by the first Garda Commissioner Michael Staines in 1922 that, "The Garda Síochána will succeed not by force of arms or numbers but on their moral authority as servants of the people".

The challenge facing the founders of the Free State as far as policing was concerned was whether they could retain the existing RIC model but render it sufficiently "Irish" in character so as to overcome the deep hostility that was felt towards the force. In this respect we can see how the Free State authorities sought to create a police force based on public consent, while retaining a model, whose essential character was defined by the absence of such consent. That this legitimacy crisis was ultimately resolved without any major structural changes of the policing system is certainly one of the remarkable stories of modern Ireland.

The adoption of the policing model of the Royal Irish Constabulary would be particularly likely in the circumstances under which the Free State emerged. The Anglo-Irish Treaty, which brought to an end the hostilities between the provisional Irish government and the British government was ratified by a majority of only seven in Dáil Éireann in January 1922. The outbreak of civil war shortly afterwards ensured that there would be no major changes in the system of control. Of central importance to the British government was an orderly retreat from Empire and a great deal of military assistance was given to the new government in its attempt to stabilise the political situation. Guns, transport vehicles, even furniture were all provided by the RIC to the nascent Civic Guard.

Allen[42] suggests that "had it been politically possible he (Michael Collins) would have retained the RIC, shorn of its imperialist traditions and answerable to a native government". In fact, this is largely what happened. But it was a delicate balancing act, which failed on one occasion. The understandable perception of an

---

[42] Allen *op. cit.,* p. 13

excessive influence of ex-RIC men in the new force caused severe disruption within the ranks of the new Civic Guard in the summer of 1922. As a consequence of the so-called "Kildare Mutiny" the force had to be disbanded and then re-constituted[43].

A Police Organising Committee was appointed by the provisional government to advise it on the establishment of a new force. The presence of a large number of RIC officers on this committee would ensure continuity between the forces. In training men for the new police the paramilitary style of the old force would be replicated through an emphasis on drill instruction. For instructions in law enforcement, the RIC *Constabulary Manual of Law and Police Duties*, first published in 1866, would be relied upon.

Those who were opposed to the Anglo-Irish treaty attempted to capitalise on the similarities between the two forces in their attempts to encourage public opposition to the institutions of the Free State. A proclamation posted in Munster by the anti-treaty IRA read, "The Civic Guard has been organised by the Provisional Government as a police force of a semi-military character ... a continuance of the old RIC".

The Garda Síochána was to remain colonial in structure but members of the force were to be "Irish in thought and action". The definition of Irishness was to lay great emphasis on adherence to Roman Catholicism, the choice of a gaelic name and the encouragement of the use of the native language by the members, the development of sporting prowess in gaelic games, the adoption of a new and distinctive badge, and the maintenance of strict personal and moral discipline including sobriety. The emphasis on cultural symbolism would be central to the definition of the Garda Síochána as it was to the emerging state. As McNiffe [44] concludes, "Independent Ireland from 1922 to 1952 supported Gaelic games, the Irish language and the Catholic Church. Both the Garda Síochána authorities and the men themselves tended to do likewise". Furthermore, the recruits to the Garda Síochána were almost identical to those typically recruited to the RIC, with regards to age, height, marital status and county of origin.

Also however, the fact that the vast majority of Garda Síochána members were unarmed distinguished them from the RIC. The decision to maintain the force as a largely unarmed one was, as McNiffe[45] suggests, "the most significant decision taken by any government concerning the Garda Síochána in the period 1922-1952". There was a combination of idealism and pragmatism in this decision but ultimately it was an extremely wise course of action. Firstly, the politically divided community of civil war Ireland having been at one time united in the face of the armed RIC

---

[43] For the events known as "the Kildare Mutiny" see Brady *op. cit.,* Chapter 4, Allen *op. cit.,* Chapter 3, McNiffe *op. cit.,* Chapter 2

[44] McNiffe *op. cit.,* p. 139

[45] McNiffe *op. cit.,* p. 96

would more readily be reconciled to an unarmed force. This also ensured that the anti-treaty IRA could not credibly include the Civic Guard in its list of legitimate targets during the civil war. Consequently, there were few injuries to the guards during the civil war although two members of the force were shot dead.

The distinctiveness of the Garda Síochána, and the basis upon which it sought to acquire public consent, would lie in its unarmed status and its reflection of cultural attachment to the majority of the population. It could be argued that the Garda Síochána represented a re-invention of the RIC. That it ultimately acquired public acceptance can be attributed to a number of factors but it must also be considered as part of a process of cultural reaction and transformation that occurred upon independence. To paraphrase the literary critic Declan Kiberd,[46] in the process of "Inventing Ireland" the founders of the new state were attempting to redefine an independent nation through institutions it had inherited under occupation.[47] The adoption of the old policing structure would reflect both the political volatility of the period and this general lack of imagination.

Particularly notable by its absence was any formal process of external democratic accountability whereby the public could hold its servants to account. Pointing to the "sterility" of the Dáil and Seanad debates which preceded the enactment of the 1925 Police Forces Amalgamation Act, Walsh[48] points out that, rather than simply retaining the highly centralised colonial system, "no one suggested the alternative of several localised forces, along contemporary British lines". This absence of local control over policing is one of the most significant legacies of this period. The limited role in the policing system permitted to the Irish public today is the result of a process, which began with the Fielding brothers in the eighteenth century and which would be perpetuated by the Free State authorities and all subsequent political leaders as they sought to concentrate and retain as much political power in the centre, amongst themselves. For political leaders, their primary concern was ensuring not so much that the Garda Síochána would be answerable to the general public, but that the leadership of the Garda Síochána would be loyal to whichever political party was in power.

Structurally, the garda remained, in the words of Salmon,[49] "a great, top-heavy, over-centralised bureaucracy in its Phoenix Park headquarters". In the absence of

---

[46] Kiberd, D. (1995), *Inventing Ireland: The Literature of the Modern Nation,* London: Johnathan Cape, p. 263

[47] As Kiberd *op. cit.,* p. 263 puts it, describing the extreme conservatism of the new statesmen, "the retreat from revolution had begun. Soon judges and lawyers would once again be donning the gowns and wigs of the British system; and the newly-liberated people would be employing the unmodified devices of the old regime upon themselves. War and civil war appeared to have drained all energy and imagination away, there was precious little left with which to re-imagine the national condition"

[48] Walsh (1998), p. 11

[49] Salmon, T. (1985), "The Civil Power and Aiding the Civil Power: The Case of Ireland", in Roach, J. and Thomaneck, J. (eds.), *Police and Public Order,* London: Croom Helm, p. 92

any effective system of external accountability, control of the force rested primarily with the Garda Commissioner. The problem with this of course is that the consent sought by the Garda Síochána from the people rested on an ideological basis encapsulated in the words of Michael Staines. Such claims to "moral authority" could only be supported by presenting members of the force as models of discipline and loyalty. Given the importance of such romantic imagery to the public status of the force, the commissioner could hardly be expected to "wash the forces dirty linen" in public.

The founders of the Irish State had achieved a notable success in creating a publicly acceptable policing system out of the ashes of a civil war. In the process of its formation however, the Garda Síochána had been placed on an unfeasibly high pedestal. It was a lofty height from which it could only descend.

The Garda Síochána would emerge from a period of turbulence into a period of relative calm. It was, up until the end of the nineteen fifties at least, a period characterised by low crime rates, high emigration, and an extremely authoritarian social climate, encouraged by a re-invigorated Catholic church which, post-independence, would assume a great deal of authority over many of the affairs of the evolving Republic.[50] The restrictions on individual and moral freedom characteristic of this period would help maintain a high level of social control. The Garda Síochána was little prepared for the challenges it would soon face however.

AN GARDA SÍOCHÁNA – CRISIS IN AUTHORITY

In recent decades the combination of a number of factors have placed great strain on the Garda Síochána and they have also contributed to a decline in public confidence in the force. The persistence of high crime rates since the early nineteen sixties have called into question the ability of the Garda Síochána to fulfill its crime control mandate. The abuse of power by members of the force and the absence of sufficient accountability mechanisms has led to an intensification of public demands for greater scrutiny of the police. The persistence of a heroin crisis in some of the state's most economically deprived communities has led to accusations in such areas of police partiality in its application of the law. Finally, internal wrangling within the garda ranks, primarily over issues concerning pay and representation, have led to an unprecedented breakdown in internal discipline within the force and significantly undermined it in the view of the general public.

---

[50] Indeed, to refer to this period as one characterised by low crime rates is to overlook the outrageous crimes being perpetrated against those within state/church institutions. It is a matter deserving of further research as to the response of the Garda Síochána to this criminal wrongdoing. It is highly likely however that the culture of non-accountability which allowed figures in church authority to evade public scrutiny during this period also determined the limits of police action

Increase in crime

The exaggerated claims as to the crime control capacity of the police, identified above as a significant factor justifying the emergence in the eighteenth century of a professional state crime control agency, have come back to haunt modern police forces. An increasing body of research has revealed that the impact of the police on crime rates is minimal.[51]

In Ireland low crime rates were a pre-1960s phenomenon. Information on crime statistics are contained in the Garda Commissioner's annual report. The first report in 1947 recorded just over 15,000 indictable offences, a figure which remained consistent up until 1961.[52] During the next thirty years crime rates have multiplied six-fold. Simultaneously however, police detection rates declined in relation to this increase in crime, thus the police became increasingly ineffective in terms of crime control. Recent reports of a reduction in crime in the Republic must be greeted with caution. Firstly, the fact that these reports are based on garda statistics is problematic. The obvious point here is that an organisation with a vested interest in the crime rate should not be able to control the means by which its own performance is determined. Crime figures can be manipulated for political purposes, either by the police as they seek more resources, or by politicians, as they attempt to justify criminal justice policies or try to divert attention from other social problems.[53] Secondly, a minor change in police recording practices can significantly alter the overall recorded rate of crime. Also, the apparent decrease in crime could merely be the consequence of a declining reporting rate. This would reflect badly on the Garda Síochána as it would be a possible indication of declining public confidence in them. A recent survey by the Central Statistics Office[54] is revealing in this respect. This is the first survey conducted in the Republic of Ireland that can enable us to consider the viability of garda statistics.

While the report was significant in terms of indicating the "dark figure" of crime, that is those crimes not reported to the Gardaí, it also suggested a wide-spread lack of confidence in the ability of the Gardaí to respond to crime. The survey revealed that 60% of thefts from vehicles, 60% of cases of vandalism, 40% of bicycle thefts, 40% of violent thefts, 50% of non-violent thefts and 40% of assault cases went unreported. Approximately thirty per cent of burglaries, thefts from motor vehicles and assaults were not reported due to a belief that the gardaí

---

[51] See F/N 12 *op. cit.*

[52] The following figures are taken from McCullagh (1996), *op. cit.,* p. 2. Indictable offences are generally regarded as those meriting trial by judge and jury. Non-indictable offences usually are tried in the absence of a jury

[53] For a discussion see Maguire, M. (1997), "Crime Statistics, Patterns and Trends: Changing Perceptions and their Implications", in *Oxford Handbook,* p. 161; O'Mahony, P. (1993), *Crime and Punishment in Ireland,* The Round Hall Press p. 10; Connolly (1998), *op. cit.,* p. 182

[54] Central Statistics Office (1998), *Quarterly National Household Survey: Crime and Victimisation Sept-Nov 1998,* Dublin: Government Publications

would not or could not do anything about the crime. The survey found that the most common reason for not reporting a crime was that it was not serious enough or that there was no financial loss. Over two thirds of those surveyed rated the work done by the gardaí in controlling crime in their neighbourhood as good or very good however. Therefore, while people do not necessarily blame the Garda Síochána, this survey reveals a public increasingly prepared to accept crime as a fact of life. Given however, that the police mandate is largely premised on their crime control capacity this survey raises serious questions as to the function served by the Garda Síochána in contemporary Irish society.

As Rawlings[55] has argued, "the consequence for the police in assuming this expertise on crime has been the assertion that crime control is possible". When this is seen not to be the case, a public brought up on the "myth of sovereign crime control",[56] will obviously lose a certain degree of confidence in the police and begin to question their role.

Police powers and abuse

Another central historical premise upon which state policing rests is that state officials can more easily be held accountable for the extensive resources and legal power regarded as necessary to the policing task. The potential for abuse in this area must be considered in light not only of these extensive legal powers but also in terms of the diffuse role performed by the police in society, and also in terms of the extent of discretionary power inherent in everyday police work. Serious concerns have arisen in the Republic of Ireland both regarding the abuse of police powers and also the failure of the existing accountability mechanisms to hold the police to account. The shooting of John Carthy and the ongoing controversy in Donegal have exacerbated these concerns.

The garda role encompasses crime control, public order, state security, economic and social regulation, public administration and accident and emergency.[57] The legal powers conferred on the individual garda member are based both in his status as a peace officer under English common law and as a result of Irish legislation. The former powers include powers to arrest for breach of the peace, the power to use no more force than is reasonably necessary to restore order, and the duty to prevent a breach of the peace. These powers have been superceded by a huge array of powers conferred on members of the gardaí by statute. They include power to use force, even lethal force, to affect an arrest, powers of entry and search, powers of detention for questioning, the power to seize material and also a large array of public order powers.

---

[55] Rawlings *op. cit.,* p. 143

[56] Garland (1996), *op. cit.*

[57] Walsh (1998), *op. cit.*, p. 51

Both in law and in practice, the individual police officer has a great deal of discretion in the exercise of such powers. Although his position in a hierarchical structure would suggest that he is never entirely independent in the exercise of these powers, the reality of everyday police work allows a great deal of latitude to the individual officer in terms of how he chooses to employ them. The low visibility of everyday police work renders the police force a unique institution in that "within it discretion increases as one moves down the hierarchy".[58] Furthermore, police powers are generally exercised out of the public gaze upon citizens who would be unlikely to formally complain.

While it has been recognised that a certain degree of police discretion is inevitable and indeed desirable, research has also shown that the police, in exercising their discretionary powers, are prone to discriminate between certain groups on the basis of their own prejudices.[59] The identification of institutional racism within the London Metropolitan Police has been raised in the context of the death of Stephen Lawrence and the disproportionate use of police "stop and search" powers in areas populated by black people.[60] Closer to home, research in Northern Ireland has revealed high degrees of anti-Catholic sentiment within the RUC and this is reflected in their relations with that section of the community.[61] Those generally exposed to the most intensive policing have been referred to as "police property" groups.[62]

In Ireland such groups would include the homeless, drug users, travellers, young people; generally people who spend a great deal of their time out on the streets and thus are more exposed than the general population to the police on the beat. Also, however, a group becomes defined as police property in a context where the dominant powers of society call upon the police to maintain social control over such categories of people.

Sectarianism within the Royal Ulster Constabulary reflects the deeply sectarian nature of the northern statelet since its establishment.[63] Racism within the London Metropolitan Police is a reflection of the high levels of racism which has been

---

[58] Wilson, J. (1968), *Varieties of Police Behaviour,* Cambridge Mass: Harvard University Press, p. 7, Quoted in Reiner (1997), *op. cit.,* p. 1009

[59] Reiner (1997), *op. cit.,* p. 1008

[60] *The Stephen Lawrence Inquiry: Report on an Inquiry by Sir William MacPherson of Cluny* (Feb. 1999), The Stationary Office: London

[61] McVeigh, R. (1994), *Its Part of Life Here: The Security Forces and Harassment in Northern Ireland,* Belfast: Committee on the Administration of Justice; Ellison, G. (1997), "Professionalism in the Royal Ulster Constabulary: an examination of the institutional discourse", unpublished DPhil Thesis, Univ. of Ulster; Royal Ulster Constabulary (1997), *Survey of Religious and Political Harassment and Discrimination in the RUC*

[62] Lee, J. (1981), "Some Structural Aspects of Police Deviance in Relations with Minority Groups", in Clifford Shearing (ed.), *Organisational Police Deviance,* Toronto: Butterworth

[63] O'Leary, B. and McGarry, J. (1996), *The Politics of Antagonism: Understanding Northern Ireland* (2nd ed.)

identified within English society, much of it directed against the Irish community. Also however, the increasingly multi-racial nature of Irish society is manifesting itself in growing levels of racism and intolerance exhibited by Irish people towards asylum seekers and refugees.[64] This is a factor of Irish life the Garda Síochána will increasingly have to confront and adapt to. However, an issue of equal importance, and one that has generally been overlooked in the policing context relates to the position of the Garda Síochána within the Irish class structure. The rural origin of most garda members often renders them ill prepared for the circumstances of urban working-class life. The low level of support for the Garda Síochána, which has been identified in many working-class areas of Dublin, can only be compounded by the perception that they are being policed by people with whom they often cannot identify.[65] Also, rural/urban prejudices are exacerbated by this imbalance between the police and the policed. Such prejudices are often exhibited through the emergence of derogatory epithets in police discourse used against those with whom they frequently come into contact.[66] Farrelly[67] found that many young people from a deprived inner city Dublin community believed that they were viewed in derogatory terms by many of the garda members they encountered.

Although such prejudices are indicative of a more general problem at the heart of Irish society, in the policing context, the potential for such prejudices to be translated into the abuse of power is magnified. The extensive powers vested in the police are generally exercised on the beat or in a police station, areas that are often invisible to public scrutiny. Furthermore, the existing legal mechanisms of holding the police to account for the use of such powers do not appear to be effective.

The huge array of discretionary powers available to gardaí on the beat has been significantly enhanced by the introduction of the Criminal Justice (Public Order) Act 1994 and the Criminal Justice (Drug Trafficking) Act 1996. Regarding the Public Order Act, Walsh[68] argues that, "There can be little doubt that this Act substantially enhances the public order powers and role of the Garda Síochána".

The 1996 Criminal Justice (Drug Trafficking) Act permits the Garda Síochána to detain a person for up to seven days for questioning. Before a person can be detained for this period, permission must be obtained from a judge of the District Court who must be satisfied that there are grounds for such an extension. Garda reluctance to divulge information about an ongoing investigation could render this judicial intervention a "rubber stamp" exercise however. Ryan[69] argues that

---

[64] Mc Laghlin, M. and O'Connell, M. (2000), *Cultivating Pluralism,* Oak Tree Press
[65] The Report of the National Crime Forum (1998), considers the alienation towards the Garda Síochána in many deprived urban areas. See Chapters 2 and 8
[66] For a list of such epithets in other policing contexts see Reiner (1997), *op. cit.,* p. 1010
[67] Farelly, J. (n.d), *Crime, Custody and Community*
[68] Walsh (1998), *op. cit.,* p. 159
[69] Ryan (1997), "The Criminal Justice (Drug Trafficking) Act 1996: Decline and Fall of the Right to Silence", *Irish Criminal Law Journal*

the ultimate effect of the Act is that "the legislature has conferred the necessary inquisitorial powers not on judges, or on public prosecutors, but on the state's investigator's, An Garda Síochána, and the venue for the exercise of these powers is not a courtroom, or a prosecutor's office, but the garda station".

The procedure for dealing with complaints against the police remained internal to the force until the enactment of the Garda Síochána (Complaints) Act 1986. This Act established a Garda Síochána Complaints Board. The Complaints Board was established following public disquiet surrounding the Criminal Justice Bill of 1983. The powers to be made available to the Garda Síochána in the Bill provoked widespread public concern about the impact these enhanced police powers would have on civil liberties.[70]

While the gardaí had justified these enhanced powers as necessary in the fight against crime, public concerns had also been fuelled by a series of cases in the mid-1970s and early 1980s which raised questions about police interrogation methods. Speculation as to the existence of a so-called Garda Síochána "heavy gang", specialising in the use of violence and oppressive tactics as a means of extracting confessions or intelligence from detainees in custody, was reinforced by a number of high profile cases which had failed due to the courts not being satisfied that the alleged confessions had been made voluntarily.[71]

The treatment of prisoners in custody is determined by the provisions of the Criminal Justice Act 1984 (Treatment of Prisoners in custody in Garda Síochána Stations) Regulations 1987 and the Criminal Justice Act 1984 (Electronic Recording of Interviews) Regulations 1997 and the Judges Rules. Keane[72] how-ever, in a consideration of the practical application of these safeguards concludes that they are not adequate. With regards to the long-running saga over the introduction of the electronic recording of interviews in garda stations, Keane suggests that, "as a watchdog" the measures finally produced were "toothless". In 1997 trial applications of such technology were initiated in four garda stations. However, suspects were unwilling to volunteer to be recorded. Accordingly, mandatory recordings were introduced for certain offences. The recording of statements in custody is a reform which has the potential to lead to a decrease in challenges to the validity of such statements in court and similar allegations of

---

[70] The powers included (inter alia) the detention of a suspect in garda custody for up to twenty hours, the powers to search, photograph, fingerprint, palm print, to take skin swabs and hair samples from a suspect. For a fuller account see Walsh (1998), *op. cit.,* p. 261

[71] See generally for the period Dunne, D. and Kerrigan, G. (1984), *Round Up the Usual Suspects, Magill*; Joyce, J. and Murtagh, P. (1984), *Blind Justice*, Dublin: Poolbeg Press; Walsh, D. "Miscarriages of Justice in the Republic of Ireland", in Walker, C. and Starmer, K. (1998), *Justice in Error* (2nd ed.), London: Blackstone Press; Kerrigan, G. (1996), *Hard Cases*, regarding the so-called Shercock case in which an elderly man died in police custody having received a severe beating while in custody, Gill & Macmillan; O'Mahony, P. (1996), *op. cit.*, p. 150

[72] Keane (1997), "Detention Without Charge and the Criminal Justice (Drug Trafficking) Act 1996", *Irish Criminal Law Journal*

police abuse of suspects, thus it favours the police. Although the introduction of such a safeguard was first recommended in the O'Briain report in the late 1970s, at the time of writing, an adequate system remains elusive. [73] In August 1999 the then Minister for Justice made a committment to introduce recording devices in 200 of the 700 garda stations throughout the state within a period of eighteen months at a cost of ten million pounds. That deadline passed with just eleven out of the proposed 200 stations fitted with the equipment however.

Regarding the effectiveness of the Garda Complaints Board, Walsh,[74] in an in-depth consideration of the practical operation of the complaints mechanism, argues that the Garda Complaints Board, which is intended to be independent of the police, is unlikely to be representative of those who would be most likely to have a grievance with the Garda Síochána and that its procedure is too slow and cumbersome. The proof of the pudding is in the eating. In 1994, out of 136 complaints alleging criminal wrongdoing, there were no prosecutions. In 1995, out of a total of 154 such citizen complaints only one prosecution resulted. Although such complaints are passed to the Director of Public Prosecutions to decide whether or not to prosecute, Walsh suggests that a contributory factor in the low success rate might be a lack of enthusiasm among garda members when called to investigate their fellow members. Furthermore, he suggests that the low success rate could lead one to conclude that "The general picture is still one of the Garda Síochána being seen to investigate complaints against themselves ... the sceptics can point to a very low success rate as evidence that the force is not really serious about prosecuting its members for criminal offences committed in furtherance of their policing objectives". In 1998, the Board received 1,400 complaints, of which 596 were processed to a conclusion in that year. The Director of Public Prosecutions directed prosecutions in nine cases, seven of which were completed with no convictions resulting.[75]

Walsh's scepticism about the Garda Complaints Board was echoed by the International Committee for the Prevention of Torture (CPT) in its 1995 report. Concerned about the presence of garda members on the board it concluded that this could "damage public confidence in the capacity of the complaints system to deal objectively with complaints about police conduct".[76] More recently, the most damning indictment of the Garda Complaints Board was issued by its own chief executive. Expressing his disillusionment with the system over which he

---

[73] Report of the Committee to Recommend Certain Safeguards for Persons in Custody and for Members of the Garda Síochána, Dublin: Government Stationery Office, 1978

[74] Walsh (1998), *op. cit.,* p. 348

[75] Information from Garda Síochána website

[76] *Committee for the Prevention of Torture and Inhuman or Degrading Treatment or Punishment, Report on Irish Places of Detention* (December 1995), Strasbourg: Council of Europe, quoted in O'Mahony, P., "The Garda Síochána and the ethics of police interrogation" (1996), *Irish Criminal Law Journal,* p. 51

presided, Sean Hurley suggested that it was, "very dangerous to have the notion of a complaints authority and not the reality of one ... it's worse than having none at all"[77]. Hurley's comments followed reports to him by solicitors that their clients were reluctant to use the Complaints Board for fear of retribution by garda members.

The judiciary has often performed an important supervisory or disciplining role over the gardaí in the exercise of their duties. This has particularly been the case through the use of the so-called *exclusionary rule*, whereby evidence obtained unlawfully by the police in the course of their investigation can be ruled inadmissible at trial. This could indirectly lead to the police refraining from such practices. From a consideration of the existing case-law however, Walsh[78] concludes that, despite the accountability potential of this rule, the Irish judiciary has been reluctant to apply it for such purposes. He suggests that, in taking this course of action, the judiciary has struck a balance between, on the one hand, "the need of the individual and the general public for a police force which can tackle crime efficiently and effectively and, on the other, the need to ensure that individuals and the general public are protected against over-zealous police practices".

Variations between the approaches of individual judges when it comes to the sanctioning of garda members renders judicial intervention an unreliable method of police accountability. In the recent high profile case of Paul Ward, for example, who was convicted for his role in the murder of crime correspondent Veronica Guerin, the Supreme Court was highly critical of the behaviour of the Garda Síochána during the investigation. Despite this however, they still went on to uphold his conviction. It might be argued that the public policy considerations of ensuring a conviction took precedence over the rights of suspects on this occasion.

A comprehensive analysis of the various issues surrounding police accountability to the law is beyond the scope of this chapter. The principal fault-line which appears to run through the existing legal accountability processes however, seems to lie in the fact that they are dependent on garda co-operation for their effectiveness. This, as has been pointed out above, appears to be the case regarding judicial intervention in the request by gardaí for permission to detain a suspect for seven days under the Criminal Justice (Drug Trafficking) Act 1996.[79] Regarding the potential for garda members to be prosecuted in the ordinary courts for criminal wrongdoing, it is the gardaí themselves who are appointed to investigate complaints against themselves. Furthermore, Walsh suggests that the special working relationship between the Director of Public Prosecutions (DPP) and the Garda Síochána might militate against the DPP initiating criminal

---

[77] *Sunday Tribune,* 16 April, 2000

[78] Walsh 1998 *op. cit.,* p. 366

[79] Ryan *op. cit.,* p. 33

procedures against members of the force, preferring to opt instead for the disciplinary mechanisms internal to the force.

It is clear that the various procedures which exist to ensure that the Garda Síochána can be held publicly accountable for the use of their powers have failed to assuage public concerns in this area. A study by Bohan and Yorke[80] which looked at public perceptions of the Garda Síochána found that 40% of respondents felt that, "in court, some gardaí would rather cover up the facts than lose face" while 57% agreed that "the Garda Síochána sometimes exceed their powers by abusing suspects physically or mentally". In 1995 the Council of Europe Committee for the Prevention of Torture[81] report on Irish places of detention concluded that, "persons held in certain police establishments in Ireland, and more particularly in Dublin, run a not inconsiderable risk of being physically ill-treated". Since 1990 there has been an immense increase in complaints made by the public against Garda Síochána members to the Garda Complaints Board; from 750 in 1990 to 1,400 in 1998. A significant number of these fall within the category of abuse of authority.[82] An almost 100% increase in complaints against the Garda Síochána should be a serious cause for concern. The shooting of John Carthy and the ongoing revelations about alleged malpractice among garda members in Donegal have intensified matters in this area.

Prevailing public concerns coupled with the anomaly of a police account-ability process largely dependent on the police for its success strengthens the argument for an independent process of police complaints. Increasingly, com-mentators on this subject are looking to the Police Ombudsman system recently introduced into Northern Ireland under the Police (NI) Act 1998.[83] The Report of The Independent Commission On Policing For Northern Ireland (The Patten Report) regarded such a system as central to the new accountability mechanisms for the new Northern Ireland Police Service (NIPS).[84] In response to recent speculation about reforms in the complaints procedure in the Republic, the Garda Commissioner stated that he was not opposed in principle to external investigation of members of the force.[85] However, the commissioner stated that he was opposed to external investigations of criminal allegations against members of the force. The position adopted by the Garda Commissioner in this respect is

---

[80] Bohan, P. and Yorke, D. (1987), "Law Enforcement Marketing: Perceptions of a Police Force", Vol. 2, *Irish Marketing Review*, pp. 72-86

[81] CPT Report (1995), *op. cit.*

[82] In 1994 64% of complaints alleged abuse of authority by a member of the force

[83] Section 50-65. This initiative was introduced on the foot the recommendations of Dr Maurice Hayes, see "A Police Ombudsman for Northern Ireland" (January 1997). An Ombudsman was appointed in October 1999

[84] The Report of the Independent Commission on Policing for Northern Ireland (September 1999), *A New Beginning: Policing In Northern Ireland*, p. 37

[85] *Irish Times*, 29 November, 2000

consistent with the powers of the Ombudsman in Northern Ireland who is restricted in terms of her independence to investigate allegations of criminal wrongdoing against members of the police. Unless the Ombudsman calls in her investigators as a matter of public interest,[86] there will continue to be cases where allegations of criminal wrongdoing by police officers will be investigated by the police themselves.

As Northern Human Rights Commissioner Brice Dickson[87] argues however in the context of policing north of the border, "There is a strong argument for insisting that the responsibility for *all* criminal investigations against police officers is transferred automatically to completely independent investigators". This argument, despite the resistance of the Garda Commissioner, remains persuasive in the south also. Particularly in the context of increased revelations of police misconduct. Furthermore, as contact intensifies between the two forces on the island into the future, something which is also recommended in the "Patten Report" and which is ongoing anyway in the context of European and international policing developments, having diverging standards of police accountability between the Garda Síochána and the Northern Ireland Police Service will become increasingly unsustainable.

Policing the public interest

In focusing on the question of ensuring that the police are held accountable to the law in the exercise of their powers, we are considering only one side of the accountability coin. An equally important consideration is ensuring that the policing process is subject to direction and carried out in such a manner as to be democratically sustainable, that is that it occurs in the interests of the public as a whole and not on behalf of specific social groups or classes.

The problem in this area of course relates to the fact that the public is made up of a diversity of interests. Professional police forces moreover have developed hand in hand with social inequality. Critical studies and a great deal of experience have revealed the extent to which police forces can become tools of power for a specific ruling faction. Comparative studies of policing remind us that liberal democratic regimes such as the Republic of Ireland, where the police do not operate simply as a tool of repression, are the exception rather than the rule.[88]

---

[86] Police (NI) Act 1998, s. 55 (6). This might occur in cases where allegations arise otherwise than through a complaint by a member of the public; matters such as corruption, fraud, extortion, domestic violence etc

[87] Dickson B, "Policing and human rights after the conflict", in Michael Cox, Adrian Guelke and Fiona Stephen (eds.) (2000), *A Farewell to arms? From long war to long peace in Northern Ireland,* Manchester University Press p. 112

[88] Bayley, D. (1985), *Patterns of Policing*, New Brunswick, NJ: Rutgers University Press; Mawby, R. (1991), *Comparative Policing Issues,* London: Unwin; Marenin O (1996), *op. cit.*

The complexity of modern policing in a liberal democracy means, however, that policing can involve a combination of what Marenin[89] refers to as the maintenance of both "specific order" and "general order". The first refers to the particular interests of dominant political and economic groups and the second refers to the interest of all in living in conditions of public tranquillity and personal security. That is, the policing function involves the police engaging in class control and traffic control.

The emergence of the Garda Síochána in a state which remained divided along civil war political lines, led to a recurrence of controversies concerning political interference with the force. This interference did not generally amount to one ruling faction attempting to use the police to establish a particular type of governance or distinct political system. The inherently conservative nature of Irish politics and the absence of any significant ideological distinction between the principal political parties ensured this. Once concerns of a possible fascist plot to overthrow the state in the nineteen thirties were shown to have been more imaginary than real, political interference with the force tended to be opportunistic and to ensure short-term political leverage for one political party or specific politician. Such controversies, which have occurred intermittently up until the present time, were often rooted in the political temptation to exploit the powers vested in the minister to appoint and remove the commissioner and senior officers, and the control enjoyed by the government over the finances of the force.

The Garda Síochána did serve a specific ordering function however. This was perhaps inevitable in a society where significant economic divisions persisted. The police are, in theory at least, empowered to respect due legal process and to apply the law impartially. It is clear however that some laws are enforced more energetically than others and some sections of society, the police property groups referred to above, are policed more heavily than others. The recent popularity among politicians of the rhetoric of "Zero Tolerance" lay in its ability to distract the public from the reality that white collar crime, the crimes of the better off, have always been tolerated more than the sorts of crimes generally engaged in by the poor.[90] Not only are the poor and other politically marginal groups most vulnerable to intense policing, they also tend to suffer most from crime.[91] The poor in society therefore, tend to be "over policed and under-protected".[92] Furthermore,

---

[89] Marenin, O. (1983), "Parking Tickets and Class Repression: The Concept of Policing in Critical Theories of Criminal Justice", *Contemporary Crises,* 6/2 pp. 241-266

[90] McCullagh (1996), *op. cit.,* ch. 3

[91] Local crime surveys in Britain have revealed the extent to which crime is concentrated in areas characterised by poverty and how particular forms of crime are suffered disproportionately by specific social groups within those areas; young males and young women in particular. See Maguire *op. cit.,* and Young, J., "Left Realist criminology; Radical in its Analysis, Realist in its policy", in *The Oxford Handbook* (1997), *op. cit.*

[92] Reiner (1997), *op. cit.,* p. 726

the poor lack the material resources to buy into the expanding private security industry. Finally, by virtue of their political marginality, the poor have a limited ability to determine the prioritisation of policing and thus the way in which police resources are employed.

It is in such circumstances that the role of public representatives in influencing policing policy becomes so important. Again however, marginalised sections of Irish society have been poorly served by successive Ministers for Justice in this respect. The minister for justice is legally empowered to ensure that the policing process reflects public priorities. The minister, for example, enjoys the power to direct the manner in which the force shall be distributed and stationed throughout the state. This power enables the minister to direct the garda commissioner to increase or reduce the concentration of the force in particular areas or localities. The deployment of the police therefore, although it may have a limited effect on crime rates, does have a symbolic relevance. The failure of ministers to exercise these powers in the interests of marginalised social groups or classes is in itself an indication of the way in which political priorities impact upon policing.

For example, during the recent BSE infection of British cattle, something that could have had a detrimental impact on the Irish beef industry, a significant number of police became instantly available to police the border with Northern Ireland. Many of these police were simply lifted from economically deprived areas of Dublin.

This politics of policing policy can also be illustrated with reference to the policing of a heroin problem in Dublin.[93] Community activists in Dublin's inner city have long campaigned for a diversion of police attention from illegal street traders in tobacco and other goods to the clearly more harmful, and equally open, heroin dealing. The allocation of resources in this respect is, it might appear, being determined by local business interests.

It is arguable that the many deaths which have resulted from the heroin trade render it the most pressing policing issue confronting the Irish state. These deaths have occurred however in the most politically and economically deprived communities in the state. The north Dublin inner city, for example, has one of the most acute heroin problems in the state. It also however, records the lowest attendance at election time.[94] It has been argued that it is due to its relative political insignificance that successive governments have permitted the heroin problem to fester and that the policing process as it affects such communities has been concentrated towards containing the problem in such areas rather than addressing it fundamentally. Reflecting this deeper class division in the state, the role of the

---

[93] Connolly (1998), *op. cit.*

[94] In the recent general election voter turnout for this area was 28%, the lowest recorded in that election throughout the state

Garda Síochána has often involved acting as a form of buffer, policing the margins of Irish society.

An apparent shift in government policy in recent years has resulted in a greater engagement by the state with the drug problem. This has been prompted by a number of factors. These factors included firstly, the MDMA or ecstasy-related deaths of a number of middle-class children. Secondly, direct links began to be made between the growth in drug use and property crime against the middle-class.[95] Finally, the shooting by organised criminals of a prominent crime correspondent in June 1996 provoked a major security reaction by the state.

The numerous deaths of members of the Dublin "underclass" does not appear to have been the primary factor which has galvanised the state into recent action. It is submitted that it was when the heroin problem was beginning to impact on middle-class society that the political establishment responded. The manner in which the drugs crisis has been policed in the past appears to have reflected the way in which the crisis has been perceived and prioritised by middle-class society. In this respect, it reveals the politics of Irish policing. The poor have generally been at the receiving end of a policing process that serves primarily the interests of others as the allocation of police resources tends to reflect the concerns of the most powerful. To suggest that the Garda Síochána has ever enjoyed "moral authority" among the poorer sections of Irish society, particularly the urban underclass, is extremely contestable.

It is the very absence of such authority that prompted the emergence of community self-policing initiatives in response to the heroin trade. To invalidate such activity by portraying it as subversive of the state is to ignore the extent to which it represents a rejection of a state policing process, the democratic legitimacy of which was, in itself, questionable. This community based anti-drugs activity revealed a public increasingly demanding a greater say and input into how and why they were being policed.

Blue Flu

Although the garda member enjoys a great deal of latitude in the exercise of his/her powers, s/he remains part of a hierarchical organisation and is bound to a strict disciplinary code.[96] Since the inception of the force, great emphasis has been placed on maintaining discipline within the force as a means of acquiring and maintaining public support and consent. The presentation of the Garda Síochána

---

[95] A report produced by the Garda Research Unit found that drug users were responsible for 85 per cent of detected aggravated burglaries, 84 per cent of detected offences of larceny from the person and from unattended vehicles and 82 per cent of ordinary burglaries, Keogh (1996), *Illicit Drug Use and related Criminal Activity in the Dublin metropolitan Area*

[96] For a detailed consideration of the internal Garda Síochána disciplinary procedure, see Walsh (1998), *op. cit.,* ch. 8

as a highly disciplined, unified and loyal public service has always been central to the retention of its public service image.

On a number of occasions however, such discipline has broken down, particularly in relation to issues of pay, conditions and the means by which garda members can articulate their grievances.[97] Garda members are restricted from entering trade unions or associations, where the object of such association is "to control or influence the pay, pensions or conditions of any police force".[98] A number of representative bodies have been permitted within the force however to ensure that members are properly represented in matters affecting their welfare and efficiency.[99]

Recommendations of the Conroy Commission (1970) and the Ryan Committee (1979)[100] went some way towards resolving outstanding grievances in relation to pay and conditions within the force. The latter committee however, headed by Professor Louden Ryan, drew attention to what he saw as an "increased preoccupation with money among gardaí".[101] Issues relating to pay surfaced again in the late 1980s and again more recently. The increased wealth within Irish society, associated with the growth of the Irish economy or so-called "Celtic Tiger" in the mid- 1990s, coupled with the high cost of living, particularly in Dublin, has led to inevitable tensions within the force. Ongoing political tensions within the Garda Representative Association (GRA) however also came into the public arena at this time. Attempts by the Garda Commissioner, independent mediators and successive ministers for justice to resolve this dispute continued with little success.[102]

In 1994 the GRA split into three. The acrimony involved in this ongoing dispute, unprecedented in extent and bitterness, was regularly displayed on television.[103] As O'Mahony[104] suggests "The ramifications of this unseemly and rancorous dispute are highly damaging to the public perception of the Garda Síochána (and) ... to its future ability to manage itself". At the root of this dispute is disagreement over money. Of course, members of the Garda Síochána are as fallible as the rest of the members of a society that is becoming increasingly

---

[97] McNiffe *op. cit.,* ch. 11

[98] A garda member below the rank of chief superintendant is statutorily prohibited from resigning his membership or withdrawing his labour without giving one month's notice to his chief superintendant. Walsh (1998), *op. cit.,* p. 32

[99] These include the Garda Representative Association (GRA), the Association of Garda Sergeants and Inspectors (AGSI), the Association of Superintendants and the Association of Chief Superintendants. Walsh (1998), *op. cit.,* p. 33

[100] Commission on the Garda Síochána (Conroy Commission) (1970), Report of Garda Committee of Inquiry (Ryan Committee) (1979)

[101] McNiffe *op. cit.,* p.167

[102] See outline of the dispute in O'Mahony (1996), *op. cit.,* and Walsh (1998), *op. cit.,* p. 36

[103] O'Mahony describes how at the 1994 GRA annual conference a private security company was hired to police the conference and ensure unruly elements were not allowed to disrupt the proceedings (1996), *op. cit.,* p. 139

[104] O'Mahony (1996), *op. cit.,* p. 140

materialistic. However, as O'Mahony puts it "it is acutely disappointing that their special privileges and responsibilities and their symbolic role and importance as guardians of the peace could not persuade them to refrain from complete immersion in the mire that is the duty-free zone of modern self-serving industrial relations". This "dismantling of the mystique" of the Garda Síochána, both for gardaí and the public, was recently advanced further in the context of a mass breach of discipline by the force.

In 1999, in a dispute over pay, over ninety per cent of garda members, claiming ill health, failed to attend work. Ignoring the Garda Commisioner's appeals for discipline this so-called 'blue flu' revealed a police force for which discipline appeared to account for little and public service for less still.

RESPONDING TO THE CRISIS

The response of the Garda Síochána to this undermining of its authority has co-incided with a specific governmental response. Two distinct lines of governmental action can be identified. They are neatly described by Garland[105] as "a *sovereign state strategy* stressing enhanced control and expressive punishment and an *adaptive strategy* stressing prevention and partnership". A principal factor that has contributed to the predominance and persistence of the former approach over time has been the conflict in Northern Ireland. The prevalence of this factor has resulted in the Garda Síochána and the government forming a punitive alliance in defence of what Garland[106] refers to as the "the myth of sovereign crime control".

Denial

The traditional reaction is premised on a *denial* that the crime problem is beyond the capacity of the Garda Síochána to cope. The consistent growth in crime since the 1960s, and the simultaneous decline in police effectiveness, has led the police to assert, as Rawlings[107] puts it, "that the failure is because access to adequate strategies, techniques, legal powers or financial resources is being obstructed".

Furthermore, the deflection of criticism concerning growing crime rates and police abuses of power has become heavily dependent on the management of crime statistics, a renewed emphasis on public relations and the compliance of the media. The Garda Síochána has invested heavily in recent years in its public relations department and it also maintains tight control over information about crime. As has been suggested above, it is obviously inappropriate that an organisation, the performance of which is judged largely in terms of its effective-

---

[105] Garland, D. (2000), "The Culture of High Crime Societies. Some Preconditions of recent 'Law and Order' Policies", *British Journal of Criminology* 40, p. 348
[106] Garland (1996), *op. cit.*
[107] Rawlings (1995), *op. cit.,* p. 143

ness in responding to crime, should control the means by which crime is recorded. The importance of this factor was highlighted recently in light of the crime study conducted by the Central Statistics Office. A newspaper report revealed that the Department of Justice requested a copy of this study prior to its publication so that the minister could be briefed on, "any unexpected issues that may be identified in the survey".[108]

The first indication of a concern with garda public relations came about in the mid-1960s with the securing of a five-minute slot on the national broadcasting station, Radio Telefís Éireann (RTE) called *Garda Patrol*.[109] In 1971 the Garda Press Office was established. This currently plays a crucial role in managing and disseminating information about crime to the public. The role of the media becomes extremely important at this stage. To the media crime reporting is a crucial asset in circulation wars and crime correspondents enjoy a high media profile. However, their sources are primarily members of the Garda Síochána themselves. As a consequence, Corless[110] argues, "journalists have found themselves under pressure to toe a garda line on stories. If they don't toe that line to their source's satisfaction, they're cut out of the leaks loop. And if the stories dry up, where does that leave the jobbing hack".

This emphasis on media management was recently exhibited in the John Carthy shooting. The media were kept away from the scene of the siege so initial reports of the shooting which emanated from garda sources were not only extremely distressful to the family, they were also clearly factually incorrect. A subsequent current affairs programme *Prime Time* which highlighted many of the inconsistencies in the original police version of events, led to a further series of stories that were also heavily biased towards the garda position. Most recently, the Coroners inquest into the shooting was followed by the publication of a lengthy internal garda inquiry into the incident.[111] A central focus of this report was the discrediting of information that did not reconcile with that presented by the Garda Síochána. Unsurprisingly, the report completely exonerated the Garda Síochána.

The ideological basis upon which state-agency policing is based, which emphasises professionalism and crime control capacity, coupled with the ex-aggerated assumption of "moral authority" throughout its history by the Garda Síochána, has produced within the force a hyper-sensitivity and defensiveness to criticism of any form from any quarter. For example, although the Garda Síochána has consistently sought greater powers or latitude in prosecuting crime it has seldom appreciated the democratic requirement for such measures to be tempered by a reliable and transparent accountability system. Public demands for

---

[108] *Sunday Tribune,* 9 January, 2000
[109] McNiffe *op. cit.,* p. 163
[110] Corless (2000), "Partners in crime", *Magill,* September
[111] Coroners Report into the shooting of John Carthy (2000), Garda Síochána Internal Inquiry (2000)

greater police accountability are generally treated with derision, and perceived as reflecting a public unappreciative of the difficulties encountered by the force. A constant backdrop employed by the Garda Síochána in resisting accountability demands is its national security role.

States of emergency

The political unrest in Northern Ireland throughout the last three decades has impacted on the southern criminal justice system in a profound way.[112] A greater availability of guns has contributed to an increase in armed robberies in the south. garda resources that might be used in relation to ordinary crime have been diverted in response to questions of state security, the preservation of which is also the responsibility of the Garda Síochána. The Garda Síochána has had to carry out commitments in relation to cross border policing. They have had to deal with kidnappings, assassinations, sieges, manhunts, hostage taking and jail riots related to the northern conflict. Extensive public disorder in the Republic following controversial events related to the conflict has often led to breakdowns in relations between the gardaí and the southern public. This occurred in January 1972 in response to the shooting of thirteen unarmed civil rights protesters by the British army in Derry. Significant unrest occurred in 1981 as ten republican prisoners died on hunger strike in prison in the north. The Garda Síochána also encountered significant public opposition as they attempted to enforce extradition treaty agreements between the British and Irish governments.

The extensive policing powers available to the Garda Síochána have often been enacted in response to the northern crisis and the declared state of emergency in the Republic. They range from the amendments to the Offences Against the State Act (1939) including the Emergency Powers Act (1976) which extended garda powers of arrest and detention, to the legislative changes of autumn (1998) which followed the Omagh bombing in the summer of that year. Many of the legal cases which have embroiled the Garda Síochána in controversy were related to the northern conflict. Indeed, the ongoing controversy surrounding gardaí in Donegal includes allegations that some members falsified IRA arms finds as a means of obtaining promotion within the force.

The most serious of all the controversies emanating from the northern conflict however and one which has remained festering silently underneath the surface of Irish politics for twenty-five years relates to the so-called Dublin-Monaghan car-bombings of 1974.[113] This atrocity constitutes the largest unsolved mass murder in the history of the state and the greatest single loss of life in the history of the

---

[112] O'Halpin (1999), *op. cit.*; see related comments by the Chairman of the National Crime Forum, National Crime Forum Report (1998), *op. cit.*

[113] Mullan, D. (2000), *The Dublin and Monaghan Bombings, the truth, the questions and the victims' stories,* Wolfhound

so-called "troubles". It was carried out by loyalist paramilitaries allegedly in collusion with elements of the British secret service. While allegations of collusion between the British army and loyalist assassins are not new,[114] serious questions remain regarding allegations of collusion between senior garda officers and the Royal Ulster Constabulary in covering up this crime.[115]

The northern conflict has also resulted in significant loss of life for members of the Garda Síochána. At least eleven members of the force have lost their lives in the course of their duty at the hands of republican paramilitaries. The most recent of these was the death of Detective Garda Jerry McCabe who was shot dead by members of the IRA in June 1996.

The conflict in Northern Ireland has also however served as a major impediment to police accountability, operating as a permanent reference point for the force in its attempts to deflect criticism. In this respect the northern conflict has facilitated the persistence of a culture of non-accountability within the force. Throughout the past thirty years of conflict, the Garda Síochána has consistently employed its state security role as a means of hampering open debate and discouraging criticism. This was reflected recently in the garda response to the media coverage of the shooting of John Carthy. The media, deciding that the public had a right to know the names of those involved in the Garda Emergency Response Unit that carried out the shooting, incurred the wrath of the editor of *Garda Review*, the official publication of the Garda Representative Association. The editorial accuses the media of forgetting "all too quickly that the members who were attached to the unit concerned are the members who on a daily basis offer this State protection from those who seek to destroy it".[116]

The persistence of a declared state of emergency, although more imaginary than real as far as the Republic of Ireland is concerned, has also resulted in politicians in Dáil Éireann being extremely reluctant to criticise the force.[117] Walsh,[118] in a study of policing debates in Dáil Éireann, quotes from a former minister for justice who was answering criticism of the garda in the context of a bungled kidnapping operation, to illustrate this point, "There is nothing between us and the dark night of terrorism but that force. While people in this house and people in the media may

---

[114] Walsh, D. (2000), *Bloody Sunday and the Rule of Law in Northern Ireland,* Gill & Macmillan ch. 7. Davies, N. (1999), *Ten-Thirty-Three: The Inside Story of Britain's Secret Killing Machine in Northern Ireland*

[115] Mullan *op. cit.,* p. 248

[116] *Irish Times,* 25 October, 2000

[117] Although, as has been shown above, both loyalist and republican paramilitary groupings have carried out armed actions in the Republic, no significant threat to the state has existed since the 1930s. In a recent policy statement however, the garda commissioner reaffirmed that "the security of the State is the primary concern of the Gardaí", *Communique* (1995), see discussion in O'Halpin *op. cit.,* p. 313 regarding the position adopted by the IRA in relation to the southern state

[118] Walsh (1998), *op. cit.,* p. 401

have freedom to criticise, the government of the day should not criticise the Garda Síochána. We all know that there were mistakes made in the operation but it is obscene that the Government and the minister responsible should be the first to lead the charge in the criticism of the Garda Síochána".

As has been argued above, the relationship between public representatives and the Garda Síochána has generally not been pursued by concerns about advancing public accountability or revealing the impotence of the policing arm of government. In this respect it is important to acknowledge that the state has an important interest in preserving the image of its own crime control ability. As Garland[119] points out, "Over time, the control of crime and the protection of citizens from criminal depredations have come to form a part of the promise which the state holds out to its citizen-subjects". Excessive criticism by government of the performance of the police is in itself therefore self-defeating. It is in this way that we can understand the dramatic reactions of the state on occasions such as the aftermath of the Omagh bombing. The legislative changes introduced in the wake of Omagh reflected more a need on behalf of the state to be seen to be doing something rather than a specific police need for the measures introduced. Another recent symbolic expression of state power in the Republic came about in the aftermath of the murder of crime correspondent Veronica Guerin in July 1996.

This murder led to the passage of one of the most draconian legislative measures ever introduced into ordinary Irish law. The introduction of seven-day detention powers for drug suspects mirrored the existing powers available under the Emergency powers Act of 1976 to deal with subversives. The Taoiseach of the day, in his support for these enhanced police powers, in a neat rhetorical flourish closed the illusory gap between emergency and ordinary police powers by suggesting that "drug dealing was a form of modern day terrorism".[120]

The Garda Síochána then, in its pursuit of increased powers or resources or legal changes, forms a punitive alliance with politicians seeking to sustain the illusion of sovereign crime control and to conceal the fact that they have little imaginative alternative. Come election time, politicians of all shades compete for votes by tapping into public fears of crime, each outdoing the other in "Law and Order" rhetoric. This punitive culture is increasingly being influenced by developments in the United States The recent importation from the US of "Zero Tolerance" of crime, however unsustainable in reality, proved particularly successful electorally. Here, and again in the Carthy case where the gardaí sought the assistance of the United States Federal Bureau of Investigation (FBI), we can witness the force looking to inappropriate and generally discredited policing models. This transatlantic seepage supports the prevailing punitive climate in Ireland.

---

[119] Garland (1996), *op. cit.*
[120] Government Press Release, 19 July, 1995

The failure of the punitive

It is widely accepted within criminological literature that traditional responses to crime, involving increases in police numbers, innovative technology or enhancement of police powers, have a minimal impact on crime rates.[121] Although developments in technology and internal re-structuring of the force can certainly enhance the efficiency of the police organisation as currently constituted, it will not necessarily have any significant impact on rates of crime. Innovative crime control tactics or strategies such as short-term intensive (zero tolerance) policing or the recent establishment of the Criminal Assets Bureau for example, established to target the proceeds of crime,[122] may have some impact in specific situations. But they are unlikely to have any impact on the overall levels of crime.

Developments in technology and the enhancement of police powers can however intrude significantly on civil liberties. Indeed the punitive response is often counter-productive as increased police powers exercised in a climate where results are expected can contribute to the abuse of such powers. The increased tension between police and community that result from such abuses further undermines the policing process which, to be effective, is dependent on public co-operation and assistance. Furthermore, what might be regarded as progress as far as the police are concerned might not necessarily reconcile with public require-ments. For example, the increased motorisation of policing has often broken down many of the traditional contacts between the police and the public thus contributing to a further alienation of the latter from the policing process.

The primary traditional ways the police deal with crime are neither reducing crime nor reassuring the public. The police devote most resources to traditional approaches that no longer work, if they ever did.[123]

The denial/punitive cycle continues however. The current government was elected on a strong "law and order" agenda, encapsulated in the slogan "zero tolerance of crime". Exaggerated claims that the government is winning the "fight against the drug barons" are supported by apparently plummeting crime statistics. In 1998, announcing a fourteen percent decrease in the rate of reported crime, the then Minister for Justice declared that "it showed our crime policy is working extremely well".[124]

As Garland[125] points out however, "Punitiveness may pose as a symbol of strength, but it should be interpreted as a symptom of weak authority". As crime is the product of deeper social forces, the Garda Síochána should not be seen as

---

[121] Bayley, D. (1994), *op. cit.*; Morgan and Newburn *op. cit.*
[122] McCutcheon, J.P. and Walsh, D. (1999), "Seizure of Criminal Assets: An Overview", 9 *Irish Criminal Law Journal,* pp. 127-132, Round Hall Sweet & Maxwell
[123] Bayley (1994), *op. cit.*
[124] *Irish Times,* 24 April, 1998
[125] Garland (1996), *op. cit.,* p. 445

a vehicle for reducing it substantially. The police, as Reiner[126] suggests, should be seen primarily as "managers of crime and keepers of the peace".

Adapting to the crisis-appeals to community

In recent times we have witnessed the development of a more pragmatic crime control strategy which, although never publicly acknowledged as such, rests on an increased awareness of the limitations of the crime control capacity of the state and gardaí and of the traditional responses to crime. One of the clearest manifestations of this countervailing tendency is an increased emphasis on inter-agency responses to crime and appeals for community participation in crime control.[127] Public attitudes about crime, their experience of victimisation and their proposed solutions are being sought through public consultation exercises such as the recently established National Crime Forum.[128] Actual community involvement in crime control is being sought through the establishment of models of community policing or Community Policing Fora.[129] A number of factors have contributed to this, as yet, tentative shift in focus.

Firstly, the costliness and apparent futility of the traditional approach to crime control have combined with the development of a more "managerial science" approach to policing. This emphasis on managerialism was reflected in the recent report of the steering group on the Efficiency and Effectiveness of the Garda Síochána[130]. This new approach, with its focus on policing as service delivery, is increasingly about emphasising the service requirements of the "consumer". A new discourse has emerged to complement this shift in emphasis. Policing is now about the quality of service delivery, and the efficient use of resources. The language and style of consumerism is reflected in the development of *Corporate Strategy Policy Documents, Market Research and Consumer Panels and Charters.* Police performance is increasingly to be judged in terms of the measurement of "outputs" rather than "outcomes".[131] Policing involves "the management of risk" as more modest policy objectives subtly displace the grander claims to crime control.

Secondly, we have seen a creeping acknowledgement of the futility of the traditional approach among government and senior garda officials. The Department of Justice, in a recent policy document alluded to the tentative nature of this shift stating that, "despite a growing acceptance that long-term solutions to crime will not be found by concentrating only on law and order responses, the

---

[126] Reiner (1997), *op. cit.,* p. 1037

[127] Crawford, A. (1997), *The Local Governance of Crime: Appeals to Community and Partnership*

[128] National Crime Forum Report (1998), *op. cit.*

[129] Connolly (1998), *op. cit.*; Connolly, J. (2000) (unpublished), *Report on the Establishment of a Community Policing Forum in North Inner City Dublin*

[130] Strategic Management Initiative (1997), *Report of the Steering group on the Efficiency and Effectiveness of the Garda Síochána,* Government Publications

[131] Garland (1996), *op. cit.*

implications of this insight are not, as yet, fully reflected in policy and strategy".[132] Thus the head of the Drug Squad could assert in 1995 that "we are committed to tough, unrelenting law enforcement although it is very clear to us that something more effective is required".[133]

This internal soul searching within the force has coincided with an ongoing process of the de-centralisation of political power within the state, a process that has inevitably begun to impact on the most centralised of all state agencies, the Garda Síochána. A central component of the new adaptive strategy has been a renewed emphasis on community participation in crime control. As has been discussed above however, since the eighteenth century, the role of the public has been clearly circumscribed in the policing process. In Ireland, much lauded models of Community Policing have promised a great deal but provided little by way of a real community input. Existing community policing schemes such as Neighbourhood Watch and Community Alert afford very little role to the community in determining policing policy and the manner in which local police resources are allocated.[134]

Current pressures for decentralisation of police power however are being most consistently articulated in terms of local community demands for more input into local police policy, particularly in the context of the drugs problem.[135] For communities that have experienced antagonistic police/community relations however, the public participation envisaged in the recent community policing strategies becomes contingent on the community having a real input into the priorities upon which this new policing arrangement is based.

An important factor which has complemented these local policing demands in recent times has been the increased receptiveness of many middle-ranking gardaí to such calls. In north inner city Dublin for example, members of the local drug squad have been particularly prominent in forging new relations with the local community. These individual initiatives have proven extremely important in addressing local alienation towards the police and developing more formalised links between the police and the local community. The recent establishment of a Community Policing Forum (CPF) in north inner city Dublin has been able to build upon these existing informal police community links which have been developed between local community representatives and individual gardaí in recent years.[136]

---

[132] Department of Justice (1997), *Tackling Crime, A Discussion Paper,* p. 144. The fact that this thoughtful and well-informed document emerged two months prior to the publication of the grossly authoritarian Strategic Management Initiative report *op. cit.* reveals the contradictory manner of current policy formation

[133] Quoted in O' Mahony (1996), *op. cit.,* p. 137

[134] Connolly (1998), *op. cit.*

[135] See Dublin Citywide Drugs Crisis Campaign (1995), *Responding Together*

[136] Connolly (1998), *op. cit.,* p. 192; Connolly (2000)

In 1995 an Inter Agency Drugs Project (IADP) was established. The primary objective of this two-year pilot programme was to bring statutory and voluntary agencies together with the local community in Dublin's north inner city in order to form a common approach to the drugs problem. In 1997 the IADP was merged with the government established local Drugs Task Force.[137] One of the primary recommendations of the IADP had been the establishment of a local Community Policing Forum. In 1999 a one-year pilot program to establish such a forum was initiated. After a process of intense consultation with the local community, involving over sixty local meetings and the distribution of over four thousand information leaflets, the first meeting of the CPF took place in a local garda station in December 1999. The primary aim of the CPF is to co-ordinate a common community/police and local authority strategy against the dealing of heroin in the immediate area.

Community policing for communities such as those of inner city Dublin should be seen as part of a shift towards community empowerment and should be understood in relation to the wider complexity of power relations. Community representatives are articulating local expectations that those who reside in such communities will have a say in the reasons why and the manner in which their area is policed. The Community Policing Forum in the north inner city is a pilot initiative and it remains at an early stage in its development. It is too early therefore to judge whether it represents such a transfer in policing power from state to community. Nevertheless, in the process of its formation, it has sought to overcome the historical tensions between the Garda Síochána and the local community and to create a sustainable model of community policing. The drugs crisis and the attendant phenomenon of local community self-policing has provided a backdrop to, and has served as a catalyst for, this new engagement of state and community. In the context of the CPF, and perhaps for the first time in the history of the state, the Garda Síochána is engaging in a process not only of intense consultation with the local community, but local people appear to be having some impact on the way in which policing resources are being deployed in their area.[138]

CONCLUSION

That the Garda Síochána emerged from the turbulence of civil war Ireland to

---

[137] Thirteen Drugs Task Forces had been established throughout the state as part of a new government initiative to tackle the drugs crisis. See O'Mahony, P. (1997), *Evaluation of north inner city Inter Agency Drugs Project,* Dublin, EHB and Copenhagen: WHO

[138] A local survey is currently being undertaken, one of the objectives of which is to ascertain local views of the Community Policing Forum, Connolly (unpublished), *Community Policing Forum Panel Survey-October/November 2000*

assume a largely unquestioned authority among the population is one of the remarkable achievements of Irish State building. In the process of its formation, the Garda Síochána would lay great emphasis on its unarmed status and, through a process of ideological transformation, would obtain the consent of the public. However, it inherited a model of policing which had been formed to maintain a distance between police and people. This model remains an anachronism in the circumstances of contemporary Ireland. Although the Garda Síochána retains a great deal of goodwill and support among the Irish population, its response to the public disquiet which has followed the shooting of John Carthy suggests that it is taking its position in Irish society for granted. In this respect, it appears to be hoist on its own petard, unable to appreciate the fickleness of a public increasingly sceptical about public institutions. The ongoing developments concerning the gardaí in Donegal have the potential to plunge the force into a crisis un-precedented in its history. Rather than adopting its traditionally defensive position in relation to the ongoing revelations there, engaging in media management for the purposes of damage limitation, the Garda Síochána now needs to be at the forefront of efforts to expose the full details of the issues involved. The development of such a culture of accountability will inevitably coincide with the creation of structures and processes of police accountability. The latter will result in the Garda Síochána becoming more exposed to independent scrutiny than heretofore, be it in the form of an independent Police Ombudsman or through the establishment of localised Community Policing Fora. It will be by endorsing this democratic imperative that the Garda Síochána will best secure its position as a public policing service into the future.

30

The Psychology of Police
Interrogation: The Kerry Babies Case*

Paul O'Mahony

SOCIAL PSYCHOLOGY AND THE LAW

Social psychology is the study of the individual in his or her social context. While this is an exceedingly wide brief, the academic discipline has tended to concentrate on a number of specific areas such as: the study of attitudes and prejudice; group processes, including leadership, power relations, decision-making and conformity to social norms; the conditions under which people attribute causal control of outcomes to human agents, including themselves; and the social constructive effects of individual and shared perceptions and expectations, that is how our expectations help confirm or even bring about what we anticipate. In recent decades, social learning theory (Bandura 1977) and cognitive science (Fiske and Taylor 1984) approaches and methods have become dominant in social psychology. These orientations place special emphasis on the study of the role of thoughts and feelings and thought processes, such as attention, memory and inference, in social behaviour, with a special focus on the errors and biases that have been found to be characteristic of human information processing.

Research by Brown et al (1977) indicates the pervasive influence of subtle but none the less powerful cognitive biases in the legal domain. They conducted an experiment in which subjects received either biased or unbiased instructions prior to examining a police line-up of suspects. The subjects were told that the

* Based in part on "The Kerry Babies Case: Towards a Social Psychological Analysis", in *Psychology at Trinity College Dublin*, (1992) special commemorative edition of *Irish Journal of Psychology* 13, 2

perpetrator either "might be" or "is" in the line-up. Seventy-eight percent of those that had the idea implanted that the perpetrator was definitely in the line-up (from which he was in fact absent) went on to identify an innocent person as a perpetrator. Only 33% of the people receiving the "might be" instructions did this. There can be little doubt that priming of this kind, ie implanted ideas which shape how the influenced person attends to, encodes, remembers and analyses new information, can have an extremely prejudicial effect.

Given the subject matter of social psychology, it is difficult to disagree with Saks and Hastie (1978) when they write that "there is a strikingly good fit between many of the behavioural questions with which lawyers, judges and litigants must deal and knowledge uncovered by social psychological research". This reflects not only the obvious general relevance of the study of human social behaviour to the law but also the fact that many of the processes at the heart of legal practice are psychological in nature. For example, the scientific study of persuasion (see, for example, Eagley and Chaiken 1993) is of central importance to an understanding of the criminal trial, involving as it does such diverse issues as what determines the credibility afforded to a witness by judge and jury, the biasing effects of certain forms of question and questioning, and the group dynamics involved in jury decision-making. Another area ripe for psychological study that has received considerable attention is the accuracy and reliability of eyewitness testimony, especially that relating to facial recognition and other forms of identification (eg Buckout 1974; Shapiro and Penrod 1986).

Potentially the most significant of all the areas, in which psychological knowledge can prove crucially relevant, is that of the police interrogation leading to an admission of guilt. A large majority of criminal convictions are achieved on foot of a confession or guilty plea. Law enforcement and the work of the criminal courts would be rendered immeasurably more difficult if all prosecutions were contested and if suspects' own freely given admissions of guilt were not acceptable as evidence of guilt. However, the criminal justice system's heavy reliance on confessions generates a real risk of miscarriages of justice.

This risk has long been recognised in law and there are many safeguards in criminal procedures designed to ensure that the police do not use methods of interrogation that tend to extract false admissions of guilt from the innocent. Torture and physical brutality are unambiguously prohibited in most jurisdictions and in international conventions. It is now generally agreed that physically oppressive methods can be as successful at eliciting confessions from the innocent as from the guilty. Modern criminal procedures and legal systems, at least in developed democracies, offer police suspects and detainees considerable protection from torture and other forms of oppression. Modern concepts of human rights and especially the key notion of presumption of innocence underpin the criminal justice system in Ireland and have gradually been implemented as a result of increasing repugnance towards the inherent injustice and arbitrariness of previously widely practised methods such as trial by ordeal and the third degree form of torture invented by the Inquisition (Ruthven 1978). Prolonged isolation, starvation, sleep deprivation and threats of harm or promises of immunity or leniency are also explicitly recognised as unacceptable interrogation techniques. These methods are outlawed because of their intrinsic abhorrence and the relatively strong likelihood that they will promote false admissions and lead to wrongful conviction and punishment.

In Ireland the regime governing police interrogations is defined by section 4 of the Criminal Justice Act 1984, section 30 of the Offences against the State Act 1939 and the Criminal Justice (Drug Trafficking) Act 1996. Under the former Act a person suspected of an offence punishable by five years or more imprisonment can be held for six hours for interrogation extendable by a further six hours at the direction of a police superintendent. There are rules governing the amount of rest, food and drink that must be provided to the suspect; the number of officers who can be involved in the interrogation; and access to a solicitor. While these same rules apply under the Offences against the State Act 1939 and the Criminal Justice (Drug Trafficking) Act 1996, the allowable period for detention under these Acts is extendable to seven days and the right to silence is restricted in certain defined circumstances.

Apart from the provision for seven-day detention and restrictions on the right to silence, this regime of constraints on police interrogation methods must be considered weak, because it does not insist on audio- or video-taping of interviews and because it does not provide the suspect with a right to have his or her solicitor present throughout the interrogation. According to one senior counsel (White 2000), "the appalling disregard demonstrated by the present regime of incommunicado interrogation of persons in police custody in the Irish Republic for, first, the protection of the dignity of the citizen as a human person, and, secondly, for truth in the criminal process, is apparent from a comparison of the protection afforded suspects during interrogation at English law and in the United States". The main additional protection to which he refers is the right to have a lawyer present during interrogation, if necessary a state-funded, independent lawyer. The significance of ensuring more effective regulation to prevent the production of false admissions in police custody is greatly increased by the fact that under Irish law a person can be convicted solely on the basis of a confession, even if he or she later retracts this confession, claiming that it was the result of coercion or trickery, and even if there is a complete absence of corroborating evidence.

INTERROGATION METHODS, FALSE ADMISSIONS AND MISCARRIAGE OF JUSTICE

In Ireland, people should be especially sensitive to the human rights dimension of police interrogation because of the infamous "Irish" miscarriages of justice in

Britain, such as the Guildford Four and Birmingham Six cases. These cases and others like them were an ironic confirmation of Lord Denning's "appalling vista" of a level of law enforcement abuse and corruption that, in his view, could not be accepted as true precisely because of what this would imply about the quality of English and Welsh criminal justice. These cases convulsed the legal system in England and Wales, leading eventually to the Royal Commission on Criminal Justice (1993). However, in Ireland we have had numerous home-grown examples of miscarriages of justice related to the conduct of police interrogations such as the Lynch case, the Sallins Train Robbery case, and the Kerry Babies case, the latter of which gained considerable international attention.

These cases have at various times led to acute public disquiet about police interrogation methods. A report by Justice Barra O'Briain (1980) expressed concern over the fact that up to 80% of serious crimes were being solved by self-incriminating statements made in garda custody, statements which would often later be withdrawn. This report made useful recommendations but was largely ignored. Brewer and colleagues (1988) have described this report as "little more than a sop to public opinion whose advice was almost totally ignored" and they have suggested that "the price for such complacency was clearly paid by the Garda Síochána in the Kerry Babies case". The Kerry Babies Case, in which the police, using a variety of more or less subtle but none the less effective psychological tactics, were able to persuade every member of an ordinary farming family to falsely admit, in considerable descriptive detail, to involvement in the murder and the well-planned disposal of a baby, led to a large-scale judicial inquiry and a detailed published report (Report of Tribunal 1985). Unfortunately this long, expensive, intense, and contentious tribunal was a major missed opportunity. It achieved little because it paid scant attention to the role of subtle forms of psychological coercion and because it did not confront directly the specific faults and dangers of police interrogation as practised in Ireland and as clearly exposed by the case. Because of its central importance this case will be examined in greater detail below.

More recent cases indicate that the problem is still with us and still requires strong remedial action. The successful appeals of Peter Pringle and Vincent Connell in 1995, particularly the latter, since it refers to a more recent interrogation, are worrying. Pringle was released after serving fifteen years in prison for the capital murder of a garda. He was released following an appeal which found that Pringle's conviction was "unsafe and unsatisfactory". A retrial was ordered but was later dropped by the state's prosecution service. Pringle's original conviction had relied fundamentally on the interpretation of a few words, which the police said he did, but Pringle said he did not, utter. The police said he had told them: "I know that you know I was involved", but Pringle claimed that he had actually said: "I know that you think that I was involved". It was a considerable help to Pringle's case that a Supreme Court judge had written an extraordinary letter to him in prison stating that he always believed Pringle had been treated unfairly and stating that "the evidence was not sufficient to convict you of murder". This case, which hinges on one disputed word, provides an eloquent and unanswerable argument for the routine taping of interviews as at least one part of the solution to the general problem.

The Court of Criminal Appeal quashed the conviction of Vincent Connell for the murder of Patricia Furlong on the grounds that the statement of admission, which was the only substantial evidence against Connell, was taken in breach of custody regulations and statutory prohibitions about length of interrogation. Several of the interviews lasted well over the four hours permitted by law. The court also found that Connell had been denied proper access to a solicitor and found it "inexcusable" that a garda cousin of Connell's had been lied to when he enquired whether a solicitor had made contact with Connell. The court was of the opinion that the accused might well have avoided making self-incriminating statements, if the proper procedures had been adhered to.

The case of Damien Marsh, accused of stabbing an English tourist to death on O'Connell Bridge, St Patrick's Day 1994, demonstrates that garda interrogation methods remain under a cloud of suspicion and that the need for some form of electronic monitoring and independent regulation remains urgent. According to the gardaí, Marsh had made a confession of guilt. However, the admissibility of the supposed confession was challenged by the senior counsel for the defence. It emerged that the original copy of Marsh's statement had disappeared from garda files and had not been recovered. But most significantly, the two gardaí present during the interrogation totally contradicted each other in their evidence to the court. At the heart of the matter, one officer claimed that the other had taken down Marsh's statement line for line, all the time stopping to read back to Marsh what he had said. However, the other officer, in his evidence, purported to have written nothing whatsoever in the course of the interview, completing the written version of the statement at a later time. After this shambles of garda self-contradiction, it is not surprising that the prosecution simply dropped the case against Marsh.

In another recent case, *The People v Ward*, the Special Criminal Court ruled alleged confessions inadmissible in evidence, pointing to police manipulation of visits to the suspect by family members as "a cynical ploy which it was hoped might break down the accused". Mr Justice Barr, delivering the judgement of the court, stated that "the court is not making a finding that the verbal admissions were in fact planted by the police as alleged, but the evidence suggests such a possibility and the accused must be given the benefit of the element of doubt which exists".

The most extraordinary recent case is that of Dean Lyons, who admitted, under the pressure of police interrogation, to the murder of two women living in a house attached to Grangegorman psychiatric hospital in Dublin. The murders, which involved mutilation and stabbing, were particularly brutal and occurred on 6 March 1997. Dean Lyons was arrested on 25 July and, after several hours of questioning by detectives, made statements of admission that led the DPP to charge him with the murders. Following two further similarly brutal murders in Roscommon on 16 August 1997, Mark Nash was arrested. He admitted to the Roscommon killings and also volunteered statements admitting to the Grangegorman murders, at the same time providing accurate and highly specific detail about the house and the way the women were killed. This was information that had not been released to the public.

Dean Lyons, who had a history of psychiatric problems and was using heroin and living rough in the Grangegorman area at the time of his arrest, was in prison on the Grangegorman murder charges at the time when Nash was arrested and confessed to the Grangegorman killings. Lyons remained in prison for seven more months until the Chief State Solicitor eventually withdrew the murder charges against him.

The findings of an internal garda inquiry into the case have not been published; nor has there been any explanation of how accurate details of the Grangegorman murders came to be in Lyons' statement to the police. While Nash has been convicted of the Roscommon murders, he has not been charged with the Grangegorman murders. Dean Lyons has since died in England, having left Ireland, according to his family, because he feared the garda.

A disquieting aspect of this case is that part of Lyons' interrogation was video-taped, but obviously to no good effect. According to Jim Cusack, Security Correspondent of *The Irish Times*, the tape of the interviews shows Lyons to be confused and incoherent and ready to admit to every charge put to him. He was suffering acutely from heroin withdrawal syndrome during these interviews. Later, further statements were taken without being recorded on audio- or video-tape. It is these statements that contained incriminating detail about the murders. This case clearly indicates that the taping of interrogations is not a perfect shield against the machinations of corrupt or over-zealous and under-critical police interrogators. As White argues, the additional protection of the presence of a lawyer for the duration of interrogation is required, most urgently when the suspect is highly suggestible or vulnerable because of addiction or other physical and emotional problems.

THE KERRY BABIES CASE

The Kerry Babies case concerned two babies. One, the Cahirciveen baby, was found, dead from multiple stab wounds, amongst rocks on a County Kerry beach near Cahirciveen on 14 April 1984. In the early hours of the previous day, Joanne

Hayes had given birth to another baby at her home about fifty miles away. Her baby had not survived the night and its body had been wrapped in bags and hidden in a water hole on the Hayes farm. This was not known at the time of the discovery of the Cahirciveen baby. Unusually for a case of infanticide, the Investigation Section of the Technical Bureau from Dublin became involved in and eventually ran the inquiry into the death of the Cahirciveen baby. By the end of April, the police had learnt of Joanne Hayes' pregnancy and the unexplained circumstances of its ending and suspicion with respect to the Cahirciveen Baby now centred on Joanne Hayes.

On 1 May Joanne and her sister, two brothers, mother and aunt were interrogated. In the course of these quite lengthy interrogations all family members signed statements which amounted to confessions of involvement in the murder and disposal of the Cahirciveen baby. Some of the admisssions were of considerable detail, including the identification of a kitchen knife as the murder weapon. On the night of 1 May Joanne Hayes was charged with the murder of the Cahirciveen baby.

Garda evidence does not dispute the fact that for many hours before confessing to the murder of the Cahirciveen baby, Joanne Hayes had forcefully proclaimed her innocence of that murder, yet had admitted to the birth and death of her own baby and accurately described its location on the Hayes farm. On the day of the interrogations, several gardaí searches were made of the Hayes farm, but these were perfunctory and failed to find the baby's body. Joanne Hayes was not permitted to accompany these searches even though she asked to do so many times. The baby was eventually discovered on the evening of 2 May.

Despite the unexpected discovery of Joanne Hayes' baby the police investigators did not abandon their conclusion that Joanne Hayes had murdered the Cahirciveen baby. Their investigation of the crime continued to focus on Joanne Hayes, relying on the assumption that she had in fact given birth to twins, one of whom was the Cahirciveen Baby. This approach did not change, even when it emerged that the Cahirciveen Baby was of blood group A, whilst Joanne Hayes and Jeremiah Locke, who was generally agreed to be the father of Joanne Hayes' baby, were of blood group O. The only substantial evidence for the twins theory was the statements of the Hayes family which spoke of a baby being stabbed and thrown into the sea, a baby clearly different from the one found on the farm. Although the Hayes family statements mention only one baby, if their statements about the stabbed baby were true, the police reasoned, Joanne Hayes must have had two babies that night.

The illogicality of this reasoning escaped notice or was ignored for almost five months, during which the gardaí steadfastfully adhered to their belief in Joanne Hayes' guilt in the murder of the Cahirciveen baby, until the Kerry State Solicitor received a letter from the office of the Director of Public Prosecutions, dated 20 September, which said: "This amazing case has been carefully studied ... The accused stand charged in respect of a baby which, on the evidence, was not the baby of Joanne Hayes. Even if she were charged in respect of a baby unknown you could not possibly run a prosecution on this evidence. All charges should be withdrawn at the first opportunity". On 10 October all charges were withdrawn.

THE TRIBUNAL

On 13 December 1984 the Minister for Justice nominated Mr Justice Kevin Lynch as the sole member of a tribunal, which was to inquire into

1) the facts and circumstances leading to the preferment, on 1 May 1984, of criminal charges against Joanne Hayes, Edmund Hayes, Michael Hayes, Kathleen Hayes and Bridie Fuller, Dromcunnig Lower, Abbeydorney, County Kerry, in connection with the death of an unnamed male infant and subsequent events which led to the withdrawal of those charges at Tralee District Court on 10 October 1984

2) related allegations made by Joanne Hayes, Mary Hayes, Edmund Hayes and Michael Hayes in written statements to their solicitor on 23 October 1984 and by Kathleen Hayes in a written statement to her solicitor on 24 October 1984 concerning the circumstances surrounding the questioning and the taking of statements from those persons on 1 May 1984

3) any matters connected with or relevant to the matters aforesaid which the tribunal considers it necessary to investigate in connection with their inquiries into the matters mentioned in 1) and 2).

The establishment of the tribunal followed the failure of an internal garda inquiry to allay widespread public and political disquiet about the case. However, the broader historical context is also relevant. Since 1977 allegations had been published in the press about the operation of a "heavy gang" within the Garda Síochána. This "heavy gang" was frequently identified with the Investigation Branch of the Technical Bureau, the same unit which was involved in the Kerry Babies case. An indication of the serious concern over these kind of issues was the statement in an internal report of 1977 by the then Deputy Commissioner of the garda that: "One of the main weaknesses of the force today is our anxiety to impress; to be the first with the news good or bad, resulting in jumping to conclusions and then trying to find facts to support them". This statement turns out to be an uncannily apt description of police reasoning in the Kerry Babies case.

In 1979 the Supreme Court ordered the release from prison of Christy Lynch, who had been convicted of murder on the basis of his own confession and had served three years. The Supreme Court concluded that Lynch had been subjected to "oppressive questioning", which had effectively pressured him into making a false confession. On the face of it the Kerry Babies case echoed the Lynch case, offering even more startling and clearcut evidence of the systematic extraction of false confessions by gardaí. It is against this background that the tribunal was set up with the investigation of gardaí interrogation methods as one of its most obvious priorities.

The tribunal sat for 77 days, 34 in Tralee and 43 in Dublin. It heard 109 witnesses who were asked a total of 61,000 questions. The tribunal itself became a *cause celebre*, provoking a great deal of critical comment and protest, most especially because of its exposure of the personal and sexual life of Joanne Hayes and because of its adherence to an adversarial model, which pitted the Hayes family against the gardaí in a legal contest akin to a criminal trial. The journalist Gene Kerrigan (1985), an astute observer of the process, wrote that "the first and paramount term of reference was that an inquiry be held into the methodology and behaviour of the gardaí in obtaining the confessions. Instead the tribunal became a contest between the gardaí and the family in which every weapon, no matter how absurd, was allowed".

Legal representatives of the gardaí expended much time and energy in discrediting the Hayes family and attempting to undermine their evidence. In addition gardaí witnesses were allowed to develop, on the witness stand, lines of thought, which attempted to make the known and agreed facts of the case more consistent with the gardaí view that the Hayes family statements about the Cahirciveen Baby were largely true. These theories relied on the possibility that Joanne Hayes had had twins and they included the superfecundation theory, which held that there were two separate fathers, one of each baby, and the "Azores Baby" theory, which held that Joanne Hayes had had twins of which Jeremiah Locke was the father, but the Cahirciveen Baby was not one of those twins, so that there was a third, as yet undiscovered, baby murdered and disposed of in the manner described by the family. Justice Lynch himself was later to call these theories "unlikely, far-fetched and self-contradictory".

THE FINDINGS OF THE TRIBUNAL

Mr Justice Lynch found that Joanne Hayes was not the mother of the Cahirciveen Baby. However, he decided that she had killed her own new-born child. The justice described what he supposed happened as follows: "Joanne Hayes got into a panic and as the baby cried again she put her hands around its neck and stopped it crying by choking it and the baby did not breathe again ... (she) used the bath brush from the bathroom to hit the baby to make sure it was dead". The justice also found that the child's birth and the manner of its death were known to the whole family and that they conspired to keep it a secret. He concluded that Joanne Hayes alone had concealed the dead baby on the family farm and that she had not told any member of the family what she had done with it, so that, when the finding of the Cahirciveen Baby was described in the newspapers, the Hayes family members, apart from Joanne, were worried that it might actually be Joanne Hayes' baby. The Hayes family denials of Joanne Hayes' pregnancy in the early part of their interrogations on 1 May caused, according to Justice Lynch, the gardaí's strong suspicions of the involvement of the Hayes family with the Cahirciveen Baby to progress into "positive and certain belief".

The justice decided that there was no assault on or physical abuse of any member of the Hayes family by any garda. He describes the younger Hayes family members' confessions with respect to the Cahirciveen Baby as "not true in relation to involvement with that baby". However, they do contain, according to his view, "large elements of the truth of what happened to the Tralee Baby (Joanne Hayes) transposed to the Cahirciveen Baby, with additions as to the stabbing and a journey to fit involvement with the Cahirciveen Baby". The statements of Joanne's mother and aunt he describes as largely true. But they refer, he believes, to the Tralee Baby, not, as the gardaí believed, to the Cahirciveen Baby. Because of this conclusion, Justice Lynch finds no need to explain why the mother and aunt signed their statements, but he offers four reasons why the younger family members signed what he calls their confessions:

1) the obvious belief of the gardaí in the involvement of the Hayes family with the Cahirciveen Baby gave rise to pressure on them to confess to such involvement". (This links with the justice's conclusion that the justifiable suspicions of the gardaí were converted into certainty by the fact that the Hayes family all lied at the start of their interrogations.)
2) the Hayes family's belief that they were in custody and not free to leave "until they should have satisfied the gardaí as to their role in the birth and death of the Cahirciveen Baby" added to the pressure on them to confess
3) the failure of the gardaí to find Joanne Hayes' baby on the Hayes farm "put further pressure on her to confess that her baby was not on the lands and therefore must be the Cahirciveen Baby"
4) as a result of "their guilty consciences relating to the birth and death of the Tralee Baby".

It is the clear implication of this reasoning that the gardaí are exonerated of any serious, systematic manipulation of the Hayes family, leading to false confessions. The justice here appears to address the core question of false confessions, but he offers a version of events that, at least superficially, actually explains them away. The responsibility for the false confessions, according to this view, is firmly placed on the Hayes family itself. The justice severely criticises the gardaí for allowing the family to believe they were under arrest and for the shabby conduct of the search of the farm, but the former is not criticised as a deliberate ploy to enhance the chances of obtaining confessions and the latter is regarded as an incidental, if unfortunate, failure, which inadvertently added to the pressure on Joanne Hayes to confess.

On close analysis, this explanation of the false confessions must be dismissed as superficial. It is nothing more than a restatement of the fact that the gardaí belief that the Hayes family were guilty put pressure on the Hayes family to confess. There is no examination of the various forms this pressure must actually have taken. The factors considered by the justice may help explain why the Hayes family members yielded to pressure, but they do not clarify the nature of that pressure.

In fact, the version of events offered by Mr Justice Lynch can be seen as an attempt to explain how it was not impossible for the Hayes family to sign false confessions without being subjected to police techniques, which promote the signing of confessions whether true or false. Mr Justice Lynch provides this "possibility explanation", albeit of limited plausibility, at terrible cost to the Hayes family. In O'Halloran's (1985) words, Mr Justice Lynch's report is "utterly damning" of the Hayes family. Largely on the basis of supposition and with minimal evidential support, he finds that the Hayes family are complicit in the killing of a baby and that they conspired to make false allegations against the gardaí and to perjure themselves before the tribunal. Meanwhile, according to Brewer and colleagues (1988), the tribunal "failed to come up with an answer to the central question of how a whole family had confessed to a murder it had not committed or even known about ... which leaves the problem of the Garda Síochána's accountability as one of the gravest for state-society relations in the Republic".

RELEVANT PSYCHOLOGICAL RESEARCH: LYING

The matter of lies and the related question of the credibility of witnesses are central to the Tribunal of Inquiry into the Kerry Babies Case. The fact that the Hayes family lied from the outset of the garda interrogations was of great moment. According to Justice Lynch, these lies were obvious to the gardaí and immediately convinced them that the Hayes family were guilty in respect of the Cahirciveen Baby. These lies, then, were a crucial part of the process which eventually led to the signing of false confessions. These early lies also stereo-typed the family as liars and so helped undermine their general credibility throughout the course of the tribunal. Special significance was placed on the fact that the family would lie so readily. Justice Lynch stated that he was satisfied that a jury, trying a case based on the family's allegations against the gardaí, would have no hesitation in rejecting all charges because of "the broad unreliability so far as truthfulness is concerned, of the Hayes family". A psychiatrist, called before the tribunal as an expert witness for the gardaí, went so far as to label or, as perhaps he would claim, to diagnose Joanne Hayes a "psychopathic liar". This psychiatrist had never examined Joanne Hayes or even spoken to her.

Lying and credibility are topics that have received substantial attention in the psychological research literature. The early classic study of children's dishonesty in the classroom by Hartshorne and May (1928) set the tone for much of the work that followed. This was to emphasise the ubiquity and mundane naturalness of lying and the fact that it is tied closely to features of the situation rather than to a particular stable personality disposition. As Saxe (1991) points out: "Each of us has ways of justifying lies, and in part, the behaviour (lying) results from seeing the world in a way that makes the behaviour acceptable". Even Justice Lynch can be accused of a minor but significant deception when introducing himself to Joanne Hayes' Aunt Bridie prior to taking evidence from her in Tralee General Hospital. He said "The Dáil, Senate and Government have asked me to investigate, as best I can, the birth of your niece Joanne Hayes' baby in Abbeydorney last April". This is an obvious distortion of what the Justice was asked to do and is a clear demonstration that telling the truth, the whole truth and nothing but the truth is no easy matter. However, if lying, in the broad sense of not always telling the truth and only the truth, is a commonplace, it is inevitable that our capacity to detect lying will be severely restricted and that the implications one can reliably draw from uncovered lies will often be quite limited.

Lewis et al (1989) studied three-year-old children, who were instructed not to peek at a toy, while the experimenter was out of the room. On later questioning, many children lied about peeking at the toy and the researchers concluded that even at a very young age children are socialised into deception, learning to successfully mask their emotions in order to hide the lie. They remarked that "deception is a frequent activity in the life of individuals. It may take the simple form of agreeing with someone with whose opinion, in fact, we do not agree or other forms such as lying about a serious transgression".

Ekman and O'Sullivan (1991) have cleverly exposed the limitations, as detectors of lies, of a variety of professional groups, including judges, psychiatrists and policemen. Subjects in this study were shown videotapes of people either lying or telling the truth in describing their feelings. Only one occupational group was able to discern liars at a rate better than chance. Interestingly, the successful group were members of the US Secret Service, who spend much of their time interrogating suspects who have made threats of violence against the US president. According to Ekman and O'Sullivan, most secret service suspects are being truthful when they deny, during interrogation, that their threats against the president are serious. The secret service agents are focused especially on signs of deceit, because their goal is to identify the rare person whose denial is a lie. The members of the regular criminal justice professions, on the contrary, believe that everyone lies to them and so they have not developed special skills at the detection of lying. While mistrust of a suspect's denials and techniques to undermine denials are essential professional tools of the policeman, it would appear that policemen as well as judges are not necessarily well qualified to assess credibility per se.

Of course, credibility is not synonymous with truthfulness. A highly credible person is a person who will tend to be believed whether or not they are telling the truth. The determinants of credibility and its influence have been of major interest to social psychologists studying persuasion and in recent years there has been considerable research on credibility within the court setting. Mehabrian and Williams (1969) have compiled some of the qualities associated with credibility in witnesses and the following have been found to enhance the believability of testimony: a conversational tone, a moderate to slightly rapid rate of speech, a lower pitch, a variety of intonation, eye contact, moderate use of gestures and a somewhat extroverted style. The important point is that, while the factors that enhance credibility may or may not in actuality be correlates of truthfulness, they can never have a direct or intrinsic relationship with truth. They are connected with persuasiveness, not veracity. When assessing credibility it needs to be borne in mind that a practiced and sophisticated witness may well be aware of the effects of factors such as lower pitch and may be capable of cynically engineering them in order to construct a fraudulent credibility.

Justice Lynch certainly uncovered lies told by both the Hayes family and the gardaí. However, his treatment of the lies of these two groups could not have been more different. The Hayes family were involved in "bare-faced lies" and "blatant perjury". The lies of the gardaí he called "an exaggeration over and above the true position" or "a gilding of the lily" or "wishful thinking elevated to the status of hard fact". The most important of the garda deceptions was what Justice Lynch called an agreed line of defence before the tribunal which "required every garda witness to say that he or she still firmly believed that Joanne Hayes was the mother of the Cahirciveen Baby". This collective deception was very important to the gardaí and had great benefits for them. It served two purposes: first, it made an implicit claim to the effect that there had been no false confessions, a claim which enabled the legal counsel for the gardaí to divert the tribunal down many fruitless avenues in the search for evidence that this claim might somehow be tenable; and second, it suggested that the gardaí were genuinely unaware of any undue pressure on the Hayes family, for otherwise how could they be so convinced that the confessions were in fact true.

Presumably Justice Lynch treated what he himself thought to be a form of garda conspiracy so leniently because he did not wish to challenge the general credibility of the gardaí. He did not wish to label and condemn the gardaí as liars, as he had the Hayes family, because then he might find himself in a position where he could only believe the gardaí when they were giving evidence against themselves. For, in an highly revealing passage, Justice Lynch says of the Hayes family that the fact that they had lied did not mean they would always lie, for "insofar as they say things which are not in their interest, they are probably telling the truth because they would not falsely and unnecessarily expose themselves to criticism and unpleasant consequences by lies against their own interest". The extreme irony of this folk psychological theory is that it is just such inexplicable, false and unnecessary confessions against their own interests by the Hayes family that the tribunal had been set up to investigate.

One of the fundamental tenets of social psychology is the centrality of the individual point of view, the unique significance of the personal perspective. An event is perceived and experienced differently by the different participants involved. It follows that the participants' subjective accounts of the event will often conflict, yet remain sincere and in a key sense valid. This concept is highly relevant to the interpretation of lying, for, as Saxe (1991) writes, "understanding the lie from the perspective of the miscreant (ie the situation from his or her vantage point) may be essential in order to deal with it". Empathy with the liar is necessary in order to ascertain why a lie was told, but also to understand how what appears to be a blatant lie may in fact be an individual's sincerely held, if idiosyncratic and questionable, belief. The tribunal's confused, moralistic stance on lies demonstrated a lack of understanding of the banality of lying and a lack of willingness to empathise with the liar, unless, that is, the liars were gardaí.

INTERROGATION AND TECHNIQUES OF PERSUASION

While a psychological perspective on lying would have been invaluable to the tribunal, the psychological findings on persuasion, compliance and suggestibility are clearly indispensable for the proper understanding of false confessions and, arguably, should have comprised the main substance of concern for the tribunal. There has not been a large amount of research on the specific mechanisms governing false confessions under the pressure of police interrogation, presumably because of restricted access and the inherent secrecy of the process. However, there is much research on related areas which provide key insights into how people can be quite easily manipulated into making false confessions.

Of course, it is universally accepted that torture and threats of violence can intimidate people into signing false confessions, but this is not what is at issue here. The present concern is with more subtle, psychological methods of persuasion, such as those which can undermine a suspect's grasp of reality and lead to a situation, such as Joanne Hayes describes, where, "I didn't think my mind was my own ... in the end I was convinced I had done it (stabbed the Cahirciveen Baby)".

The classic social psychological experiments of Asch (1956) and Milgram (1974) have an obvious relevance. Asch's work indicates that pressures to conform with the group can cause individuals to agree to patently false statements, even those that go against the evidence of their own eyes. In an experimental context where six confederates of the researcher expressed patently false judgments about the comparative length of lines in the presence of a subject who had yet to make his or her judgment, Asch found that many subjects acquiesced to the pressure to conform and agreed with the evidently wrong majority judgment. People are, generally speaking, reluctant to express a view contrary to that of the majority. Partly, this is because we tend to look to others for confirmation of our understanding of the world and actively seek consistency between our own views and those of others and, therefore, can be easily brought to question the accuracy of our own views. Partly, it is because humans crave the acceptance and approval of others and are loath to risk rejection because of what they fear may be seen as eccentric, unacceptably different views.

Milgram's work showed that in certain structured situations most people can be induced to comply with the instructions of an authority figure, even when called upon to behave in a manner of which they would normally strongly disapprove (eg inflicting a dangerous electric shock on someone who fails a simple learning task). The Asch and Milgram studies, and the many inspired by them, serve to emphasise the immensely important role of situational factors and social expectations in determining individual behaviour. In legal settings, Loftus and Palmer (1974) have shown how even minor situational manipulations of seemingly trivial variables can have momentous effects. They varied the intensity of the descriptive term used to ask a question about a collision of cars and found that this had a marked effect on the estimate of vehicle speed. The use of the words "contacted", "hit", and "'smashed" resulted in average estimates of 31.8, 34, and 40.8 mph, respectively.

While these studies provide evidence about the social influence processes which lead people in general to conform with group views or submit to the will of authority figures, Kassin and Wrightsman (1985) have made a useful distinction among three different types of false confession, which they name voluntary, coerced-compliant and coerced-internalised. Voluntary false confessions are not central to the concerns of this paper because they are not a function of police behaviour; but they are obviously an important part of the backdrop to forced false confessions. Many people have falsely confessed to crimes, most often particularly infamous crimes. For example, two hundred people voluntarily confessed to the kidnapping of the Lindbergh baby. As Kassin (1997) argues, there are many possible motives for such a confession, which reside largely within the individual, including "a pathological need for fame, acceptance, recognition, or self-punishment".

Coerced-compliant false admissions, on the other hand, are made in response to a situation in which considerable pressure is placed on the suspect. The suspect is still clear in his own mind that he is innocent, but is brought to the point where he will more or less rationally decide to falsely admit to guilt in order to escape an extremely aversive situation or gain a promised reward. According to Kassin (1997), these kind of false confessions are the easiest to understand "as they arise when a suspect comes to believe that the short-term benefits of confessing (eg being left alone, fed or released) outweigh the long-term costs (eg prosecution, loss of reputation, incarceration)". Bordens (1984) has provided evidence for this process in role-playing studies, in which subjects playing the part of an innocent suspect have often been found to plead guilty in order to cut their losses. The intrinsic benefits of compliance, including winning approval and achieving at least a short-lived resolution of the distressing conflict between the suspect's and the interrogators' inconsistent views of the world are also strong motivating factors, which facilitate a coerced-compliant false confession. While torture and brutal treatment are obviously likely to lead to coerced-compliant false confessions, the key point is that the deliberate creation of an unpleasant and tense psychological environment and the subtle manipulation of the suspect can also produce them with ease.

Gudjonsson (1992) and Kassin (1997) have analysed police manuals on interrogation, including *Criminal Interrogation and Confessions* (Inbau et al 1986), the most popular and influential of such manuals. These manuals clearly advise police on how to exploit their control of the interrogation situation in order to provide powerful opportunities to condition and shape the suspect's response without resorting to physical oppression. In the first place *Criminal Interrogation and Confessions* recommends that interrogations take place in a physical environment that promotes psychological feelings of social isolation, sensory deprivation and lack of control. Inbau et al then describe a nine-step procedure, instructing interrogators to, on the one hand, confront the suspect with his guilt, interrupting all statements of denial, and, on the other, offer the suspect sympathy and plausible, face-saving explanations for the alleged crime. The manual explicitly recommends the deliberate manipulation of the suspect so as to minimise the perceived negative consequences of confession and maximise the experience of anxiety resulting from continued denial.

It should also be borne in mind that suspects may be unaware of the practical and legal consequences of a false confession. However, the police are well aware that they need only apply enough pressure to obtain admissions in the interrogation situation and do not have to be too concerned about future retractions, which can convincingly be attributed to a cynical legal ploy on the part of the accused and defence counsel. The suspect may mistakenly think, at the time of making admissions, that their confession can be easily and completely nullified by later retraction. However, the law and jurors tend to place greater weight on a confession than on a retraction. A confession, which can and does lead to a serious charge such as murder, appears to be more genuine because of the very seriousness of the consequences of the confession. This reasoning mirrors the process by which Justice Lynch placed more faith in statements by the Hayes family that were obviously against their own interests. However, the appearance of genuineness is spurious because it relies on hindsight and does not take proper account of the mental processes of and the pressures on the accused at the precise time he made the admissions. Furthermore, many suspects may be unaware that, in Ireland, an accused can be convicted solely on the basis of a retracted confession.

Actual police practice can involve fraudulent claims that the police are in possession of evidence which incriminates the suspect or that an accomplice has implicated the suspect or other forms of trickery which heighten the suspect's sense of hopelessness, confusion and distress and thereby correspondingly increase the attraction of a confession with its prospect of immediate release from a bizarre and terrifying situation. Leo (1996) has examined 182 live and videotaped interrogations in Californian police stations and has described the "systematic use of deception, manipulation and betrayal of trust in the process of eliciting a suspect's confession". While police refusal to accept any account of events that does not involve an admission of guilt is at the core of this methodology, the approach is most powerful and most likely to procure false admissions when conjoined with a seemingly sympathetic reconfiguring of the consequences of the confession that overstates the benefits and understates the costs.

The third type of false confession, the coerced-internalised, results from a process akin to the religious cult conversion attempt or the high intensity sales pitch or the "brain-washing" of American prisoners of war during the Korean War, all of which have been extensively studied (Cialdini 1988). Lifton's (1963) analysis of the overall strategy of thought reform methods in Korea helps explain intensive methods of interrogation. He has described techniques which lead to depersonalisation, to a weakening of an individual's prior frame of reference, and eventually to a state of hypersuggestibility. Lifton's analysis helps explain how a suspect might sign a false confession, not only as a matter of transient, superficial compliance under psychological duress, but also because he himself has become convinced of the truth of the allegations against him. The very act of making false admissions itself reinforces the process because especially under conditions of uncertainty we look to what we ourselves are saying and how we are behaving as an essential guide to what we can believe of ourselves (see, for example, Bem's theory of self-perception 1972). Furthermore, cognitive dissonance theory (Festinger 1957) predicts that a genuine shift in belief, such as towards believing that you actually did something you initially knew you did not do, is more likely when the apparent reasons for making admissions are weak and intangible. So, for example, if you have been tortured into an admission, your confession will very likely be coerced-compliant as opposed to coerced-internalised, because you are very aware of strong extraneous reasons for making the confession. However, if you have been driven to make admissions by many subtle, covert and unrecognised psychological pressures, you will be unable to explain to yourself why you made the confession and will be more likely to resolve the conflict between your confession and your actual innocence by shifting to a belief that you are in fact guilty.

The essence of extremely forceful psychological methods of interrogation is in the profound disorientation of the target's sense of self and of the world. The techniques employed restrict the target's mental focus to the here and now, which is firmly controlled and dictated by the interrogators. The aim is to detach the target from his past and future and dislodge him from his normally secure anchorage in a predictable social world, a comfortable set of relationships and an accepted order of values. The methods are continuous with those that lead to coerced-compliant false confessions, only more extreme and more aggressively confrontational across a wider variety of personal domains. These methods exploit the fallibility and malleability of memory and the fact that, as Koffka (1935) states "remembering appears to be far more decisively an affair of construction rather than one of mere reproduction". Forceful psychological methods induce a degree of self-doubt and confusion that undermines the individual's faith in his own perception of the world and brings him to almost gratefully accept the interrogators' version of the world as a form of genuine enlightenment. These methods can be effective with almost anyone other than the exceptionally defiant and independent-minded. Forceful psychological methods of interrogation are highly deliberate and involve, as in the case of Korean brain-washing, a conscious process of implantation of an entirely new set of ideas or specific new memories to replace those that have been challenged and placed in doubt by the disorientation phase.

Recent psychological research, much of it concerned with so-called *false memory syndrome* (eg Loftus and Ketcham 1994), has demonstrated the effectiveness of such a process. For example, Ceci and Huffman (1997) found, in an extensive series of experiments with pre-school children, that it was possible to implant in children's minds false beliefs that they had witnessed events which did not in fact happen. Repeated suggestions over long intervals were shown to be especially effective at inducing false beliefs. It proved impossible in debriefing sessions for either the experimenters or the parents to convince a proportion of the children that the events, featuring in implanted false memories, had not actually occurred. Ceci and Huffman argued that one mechanism underlying false beliefs is the misattribution of the perceived familiarity of the implanted event. Some children confuse familiarity due to imagining the event with that due to actually experiencing it. Younger children and highly suggestible adults more quickly forget the source of their information.

On the other hand, the full force of psychological methods is not required in order to engineer a coerced-internalised false admission, in which a suspect's memories of his own actions are altered or compromised. Individual factors play an important role because people differ markedly in level of suggestibility, that is in their susceptibility to social influence and their predisposition to comply with authority. Gudjonsson (1991) has constructed a self-report measure of individual differences in compliance and found that it successfully discriminated between twenty police suspects who refused to make admissions (resisters) and twenty who made self-incriminating admissions that they later retracted (retractors). Gudjonsson (1991) has also developed an instrument to measure what he terms interrogative suggestibility. This measures both the extent to which a person tends to yield to misleading questions and the extent to which he displays a general shift in memory in response to suggestive pressures. Gudjonsson found that resisters had lower and retractors higher suggestibility scores relative to the general public. Some factors such as sleep deprivation have been shown to increase the suggestibility scores of normal subjects but high suggestibility as a stable characteristic of individuals is associated with low self-esteem, lack of assertiveness, high levels of anxiety and a poor memory (Gudjonsson 1992). In short, the highly suggestible and compliant suspect is especially vulnerable and much more likely to make a coerced-internalised false confession in the face of the kind of police interrogation methods that are designed to elicit coerced-compliant confessions.

Joanne Hayes described how she felt her mind was no longer her own and how she came to internalise as true that she had stabbed the Cahirciveen baby. It seems probable that Joanne and other members of the Hayes family were relatively suggestible people and that their suggestibility was greatly increased by the overwhelming experience of shame at what had happened to Joanne's baby and anxiety at suddenly finding themselves treated as suspects in a notorious and highly publicised case of infanticide. Police strategies used in this case, such as refusal to accept all denials, failure to explain fully to the suspects their right to leave the police station, the surreptitious supply of details of the crime to the unwitting suspects and the alternation of offers of sympathy and understanding with threats about future consequences, fall short of what can be termed highly forceful methods likely to obtain a coerced-internalised false confession. However, they were, manifestly, powerful enough to elicit coerced-compliant false confessions and, in the case of the highly distressed, anxious and suggestible Joanne Hayes, to promote at least a temporary, internalised belief in her own guilt in respect of the Cahirciveen infanticide.

CONCLUSION

If the tribunal had attempted a full examination of police interrogation methods in the Kerry Babies case, its emphasis would undoubtedly have been on the use of subtle psychological pressure and techniques of persuasion and on how to regulate their use. While such a focus would have been informative and valuable, it is unlikely that many specific techniques, allowable within the current regime governing interrogation, would have been identified as illegal or always inappropriate. Police involved in criminal investigations must have some weapons at their disposal to counteract and expose the expected evasions and denials of guilty suspects. Police must be allowed to confront, contradict, undermine, pressurise and, in strictly limited ways, trick suspects. However, the need at policy level is to create structures and rules that ensure that the use of techniques of interrogation and the manipulation of the detained suspect's environment and state of mind never amounts to the kind of psychological duress that can lead to coerced confessions of the compliant or internalised variety. The first step towards solving these problems is to admit that we have such problems. The crucial questions are how to open secretive interrogation processes to scrutiny and which safeguards to put in place in order to ensure that acceptable pressure on suspects to admit to the truth does not become unacceptable pressure to admit to the crime, whether true or false.

The protection of the detained suspect's physical and mental condition, including the provision of access to food, drink, medication, rest and sleep is absolutely essential. The video-taping of interrogations is also a useful measure. However, as the Dean Lyons case indicates, recording is a necessary but by no means sufficient safeguard, primarily because so much can happen off tape. Also, as White (2000) argues, there is an irrefutable case for insisting that interrogations take place in the presence of a defence lawyer. There is also a strong case for a change in the law such that retracted confessions without corroborating evidence will no longer be a sufficient basis for a conviction. At the very least it should be required, as in Scotland, that the retracted confession contain "special know-ledge" that was previously unknown to the police, such as the location of a murdered victim's body. In the absence of such legal changes, it would certainly be useful to introduce routine scientific testing of the suggestibility and compliance of suspects who have retracted confessions and make the findings available to judge and jury.

Equally as important as legal and procedural reform is the matter of police culture. Outright, wilful corruption, including framing suspects by concocting confessions and falsifying evidence, is the extreme end of a continuum which begins with over-zealousness and small carelessnesses with regard to truth in the criminal justice process. The Kerry Babies case is an exemplar of the dangers of rigidity of thought, groupthink and, in the former deputy commissioner's words, "jumping to conclusions and then trying to find facts to support them". Education and training within the Garda Síochána should actively encourage the kind of lateral and critical thinking and self-interrogation that is required in order that biased, one-sided and expedient reasoning is quickly recognised for what it is, if not avoided altogether. It is particularly difficult for the police to abide by the presumption of innocence since they are in the business of making accusations of guilt and must frequently operate on an often heuristically fruitful presumption of guilt. However, training should alert all gardaí to the existence of suggestibility and educate them in the conscientious and legitimate use of the various subtle but powerful psychological means of persuasion. Most importantly, the force should attempt to inculcate in all its members a sense of values that sustains truth and justice as the cardinal virtues of policing and abjures all methods of investigation and interrogation that might sacrifice these virtues for the sake of seeming effectiveness.

REFERENCES

Asch, S. E. (1956), "Studies of independence and submission to group pressure", *Psychological Monographs,* 70, 9, Whole no. 416

Bandura, A. (1977), *Social Learning Theory,* Englewood Cliffs: Prentice Hall

Bem, D.J. 1972 "Self-perception Theory", in L. Berkowitz (ed.), *Advances in Experimental Social Psychology (Vol. 6),* New York: Academic Press

Bordens, K. S. 1984, "The effects of likelihood of conviction, threatened punishment and assumed role on mock plea-bargaining decisions", *Basic and Applied Social Psychology* 6, 93-110

Brewer, J., Guelke, A., Moxon-Browne, E., Hume, I. and Wilford R. (1988), *The Police, Public Order and the State,* Basingstoke: Macmillan

Brown, E., Deffenbacher, K. and Sturgill, W. (1977), "Memory for faces and the circumstances of encounter", *Journal of Applied Psychology* 62, 311-318

Buckout, R. (1974), "Eyewitness Testimony", *Scientifice American,* 231, 6 23-31

Ceci, S. J. and Huffman, M. L. (1997), "How suggestible are pre-school children? Cognitive and social factors", *Journal of the American Academy of Child and Adolescent Psychiatry* 36, 948-958

Cialdini, R. B. (1988), *Influence: Science and Practice,* Glenview Ill.: Scott, Foresman

Eagley, A. H. and Chaiken, S. (1993), *The psychology of attitudes,* Fort Worth: Harcourt Brace Jovanovich

Ekman, P. and O'Sullivan, M. (1991), "Who can catch a liar", *American Psychologist* 46, 913-920

Festinger, L. 1957, *A Theory of Cognitive Dissonance,* Stanford: Stanford University Press

Fiske, S. and Taylor, S. (1984), *Social Cognition Reading,* Mass.: Addison-Wesley Publishing

Gudjonsson, G. H. (1991), "Suggestibility and compliance among alleged false confessors and resisters in criminal trials", *Medicine, Science and the Law* 31 147-151

Gudjonsson, G. H. (1992), *The Psychology of Interrogations, Confessions and Testimony,* London: Wiley

Hartshorne, H. and May, M. (1928), *Studies in the nature of character,* New York: Macmillan

Inbau, F., Reid, J. and Buckley, J. (1986), *Criminal Interrogation and Confessions,* Baltimore: Williams and Wilkins

Kassin, S. M. and Wrightsman, L. S. (1985), "Confession Evidence", in Kassin, S. M. and Wrightsman, L. S (eds.), *The Psychology of Evidence and Trial Procedure,* Beverly Hills: Sage

Kassin, S. M. (1997), "The Psychology of Confession Evidence", *American Psychologist* 52, 3 221-233

Kerrigan, G. (1985), "The Kerry Babies Case", *Magill,* 30 May 16-51

Koffka, K. (1935), *Principles of Gestalt Psychology,* New York: International Library of Psychology, Philosophy and Scientific Method

Leo, R. A. (1996), "Inside the interrogation room", *The Journal of Criminal Law and Criminology* 86, 266-303

Lewis, M., Stanger, C. and Sullivan, M. (1989), "Deception in 3-year-olds", *Developmental Psychology* 25, 3 439-443

Lifton, R. (1963), *Thought Reform and the psychology of totalism,* New York: Norton

Loftus, E. and Palmer, J. (1974), "Reconstruction of automobile destruction: an example of the interaction between language and memory", *Journal of verbal learning and verbal behaviour* 13, 585-589

Loftus, E. and Ketcham, K. (1994), *The myth of repressed memory: False memories and allegations of sexual abuse,* New York: St Martin's Press

Mehabrian, A. and Williams, M. (1971), "Nonverbal concomitants of perceived and intended persuaviseness", *Journal of Personality and social psychology* 13, 37-58

Milgram, S. (1974), *Obedience to authority,* New York: Harper

O'Brian, B. (1980), *Report of the Committee on Criminal Procedures,* Dublin: Stationery Office

O'Halloran, B. (1985), *Lost Innocence,* Dublin: Raytown Press

Report of the Tribunal of Inquiry into the Kerry Babies Case, (1985), Dublin: Stationery Office

Report of the Royal Commission on Criminal Justice, 1993, London: Home Office

Ruthven, M. (1978), *Torture: The Grand Conspiracy,* London: Weidenfeld and Nicolson

Saks, M. and Hastie, R. (1978), *Social psychology in court,* New York: Van Nostrand Reinhold

Saxe, L. (1991), "Lying", *American Psychologist* 46, 409-415

Shapiro, P. N. and Penrod, S. (1986), "Meta-analysis of facial identification studies", *Psychological Bulletin* 100, 2 139-156

White, J. P. M. (2000), "The Confessional State – Police Interrogation in the Irish Republic: Parts 1 and II", *Irish Criminal Law Journal* 10, 1 17-20 and 10, 22-6

SECTION 6

THE PENAL SYSTEM

31

Introduction

Paul O'Mahony

How a nation reacts to crime and specifically how it punishes or fails to punish criminals reflect the core values of a society and are definitive of that society's essential character. As Nelson Mandela (1994) has said: "no one truly knows a nation until one has been inside its jails. A nation should be judged not by how it treats its highest citizens, but its lowest ones". But no comprehensive understanding of the current state of prisons is possible without an examination of the historical roots of the penal system. As Nagel (1973) points out in reference to America's legacy of nineteenth century prisons: "the endurance of these monolithic structures is surpassed only by the tenacity of the assumptions and attitudes on which they were founded".

In fact, the origins of the modern Irish prison system are to be found in the establishment of Mountjoy Prison in 1850, one of sixteen prisons built at that time in Britain and Ireland on the so-called penitentiary model of Pentonville Prison in London. Partly inspired by the design of Bentham's (1789) panopticon, in which a single unobserved warden in a central circle building could oversee hundreds of prisoners in their cells in the surrounding prison, Mountjoy was and still is a grim, forbidding stone building designed to sustain a regime of solitary confinement. In the "silent and solitary" penitentiary system, prisoners were fed through a hatch in their cell doors, worked alone in their cells at cobbling or some similar activity and were allowed nothing other than religious reading material to break the endless monotony. They left the cell only for an hour's silent outdoor exercise each day or to attend church. This regime was intended to induce penitence and spiritual renewal in the punished criminal, not just to deter him from future crime.

The penitentiary system was not only the fruit of almost a hundred years of protest, critique and proposal by religiously inspired philanthropists, such as John Howard, but was itself explicitly founded on religious ideals and methods. According to Ignatieff (1978), the system reflected the view that "salvation was not only God's work. It was the State's work too." The architectural, legal and organisational legacy of the penitentiary system, if not its full-blown religious ideology, is still very powerful today. The Victorian buildings and many of the rules, concepts and secular ideals of the penitentiary, though much modified and sometimes ostensibly repudiated, are still a formidable presence in the current Irish system.

However, the intervening 150 years have witnessed a gradual process of softening of the original, very severe prison regime. Corporal punishment, such as birching, and dietary punishment, including bread and water starvation diets, have been abandoned. The harsh discipline and conditions of forced and often deliberately punitive and unproductive labour, as on the treadmill or crank, have been abolished or greatly alleviated. There have also been progressively tighter restrictions on the power of the prison authorities to totally isolate the individual offender. At a more mundane level, but equally crucially, creature comforts such as mattresses, permission to smoke cigarettes, decent food, radios and more recently televisions and in-cell sanitary plumbing (for most but by no means all Irish prisoners) have been introduced. Interestingly, the original planners of Mountjoy Prison were enlightened enough to provide integral sanitation in each cell, as well as a unique dual chimney system to facilitate the flow of fresh air through the whole prison. However, because it very frequently blocked up, the plumbing system was soon removed and has yet to be replaced by a modern system (Carey 2000).

The gradual process of humanisation of the prisons regime, which has continued throughout the last 150 years, undoubtedly reflects changing value systems and rising standards of comfort and material well-being in society outside of prison. While it is a part of what has been called by Norbert Elias (1938) "the civilising process", it has not transformed the prison into a place where offenders "suffer no hardship greater than that which is inherent in the deprivation of liberty" (Department of Justice 1994). Rather, it has led to a somewhat sanitised modern prison system that in the words of David Garland (1990) "provides a way of punishing people – of subjecting them to hard treatment, inflicting pain, doing them harm – which is largely compatible with modern sensibilities and conventional restraints upon open physical violence".

But the Victorian reforms also brought very significant legal innovations which provided a structure of laws and specific mechanisms for the surveillance and control not just of prisoners but of the penal system itself. A comprehensive code of prison rules and a system of inspection were introduced and, eventually, visiting committees were established in order to provide a modicum of democratic oversight and community involvement. This legal framework afforded meaningful rights to the punished and placed strict constraints on those authorised to punish on behalf of the state. For the first time in history there was the makings of a satisfactory answer to the question "Who guards the guards?". The new penal code of the mid 1800s, which, to a very considerable degree, shaped the present Irish prison ethos, was the vehicle by which society was able to leave behind the arbitrary and brutal oppression of the "bloody code", which relied on the death penalty, corporal punishment, transportation, forced labour, and ritual public humiliation, and move forward to the modern legal framework of human rights, which underpins the protections Irish prisoners now enjoy.

The generally more humane quality of modern imprisonment in Ireland, notwithstanding some vestiges of a grimmer era, such as the slopping out of night waste, and notwithstanding the continuing potential for human rights abuses and the failure to achieve the declared aim of a regime that merely punishes by depriving liberty, should be acknowledged and valued not only by the prisoner but by all citizens who cherish human rights and the preservation of human dignity. However, from the penal policy-making perspective, one of the most significant changes since 1850 has been the sad slide from the heights of official confidence and optimism about the role and potential effectiveness of prison to, until very recently, a climate of widespread scepticism and fatalism about prison. The initial clarity and certainty about the positive effects of imprisonment, which underpinned the Victorian reform movement, has long since been supplanted by a sense of defeatism. The decline of faith in prison was in large measure due to the continual failure of the religiously inspired penitentiary system and later "scientific" alternative rehabilitative endeavours, based on medical, psychological and educational treatment, to meet the key goal of reforming the criminal into an honest and useful citizen. It also reflects a considerable truth in Mattick's (1974) statement that "if men had deliberately set themselves the task of designing an institution that would systematically maladjust men, they would have invented the large, walled, maximum security prison".

Be that as it may, Ireland, like most Western modern industrial states, has abandoned corporal and capital punishment, and has placed imprisonment at the centre of the system of criminal sanctioning. Imprisonment is now the ultimate form of punishment, the punishment of last resort. Imprisonment is the severest punishment available to sentencers and as such it is inevitably the sanction of first choice for almost all serious crimes. In addition, all of the alternative non-custodial sanctions available for less serious crime such as probation, community service and fines, depend on the availability of imprisonment as a kind of enforcer, the final deterrent for incorrigible, persistent, petty offenders, who are unable or refuse to comply with court orders.

In this context, the discourse on prisons remains vexed and riven by paradoxes. The current much improved system is the product of a gradual evolution, but this progress has served only to point up the prison's seemingly ineradicable potential for human rights abuses and, in many respects, its inherent futility and injustice (O'Mahony 2000). The prison discourse is constituted, according to Rotman (1995), by a never-ending cycle of "exposes, reports, proposals, then more exposes", all characterised by "despair about on-going problems, a lofty idealism and a dogged optimism that prisons could be improved". Much of this critical discourse focuses on the purposes of punishment and imprisonment and on how society can justify and legitimate the intrinsically negative and morally questionable infliction of pain. The apparent relative failure of prisons to reduce crime and recidivism and to reform offenders (Martinson 1974) and their potential for inflicting damage on inmates and their families and augmenting rather than diminishing their criminal tendencies have meant that prisons are often portrayed as a necessary evil. However, given the clear evidence for at least a comparable level of efficacy for community-based sanctions, the necessity of prison can be questioned in the case of many types of less serious crime. One British review of the evidence has concluded that "custody is the most expensive disposal and once the prisoner is released, is no more successful at preventing future crimes than other (non-custodial) disposals" (Home Office 1998).

Critics of the prison, however, range across the whole spectrum, from those who would reduce the use of imprisonment or abolish it altogether to those who would greatly extend its use and increase the severity of its punitive effect (Hawkins 1976). A leading abolitionist, Mathiesson (1990), has declared that "the prison does not have a defence, the prison is a fiasco in terms of its own purposes". In fact, there is a tangled web of interrelated objectives behind any sentence of imprisonment. As Hart (1968) puts it: "men punish and always have punished for a vast number of different reasons ... and any morally tolerable account of punishment must exhibit it as a compromise between distinct and partly conflicting principles".

Imprisonment is aimed, to varying degrees in different cases, at: retribution, that is the rebalancing of the benefits an offender might have gained from crime by the application of a quantifiable disbenefit; the reform and rehabilitation of the offender; a publicly visible form of punishment; deterrence both of the punished individual and the public at large; the exclusion of offenders from open society; direct prevention of crime by incapacitation of the offender for the period of imprisonment; and the expression of community values and social disapproval. It is manifestly obvious that imprisonment very frequently fails at some of these objectives, especially rehabilitation, reform and individual deterrence; but, equally, it is undeniable that it has meaningful success in terms of incapacitation, social exclusion, imposing retribution, declaring social disapproval and deterring some citizens from ever getting involved in crime.

Analysis of the current Irish prison system is limited by a dearth of up-to-date official statistics and a lack of in-depth research. However, it is possible to give outline answers to some of the key questions raised by this brief discussion of the history and purposes of imprisonment. The following key questions, which all relate to how Irish society uses imprisonment as the ultimate response to crime, will be briefly addressed: in what kind of conditions are prisoners held?; what kind of people are imprisoned?; for what type of crimes?; for what type of sentences?; and what is achieved by their imprisonment?

First, however, it is useful to briefly describe the prison plant and the trend in prison numbers. There is a considerable range of different types of prison and prison regime. There are presently seventeen different institutions, including three medium-sized modern closed facilities (Wheatfield, Castlerea, Midlands Prison), one modern remand prison (Cloverhill), three small open prisons (Shanganagh for juveniles and Loughan House and Shrelton Abbey for adults), a training prison with special work and training facilities, which is designated as drug-free and semi-open though it is behind the walls of the Mountjoy Complex (Training Unit), a prison for young male offenders (St Patrick's), a modern women's prison (Dochas, within the Mounjoy Complex), a high security prison (Portlaoise), until recently mainly used to hold subversive or political terrorist prisoners, two long stay prisons (Curragh and Arbour Hill), which hold mainly sex offenders and murderers, and four older prisons (Mountjoy, Cork, Fort Mitchel and Limerick). There is a small unit for female prisoners in Limerick prison. Mountjoy Male and Female is the principal committal prison, receiving new arrivals into the system, but St Patrick's is the juvenile committal prison and Cork serves as a regional committal prison.

In 1961, the daily average number of prisoners in the country, including unconvicted remand prisoners, was only 447. But in the following four decades the Irish prison system has witnessed phenomenal growth. Ireland, among the Council of Europe countries, had the most rapid growth in its prison population in the seventeen year period to 1987 (Tournier and Barre 1990). The number of Irish prison places increased by 156% in this period compared to an increase of only 19.8% in the UK, which suffered even greater increases in crime than Ireland during the seventeen years. In Europe, only the Iberian countries have witnessed a comparable growth in prison numbers. Ireland's increasing use of prison, in fact, most closely mirrors what has been called the "incarceration binge" (Hoelter 1998) in the USA, where the total number of people held in jails in 1997 was 1.78 million, which represented a 262% increase over the 1980 figures.

On 1 June 2000 there were 2,940 people in custody in Irish prisons, including eighty-seven females. This represents a 51% increase since 1987 (with almost all of the expansion occurring since 1996) and an enormous 658% increase since 1961. This level of increase far outstrips the increase in the number of recorded indictable crimes between 1961 and 2000, which is of the order of about 400%.

Despite a particularly rapid expansion of prison places since 1996, involving the opening of about 1,000 new prison beds in four new prisons, the system is still afflicted by chronic overcrowding. In June 1999 the system as a whole was 19% overcrowded, but this problem was concentrated in the older prisons with the worst material conditions, that is Mountjoy, Limerick and Cork, which were, respectively, 41%, 69% and 84% above their design capacity. The current plan is to increase the capacity of the prison system to 4,000 within the next few years, but these current trends suggest that even this level of expansion will fail to solve the overcrowding problem, because, in spite of falling crime figures, more offenders are being sent to prison, more offenders are receiving long sentences, and more unconvicted and untried defendents are being refused bail and held in custody. The increased accommodation is also being used to reduce the number of prisoners who are being given unprogrammed early release in order to free up prison places. In 1995, 558, or about 21% of all offenders sentenced to imprisonment, were actually serving their sentences at liberty under the early release scheme. By 1998 this proportion had been reduced to 15% and by 2001 to 6% or less than 200 offenders (*Irish Prison Service News* 2001).

In what kind of conditions are prisoners held?

There are a few areas of the Irish prison system, like Dochas, the new women's prison, which provide exemplary conditions and services. The generally small size of prisons and humanitarian ethos of management mean that most Irish prisoners escape the worst excesses associated with the utterly brutalising prison regimes that are familiar from some larger countries, such as the USA. However, the large, older Irish prisons continue to be overcrowded and drug-ridden and afford a very low standard of accommodation and facilities. Conditions are insanitary, lock-up times are unconscionably long, and there is a chronic shortage of medical and psychiatric and general rehabilitative services, purposeful work, educational and training activity and recreational facilities. This is in spite of the fact that the Irish prison system is one of the most expensive in the world, presently costing over £50,000 per prisoner per annum. The system also has one of the most favourable prison officer-prisoner ratios in the world, yet continues to have an enormous prison officer overtime bill. In 1997, the Prison Service Operating Cost Review Group concluded that the costs of the system were "significantly out of line with those in other jurisdictions" and that prison management was "underdeveloped and ill-equipped to provide a service in the most cost effective manner".

Furthermore, some of the newer prisons have been built to an unacceptably low standard. The remand prison, Cloverhill, which holds legally innocent people, has been designed to be overcrowed with small three-man cells and a paucity of facilities. One Irish prison architect (Clancy 1994) has argued that "even in recently built accommodation the design of the cells and other spaces within the compound tends to be depressingly grim and it is hardly surprising that drug abuse and suicides are common".

What kind of people are imprisoned?

It is a fact of fundamental importance about Irish prisons that they are full of those who, by accident of birth, come from communities that suffer from chronic unemployment, low income, poor nutrition, deficient education, bad housing, and a whole series of related personal problems such as family breakdown, alcoholism and drug addiction (Hannon et al 2000, O'Mahony 1993, 1997). Many prisoners themselves have alcohol, heroin addiction or psychiatric problems and a large number come from disturbed family backgrounds. The vast majority of prisoners have left school without qualifications or before the legal school leaving age and have a poor employment record. While this profile of multiple disadvantage is typical of prisoners around the world, one study (O'Mahony 1997) has suggested that the prison population in Ireland come from the most deprived groups and lowest socio-economic classes to a far more concentrated degree than is the case in Britain. In many of the larger prisons, medical, social work, rehabilitative and psychiatric services appear to be overwhelmed by the problems they face.

For what type of crimes?

Morgan (1994) has described three modes of imprisonment, the *custodial*, the *coercive* and the *punitive*. *Custodial* imprisonment refers to the holding in custody of as yet unconvicted people remanded to a court and illegal immigrants. *Coercive imprisonment* refers to the detaining of fine-defaulters, debtors and those in contempt of court or otherwise non-compliant with a court order. Finally *punitive* imprisonment refers to the direct use of imprisonment by a court as punishment. The first point of note, then, is that not all prisoners are imprisoned for crime or as a punishment for an offence that the court considered deserving of imprisonment.

On 1 June 2000, 322 of the 2,940 total of prisoners in custody, or 11%, were unconvicted and on remand and detained in Morgan's *custodial* sense. Remands are a growing proportion of the prison population as a consequence of the change in the bail laws and the opening of Cloverhill as a designated remand prison. In January 1994 (the last date for which there are full statistics available) there were only sixty-two remand prisoners in the system, which was less than 3% of the then prison population. However, remands represent a much larger proportion of the committals to prison than of the detained population because they tend to spend a short period in prison. In 1994, there was a total of 4,664 committals under remand, amounting to 40% of the number of committals, which stood at 11,530. Again out of this total of 11,530 committals, 2,173 (19%) were fine defaulters and 270 (2.3%) were debtors, in contempt of court or in default of sureties. Although the exact breakdown is not available, it is certain that these *coercive* uses of imprisonment, while very substantial in terms of committals, constitute a much smaller proportion of the detained population because of their normally very short stays in prison. It is reasonable to speculate on the basis of these figures that about 20% of the detained prison population in 2001 are either *custodial* or *coercive* prisoners. However, the indications are that only a minority (around 40%) of the people annually committed to prison are *punitive* prisoners, that is offenders sent directly to prison as punishment.

The majority of convicted Irish offenders are sent to prison for relatively minor acts of property theft. Table 1 provides a breakdown of the offence type for the 6,866 non-remand committals to prison in 1994 and includes those in prison for failure to pay a fine.

Table 1: breakdown of offence types

	Committals 1994		Detained January 1994	
	No.	%	No.	%
Offences against the person	705	10	505	26
Offences against property with violence	668	9	520	27
Offences against property without violence	1957	29	562	29
Miscellaneous non-violent *including:*	3536	52	363	18
Road Traffic Acts offences	*1765*	*26*		
Drunkenness	*205*	*3*		
Debtors, contempt etc.	*270*	*4*		
Other non-violent	*1296*	*19*		
Total	**6866**		**1940**	

In 1994, therefore, when the crime total was 101,036, about sixty-eight people were *punitively* or *coercively* committed to prison for every 1,000 indictable crimes recorded. This compares with a figure of about fourteen per 1,000 in England and Wales (Home Office 1995), which is almost five times less. The imprisonment under conviction rates per head of population for the two jurisdictions (137 and 179 per 100,000 for England and Wales and Ireland respectively in 1994) are far less dramatically different because England and Wales has about three times more crime. The detention rate, that is the number of peole held in prison per 100,000 of population, is actually lower in Ireland (in 1994, 60 versus 120 per 100,000). However, this mainly reflects the wide use of unprogrammed early release, the high proportion of short sentences, and the very large number of fine-defaulters sent to prison for extremely short periods in Ireland. The current expansion of prison places, which is putting an end to unprogrammed early release means that detention rates in Ireland will more truly reflect imprisonment rates and will quickly converge with and possibly surpass the detention rate in England and Wales.

Nonetheless, imprisonment rates clearly point to a comparative Irish overuse of prison, particularly in regard to the breadth of use as opposed to the harshness of individual sentences. The proportion of indictable crime that is violent and serious is not lower in England and Wales than in Ireland and, as Table I indicates, the majority of those sent to prison in Ireland have not committed serious crime. Yet, the figures show that in Ireland one person goes to prison for about every fourteen reported indictable crimes, whereas in England and Wales one person goes to prison for about every seventy reported indictable crimes. This enormous discrepancy has undoubteldy increased since 1994 because Irish levels of committal to prison under sentence have increased whilst the level of reported indictable crime has substantially decreased by about 20%.

Irish sentencing patterns have clearly become anomalous in the broader Western European context. Neighbouring countries like England and Wales have experienced growth in crime rates almost exactly parallel to those in Ireland, but from a much higher base. However they have adjusted their sentencing practice by restricting the use of imprisonment and turning to fines and community based sanctions to a far greater extent than Irish courts.

Only 19% of people punished by imprisonment in Ireland in 1994 had committed a violent offence, whether against the person or property. Eighty-one percent were imprisoned for non-violent offences, including substantial numbers for debt and drunkenness and an extraordinary 26%, or more than a quarter of the total, for traffic offences, not including dangerous or drunken driving. It cannot even be assumed that all the 19% sentenced for violent crime have committed serious offences, since 272, out of 1373 such committals (20%), received a very short sentence of under three months. The detained population figures reflect the accumulation over time of long-sentence prisoners but, even so, as Table 1 illustrates, almost half (47%) of the detained, sentenced population in 1994 were being punished for non-violent offences.

For what type of sentences?

Figure 1 illustrates the distribution of sentence lengths received by all committals under sentence for the year 1994 and by the detained, sentenced population on 1 January 1994. This indicates two very disparate profiles. The prison at this time held predominantly longer stay prisoners (81% with sentences over one year and

29% with sentences over five years), but this is clearly a poor guide to the use of imprisonment by the courts, since the much larger number of committals to prison by the courts were overwhelmingly on short or very short sentences. In recent years, the numbers of prisoners serving a life sentence for murder or a long sentence for sex offences have grown notably, to stand in June 2000 (*Irish Prison Service News* 2001) at 104 and 354, respectively. Indeed, the proportion of the detained population imprisoned for offences against the person increased from 26% in 1994 to 35% in 2000.

Figure 1: sentence lengths

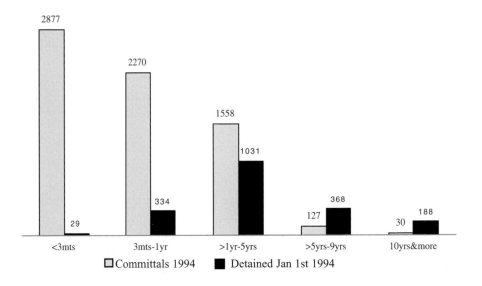

Life sentence and long-sentence prisoners, such as most sex offenders, obviously accumulate within the system. However, the fact remains that, in general, sentences to imprisonment are overwhelmingly short, that is one year or less (75%), and the largest category by far is sentences under three months (42%). This latter category, of course, includes sentences of imprisonment imposed *coercively*. There is obviously a huge and rapid turnover of offenders with very short stays in prison of a few days or weeks. Remission of 25% of sentence (33% for females) and unprogrammed early release also have a marked effect on reducing lengths of time actually spent in prison.

What is achieved by their imprisonment?

Finally, there is little evidence that imprisonment in Ireland reduces crime, deters prisoners from future crime or reforms and rehabilitates many of them. The massive increase in the use of imprisonment over recent decades has for the most part coincided with a continuing increase in recorded serious crime. Most especially, the use of imprisonment has had a negative impact in the crucial area of drug-related crime. The prison, so far from reducing the incidence of drug use amongst offenders, has almost certainly contributed to its increase and to the growth of drug-related crime, which has come to dominate the Irish crime scene (Keogh 1997).

There is no available evidence on what proportion of first committals to prison never return to prison but, according to 1994 figures, 60% of sentenced adults and 43% of sentenced juveniles had served a previous sentence. Hannon et al (2000) found that while less than 5% of a large random survey of male prisoners had spent five years in prison under their current sentence, 26% of them had spent more than five of the last ten years in prison under various sentences. A random sample survey of 108 Mountjoy prisoners (O'Mahony 1997) indicated that 77% had spent time in St Patrick's, the juvenile detention centre, and 93% had served a previous sentence. In fact, more than half of the sample had more than ten previous convictions and the sample as a whole had an average of fourteen convictions and ten separate episodes of imprisonment. Evidently, while an unknown but probably quite small number of people are sent to prison once and never return, the people against whom imprisonment is typically used are highly recidivist. They are not appreciably deterred or reformed but are far more likely to be confirmed and hardened in their criminality by prison.

In conclusion

There is a growing awareness that it is unrealistic to look to prisons to transform, or even to scare, offenders into being conformist, aimiable, socialised citizens. Prisons cannot entirely undo the powerful formative influence of the family and neighbourhood and of the social, economic, and subcultural factors which profoundly shape criminal motives and careers. Furthermore, the figures just examined indicate that the Irish use of imprisonment is seriously skewed with the majority of sentences imposed being very short and for relatively petty crimes. The Irish courts clearly do not use imprisonment as the last resort. In 1994 27% of prison committals were under twenty-one years old and there is evidence (O'Mahony 1997) that over a fifth of prisoners' first convictions, involving mostly non-violent crime, were punished by a term of imprisonment or detention. Short sentences can only be useful *coercively* or as a deterrent, but the overwhelming evidence is that this use of imprisonment actually serves to undermine the deterrent effect of imprisonment. The vast majority of people passing through the prisons are there for too short a time to be able to benefit from training, therapeutic, educational and rehabilitative programmes. Indeed the constant demands on the system posed by short-term prisoners are very likely to deflect energies and resources away from the provision of effective services to long stay prisoners.

However, prison can provide some opportunities for positive personal development. It is possible to devise programmes, such as the CONNECT project (Integra Support Structure 1999), to which the government has committed £46 million over the next six years, which represent a realistic opportunity for improving the employability and social attitudes of offenders. This programme operates an individualised system of planned personal development, which aims at the *habilitation* of undereducated and inadequately socialised offenders. The programme stresses participative, partnership approaches and the empowerment of the individual offender and so represents a real chance to overcome past attitudinal barriers to the success of offender rehabilitation. The focus is on interpersonal and basic cognitive skills as much as on narrowly defined vocational training, and the programme, very crucially, involves an element of job placement and throughcare on release from prison.

It is evident that prison cannot fulfill all of the positive expectations held for it and, equally, that many of the destructive side-effects of imprisonment for the personality and prospects of the prisoner, for his family, and for the fabric of society are avoided only with extreme difficulty. It is also evident that the overcrowding and poor material conditions in many Irish prisons and the manner in which the Irish courts make use of imprisonment work to the detriment of plans to improve the ethos and effectiveness of prison. While drug treatment, sex offender therapy, anger management groups, the CONNECT project, and other similar positive developments are starting to overturn previous defeatist attitudes about rehabilitation in prison, it still remains true that, as the Webbs (1922) have stated, "the most hopeful of 'prison reforms' is to keep people out of prison altogether" .

REFERENCES

Annual Report on Prisons (several years), Department of Justice, Dublin: Stationery Office

Bentham, J. 1789, *An Introduction to the Principles of Morals and Legislation,* London

Carey, T. 2000, *Mountjoy: The Story of a Prison,* Cork: Collins Press.

Clancy, F. 1994, "Prison Design and Construction", in the October edition of *Build*

Department of Justice 1994, *The Management of Offenders: a Five Year Plan,* Dublin: Stationery Office

Elias, N. 1938, *The Civilising Process: The History of Manners,* Oxford: Basil Blackwell

Garland, D. 1990, *Punishment and Modern Society,* Oxford: Clarendon Press

Hannon, F., Kelleher, C. and Friel, S. 2000, *General Healthcare Study of the Irish Prisoner Population,* Dublin: Stationery Office

Hart, H.L.A. 1968, *Punishment and Responsibility,* Oxford: Oxford University Press

Hawkins, G. 1976, *The Prison: Policy and Practice,* Chicago: University of Chicago Press

Hoelter, H. 1998, "Lessons Learned from America: Stopping the Incarceration", Binge Lecture to the Law School Trinity College Dublin, February 1998

Home Office 1995, *Digest 3 Information on the Criminal Justice System in England and Wales,* London: HMSO

Home Office 1998, *Reducing Offending: An assessment of research evidence on ways of dealing with offending behaviour,* London: HMSO

Ignatieff, M. 1978, *A Just Measure of Pain,* p 56, London: Penguin Books

Integra Support Structure 1999, Proceedings of the 1998 Integra Conference, Dublin *Including Prisoners and Ex-offenders in Employment and Society,* Dublin: Integra Support Structure and WRC Social and Economic Consultants

Irish Prison Service News 2001, April, Volume 1, Part 5, Dublin: Irish Prison Service

Keogh, E. 1997, *Illicit Drug Use and Related Criminal Activity in the Dublin Metropolitan Area,* Dublin: Garda Headquarters

Mandela, N. 1994, *The Long Walk to Freedom,* London: Little Brown

Martinson, R. 1974, "What works?: Questions and answers about prison reform", in *The Public Interest* 10, 22-54

Mathiesen, T. 1990, *Prisons on Trial,* London: Sage

Mattick, H. 1974, *The Prosaic Sources of Prison Violence,* Occasional Papers Chicago: University of Chicago Law School

Morgan, R. 1994, "Imprisonment", in *Oxford Handbook of Criminology* (eds. Maguire, M., Morgan, R. and Reiner, R.) Oxford: Clarendon Press

Nagel, W. 1973, *The New Red Barn: A Critical Look at the Modern American Prison,* New York: Walker

O'Mahony, P. 2000, *Prison Policy in Ireland; Social Justice versus Criminal Justice,* Cork: Cork University Press

O'Mahony, P. 1993, *Crime and Punishment in Ireland,* Dublin: Round Hall

O'Mahony, P. 1997, *Mountjoy Prisoners: A Sociological and Criminological Profile,* Dublin: Stationery Office

Prison Service Operating Cost Review Group 1997, *Report*, Dublin: Stationery Office

Rotman, E. 1995, "The Failure of Reform: United States 1865-1965", in *Oxford History of the Prison* (eds. Morris, N. and Rothman, D.) Oxford: Oxford University Press

Tournier, P. and Barre, M. 1990, "A Statistical comparison of European prison Systems", in *Prison Information Bulletin* No. 15, Strasbourg: Council of Europe

Webb, S. and B. 1922, *English Local Government: Prisons,* London: Longman

32

Punishment in Ireland:
Can We Talk About It?*

Patrick Riordan

Events in Ireland in the past year have brought the topic of punishment into the headlines. The publicity surrounding a particularly brutal incident of incest led to cries for stiffer penalties followed by a rushed change in the legislation. At the same time we have seen widespread dissatisfaction with variations in sentencing and frequent protests at too lenient sentences. In fact it is now quite common, after a judge has imposed sentence, to see victims and their relatives being questioned in the media, as to whether they are satisfied with the sentence imposed. There seems to be a growing public sense that the victims of crime are or ought to be important players in the whole drama of conviction and sentencing.

All of these developments take place against the background of almost total silence concerning the rationale of punishment in general. The demand for stiffer penalties for particularly abhorrent crimes has received wide publicity, and politicians have not been slow to see their opportunity to serve their constituents. However, there has been very little discussion about punishment in general, and the reasons behind the assumption that punishment is an appropriate response to crime. Why does society punish those convicted of crime? What is the point of punishment? What are the appropriate forms and measures of punishment?

Other countries have seen a lively debate on these questions, largely because of the collapse of the conventional wisdom of the 1960s that punishment was essentially about the rehabilitation of criminals. This debate has spawned a

---

* *Administration* 41, 4, 1993–94, 347–61

considerable literature, also on the philosophical issues involved, but so far the debate has hardly impinged on the public agenda in Ireland. The early 1980s saw a number of investigations into our penal system, followed by the publication of reports, culminating in the Whitaker Report of 1985.[1] But while these discussed the whole penal system in great detail, they hardly raised the philosophical issues. The Whitaker Report contents itself with reproducing "traditional" views, and with noting the foremost concerns in the "public mind", even though it mentions some qualifications to these received opinions.[2] But are the traditional views, however qualified, adequate to answering the basic questions as to why we have duties and rights to punish? It is vitally important for the integrity of our legal and penal systems that we address these issues. Otherwise there is the danger that in responding hurriedly to demands arising from particularly horrific crimes and events, we will undermine the moral basis of our existing institutions. The Whitaker Report expressed this concern in the following terms:

> It is to be hoped, in any event, that society, while taking all proper steps to protect itself, will continue to educate itself to be less sensitive to the stimulus of horror and indignation, less prone to emotions of fear or vengefulness, and more aware of the contribution to crime made by the deficiencies in its own structure and operations.[3]

In this paper I want to address the questions surrounding the problem of justifying punishment. In doing so, I will briefly survey some of the relevant philosophical debates. I want particularly to focus on two issues which are highlighted by the recent developments I have mentioned. The first issue concerns the role of victims and their families in the punishment of the offender. If victims are to have a say, what then distinguishes punishment from revenge? Or should there be any distinction between these two, other than in terms of efficiency or humaneness perhaps? The second issue concerns the basis for determining the appropriate scale of punishment. With what reasons can we determine whether or not the punishment fits the crime? But to address these two questions, I must first situate them in the general discussion of the justification of punishment.

---

[1] Sean McBride (ed.), *Crime and Punishment: Report of the Commission of Enquiry into the Irish Penal System* (Dublin: Ward River Press, 1982); Council for Social Welfare, *The Prison System* (Dublin: 1983); Joint Working Party, Irish Council of Churches and the Irish Commission for Justice and Peace, *Punishment and Imprisonment, with special reference to prisons and places of detention in the Republic of Ireland* (Dublin: Dominican Publications, 1985); David Rottman, *The Criminal Justice System: Policy and Performance* (NESC Report 77, Dublin: Stationery Office, 1984); T.K. Whitaker (Chairman), *Report of the Committee of Inquiry into the Penal System* (Dublin: Stationery Office, 1985)

[2] Whitaker, p. 39

[3] Whitaker, p. 29

WHAT IS PUNISHMENT?

Philosophers have listed the following five essential elements of punishment.[4] It is held that punishment

1) must involve consequences normally considered unpleasant
2) must be for an offence against legal rules
3) must be imposed on an offender for an offence in which s/he is presumed to have acted voluntarily
4) must be intentionally administered by officers who in the relevant society are regarded as having the right to do so
5) must be imposed and administered by an authority constituted by a legal system against which the offence is committed.

These five characteristics are used to distinguish punishment from other activities and social institutions which appear very similar to it. So, for instance, points (4) and (5), specifying that punishments are imposed by disinterested persons acting in a representative capacity, allow us to distinguish cases of punishment from cases of revenge. Revenge is taken by a very interested person, either the victim of some wrong or a member of the victim's family. Constitution of the punishing authority by the legal system (5) allows us to distinguish cases of punishment from instances in which summary justice is administered by policemen taking the law into their own hands. The fact that punishment is imposed for a breach of the law (2) allows us to distinguish imprisonment as punishment from instances of protective custody or quarantine. And while fines may often seem similar to taxes, and even be treated as such by some citizens (parking fines as a tax on a particularly good parking slot), this same characteristic (2) is the basis for a distinction between fines as punishment and taxes. Philosophers tend to agree on the third characteristic, that punishment requires the assumption that the offender acted voluntarily in committing the crime. Punishment therefore treats the one punished as a free and responsible human being. Rhetoric which refers to criminals as "vermin" and "animals" denies their humanity and contravenes this third element of punishment: if the criminal is not to be held responsible (as a human agent) for the crime, then whatever is done to him is not punishment. However, it is the first characteristic which highlights the need for justification. Punishment requires a justification because it usually involves a direct imposition of pain or something unpleasant on people. Those punished are deprived of some good: money, property, companionship, liberty, respect, or life itself. Normally it

---

[4] There is a useful summary in Nigel Walker, *Why Punish?* (Oxford: Oxford University Press, 1991); Walker draws on Anthony Flew, "The Justification of Punishment", *Philosophy* 3 (1954), p. 291ff; see also H.L.A. Hart, *Punishment and Responsibility: Essays in the Philosophy of Law* (Oxford: Oxford University Press, 1968)

would be considered morally wrong directly to deprive someone of some good: why is it not only good but sometimes even morally obligatory to do so in the case of punishment? Why is it that some people and institutions have both the right and the duty to punish?

THE JUSTIFICATION OF PUNISHMENT

There are certain stock attitudes and answers which recur frequently in public debate and which reflect the various theories of punishment. Five such theories are usually distinguished.[5]

1) "That'll teach him! He needs to be taught a lesson." Namely, that crime doesn't pay, that the criminal loses out in the long run, and so will have reason not to repeat the crime. This view reflects the understanding of the aim of punishment as *internal deterrence*, the point being that the person convicted of crime (convict) is to be deterred from further crime.

2) "I'm going to make an example of you", and so the convicted criminal is given the maximum or an exemplary sentence as a warning to all other would-be criminals that crime does not pay. The criminal is punished in order to deter others from crime. This is the theory of *external deterrence.*

3) "He ought to be locked up, put away! Society needs to be protected from the likes of him!" According to this view, the point of punishment is to protect society and to incapacitate those who pose the greatest threat to victims of future crime. This reflects the *social defence* or *incapacitation* theory.

4) "Criminality is like an illness; the criminal is sick, and ought to be treated in such a way that he can be reformed. Punishment is justified only if it is rehabilitative, enabling the convict to re-enter society and play a normal, law-abiding role." This theory sees punishment as *rehabilitation.* However, in so far as advocates of this view understand crime in terms of social or psychological causes, they presuppose that the criminals were not "free" in their acts of crime, and so are not to be held responsible. If this is the case, then rehabilitation is not punishment, and this theory does not provide a justification for punishment.

5) "The convict has broken the law, and so he deserves to be punished." This is the theory of *retribution* which is often formulated in terms of deserts. However, it often also considers punishment in terms of "payment", paying a debt to society. The retributivist explains this by pointing out

---

[5] See for example R.J. Gerber and P.D. McAnany (eds.), *Contemporary Punishment: Views, Explanations, and Justifications* (Notre Dame, Indiana: University of Notre Dame Press, 1972); see also C.L. Ten, *Crime, Guilt and Punishment* (Oxford: Clarendon Press, 1987)

that the criminal has disturbed a pre-existing order of justice, and so ought to be punished in order to right the wrong and to re-establish the order of just relations.

REHABILITATION?

In the optimism of the 1960s, rehabilitation became established as the dominant rationale of the penal systems in both the United Kingdom and the   States. With the growing influence of the human sciences of sociology and psychology, society was seen more and more as a construct which could be remade, and individuals' behaviour was considered changeable by conditioning. The proper programme of treatment would rehabilitate the offender and make him or her capable of life in society. Of course professionals with the appropriate expertise would be required in order to design and administer the requisite reform programmes. One of the consequences of this development was a division in the personnel of penal institutions. On the one hand were those considered to have the competence and responsibility for rehabilitating the criminals, and on the other were those whose sole function was now understood in terms of security. Of course those undergoing rehabilitation were still being constrained and held against their will in penal institutions. Somebody had to turn the key. This resulted in a deterioration in the morale of prison officers. Without a respectable public philosophy to explain their function in terms of punishment, they could only begin to see themselves as the dominant theory saw them, namely, as the keepers of human warehouses. This was dehumanising both for the officers themselves and for the inmates in their care. The dissolution of the reform model left a vacuum which has not yet been filled.[6]

Another worrying aspect of the rehabilitation model was the practice of indeterminate sentencing in the United States. Since the point of punishing was to rehabilitate the offender, then the reform programme would have to be implemented until it achieved its effect. Parole boards were constituted to review prisoners' progress. In effect, these boards had the power to keep prisoners in jail indefinitely. At the same time, prisoners learned the game of satisfying the expectations of parole boards. Reflection on the violation of prisoners' human rights in this system, as well as on the basic failure to reform, have led to the abandonment of the rehabilitation model.

There seems now to be widespread agreement that rehabilitation is not the same as punishment. While it may be possible to offer prisoners opportunities of rehabilitation while they are being punished, it is clear that society sees some

---

[6]   A.E. Bottoms and R.H. Preston (eds.), *The Coming Penal Crisis: A Criminological and Theological Exploration* (Edinburgh: Scottish Academic Press, 1980)

point in punishment other than the purpose of rehabilitation. Whitaker notes that punishment as distinct from deterrence, rehabilitation and incapacitation, remains foremost in the public mind as the principal objective of imprisonment.[7] But if rehabilitation does not justify punishment, what does?

A common element in the deterrence and incapacitation theories is that they explain punishment by reference to its consequences. As a result, they are often spoken of as utilitarian theories. The point is to prevent crime, and so the effectiveness of punishment could be measured by variations in the crime rate. There are three questions which are usually raised to challenge this view. Firstly, if the reduction of the crime rate provides the explanation and justification of punishment, why is it that only the convicted criminal may be punished? Why not punish scapegoats if it proved to be effective? Secondly, while punishment might be good for society, why is it also good for the persons punished? Thirdly, on what basis do we implement a scale of punishments, and try to fit the punishment to the crime? These three sets of questions pose problems for any exclusive reference to consequences in the justification of punishment. The fining, flogging or hanging of scapegoats could be efficient as a deterrent; potentially dangerous people could be locked up at the discretion of the police in order to protect society – "do it to them before they do it to you"; reformatories and psychiatric hospitals would have plenty to do in rehabilitating the maladjusted. But would these be instances of justified punishment? And if reform is the point, should we keep prisoners locked up until they are reformed, no matter how minor the offence? Should we enlarge penalties until the crime rate is negligible?

RETRIBUTION?

Advocates of these theories attempt to solve the difficulty by appealing to an element of the fifth, retributive theory, specifying that only convicted criminals may be punished.[8] But retributivism proposes more than this. It wishes to justify punishment in terms of deserts and justice, and it seeks to explain further why it might be considered good for the convict to be punished.

According to the retributivist explanation of punishment, a person, by wantonly, intentionally or negligently inflicting harm, disrupts a pre-existing order of justice.[9] Punishment is a restoration of that order by depriving the criminal of the advantage he gained by his crime. What the criminal gains in the act of committing crime is the advantage of indulging a wrongful self-preference, of permitting himself an excessive freedom in choosing, this advantage being something that his law-

---

[7] Whitaker, p. 39

[8] This is H.L.A. Hart's solution, *op. cit.*

[9] I am relying here on John Finnis, "The Restoration of Retribution", *Analysis* 32 (1972), and also on Chapter X of his *Natural Law and Natural Rights* (Oxford: Clarendon Press, 1980)

abiding fellow citizens have denied themselves in so far as they have chosen to conform their will to the law, even when they would prefer not to. The advantage arises from the fact that the crime is a free and responsible exercise of freedom. The advantage is lost when the criminal has the disadvantage of having his wayward will restricted in its freedom by being subjected to the representative will of society through the process of punishment. So punishment is essentially a subjection of the criminal's will, rather than an infliction of pain or a deprivation of some good. Punishment is seen also as a restoration of an order of fairness. The relevant order is not simply the relationship between the criminal and the victim; no one else should be unfairly disadvantaged by attempting to live in strict accordance with the basic order of fairness and the structure of reciprocal rights and obligations which is expressed in the laws of society.

Proponents of a retributivist theory of punishment argue that this theory is preferable to utilitarian theories in being able to offer answers to the three questions posed above. Firstly, why may only those convicted of a crime be punished? Because punishment is a restoration of a just order of relations which had been distorted by the crime, and which remains disrupted as long as the offender retains the benefit (act of freedom) which other participants in the order have denied themselves. Pure utilitarians cannot answer this question from their own theory, since the penalising of scapegoats might well be more effective than the punishment of offenders. Secondly, why is punishment good for the one punished, and not only good for society? Because it is good for anyone to be a member of a human society on an equal footing with every other member, enjoying the same benefits and carrying the appropriate burdens. A pure utilitarian, who says that each person is to count as one and only one, will allow the good of several others to outweigh the good of the offender. And if the good of the offender is to be calculated in terms of utility, punishment must seem to be a disutility to the one punished in each case. Thirdly, why make the punishment fit the crime? The crime was a disruption of a just order of relations in society, and the enormity of the crime is proportionate to the benefits and burdens in terms of which citizens co-operate. The more important or essential the values at stake, the more grievous the punishment. The pure utilitarian, by contrast, makes the punishment fit, not the crime, but the expected consequences, eg reduced crime rate or reform of the prisoner.

CONDITIONS FOR JUSTIFIABLE PUNISHMENT

Two presuppositions of the retributive theory, when they are made explicit, provide us with interesting conditions for justifiable punishment. Firstly, it is presupposed that the criminal is free in the criminal act, that the criminal has a choice, and therefore can be held responsible. Secondly, it is presupposed that the crime disturbs a social order which is just in relevant respects. The punishment is intended to restore the relevant balance of rights disrupted by the crime. However, in many cases and situations, it might be argued that one or both of these conditions is not met, that the criminal cannot be held responsible or that the order of relations in society is not just in some relevant respects. For instance, where we find a high statistical correlation between crime, and social and economic deprivation, then we must raise serious questions about the legitimacy of our penal policy. In this case, those who become involved in crime happen to be excluded from participation in a social order which confers benefits on its other members. Whitaker cautiously refers to these questions again and again in drawing attention to the fact that Irish society is increasingly aware of its own responsibility for the level of crime.[10]

PUNISHMENT AS COMMUNICATION

Recent presentations of a retributivist view of punishment rely on a model of communication to explain their theory.[11] Punishments are actions undertaken deliberately by a disinterested person, acting in a representative capacity, in order to bring about unwelcome consequences that shall be recognised as such by the person being punished for some wrong which that person did. The positive elements of the various theories above can be drawn together into an analysis of punishment as communication in a complex dialogue. To the convict, the punishment is a form of reprobation, communicating society's condemnation and disapproval of the deed in unmistakeable terms. To law-abiding citizens and upright members of law-enforcing agencies, it is a recognition of their sacrifices in upholding and conforming to the requirements of the law. To the observer, it is a denunciation and possibly a warning, indicating what the values of society are and underlining the authorities' willingness and determination to uphold them. To the victim, it is a disavowal and a vindication, conveying the message that the misdeed, although perpetrated by a member of society, is not to be interpreted as being in any way an action of society. The point of punishment is to make the criminal understand that the reprimand is really meant, and so as something unwelcome, it is translated into the interests and value system of the criminal so that it cannot be misunderstood. However, not only the criminal, but all potential criminals, the victim and potential victims, law-abiding members of society and law enforcement officers, should get the message that society through its officers is determined to vindicate its values.

---

[10] Whitaker, p. 29. See also p. 30

[11] See J.R. Lucas, *On Justice* (Oxford: Oxford University Press, 1980), especially Chapter 6: "Punishment"

RETRIBUTIVISM ASSESSED

There are various forms of retributivism.[12] How successful is the version presented above in answering the questions raised? Does it provide us with a viable theory which could function as a public philosophy in making sense of and justifying our penal practices? The retributivist theory has received a lot of attention recently. Once decried as a cover for revenge, as a shameless avowal of society's right to perform the same heinous acts which it forbids its members to do, it is now being promoted by some as the solution to the vacuum left by the bankruptcy of the rehabilitation theory. The language of retribution has been adopted into law in some American states since the 1970s. It is the language of deserts and just deserts, of paying a debt to society, of redressing the balance, of the restoration of social order. However, it is not always clear what these terms mean, and so we find a considerable literature in recent years discussing these elements of the retributivist theory. They seem to have intuitive rightness. However, the revival of retributivism in some quarters has been associated with demands for the (re-)introduction of the death penalty and other "law and order" agenda. This has led some critics to be wary of the intuitive appeal of retributivism. And so the questions are asked with some urgency: are these intuitively appealing ideas merely metaphor? Is there a rational basis for them? David Dolinko discusses recent attempts to answer this question.[13] Common to these attempts is the conviction, expressed by Herbert Morris, that wrongdoers deserve punishment, because punishment eliminates the unfair advantage which the wrongdoers have gained in their criminal act.[14] In other words, it is agreed that punishment restores the balance of benefits and burdens in society. What is disputed in the literature surveyed is the nature of the unfair advantage presumed gained by the criminal, and the nature of social order as a balance of rights.

THE ROLE OF THE STATE

Every version of retributivism relies on some understanding of the nature of social order, and of the role of the state in this regard. It is worth considering one recent discussion of a retributivist justification of punishment for the sake of its clear position on these issues. Richard Swinburne has argued that there is no essential

---

[12] John Cottingham, "Varieties of Retribution", *Philosophical Quarterly* 29 (1979), pp. 238-46

[13] David Dolinko, "Some Thoughts About Retributivism", *Ethics* 101 (1991), pp. 537-59. Dolinko surveys the following works: George Sher, *Desert* (Princeton NJ: Princeton University Press, 1987); Jean Hampton, "The Retributive Idea", in Jeffrie Murphy and Jean Hampton, *Forgiveness and Mercy* (Cambridge: Cambridge University Press, 1988); Michael Moore, "The Moral Worth of Retribution", in Ferdinand Schoeman (ed.), *Responsibility, Character and the Emotions* (Cambridge: Cambridge University Press, 1987)

[14] Herbert Morris, "Persons and Punishment", *Monist* 52 (1968), pp. 475-501

difference between revenge and punishment. He insists that victims have the right to effect retribution. He maintains that the primary justification of punishment is as a substitute for revenge in circumstances where it is better that some authority act as the agent of the victim in exacting his revenge'.[15] In both revenge and punishment, there is an infliction of harm as a retribution for wrongdoing; the difference between them is simply a matter of who inflicts the harm, the victim or the state. In the latter case, the state's only justification for punishing is that it acts as agent of the victim (of course it is allowed that the state can be victim too, and can take revenge on its own behalf, eg in the case of treason). Swinburne makes this point strongly. He can see no other basis for justifying the state's action in punishing than that it acts as agent of the victim. He is relying here on an interpretation of Locke's analysis of the origins of the state in the consent of citizens who hand over some of their natural rights, including the right to punish.[16] Does Locke's text allow the reading which Swinburne offers? In support of Swinburne's interpretation is the fact that Locke asserts the right to punish as a natural right, existing in the state of nature, before the institution of political power. However, Locke insists that everyone in the state of nature has the right to punish any transgression of the law of nature, not only those transgressions of which they are the victims. However Locke says that punishment has two aspects: one of those aspects' is reparation, ie the return to the victim of whatever was lost in the crime, along with some compensation for the bother of recuperating the loss. In the state of nature, only victims can exact reparation. In the making of the social contract, the right to punish is handed over to the constituted political power. To the extent that punishment still entails an element of reparation to the victim, the state could be thought to act as representative of the victim in exacting reparation. But in so far as it is enforcing natural rights, or laws made consistent with natural rights, it acts not merely as representative of victims, but as agent of all citizens who are united in their concern for rights. Calver summarises Locke's view as follows:

> the magistrate has two separate tasks to perform. He must determine the appropriate penalty for an offence, and he must also set the amount of compensation due to the victim of the offence. An injured individual has the right to demand compensation or he may waive his right; however he cannot determine what the level of compensation is to be. The magistrate may also exercise his right to remit punishment, but he has no power to decide whether compensation is to be made.[17]

Of course the issue here is not the interpretation of Locke. Rather it is a matter of clarifying the fundamental issue of the role of the state in any version of retributivism.

---

[15] Richard Swinburne, *Responsibility and Atonement* (Oxford: Clarendon Press, 1989), p. 94

[16] John Locke, *Two Treatises of Government*, ed. Peter Laslett (Cambridge: Cambridge University Press, 1960)

[17] Brian Calver, "Locke on Punishment and the Death Penalty", *Philosophy* 68 (1993), pp. 211- 29, at p. 223

I began this paper by commenting on two disturbing features in recent public discussions related to penal policy. One was the focus on the demands of victims; the other was the unreflected cry for stiffer penalties. I hope that it is now clear that the concentration on the wishes of the victims and their families has important implications concerning our view of the social fabric and the role of the state. The two contrasting versions of retributivism presented above clarify the problem. Is punishment essentially a dialogue between offender and victim (and his agents), or is punishment a communication which involves a wider circle of participants, including the victim? Retributivism sees punishment as the restoration of social order. One version of retributivism which links revenge and punishment takes a narrow perspective on the order to be re-established. The balance to be restored is that between the criminal and the victim; the victim has been wronged and is entitled to right that wrong by exacting revenge on the criminal. When the state punishes, it acts as agent for the victim. The other version offers a broader perspective on that order. There is a balance of benefits and burdens between all the members of society which is to be maintained. Within this order, the criminal has his or her proper place, as has the victim, but there are others also, for instance law-abiding citizens who forgo the freedom of wrongful self-preference and law enforcement officers who accept personal risks for the sake of that order. On this view, the state and its officers and institutions involved in punishment are acting as agents of society and all its members, and not simply acting as representatives of victims. It is because of its responsibility for the common good of society that the state has both the right and the duty to punish. So while victims and their families have something to say in the drama of punishment, they are neither the only nor the main speakers in that drama.

IRISH ISSUES

Has the hope expressed in the Whitaker Report been realised or frustrated? That hope was that society would educate itself, so as to be less vulnerable to manipulation by feelings of horror and indignation and less likely to act out of fear or desire for revenge.[18] What has been shown by recent experience? Are we at the mercy of events and subject to the immediacy of response to crises highlighted by the media? I have suggested that recent events raise two serious questions for public life in Ireland which in turn raise more fundamental and even philosophical questions. The questions concerned the rationale of punishment and the proportion to the crime, and the role of victims in punishment. I hope I have shown that both of these issues lead us into questions about the constitution of society, the function of the state, and the nature of the common good. Also, they

---

[18] See note 3 above

involve questions about the justification of punishment in general, and require us to take a stance on questions being debated in the discussion of retribution. If there is no satisfactory utilitarian justification for punishment, must we not espouse some version of retributivism? But then in order to have a rational basis for our schedule of penalties, to make the punishment fit the crime, we would need a public philosophy of the common good, some articulation of the benefits and burdens, rights and duties, which are essential to our membership of society. It is clear from other areas of Irish social life that we can no longer rely on a shared understanding of these matters. All the more reason then to encourage a public debate on these issues. In giving victims pre-eminence in media comment on punishments meted out, we are in danger of further undermining the fabric of shared meanings and commitments which hold together a social order understood as a balance of benefits and burdens. To counterbalance this trend, which is very understandable in the light of previous neglect of victims in the context of the focus on the criminal, we must articulate an understanding of the common good which is capable of sustaining the commitment of citizens to the common project.

But, of course, a shared understanding of the common good would not be sufficient on its own to guarantee the justifiability of our penal system. There would indeed have to be an adequate analysis of the pre-existing order of justice which is disrupted by crime, if we were to attempt to justify penal policy as restoration of a disturbed order. However, the more critical condition is that the social order which is disrupted by crime would have to be just in relevant respects for punishment to be justified. As long as crime continues to be correlated with social and economic deprivation, we must seriously doubt the justice of the pre-existing order, and correspondingly, doubt the moral justifiability of the punishments administered for the sake of a restoration of the balance of benefits and burdens disturbed by crime. Until such time as an articulate understanding of the common good is translated into effective programmes to incorporate the marginalised and alienated into the balance of benefits and burdens which constitutes Irish society, our penal policy will continue to be dominated by the objective of protecting those who are included in the social fabric from those who are effectively excluded.

33

The Irish Prisons Service, Past, Present and Future – A Personal Perspective

Sean Aylward

The establishment of the Prisons Agency should create an opportunity to manage change in the prison service *through a dynamic and energetic style of management* (McAuley 1997, p. 49)

INTRODUCTION

The Irish Prisons Service is actually one of the oldest public institutions in the country, dating from the decision in 1854 to establish a three-man board, the Convict Prisons Board, to manage convict prisons in Ireland. Its first chairman and director was Sir Walter Crofton and the other two members were Captain Knight and John Lentaigne (Carey 2000). The first prisons to be managed by the new board were Mountjoy (opened in 1850), Spike Island (1847) and Smithfield. Walter Crofton was to lead a major programme of reform in the Irish prison system.

Prior to the establishment of the Convict Prisons Board, prisons in Ireland constituted county jails, debtors prisons, bridewells, manor prisons and felons prisons. These institutions, many of which were dens of squalor, unlit and un-heated, were locally controlled by the grand juries and local authorities. The burden of maintaining and financing these prisons led to increasing pressure on central government to take over the administration of prisons. Furthermore, the emergence of powerful penal reform pressure groups towards the end of the eighteenth century, led by such influential figures as John Howard and Elizabeth Fry, provided the catalyst for change which was eventually to lead to the centralisation of the administration of prisons in Ireland in 1877.

The transportation of convicts to America and Australia, as an alternative to the gallows, was a regular occurrence in Ireland in the eighteenth century and the first half of the nineteenth century. There was relatively little emphasis on imprisonment as a form of punishment and the longest sentence of imprisonment at this time was two years. In the period 1791 to 1853, 39,000 Irish convicts were transported to Australia (9,000 of whom were women, a much higher proportion of female offenders than feature in crime figures in the modern period (Hughes 1987). Much smaller numbers were transported to the colony of Virginia and elsewhere in North America and to the sugar plantations in Jamaica and Barbados. However, the American Revolution of 1786 put an end to most of the transportation to the Americas.

The appointment of the Molesworth Committee in 1837 and the subsequent publication of the committee's scathing report the following year ultimately led to the abolition of transportation as a system of punishment in 1853. For the first time, long-term prisoners would be held in Irish jails which, in 1853, consisted of about thirty-eight prisons and ninety-eight bridewells run by grand juries and local authorities.

Table 1: extract of prison statistics from 1852

Prison	No. in custody 31 Dec 1852	Deaths	Pardons	Transported
Mountjoy	493	5	1	34
Spike Island	1,882	190	5	845
Smithfield	812	9	0	28
Fort Camden	132			
Fort Carlisle	71			
Newgate	300	13		14
Philipstown	31			
Grangegorman	Not available	2		375
Ennis	267	12		Not available
Maryborough	73	1	6	
TOTAL	**3,563**	**232**	**6**	**1,296**

The number of deaths in custody on Spike Island is especially notable

The combined effect of abolition of transportation to the colonies, the agrarian conflict in Ireland and the Great Famine had a dramatic impact on the prison system as the numbers in custody grew at an alarming rate. In 1849 there were over 100,000 persons imprisoned in Ireland (Carey 2000). The appalling conditions of the prisons, coupled with the acute distress caused by famine, led to disease and death for large numbers among prisoners. In 1849, over 1,300 prisoners died (Carey 2000). Prison statistics for 1852 show a very disturbing picture.

REFORM OF THE PRISON SYSTEM

Reform of prisons in Ireland in many respects commenced with the appointment of two Inspectors General for all prisons in 1822. Their main functions were to exercise greater control over boards of superintendence of prisons, to ensure that misconduct was reported and that the dietary plan was adhered to (as much for financial control over costs as for concern about adequate sustenance for the prisoner).

The early part of the nineteenth century also saw a change in the nature of imprisonment and punishment. Hard work for prisoners was seen as a way society could exact retribution for the crime committed by the prisoner as well as acting as a deterrent to potential criminals. Prior to that prison was simply a place to confine criminals pending sentence and transportation. There was no system of separation and people of all ages, both sexes, and thieves and murderers mingled together in the one jail. Corruption and exploitation in the local jails was rampant. If a prisoner had sufficient means then he could ensure a reasonably comfortable existence for himself in prison.

Crofton's programme for prisoners was based on the notion of criminal reform and separation of the criminal. A key tenet of the Crofton philosophy was to "restore the prisoner to society with an unimpaired constitution, and with sufficient health and energies to enable him to take a respectable place in the community" (Carey 2000). This was heady stuff for the 1850s. For a new prisoner entering the Crofton system the regime facing him was harsh. The aim was to crush the criminal mind and remould it. It had elements of classic military recruit training to it. There were three stages in the process.

(i)   A prisoner would serve the first nine months of his sentence in isolation in Mountjoy Prison. Such was the emphasis on separation that even attendance at church in the prison offered no respite as each pew was divided into individual boxes for all the world like upright coffins.

(ii) The next stage in the Crofton regime was labour in association on Spike Island in Cork Harbour (now Fort Mitchel Prison) where prisoners were allowed to converse and work in the open air. A system of "marks" was introduced as each prisoner was given the chance to work out his own redemption through labour on the principle that "the fate of every man should be placed in his own hands". Under this system the accumulation of marks corresponded with a reduction in the time spent in custody.

(iii) The final stage was spent in "intermediate" prisons. This was where the prisoners learnt the final lessons under the Crofton system – that they should lead a good, honest life and that they should emigrate. Emigration afforded the "reformed" prisoner the opportunity to work in a country where labour was scarce, unlike Ireland where there was a vast labour surplus.

The Crofton system attracted considerable international attention at the time and such was its contribution to prison management that elements of the system were copied by other jurisdictions. For example, the Irish marks system was copied by twenty American states (Aylward 2001). However, the winds of change in Irish prison reform, which sprang up suddenly under Walter Crofton, were beginning to decline in strength, and by the mid-1880s the Crofton system was in decline as reported recidivism among prisoners increased.

GENERAL PRISONS BOARD

Despite the comprehensive detail of the Crofton system there was, in fact, a huge disparity in terms of the strictness of the regime from jail to jail with the local grand juries, composed of the local members of the respectable rate-paying classes, retaining a large degree of autonomous control over their prisons. Centralised management of the penal system was seen as the key to prevent criminal elements migrating to areas where sentences were seen to be more lenient and which had better prison conditions. The creation of the General Prisons Board in 1877, under the General Prisons (Ireland) Act, represented a desire by government to bring together under a single statutory board powers that previously were distributed among the Convict Prisons Board (1854), an inspectorate of local prisons (1786) and innumerable local authorities.

The new board was given the task of establishing a uniform code for the management of prisons and prisoners. Visiting committees consisting of justices of the peace were set up for every prison and these committees were to report on any abuses of prisoners and other matters to the lord lieutenant. Visiting committees are still in existence today and act in many respects as a watchdog over the prison for the Minister for Justice, Equality and Law Reform.

The board set about its work with some enthusiasm. Indeed such was its zeal that by 1914, the annual prison population had fallen to just over 10,000. There were just Mountjoy, Maryborough Convict Prison (now Portlaoise Prison), fourteen local prisons, one borstal, one Inebriate Reformatory and five bridewells in operation. In 1910, *half* the prisoners in custody were women, reflecting perhaps the appetite of the authorities for repressing begging and female prostitution as well as Edwardian concerns about instances of dishonesty among the vast army of female domestics (Eggleston 2000).

IRISH PRISONS 1922–1999

The advent of independence from the United Kingdom under the 1922 Treaty did not change the core structure of our prisons one iota; barring of course changes of personality in certain key positions like the Governor of Mountjoy. (Sean Kavanagh, the Mountjoy governor from 1928 to 1962 was an inmate there during the War of Independence 1918-21). In 1928, ostensibly as a cost-cutting measure, the General Prisons Board was abolished and its functions were absorbed into the then Department of Home Affairs, later the Department of Justice. For the next fifty years very little happened in terms of organisational change in our prisons with the exception of the introduction of the Prison Rules, introduced in 1947 and still in force to this day.

During the period 1928 to 1956, the Prisons Service severely contracted in size as the general prisoner population decreased. Our prison buildings, a sprawling Victorian estate, received very little investment over this period. The contraction in scale in our prisons also reflected a static Irish demography – low birth rates/ high emigration and very low levels of reported crime (Aylward 1999). As the service contracted, prisons at Galway, Tralee, Drogheda, Waterford and Kilkenny were shut down. In 1956 alone, three prisons were closed, Cork Prison was handed over to the local university, the Borstal Institution in Clonmel was transferred to the old Female Prison in Mountjoy and renamed St Patrick's Institution. Sligo Prison closed in the same year. In fact, by 1956, the only prisons in use were Mountjoy, St Patrick's, Portlaoise and Limerick. The latter two prisons were actively considered for closure and only escaped that fate for local political reasons.

Ireland had, over the thirty years in question, virtually the lowest crime levels in the developed world. My own theory is that the safety valve of emigration in the 1930s through to the 1950s removed from the state the young men who would constitute the bulk of the prison inmate population in every country. Our young women, of course, emigrated in even greater numbers over the period. In the words of John B. Keane's famous song, "many young men of twenty said good bye".

As emigration declined, the prisoner population started to increase in the late 1960s. With the outbreak of the Northern Troubles from 1969 and the growth in drug related crime in Dublin, particularly from the late 1970s on, the prison system here suddenly came under unprecedented pressure, largely due to what has often been described as the "tyranny of numbers" (Whitaker Report 1985).

The overcrowding crisis reached a particular climax in May 1972, with an unprecedented riot in Mountjoy Prison by subversive prisoners. Portlaoise swiftly became the main place of custody for persons tried and convicted by the Special Criminal Court The number of persons in custody continued to grow and by 1980 there were about 1,200 persons in prison. Around this time, Spike Island and Loughan House were opened to hold juveniles. By 1985, the total number detained at any one time had increased to about 1,900.

The extensive use of prison officer overtime as a coping mechanism to deal with the new tyranny of numbers and as an alternative to the recruitment of prison officers became endemic throughout the system. The Temporary Release (TR) system, originally introduced as a flexible humanitarian and reforming mechanism under the Criminal Justice Act 1960 was later to be used extensively to release early or "shed" prisoners to preserve order in vastly overcrowded prisons. The "revolving door", as it later came to be known, was used to keep prison numbers in check – a crude and arbitrary system which rightly attracted considerable public opprobrium. It is only with the extensive prison building programme of the last three years that this "revolving door" has ceased to spin, with the consequent reduction in unplanned temporary releases. This decline in TRs has coincided with a reduction in national crime levels, which must have benefited from this development (see Figure 1)

Figure 1: indictable offences recorded 1985 to 1999

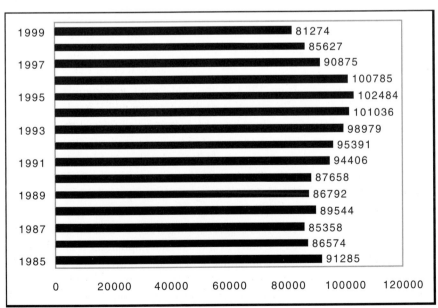

Source: Garda Síochána *Annual Report* 1999

The mid-1970s brought equality of opportunity for female prison officers and they are now eligible for promotion to the highest grade in the service. Up to the mid-1970s only basic grade posts were open to female officers. The highest grade then available to female officers were the two posts known as Matron and Assistant Matron of the Women's Prison in Mountjoy.

In 1981, there were 1,215 persons in custody in prisons and institutions around the country. The number of staff in the service was 1,444. In 1981, it cost £15,000 per annum to keep one male prisoner in custody in Mountjoy Prison and over £40,000 to keep a juvenile in Loughan House. The current cost of keeping a person in custody is about £54,000. In the ten years to 1994, for example, the average daily male prison population increased by approximately 26% while in the four years from 1994 to 1998, it increased by 29%. Table 2 charts the more recent rises in the prison population.

Table 2: snapshot of prison population on second Wednesday in July 1996-2000

Date	In custody	% change over prev year	On temp release	% change over prev year	Total serving sentence	% change over prev year	% on temp release
12 Jul '96	2,224	–	506	–	2,730	–	18.5
9 Jul '97	2,470	+11.1	529	+5.5	2,999	+9.9	17.6
8 Jul '98	2,645	+7.1	403	-23.8	3,048	+1.6	13.2
14 Jul '99	2,822	+6.7	413	+2.5	3,235	+6.1	12.8
12 Jul '00	3,009	+6.6	219	-4.7	3,228	-0.2	6.8

PRISON REGIME

The regime for prisoners from 1922 to the mid-forties was quite rigorous. It reflected perhaps the narrow perspective of the Victorian and Edwardian middle class. There was no evening recreation, and segregation was strictly enforced. Smoking, and access to radios, papers and magazines was strictly prohibited. Convicted prisoners were supplied with exclusively grey clothing and those on remand wore blue prison clothes and brown ankle boots (Prisoner D83222, 1946).

There was a general relaxation of the regime in the period after the second world war. Evening recreation was introduced from 5.30 to 7.30 pm with a late supper. Smoking was allowed – four cigarettes on a weekday and six on a Sunday. Towards the end of the 1950s the daily average prison population was 400 (today it is in the region of 3,000). Prison numbers in Mountjoy were also very low at this time.

Rehabilitation of prisoners became an issue of public debate in the late 1960s and early 1970s. The only qualified professionals in the prison service until that time were part-time chaplains and doctors. As the service expanded they were joined by various other professionals such as welfare officers, teachers and psychologists.

In 1987, Ireland, along with other Council of Europe countries, adopted the European Prison Rules (EPR) which were an adaptation to European conditions of the UN Standard Minimum Rules for the Treatment of Offenders. But, as well as being a set of standards, the EPR provide the philosophical basis and the guiding principles for the management of Irish prisons.

AN INDEPENDENT PRISONS AGENCY – HISTORICAL GENESIS

A developing pattern of poor industrial relations in the 1980s culminated in the establishment of the Committee of Inquiry into the Penal System which published its report in 1985 (Whitaker Report 1985). This major enquiry was fortunate to have as its chairman Dr Ken Whitaker, a former Central Bank Governor and Secretary of the Department of Finance. The report when produced was scarifying about the lack of investment in prison infrastructure over the years and also quite critical about the lack of modern management systems. The Inquiry Team reported that it was "in no doubt as to the desirability of constituting the prisons administration as a separate executive entity and of identifying its Director as the manager responsible for the efficient running of the system" (Whitaker Report 1985, p 123). At the time, the government and the justice department leader-ship publicly took the view that the improvement of prison conditions and a new focus on offender rehabilitation should be tried first, before the nettle of institutional reform would be grasped.

The Whitaker Report was followed, after a very long public silence, in 1994 by the *Management of Offenders – A Five Year Plan* published by the Department of Justice. That plan failed to reach a conclusion on the question of an independent prisons agency but clearly concluded that there was a need: "to change the management structure for prisons, and to involve other interests in the general direction of the prison service" (Department of Justice 1994). In other words, persons from outside the Department of Justice should be represented in the administration of prisons.

Against this background – and with the impetus of a commitment in the government programme – *A Government of Renewal* – to examine the establishment of a Prison Board, the organisation of the prison service was soon to be reviewed again. Growing concern in political circles about the criminal justice system as a whole led to the landmark government decision of 12 November 1996 to establish an independent prisons agency to run the prison service on a day-to-day basis. The agency would be overseen by an independent Prison Board. The intention was that the prisons service should move from being a functional area of the Department of Justice, Equality and Law Reform to independent executive agency status. The new agency – to be known as the Irish Prisons Service – would be established on an administrative basis pending the enactment of legislation to put it on a statutory footing.

An Expert Group was convened under the chairmanship of Dan McAuley, chairman of Irish Cement and former chief executive of the Federated Union of Employers. The group published its report, *Towards an Independent Prisons Agency*, in February 1997. The group made recommendations on

(i) the role, functions, structure, management and legal framework of the agency

(ii) the composition and functions of the Prisons Board

(iii) partnership arrangements between management and staff of the agency

(iv) an Inspector of Prisons and a Parole Board.

The Expert Group concluded that, having regard to the government decision of 12 November 1996, "the rationale for the establishment of the new agency is that significant change and development in the prison system is necessary and that this can be achieved more effectively through an independent agency" (Expert Group 1997). The Expert Group report constitutes the framework within which the Prisons Service legislation will be drafted.

The Expert Group recommended that the new agency should be under the control of an independent board whose members should be appointed by the minister. The establishment of the board would ensure that the agency would be operationally independent in performing its day-to-day functions and activities. The report also recommended the appointment of a director general who would be responsible and accountable to the board for the day-to-day management of the prisons services. As spring 1997 moved to summer the country moved towards a second general election and a change in the political administration. The report was shelved pending the elapse of a "bedding in" period for the new administration.

APPOINTMENT OF INTERIM PRISONS BOARD

In December 1998, John O'Donoghue, the new Minister for Justice, Equality and Law Reform who succeeded Nora Owen as Justice Minister in June 1997, announced that the government had decided to establish a Prisons Authority Interim Board to prepare for the establishment of a statutory Prisons Authority. The government decision also provided for the appointment through open public competition of a director general for the Prisons Service in advance of the enactment of the Prisons Service establishment legislation.

An Interim Prisons Authority Board was appointed under the chairmanship of Brian McCarthy, Chairman of FEXCO. It now includes the director general as well as eleven other members with a mix of business and administrative experience. The board will act on a non-statutory basis until the amending legislation to establish it on a permanent and statutory footing is passed by the Oireachtas. Following the enactment of the legislation, the statutory board will be given responsibility for the day-to-day management of the Prisons Service. However, before we get to that stage some very important work must be completed in preparation for the changeover to the new structure. That preparatory work will necessitate the preparation of

- guidelines in relation to the management, administration and business of the Prisons Service
- a statement on the steps involved in the transition to the statutory Prisons Authority including the senior management structure for the Authority
- a strategy statement and business plan
- annual budgets and key objectives and targets for the Prisons Service.

As the person who was on 15 July 1999 given the task to lead the service through this transition period I have been very preoccupied with this preparatory work. However, my first and most abiding priority as director general has been and will be to ensure continuance of the Prisons Service as one of the essential bulwarks of civil society.

The concept of the Prisons Service as a learning organisation has been repeatedly emphasised by me since my appointment as director general. I have tried to sustain and promote this concept at every suitable opportunity. Where we have inaugurated positive change in the organisation we have gone out of our way to celebrate and publicise that change. We have tried to ensure that in the minds of staff and the wider public these developments are seen as important and not reversible.

I think it was John Maynard Keynes who said that every senior statesman is living off the intellectual capital with which he entered politics in his youth. This tendency is very marked in the leadership grades in traditional hierarchical organ-isations. "Been there, done that, wore the T-shirt" would, in a phrase, summarise the perspective of many managers I have met in these services over the years. The Prisons Service has no immunity to this tendency to intellectual depletion. Growing and developing a leadership culture will be an abiding challenge for us over coming years.

Over the past few years we have tried to show that the Prisons Service is now looking to its staff at all levels *to act as people who remain open to new ideas* and to the philosophy of making a difference every day for people, for the prisoner and the wider community. The phrase, "making a difference", was indeed repeatedly deployed by me when addressing the Prison Officers' Association at their annual delegate conference in Westport in May 2000.

In my speech on that occasion I spoke about change in the Irish Public Service – the Strategic Management Initiative where individual managers and staff alike are expected to take personal responsibility for delivering results against planned targets and using modern management techniques to achieve greater levels of efficiency. I highlighted the genuine expectation of change which I had observed on my visits to the various prisons around the country. I suggested that this expectation could be harnessed to organise ourselves better, to eliminate inefficiencies and the corrosive overtime culture in the organisation.

I went on in my address to the POA Annual Conference to talk about how the new vision for the service would free up staff from traditional lock and key duties and deploy them on more productive duties with much greater job satisfaction. I set out for them a new scenario for the organisation as a service which

1 not only fulfils its custodial role effectively but gives equal and substantial weighting to care and rehabilitation of offenders
2 provides a safe, secure, just, and positive environment and which operates effective programmes as part of a *structured sentence management* approach
3 actively and fully involves prison officers in all aspects of the care and rehabilitation of offenders through multi-disciplinary team working
4 must become much more flexible in its working arrangements and must make far greater use of beneficial information technology such as electronic lockings and closed circuit CCTV
5 is to be an organisation which aspires to the highest ethical standards and is prepared, at all times, to shoulder its responsibilities and demonstrate accountability for its actions.

I told my Westport audience that the achievement of these five aspirations was not something which could be achieved overnight, and that realistically, full implementation of a vision such as this would require up to five years to implement.

That Westport statement still encapsulates my message as director general and my expectation of the organisation. Only time will tell whether the optimism and hopefulness I expressed on that occasion was well placed.

Our ambitions for the service, of course, go a lot further than "keeping the show on the road". I want to leave the area better than I found it. We want to end up, in a phrase, with *a prison system to be proud of.* Taking pride is at the core of the internal discipline of all uniformed services. The internal myths and folklore of Irish prisons have pride as their essential touchstone. Pride lies behind all the folklore of the service, even the "war stories" about pranks, escapes and escapades down the years where prison discipline and adherence to procedure went out the window.

Of course, no organisation, however strong its ethos and traditions, can depend indefinitely on personal charisma and last minute decision making to cope. Eventually that engine runs out of gas. The organisation cannot run on goodwill and good luck forever. The organisation requires a deeper managerial system than simple loyalty to the state and the formal hierarchy.

Over the past two years, with my transition team, I have sought to embed in the organisation a forward planning focus, proactive in terms of policy development, including emergency response arrangements which traditionally have been left to local managements to organise on an ad hoc basis.

Going around the country to our different prisons one is struck over and over again by the intensely local and individual character of these institutions, manned invariably by locally born officers and with a whole set of individual arrangements and work practices. Simple basic things like clocking-in arrangements have proved to be intensely local, idiosyncratic and informal in practice and based on requirements and agreements whose origins are very obscure – lost all too often in the mists of time.

Personally, I do not want to undermine justifiable pride in positive features of local administration – like the hurley repair workshop in Cork, the Braile printing at Arbour Hill, the positive charitable work on behalf of the community at Portlaoise or the enormously good humoured coping culture at Mountjoy. My task like that of many new CEOs has been to standardise the service we deliver. In our case to make consistent across the service our management of the staff who serve the organisation and the offenders whose sentences we manage on behalf of the community. Standardisation is not just a commercial concept. Justice and efficiency alike are impossible without consistency.

PRISONS – THE WAY AHEAD

The roots of modern Irish penology still lie in the Victorian era. I make no apology for that. The leading Victorian prison reformers were really far more advanced in their thinking than many present day commentators on crime and punishment issues.

The nineteenth-century prison reformers like Howard and Crofton really believed in rehabilitation of the individual offender in the custodial setting. They seriously addressed healthcare and substance abuse problems (largely alcohol abuse) in prison inmates and they worked assiduously towards the offender returning to a useful and law abiding role in society. I have no compunction in lauding those approaches in the present day while linking their objectives to modern day techniques and technologies like for instance group therapy and electronic monitoring. Clearly the prison in the modern era must do more than simply warehouse offenders, exacting retribution on behalf of outraged victims and their families.

Four key issues (drug addiction, lack of sex offender treatment, bad conditions in Mountjoy and other prisons, and high recidivism rates) have long been the subject of public criticism in respect of the prisons service. We have resolved, as far as possible, to seek "early wins" in relation to all four. Kotter (1995) argues that organisational renewal risks losing momentum if there are no short-term goals to meet and celebrate. I agree with him that "when it becomes clear to people that major change will take a long time, urgency levels can drop", and that "commitments to produce short-term wins help keep the urgency level up" (Kotter 1995, p 66).

DRUG TREATMENT FOR PRISONERS

There has been a plethora of reports in recent years, including O'Mahony (1997), Allwright et al (1999) and Hannon et al (2000) which confirmed high levels of drug dependency among prisoners and drug misuse while in prison.

Over the years prison authorities, including myself as head of operations from 1993 to 1997 tended to focus less on treatment approaches and more on the anti-contraband, enforcement approach. Initiatives taken by prison management down the years included progressively tightening up arrangements in visiting areas, increased use of closed circuit television cameras (CCTV), searches of prisoners and their cells etc.

I think that as a country, and especially as administrators in the criminal justice system, we were collectively in denial about the extent of the illegal drug problem nationally through most of the 1980s and 1990s. We failed to recognise the extent of heavy drug addiction in our society at a time when it was cutting such a swathe through whole communities, particularly local authority housing areas in the north and south inner city of Dublin and in the city's northern and western suburbs. The drug problem was, in reality, fuelling most property crime in the state over this period and was hugely concentrated among the offender population regularly passing through the prisons.

The healthcare issue was the first symptom of the problem of drug abuse in Irish prisons. This issue emerged through what, in retrospect, can only be called the virtual panic response in the prisons to the AIDS virus in the inmate population. Prisoners who were around at the time have described to me their being hurriedly blood sampled by frantic medics. The prisoners with positive results to the test were hurriedly told the bad news. They were then told to throw their worldly goods into a large black plastic bag and were escorted with it out of the prison in the middle of the night to quarantine landings in Arbour Hill Prison. The prisoners escorts were terrified, prison officers wearing head to toe overalls – which were described to me as "space suits with glass visors". The distress experienced by both parties can only be imagined.

In a matter of months, far more humane and less terrifying protocols were developed to manage the prisoners with drug related illnesses like Hepatitis C and the HIV virus. Humane detoxification for heroin dependent prisoners took a lot longer to arrive in the Dublin prisons, the main locus of the addiction problem. Eventually 7, 12, and 14 day methadone based detoxification regimes were introduced in the 1990s via the medical officers in the main Dublin prisons (these medical officers were all GP's who worked in the prisons on a part-time basis). We still experience the criticism that prisoners serving short sentences who have been on long-term methadone maintenance on the outside are knocked off methadone in prison and relapse in that setting into injecting behaviour. Thus the argument goes, they return from prison to their communities in a more damaged state than they were in before committal.

SUPPORTING ABSTINENCE FROM DRUGS IN PRISONS

In 1996, I was actively involved with Governor Bernard Power in instituting a drug-free prison initiative at one of our smaller prisons, the ninety-six person Training Unit at the back of Mountjoy Prison. This drug-free unit enables those prisoners who do not have a background of drug abuse and those who have demonstrated the desire to stop taking drugs to be detained in a drug-free and secure environment. In that setting, mandatory urine testing was put in place and all prisoners involved are excluded from access to prescribed mood altering medication.

EARLY DRUG TREATMENT INITIATIVES

In that same year 1996 we also opened the Mountjoy Treatment Facility at the prison's Health Care Unit. This unit was the first of its kind in a prison environment in the state. It is modelled on hospital based units in the community and is aimed at weaning addicts off drugs by gradually reducing dosages of substitutes such as methadone. A detoxification and therapeutic counselling programme lasting six weeks is provided to offenders in groups of nine at any one time. Over two hundred and fifty offenders have successfully completed the programme in the Drug Treatment Unit to date. A second drug treatment programme commenced earlier this year in Mountjoy Prison. This unit provides an additional nine treatment places at any one time. The main emphasis is on offering detoxification and intensive therapeutic counselling over six weeks to prisoners nearing release, with a view to returning them drug free to a structured drug treatment programme in the community.

A review of the first 12 months of the programme (Crowley 1999) found that out of 88 prisoners accepted into the programme, 36 had returned to drug use one year later. When reviewed 18 months later – up to February 1999 – a further 15 patients had relapsed thus giving a total number of 51 prisoners out of 88 who had relapsed. Sixteen patients could not be followed up, but if those had also relapsed this would give us a 12 monthly relapse rate of 78%. This relapse figure is shockingly high, but is favourable when viewed in comparison to in-patient detoxification programmes internationally which have on average a 90% relapse rate. The fact is that the majority of addicts may become drug free and relapse several times before succeeding in becoming drug free for an extended period.

THE WAY FORWARD

An Action Plan on Drug Misuse and Drug Treatment in the prison system was published just prior to my appointment in July 1999. This plan provides a broad general strategy to raise the level of treatment for drug addicted offenders. It includes the expansion of detoxification facilities, the creation of more drug-free areas and the provision of methadone maintenance. The provision of addiction counselling support services is central to the plan.

Towards the end of 1999, following discussions with our minister, I established a National Steering Group for Prison Based Drug Treatment Services, under my chairmanship, with a view to implementing the Action Plan. The Steering Group comprises representatives from the Prisons Service, the Department of Justice, Equality and Law Reform, Eastern Health Board, and the Probation and Welfare Service. The group invited, via public advertisements, submissions from the general public as well as from special interest groups in relation to the review. Twenty-two submissions were received in response to the advertisement in the national press.

The Steering Group presented its first report in July 2000. The report covered in some detail the needs of Mountjoy Male Prison, Dochas Centre (Mountjoy Female Prison), St Patrick's Institution and Cloverhill Prison. It proposes a systematic and partially centralised approach to drug treatment services in the prison system as a whole based to a considerable degree on the Mountjoy Prison complex. The report also called for a multidisciplinary approach to the drug problem in prisons with substantial Eastern Regional Health Authority input. One of the most significant conclusions of the report was that the Prisons Service must replicate in prison, to the maximum extent possible, the level of medical and other supports available in the community for drug dependent people. The approach put forward included recommendations on methadone maintenance and the more extensive use of doctors, nurses, psychologists, and psychiatrists. Although its implementation will be expensive, I am confident that it will prove to be a justifiable investment. The over-riding emphasis is on "through-care" for prisoners and consultation with community interests in the drug treatment area.

On production of the report in July 2000, the minister put a memorandum to government seeking its endorsement for the staffing and strategy recommendations which the group put forward. Following consultations with departments over the period August to September, the memorandum was considered by government at its meeting on Wednesday, 18 October 2000.

The Government then decided to

(1) approve, in principle, the implementation of the recommendations made in the *First Report of the Steering Group on Prison Based Drug Treatment Services*

(2) note that the precise staffing and other expenditure related proposals arising will be the subject of direct negotiations between the Departments of Justice, Equality and Law Reform, Finance and Health and Children as well as the Prisons Service and Health Boards.

While the "devil is in the detail" which will have to be negotiated with the Department of Finance, this government decision represents a landmark step in tackling the drug problem in our prisons. We have moved from diagnosis to prescription in relation to the drug problem in prisons. Now we have to deliver the treatment.

In advance of these planned initiatives we have ploughed ahead with extending methadone maintenance to prisoners who were compliant methadone programme participants before they came into our custody. We now have almost 300 prisoners on methadone maintenance, under medical supervision, on a daily basis. That is just under 10% of the daily prison population nationwide. We are also working, in tandem with the Probation Service, to enhance co-operation with relevant local services in the drug treatment area to ensure effective throughcare arrangements for prisoners in this category.

SEX OFFENDER TREATMENT

The number of sex offenders in custody in Irish prisons has increased dramatically since the mid-1990s. In 1994, there were 183 sex offenders in custody. By September last year, the number of persons on remand or under sentence in respect of sex offences was 390 which accounted for approximately 1 in 7 of all prisoners in custody and a very much higher proportion of our long-term prisoner population. I believe the trend of committals in this area will continue to rise as disclosure of offences in this area also increases. Because of the length of sentences for offences of this type the "silting up" effect will also occur with overall numbers in this offender group in our custody. In a few short years we have moved from having only one prison occupied by sex offenders, Arbour Hill, to two prisons: Arbour Hill and the Curragh, with significant populations of sex offenders in Wheatfield, Castlerea, Cork and Limerick Prisons.

The rapid increase in sex offence convictions was attributable at least in part to the sterling work of the Rape Crisis Centres around the country and spokes-women like Olive Braiden who encouraged reporting such offences. There was also a statistically significant impact from prosecutions in respect of paedophilia-related offences. The taking of successful prosecutions in respect of such child abuse offences, including prosecutions in respect of offences committed many years previously, continues apace. The court lists for the next two years up to October 2002 are full of such cases. While it is expected that the prison system will continue to receive growing numbers of sex offenders in future years, it is, I think, unlikely that the dramatic rate of increase in committals for sex offences between 1995 and 2000 will be sustained. As a group, sex offenders have placed quite complex demands on the prison system over recent years. These demands include the following requirements:

(i) in terms of numbers alone, *the need to provide suitable and secure prison places* for some hundreds of sex offenders added to the already difficult overcrowding problem over the late 1990s. It necessitated greater use of early release of other prisoners to maintain prisoner numbers overall at manageable levels

(ii) in most prisons here and abroad, *sex offenders have had to be segregated* from the general prison population to ensure their safety. This entails detailed planning of their every movement around the prison and every aspect of their involvement in prison life. They can attend workshops, education units, religious ceremonies and recreation halls *only* when those areas are clear of prisoners who might pose a threat to them. The only prison we have where sex offenders mix freely with the general offender population is Castlerea Prison (where they constitute a majority in a carefully selected prisoner population)

(iii) the need to develop and provide a variety of specialist therapeutic interventions aimed at rehabilitation of sex offenders.

It was in the area of relapse prevention that we decided to focus our efforts for an "early win" in respect of sex offenders. Media coverage and commentary about the issue of sex offender treatment programmes frequently implies there is only one form of rehabilitation programme in place for sex offenders in Irish prisons and that it reaches a very limited number of prisoners annually. This assertion is quite incorrect but is unfortunately difficult to refute.

There are actually three forms of direct therapeutic intervention available to sex offenders within the Irish prison system at present. All three are aimed at enabling such offenders gain some measure of control over their personal tendencies towards offending behaviour.

The first intervention method is individual counselling from the Prison Psychology Service and from the Probation and Welfare Service. This is a largely demand-led service to individual prisoners who ask for help. The second intervention is a multi-disciplinary Thinking Skills Group Work Programme which focuses on issues such as anger management, evasion of personal responsibility and relapse prevention. This programme has been in place in Cork Prison and Arbour Hill Prison since 1998 and has just started in the Curragh Prison. The third intervention, which tends to receive most media coverage, is an extremely intensive offence focused group work programme, which up to now has only been available at Arbour Hill Prison. This programme is delivered by officers of the Probation and Welfare and Prison Psychology Services. Additionally, prisoners in this sex offender group (and indeed all other categories of offender) have access to psychiatric services which are provided to prisons on a sessional basis as well as in response to particular individual crises. The providers in this respect are usually forensic psychiatrists attached to the Central Mental Hospital, Dundrum.

A Working Group, which we set up in 1999, comprising representatives of all the relevant agencies and prison disciplines is currently overseeing the introduction of a number of new interventions for sex offenders in the Curragh Prison. Prisoners and staff at the Curragh have now been involved in the inception of new prisoner programmes there, one exclusively involving specialist staff (as in the intensive Arbour Hill programme) and the other programme on the same pattern as the Thinking Skills Programmes in Cork and Arbour Hill which are delivered by multi-disciplinary teams including specially selected and trained prison officers. I personally attended the inaugural meeting of the group and one or two other meetings to signal my personal interest in its success. I also intervened personally to ensure the co-operation of the Prison Officers Association (POA) when an industrial relations difficulty threatened to "scupper" the Curragh programme during late October 2000.

The first step being promoted by the Curragh Project Group involves the expansion of generic therapeutic services in the prison. The Probation and Welfare Service and the Psychology Service are currently recruiting extra staff and it is now agreed that the Curragh will have priority in the allocation of resources. Already a member of the Prisons Psychology Service has taken up an assignment to the Curragh since September 2000. He joined a probation officer who had also been assigned to duties there since the summer. They will be joined in their work with offenders at the Curragh by further members of their services as the "roll out" of support services for sex offenders at the prison continues.

The Thinking Skills course referred to earlier was introduced in Arbour Hill and Cork prisons early in 1998. Following a number of months staff training that course has just been extended to prisoners at the Curragh. The course is designed to target a range of offenders, including sex offenders, particularly with a view to motivating the latter group to engage in the more intensive programmes. The course is run by multi-disciplinary teams, including prison officers, Probation and

Welfare staff and teaching staff under the guidance of the Department's Psychology Service. The skills taught in this programme include general strategies for recognising problems, analysing them and considering non-criminal alternatives, how to consider the consequences of their behaviour, to think before they act, how to go beyond their own view of the world and consider the thoughts and feelings of other people and how to develop the ability to control their own behaviour and avoid acting impulsively. This programme is considered by my colleagues to be the preferred first line of approach to rehabilitating sex offenders in custody. This is because in many cases it builds up their frequently low personal motivation to address offending behaviour in depth.

The Intensive Sex Offenders Treatment Programme was introduced in the Curragh in late December 2000 and will initially be operated exclusively by the Probation and Welfare Service and Psychology Service, in the same mode as the current Arbour Hill programme.

However, at the Curragh and elsewhere that programme is going to be augmented, if not replaced ultimately, by intensive rehabilitative programmes for sex offenders to be *delivered by multi-disciplinary teams.* This multi-disciplinary model has been operated satisfactorily in prisons in Great Britain and North America over the last ten years or so. With the objective of replicating this approach we decided to contract in the services of a research psychologist as an additional resource to work on this project alongside the existing disciplines in the Prisons Service. Our objective is to put in place a wider range of rehabilitative programmes for sex offenders than are currently available and to ensure they operate on independently accredited selection, training and service methods. We also intend that these programmes should reach *every* sex offender in custody who is willing to participate at some level in their personal rehabilitation and relapse prevention. In September 2000, following a public competition in this respect, a contract was awarded to an experienced psychologist, Dr Francesca Lundstrom, to carry out this research task. It will be completed by her in 2001. In addition, a major review of the effectiveness of the present intensive Arbour Hill Sex Offender Programme is currently underway between the Prisons Psychology Service and the Department of Psychology, University College, Dublin, under the leadership of Dr Alan Carr.

In a prison setting it is beneficial to have a team approach to the therapeutic side of the rehabilitation of sex offenders. It is not about doing anything on the cheap but informing the whole institution about the way to approach offenders. It has deeper philosophical value than simply saving a few bob or using somebody to deliver a programme who is not as high up the formal skill ladder. It is something that helps to inform the whole prison.

MOUNTJOY COMPLEX REDEVELOPMENT.

Mountjoy Prison is now over150 years old and is in need of drastic refurbishment to bring it up to modern standards and provide up-to-date facilities for the custody and care of offenders committed there. The Mountjoy complex includes the main male adult prison, the equally old St Patrick's Institution building, the Training Unit and the new Dochas Centre (Women's Prison). This complex covering eighteen arcres of the North Inner City of Dublin still holds more than 1 in 3 of all the prisoners in custody in this state. Until recently it held half of them.

In early 2000, with the approval of our minister, I established a multi-disciplinary group, chaired by Governor John Lonergan, and comprising senior members of the Prisons Service, representatives from the Department of Justice, Equality and Law Reform, Probation and Welfare Service, City of Dublin Vocational Education Committee, Prisoners Aid through Community Effort (PACE), and the Architectural Design Team from the Office of Public Works, to devise a comprehensive plan for the redevelopment of the entire Mountjoy complex.

The group submitted its first report in May 2000 (Mountjoy Group 2000). Its more significant recommendations include the following.

- The overall new Mountjoy design should facilitate maximum flexibility in the use of facilities
- It should promote a balanced prison regime of custody, order, care and rehabilitation
- The complex should continue as a committal facility for men and women aged eighteen and upwards; (ie sixteen and seventeen year olds should be accommodated elsewhere)
- Capacity to be 870 prisoners in toto, all to be held in medium security conditions (reduction in present capacity of approximately 200)
- Facilities for prisoner assessment as part of prisoner management programme
- Special focus on eighteen to twenty-three year olds
- Commitment to a drugs free and drug dependency treatment policy
- An appreciation of special needs such as medical, psychiatric, ethnic/ culture requirements for prisoners
- A positive and progressive regime.

The group presented a second report in February 2001 which contains outline architectural design and development plans for the complex. The core of the proposals is to demolish most of the old Victorian buildings and replace them with modern, high density housing units with suitable facilities for recreation, education and rehabilitation work with offenders.

REDUCING RECIDIVISM, WORK/TRAINING – CONNECT PROJECT

The purpose of the longstanding work/training activity in Irish prisons is to provide occupation for prisoners during their time in custody *and* to provide training so that inmates who are motivated to do so can acquire marketable skills to help them get employment after they leave prison. The work/training programme is intended to operate in a complementary manner with the other prison programmes and regimes including education, psychology, welfare etc. Even the most right wing commentators on crime and punishment tend to support such programmes.

A wide range of vocational activities is provided for our inmates across the Irish prison system – metalwork, woodwork, construction activities, farming, horti culture, computers, printing, electronics, clothing manufacture, Braille production, catering, laundry, driving instruction, health and safety training, craft activities etc. All staff engaged in work and training are members of the Prisons Service. Clearly a working life is generally incompatible with an offending life style. Getting prisoners on to the track of a working life is the optimal rehabilitation objective. In the past, high levels of unemployment nationally made employment prospects for convicted persons very bleak indeed. That has all changed now with the very tight labour market which currently prevails in the country.

CONNECT project

Over the past three years we have sought to expand the range of rehabilitation options for prisoners through the development of a pilot programme called CONNECT. This is an action-research project taking place since 1998 in Mountjoy Prison and the nearby Training Unit, funded by the EU Integra Employment initiative. Various agencies of the Department of Justice, Equality and Law Reform, including the Prisons Service itself and the Probation and Welfare Service, have collaborated in conducting the project with the National Training and Development Institute (NTDI), part of the REHAB Group. The lead player at Prison Headquarters, Martin Hickey, happens to also serve part-time as a member of my transition team.

Our objective in CONNECT was to find how to create new effective pathways for people in prison to follow to achieve labour market participation after their release from custody. The scope of what we were trying to achieve can best be understood by taking a brief look at the profile of the prisoners we were dealing with. A 1996 study of Mountjoy prisoners (O'Mahony 1997, chapters 3 to 6), a broadly representative sample at the time of the inmate population as a whole, showed that:

- 49% were aged between nineteen and twenty-six
- 56% came from six socially disadvantaged areas of Dublin

- 27% were from families broken by separation when they were still young
- 50% of the married prisoners were separated from their families
- 80% left school before sixteen years of age
- 88% were unemployed just prior to imprisonment
- 27% had never held a job
- 63% had a serious heroin dependency
- 70% were in prison for property crimes – robbery, burglary, larceny
- 89% were acknowledged recidivists.

Essentially what the Mountjoy-based project sought to achieve was to make a bridge between life in custody and participation in the labour market after release. It dealt with the prisoners as they presented themselves, no selection criteria were applied except the core requirement that people had to want to participate. Through CONNECT we addressed core issues affecting prisoners including personal decision-making capacity, coherence among our support services and linkages "from inside to outside".

The project had three stages for the participants.

(1) *Options*: is a pre-vocational training programme designed to provide personal development training and job seeking skills for participants. The programme aims to challenge the thinking of those taking part and to encourage them to think of the future in terms of the type of work/training/education they would ultimately like to take part in. It examines with the prisoners how they can use their time in custody to optimum personal benefit. Twelve participants take part in each module of the programme five days a week for fourteen weeks.

(2) The *Vocational Needs Assessment* and *Individual Planning Process* (IPP). The IPP is designed to elicit the needs of each individual in a holistic way. It assesses needs in all areas of the individual's life and culminates in a report detailing the personal strengths *and* areas in need of development for the individual. This information is fed back to him/her by the IPP Mentor, usually a prison officer.

(3) The introduction of the participants to *Vocational Training Programmes* certified by external bodies in the areas of high labour-market demand at present, for example industrial cleaning, bakery, catering, welding, construction and computers.

A total of 174 prisoners, both men and women, have participated to date in the pilot CONNECT Project in 15 separate modules. Of the participants, 76 have been released. Of the 76 released, 26% went out to jobs, 7% went out to further training, 5% went out to residential drug treatment, 58% dropped out of contact with the services. Of the 76 who were released only 4% have been returned to prison (Source, NTDI/Irish Prisons Service).

Thanks to the recent investment made in providing additional prison spaces we are bringing to an end the chronic overcrowding which has bedeviled the system for so many years. We are now in a position to create an environment in which sentence planning and rehabilitative programmes such as CONNECT can succeed and be mainstreamed throughout the service.

I am particularly delighted with the lead role played by basic grade prison officers in this project. This is in keeping with our objective to transform the role of the basic grade officer away from lock and key duties to more challenging, value-enriched tasks. The symbolism of the prison officer carrying out mentoring roles and the intuitive logic of emphasising career development for prisoners made CONNECT a flagship project for us. Thanks to the efforts of my colleague in the Department's Equality Division, Assistant Secretary Sylda Langford and of course our minister himself, the National Development Plan has provided the resources for us to implement the CONNECT Project throughout our prison system. A public competition was held during Autumn 2000 to procure our long-term external training partner. The National Training and Development Institute (NTDI), who had been on board during the pilot phase, won the competition and following exchanges of contracts, CONNECT 2000-2004 was formally launched by the Minister for Justice, Equality and Law Reform on 1 November 2000 at a ceremony in the Dochas Centre (Women's Prison, Mountjoy, Dublin).

CONCLUSION

We in the Irish Prisons Service have to respond to the challenges which face us in a more open and imaginative way more than we would have done in the past.

Public opinion is a real force at this juncture in the debate about criminal justice in the modern era. We have to ensure that public opinion is as well informed as possible about what the prison system is doing on behalf of the community in promoting its long-term health and safety. When things go wrong for us (and things often do go wrong in prisons adminstration) we have a duty to explain what happened, insofar as security or legal constraints allow. We have a duty also to work to prevent a repetition of mistakes made. Prisons administration is an area where few mistakes go unpunished in terms of public opprobrium.

Prisons administration is *always* going to be at the unglamorous end of public service. Some commentators have described prison management as the impossible job in public service. Derek Lewis, the businessman who briefly headed up the English Prison Service in the early 1990s, described his tenure as "the longest toughest most traumatic time of my life". Individual traumas aside, the Irish Prisons Service will I hope in years to come be increasingly regarded as an essential service where the quality of our input has substantial relevance to the overall quality of life in the wider community. The core mission for our organisation will be to deliver a quality service in the future.

I will close with a quotation from Winston Churchill, of all people, which is frequently cited but rarely given in full form. It deserves repetition here: "the convict stands deprived of everything that a free man calls life ... the mood and temper of the public in regard to the treatment of crime and criminals is one of the most unfailing tests of the civilization of any country. A calm and dispassionate recognition of the rights of the accused (and) ... of convicted criminals against the State ... and an *unfaltering faith that there is treasure if you can only find it, in the heart of every man* – these are the symbols which in the treatment of the crime and criminals mark and measure the stored up strength of a nation and are the sign and proof of the living virtue in it" (Winston Churchill, Home Secretary, 1910).

REFERENCES

Allwright, S., Barry, J., Bradley, F., Long, J. and Thornton, L. (1999), *Hepatitis B Hepatitis C and HIV in Irish Prisoners: Prevalence and Risk,* Dublin: Stationery Office

Aylward, S. (1999), "The Irish Prisons Service in the New Millennium", *Communique,* Journal of An Garda Síochána.

Aylward, S., "Driving for Results and Delivering the Vision", The Role of the CEO in the Independent Irish Prisons Service, Start up Phase 1999-2000, A Personal Account. Thesis presented for Master of Science course in Public Service Management, IMI/TCD

Carey, T. (2000), *Mountjoy: The Story of a Prison,* The Collins Press, Cork.

Crowley, D. (1999), "The Drug Detox Unit at Mountjoy Prison – A Review", *The Journal of Health Gain* 3 (3) 17-19

Department of Justice (1994), *Management of Offenders, A five year Plan,* Government Publications Office

Eggleston, C. The Liam Minihan Memorial Lecture, Marino Institute, Dublin, 19 October 2000

Expert Group on Prisons (1997), *Towards an Independent Prisons Agency,* Dublin: Stationery Office

Hannon, F., Kelleher, C. and Friel, S. (2000), *General Healthcare Study of the Irish Prisoner Population,* Dublin: Stationery Office

Hughes, Robert (1987), *The Fatal Shore.* London: Collins Harvill, pp 59-67

Kotter, John P. (1995), "Why Transformation Efforts Fail", *Harvard Business Review,* March/April 1979, pp 106-114

Mountjoy Group (2000), First and Second Reports of the Working Group on the Redevelopment of the Mountjoy Complex, Internal Document, Department of Justice

O'Mahony, P. (1997), *Mountjoy Prisoners: A Sociological and Criminological Profile,* Dublin: Stationery Office

Prisoner D83222, (1946), *I Did Penal Servitude,* Dublin: Metropolitan Publishing Company

Whitaker Report (1985), *Report of the Commission of Inquiry into the Penal System,* Dublin: Stationery Office

34

The Social Analysis of the Irish Prison System

Ciaran McCullagh

Introduction

In this chapter we examine the way in which the Irish prison system operates. We do this by outlining its main features, by considering the likely future development of the system, and by looking at explanations that can be offered for the kind of penal expansion that is currently being experienced in Ireland. The level of punishment of offenders who come from seriously deprived backgrounds is increasing and that is a phenomenon that requires some explanation. The Irish penal system can with only slight exaggeration be characterised as mainly a means through which the poor are punished.

A democratic deficit?

However before getting on to these issues, it is necessary to make a preliminary observation. The information through which we can describe, comprehend and assess the Irish prison system is drawn largely from the annual reports on Prison and Places of Detention published by the Department of Justice, Equality and Law Reform. Though there have been criticisms of the manner in which the figures have been compiled and the manner in which they have been presented (see for example, Rottman 1984) these have proved of some use. These reports have been published in a fairly consistent if not always timely fashion up to 1994.

Since then however the situation has deteriorated to a significant and worrying degree.

The 1994 report was published in 1997. It was December 2000 before a report covering the years 1995 to 1998 was published. Its contents were a considerable deviation from those of previous ones. The number of statistics was significantly reduced and they were organised into categories that are less comprehensive and less informative than those used in previous reports. This concern with the quality of prison reports is not merely a pedantic one.

Open and accessible information on what is happening in the institutions in which citizens are deprived of their liberty is a fundamental requirement of a democratic society. Its absence means that we are deprived of an important means through which we as citizens can call the state to account. This is particularly important in that the Irish prison system does not have independent external oversight.

FEATURES OF THE SYSTEM

When we analyse these reports and combine them with other kinds of knowledge and research on the prison system we can point to the following key features of the system in Ireland.

1 Increased numbers

The most striking feature of the system is the significant increase in the numbers incarcerated. The inadequate nature of prison reports makes it difficult to demonstrate this in a consistent fashion. The most recent reports show that committals to prison have risen from 9,928 in 1995 to 11, 307 in 1998, a percentage increase over the period of 14%. The extent of the increase in committals to prison can be gauged from the fact that the corresponding figure for 1991 was 7,952 and for 1981 was 6,327. However the 1998 figure is indicative rather than fully informative as it includes men, women and juveniles and, perhaps more importantly, it does not distinguish between those committed under sentence, those committed for non-payment of fines and those committed on remand.

An alternative way of making the point about increased numbers is to use the figure for the Daily Average Population in prison and places of detention. This is the number who are in prison on a particular day of the year. In 1991 this figure stood at 2,185. In 1994 it was 2,121. In 1998 it was 2,610 and on 1 June 2000 it was 2,940. These figures confirm the rise in the prison population (38% since 1991) and suggest that this rise accelerated in the mid-1990s, particularly between 1996 and 1997.

2 Remand Prisoners

Prison reports would suggest that those on remand constitute a significant part of the prison population. Remand prisoners are either awaiting trail or awaiting sentence. In 1991 their numbers stood at 3,517, while the number of convicted committals was 4,435. This means that remands made up 42% of committals to prison. In 1994 the number of remand prisoners was 4,729, while the number of committals under sentence was 6,506. The most recent report does not contain comparable figures. But it shows that 322 prisoners were on remand on 1 June 2000. This represented 11% of the prison population on that day.

The situation in relation to remand prisoners has always been problematic. Until the 1996 Bail Referendum and the regulations based on it introduced by the minister in 1998, the right to bail was almost absolute in the Irish courts, with only a limited number of exceptional circumstances in which bail could be refused. These included where there were reasonable grounds to believe that the accused would not turn up for trial or would attempt to interfere with witnesses or evidence, if granted bail. This did not prevent substantial numbers being held on remand (see McCullagh 1990). O'Mahony (1993:103) has suggested that the length of time remand prisoners spend in prison is short, with the average length of stay being ten days. Until recently they have shared a prison regime that, with some minor exceptions, was effectively speaking the same as that for convicted prisoners. The opening of a remand prison at Cloverhill in Clondalkin has formally segregated them from convicted prisoners though media reports on the new prison suggest that conditions there are far from ideal.

A more worrying aspect of remand prisoners is that prison statistics show that significant numbers of remand prisoners are not recommitted to prison after they have been sentenced by the courts. In 1994, for example, 4,729 prisoners were either in custody on remand on 1 January or else committed on remand during that year. Yet 2,387 of these (50% of the total) were "brought up (in court) and not re-committed". These kinds of figures lead to concerns that many offenders are being remanded in custody unnecessarily (see Mc Cullagh 1990).

3 Fine defaulters

The number of fine defaulters in Irish prisons is also a striking feature of the system. In 1991 the number committed in default of fines was 769, or 28% of all committals under sentence of imprisonment. In 1994 the figure was 2,173, or 38% of those committed to prison. The most recent figures suggest that the number of committals to prison for failure to pay a fine has declined somewhat. The Minster for Justice told the Dáil that 1,610 people were committed to prison for non-payment of fines in 1996, but it is not possible to ascertain what percentage this represents of all those committed under sentence (see Report of the Dáil Sub-Committee 2000).

The imprisonment of fine defaulters raises serious questions about the use of prison. These are offenders whose initial offences were not enough to merit prison sentences. They were subsequently imprisoned either because they were unwilling or unable to pay the fine imposed by the court. As the level of fines is generally relatively low in Irish courts, it is likely that many offenders do not have the necessary means to pay them.

This creates an invidious situation for such offenders. Research indicates that disadvantaged offenders are more likely to receive an immediate prison sentence than a fine. Bacik and her colleagues (1998) found, for example, that defendants from poorer parts of Dublin were less likely to be fined and more likely to be sent to prison. As the Dáil Sub-Committee on Crime and Punishment (2000: 10) concluded, this means that "the poor are doubly disadvantaged. They are more likely to be jailed than fined in the first instance, but even if fined they may end up in custody anyway in the event of non-payment". For poorer offenders the imposition of a fine may merely be a temporary hiccup on the route to prison.

4 Overcrowding and early release

The main impact of the increase in prison numbers has been overcrowding in the system. There has not been enough space in the prisons to accommodate the extra inmates. The problem is most severe in Mountjoy but there are also significant problems in St Patrick's Institution for Juvenile Offenders, and in Cork Prison. In 1998, for example, Mountjoy had a "design capacity" for 607 inmates and a daily average population of 807. Moreover the problem is not confined to the older prisons. Wheatfield is a purpose built prison that opened in 1989. It was designed to accommodate 320 prisoners yet the daily average population for 1998 was 360.

Such overcrowding produces dismal living conditions for inmates. The extra numbers have been accommodated by adding extra bunks to two and three prisoner cells or through having mattresses on cell floors. Some prisoners in St Patrick's have spent their entire sentences sleeping on such mattresses (*Annual Report on Prisons* 1995-1998: 62). It also prevents prison services such as education and work training from working with an acceptable level of efficiency and effectiveness.

The problem of overcrowding has been alleviated, though not eliminated, through the provision of extra places in individual prisons and through the opening of the remand prison. Overcrowding continues, for example, to be a problem in Mountjoy. On 2 May 2000 there were 675 male offenders in the prison, that is 128 more than its design capacity for male prisoners.

This in effect means that the system continues to rely on early release procedures, through which prisoners are freed before their sentences are complete. This is known in administrative and legal terms as "temporary early release" but more colloquially it is known as the "revolving door". Originally temporary release had a marginal role in the prison system and was intended as part of a planned rehabilitation strategy. Now it has become the major means through which prison overcrowding is deal with. Its implications have been that, according to prison authorities, prisoners are often freed "at far earlier stages than would otherwise be considered desirable" (*Annual Report* 1995-1998: 21). It has also arguably had an effect on public confidence in the judicial and legal system in that for most offenders there may be little relationship between the sentence of the court and the sentence they actually serve.

According to prison authorities the provision of extra places has reduced the use of early release. In May 1998, 455 offenders were on temporary release, compared to 558 the previous May. Official figures also show that although the number on temporary release has halved between 1998 and 2000, it continues to be an issue. The Minster for Justice claimed that the "revolving door" would close by autumn 1999 (*Irish Times*, 2 June 1999). The available figures would suggest that this target has not yet been achieved.

In the same speech the minister also extended the types of prisoners who would not qualify for temporary release. These had included those serving sentences for drugs trafficking, armed robbery and sex offences. He has now added those convicted of violence against women, attacks on the elderly, car theft and serious public order offences. The precise impact of these changes is difficult to evaluate from prison statistics but the numbers serving sentences for some of these offences appears to be relatively small so its impact on temporary release may be less significant than the publicity surrounding the announcement might have suggested.

However the decision by the minster to deny early release to certain categories of offenders illustrates the political nature of the prison system in Ireland. It is reasonable to argue that the decision to give temporary release should be an integral part of the rehabilitation process and of what the National Crime Forum Report (1998) called "a planned programme" of sentence management. In such a scenario the granting of early release should be based not on offence but on the stage that a prisoner's rehabilitation had reached. The minister's decision effectively undermines whatever potential there was for a comprehensive planning of programmes aimed at the prevention of further offending. The nature of the offences chosen for exclusion from temporary release would suggest that a desire by the minister to be seen to be tough on crime has outweighed a desire to institute programmes to change the motivations and the behaviours of prisoners.

5 The experience of prison: the views of inmates

The figures show increases in prison numbers but what is it like to be in prison? There are only two sources on the experiences of prisoners and they are both limited in that that they both relate to one prison, Mountjoy. The first is the responses of prisoners to O'Mahony's (1997) survey. Their general tone was critical. The most common complaints were about hygienic conditions, the attitudes and behaviour of prison officers, and the dominance of drugs in the prison. Where hygiene was concerned the main problem was the inadequacy of conditions of facilities and the lack of in-cell sanitation. There were also complaints about mice and cockroaches and the generally dilapidated state of the place. The main complaints about prison officers related to the lack of respect prisoners experienced from them. In addition some complained that prison officers were deliberately provocative. They caused tension and unnecessary aggravation through, for example, verbal abuse. However this aggravation did not generally result in physical ill-treatment. Only one respondent spoke of being physically ill-treated by prison staff.

This is borne out by the report of the European Committee for the Prevention of Torture and Inhuman or Degrading Treatment (1999). The members of the committee visited a number of prisons in Ireland in 1993 and again in 1998. They found that the majority of prison officers treated prisoners in a humane way. But they expressed concern at a number of complaints they received about physical ill-treatment and verbal abuse by prison officers. They claim that the authorities acknowledge the existence of "rogue officers" specifically in Mountjoy and Limerick prisons.

But the committee was concerned that "little effective action" had been taken against them. A new disciplinary code had been introduced for prison officers. But the committee found that the Department of Justice, Equality and Law Reform and the Prison Officers Association had come to an agreement that "disciplinary complaints against an officer arising from an allegation against a prisoner would be dealt with by way of a circular outside the Code".

A number of prisoners complained about the presence of drugs in the prison and the absence of drug addiction treatment. They said that it was difficult to avoid drugs, either in terms of their availability or in terms of the health hazards associated with them. These included the dangers of used syringes and of sharing facilities with prisoners with either hepatitis or HIV. There was also a lack of services for drug users, whether these were counselling services, needle exchange or methadone maintenance.

The second source is a recent account given to journalist Paul Howard (1998) by an anonymous offender. He had spent a significant part of his adult life either in St Patrick's Institution or Mountjoy and his account confirms many aspects of O'Mahony's survey. It shows that relationships between staff and prisoners are not inevitably antagonistic or conflictual and he did not see or experience any brutality from prison officers. Any of the fighting that he witnessed was between prisoners. In his account boredom, loneliness, depression and drug use are the dominant features of prison life. Most of the inmates spend their time in "daily idleness". Drug smuggling is widespread, sophisticated and generally successful. So too is self-directed violence, whether this is in the form of suicide, self-injury and self-mutilation. This is some distance from popular perceptions of the place as a "holiday camp".

5 What did they do, why are they there?

In the normal course of events it should be possible to see from the published prison statistics the nature of the offences for which prisoners committed under sentence were found guilty. However the inadequate nature of recent reports means that we have to rely on the figures for 1994 for some indication of this. These show that two types of offence account for over half of those committed to prison on conviction – offences against property without violence (primarily larceny and car theft) and offences under the Road Traffic Act. A total of 6,866 offenders (the figure includes men, women and juveniles) were committed to prison. Fifty-four per cent of these were committed for the two above offence types. However, as the report of the Crime Forum (1998: 149) pointed out, the majority of offenders under the Road Traffic Act do no get to prison because they pay the relevant financial penalties before committal.

Ten per cent of offenders were committed for crimes against the person. The vast 'majority of these were committed for assault. If we can judge by length of sentence many of these assaults were of a less serious nature. For example, of the 286 males committed to prison for assault, 164 (57%) were given sentences of six months or less. Eight of the sixteen women were given three months or less and thirty of the seventy-three juveniles were given six months or less. O'Mahony (2000: 30) also argues that many of the assaults were of a minor or technical nature so they cannot be regarded as "truly serious".

There is little in these figures that differs radically from those in previous prison reports. The public and media perceptions may be that prison is full of violent offenders. The fact is that the bulk of the prison population in Ireland is made up of petty if persistent offenders who mainly commit crimes against property without violence.

6 Drugs and prison

Two other features of the prison system are noteworthy. One has already been alluded to. This is the presence in the prisons both of serious drug addicts and of a dependable supply of illegal drugs to meet their needs. The increase in inmates with drug problems reflects the way in which the crime situation in Ireland has been transformed since the late 1970s by the increased availability and use of hard drugs, principally heroin. Dublin in particular has had an epidemic of drug use, mainly in disadvantaged areas. This has impacted on the nature of crime in a number of ways. Most pertinent for our purposes has been the creation of the phenomenon of addict crime. According to one study (Keogh 1997) over 90% of heroin users finance their habit through crime. It is probably overly simplistic to argue that drug use causes crime as arguably many of these individuals might have engaged in crime without the added pressure of drugs. But it is undoubtedly the case that drug use has intensified their level of criminal activity.

This level of drug use has had knock-on effects on the prison system. O'Mahony's (1997) study of the population of Mountjoy found that almost two-thirds of male and female prisoners had significant histories of heroin use. Moreover imprisoning such people has not significantly impeded their access to drugs. O'Mahony found that almost half the prisoners had used heroin in the prison. The conditions under which they used it are particularly problematic. It is used intravenously and, in the absence of sterile needles, the spread of hepatitis and HIV infection has been facilitated. Another study of drug users in the prison system found that 55% of those who inject said that they shared drug-injecting equipment (Alwright, Bradley, Long and Thornton 1999).

This level of drug use has impacted on prison life in a number of ways. A notable impact for prisoners has been the high level of security and surveillance of prison visits and the consequent dehumanisation of interaction between prisoners and their families. In Cork prison, for example, a heavy perspex wall separates prisoners and visitors. It allows visual contact but prevents physical interaction. According to officials this has prevented the smuggling of drugs into the prison. A recent newspaper report (*Irish Examiner*, 5 September 2000) indicated that prison officials had made 622 seizures of drugs in the prison system, including thirty-one in Cork prison. The report went on to quote "informed sources" as claiming that such seizures were only a fraction of the drugs being smuggled into prisons.

It has also impacted on prisoners in that one in five prisoners who inject drugs claimed that their drug use started in prison (Alwright, Bradley, Long and Thornton, 1999). There is also the risk to the lives of drug users in prison. According to the figures produced by the National Steering Group on Deaths in Prison (1999:37-39), nine people died in prison between 1990 and 1997 as a result of drugs overdoses and most of those who died in prison in 1995 and 1996 had heroin addictions.[1]

Finally the presence of drugs and drug addicts in the prisons has also impacted on the working conditions of prison staff. It has created difficulties and anxieties for them in terms of the fear of being attacked with infected syringes and the worry about being pricked by needles in searches of cells. A knock-on effect of this has been the use of "non-touch techniques" in the treatment of prisoners with viral diseases. This in turn has made prisoners reluctant to be tested for such diseases. For them the treatment is worse than the disease.

---

[1] There would appear to be a problem here in that, while the text of this report gives the number of deaths from drug overdoses as eight, the tables in the report give a figure of nine

7 Sex offenders in the system

The other feature has been the increase in the number of those committed to prison for sexual offences. In 1994, seventy-six people, all male, were committed to prison for sexual offences (1% of the total committed to prison in that year). The figures for those in prison on 1 June 2000 while not directly comparable show that 14% of the prison population is now made up by those imprisoned for sexual offences. Again all of these are male. According to the Annual Report for the years 1995 to 1998 (2000: 23) "the most significant change in the profile of the prisoner population ... was the growth in the number of persons on remand or serving sentences in respect of sexual offences". Roughly equal numbers have been convicted for offences against adults and against children.

These offenders, particularly those who sexually assaulted children, place particular strains on the system, most notably in the need to segregate them from others prisoners for safety reasons and in the need to provide treatment programmes for them. Two prisons have been reserved for such offenders, Arbour Hill and the Curragh. Only one of these, Arbour Hill, provides a sex treatment programme. This caters for a maximum of ten inmates each year. The Curragh currently holds just under one hundred male sex offenders but has no treatment programme targeted for them. They also differ in other ways from those in other prisons. They tend to be somewhat older and from more advantaged social backgrounds (O'Mahony 1997: 140).

8 The social background of prisoners

We do not have comprehensive information on the social backgrounds of people in prison. Our knowledge is confined to a number of surveys of the prison population in Mountjoy (see, for example, O'Mahony 1993 and 1997). It could be argued that these results might not be typical, as all prisoners are not imprisoned in Mountjoy. But O'Mahony maintains that they reflect the "majority profile" for the Irish prison population. The picture that these surveys paint is one of economic, social and personal deprivation. Indeed there had been little change between the 1986 survey and the 1996 one, other than an intensification of the levels of social deprivation of those sentenced to prison.

This deprivation can be seen at a number of levels. The majority of prisoners were from lower working-class backgrounds. When they were classified according to their "best ever job", 94% were either unskilled or semi-skilled manual workers. Eighty-eight percent of them had been unemployed prior to their committal to prison and 44% had either never worked or else never had a job that lasted more than six months. Equally for many there is little evidence of a work culture in their background. Only 39% grew up in homes where the father had a history of continuous employment and 32% came from homes with no working parent. Educational disadvantage is indicated by the number (50%) who left school before the legal minimum age of fifteen and 80% had left school before they were sixteen. One-third had never been beyond primary school level and more than a quarter had literacy problems.

They also had significant histories of the abuse of both legal and illegal drugs. If the drug of abuse was not heroin then it was alcohol. Only eleven of the one hundred and eight prisoners interviewed did not have experience of illegal drugs like heroin or problems with legal ones like alcohol.

In summary then those who get sent to prison in Ireland are primarily young males with significant histories of early school leaving, of unemployment that is intergenerational in nature, and of serious drug problems. How we characterise them in terms of their social background is an important exercise. O'Mahony (1997) has suggested that their level of adversity may lead to them being most accurately classified as marginal working class.

9 The case of the missing white collar criminals

It might be convenient to conclude from this that the explanation of crime and the understanding of the prison system should focus on why people from these kinds of backgrounds commit crime. However it is equally plausible to argue that it is not so much these kinds of people that commit crime but it is these kind of criminals who get caught and when caught get sent to prison. As I have argued elsewhere (McCullagh 1996) the crimes of others, such as the middle and upper classes in Ireland, have largely been ignored by the criminal justice system. This means that a full accounting of who we imprison requires to be balanced by some accounting of those whom we do not. For example, despite the fact that tax evasion has been a criminal offence since 1945 and given that it is not unknown in Ireland, we have managed to keep these kinds of offenders out of prison. We have also managed to keep employers who tolerate dangerous working conditions that result in deaths of their employees out of prison and for the most part we have been reluctant to imprison people who have been involved in corporate fraud, particularly that against the European Union (O'Toole 1995). It follows from this that the composition of the prison population is as much a reflection of the differential ways in which the crime of different social classes in Ireland is dealt with as it is of their propensity to commit crime.

10 International comparisons

We have seen how the numbers being incarcerated in the prison system are rising but how do we compare in this regard with the experiences of other countries. International comparisons are complicated by differences in how countries compile prison statistics and by the statistical measure of comparison. However if we bear these in mind we find that the Irish use of prison is by these standards extensive. We have one of the lowest crime rates in Europe. In 1998, for example, only Portugal and Greece had lower rates. Yet our use of prison was high. Measured in terms of prison population per 100,000 recorded crimes in 1996 we had the third highest rate of imprisonment. Only Northern Ireland and Spain had higher rates (figures in Dáil Sub-Committee Report).

More conventional measures of prison population relate the numbers in prison to the size of the population rather than to the level of crime. Two measures are important here. The detention rate is one. This refers to the number of people in prison (per 100,000 of the population) at a given point in time. The other is the imprisonment rate. This is the number of people sent to prison in one year. The distinction between the two may seem academic but the differences between the two measures reveals important aspects of the use of prison.

The detention rate is the one most often used in international comparisons (see Walmsey, 2000). Ireland's detention rate (which includes sentenced and remand prisoners) in November 1999 was 80 per 100,000 of the population. This suggests that while the use of prison has increased significantly (in 1992 it was 70 per 100,000), by European standards imprisonment is used in moderation.

However when we look at the imprisonment rate we find that in 1992 Ireland's rate was the highest of any country in the Council of Europe. The rate, at 328 per 100,000 was more than twice the rate in Italy and France and four times that of Greece. The Irish use of prison becomes more pronounced if we look only at convicted prisoners. In 1992 the only European country with a higher imprisonment rate for prisoners under sentence was Norway. The Irish imprisonment rate for convicted sentenced prisoners (174 per 100,000) was strikingly different than that of other European countries such as France (34 per 100,000), Italy (24 per 100,000) and Portugal (12 per 100,000) (see O'Mahony 1997: 169).

Consideration of these two rates presents us with an anomaly. The detention rate in Ireland is low but the imprisonment rate is high. The apparent contradiction is resolved by the realisation that while we imprison higher proportions of our population than other European countries, we keep them in prison for shorter periods of time. This is due to the greater prevalence in the Irish system of short sentences and the fact that overcrowding means that many do not serve their full sentences. According to O'Mahony (1997:170) "if Irish prisoners were held for close to the full term of their sentences the sentenced detention rate would be far higher than the present high rate and easily one of the highest, indeed probably the highest, in Europe".

The Minister for Justice has argued that increases in the number of prison places (from 2,000 to 3,200) will reduce the use of early releases and ensure that offenders will serve their full sentences (*Irish Times*, 2 June 1999). The absence of recent statistics makes definitive conclusions impossible but if the minister's claims are true Ireland may have achieved the unusual distinction of being one of the most punitive societies in Europe.

Two other points emerge from international comparisons. The first relates to the age profile of prisoners. Almost one-third of Irish prisoners are under twenty-one. The detention rate for juveniles in Ireland is, after England and Wales, the highest of those countries in the Council of Europe. The second is the issue of cost. International comparisons suggest that the cost of holding someone in prison in Ireland for a year is especially high. It stood (in 1998) at £58,400, the bulk of which is accounted for by wages for prison staff. Ireland is also high in its employment of prison officers. The ratio of officers to prisoners is one to one. In other prison systems there is one officer for every three to four prisoners. Indeed in June 1999, the staff (including teachers) in the prison system exceeded the number of prisoners by 101 (*Irish Independent*, 25 June 1999).

WHY DO WE PUNISH?

So far we have looked at the key features of the prison system in Ireland. It is now appropriate that we turn to the question of what we as a society hope to achieve by this amount of punishment? The fact that prison involves the confinement of people and the deprivation of their freedom means that like all systems of coercion it requires some justification and legitimation. This is normally derived from shared and agreed purposes. The use of prison however is unusual in this respect. Its use can be justified in at least four ways but these are often combined in different and not necessarily consistent and coherent ways (see Sparks 1996).

The first justification for prison is incapacitation. We put offenders into prison because their presence there prevents them from committing further crimes. This justification is often accompanied by a belief in humane containment, which basically argues that while offenders are in prison they should be treated in line with sets of acceptable and enforceable standards in areas like accommodation, hygiene and access to social educational and medical services.

The second justification for the use of prison is denunciation. We put people in prison to express our disapproval of what they do. This is a function of prison that should not be underplayed. There is a very strong belief that prison is the only kind of punishment and the only way in which the disapproval of society can be expressed. This is encapsulated in the notion of "getting off with a fine". This justification is often accompanied by a retributive element in terms of which prison is simply and solely to punish offenders for what they have done.

The third justification is general deterrence. This argues that we should put people in prison to deter others from engaging in the kinds of behaviour that we as a society wish to prevent. This is, for example, one of the most common justifications for the death penalty. The knowledge that we will be executed is held to be a deterrence against us murdering someone.

Individual deterrence is probably the most commonly recognised function of prison. Here the purpose of prison is to ensure that imprisoned individuals do not re-offend, either through fear of the prison or through undergoing a change of heart due to the prison experience. It encapsulates the hope that the experience of imprisonment will be sufficiently educational or rehabilitative to persuade or encourage offenders not to get involved in crime again. From the rehabilitative as opposed to the punitive or retributive perspective, this is to be achieved through the participation of offenders in programmes of education, behavioural modification, or personal counselling. Very often, of course, rehabilitative approaches have to coexist with essentially punitive approaches.

Apart from this well-recognised contradiction, a number of these purposes raise serious moral and political issues. Some, for example, separate the issue of punishment from the fact that the prison population is, as we have seen, mainly a marginalised working-class one. So if we put people in prison to express social disapproval then it provokes the question of whose disapproval is being expressed and why is it only the behaviour of the marginal working-class people that we wish to denounce? On the other hand if we believe in general deterrence and if we punish some to deter others, do we, as Thomas Mathieson (1990) has argued, sacrifice the poor and the stigmatised to keep the rest of us on the straight and narrow? Punishing the poor to provide a role model for others is a position that some may find morally problematic.

In point of fact the prison system tends to resist being classified in terms of a single function and its use reflects a complex and contradictory mixture of the various functions. It is in that sense that Sparks (1996: 201) argues that "it is more common than not for retributive and deterrent principles to stand side by side in the armoury of possible sentences, even when purist advocates of each insist that they are logically incompatible". In the Irish system the declared aims are rehabilitative. The report of the Expert Group on setting up the recently instituted Independent Prisons Agency to run the prison system said that one of the functions of the agency would be "to actively encourage the rehabilitation of prisoners". However it is possible to argue that the refusal of early release to certain categories of offenders means incapacitation may not be a declared principle but an implicit or operating one for certain categories of offenders.

The measurement of the effectiveness of prison has spawned a research industry in those countries, like the United States, that can afford it. General deterrence has, for example, been assessed but the relevant research shows only negligible or modest effects (see Mathieson 1990). The deterrent effect of the increased use of prison has been used in Ireland as an explanation for the falling rates of crime since 1995. But as prison numbers have also risen in times of rising crime the precise nature of its deterrent effects is by no means straightforward.

Individual deterrence is measured by the rate of recidivism, that is the previous criminal and penal involvement of the current prison population. It is one of the few functions of prison on which we in Ireland have a certain amount of information. In a typical year, Irish prison statistics would suggest that 60% of inmates have been there at least once before. Paul O'Mahony's research (1997) on Mountjoy prison suggests that these kinds of recidivism figures are not wholly accurate. His survey showed that almost 90% of prisoners had served previous terms of imprisonment. Moreover 15% of inmates had more than twenty prison terms under their belts. In any other kind of institution these figures would be taken at indicators of failure. O'Mahony (2000: 74) goes on to argue that rates of recidivism in the Irish system have the dubious honour of being among the highest in the developed world. When we combine this with the fact that the cost of keeping someone in prison in Ireland is, as we have seen, unusually high it is reasonable to conclude that the prison system here is a very expensive failure.

WHAT IS TO BE DONE?

In the face of this the question arises as to what can be done to make the prison system more effective. Proposals in this area can be divided somewhat crudely into two kinds and can be assessed by two criteria. One is the extent to which they control or reduce the excessive use of prison and the other is in terms of the contribution that they make to the rehabilitation of offenders. The first policy initiative is the one being pursued by the present government. This involves increasing the capacity of the prison system so that the revolving door will be closed. A number of new prisons and extensions to existing ones have either been built or are in the course of being constructed. They will provide an additional 1,500 places in the system by the middle of this decade. This will at certain levels improve the physical conditions in which prisoners are kept. The new women's prison at Mountjoy is a good example of this. If this is accompanied by the kind of sentence management advocated by the National Crime Forum (1998) there may be the potential for prisons to make a more positive contribution towards the rehabilitation of offenders than has previously been the case.

However the situation here is not one of unqualified optimism. The increased availability of prison spaces is unlikely to do much about the overuse of prison. If prison spaces are there they will be used. In addition the commitment to increase the number of prison spaces has not necessarily been coupled to a commitment to build better quality facilities. The example of the new remand prison in Cloverhill is a case in point. The European Committee for the Prevention of Torture (2000) praised the high standard of equipment in the prison but expressed concern at the decision to house three prisoners in cells measuring 10.4 square metres. It described these conditions as "very cramped". Paul O'Mahony (2000: 67) has claimed that the prison was "built to atrociously low standards", which "are in certain respects well below those that pertained in the original Victorian prisons". It is particularly disturbing that these are the conditions in a remand prison, that is one in which legally innocent people will be detained.

The other policy direction is the reserving of prison for serious and violent offenders and the diversion of others from the prison system towards a range of alternative sanctions such as community based projects which are influenced by and which operate on a philosophy of restitution and restoration (Whitaker 1985). The evidence from other countries suggests that such sanctions do not necessarily have higher failure rates than prison. They also operate at a lower cost and are less destructive of the individuals involved than a spell in prison. The problems with such sanctions in the Irish context are threefold.

One is that while successive Ministers for Justice have declared their support for such sanctions this has not always translated itself into more concrete action such as security of funding for the projects. It also has not produced the institutionalisation of career paths and some level of security for the staff of many of the projects. The second is that the available evidence would suggest that the courts are unwilling to make use of such sanctions. Fines are, for example, much less likely to be used in Ireland for indictable offences than is the case in a comparable jurisdiction, England and Wales (see Sub-Committee on Crime and Punishment 2000: 8). It may also be the case that there has been a proportionate decline in the use by the courts of existing non-custodial sentences. This means that there is no guarantee that extending the range of these sanctions will result in an increase in their use by the courts (McCullagh 1990, also O'Mahony 2000: 58). The third problem with such sanctions is illustrated by the experience of other countries. These have found that the availability of alternative sanctions does not necessarily result in a decline in the prison population. This is because the courts use them for offenders that they would not normally send to prison. These sanctions are used instead of existing non-custodial sanctions or else for offenders that might previously have been cautioned. The effect of this is that both the prison population and the range of alternative sanctions grow alongside each other. In this sense the major problem with alternative sanctions is that of ensuring that they are used with offenders that are genuinely at risk of going to prison.

EXPLAINING PENAL EXPANSIONISM

Our analysis of the prison population shows its two main features. One is that the prison population is composed largely of those who can be characterised as the marginal working class. The other is that the prison population numbers are rising and the authorities are prepared to build more prisons and provide more prison places to accommodate these increases. The analysis of this phenomenon can only go so far when approached from a policy perspective. A more complete account requires us to engage with a literature that deals with the social analysis of penality.

The question that we must address is why Ireland is becoming a more punitive society but also a selectively punitive one. That is, it is willing to imprison a significant segment of its population by international standards, but one that is largely young, male and significantly disadvantaged in educational, social and employment terms.

The obvious explanation is that the size of the prison population is a reflection of the level of crime, that is as crime rises so too does the prison population. There are however a number of reasons to be sceptical of this explanation. One is that while Ireland is, as we have seen, in the middle or at the top of penal tables, it continues to be at the bottom of the crime tables. Despite the changes in crime over the last thirty years Ireland continues to be a low crime country. The second is that there is no clear and direct relationship between the level of crime and the level of imprisonment (Christie 1993:92, O'Mahony 1993). They have not moved together in a consistent and statistically significant fashion, a point aptly illustrated by the drop in crime over the past six years and the significant increase in the prison population.

Sociologists of punishment have sought explanations for this kind of penal expansionism in factors external to the criminal justice system as this is normally conceptualised. These involve relating changes in the prison population to changes in economic conditions in society. Rusche and Kirscheimer (1968), for example, argue that the function of prison is to control and deter the lower class. This means that it is used to imprison them in times of economic recession when their incentive to engage in crime or to create possible unrest might be particularly pressing. So as unemployment rises imprisonment will also. Conversely, as unemployment falls so too will imprisonment as high rates of imprisonment would deprive a growing economy of a source of cheap unskilled labour. Hence for them the relevant relationship is not that between imprisonment and crime but that between imprisonment and unemployment.

Research which examined this relationship in an Irish context for the years 1951 to 1988 (Mc Cullagh 1992) found little supporting evidence. There was no strong direct relationship between unemployment and imprisonment rates over the period but to the extent that such a relationship existed it was only for the period 1980 and 1988 and only for male offenders. Extending the analysis to the current period is unlikely to support this kind of argument about the rise in the prison population. We are now in a period of low unemployment, increasing and pressing shortages of labour and rising imprisonment. It follows from this that if there is a relationship between the economy and the penal system, it is not of the kind anticipated by Rusche and Kirscheimer.

Wilkins (1990) has offered a less deterministic explanation that links the rise in imprisonment to the range of income distribution in a society. He argues that societies with a wide range of income inequalities tend to have an ideology of individualism and correspondingly in such societies people may be held more radically responsible for their behaviour. If this behaviour is successful it is applauded. If it is criminal or deviant then offenders are held to be more severely culpable for their offending than would be the case in a more equal society and punished accordingly. In this scenario radically individualistic societies tend also to be radically punitive ones. The United States is a leading example though some analyses of recent changes in Ireland have spoken about the rise in individualism here also. The growing inequality has also been documented (see Allen 2000). So this kind of analysis has the potential to explain penal expansion in Ireland though the manner in which it would apply needs more precise documentation.

Bauman (2000) has also linked the rise in the prison population to radical changes in what he characterises as post-modern society. He argues that in a globalised world change has, paradoxically, become the only constant. This creates, what he calls "genuine problems of insecurity and uncertainty" (Bauman 2000: 215) and along with this comes the demand that "something be done about it". But as the changes cannot be controlled the desire for certainty is one that can never be satisfied. In such a situation there is a transfer of anxiety. Global anxieties and uncertainties become "condensed into the anxiety about safety" (Bauman 2000:216). This is a demand that politicians can respond to and the expansion of the prison population is the inevitable and highly popular outcome. It shows that governments are doing something, "not just, explicitly, about the personal safety of their subjects, but by implication about their security and certainty as well" (Bauman 2000: 217).

The imprisonment of the poor in this model is a form of comfort blanket for a post-modern society. It represents a manner of dealing with the anxieties that such societies inevitably engender. This argument has intriguing potential when applied to Ireland. Here it is arguably the case that the experience of wealth is new and not necessarily secure. There often seems to be a sense that it is not so much a question of the Celtic Tiger being alive but a question of how soon it will die. It is also the case that much of the new wealth has been produced by the kind of economy that Bauman sees as characteristic of a post-modern society, that is one based on high tech industry and with considerable labour flexibility. Hence the space for anxieties and uncertainties is considerable and the potential for the "transfer of anxiety" is substantial. This is increased by a kind of press coverage of crime in Ireland that feeds public fears (O'Connell 1999). The political capital that this kind of situation creates has been spotted by the present government and has produced the so-called "zero tolerance" slogan that played such a large part in the most recent general election. The campaign had little relationship to the notion of zero tolerance as envisaged in the American model (see Silverman

1999) but in political terms it proved to have a lot of electoral potential. It also provided the impetus for the current prison building spree.

It could be argued that accounts such as those of Bauman and Wilkins are one-dimensional and ignore the countervailing forces that operate in a society and that can be critical of such developments. These forces have traditionally been located in the liberal middle class but, as Garland (2000) has recently argued, this has now changed. This class was the bedrock of support for liberal and non-punitive responses to crime. They saw the adaptation of a "civilized" attitude as a mark of cultural distinction, separating them from the "small-minded" petty bourgeoisie. However their liberalism has been in decline since the late 1970s and early 1980s. This has been brought on by their new experiences with crime (particularly in Ireland with car-theft) and by the increased insecurity and precariousness of their lives brought on by changes in the structure of their economic and domestic lives. They have now become enthusiastic supporters of punitive responses to crime.

In this sense then recent sociological analyses tend to be pessimistic about the future of imprisonment. But it is possible to recognise these as containing equal elements of analysis and prophecy or warning. If that is the case then they point to one of the problems for penal reformers. It is no longer enough to simply present convincing arguments for the reform of the penal system. It is also necessary to find a significant power grouping in a society to "carry" the argument in a political setting. The penal reform groups of the nineteenth century in England and the United States were part of the advancing army of the progressive middle class. If Garland's argument is correct they have now deserted this movement and there is no obvious sign of their replacement. In the absence of the access that their power provided, contemporary penal reformers will be listened to politely and then decisively ignored.

CONCLUSION

In this chapter we have outlined the significant features of the penal system in Ireland. These include the increase in the numbers being incarcerated and the problems posed for the prison system by the imprisonment of offenders with drug problems and by the increased imprisonment of sex offenders. Arguably however the most decisive feature of the system is the extent to which it continues to imprison a particularly deprived section of society, namely the marginal working class. We considered a number of explanations that have been offered for this kind of penal expansionism but the necessary empirical data is not available to assess their relevance to the Irish situation. However the underlying point is that the prison population is not some inevitable and predestined outcome of the crime situation but it is a political response to it. It is therefore at the level of the social analysis of penality that it needs to be understood.

REFERENCES

Allen, K. (2000), *The Celtic Tiger: The myth of social partnership in Ireland*, Manchester: University Press

Alwright, S., Barry, J., Bradley, F., Long, J. and Thornton, L. (1999), *Hepatitis C and HIV in Irish Prisoners: Prevalence and Risk*, Dublin: Stationery Office

Annual Report on Prisons and Places of Detention for the Years 1995-1998, Dublin: Stationery Office

Bacik, I., Kelly, A., O'Connell, M. and Sinclair, H. (1998), "Crime and Poverty in Dublin", in Bacik, I. and O'Connell, M. (eds.), *Crime and Poverty in Ireland*, Dublin: Roundhall Sweet and Maxwell

Bauman, Z. (2000), "Social Issues of Law and Order", *British Journal of Criminology* 40, pp 205-221

Christie, N. (1993), *Crime Control as Industry*, London: Routledge

European Committee for the Prevention of Torture and Inhuman or Degrading Treatment (1999), *Report to the Irish Government on the Visit to Ireland*, Internet Edition

Garland, D. (2000), "The Culture of High Crime Societies", *British Journal of Criminology* 40, pp 347-375

Howard, P. (1996), *The Joy,* Dublin: O'Brien Press

Keogh, E. (1997), *Illicit Drug Use and Related Criminal Activity in the Dublin Metropolitan Area,* Dublin: Garda Headquarters

Mathieson, T. (1990), *Prison on Trial,* London: Sage

Mc Cullagh, C. (1990), "Asking the Wrong Questions? – A Note on the Use of Bail in Irish Courts", *Administration* 38, No. 3, pp 271-279

Mc Cullagh, C. (1992), "Unemployment and Imprisonment: Examining and Interpreting the Relationship in the Republic of Ireland", *Irish Journal of Sociology* 2, pp 1-19

Mc Cullagh, C (1996), *Crime in Ireland: A Sociological Introduction,* Cork: University Press

National Crime Forum (1998), *Report*, Dublin: Stationery Office

O'Connell, M. (1999), "Is Irish Public Opinion towards Crime Distorted by Media Bias", *European Journal of Communication* 14, No. 2, pp 191-212

O'Mahony, P (1993), *Crime and Punishment in Ireland*, Dublin: Round Hall

O'Mahony, P. (1997), *Mountjoy Prisoners: A Sociological and Criminological Profile*, Dublin, Stationery Office

O'Mahony, P. (2000), *Prison Policy in Ireland: Criminal Justice versus Social Justice,* Cork: University Press

O'Toole, F. (1995), *Meanwhile Back at the Ranch: The Politics of Irish Beef,* London: Vintage

Rottman, D. (1984), *The Criminal Justice System: Policy and Performance,* Dublin: National Economic and Social Council

Rusche, G. and Kirscheimer, O. (1968), *Punishment and Social Structure*, New York: Russell and Russell (originally published in 1939)

Silverman, E. (1999), *NYPD Battles Crime,* Boston: North Eastern University Press

Sparks, R. (1996), "Prisons, Punishment and Penality", in McLoughhlin, E.

and Muncie, J. (eds.), *Controlling Crime,* London: Sage, pp 197-248

Sub-Committee on Crime and Punishment (2000), *Alternatives to Fines and the uses of Prison,* Dublin: Stationery Office

Walmsley, R. (2000), *World Prison Population List* (Second Edition), Home Office Research, Development and Statistics Directorate

Whitaker Report (1985), *Report of the Committee of Inquiry into the Penal System,* Dublin: Stationery Office

Wilkins, L. (1990), *Consumerist Criminology,* Aldershot: Gower

35

Punishing Poverty and Personal Adversity[1]

Paul O'Mahony

A nation's prison system is a cultural product, shaped by prevailing social, political, and moral values and attitudes. How a nation defines crime and reacts to it and specifically how it punishes or fails to punish criminals is a question of central importance, which reflects the core values of a society and is definitive of its essential character. As Winston Churchill [2] put it, in an often quoted phrase, "The mood and temper of the public in regard to the treatment of crime and criminals is one of the most unfailing tests of the civilisation of any country". Here in Ireland, Bishop Dermot O'Mahony[3] has recently made a similar point, when he wrote: "What we do with our prisons and how we treat those in them is one of the best indicators of the extent to which the culture of human rights has truly penetrated our society. For Christians it is a touchstone of our concern for the marginalised, the outcast and the deprived." The everyday reality of punishment in Ireland, then, is a profoundly significant indicator of the real values of our society as opposed to the normally unchallenged, and often smug and ill-founded assessments familiar from political rhetoric.

---

[1] This paper is based on the Liam Minihan Memorial Lecture presented, under the auspices of the Department of Justice Prison Education Service, at the Marino Institute of Education on 9 October 1997 and was originally published in *Crime and Poverty in Ireland*, I. Bacik and M. O'Connell (eds.), Dublin, Round Hall Sweet and Maxwell

[2] From a speech made in 1910 when Churchill was British Home Secretary, cited in the *Report of the Commission of Inquiry into the Penal System* 1985, p. 29, Dublin: Stationery Office

[3] Writing in the Foreword to the Irish Commission for Justice and Peace 1994 paper: *Human rights in prison*, Dublin: Irish Bishops' Commission for Justice and Peace

Of course, Churchill, by linking the treatment of crime and criminals with the notion of civilisation, was emphasising the absolute importance to the quality of a society of the rule of law, of due process in legal proceedings, and of the avoidance of arbitrariness, injustice, brutality and dehumanisation in the infliction of lawful punishment. He was making the point that social order and conformity with the law, though essential goals for a society, are not detached ends in themselves, to be gained at any cost.

Societies differ widely in the means by which they aim to attain these desirable ends and using just, legal, humane and constructive means is as important to the quality of civilisation as attaining the ultimate goal of a law-abiding society. The stereotypical African, Asian or Latin American post-colonialist, police and military dictatorships are, unfortunately, not figments of journalistic or artistic imagination, but do exist and do savagely oppress their populations. They oppress using the apparatus of state power, including the law and law enforcement agencies, and by being generally contemptuous of human rights concerns and civil liberties. Closer to home, the now historical, but enduringly relevant, murderous, but in their own terms technically legal, state regimes of Nazi Germany and Stalinist Russia chillingly drive home Churchill's message.

In this context, the foundation of Mountjoy in 1850, on the penitentiary model of Pentonville, must be seen as a watershed in the progression of Irish civilisation. This was a pivotal event in Irish penal history because it marked a sharp divide between the medieval approaches to punishment, which still predominated in the early 1800s, and the modern penal era of self-imposed state restraint and regulation. A central premise of the new approach was the optimistic view that man, even criminal man, was the perfectible creature of a benevolent Christian God.[4] But the most revolutionary and enduring achievement of the reforms was the new legal, administrative and conceptual framework which was to put the business of state punishment on a radically new, more principled and more humane footing[5].

The historical context of the radical reforms of mid-nineteenth-century Ireland was an international one with its roots in the Enlightenment. Reforms occurred throughout the developed world and are usually thought to have been stimulated by Beccaria's 1764 "Essay on Crimes and Punishments".[6] Traditional systems of punishment had been notable mainly for arbitrary cruelty, oppressiveness,

---

[4] Michael Ignatieff, in *A Just Measure of Pain,* 1978, London: Penguin Books, referring to the penitentiary, describes the immensely influential penal reformer John Howard (1726 to 1791) as believing that "salvation was not only God's work. It was the State's work too, and for the first time, Howard insisted, a technology of salvation existed for earthly use", p. 56-57

[5] Ignatieff, *ibid.*, at p. 78, describes the new penitentiary rules of 1842 as "an enumeration of the inmates' deprivations but also a charter of their rights. They bound both sides of the institutional encounter in obedience to an impartial code enforced from outside. As such they reconciled the interests of the state, the custodians, and the prisoners alike"

[6] Beccaria c 1764 (in English, 1767), *Of Crimes and Punishments,* London: J. Almond

financial and moral corruption, and inherent, far-reaching injustice. They had employed physical pain and the death penalty, often for trivial property offences,[7] and had failed to provide any rights for the punished or any restraints on the punishers. Punishment was exercised on the powerless at the whim of the powerful.[8]

Beccaria saw that penal measures, at that time, were often disproportionately harsh and applied in a prejudicial and selective manner. He argued that punishment should be made proportionate to the seriousness of the crime, should reflect the properly tested and established guilt and culpability of the offender, and should tend to the minimum necessary. Beccaria also prioritised the principle that all men are equal before the law and insisted that it be enshrined and realised in actual procedures and legal systems. The 1850 Mountjoy penitentiary and the legal philosophy behind it reflected many of these ways of thinking and represented a huge step towards achieving human rights within prisons.

The last 150 years have seen many new theories of punishment and many approaches to the rehabilitative treatment of prisoners. The original religious mission behind the penitentiary faded quite quickly to be replaced by treatment models based on medical, psychological, vocational, and educational theories. In every case, initial enthusiasm and energy faded just as quickly as the mid-nineteenth-century religious ideology.[9] The present situation might be described as a typical post-modern, pluralist one, in which numerous views, theories and practices, many lingering on from the past, coexist – for the most part peacefully – within the system. They coexist peacefully, if rather uneasily, because the undeniable contradictions between them are largely unspoken.

On the other hand, the recent growth in crime, the increasing public concern about it, and the evident failure of the prison system to rehabilitate – whatever methods it tries – have lead to a widespread atmosphere of disillusion and defeatism about prisons. This atmosphere and the broader context, in which we now take so many of the comforts and safeguards of our civilisation too much for granted, have engendered a collective amnesia about the long struggle to gain civil liberties and humane forms of state punishment. As a result, in some quarters, there have been strident demands for a return to more brutal methods and to a reliance on pure deterrence, fear and harsh punishment. Indeed, in recent years there has been considerable evidence, particularly in the USA, but also quite manifestly in this country, that there is a new willingness in the public and

---

[7] According to Brian Henry (in *Dublin Hanged,* 1994, Dublin: Irish Academic Press) of 238 people hanged in Dublin between 1780 and 1795, only thirty were convicted of murder, two of intent to murder, two of rape, and one of stabbing. All the remainder were convicted for burglary, robbery, and theft of items including a cow, a hat and coat, a watch and a guinea, and six hams

[8] See Foucault, M. 1977, *Discipline and Punish: The Birth of the Prison,* London: Allen Lane

[9] See Garland, D. 1985, *Punishment and Welfare: A History of Penal Strategies,* Aldershot: Gower

political mind and amongst some criminal justice professionals to return to the era of unforgiving, unrestrained retribution.[10]

Some jurisdictions are experimenting once again with penal methods, like chain gangs and the modern equivalent of the stocks, which are explicitly designed to degrade, shame and humiliate. In America there has been a return to the use of excessive punishment for petty crime with the introduction of the "three strikes and out" laws. When faith in the institution of prison reaches a low ebb, radical change becomes a real possibility and the danger is that the current zeitgeist, which favours a simplistic view of crime and a naive dependence on deterrence through ever harsher methods, might usher in changes that undermine the core, civilised values that have been embodied in our system since 1850.

In this context, it is obviously timely to address in a fundamental way, as they did in the early nineteenth century, the crucial activity of state punishment and its inextricable connection with the quality of our civilisation. We need to ask what do we want prisons to do, for the prisoner and for society, in the profoundly altered conditions of modern life? We also need to examine what are the actual effects and the current realities of prison. Henry Fielding once called the pre-penal reform prisons "Seminaries of vice and sewers of nastiness and disease". It is hardly an exaggeration to suggest that currently our prisons, with their problems with drugs, drug-related illness, overcrowding and recidivism, are in greater danger of again fitting that description than at any time since 1850. In Ireland, the need for a thorough self-examination on these issues is more urgent than elsewhere because of the evidence that we greatly overuse imprisonment when compared with our European neighbours. We send more of our citizens to prison every year than almost any other European country, yet we have one of the lowest crime rates in Europe.[11]

My task here, however, is to look at only one strand of the evidence that might be useful to a broader understanding and to a constructive critique of our penal system. I intend to look at some of the results of a survey I undertook in 1996 of the social and criminal histories of 124 Mountjoy prisoners.[12] This was a representative, random sample survey, involving one fifth of the total population of the prison – a large enough sample from which to make reliable generalisations to the whole Mountjoy population. Who prisoners are, and where they have come from, as well as what they have done, is vital information that provides insight into not only how our criminal justice system works, but how our society works.

---

[10] For an analysis of the Irish situation see O'Mahony, P. 1996, *Criminal Chaos: Seven Crises in Irish Criminal Justice*, Dublin: Round Hall Sweet and Maxwell

[11] See Council of Europe 1992, *Penological Information Bulletin No. 17*, Strasbourg: Council of Europe and Young, W. and Brown, M. 1993, "Cross-national comparisons of imprisonment", in *Crime and Justice: an Annual Review of Research*, Vol. 20, Chicago: University of Chicago Press

[12] For a full account of this study, see O'Mahony, P. 1997, *Mountjoy Prisoners: A Sociological and Criminological Profile*, Dublin: Stationery Office

The profile of prisoners is an important guide to the essential qualities of a penal system and to the use a nation makes of imprisonment, but it also reflects important broader social realities. For example, women prisoners today make up only about 2% of Irish prisoners, but, in the middle decades of the nineteenth century, they constituted more than a third of all prisoners. In 1873 there were 12,935 female committals to prison; 120 years later, in the Republic of Ireland, there were less than 500.[13] The implications of these dramatic differences are by no means clearcut, but it is obvious that they denote profound changes not only in the operation of the criminal justice system but also in the attitude of society to women and, perhaps, in the behaviour of women. Similarly, changing patterns in the use of prisons to house the insane and mentally disturbed, political dissidents, the poor, and the homeless reflect important changes in social and political conditions, values and priorities.

Currently in the US a young Afro-American male is seven times more likely to end up a prisoner than his white counterpart.[14] Afro-Americans form nearly half the US state prison population but only around 10% of the general population.[15] It has been estimated that about 20% of this excess is due to racially based discrimination in criminal justice procedures, but the remaining 80% is due to the greater involvement in crime of Afro-Americans.[16] That is a plain description of the facts, but the implications of the facts are far from plain. These facts inevitably raise the question of the crime-proneness of the black man, but they do not prove that the black male has any innate tendency to crime with a biological or genetic basis. Nature and nurture undoubtedly interact in complex ways to produce criminality. Inherited temperament and mentality can play an important role in the development of criminal behaviour patterns,[17] but criminality is an acquired characteristic – primarily a learnt response to the environment. Our understanding of the evolutionary process indicates that such acquired characteristics are not inherited. On the contrary, while the facts indicate the deep involvement in crime of young black Americans, they also point to the possibility that society, because of the way it is structured, actively engineers situations which create this kind of crime. The prevalence of crime in the Afro-American population is so excessive that we are unavoidably drawn towards social process explanations, which, for

---

[13] The figures are from Anonymous 1875, "Irish Prisons", *Dublin University Magazine,* p. 641-53 Vol. 62 and the Department of Justice *Annual Report on Prisons* 1993, Dublin: Stationery Office

[14] US Department of Justice Bureau of Justice Statistics, *Bulletin,* August 1995

[15] US Department of Justice 1993, *Survey of State Prison Inmates* 1991, Washington DC: Bureau of Justice Statistics

[16] According to a study by the US National Academy of Sciences, cited by Norval Morris in his chapter "The Contemporary Prison", in *The Oxford History of the Prison,* 1995, New York: Oxford University Press, p. 242

[17] See, for example, Mednick, S. and Volavka, J. 1980, "Biology and Crime", in *Crime and Justice: An Annual Review of Research,* Vol. 2, Chicago: University of Chicago Press

example, link black crime to how race is socially constructed in the US and to the fact that minority racial status there is almost synonymous with social and economic disadvantage. In other words, the inherited characteristic of dark skin colour may be a contributory factor in the development of criminality, but mainly because of its social meaning and not because of any intrinsic link between skin colour and crime-proneness. Strongly confirming this conclusion, it is found that when Afro-Americans move into the middle-classes, their children are not any more involved in juvenile delinquency or crime than the children of their white neighbours.[18]

Another example, of how revealing of a society the profile of prisoners can be, is found very close to home in Northern Ireland. There, an astonishing 73% of all prisoners sentenced to immediate custody in 1994 were convicted of politically motivated and sectarian crimes.[19] This is a key, defining fact about Northern Irish society, just as revealing and provocative as the facts about the racial identity of prisoners in the US.

What then are the important and revealing characteristics of the Irish or more specifically the Mountjoy prison population and how do they reflect on Irish society? It is quite easy to produce a thumbnail sketch and many people are by now very familiar with this outline picture. Indeed, prisoners in the Republic of Ireland tend to share a familiar set of characteristics with the prisoners of most developed countries – they tend to be young, urban, under-educated males from the lower socio-economic classes and the so-called underclass, who have been convicted predominantly for relatively petty crimes against property without violence. Very few offenders are imprisoned for white collar crime. As in many other countries, a large number of prisoners are dependent on alcohol or opiate drugs and many have psychiatric problems and disturbed family backgrounds.

However, it is worth looking at this profile in more detail because the facts about who prisoners are are even more challenging and subversive of the legitimacy of our current approaches to crime and punishment than the facts about the level of civilisation of the system, as indicated by prison conditions and the human rights record. The conditions of imprisonment and the purposes, priorities and effectiveness of regimes and the extent to which they embody fairness, decent treatment and respect for due process, are vitally important. But looking closely, at who prisoners are, forces us to probe the whole issue of where crime comes from and to question and, perhaps, even abandon the customary, glib, comfortable assumption that criminal responsibility begins and ends with the guilty individual.

---

[18] Norval Morris in his chapter "The Contemporary Prison", in *The Oxford History of the Prison,* 1995, New York: Oxford University Press p. 241

[19] Northern Ireland Office 1996, *Digest of Information on the Northern Ireland Criminal Justice System,* No. 2, Belfast: HMSO

The characteristics and circumstances of prisoners are not just interesting in themselves, they are also interesting because they inevitably draw us on to conclusions about the causes of crime and, most importantly, about the contribution of society to those causes. This is considerably more uncomfortable than asking how the system measures up to civilised ideals, because it raises the unwelcome possibility that it is society as a whole and not just the penal system that needs to change. This process raises fundamental issues of social justice, which cannot be solved simply by ensuring that the penal system is run in a just and decent manner. As the philosopher Riordan[20] has argued: "As long as crime continues to be correlated with social and economic deprivation, we must seriously doubt the justice of the pre-existing order ... until such time as an articulate understanding of the common good is translated into effective programmes to incorporate the marginalised and alienated into the balance of benefits and burdens which constitutes Irish society, our penal policy will continue to be dominated by the objective of protecting those who are included in the social fabric from those who are effectively excluded".

The most important fact, then, about the profile of the typical Mountjoy prisoner is that it is unambiguously one of relatively severe personal and social disadvantage. There are a number of important indicators of this relative deprivation. An obvious place to start is with the material background, ie the family home of the prisoner, and the location, type and income level of that home.

There is some diversity amongst Irish prisoners – for example, in the course of my interviews of 108 prisoners in Mountjoy, I met an Indian and a Jamaican prisoner – but by and large Mountjoy prisoners are remarkably similar in their background. They are overwhelmingly young, in their mid to late twenties, and 56% of them come from just six districts in Dublin noted for their concentration of low quality corporation housing and accompanying socio-economic deprivation. Most of the others come from similar less favoured housing areas in other parts of Dublin. One-third came from rented inner city corporation flats and the majority of the rest from rented corporation housing. Only one in five came from owner-occupied housing in a country were over 70% of people are owner-occupiers.[21]

They also come from exceptionally large families with an average of seven children. Only about 10% of the prisoners came from families with less than four children. This is an important fact when placed alongside the information on housing and income, because it points to a level of unavoidable overcrowding and

---

[20] Riordan, P. 1994, "Punishment in Ireland: Can we talk about it?" *Administration* 41 No. 4, p. 360

[21] See *Ireland for All: CORI Socio-economic Review for 1996,* p. 46, Dublin: Justice Commission, Conference of Religious of Ireland

to the inevitable spreading thin of scarce resources, both material, emotional and psychological, in a large family.

And what about the income levels of the prisoners' families? Only about 15% of the prisoners had fathers who had ever held what might be termed relatively secure, well-paid, skilled jobs in the top four employment categories. At the opposite end of the scale, a similar number of fathers were chronically unemployed and described as without any occupation. The large majority of the fathers were in categories five and six, that is semi-skilled and unskilled labouring. But this fact undoubtedly exaggerates, in several ways, the benefits to the prisoners' families of the occupation of the father. Many of the fathers with a named occupation were in fact further described as mostly unemployed or in casual employment only. And many of them had separated from their families and were not providing much or any financial support.

When a close analysis of the situation was made it was found that 32% of the prisoners were brought up in families where normally there was no parent in employment, and a further 20% in families where only the mother worked – almost invariably in low paid, physically exhausting work such as cleaning offices. When one considers the average family size of seven children, it becomes clear that for a great many Mountjoy prisoners family life must have been a situation of considerable hardship and sometimes extreme want. Clearly, the supervision and practical and emotional support of a large family of children becomes highly problematical, when a mother is forced to cope alone or to go out early in the morning to an exhausting menial job, in order to raise money. All told only 9%, less than one in ten, of the prisoners had a parent or parents living in the home, who were continuously employed in jobs providing reasonable remuneration.

There was also evidence of an unusual degree of disruption in the family background of these prisoners. While 12% had lost a parent to death when still a child, a remarkable 27% came from unconventionally constituted families, mainly families broken by desertion, separation or divorce. Another sign of a disrupted and probably of a disruptive family background was the fact that 15% of the prisoners had a father who had been imprisoned. The general presence of models for criminality in their home environment is even more strongly indicated by the fact that 44% had a sibling who had been in prison.

The Mountjoy study provided no data on the role of problems such as alcoholism and domestic violence in the prisoners' parental homes, but it is probably reasonable to speculate that they had more than their fair share of such problems also. But it is, anyway, clear from the information in the study that Mountjoy prisoners come, overwhelmingly, from a background marked by egregious material poverty and, also, often by family instability and concomitant social and psychological stress.

If the family background of these prisoners can, very frequently, be aptly described as one inextricably snared within the vicious cycle of economic and socio-cultural deprivation, it is perhaps not too surprising that a similar aura of failure and inadequacy haunts the all important area of their personal development. The evidence was clearcut that these people had failed within the educational system and that the normal educational system had failed them. Eighty percent had left school before the age of sixteen and one-third had not attended school beyond the primary or special school level. Twenty-nine percent of the sample claimed to have some difficulty with reading and 21% admitted to functional illiteracy. Only about a quarter of the prisoners had ever taken any form of public examination and in many cases these exams were taken through the prison education system. A tiny 4% of Mountjoy prisoners had progressed to the Leaving Certificate level or beyond, again mostly through the prison education system. In stark contrast, figures show that almost 80% of young people in Ireland now progress to the Leaving Certificate level and that almost half of all Irish adults have attained a Leaving Certificate.[22] Pointing up the highly specific and socially aberrant nature of these prisoners' educational failure is the fact that even amongst the lowest socio-economic group in society generally, ie unskilled manual labourers, more than half of children complete the Leaving Certificate.[23] Given the paramount importance of education in modern life, the significance of these prisoners' failure to benefit from the educational system, whatever the root causes of this failure, is undeniable. For example, an ESRI study[24] found that 75% of impoverished households in Ireland were headed by a person with no educational qualifications and a further 19% by persons with only junior cycle qualifications. Educational failure is directly related to long-term unemployment and another ESRI study[25] found that in a five year follow-up period those with no qualifications continued to have an unemployment rate of about 60%, while the unemployment rate of those with the Leaving Certificate dropped from 32%, shortly after entering the labour market, to only 10%, five years later.

There are, of course, individual-centred explanations at hand to explain educational failure. Attention deficit and hyperactivity syndrome, other forms of learning disability, measured low IQ and the putative, underlying lack of intelligence, are all factors that are usually seen to belong definitively to the individual. These personal problems are not normally thought to have a moral

---

[22] OECD 1996, *Education at a glance,* Paris: OECD

[23] ESRI 1996, *School Leavers' Survey,* Dublin: ESRI

[24] ESRI 1994, *Policy and Poverty in Ireland,* Nolan, B. and Callan, T. (eds.), Dublin: Gill and MacMillan

[25] The study by Damien Hannon, entitled *School to work and adulthood transitions in Ireland,* is cited in *Early School Leavers and Youth Unemployment,* Report No. 11 of the National Economic and Social Forum, January 1997, p. 23

dimension or to be blameworthy, but the customary focus on them tends to favour an individual-centred explanation of educational failure and to deflect attention away from the broader social failure to cherish all the children of the nation equally – through the provision of resources and educational structures equal to the task of educating socio-culturally disadvantaged and excluded children to the limits of their capacity. Individual-centred explanations of educational failure also tend to engender a climate of resignation and defeatism, predicated on the view that the core problem lies essentially within the person and is, in the final analysis, intractable. In reality, every year in Ireland[26] several thousand children from a disadvantaged background drop out of school early without any qualifications and long before they reach their full potential. Personal limitations and disabilities as well as parental attitudes play some role in this attrition process, undermining children's motivation for education, but the main causes are to be found in social structures and in the failure of the educational system to develop effective programmes targeted on socially disadvantaged children. There is ample and irrefutable evidence[27] for a very strong link in Ireland between severe socio-economic disadvantage and educational disadvantage and the government has in recent years acknowledged and begun to address this problem.[28] Truanting, which was a practice for 63% of these prisoners and undoubtedly contributed significantly to their failure within the education system, is often seen as the expression of personal choice and willfulness, but it is also seen to have some social causes. Nevertheless, the social response to the major problem of school absenteeism, particularly amongst less able and more disadvantaged children, has been grossly inadequate.

The work and work training experience of the Mountjoy prisoners was slightly more positive than their educational experience, but still indicative of serious problems. Just over half had some form of skills training, though again much of this was within the penal system. However, much of the training appears to have been of little practical value and to have little altered these people's life chances and employment opportunities. Many, who had done various training courses, said they had never held a proper job. Just 9% had successfully completed specialised work training and could be counted as skilled or semi-skilled workers.

In fact, a little more than a quarter of the whole sample claimed to have never in their lives held a proper job and, including these, 44% had never held a job for more than six months. On the other hand, a similar number of prisoners (43%)

---

[26] See Dermot Stokes 1995, *Youthreach: An Overview – Developments and Future Trends,* Department of Education

[27] See Kellaghan, T., Weir, S., O'Huallachain, S., Morgan, M. 1995, *Educational Disadvantage in Ireland,* Dublin: Combat Poverty Agency

[28] Most notable in this regard is the 1996 Department of Education Programme, *Breaking the Cycle of Educational Disadvantage*

had been in a job for at least one year. Best ever jobs for those who had worked were predominantly in the lowest, unskilled category and 94% of prisoners were categorised in the two lowest socio-economic classes, according to their descriptions of their best ever job or lack of work experience. In many cases, experience of working life was a thing of the past and mainly confined to the late teenage years. Many of the people who had held a job for a considerable period had, for one reason or another, veered off the employment path and, in recent years, tended not to work. As many as 88% of the sample had been unemployed prior to their current imprisonment.

Table 1: prisoners' exposure to adversity

Indicator of Adversity	% of Prisoners positive for indicator
Family size – four or more children	91%
Left school by fifteen	79%
Father in social class six or chronically unemployed	61%
No parent working or only mother working in family home	53%
No substantive work or educational qualification	45%
Loss of parent before fifteen	37%
Illiterate	29%
Parent imprisoned	15%
Heroin user	66%
Never held a job lasting more than three months	40%
Has made a suicide attempt	30%
Has hepatitis or is HIV positive	29%

The highly distinctive profile of disadvantage of prisoners is not by any means confined to family background, poverty and educational and employment problems. Prisoners are distinctive by virtue of a whole raft of other personal, social and health problems (see Table 1). But these problems, like their employment experience and criminal conduct itself, involve an element of autonomous adult action, that is a degree of what we would normally label free choice, and this fact often obscures the fundamental preconditions for the problems, which are found in socio-economic disadvantage.

The problems of personal adversity experienced by these prisoners unequivocally indicate lives of some turmoil and often considerable emotional and physical devastation. For example, 77% of the Mountjoy sample had used illegal drugs other than cannabis and two out of every three prisoners interviewed had used heroin. About the same proportion had had or still had a serious drug addiction. About a third of all prisoners suffered from either HIV or hepatitis or both. More than a third had experienced a life-threatening drugs overdose and almost a quarter had made a very deliberate and serious attempt on their own life mainly when outside of prison. One in five had been a patient in a psychiatric hospital outside of the prison system. In addition, the majority of the small proportion of non-drug using prisoners had long histories of alcoholism.

This is an appalling picture of the toll exacted by the lifestyle of these prisoners. And a similar disastrous pattern is apparent in their social relations. Whereas, based on their age, one might expect far more than half of these men to be married, only 8% were currently married. Including these, one-third were in some sort of stable relationship. The remainder were almost evenly split between those who had parted from a long-term partner and those who had never had such a partner. On the other hand, almost three out of every four prisoners had at least one child. Almost 60% of the prisoners with children were not involved with their families and were not active fathers. Even in the married group, all but one of whom had children, an extraordinary 58% were separated from their wives and children. These figures not only point to disordered and chaotic personal lives, but also suggest that the attitudes and behaviour of many of these prisoners are already making a significant contribution to the next generation of troubled and troubling youth.

There are two more aspects of the Mountjoy study, which help elucidate the extent to which the Irish prison system is targeted, not exclusively but to an exceptional degree, on people from the most disadvantaged, dysfunctional and excluded groups in Ireland. Firstly, the results for this group of prisoners were contrasted with those for a similar representative sample of prisoners I had interviewed in Mountjoy,[29] almost precisely ten years earlier, and with samples from other prison systems.[30] The disconcerting conclusion to be drawn from these comparisons was that on numerous criteria the current Mountjoy prisoners are found to be worse placed.

For example, drug abuse is far more rampant and destructive than was the case in 1986 and casual fatherhood is much more prevalent. The percentage of prisoners, who had used drugs other than cannabis, had increased from 37% to 77%. Despite a lower marriage rate in 1996, 72% of the sample had fathered

---

[29] O'Mahony, P. 1993, *Crime and Punishment in Ireland,* Dublin: Round Hall

[30] Most importantly, those described in US Department of Justice 1993, *Survey of State Prison Inmates 1991,* Washington DC: Bureau of Justice Statistics; Dodd, T. and Hunter, P. 1992, *The National Prison Survey 1991,* London: HMSO; and Wozniak, E., Gemmell, M. and Machin, D. 1994, *The Second Prison Survey,* Scottish Prison Service Occasional Papers No. 10, Edinburgh: Central Research Unit

children, compared with 42% in 1986; and 59% of prisoners with children had no involvement with them, compared with 50% in 1986. While the national economy has experienced a period of significant growth and there has been real improvement in the provision of training and educational services over the decade in question, the position of prisoners generally appears to have disimproved. In 1996, a slightly greater proportion of the prisoners had left school before the age of sixteen than in 1986 (80% compared with 78%). In 1996, 88% of prisoners had been unemployed prior to their imprisonment compared with 79% in 1986, and 27% had never had a proper job compared with only 7% in 1986.

Interestingly, comparisons with England and Wales suggest that the Irish prison population may be drawn in a much more concentrated way from the socially, educationally and economically disadvantaged sector of society than is the case elsewhere. For example, in England and Wales only 49% of prisoners were unemployed prior to imprisonment (compared with 88% in Mountjoy), only 6% had never worked (compared with 27%), and only 43% had left school before the age of sixteen (compared with 80%). An interesting general indicator was that only 41% of prisoners in England and Wales were classified as falling in the two lowest socio-economic classes compared with 93% of Mountjoy prisoners. The case can be made that we are more similar, in the extent to which we deploy prison as a means to control a specific underclass and their particular crimes, to the American situation, where the ghetto-dwelling, black man is seven times more likely to end up in prison than his white fellow citizen. Because in Ireland the issue is class and there is a lack of visible race differences between the classes, the facts of the highly selective action of the penal system are less conspicuous. However, it is even possible that, for the small sector of the Irish population that appears predestined to fill our prisons, the odds stacked against them are even greater than for the socially excluded Afro-American.

Secondly, I made a series of statistical analyses examining the relationships between early childhood disadvantages such as a broken home and later adversities such as becoming a heroin addict and aspects of the prisoners' criminal and prison careers. Table 2 illustrates one such analysis – of the important relationship between early school leaving and criminological variables. While the least educated group are somewhat anomalous, these figures show a remarkably powerful and consistent tendency for early school leaving to be associated with earlier first conviction and the accumulation of a greater number of convictions. These analyses in general confirmed strong links between childhood disadvantage and both later personal problems and, significantly, the seriousness of a criminal and penal career. For example, less than half of the prisoners with two or less childhood background disadvantages, such as a chronically unemployed or absent father, suffered two or more current personal adversities, such as HIV status. On the other hand, 91% of prisoners with six or more background disadvantages suffered two or more current personal adversities. It was also clear that the more disadvantaged the child, the earlier he gets into trouble with the law and the more serious is his subsequent criminal and penal career. Prisoners who had experienced six to eight of the background disadvantages under examination, when compared with those who had experienced two or less, received their first conviction at a much earlier age (15.4 years versus 18.2), had many more convictions (an average of 15.7 versus 8.9), were more likely to be using heroin in prison (81% versus 56%), more likely to have been imprisoned as a juvenile (83% versus 53%), and more likely even to have been placed in a padded cell (57% versus 32%).

Table 2: the influence of early school leaving

Left School	Before 11 yrs	At 11 or 12	At 13 or 14	At 15 or 16	Over 16 yrs
% of prisoners	12%	10%	28%	43%	7%
Mean age of first conviction	16.9 yrs	14.3 yrs	15.8 yrs	17.5 yrs	18 yrs
Mean number of convictions	15.4	16.1	13.5	12.7	7.6

What is striking is that these differences, linking degrees of disadvantage in childhood to degree of criminality and to continuing relative disadvantage in later life and within the criminal justice system are clearcut, even amongst a group of prisoners who as a whole are unusually disadvantaged by the standards of the general population. Comparisons between prisoners' levels of disadvantage and general population norms would, of course, be far more striking, but analysis within the prison population itself amply illustrates the powerful, cumulative, malign effect of childhood adversities. There are no Irish large-scale, prospective studies mapping the role of childhood disadvantage in the genesis of crime, but the present results are suggestive of a very similar picture to that depicted by Kolvin et al[31] in their thirty year follow-up study of a cohort of 1,142 children born in Newcastle UK in 1947. Kolvin et al found a "dramatic increase in the rates of delinquency and criminality in relation to the severity of deprivation in the family of origin". Sixty percent of males from multiply deprived backgrounds ended up with a criminal record compared with only a sixth of those from non-deprived backgrounds.

Of course when focusing on prisoners' adult lives, for example on their negative employment experience or their drug use, we have already crossed the Rubicon that seems to divide unambiguously adverse factors that are visited on

---

[31] Kolvin, I., Miller, F., Fleeting, M. and Kolvin, P. 1988, "Social and Parenting Factors Affecting Criminal Offence Rates", *British Journal of Psychiatry* 152, pp. 80-90

innocent children and adverse factors that are perceived to involve a contributory element of adult choice and willfulness. We have moved from a picture, with which everyone readily sympathises, of the powerless child who cannot resist the forces that shape and condition him, such as poverty or negligent and brutal parental attitudes, to a realm where it is quite plausible to partially attribute failure – to conform with societal standards and succeed legitimately in life – to anti-social attitudes, wrong choices and personal moral flaws, such as selfishness, fecklessness, dishonesty or laziness. We are all familiar with the stereotype of the work-shy gurrier, who supplements his dole with various illegal scams and actively chooses to live parasitically and dishonestly on society. Many Mountjoy prisoners could be said to fit this particular stereotype or other equally negative stereotypes, such as the hedonistic drug user, bent on self-destruction and indifferent to the havoc he may cause to others in order to satisfy his addiction. The victims of muggings and burglaries find it difficult to deeply consider the root causes of criminal behaviour and are rarely inclined to probe issues of motivation and causality beyond the immediate criminal motive – the obvious readiness to take unfair and dishonest advantage of others. In this, they are in agreement with the legal system, which concerns itself with the matter of guilt, entirely in the relatively straightforward form of proving the identity of the perpetrator and establishing criminal intent, but essentially ignores the formative influences on the criminal.

While it is widely accepted that family background and harsh social conditions may make crime more likely, the contribution of immediate personal choice is always emphasised and prioritised in both the legal system's response to crime and in common perceptions of criminal conduct. The core failure is seen to reside in the individual – in the selfishness or malevolence of the attitudes and values that shape his or her choices. While, theoretically, many people understand that criminal behaviour is learnt behaviour and, therefore, the byproduct of a complex socialisation process, few people appreciate that shortcomings in socialisation are often inextricably linked to wider social conditions and social and economic structures imposed on powerless people, families and whole communities.

The courts, especially in the case of first offences, sometimes mitigate sentences because of a background of obvious disadvantage, but in the final analysis the courts must, and do normally, respond to criminal behaviours as such and ignore the factors and conditions in a personal life history which led to the behaviour and formed the criminal intent. This is how things must be, for in a sense the courts are a system designed to play an active role in the socialisation of anti-social individuals and to remedy the inadequate socialisation of criminals. The courts act in order to influence behaviour, by declaring which behaviours are intolerable, and by deploying sanctions to change people's attitudes to and proclivities for those behaviours.

But the penal system is in no way equipped to comprehend or address the burden of disadvantage that most criminals carry. The courts and prisons cannot be expected to cope with the underlying paradox that the reason why an individual is inadequately socialised (and has learnt to make criminal choices) is primarily related to inadequate parenting and an unstable and inadequate home background, which are, in turn, often largely the result of conditions of harsh deprivation and social disadvantage.

Many prisoners are not, by normative, middle-class standards, altruistic, philanthropic or even congenial people. As adults they frequently display expedient consciences, anti-social, parasitic and aggressive attitudes and a commitment to forms of conduct designed to advantage themselves at the expense of vulnerable others. Mind you, if you think about it, you can find such personality configurations amongst "the highest in the land". It is always incumbent on us to remember that the strong link between deprivation and crime refers only to the kind of crime we tend to punish with imprisonment and not to crime in general or immoral conduct as such, which are unlikely to be strongly related to deprivation.

Most of the prisoners interviewed in the Mountjoy study had embarked on an extraordinarily extensive criminal career, involving scores and sometimes hundreds of crimes, hurting many innocent people. On average they had received fourteen convictions and been sent to prison on ten different occasions following conviction. Many people, who have had similarly disadvantaged backgrounds, sometimes including the brothers of prisoners, respect the law and respect other people's persons and property. It is not surprising then that, while being "tough on crime" is an inevitably popular political slogan, there is far more ambivalence about being "tough on the causes of crime". People see the correlational link between deprivation and crime but, perhaps understandably, resist any implication that there is a causal link that explains individual criminal behaviour, to the extent that it might partly excuse it. Causal chains in this area are, anyway, multifactorial and highly complex and, in the individual case, almost inevitably obscure. Because there is no necessary, inevitable link between deprivation and crime, people can easily conclude that, despite the impressive correlational evidence, there is in fact no significant relationship between deprivation and crime that needs to be addressed.

However, the concept of socialisation is the key to understanding many of the important causal chains between deprivation and crime and, perhaps also, to understanding why it is not appropriate to always focus only on the matter of immediate criminal intent and criminal responsibility. Social and economic disadvantage and marginalisation operate on various levels to undermine positive socialisation of the young, and thereby contribute crucially to delinquency and criminality. Poverty and adverse social conditions undermine the material, practical and psychological capacity and motivation of parents to provide the kind of environment which fosters pro-social behaviour and sound moral development. The experience of being marginalised and excluded from many of society's benefits provides severely disadvantaged communities with a collective rationale for an oppositional, subcultural value system, that is anti-authority, sceptical of the moral claims of the more comfortable majority in society, and tolerant of dishonest means for achieving otherwise unattainable benefits. The undeserved personal experience of harsh conditions and the young person's growing consciousness of a stigmatised, inferior social role lead to disaffection, anger, boredom and lack of self-esteem. Social conditions can also engender, within families and communities, a sense of hopelessness and defeatism, which lead to what has been termed an "optimism deficit", whereby people believe that even genuinely available opportunities, such as education, are "not for them". These negative psychological processes prepare the ground for and greatly increase susceptibility to both crime and drug addiction. Finally, it also seems self-evident that poverty and inequality are important direct causes of crime in themselves, over and above the issue of socialisation, since, in an acquisitive, consumerist, increasingly affluent and exhibitionist society, they provide immediate, material motivation for self-gain crime.

The catalogue of severe problems that afflict many prisoners has nothing to do with coincidence. There are layer on layer of difficulties, but they are not isolated and unconnected problems that, by some statistical freak of chance, have been heaped on these particular misfortunates. These problems are all linked and all find their roots in a disadvantaged childhood and, to some extent, in a lack of inherent personal resilience and special resources, such as high intelligence, which might help a person overcome the worst of backgrounds. The problems of school failure, poverty, dysfunctional family life, inadequate or inappropriate child-rearing and discipline, drug abuse, anti-social attitudes and fraught inter-personal relationships propagate, potentiate and propel each other.

Criminal behaviour is just one part of the package, one florid expression of a ghastly deprivation syndrome. Turning to alcohol or drugs for oblivion or excitement in a harsh, boring, ungiving and hopeless environment, just like turning to crime for material gain or status amongst peers, is essentially a predictable response to an inescapable, overpoweringly negative social context. It is a sign of inadequate social and personal resources and of insufficient opportunities for more positive development. Prisoners are often reckless about harming others, but they are as reckless about harming themselves and their own loved ones. Their problem behaviours are inextricably intertwined – for example drugs and crime quickly begin to feed off each other and lead to illness and increased alienation – and are rooted in and fostered by their personal history of social, educational, economic and emotional deprivation.

We end up with individuals who are both damaged and, in large part because of this damage, damaging – damaging to selves and others. The criminal justice system, naturally enough, is primarily a response to their propensity to damage others. We as a society, and especially our criminal law, have quite demanding expectations of all adults (that is everyone over the age of criminal responsibility, which astonishingly is still only seven years and about to be raised to only ten years). We expect them to overcome their history of disadvantage and failure; to bury their feelings of inadequacy, inferiority and worthlessness – even though these are endorsed daily by society; to suppress resentment brought on by comparison of their situation with how others are situated; and to accept their place and conform in whatever limited, socially acceptable role may be available to them. We expect them to buy into the myths of the "just world" and the level playing field. These expectations are a particularly heavy burden for the impoverished and socially marginalised, who must transcend the pain of their own exclusion from the first eleven and almost every other team that counts, and who must learn to accept that their lowly status in life is both fitting and deserved in a purportedly "just and fair" society. Adults, from the most disadvantaged backgrounds, are expected to conform to normative codes of behaviour without obtaining any of the more tangible rewards that better placed people automatically gain from being law-abiding. In a sense, they alone are called on to demonstrate lawful conduct purely for its own sake, in a system designed primarily to protect the status quo, with all its inbuilt inequalities.

The cut and dried, condemnatory approach towards criminal behaviour, favoured by so many people today, might be appropriate and, indeed, the only possible approach for the criminal justice system. But for society as a whole, which must look at the broader picture and endeavour to take collective, political action that is preventive of crime, it is essential to focus on social structures and how they impact on crime through the creation of conditions of stark disadvantage.

We need to undertake a process of rethinking criminal justice issues in their proper context, which is the whole social system. We tend to focus solely on the individual criminal and how to punish, rehabilitate and deter him (or her). This is at best a partial and very limited view. We need urgently to also focus and reflect on the social setting which constitutes the formation of a disproportionately large number of our current prisoners. We need to focus especially on the deep-rooted inequities of our society and the inequalities of power, wealth and opportunity that have played and continue to play a powerful role in generating crime. Eliminating the worst of these inequalities will not abolish crime, which can arise in all sorts of circumstances for all sorts of reasons, but it could put an end to the existence of the deep divisions and deprived conditions which currently perpetuate anti-social and actively criminal subcultures amongst some of the most deprived groups in society. On the other hand, without a sophisticated and compassionate understanding of the role of social factors in crime, and without the active pursuit of social justice, most of our efforts at reducing crime are likely to be superficial and doomed to failure.

Irish society uses prison selectively to punish those already egregiously disadvantaged by the structures and strictures of Irish society. This is not to suggest that the crimes of the marginalised groups, who form the core of the Irish prison population, do not deserve to be sanctioned by imprisonment, nor is it to suggest that middle-class people, who commit similar crimes, tend not to be sanctioned with imprisonment, though this is a real possibility.[32] However, it is to suggest that there is a whole vast realm of crime – crime of dishonesty specific to the powerful and the privileged – that is not only rarely punished by imprisonment, but is rarely punished at all. As GB Shaw[33] has argued: "The thief who is in prison is not necessarily more dishonest than his fellows at large, but mostly only one who through ignorance or stupidity steals in a way that is not customary. He snatches a loaf from the baker's counter and is promptly run into jail. Another man snatches bread from the tables of 100 widows and orphans and simple credulous souls, who do not know the ways of company promoters, and likely as not he is run into parliament."

The increasing population of sex offenders in prison, who now number over 300, are an exception which confirms the rule that prisons are used to an inordinate extent, in Ireland, to control the very lowest echelons of society. Imprisoned sex offenders, when compared with other prisoners, are a far more socially mixed group, containing people from all classes and all walks of life and many who have benefited from considerable social advantages, such as a professional education. However, the tendency to pursue, convict and imprison sex offenders is a recent development and at present only a tiny proportion of rapists and child sex abusers are caught and imprisoned.[34] It is a salutary thought that if all sex offenders, who by the present standard deserved imprisonment, were actually imprisoned, then the current social class imbalance in the prison population would almost entirely disappear. If the perpetrators of domestic violence and the, overwhelmingly middle-class, white-collar criminals were also imprisoned in numbers proportionate to the prevalence and seriousness of such crimes in Irish society, then the class bias in our penal system would almost certainly be reversed.

Despite what Churchill said, it is not possible to have a civilised, good and just penal system within a society which lacks many of the basic qualities of a good

---

[32] For example, see O'Connell, M., Bacik, I., Kelly, A. and Sinclair, H., "Crime and Poverty in Dublin: An analysis of the association between community deprivation, District Court appearances and sentence severity", in I. Bacik and M. O'Connell (eds.) *op. cit.*

[33] Shaw, G. B. 1922, Preface to *English Local Government: Prisons,* Sidney and Beatrice Webb, London: Longman

[34] National Women's Council of Ireland 1996, *Report of the Working Party on the legal and judicial process for victims of sexual and other crimes of violence against women and children,* Dublin

and just civilisation. Our prisons may be the most significant test, as Bishop O'Mahony said, of how we treat the marginalised, outcast and deprived, but an equally serious and urgent concern should be with how our society can be reconstructed so as not to produce thousand upon thousand of marginalised, outcast and deprived people.

36

The Probation and Welfare Service: its Role in Criminal Justice

Patrick O'Dea

Alternative sanctions to custody and the Probation and Welfare Service (PWS), which administers most of these sanctions, play a large role in the Irish criminal justice system, as is evidenced by the fact that there are around 5,000 offenders on a daily basis serving community based sanctions under the supervision of the Probation and Welfare Service (PWS). That is about 2,000 more than the average number of persons who are in custody.

The roots of probation in Ireland are shared with those in Britain, because this country had been under British rule up to 1922. The origins of probation are in the informal system of supervision of people who came before the courts most commonly on charges of drunkenness. From 1840, courts in Britain developed practices of discharging such offenders with conditions as to their behaviour and supervision.

Philanthropic agencies were the first to provide care and supervision to those offenders, who had been conditionally discharged. The Church of England Temperance Society appointed its first Police Court Missionary in 1876. This informal system of supervision was given legal force by the Probation of Offenders Act 1907.[1]

---

[1] McWilliams, W. 1983, "The Mission to the English Police Courts 1876-1936", *Howard Journal* 22: 129-147

The history of probation in England before the Probation of Offenders Act 1907 is well documented. The same is less true of Ireland.[2] It must be said that despite the existence of the Probation of Offenders Act 1907, probation as a disposition only came into extensive use in the late 1960s.

There was one probation officer at the time of the establishment of the Irish state, (1922). She remained in position under the new authority. As before, charitable societies also continued to work with offenders who had been conditionally discharged. The Salvation Army had a presence in the Dublin courts until the 1970s. The new Irish state viewed probation as an area mainly for voluntary effort. The Society of Saint Vincent de Paul and the Legion of Mary assisted in the "befriending" of offenders, as did the Protestant Discharged Prisoners Aid Organisation. As late as 1962, the then Minister for Justice, Charles Haughey, was exhorting people interested in youth welfare to get involved in the care of offenders. An even later Minister for Justice, Michael O'Morain, expressed the view in 1968 that work undertaken by voluntary agencies was more effective than anything done by an official probation service[3].

For the decades 1940-1960, the Probation Service consisted of seven officers, based in the Dublin Metropolitan area. These officers were until 1957 unestablished, ie, without security of tenure or pension rights. As McNally[4] suggests: "There appeared to be a lingering doubt as to the appropriateness of professionalising Probation as opposed to harnessing the missionary zeal for reclamation evident in the original Police Courts Mission".

In 1969 an internal Department of Justice examination of the PWS took place. Its report[5] recommended expansion and following the report's implementation three senior probation and welfare officers (PWOs) and twenty-seven PWOs were appointed. By 1972, the PWS had become available to courts outside Dublin and the appointment of officers was undertaken on a national basis. As the PWS established a presence in an increasing number of courts, the rate of referrals grew and pressure for further expansion built up. The political context of the late 1970s expansion of the PWS was significant. This was the election in 1977 of a Fianna Fáil government under Taoiseach Jack Lynch, whose policy was to invest money in public sector job creation. The PWS availed of this opportunity for expansion. The number of basic grade PWOs increased from 7 in 1964 to 30 in 1972 to 54 in 1977 and 119 in 1980. In 1980, the Probation Service was reorganised on a regional basis and renamed the Probation and Welfare Service.

[2] McGowan, J. 1993, "The Origins and Development of the PWS from 1907 to the Present Day", Dissertation submitted to UCD for Master of Social Science

[3] *Ibid.*

[4] McNally, G. 1993, "History of Probation Service", *The Probation Journal*, PWS

[5] Department of Justice 1969, "Internal Examination of the Probation Service," unpublished

During the 1990s the government approved 91 new posts, most of which, however, have never materialised. This was largely as a consequence of temporary embargoes and restrictions on public service numbers. Staffing levels varied from 134 PWOs in 1991 to 148 in 1997, demonstrating only a relatively small increase from the complement of PWOs in 1980.

THE PHILOSOPHY OF PROBATION PRACTICE

The Probation of Offenders 1907 legislation directs probation officers to, "advise, assist and befriend" offenders. The shape and content of that "advice, assistance and friendship" have changed over time to accord with the prevailing philosophical paradigm underlying practice. The early decades of the last century saw probation work with offenders that was religious in outlook. The probation endeavour was devoted to the saving of souls. By the late 1930s there had been a philosophical revolution. The view was that the offender was susceptible not to grace but to cure through scientific treatment. The offender had become more a patient than a sinner. As McWilliams writes: "Between the late 1930s and the 1960s the probation system in England was transformed from a service devoted to the saving of souls through divine grace to an agency concerned with the scientific assessment and treatment of offenders".[6]

The obligation in the probation statute to "advise, assist and befriend" has generally taken the form of the provision of a social casework service to offenders. Offending behaviour per se was within the treatment framework but its aetiology and ontology were not necessarily of central concern. An assumption of the approach was that an improvement in offenders' general human functioning would itself take care of offending behaviour.

However, in the post World War II era, disillusionment with the effectiveness of offender treatment programmes grew. A body of research accumulated, most notably epitomised by Martinson's 1974 paper reviewing research on the effectiveness of a large number of treatment programmes, that inspired what might be labelled the "Nothing Works"[7] school of thought. Martinson's and other reviews of the offender rehabilitation literature came to a firm conclusion that there was little evidence for the effectiveness of treatment programmes especially when evaluated in terms of their capacity to reduce reoffending and recidivism.

More recent close examination of the research literature on offender treatment

---

[6] McWilliams, W. 1986, "The English Probation System and the Diagnostic Ideal," *Howard Journal,* Vol. 25, No. 4

[7] See for example: Lipton, D., Martinson, R. and Wilks, J. 1975, *Effectiveness of Correctional Treatment: A Survey of Treatment Evaluation Studies,* New York: Praeger; Martinson R. 1974, "What Works? Questions and Answers about Prison Reform", *The Public Interest* 23, 22-56

has been far more positive[8] and indicates that some treatments do work. In recent decades treatment programmes themselves and the methods for evaluating them have grown in sophistication and current research on offender treatment programmes not only reveals that some treatments reduce recidivism, but also contributes to our understanding of the conditions necessary for effective interventions.

Research[9] points to primary principles of effective treatment, where reducing recidivism is the goal. Two of these are 1) The Risk Principle and 2) The Need Principle. The Risk Principle advocates that the level of treatment should match the risk level of the offender, ie higher risk offenders should receive higher levels of treatment. Methods for the assessment of risk levels and the prediction of recidivism are consistently improving. The Need Principle identifies two categories of offender need, criminogenic and non-criminogenic needs. Probation practice should address primarily those problems and areas of need that maintain or support people in offending behaviours and not other non-offending related personal needs. According to this view, addictions and unemployment are criminogenic factors. Non-criminogenic needs, such as self-esteem or anxiety, are unlikely to impact directly on future criminal behaviour.

Research[10] has also highlighted that cognitive-behavioural techniques are a dramatically more effective approach to reducing re-offending than methods based on so-called humanistic approaches. Cognitive behavioural techniques are designed to assist someone to modify their thinking and actions. These techniques have not been developed solely to deal with offending but have a wide application in therapy with a diverse range of behavioural and psychological problems. Cognitive behavioural techniques derive from an eclectic theoretical approach within psychology, which draws on behaviourism,[11] cognitive theory,[12] and social learning theory.[13] Behaviourism stresses the role of external factors in shaping and

---

[8] See for example: Andrews, D.A., Zinger, I., Hoge, R.D., Bonta, J., Gendreau, P. and Cullen, F.T. 1990, "Does Correctional treatment work? A Clinically relevant and psychologically informed meta-analysis", *Criminology* 28; McGuire, J. 1991, "Things to do to make your programme work", in *What Works, Effective Methods to Reduce Reoffending*, Conference Proceedings Manchester: Greater Manchester Probation Service; McIvor, G. and Roberts, C.H. 1991, *Towards Effective Policy and Practice, Supplement to National Standards and Objectives for Social Work Services in the Criminal Justice System*, Scottish Office Work Services Group

[9] Bonta, J. 1997, *Offender Rehabilitation from Research to Practice*, Ministry of Solicitor General, Canada, Report 1997

[10] Chapman, T. and Hough, M. 1998, *Evidence based practice: a guide to effective practice*, edited by M. Jane Furness on behalf of HM Inspectorate of Probation, Home Office

[11] Skinner, B.F. 1938, *The Behaviour of Organisms: An experimental analysis*, New York: Appleton-Century-Crofts

[12] Meichenbaum, D.H. 1977, *Cognitive-Behaviour Modification: An Integrative Approach*, New York, NY: Plenum Press

[13] Bandura, A. 1977, *Social Learning Theory*, New Jersey: Prentice Hall

reinforcing an individual's action. Cognitive theory stresses the importance of an individual's thought processes such as reasoning and problem-solving. Social learning theory holds that while the environment is a key factor, learning may also occur indirectly, through observation and modelling of the behaviour of others.

ORGANISATION OF THE PWS

The PWS is part of the Department of Justice, Equality and Law Reform. Significantly the agency has no existence in law as a corporate entity or a distinct agency in the criminal justice system. The PWS operates independently on everyday professional matters. Beyond that, the functions of finance, personnel, staffing and information technology are provided through the Department of Justice, Equality and Law Reform. The PWS has a reporting relationship with the Prisons and Probation and Welfare Policy Division of the Department of Justice, Equality and Law Reform. The Exchequer provides funding for the PWS through the Prisons Vote. A change to these organisational features and to the corporate status of the PWS is one of the principle recommendations of the Expert Group on the Probation and Welfare Service that reported in 1998.[14]

The organisational structure of the PWS is built on a team basis. Teams consist of approximately six probation and welfare officers (PWOs) headed by a senior probation and welfare officer (SPWO). Most teams have responsibility either for offenders in a specific community defined by a bounded geographic area or for offenders in a specific detention centre. There is also a small number of teams with specialist functions and responsibilities, eg one team covers statistics and research and one has responsibility for the Intensive Probation Supervision schemes. There are nine assistant principal probation and welfare officers (APPWOs) who constitute the next layer of management. Generally, APPWOs have responsibility for a number of SPWOs and their teams, and other varying areas of responsibility.

PWS operates a hierarchical model of organisation. Responsibility for the management and direction of the PWS is concentrated in the office and person of the principle probation and welfare officer. However the management practice in the PWS should in time reflect the more recent developments in public service management. A key element of this approach is partnership.

The legal framework and statutory basis for the work of the PWS is found in its responsibility for implementing orders made by the courts under the following range of legislation:

Probation of Offenders Act 1907
Childrens Act 1908, as amended Section 67
Criminal Justice (Administration) Act 1914

---

[14] Expert Group on the Probation and Welfare Service, 1998, *First Report*, Dublin: Stationery Office

Criminal Justice Act 1960
Misuse of Drugs Act 1977, Sect. 28 (2)
Criminal Justice (Community Service) Act 1983

The Service also has responsibility to provide social reports in family law cases in the civil courts under the following legislation:

Family Law Act 1995
Family Law (Divorce) Act 1996.

STAFFING AND RESOURCES

Hopelessly inadequate staffing levels have seriously undermined the capacity of the PWS to deliver services. Though its client/offender base is considerably larger than that of the Prisons Service, the PWS receives less than 10% of the Prisons Vote. For example, in 1998 the PWS received only £15.9 million out of the £183 million total for the Prisons Vote. On a daily basis, the PWS has responsibility for 2,000 more offenders than does the prison system. A recent European comparative study[15] examined the budget of the probation service system in relation to that of the prison system in a large number of European countries. This study confirms the picture of an underdeveloped Irish probation system. It concluded that "Ireland's and Finland's probation services are Europe's poor cousins with 7.8% and 7.5% of the amount of their county's prison budget respectively." By comparison, the Austrian percentage was 14%, the Scottish 20% and the Swedish 25%.

Reflecting the underlying failure to resource the PWS, a number of authoritative reports have expressed profound concern about the level of funding available to the PWS. For example, the final report of the Expert Group on the Probation and Welfare Service[16] commented as follows: "Without adequate resources to develop and expand to meet ongoing needs, the Service cannot offer the courts or the community the type of services which we believe are required. Lack of resources leads to staff shortages, high workloads, lack of back-up facilities and low morale. This can in turn lead to a loss of confidence by the courts in the system. The issue of inadequate resources urgently needs to be addressed".

This echoes the sentiments of the Whitaker Committee expressed as long ago as 1985: "A more general difficulty in making use of non-custodial alternatives is the limited resources of the Probation and Welfare Service. At present the staff of 169 must service 11 custodial institutions, provide social enquiry reports ordered

---

[15] *Probation and Probation Services: A European Perspective*, A. van Kalmthout and J. Derks (eds.) 2000, Nijmegen: Wolf Legal Publishers
[16] Expert Group on the Probation and Welfare Service, 1999, *Final Report*, Dublin: Stationery Office

by the courts, supervise offenders on temporary release and supervise persons placed on Probation or Community Service Orders. A progressive strengthening of the service is essential for more effective and extensive use of alternatives to imprisonment".[17]

The representative body for basic grade PWOs has also been very forthright in its criticism of the ongoing resourcing situation: "The PWS Branch of IMPACT believe that this state is effectively without an adequate, developed and efficient system of community supervision of offenders. Comparisions with similar jurisdictions indicate that Ireland is seriously under-resourced in this way. Broken promises over many years and a recruitment system that is slow and cumbersome have contributed to this neglect".[18]

Unfortunately the deficit in staffing of the PWS in the decade and a half since 1985, when the Whitaker Committee first noted the inadequate resourcing, has got worse not better. The Expert Group on the PWS in part attributed this to the fact that "while the PWS deals with a far greater number of offenders than prisons do, its success in convincing government and the broader public of its pivotal place in the management of offenders has been poor".[19] Statistical data for the 1990s show that although the PWS was a major player in the criminal justice system, the 1997 staffing level was only 148 PWOs. This was only a tiny increase on the figure for 1990, which was 134 PWOs. At the same time, the volume and complexity of work undertaken at the end of the nineties have developed to an entirely different order than existed even as recently as the start of the decade. Developments include an immense growth in the annual number of referrals to the PWS from 3,789 (in 1990) to 6,069 (in 1997).

The government and Department of Justice, Equality and Law Reform, therefore, know because they have been frequently informed, that the PWS is without the capacity to carry out its statutory obligations. It is known that there has been a significant increase in the workload of the service in recent years, without a corresponding increase in the number of staff to meet work demands. Consequently, the highly unsatisfactory situation obtains whereby, on the one hand, not all offenders on statutory bonds are being adequately supervised and, on the other, court cases are being remanded for much longer periods for the purpose of acquiring pre-sanction reports.

The profound and persistent political failure to develop the Probation and Welfare Service ignores the basic recommendation of a number of authoritative reports on the management of offenders, including reports by the Department of

---

[17] Department of Justice 1985, Report of the Committee of Inquiry into the Penal System, Dublin: Stationery Office

[18] PWO Branch IMPACT 1998, Submission to Expert Group on PWS

[19] *Op. cit.,* Note 15

Justice itself.[20] These reports have each highlighted the need to develop community sanctions in this jurisdiction.

It is quite clear that, if community sanctions are to take their proper place at the centre of the criminal justice system, the process of fitful growth of the PWS must be replaced by a managed, substantial growth in staff numbers. The Expert Group on the PWS recommended that "the number of staff serving be brought up to levels previously approved by government decisions. This will mean an increase in the number of basic grade officers serving from 148.5 (at 31-12-1997) to 225, with appropriate increases in the number of senior staff and clerical support". They also recommended that the current system for the recruitment of staff be streamlined. There are also implications for training. Most PWOs, in line with the personnel from other social work agencies, hold the National Qualification in Social Work. There is a widespread view among PWOs themselves that probation practice and criminology are inadequately presented on the qualifying courses for this professional qualification. Recruitment as well as the functional capacity of PWOs could be facilitated and improved if these courses provided more coverage of areas of special relevance to the work of the PWS.

The PWO branch of IMPACT (the public service union) commenced industrial action on 10 May 1999 to secure implementation of the recommendations of the Expert Group. The Department of Justice agreed to commit itself to immediately increase the establishment figure of basic grade officers to 193.5, thereby allowing for the recruitment of thirty-three new permanent PWOs. Though recruitment in line with this agreement has been advanced, an increase in the number of basic grade PWOs has as of now failed to materialise. The beneficial effect of recruitment has been lost to the general attrition rate as officers regularly leave or retire from the service. Unfortunately, inadequate staffing levels remain a very serious feature of the PWS and continue to seriously undermine the delivery of service.

THE WORK OF THE PWS

The work of the Probation and Welfare Service now falls broadly into the following categories.

1   Preparation of (pre-sanction and review) reports for the courts

---

[20] Including the following reports: Department of Justice 1985, *Report of the Committee of Inquiry into the Penal System*, Dublin: Stationery Office; Department of Justice 1994, *The Management of Offenders: A Five Year Plan*, Dublin: Department of Justice; Department of Justice 1997, *Tackling Crime, Discussion Paper*, Dublin: Stationery Office; *National Crime Forum Report* 1998, Dublin, Institute of Public Administration; Expert Group on the Probation and Welfare Service 1998, *First Report*, Dublin: Stationery Office; and Expert Group on the Probation and Welfare Service 1999, *Final Report*, Dublin: Stationery Office

2   Supervision of offenders in the community (probation, community service, supervision during deferment, temporary release, etc)

3   Welfare services to offenders in prisons and places of detention

4   Services to a range of special projects, hostels, workshops, special schools etc.

5   "Non-criminal" work, ie family law courts assessments, and adoption.

The most recently published report of the work of the Probation and Welfare Service for 1997, shows the scale of services provided in that year, including the following: 5,953 pre-sanction reports, (Probation and CSO) prepared for the courts; 36 victim reports; 1,506 probation orders; 1,992 supervisions during deferment of penalty; 1,167 community service orders; 89 offenders supervised on early release from prisons and special schools; 85 offenders helped on a voluntary basis; and 18 referrals from other jurisdictions, most particularly the United Kingdom.

The PWS also provides the welfare service to thirteen custodial institutions, as well as to hostels, workshops and special projects financially supported by the PWS. There are also Staff Development and Research/Statistics sections in the Probation Service. In total, 190 professional personnel of all grades (PWOs and management grades) provide that level of service

Court reports

PWOs provide around 6,000 reports to the courts currently each year. At one level the requests for pre-sanction reports has been related to a court's consideration of a community sanction. In other cases especially at the level of the higher courts (Circuit and Central Criminal) pre-sanction reports assist judges in consideration of custodial sentences. In addition, in many cases where serious offenders receive prison sentences, they are referred to the PWS for progress reports at a specified later date in the course of their sentence. Community sanction with partial suspension of prison term has often been considered at the review stage (although a Supreme Court judgement in November 2000 may lead to the abandonment of this particular mechanism).

The PWS provides guidelines for the preparation and presentation of pre-sanction reports.[21] As these guidelines explain, the request for the report provides the opportunity for the PWS to assist the court in determining the most suitable method of dealing with the offenders. Reports do more than just collate relevant background information, they examine the offender's attitude to the crime and assess the strength of motivation to address the offending behaviour, both issues of major concern to the court.

---

[21] The PWS 1999, *Service Practice for the preparation and presentation of Pre-Sanction Reports,* Dublin: PWS

Offenders, whether guilty of petty or serious crime, are capable of attitudinal and behavioural changes and may also become engaged in making reparation to their victims or the local community. The report highlights how the offender can deal with offending patterns, and can improve or remedy defects in coping skills and social functioning. It specifies what interventions will be put in place, and outlines proposals for the safe management of the offender by means of a community sanction.

Experience shows that the courts expect and will be well disposed towards a properly researched and formulated plan for dealing with offenders while taking into account the seriousness of the offence and the need to protect the community. The report conveys to the court the likely response of the offenders, when a conclusion is reached that a community sanction would be suitable in the particular circumstance of the case. It is worth noting, however, that although the PWS discourages the practice, probation orders may be made without the court seeking or considering a pre-sanction report.

The PWS guidelines on the Criminal Justice (Community Service) Act 1983, "The Management of the Community Service Order", advises on the preparation and presentation of reports in relation to community service. The guidelines advise that in preparation of the report, the probation officer should pay particular attention to a) the suitability of the offender for community work with reference to his attitude to the offence and the injured party and b) the availability of suitable work.

The guidelines put forward the following criteria and issues for consideration in the selection of suitable offenders for community service: permanency of residence; work record; sufficiency of free time to complete CS work; health; psychiatric and emotional problems; motivation to complete CSO; alcohol and drug problems; record of violence or sexual misbehaviour; understanding of the demands of the order and of implications of failure to complete.

Probation

The founding father of criminology in the UK, Leon Radcinowicz, said of the probation order that it was the single most important rehabilitative sentence of the twentieth century.[22] A probation order is the main base of the work of the Probation and Welfare Service. The objective of probation is to enhance public safety through a "rehabilitation" programme of work with an offender that can reduce the likelihood of future offending.

The PWS document "The Management of the Probation Order (Policy and Procedure)"[23] states that

---

[22] Smith, G. 1998, HM Chief Probation Inspector, "Recent Developments in the Probation Service in England and Wales", *Penological Information Bulletin No. 21*, Council of Europe

[23] The PWS 1986, *The Management of the Probation Order (Policy and Procedure)*, Dublin: PWS

1) The Probation of Offenders Act 1907 as amended by the Children's Act 1908, Criminal Justice Administration Act 1914, and the Criminal Law Amendment Act 1936 places at the disposal of Criminal Courts the machinery for supervising offenders

2) The Act may be applied in the case of any person charged before a court of summary jurisdiction with an offence punishable by such a court. The original 1907 probation legislation describes the probation function as being "to advise, assist and befriend" the offender.

Using probation orders, the courts can conditionally discharge offenders who give a formal undertaking to be of good behaviour for a specified period of time (up to three years) and to follow the advice and directions of a probation officer. The general conditions attaching to a probation order are expressed in the language of the Edwardian era, ie that "the person a) be of good behaviour, b) does not associate with thieves or other undesirable persons, c) does not frequent undesirable places, d) does lead an honest and industrious life, e) shall abstain from intoxicating liquor".[24]

The court may impose additional conditions to such an order (eg an order to attend for addiction treatment), residence conditions, payment of compensation etc. Probation officers are charged with the duty of supervision, on behalf of the courts, of the conduct of offenders given to their care. Section 4 of the Probation Act outlines the duties of a probation officer as to visit or receive reports from the person under supervision; to see that he observes the conditions of his recognisance; to report to the court as to his behaviour; to advise, assist and befriend and when necessary to endeavour to find him suitable employment.

It is this duty to "advise, assist and befriend" which allows for the flexible range of "social work" practised within the legal framework of the probation bond. However, it is obvious that if probation supervision is to reduce re-offending, the PWS must ensure that its practice is informed by "what works" research. Research raises doubts about the effectiveness of loosely defined, unstructured individual casework with offenders on supervision.[25] Individual casework, the traditional hallmark of probation supervision, remains the dominant mode of work in the Irish PWS. However within that mode of work with offenders, some probation practitioners have increasingly come to target offending behaviour and the means by which an offender can modify his/her offending behaviour.

Evidence based practice research, as McIvor[26] indicates, has highlighted that "interventions which have proved ineffective in reducing the frequency or

---

[24] The Probation of Offenders Act 1907

[25] Lipsey, M.W. 1990, "Juvenile delinquency treatments: A meta-analytic inquiry into the variability of effects", in K.W. Wechter and M.L. Straf (eds.), *Meta-analysis for Explanation: A Casebook*, NY: Russell Sage Foundation

[26] McIvor, G. 1995, "Rehabilitation and Community Sanctions", in *The Management of Offenders, A Five Year Plan*, IMPACT

seriousness of re-offending include those which are unstructured and unfocused, which are applied inconsistently, and which are imposed upon offenders rather than being negotiated as part of a contractual agreement and implemented with the offender's consent. Traditional methods of relatively unfocused casework and counselling appear to be ineffective as do various psychotherapeutic models of intervention". There is a clear onus on the PWS to leave these ineffective methods behind and to develop training systems and work methods that support approaches of proven value.

It is not possible to overstate the difficulty and complexity of the task since probation orders tend to be used with offenders with personal problems such as alcohol or drug addiction problems, a history of family disharmony or child sexual abuse, personality disorders, and housing or other social problems. As well as directly monitoring and challenging probationers' offending behaviour, probation officers undertake individual and family counselling with offenders and refer to and liaise with specialist agencies, such as training centres and special schools.

If the probationer fails to comply with the probation conditions, the probation officer must "swear an information" before the court. This usually results in the issue of a warrant for the arrest of the accused. The gardaí have responsibility to execute the warrant through arrest of the offender. It cannot be surmised what the level of co-operation by offenders with their supervising probation officers is, because the statistics on breach of probation bond are not recorded in PWS annual reports. Anecdotal evidence might suggest that less than 10% of offenders on probation are brought back to court for not complying with their court orders. However in practice the breach procedure is cumbersome enough to be off-putting and this estimate figure might be in part a reflection of that reality.

Supervision during deferment

While a probation order is a final order of the court, supervision during deferment of penalty has a rather special, more ambiguous status and basis. An increasing practice in the courts is for judges to adjourn cases on bail for a fixed period, after a full assessment and pre-sanction report, in order to review progress in open court on the return date, that is the date set for reappearance before the court. The rationale for this procedure is that it is arguably more appropriate than a final court order of probation in circumstances where there remains continuing doubt as to an offender's ability to engage with and satisfy the requirements of a community sanction.

Deferred supervision is used frequently, but by no means solely, in cases involving "chaotic" drug abusers. It is also used extensively in the higher courts. Recognisances for such adjournments can include requirements to maintain a nominated place of residence, or to co-operate with supervision, or to attend for specific forms of treatment, or other conditions similar to those on a probation recognisance. The court usually expects a written progress report of the defendant's compliance with supervision to be produced on the return date, if a case has been deferred on recognisances involving a condition of supervision. The judge then decides whether to continue supervision by the PWS or dispose of the case by way of a custodial or a non-custodial sanction. While there is no legislative base for this procedure of adjournments and periodic review, and it might be termed a judge-made remedy, it has become more popular with the judiciary than the probation order. The PWS finds itself involved in an ever-increasing number of such supervision.[27]

For example, the comparative frequency of the two approaches varied as follows:

1992	1,062 (Sup. During Def.)	1,039 (Prob.)
1994	1,589 (Sup. During Def.)	1,044 (Prob.)
1997	1,992 (Sup. During Def.)	1,506 (Prob.)

Intensive Probation Supervision

The Intensive Probation Supervision (IPS) programme has been operating in Dublin and Cork since 1992. Current schemes under the Intensive Probation Supervision programme are known as the Bridge Project and the Grattan House Project, based in Dublin and Cork respectively. These are innovative community-based alternatives to imprisonment. IPS represents new thinking and a new approach to working with young adults, ages eighteen to twenty-six years, who are serious or persistent offenders. The programme utilises specific group and individual approaches that have been based on "what works"[28] research. The general approach incorporates theoretical insights and practical techniques from cognitive behavioural and social learning theory and practice,[29] and from the literature on the psychology of criminal conduct.[30] However, specific approaches and techniques have been developed and elaborated by PWOs in response to the particular Irish context.[31] The PWS and the Irish Youth Foundation fund the projects and both projects have additional finance and staff provided by the local

---

[27] The PWS 2000, *The PWS Report 1997,* Dublin: Staionery Office

[28] McGuire, J. (ed.) 1995, *What Works: Reducing Re-offending: Guidelines from Research and Practice*, Chichester: John Wiley and Sons

[29] The following are important and useful texts in the area: Skinner, B.F. 1938, *The Behaviour of Organisms: An experimental analysis*, New York: Appleton-Century-Crofts; Meichenbaum, D.H. 1977, *Cognitive-Behaviour Modification: An Integrative Approach*, New York, NY: Plenum Press; Bandura, A. 1977, *Social Learning Theory*, New Jersey: Prentice Hall

[30] Andrews, D.A., and Bonta, J. 1998, *The Psychology of Criminal Conduct*, 2nd ed., Cincinnati: Anderson Publishing

[31] Fernee, U. 1998, "Intervening Effectively with Male Offenders", *Irish Social Worker,* Vol. 16, No. 3

Vocational Education Committee. To this degree, the IPS programme is a model of integrated service delivery.

The courts refer offenders to the IPS programme, as a direct alternative to substantial custodial sentences. Offenders remain accountable to the court while participating on the programme, usually through the mechanism of supervision on deferment of penalty as described previously. In addition, referrals of persons, who have served a period of imprisonment but who are deemed appropriate for inclusion in the programme as part of an overall plan of supervised temporary release, are accepted through the prison administration.

The group work programme of the IPS programme is divided into three phases. Each phase has clearly defined aims and procedures. In phase one, staff meet with the prospective participant to carry out an in-depth assessment focusing on his/her attitude to crime, motivation and level of social skills, addiction or other personal difficulties and education/training needs. Phase two of the programme provides an integrated set of group work modules, which have been designed by staff and are implemented by the team over an ordained period. The content material of these group modules is critically reviewed in order to maintain a high level of programme integrity and ensure that a focus on criminogenic factors is maintained. Phase three of the programme is a period of re-integration when participants receive ongoing support, firstly in their efforts to meet training and employment goals, and also in relation to the management of personal difficulties. In the light of the continuing demand for effective intervention with offenders, the PWS is convinced of the worth of the IPS programme and believes that it is essential that the PWS continues to have resources to deliver and expand these projects

Community Service

Community Service (CS) has become another major component of the PWS's workload. The scheme started in 1984. CS includes the positive elements of "repaying one's debt and community reintegration of offenders". It is also punishment in the sense of deprivation of offenders' leisure time. Anyone over sixteen years is eligible for the scheme.

As the PWS policy document on "The Management of the CSO"[32] states, the Community Service Act provides for "The performance of unpaid work in the community by a person who is sixteen years or over, who has been convicted of an offence, for which the appropriate penalty would be an immediate custodial sentence, and who has given his/her consent to the court. The Act allows for a report to court, arrangement of placement and supervision by the PWS of the offender during the existence of the order of the court and makes it an offence to fail to carry out the order of the court."

---

[32] The PWS, 1998, *The Management of the Community Service Order*, Dublin: PWS

CS is a direct alternative to imprisonment and a final order of the court (subject to appeal). A CS order may be made only after conviction and when the judge has the possibility of a custodial sentence in mind. A judge first adjourns the case for a number of weeks and refers an offender to the PWS for assessment as to their suitability for a CS order. A probation officer assesses the defendant's suitability and consent for CS and the availability of appropriate work. The PWS guidelines on CS[33] advise that in preparation of the report, the probation officer should pay particular attention to a) the suitability of the offender for community work with explicit reference to his attitude to the offence and the injured party and b) the availability of suitable work. The guidelines include the criteria for the selection of suitable offenders for CS.

Offenders may be deemed unsuitable when they are abusing drugs and not in a treatment programme or unwilling to undertake such a programme. A report following assessment is made available to court for the next court appearance. If the offender is assessed as suitable, if he or she has consented to work and if CS work is available, a CS Order may be made by the court. A default sentence of detention or imprisonment is specified as is the number of CS hours the offender is required to work.

An offender must do a specified number of hours (minimum 40 – maximum 240) unpaid work in the community. The type of work undertaken includes renovating, painting and decorating community facilities, landscaping, helping out in youth clubs and senior citizen's centres and a whole range of useful work and activities in local communities which otherwise would not be done.

The offender will be supervised in that work by the PWO. If the offender fails to commence or complete the CS work, the PWO applies to court for the issue of a summons to return the offender to court. The offender can be given either extra time to complete the CS or can be committed to jail as per the default sentence of custody.

Offenders' generally positive attitudes to CS are demonstrated by the fact that over 80% of offenders successfully complete CS orders.[34] The 17% of offenders who have their orders revoked compares well with figures from other European countries. The prospects for CSO completion would appear to be best among older, first-time offenders and with offenders who have committed less serious assaults.[35]

Prisons and places of detention

PWOs also play an important role in the prison system where they have welfare and some rehabilitative and therapeutic responsibilities. At present, thirty-one

---

[33] *Ibid.*
[34] Walsh, D. and Sexton, P. 1999, *An Empirical Study of Community Service Orders in Ireland*, Department of Justice, Equality and Law Reform
[35] *Ibid.*

PWOs provide a "listening ear" and a safety valve to prisoners. Their role has been described as helping offenders to cope and work towards a resolution of personal and practical problems, counselling offenders and co-ordinating the activities of voluntary groups visiting and dealing with offenders in custody. Reflecting this role, individual social casework is the dominant mode of work by Probation and Welfare staff with prisoners.

In addition PWOs have been involved in a number of special therapeutic initiatives for sex offenders, most notably at Arbour Hill Prison, Dublin. In 1993 the Minister for Justice produced a discussion document on sex offenders called "A Proposal for a Structured Psychological Treatment Programme for Sex Offenders".[36] As a result, the first ministerial mandated Sex Offender Treatment Programme was initiated in 1994. It is a joint venture between the Psychology Service of the Department of Justice and the PWS. It is an intensive, highly structured programme, which runs for approximately one year for each group .

The PWS has the responsibility for co-ordinating the Mountjoy Drug Treatment Facility, which opened in 1996. This is both a medical and therapeutic programme provided to small groups of offenders with drug problems. PWOs in prisons have historically also provided a range of programmes for groups of prisoners including alcohol education, HIV and drug awareness, assertiveness training, and life sentence support programmes. Sadly the programmes are not uniformly available throughout the prison system. The quality, quantity and consistency of programmes vary enormously from prison to prison and place to place. Crucially these educational, supportive and rehabilitative programmes have been without topdown policy and resource support even within the PWS.

In addition Probation and Welfare Service provide in-depth reports on prisoners under review to the Department of Justice instituted Sentence Review Group. This group is similar in concept to a parole board for prisoners, who have served at least seven years of their sentences. Probation staff also provide reports in response to requests by prisoners under the Transfer of Prisoners Acts 1995 and 1997.

It is the policy of the PWO branch of IMPACT[37] to encourage a redefinition of the role of the PWS in prisons. The branch believes that the PWO should be less involved with meeting the routine welfare needs of prisoners and more with the development of a range of rehabilitative interventions designed to actively address offending. This would involve the service in taking on the role of a major rehabilitative force in the prison system, establishing an ordered structure of rehabilitation for those in custody. The branch argues that specialised group work programmes are required for the problems of alcoholism, violence and for many

---

[36] Department of Justice 1993, *A Proposal for a Structured Psychological Treatment Programme for Sex Offenders*, Dublin: Stationery Office

[37] *Op. cit.,* Note 17

special client groups (lifers to name one). An immense increase in the capacity of sex and drug offender programmes is also urgently required. It is the view of the PWO union that a properly designed and implemented structure of such re-habilitative programmes would have a major impact on the attitudes and behaviour of offenders and would make a significant contribution to public safety.

After-care/temporary release

PWOs only supervise those offenders on temporary release (TR), whose release was part of a planned programme of rehabilitation and re-integration into the community. They have had no involvement with the large number of offenders who have been on unplanned temporary release (frequently known as "shedding") in recent years due to the prisons accommodation crisis. The PWS must assess all offenders who are being considered for planned TR in advance of their release. A significant increase in the workloads of the PWS, without a corresponding increase in staffing resources, has resulted in the PWS playing a very reduced role in supervised TR compared to previously. A Dáil question, in May 2000, stated that a total of seventy-three offenders were at that time under the TR supervision of the PWS. These consisted mainly of lifers and other special cases.

In general, it can be said that supervised TR or aftercare of prisoners is a service that is largely underdeveloped in this state. This is in spite of the fact that the inadequacy or in some instances the absence of such services have been highlighted in several government reports on the penal system.

For example, the 1985 Whitaker Report[38] reviewed the aftercare services available to people discharged from prisons and recommended that, "aftercare of prisoners should be improved". More recently, the Management of Offenders document[39] recommended that "formalised aftercare arrangements for offenders should be put in place" and the Final Report of the Expert Group on the PWS[40] recommended "that resources be provided to allow the Service (PWS) provide for a comprehensive aftercare service for prisoners". Although no research has been done on the question, it is probable that the greater proportion of offenders would welcome the involvement and support of probation staff in an endeavour to cope better in the community following release from custody.

Juvenile offenders

The PWS deals with a declining number of young offenders, categorised as those under sixteen years of age. In 1992, the courts placed 269 people under sixteen

---

[38] *Op. cit.,* Note 16
[39] Department of Justice 1994, *The Management of Offenders: A Five Year Plan*, Dublin: Deptartment of Justice
[40] *Op. cit.,* Note 15

years on probation or deferred supervision and the figure for 1997 was 261. This compares with a figure of 526 in 1989.[41]

The majority of young people referred to the PWS can be helped while remaining in the community. PWOs "advise, assist and befriend" these young people and their families through difficult phases of their lives. In addition to the established practice approaches, such as one to one casework and family-orientated social work, it is envisaged that the Children Act (2001) will encourage new ways of working with young offenders in the community. For example, family conferences and a new middle range of community sanctions, such as day detention centres, are just some of the new features of the planned juvenile justice system that can be expected to impact on the mode of work of the PWS. Undoubtedly, research from other countries with longer experience of these methods can assist in the design of more effective work with young offenders and in managing the optimum selection of appropriate targets for probation involvement.

Apart altogether from the planned future services, the PWS already runs or assists in the running of a modest infrastructure of facilities for young offenders. These are four probation hostels and a growing number of training workshops which have been established under the aegis of the PWS. The Probation Service is also involved in a number of community-based programmes designed to "divert" young people away from crime. The programmes range in scope from recreational to employment-related activities.

There are five special (industrial/reformatory) schools available to the courts. They have places for up to fifteen girls and 216 boys, generally under the age of sixteen years. Three (and previously six) PWOs are assigned to work in the special schools. Their duties include regular contact with the young persons' families, individual counselling, groupwork and aftercare of the young person.

The Children Act 2001 distinguishes between children who have a need for care and protection and children who are before the court for pre-dominantly criminal behaviour. Under this legislation, the former group will have separate places of detention in a new system of high support/security places under the health boards. It has yet to be made known what relationship PWS will take up with this new system.

Community involvement

Raynor et al have argued that practice with identified offenders "needs to be complemented by a commitment to a broader engagement with the social problems associated with crime".[42] The PWS has a history of community involvement. Many probation staff are involved in various community-based initiatives and

---

[41] *Op. cit.,* Note 26
[42] Raynor, Smith and Vanstone 1993, *Effective Probation Practice*, London: Macmillan

projects in a voluntary capacity. Indeed many successful projects have evolved out of individual officers' personal, voluntary commitment and dedication. This community approach and involvement is now been developed in a more strategic and planned way by the PWS itself.

PWOs are reaching beyond those services traditionally structured to deal with crime and utilising the new opportunities arising for those concerned with social and economic factors such as unemployment, social exclusion and with the relation of these factors to crime. For example, the PWS now has representation on Local Drugs Task Forces, Local Development Partnerships, and Integrated Services Projects. PWOs have demonstrated the training, skills, commitment and professional backgrounds to do this work and thereby expand the service's community development programme in a meaningful way. The pursuit of social inclusion is stated as a fundamental objective of the National Development Plan (NDP) for the years 2000 to 2006.[43] The specific measures to arrest the "drift" of young people into unemployment, crime and substance abuse mentioned in the NDP are of special importance for the context in which PWOs operate. Importantly, the NDP also supports the introduction of more effective measures to assist with the re-integration into the community of those who have been involved in crime.

This explicit reference to crime in the NDP is significant. It is significant too that crime is framed in terms of a social problem and not solely in terms of personal irresponsibility. Social inclusion is implicitly acknowledged as a crime prevention tool. Opening employment to the traditionally socially excluded is the favoured means to address their social exclusion. The PWS is to be funded to ensure that an adequate range of progression routes are available to enable "target groups" to move in from the margins. The routes will provide both pre-employment training and personal development work.

The PWS document[44] describes an outline for the delivery of services. Investments are proposed that will contribute to an infrastructure where employability and job placement become realistic goals for the formerly marginalised. The plan is to provide a progression of opportunities for offenders and former prisoners. The PWS is to provide facilities in areas of high crime and unemployment for this purpose. Geiran,[45] while welcoming this new area of community involvement for the PWS and accepting that it has the potential to make a major impact, argues that there is a need for the PWS to develop specific evaluative tools suited to its community work so that practice can be properly assessed and placed on a strong evidence-based foundation.

---

[43] *National Development Plan 2000 to 2006,* (NDP) 2,000, Dublin: Stationery Office

[44] The PWS 2000, untitled and unpublished document on the role and implications of NDP for PWS, Dublin: PWS

[45] Geiran, V. 1998, "Community Development and the Probation and Welfare Service", Appendix 4, Submission to The Review Group of the PWS, IMPACT

Civil law

Finally, in this brief overview of the work of the PWS, mention should made of the Service's contribution in the area of civil law. The PWS is well known for its work in the criminal area. Less well known is the role the agency has had in two areas of civil law – Adoption and Family Law.

Adoption

A team of six PWOs is seconded from the PWS on a long-term basis to the Adoption Board. Their role is to act as social work advisors to the board, to assess the suitability of adoption applicants and to counsel both birth mothers and, since the 1996 Adoption Bill, birth fathers. The team foresees this role continuing. There have been some recent developments to the role, including the expansion of duties to cover 1) the assessment of Irish nationals who apply to adopt a child from abroad under Irish adoption law and 2) some involvement in the tracing process. Work around the search and re-union of adoptees and birth parents has steadily increased in recent years, although the absence of a National Contact Register is seriously impeding the provision of this service.

The Final Report of the Expert Group has recommended that in future, staff of the Adoption Board should no longer be seconded from the PWS.[46]

Family law

It is little known that for twenty years up to 1995 the PWS has provided independent assessments for the Family Law courts, at the request of members of the judiciary. These assessments related in the main to barring, custody and access order applications and occasionally to maintenance disputes. Social reports (assessments) provided in these types of cases are in-depth background reports that, for example, might examine in some depth the relationship between a couple and the implications of this relationship for the welfare of their children. Specific recommendations to the court are a normal part of such reports. The Family Law Act 1995, Section 46, has acknowledged the role of these reports as central and makes statutory provision for them in Family Law cases. The Act acknowledges that independent assessments are an essential part of any comprehensive service to the Family Law courts. It names the PWS as one of the agencies to compile social reports. However, at the present time, the PWS remains unable to undertake the work due to a lack of resources

Though provision for "social reports" now exists in statute, it is not in fact being provided for. The Family Law courts were deprived of their only consistent social reports service in 1996 when the PWS withdrew that service to the courts

---

[46] The Expert Group on the Probation and Welfare Service 1999, *Final Report*, Dublin: Stationery Office

for lack of funding. The Final Report of the PWS Expert Group recommended, that the current role of the PWS, which is to provide independent objective assessments to the courts, should be maintained. The group also recommended that the PWS would be adequately resourced to enable it to discharge its function in the Family Law courts. Ideally this work would take place under the aegis of an independently resourced and administered civil family section within the PWS. Meanwhile, adjudication in child custody cases etc, without the assistance of a neutral report, is the basis of daily decision making in the Family Law courts of Ireland.

FUTURE DIRECTIONS

It is clear that the PWS is at an important crossroads in its development. There are many recent social and economic, political and legal changes that have impacted on the work of the PWS and at the same time presented new opportunities for expansion and development. This has been recognised to the extent that an Expert Committee on the PWS has been established and has published two reports. Considerable knowledge and information are now available to guide the future direction of the PWS. The growing literature mainly from abroad on best practice models and evidence-based practice is also an important guide to that future. However probation practice must also be complemented by a commitment to engage with the broader social problems associated with crime in line with and inspired by the major socio-political movements of recent years that have focused on social partnership, the integration and strategic management of public services, and the assault on marginalisation, poverty and social exclusion.

The Final Report of the Expert Group on the PWS[47] made specific recommendations on the organisational structure of the PWS. In summary, these were

- the establishment of a statutory PWS agency with a board of directors who would have responsibility for policy and direction within a statutory framework
- the appointment of an inspectorate of probation
- a shift in political and legislative policy to facilitate an increased range of community sanctions
- the PWS to be adequately resourced to enable it to discharge its functions in Civil Courts (Family Law)
- the PWS to be resourced to a level that enables it to provide aftercare services for prisoners
- a more effective use of the professional expertise of PWO in prisons.

---

[47] *Op. Cit.,* Note 15

The next step is for this new knowledge and awareness to be applied and for these recommendations to be implemented. A key component is to establish a statutory PWS, with a board, independent of the Department of Justice, Equality and Law Reform. Such an initiative would endow the PWS with a far greater sense of professional integrity and identity. It would also ensure that the PWS becomes a leading agency within this jurisdiction's structure for the management of offenders. From a secure organisational base of this type, the PWS will be able to develop its professional practice at individual offender level and at the levels of family and community.

The importance of the community level of activity needs to be especially emphasised, because though this fact is of little interest to the court when fulfilling its judicial function of determining guilt, rehabilitation depends strongly on the kind of environment an individual lives in.

It is a priority that the PWS expose itself to outside scrutiny and not hide behind a cloak of "good works" and "moral worthiness". It is critical that the three levels of probation intervention (individual, family and community) are properly evaluated and that the results of evaluations and of evidence-based practice research inform and guide probation practice. An inspectorate of probation can provide the necessary external monitoring of probation practice at the three levels. This is consistent with the increasing emphasis in public service organisations on output-based results.

However, despite the rather obvious and urgent developmental agenda for the PWS, the government seems set to continue in its generally neglectful approach, ignoring the now voluminous evidence, arguments and research supporting rapid and substantial development of the PWS. The government appears unconvinced of the case for investment in the PWS. It also appears to lack conviction that an express policy for the management of offenders in the community is politically desirable. This demonstrates considerable lack of awareness of the high level of demand for the probation "product" from the courts. It is an attitude that has the very serious consequence of undermining the capacity of the PWS to deliver services. Given the prevailing political attitudes and the long history of neglect and under-resourcing of the PWS, it would appear that a properly managed, adequate level of investment in the PWS may have to await a radically more rational criminal justice policy.

SECTION 7

CRIME PREVENTION, CRIME REDUCTION AND TREATMENT OF OFFENDERS

37

Introduction

Paul O'Mahony

The business of crime prevention, crime reduction and treatment of offenders is immensely complex, reflecting the many different forms of crime, the diverse motives for crime, the many problems of offenders and the tangled web of causes of crime. There is also a bewildering wealth of different foci for prevention, reduction and treatment, involving many different technologies, professions and philosophies. For example, there are preventative programmes aimed at pre-school educational enrichment; community development and the improvement of housing estates; family support; substance misuse prevention; and youth training and development. Similarly, there are the many programmes that employ the various techniques of the clinical and educational professions and aim at the treatment and rehabilitation of established offenders. Such programmes include psychiatric treatment, anger management training, drugs counselling, vocational and social skills training and sex offender therapy. Moreover, not infrequently, an issue arises around whether or not an offender is so mentally ill that criminal responsibility is impaired or non-existent and whether, in Prins' (1980) phrase, he or she should be treated as "an offender, deviant or patient".

Although it needs to be borne in mind that the disease model is rarely appropriate in the area of criminal conduct, it is helpful to examine the enormous variety of initiatives to reduce crime in terms of the three categories used to describe prevention in the health area: the *primary*, *secondary* and *tertiary* levels of prevention. Breaking down the many different crime reductive approaches in this way helps clarify their objectives and their basic similarities and differences.

Primary prevention aims to reduce the general incidence of or exposure of people to risk factors for criminality. These risk factors include poverty, inadequate housing, poor educational provision and related community problems such as chronic unemployment and drug misuse. Programmes designed to impact on these areas can collectively be described as social inclusion programmes. The Partnership 2000 Document (Government of Ireland 1996) has claimed that "social inclusion will be pursued not in any residual way, but rather as an integral part of the partnership and a strategic objective in its own right". While social inclusion is an end in itself, success in this endeavour is expected to have a positive crime reductive effect, since "to minimise or ignore" the challenge of social exclusion would result in "an increase in all the attendant problems such as poor health, crime, drug abuse, and alienation".

Primary prevention also embraces family and parenting risk factors such as family breakdown or disruption, alcoholism or violence in the home, and poor discipline and neglect, all of which can impact negatively on the socialisation of children. Indeed, in recent years, as Lilly et al (1995) point out, families have been recognised as the primary site for interventions intended to have an eventual crime reductive effect, because they are "incubators for and prophylactics against crime involvement".

Many primary prevention initiatives are targeted universally or very broadly within society, for example action against poverty or programmes to improve the capacity of schools to retain students within the education system. Many others are selective, for example programmes which target at-risk families for special support or particularly disadvantaged schools. Crime reduction is generally just one of many potential, long-term benefits of primary prevention programmes.

Secondary prevention encompasses all types of early intervention with delinquents and at-risk youths, that is all remedial responses to the kinds of problem behaviour which hint at or reliably predict future involvement in offending or further more serious and persistent offending. This can include initiatives such as therapy for young schoolchildren, who are aggressive or out of control; anti-bullying and anti-truanting programmes in schools; police cautioning and diversion from the courts of young offenders; and youth development projects, such as the car maintenance and driving projects aimed at so-called joy-riders.

Tertiary prevention aims to reform and rehabilitate or, at the very least, contain and restrain people with a history of persistent or serious offending. For the most part, therefore, tertiary prevention is located within penal and criminal justice institutions. It embraces initiatives such as sex offender therapy, education in literacy and numeracy, probation supervision, community service, alcohol and substance abuse detoxification and counselling and training in interpersonal and vocational skills for offenders in order to improve their employability. Clearly not all tertiary methods focus directly on offending behaviour. Many are aimed at solving other problems for the offender or aimed at his or her positive, personal development and impact on criminality only as a byproduct of treatment. One major initiative of this type outside the criminal justice system is the methadone maintenance programme (Dack 1996) which sets out, first and foremost, to stabilise the lifestyles of drug abusing offenders in the community but also has the objective to thereby substantially decrease their involvement in crime.

The rational choice model and prevention

Of course, criminal sanctioning in itself is a form of tertiary prevention, although this fact tends to be forgotten in a context where there are so many deliberately planned, professionally based, rehabilitative programmes, which focus on the specific "pathologies" and deficits of individual offenders or groups of offenders.

It is also important to note that endeavours to reduce or prevent crime are by no means always directly focused on people. The "rational choice" model of criminal behaviour (Cornish and Clarke 1986) emphasises the "economy of crime" and is linked to many primary prevention initiatives that are focused on the environment. For example, Becker (1968) has stated that "a useful theory of criminal behaviour can dispense with special theories of anomie, psychological inadequacies, or inheritance of special traits and simply extend the economist's usual analysis of choice". According to this view, the individual will choose illegal or legal activity depending on which choice offers the highest personal return. Potential gains and potential risks are set off against each other in an essentially rational, calculated manner.

These theories hark back to the views of Beccaria (1764) and the classical school, who believe that the criminal act essentially begins and ends with the exercise of free will. This view tends to diminish the importance of, or altogether exclude from consideration, the antecedant factors and individual predispositions that might influence a person's criminal choice, such as their social and economic background. The focus of attention is shifted firmly onto current environmental factors that can influence the potential offender's choice, most especially the relative difficulty of the criminal act and the probability of being caught and punished. Despite the seemingly obvious relevance of making crime difficult and bringing criminals to justice, it is worth noting that studies of offence motivations and decisions do not offer much support to this general perspective, since they indicate that the prospect of being caught and punished plays little active part in offenders' thinking in the moments immediately prior to the commission of an offence (Light et al 1993, Carroll and Weaver 1986).

Economy of crime type theories have been very influential because they stress the role of opportunity and of features of the environment that make crime more or less likely. These theories support overtly deterrent schemes that aim to mobilise the community against crime, such as Neighbourhood Watch and the provision of personal alarm systems for the isolated elderly. They have also inspired target-hardening and so-called situational crime prevention approaches

(Home Office 1998). Hughes (1996) has stated that "situational crime prevention is arguably now the most powerful and hygienic discourse of crime prevention (if we exclude mass incarceration through imprisonment from our calculations)". Initiatives of this type include the design of "defensible space" and of more thief-proof cars and homes, the development of gated "fortress" housing estates, and the widespread use of CCTV and private security personnel. These methods are fundamentally aligned with the general deterrent, law enforcement approach to crime reduction, rather than any more constructive, preventative approach focused on people. That is to say they are almost entirely concerned with the prevention of crime by means of defence and deterrence. The aim is not so much to change potential offenders as to change the contingencies that bear on their decision-making.

Punishment as a tertiary prevention technique

The rational choice perspective or "homo economicus" model of man harmon-ises closely with the purposes, methods and philosophy of the criminal justice system itself. This reminds us that the activities of law enforcement and the penal system can themselves be reasonably described as a form of treatment of offenders, involving the application of punishment. Punishment is widely used to change people's behaviour. For example, aversion therapy is based on the carefully planned punishment of the therapeutic subject. Parents rely on punishment as well as on reward in the upbringing of children. Vehemently expressed parental dis-approval and other forms of punishment, some of which, like reduction of pocket money or restriction to the bedroom, mirror the activities of the penal system, play a central role in the formation of the child's conscience. In other words, parental punishment has a formative role in the child's development of feelings of guilt and shame about socially disapproved behaviour and development of the capacity for self-regulation and self-restraint

As Maguire and Priestley state (1995) "punishment is an effective method of behavioural change", even though "on balance, methods of behavioural change based on some form of positive reinforcement work better overall". Behavioural scientists such as Skinner (1953) have established that to be truly effective punishment should be inevitable, immediate, severe, and understood by the punished person to be the direct consequence of their conduct. There should also be viable alternative forms of behaviour to that for which the person is being punished. However, it is very significant that, as Maguire and Priestley state, "it virtually goes without saying that none of these conditions is adequately met in the criminal justice system".

In spite of the essential inefficacy of penal punishment, society and the criminal justice system itself hold crime reduction and prevention to be primary aims of all criminal sanctioning, including imprisonment, suspended imprisonment, fines, community service and probation supervision. This is an essential point because the discourse on penality is often couched in terms of a radical opposition between reform and punishment. In fact, it is extremely difficult to make a meaningful distinction between an offender, who has been changed by the unpleasant experience of imprisonment (or the active threat of imprisonment on a sentence that has been suspended) and avoids crime in order to avoid imprisonment, and a similarly "reformed" offender, who avoids crime because he or she has "seen the light" or gained improved prospects in open society through some overtly rehabilitative process. In any event, motives are almost always mixed and a change of heart does not preclude the continuing influence of a prudent concern with the threat of punishment. Carlen (1994), indeed, takes the view that punishment is an active ingredient of the rehabilitative process and that "in order to be rehabilitated, offenders would need to be convinced not only that their own behaviour had been reprehensible but also that the state's treatment of them had been just".

The failure of punishment with actual offenders may in part be because the punished person rarely accepts that the punishment is, in Carlen's sense, justified. The restorative justice ideology and movement (Consedine 1995) is an explicit attempt to rethink the whole criminal justice process in a way that centrally addresses the offender's sense of responsibility for his or her actions. It is, arguably, a system for replacing traditional punishments with a form of punishment that might be a truly effective treatment. The aim is to persuade the offender to take responsibility and avoid re-offending by confronting him or her with the consequences of the offence and obliging him or her to make restitution to the community and the victim. The process can involve victim/offender mediation and group conferencing, where parties with a stake in the issue, including the victim, community representatives, the family of the offender, the police, and service agencies, can meet to discuss the case with the offender and collectively design a suitable response. An important aspect of this approach is that consideration is given to and provision is made for the needs of the offender who, through the process, tends to be reintegrated with the community rather than ostracised from it. In a review of such restorative justice programmes the British Home Office (1998) has stated that "such evidence as we have, from a range of schemes in different countries, suggests projects involving some form of reparation and which confront offenders with the consequences of their behaviour are promising".

However, the failure of traditional penal punishment is largely due to the fact that punishment is rarely perceived as an inevitable or immediate or severe consequence of crime. Indeed, Mayhew et al (1993) have claimed that in Britain the probability of conviction following a criminal offence is as low as 3%. Nor does it appear that the greater severity of imprisonment adds to its effectiveness as a punishment. A British Home Office study (1998) has concluded that, apart from its incapacitative effect, imprisonment is no more successful at preventing future crime than non-custodial sanctions. Lipsey (1995), in a meta-analytic review of scientific evaluations of penal sanctions, concluded that explicitly punishment-based approaches such as shock incarceration, boot camps and intensive surveillance actually have a counterproductive effect and lead to a 25% increase in re-offence rates compared to less severely treated control groups.

While it is reasonable to recognise criminal sanctioning, that is punishment, as a form of tertiary prevention, the evidence is strong that punishment and imprisonment in particular are ineffective treatments, which achieve little in the way of crime reduction amongst established offenders. Indeed, the Expert Group on the Probation and Welfare Service (1998) state that "imprisoning offenders has not been a successful approach to the problem of reducing crime. Certainly if one of its purposes is to rehabilitate offenders and reduce re-offending, it has failed dramatically." On the other hand, it is reasonable to suppose that the spectacle of others being punished for their crimes may be an effective form of social control that prevents an unknown amount of crime by those not yet involved in offending. Criminal sanctioning, then, while a weak technique of tertiary prevention is possibly an effective technique of primary prevention.

The negative findings on punishment as a treatment modality led Andrews (1995) to conclude that "criminal sanctioning without the delivery of correctional treatment services does not work". This statement partially echoes and partially contradicts Martinson's (1974) extremely influential paper which assessed penal treatment programmes and gave birth to the "nothing works" doctrine. Martinson examined 231 scientific studies published between 1945 and 1967 and concluded that "with few and isolated exceptions the rehabilitation efforts that have been reported so far have had no appreciable effect on recidivism". To the contrary, Andrews believes that some forms of treatment of offenders supplemental to imprisonment can be effective. Indeed, in recent decades, there has been considerable growth of confidence in the potential of both crime preventative projects at the primary and secondary levels and treatment programmes for career criminals, including incarcerated offenders.

Evaluation of primary prevention methods

In the primary preventative arena, an increasing number of scientifically evaluated, longitudinal projects have begun to produce reliable evidence of positive impact (Greenwood et al 1996). One often cited randomised trial is the High/Scope Perry Pre-School Programme, which for many years followed up a group of fifty-eigth African-American children, exposed to a high quality pre-school programme lasting two years, and a control group of matched children, not receiving a pre-school intervention. At age nineteen arrest rates for the experimental group were 40% lower than those for the control group. At age twenty-seven, 35% of the control group, but only 7% of those who had benefited from the pre-school intervention, had been arrested five or more times (Schweinhart and Weikart 1993). There were many other comparatively positive outcomes for the experimental group, seemingly linked to the relatively short-lived "head start" intervention when they were small children.

Olds et al (1998) have followed up the first children of highly disadvantaged mothers, who received regular visits from a nurse home visitor to provide education and support in the perinatal period and for the following two and a half years. The experimental group children had 56% fewer arrests and 56% fewer days of alcohol consumption by age fifteen than the control group children. The authors claim that a cost benefit analysis proves that the programme recovers its costs by the child's fourth birthday through savings for public services. Lowering the incidence of adolescent offending is only one of the positive outcomes of this early intervention. Analysis of the results of this study point to the complex chain of intermediate causes leading to the more positive outcomes for adolescents. For example, the mothers in the experimental group, when compared with controls, had fewer alcohol and drug problems, a better employment record, fewer children, less arrests and 79% fewer verified reports of child abuse or neglect against them.

Olweus (1991) in Norway has been the pioneer of the "whole school" approach to bullying and has shown this to be effective in a thoroughly evaluated anti-bullying initiative in forty-two schools. The scheme achieved major reductions of bullying but also significantly reduced more general anti-social behaviour of schoolchildren. Scherman (1997) has reviewed seventeen home or clinic based family therapy and parent training programmes. Scientific evaluations of these programmes showed, in all but one case, measurable improvements in parenting and at least moderate, short-term or long-term reductions in the anti-social behaviour of the children. Goldblatt and Lewis (1998), in an overview of the literature, conclude that "a wide range of initiatives which target children, their families, their schools and their friends prevent criminality or reduce related risk factors". Furthermore, they argue that there is evidence that the most beneficial early intervention programmes specifically target at-risk children and their parents and schools and operate in an integrated way across a number of domains of the child's life, rather than focusing exclusively on one or two crime-related risk factors.

Evaluation of secondary prevention methods

Research on secondary prevention, that is work with delinquency or incipient delinquency, is also moderately encouraging but not so unequivocally positive as that on primary prevention. Lipsey (1992) examined almost 400 scientific evaluations of treatment programmes for delinquency. These studies involved over 40,000 juveniles, encompassed many different treatment modalities and represented all the eligible published and unpublished research from English-speaking countries since 1950. Using meta-analytic techniques Lipsey estimated the net treatment effect in terms of reduction of recidivism. While the average recidivism rate, after about six months, for the control groups was 50%, it was 45% for the groups receiving treatment – that is 10% less of the control groups than of the experimental groups had re-offended. Lipsey comments that "while not an overwhelming effect that can be annouced as a "cure" for delinquency, a net 10% average reduction cannot be called trivial – it is, for example, within the range of effects viewed as significant in medical treatment and other such domains". There was great variability in the effectiveness of the treatment modalities with some approaches having a negative effect and some showing far more than 10% improvement over controls. The better treatments had a more concrete, behavioural or skills oriented character leading Lipsey to conclude that "it is much better to target behaviour for change, and approach it in a relatively structured, concrete fashion, than to target psychological process for change and approach it using variations on traditional counselling and casework techniques".

In Ireland, the Juvenile Diversion Scheme appears to have been an extremely successful secondary prevention treatment modality (Garda *Annual Report* 1998). The Garda report states that 89% of the many thousands of young offenders annually, who, under the scheme, are given a formal or informal warning, diverted from court, and sometimes provided with comunity-based activity and training programmes or special counselling support, avoid prosecution up to the age of eighteen. An evaluation by O'Dwyer (1998) has largely confirmed these positive results. The Garda Special Projects is another important initiative in this area, which has a multi-agency dimension and attempts to integrate crime prevention with youth work practice. According to Bowden and Higgins (2000), the projects have three core features: "the creation of alternative progression/development routes; challenging young people's offending and other unacceptable behaviour through personal development or through one to one interventions; and providing leisure and recreational activities". In their preliminary evaluation, Bowden and Higgins conclude that the projects have had a positive impact and have persuaded young people to desist from crime, although, as yet, there is an overemphasis on diverting from crime and a lack of counterbalancing focus on diverting to "alternative systems such as training, education, employment and further personal or creative development".

Recent research has highlighted the absolute requirement for independent, evidence-based evaluation of secondary prevention projects, because it has shown that some interventions, which on the surface appear entirely well-intentioned and benevolent, actually have quite serious negative effects. For example, Lipsey (1995) in his meta-analysis of programmes aimed at delinquency reduction, mainly in the USA, concluded that 29% had net negative effects. Dishion et al

(1999) state that "the scientific and professional community must be open to the possibility that intentions to help may inadvertently lead to unintentional harm". In their study they draw particular attention to interventions that deal with at-risk youths in groups. They argue from the evidence that there is a very real danger that projects, which bring delinquent youths together in a context excluding the direct involvement of the family, will have long-term negative effects, actually increasing delinquancy. They put this down to the role of "deviancy training" within the teenage peer group. One study (Buehler et al 1966) has found that, within an institutional setting at least, peers provide nine times more reinforcement to each other than is provided by the adult staff, thus indicating how peers might easily undermine the positive influence of adult guidance and pro-social role models. These findings have significant implications for initiatives such as the Garda Special Projects.

The Cambridge-Somerville study (McCord 1978) of interventions with at-risk adolescents was carefully constructed to facilitate scientific evaluation and has now been followed up for over forty years. The target boys in this study received medical treatment, special academic tutoring and general mentoring and were encouraged to participate in local community groups, helped to get jobs, taught how to drive and brought to sporting events. Systematic evaluation of this major project, comparing the treated boys with matched, untreated boys, now indicates that for the most part these interventions had no effect with respect to preventing negative outcomes such as conviction for a serious crime, either in the short or the long term (thirty years of follow-up). In 150 matched pairs, both boys often had similar outcomes. However, most astonishing was the finding that, in the 103 pairs where outcomes differed, in 64 cases, that is a significant majority, it was the treated and not the untreated boy who had the more undesirable outcome. The variable that seems to explain most of this difference was whether or not the boy had been at two or more of the summer camps promoted as part of the study treatment regime. Current analysis (Dishion et al 1999) suggests that "deviancy training", ie reinforcement and escalation of deviant behaviours and attitudes, occurring amongst the groups of delinquent peers at summer camp, may account for the failure of treatment. The importance of this study as a warning about the need for caution in the design of interventions and for careful and wide-ranging evaluation of impact cannot be overstated.

Howell (1995) has identified features, in addition to the need to avoid deviancy training, that are common to the most successful programmes for juvenile delinquents. He describes them as follows:

- they are holistic, dealing simultaneously with many aspects of youth's lives
- they are intensive, involving multiple contacts
- they mostly operate outside the formal justice system

- they build on youth's strengths rather than focusing on their deficiencies
- they adopt a socially grounded approach to understanding a youth's situation and treating it rather than an individual or medical-therapeutic approach
- they have a case management approach that involves the development of individual treatment plans and provides frequent feedback, both positive and negative, to the youths on their progress
- they provide effective education, vocational training, and counselling strategies tailored to the individual needs of juveniles.

Evaluation of tertiary prevention methods

Information on the effectiveness of tertiary prevention measures is more difficult to come by and more ambiguous. As has been already argued, the application of punishment alone tends to be ineffective. However, some evidence has been accumulating for the effectiveness of correctional treatment for both serious and persistent juvenile offenders and adult offenders. A meta-analysis by Garrett (1985) examined 111 institutional or community-based residential treatment programmes, aimed at serious and persistent juvenile delinquents, and found that they produced effects that were "modest in some cases, substantial in others, but overwhelmingly in a positive direction". These programmes tended to be similar in nature to the secondary prevention programmes already discussed. Again the more focused behavioural treatments showed stronger positive effects than psychodynamic or life skills based treatments. Howell (1995) has pointed out that intensive aftercare services are crucial to the success of such residential and prison programmes and that the key objectives of programmes should be to prepare youths for stable employment, place them in real jobs and reintegrate them gradually into their homes and communities.

Losel (1995) has provided an overview of meta-analyses in the general area of treatment of offenders and mentions only two that involve incarcerated adults. One was his own study of eighteen programmes in what he terms social-therapeutic prisons (Losel and Koferl 1989). Average effect rates were 11% in terms of the criterion of reduced recidivism. This level of effect is comparable to the average level found by Lipsey (1992) in his major study of almost 400 secondary prevention programmes for juveniles. The other meta-analysis was by Andrews et al (1990) and found a similar net effect rate of 10%. However, in a comparison of prison with community-based programmes, Andrews et al found that the community-based approach was superior.

Of course, given the fact that many prisoners are undereducated and have serious substance abuse and/or psychiatric problems (Gunn 2000), many of the programmes for established offenders in prison are specialised and focus on a single problem area, such as drug misuse, psychiatric illness, basic education and literacy, sex offending, aggression, or lack of impulse control. These programmes tend to be run by various professionals, including teachers, psychologists, social workers, doctors and psychiatrists. Very often the service providers strive to attain a type and quality of programme similar to that found in open society, but they struggle in this endeavour due to poor resources and the inherent institutional constraints of the prison setting. For practical and ethical reasons randomised control trials of these kinds of treatment are very rare and there is a lack of scientifically rigorous evaluation. There is, therefore, considerable uncertainty about the effectiveness of treatments, as for example is the case with sex offender therapy, about which Prentky (1995) says "while some of the evidence is encouraging, at the present time, the most informed and dispassionate conclusion must be that the jury is still out".

Prison-based treatments can at best hope to achieve the success rates of equivalent treatments outside the criminal justice system. Often, the success rates of even model, well-resourced programmes, dealing with intractable problems like drug misuse or alcoholism in the non-offender population, are moderate to low. Expectations for treatment will therefore often be low, although there are many individual cases of great success such as totally unschooled prisoners gaining a university degree through prison education services or prisoners attaining total abstinence from drugs. In the penal system there is the additional problem of obtaining the active participation of offenders in treatment, especially if the programmes are compulsory. One tentative finding (Hepburn 1995) is that the limited evidence available indicates that "the degree to which treatment is received voluntarily does not seem to affect the outcome". This is a hopeful sign for the relatively new initiative of Drug Courts that are empowered to mandate rehabilitation treatment for drug using offenders.

Lindqvist and Skipworth (2000) point out that, for forensic psychiatry, treatment issues are especially complex and go beyond the need to respond to the disorder itself. They identify various "dynamic features" that can cause resistance to change, particularly family problems and poor sociocultural circumstances, substance misuse, and the "anti-therapeutic system dynamics" of the prison, which can cause stigmatisation and "reciprocal friction and aggression". There is often a hierarchy of offender therapeutic needs relating to immediate medical urgency or to the necessity to deal with overarching problems, such as current self-harm or drug misuse, before proceeding to developmental phases of rehabilitation, such as preparation for employment. Lindqvist and Skipworth believe that the outcome of the rehabilitation process depends on the sum of individual contributions in different areas within the treatment system and, indeed, on the interactive effects of these contributions. They state that "at best these contributions will be synergistic and complementary; at worst, the effect may be negative and associated with a detrimental outcome".

The most progressive and promising current initiatives in prison rehabilitation represent a convergence of two major developments. In the first place there is the effort to totally reconstruct the prison environment and prison culture so as to make it conducive to rehabilitation. Secondly, there is currently a new capacity to learn from social science research and best practice models about the most effective techniques, such as cognitive-behavioural therapies and participative learning, and the most effective strategies, such as holism and individualisation, that work to promote change in people and decrease the likelihood of re-offending.

There is a genuine synergy here because the holistic, individualised, flexible, client-centred, needs-based approach that has been proven successful in secondary prevention is greatly facilitated by or, perhaps, even requires a prison environment that has active, positive links with broader society and both affords the offender self-respect and a sense of responsibility and encourages the offender's active participation and motivation for self-improvement. The main issue is creating prison conditions and post-release throughcare into the community that will actively assist education, training and cognitive-behavioural programmes in the enablement and empowerment of offenders, who often have serious health, social and personal problems and are seriously handicapped by lack of education and employment experience.

Grendon prison in Britain maintains a therapeutic community which uses social and psychological processes, such as encounter groups and peer pressure, in an attempt to reconstruct the personality and motivation of offenders. This regime has survived for several decades and has had reasonably good results (Gunn et al 1978), even though it deals overwhelmingly with men who have committed serious violent offences, including sex offences, and are characterised by psychiatric problems, substance abuse problems, suicidal behaviour, intractable personality disorders, and indiscipline, including hostage-taking within the prison system (Newell 1997). Grendon therapeutic community is firmly based on four fundamental principles – Democracy, Tolerance, Communalism, and Reality Confrontation – which are the diametric opposite of normal prison values. Therapeutic consider-ations are prioritised in decision making, except when the basic safety of the environment is threatened. There is a strict demand that there be no violence, drug use, sex, or confidences within the prison and this demand is widely met, allowing the whole enterprise to be founded on trust.

Progressive prison systems in Denmark, Germany and elsewhere are attempt-ing to incorporate more and more of the positive therapeutic approaches of the Grendon model into their regimes for normal prisoners in the sure knowledge that this is the best way to combat the negative effects of imprisonment and open up realistic opportunities for the rehabilitation of prisoners. Denmark's Ringe Prison is based on the principles of openness, normalisation and responsibility. Prisoners live in small, self-governed, both sex households within the prison. They must shop and cook for themselves, with a designated prisoner allowed out to town to do the shopping. They self-manage all the normal tasks of daily living. Prisoners who enrol in potentially beneficial educational or training programmes are entitled to leave the prison to attend them. Prisoners are also permitted to form intimate partnerships with each other.

These sort of progressive regimes, which place emphasis on offender responsibility, positive socialisation, and on undoing the effects of past harmful and inadequate socialisation, indicate how it might be possible to make the punishment of imprisonment extend no further and do no more damage than the mere deprivation of liberty. At the same time they are methods that harmonise with both the new restorative justice model and the needs-based empowerment models of rehabilitation that are now in vogue and have some genuine prospect of at least modest success. Needless to say, however, prevention remains far better than cure and the powerful early interventions that impact on the family and on the social and economic environment of the child must be prioritised.

REFERENCES

Andrews, D. 1995, "The Psychology of Criminal Conduct and Effective Treatment", in *What Works: Reducing Offending,* James McGuire 1995 (ed.), Chichester: Wiley

Andrews, D., Zinger, I., Hoge, R., Bonta, J., Gendreau, P. and Cullen F. 1990, "Does Correctional Treatment Work?: A clinically relevant and psychologically informed meta-analysis", *Criminology* 28 369-404

Beccaria, C. 1764, *On Crimes and Punishment,* in English 1963, Indianapolis: Bobbs-Merrill

Becker, G. S. 1968, "Crime and Punishment: An Economic Approach", *Journal of Political Economy* 76

Bowden, M. and Higgins, L. (2000), *The Impact and Effectiveness of the Garda Special Projects*, Dublin: Department of Justice, Equality and Law Reform

Buehler, A., Patterson, G. and Furniss, J. 1966, "The Reinforcement of Behaviour in institutional Settings", *Behaviour Research and Therapy* 4

Carlen, P. 1994, "Crime, Inequality and Sentencing", in *A Reader on Punishment,* Duff, A. and Garland, D. (eds.), Oxford: Oxford University Press

Carrol, J. and Weaver, F. 1986, "Shoplifters perceptions of crime opportunities: a process tracing study", in *The Reasoning Criminal,* Cornish, D. and Clarke, R. (eds.), New York : Springer Verlag

Consedine, J. 1995, *Restorative justice: Healing the Effects of Crime,* Lyttleton New Zealand: Ploughshares Publications

Cornish, D. and Clarke, R. (eds.) 1986, *The Reasoning Criminal,* New York: Springer Verlag

Dack, B. 1996, "Drugs, Crime and Methadone", *Irish Social Worker* 14 3/4, 14-16

Dishion, T., McCord, J. and Poulin F. 1999, "When Interventions Harm", in *American Psychologist* 54 9

Expert Review Group on the Probation and Welfare Service 1998, *Report*, Dublin; Stationery Office

Garrett, P. 1985, "Effects of residential treatment of adjudicated delinquents; a meta-analysis", *Journal of Research in Crime and Delinquency* 22 287-308

Garda Síochána 1998, *Report on Crime*, Dublin: Garda HQ

Goldblatt, P. and Lewis, C. (eds.) (1998), *Reducing Offending: an assessment of research evidence on ways of dealing with offending behaviour,* Home Office Research Study 197, London: HMSO

Government of Ireland 1996, *Partnership 2000 for Inclusion, Employment and Competitiveness*, Dublin: Stationery Office

Greenwood et al 1996, *Diverting Children from a Life of Crime; Measuring Costs and Benefits,* Santa Monica: Rand Corporation

Gunn, J. 2000, "Future directions for treatment in forensic psychiatry", *British Journal of psychiatry* 176 332-338

Gunn, J., Robertson, G. and Bell, S. 1978, *Psychiatric Aspects of Imprisonment,* London: Academic Press

Hepburn, J. 1994, "Classifying Drug Offenders for Treatment", in *Drugs and Crime: Evaluating Public Policy Initiatives,* MacKenzie, D. and Uchida, C. (eds.), London: Sage

Home Office 1998, *Reducing Offending: an assessment of research evidence on ways of dealing with offending behaviour,* London: HMSO

Howell, J. 1995 (ed.), *Guide for Implementing the Comprehensive Strategy for Serious, Violent, and Chronic Juvenile Offenders,* Washington: US Department of Justice

Hughes, G. 1996, *Understanding Crime Prevention,* London: Wiley

Light, R., Nee, C. and Ingham, H. 1993, *Car Theft; The Offender's Perspective,* London: HMSO

Lilly, J., Cullen, F. and Ball, R. 1995, *Crime Theory: Context and Consequences,* London: Sage

Lindqvist, P. and Skipworth, J. 2000, "Evidence-based rehabilitation in forensic psychiatry", *British Journal of psychiatry* 176 320-323

Lipsey, M. 1992, "Juvenile Delinquency Treatments: A meta-analytic inquiry into the variability of effects", in Cook, T., Cooper, H., Cordray, D., Hartmann, H., Hedges, L., Light, R., Louis, J. and Mosteller, F. (eds.), *Meta-analysis for explanation: A Casebook,* New York: Russell Sage

Lipsey, M. 1995, "What do We Learn from 400 Research Studies on the Effectiveness of Treatment with Juvenile Delinquents", in McGuire, J. (ed.), *What Works: Reducing Offending*, Chichester: Wiley

Losel, F. 1995, "The Efficacy of Correctional Treatment: a Review and Synthesis of meta-evaluations", in McGuire, J. (ed.), *What Works: Reducing Offending*, Chichester: Wiley

Losel, F. and Koferl, S. 1989, "Evaluation Research on Correctional Treatment in West Germany: A meta-analysis", in *Criminal Behaviour and the Justice System: Psychological Perspectives,* Wegener, H., Losel, F. and Haish, J. (eds.), New York: Springer

Mayhew, P., Maung, N., Mirlees-Black, C. 1993, *The 1992 British Crime Survey,* London: HMSO

McCord, J. 1978, "A Thirty Year Follow-up of Treatment Effects", *American Psychologist* 33

McGuire, J. and Priestly, P. 1995, "What Works: Past Present and Future", in McGuire, J. (ed.), *What Works: Reducing Offending*, Chichester: Wiley

McGuire, J. (ed.) 1995, *What Works: Reducing Offending*, Chichester: Wiley

Martinson, R. 1974, "What works?: Questions and answers about prison reform", in *The Public Interest* 10, 22-54

Newell, T. 1997, Paper in Conference Proceedings "Is Penal reform Possible?", Dublin: IPRT

O'Dwyer, K. 1998, *Evaluation of the Juvenile Diversion Scheme,* Dublin: Garda HQ

Olds, D., Hill, P., Mihalic, S. and O'Brien, R. 1998, *Blueprints for violence prevention, Book Seven: Prenatal and Infancy Home Visitation by Nurses,* Boulder: Centre for the Study and Prevention of Violence

Olweus, D. 1991, "Bully/victim problems among schoolchildren: Basic facts and effects of a school based intervention programme", in *The Development and Treatment of Childhood Aggression,* Pepler, D. and Rubin, H. (eds.), New Jersey: Erlbaum

Prentky, R, 1995, "A rationale for the treatment of sex offenders", in McGuire, J. (ed.), *What Works: Reducing Offending*, Chichester: Wiley

Prins, H. 1980, *Offenders, Deviants or Patients,* London: Tavistock Publications

Schweinhert, L. and Wiekart, D. (1993), *A Summary of Significant Benefits: the High/Scope Perry Pre-School Study through age 27*, Ypsilanti-Michigan: High/Scope Press.

Skinner, B. 1953, *Science and Human Behaviour,* New York: MacMillan

Sherman, L. et al (1997), *What works, what doesn't, what's promising,* Washington DC: US Department of Justice.

38

Youth Crime Prevention

Marian Quinn

The incidence and nature of juvenile offending is an emotive subject which frequently makes headline news as drug abuse, violence and late night brawls involving teenagers appear to be on the increase. The fact that garda statistics do not always support the position that juvenile crime is on the increase (Garda Commissioner annually, and see table 1), is often offset by the creation in the media and in folk myth of such infamous figures as the fourteen year old "Little General" from West Dublin and other anti-hero types. In this context it is almost inevitable that a large sector of the public will conclude that more and more young people are out of control.

The increased level of discussion regarding young offenders which has taken place in the justice system over recent years is an indication of a deeper official commitment to developing effective responses to the needs of young people. The principles which underpin proposed legislation emphasise the importance of child-centred interventions, and inter-agency co-operation, in order to ensure a cohesive, holistic response to the problems of offending children and youth. Following increased public, professional and political concern and debate in recent years, unprecedented levels of resources are now being allocated to preventive programmes.

Nevertheless, professionals in the field are yet to be convinced of the extent to which the reality of the criminal justice system and society fully reflects this new found concern about young people. It is as yet uncertain how faithfully new developments adhere to an ethos which places primary value on the child and on the affirmation of the family. There remains suspicion in many minds that we have not moved sufficiently away from the traditional, punitive approaches which sought to blame the parents and punish the child, so as to achieve a truly child-centred model.

Table 1: trends in various measures of the incidence of juvenile offending

	1993	1994	1996	1999
Referrals to National Juvenile Office:				
male	9,608	10,460	9,318	9,118
female	1,832	2,025	1,398	1,772
total	**11,440**	**12,485**	**10,716**	**10,890**
Juveniles prosecuted				
male	4,161	2,436	3,941	3,910
female	473	303	335	350
total	**4,634**	**2,739**	**3,941**	**3,910**
Numbers Cautioned				
male	4,846	5,572	5,712	5,558
female	1,044	1,234	1,063	1,366
total	**5,890**	**6,806**	**6,775**	**6,944**

Source: An Garda Síochána 1993, 1994, 1996, 1999

In practice, there is a tendency to focus crime prevention strategies on disadvantaged young people. This approach may appear sensible given the over-representation of those from poor communities amongst known offenders and the prison population (O'Mahony 1997). However, these statistics can be influenced by many factors, such as how and why crimes are reported; the extent to which certain communities are policed; the chances of particular young people being stopped and searched by gardaí; the likelihood of particular groups having their cases processed, as opposed to being cautioned, and so on. The extent to which the assumptions and prejudices of state systems propagate the over-representation of marginalised groups amongst the offending population must be questioned. We need only consider the number of tribunals taking place, and the socio-economic profiles of those involved to recognise that crime is not exclusive to the poor.

Yet resources are scare and the targeting of programmes is a necessity. Ensuring that those most at risk are engaged in preventive programmes, without being further stigmatised through that very participation, is a constant dilemma for anyone engaged in youth crime prevention. Clearly practitioners, policy makers and researchers alike must examine carefully the criteria by which they define "at risk", and all the other assumptions which underpin interventions.

This chapter will provide an overview of the juvenile justice system, past and present, as a framework by which to understand the influences and philosophies which inform interventions with young people at risk. The general context of preventive measures will be examined by way of an analysis of risk factors, whilst interventions already established in Ireland will be discussed, with specific reference to the "what works" research.

A HISTORY OF YOUTH CRIME PREVENTION

Responses to juvenile offending vary enormously, and are heavily influenced by providers' understanding of causal factors, especially by whether causes are seen to reside in the individual young person or in factors outside the individual's control. Thus, proponents of individual responsibility can comfortably argue a punitive approach. However, those who see social and environmental factors as at the root of juvenile offending also seek solutions in these issues. Advocates of a child-centred approach will argue for a system which affirms rather than labels children, which educates rather than punishes, and which supports rather than excludes. Tensions between these two positions, that is the justice position stressing individual responsibility and the welfare position stressing the needs of the maturing child and his or her family, underlie, and to an extent, are prompting the current reshaping of the Irish juvenile justice system.

Prior to the mid-nineteenth century justice systems did not distinguish between adults and children. The process of industrialisation and urbanisation resulted in large numbers of children begging and committing petty crimes, necessitating the bourgeoisie to respond to the problem of "street urchins". The introduction of Reformatory Schools in 1858 mirrored the developments of other European countries, in that this was the first legislation which recognised that children in trouble, or causing trouble, should be treated differently from adults. The establishment of what O'Sullivan (1997) calls "Reformatory Schools for the dangerous classes, ie non-conforming and delinquent children, and Industrial Schools for the perishing classes, ie children at risk of becoming delinquent or pre-delinquent children" has been interpreted in divergent ways. Robins (1980) sees this as a progressive move, underpinned by genuine humanitarian concern. O'Sullivan (1979) however, regards the introduction of these schools as vehicles of social control, and a means by which to protect the security and property of the wealthy.

Legislation followed which broadened the scope of child-specific inter-ventions. The first juvenile court was established in Chicago in 1899, and European countries followed suit shortly after, with the rudiments of a juvenile justice system being introduced in the Netherlands (1905), United Kingdom (1908), and Belgium and France (1912). Given the political situation at the time, Ireland automatically adopted the British legislation.

The continuing predominant emphasis on punishment was challenged by various philanthropic and feminist groups, which began to recognise the differing needs of children. In addition, there was a growing understanding that criminal behaviour amongst children was the result of poverty and destitution, rather than depravity or lack of morals. A number of individual institutions were set up by volunteers, specifically for young offenders, whilst there was growing demand for preventive rather than punitive action.

Developments which took place during this period included the introduction of the Youthful Offenders Act 1854, which gave statutory recognition to the various institutions being run by religious and charitable organisations. This was seen as a significant improvement, as the courts could now refer children directly to them, whilst an inspectorate was also established to monitor them. However, the Act was limited in that children and adults continued to be subject to the same legal processes, so that, for example, a seven year old could receive the death sentence. Eventually there was a move to establish a special tribunal which would be responsible for overseeing the needs and welfare of children, resulting in the Summary Jurisdiction Over Children Act 1884. Reformers were disappointed with the scope of this measure, and children continued to appear in adult courts, whilst throughout Ireland, England and Scotland, large numbers of children continued to be imprisoned.

The new liberal government of 1906 was quick to bring in major reform of the system in the guise of the Children Act 1908, which to this day remains the single most significant piece of legislation within the Irish juvenile justice system. This progress was associated with recognition of the inadequacy of the somewhat incoherent approach to children's issues that then prevailed, and of the clear need for a special ministry to focus on and monitor the requirements of children.

The positive aspect of the 1908 Act was the separation, within the criminal justice system, of offending children from adult offenders. Thus, it states that children aged under fifteen years cannot be sentenced to imprisonment, and instead may be sent to one of the six "special schools" run by the Department of Education (referred to in legislation as reformatories and industrial schools). Special schools can be open or secure units, and are still a feature of the system. There are currently a total of 226 places, in six special, schools in the Republic of Ireland, fifteen of which are for girls. Despite the progressive tenor of the 1908 Act, the dependence on custodial sentences remained a concern to those promoting a welfare based approach to juvenile offenders.

CURRENT THINKING

The fact that the central legislation for dealing with young people who commit crime dates back to the beginning of the last century is an indication of a long-standing lack of political interest in this area. Until very recently, there was a complete absence of political and public discussion focused on the prevention of youth crime. Political knee-jerk reactions, often promoting punitive approaches to the latest so-called outbreak of juvenile offending, and designed chiefly to pacify the concerned person on the street, have been commonplace. Irish juvenile justice has been characterised by an inherent inconsistency, fluctuating uncertainly between harsh punitive responses and a response which recognises and attempts to address the needs of the child. Preventive measures have been characterised by a lack of long-term planning and coherence in policy-making and by chronic under-funding and under-resourcing. The absence of any long-term strategy or clarity regarding inter-departmental linkages has led to a complicated series of responses, with frequent overlaps, gaps and contradictions.

Policy developments and legislation in Irish criminal justice have tended to mirror the British experience, although recent years have demonstrated a growing awareness that legislation and policies from abroad cannot be simply grafted on to the Irish system. There is a new-found confidence regarding Ireland's capacity and responsibility to meet its own needs with tailor-made policies fitted to the local cultural conditions.

Perhaps in response to a growing awareness of the seriousness of the problems of juvenile crime and the inadequacy of the official Irish reaction over many years, the Irish juvenile justice system has in the last few years experienced a unique period of debate and discussion. Much of this process has been instigated at government level, and is welcomed by all those working in, and concerned about, juvenile justice. Although preventive practice has not been subject to the same level of debate, it has received unprecedented funding in recent years, enabling the expansion of existing programmes, and establishment of new initiatives.

Important legislative changes have recently been made with the Children Act 2001. This is largely the result of a highly critical review of the juvenile justice system (Government 1992), and the recognition that reform of the 1908 Act is seriously overdue. Whilst the proposals contained in the Act have elicited mixed reaction, there is nevertheless some innovation within it. The Act is discussed in some detail elsewhere in this volume, but it is worth noting here that the central aspects are:

- raising the age of responsibility to twelve, with the option of a further increase to fourteen years
- placing the Garda Juvenile Diversion Scheme on a statutory basis

- establishing structures for the supervision and monitoring of Garda Juvenile Liaison Officers
- the introduction of family group conferences.

While the Act includes some significant opportunities for developing child-centered approaches and supports for those working with young people in difficulty, these innovations are juxtaposed with proposals which appear to focus on placing blame and extracting retribution. The difference is that the spotlight has shifted from the young people themselves to their parents, without any recognition of the parents' needs, or any suggestion that substantial interventions will be established to encourage and enable positive parenting. The extent to which the Children Act is actually implemented and the resources allocated to enable its effective delivery remain to be seen. Irrespective of its final form, this is a significant piece of legislation, as it marks a major shift in the political climate surrounding juvenile justice, and indicates a new openness to challenging ideas, debate, and innovation.

Recent years have also seen the establishment of a new ministry, a junior minister with special responsibility for children. This ministry uniquely encompasses the Departments of Health, Education and Justice, and has certainly enabled (or perhaps necessitated) inter-departmental co-operation. It has also gone some way to raising the profile and status of preventive work with children and their families. Some of the developments that will be outlined below, are a direct result of the interest and commitment of this ministry. The development of the National Children's Strategy and the National Children's Office to co-ordinate the work of all departments for children is welcome. The expanded role of the Minister for Children and the appointment of an Ombudsman for Children are likely to increase greatly the possibilities for positive developments in this area.

The emphasis on inter-departmental co-operation is mirrored at every level in that there are now expectations (often underwritten in funding commitments) that projects will consult and engage with relevant agencies in the development of programmes and identification of priorities. The Taoiseach (Bertie Ahern) himself noted the need for improved consultation and partnership:

> something is missing in the way we have approached the problem (of disadvantage) up to now ... We need urgently much closer working relationships between statutory organisations ... Agencies must take more account of the real needs and experiences of end-users when designing and planning services (Taoiseach 1998).

The emphasis on integrated services has undoubtedly impacted on expectations of agencies and projects, while developments such as the local Partnership Boards and Integrated Services Project (ISP) have the potential to identify key learning for the future. However, the extent to which this vision of inter-agency co-operation is experienced locally, or at regional and departmental level, is uncertain. The absence of long-term strategies and corresponding funding, alongside the reliance on short-term pilot programmes, creates an insecure, sometimes defensive attitude amongst service providers. Many enter negotiations with other agencies with trepidation, suspicion and resistance, whilst the lack of clarity regarding the nature of meaningful co-operation or appropriate monitoring mechanisms also creates barriers.

There is a growing recognition that youth crime is influenced by a number of complex and inter-connected factors, and that effective interventions must therefore be comprehensive and holistic. A recent report notes that while there are individual elements which contribute to an effective strategy, such as parental supports, pre-school education and leisure options, these must be delivered in the context of an overall strategy, with meaningful consultation and multi-agency involvement in programme development. No single initiative "will control crime on its own. An effective crime reduction strategy is one in which an integrated package of best practice is developed and delivered consistently over time" (Goldblatt and Lewis 1998:3). Given the barriers to such an approach, strategies to ensure effective inter-agency co-operation must be integral to crime prevention practice.

RISK FACTORS

A great deal of research has focused on identifying the factors which increase a young person's risk of offending or anti-social behaviour. These indicators offer an important framework for developing preventive initiatives, as they provide a focus for interventions.

Risk factors include parents, siblings and peers who offend; poor parental supervision, and harsh or erratic discipline; lack of attachment to the family and school; truancy and exclusion from school; aggressive and hyperactive behaviour in early childhood, and drug and alcohol use (Farrington 1996; Graham and Bowling 1995; Audit Commission 1996). Gender, however, is the single most significant factor, with males being more than twice as likely to offend than girls (Graham and Bowling 1995). In addition, poverty and growing up in a disadvantaged community, is a significant factor (Audit Commission 1996). This is certainly reflected in the Dublin prison population, with nearly half the male inmates coming from five particularly disadvantaged areas of Dublin (O'Mahony 1997).

Research has found that risk factors tend to converge, so that certain groups of young people experience numerous risk factors. Individuals whose childhoods are characterised by a number of these factors are more likely to become involved in anti-social and offending behaviour, whilst those who begin to offend at an early age are more likely to become serious and persistent offenders (Graham and Bowling 1995).

Graham and Bowling (1995) identify five key factors for males as follows: delinquent peers, low parental supervision, truancy from school, delinquent siblings and school exclusion; and for females as follows: delinquent peers, low parental supervision, truancy from school, weak attachment to school and weak attachment to family. Their self-report study of young people provided clear evidence that the greater the number of factors experienced, the greater the incidence of offending (see Table 2). Eighty percent of males who experienced four or five factors had offended three or more times.

Table 2: delinquency as a function of number of risk factors

No. of factors experienced	% delinquent: males	% delinquent: females
0	20	7
1	36	13
2	62	27
3	71	35
4 or 5	81	61

Graham and Bowling 1995: 47

It should, of course, be noted that none of the identified risk factors are predictors and that the majority of people living in disadvantaged communities and the majority of early school leavers do not develop criminal careers. However, this research is important as a basis for risk assessment, which informs interventions with young people. Of course, this does indicate that some children and young people clearly have a great deal stacked against them. However, research has found that interventions which aim to reduce one risk tend to have a positive impact on other factors. So, programmes which seek to increase familial attachment can also improve school attendance, family discipline and literacy levels.

This evidence gives further credence to the "joined-up" approach. The importance of tackling a number of key factors is noted consistently (Utting 1996; Communities that Care 1999; McKeown 2000), reiterating the need for inter-agency co-operation in order to ensure an integrated, comprehensive response, as well as effective mechanisms by which to identify need and allocate responsibility. However, there is also recognition amongst practitioners and policy makers that such an approach does not always happen naturally. The impending Youth Work Act is likely to include a requirement for regional and national youth work plans, which will be developed in consultation with all agencies working with young people. However, definitions of youth work are not universally consistent and there are concerns that some of the initiatives described below will not engage in this process. There is significant potential for inter-agency conflict and an absence of coherent, integrated strategies.

YOUTH CRIME PREVENTION APPROACHES

The risk factors outlined above provide a framework by which to identify crime prevention strategies and the aims of such interventions. Traditionally, preventive measures have been considered in three phases:

> Primary prevention aims at changing social conditions and generally wants to prevent criminal offences. It can define its target group only in general and relatively imprecise terms. Secondary crime prevention, more clearly, addresses children and adolescents who are behaviourally deviant and/or socially at risk and offers support that can be more precisely described. Tertiary crime prevention wants to prevent recidivism and therefore addresses young people who have already committed criminal offences (Holthusen and Schafer 2000:21).

Within each of these stages a variety of approaches may be taken, depending on the philosophy of the practitioner and the theories which underpin such interventions. While research in this area remains sparse, there is a growing body of work which illustrates those aspects of practice which appear to promote positive change, as well as studies which highlight damaging or ineffective strategies. This is a significant advance from the belief that "nothing works", which characterised criminal justice agencies during the 1970s and 80s. The "nothing works" stance is now generally regarded as reflecting the inappropriate evaluation methods of the time as much as or more than the actual inadequacies of the interventions themselves.

Youth crime prevention can be categorised under the following four headings.

Developmental prevention

Researchers in this area have, for the most part, not focused specifically on crime, but have come to recognise that those factors which indicate risk of early school leaving, drug use, unplanned pregnancy and so on, tend to equally apply to offending behavior (Tonry and Farrington 1995). These programmes aim to reduce the risk factors, and promote protective factors, through strategies fostering positive parenting, improving the child's mental and physical well-being, and enabling educational achievement. These programmes include a wide range of methodologies, including cognitive skills training, educational and training programmes, and behaviour modification techniques.

Community prevention

These interventions are "designed to change the social conditions and institutions – such as family, peers, social norms and organisations that influence offending in communities", (Farrington 1996: 18). The key concept underpinning this strategy is that the nature and profile of a community influences the behaviour of its residents and that changing the former (both physically and socially) may therefore have an impact on the latter.

Situational prevention

These strategies aim to reduce the opportunities for crime, through the careful design and planning of buildings and environments, and through the development of effective systems for vigilance and security in communities.

Criminal justice prevention

The use of court orders, custodial sanctions and justice operated rehabilitative and support programmes make up this strand of prevention. Traditionally, the fear of such interventions was regarded as sufficient to prevent the majority of potential offenders, whilst incarceration prevented further offences by those for whom this was not an adequate deterrent. The extent of recidivism has brought an awareness that these mechanisms are no longer sufficient.

It should be noted that elements of these various approaches are frequently combined and cannot always be examined separately. Indeed, the importance of comprehensive, multi-faceted interventions has already been noted, and strategies which draw on a number of these elements are most likely to be effective in reducing crime. The interventions examined below will largely, but not exclusively, focus on developmental and community prevention programmes.

SPECIFIC INTERVENTIONS

Youth work generally, and youth crime prevention specifically, is characterised in Ireland by a dependence on pilot programmes and an absence of long-term commitment; initiatives tend to be understaffed and under-resourced, and there is an expectation that workers and the young participants will "make do" with whatever is provided. In terms of quality assurance, evaluation and monitoring are frequently seen as "add on" rather than integral aspects of the programme. Scientifically rigorous research in this area is extremely scarce in Ireland, and there is a reliance on other countries to provide vital information and frameworks. Clearly there is merit in looking beyond Irish experience in order to develop our own practice, and this is increasingly facilitated by the globalisation of inform-ation and the availability of technological supports. However, this openness to import insights has been underpinned by a reluctance to acknowledge our own experiences and a lack of confidence regarding our own abilities. This tradition is beginning to change, assisted by the increased professionalism of this area and the increasingly stringent funding criteria (necessitating the documentation of practice), alongside an acknowledgment by government and other funders of the innovation and effectiveness of many indigenous interventions.

Many of the initiatives outlined below have a multi-agency aspect to their work, in that various key agencies are involved in management, referral and/or service delivery. There is now an expectation that inter-agency co-operation, multi-disciplinary approaches, and consultative processes will form central aspects of crime prevention strategies, and many groups, agencies and individuals have endeavoured to ensure these approaches underpin their actual practice. However, the lack of definition regarding consultation or multi-agency work and the associated difficulties in monitoring the implementation of this approach have been problematic. Appropriate monitoring and evaluation at all levels of service delivery are necessary to highlight discrepancies and deficiencies and remedy them so as to facilitate more meaningful inter-agency engagement.

Current policy, and impending legislation, emphasise the prevention of youth crime and foster a comprehensive approach which reflects the complexity of risk factors associated with juvenile offending. Despite the limitations noted above, there are many effective and dynamic programmes established in Ireland, in both community and school settings, delivered by voluntary and statutory agencies. However, they are almost always delivered by practitioners characterised by personal commitment and belief in the potential for change.

The following types of intervention will be examined:

- those which aim to support families and enable positive parenting
- those which are school based, or which seek to encourage children to stay in school
- those aimed at specially targeted individuals and groups of young people
- community wide interventions.

The interventions outlined below have a variety of target groups, and frequently work with young people with diverse levels of criminal experience, from none to extensive. The main focus of this chapter is on young people who have not committed offences but are regarded as being at risk of offending and young people who have committed one or two crimes, but for whom such behaviour has not become ingrained.

FAMILY-BASED INTERVENTIONS

Family support programmes have experienced a unique period of growth in recent years, with a number of policy documents noting the importance of such interventions and a corresponding increase in funding. The *Springboard* programme was launched in 1998 (see below), while the following year saw a government commitment to establishing 100 Family and Community centres across the country

(Commission on the Family 1998). The recent Child Protection Guidelines note the centrality of family support (Department of Health and Children 1999), and a range of interventions aimed at promoting family cohesion are outlined in the National Development Plan 2000-2006 (Government of Ireland 1999). The link between family, parents and other social policy issues is noted by McKeown:

> family support work is embedded in the broader socio-economic context of disadvantage and its effectiveness cannot be separated from broader co-ordinated measures to address problems, such as poverty, unemployment, educational disadvantage as well as inadequate facilities and services which can have such a debilitating effect on families (McKeown 2000:32).

Given the risk factors outlined above, it is apparent that youth crime prevention strategies should include programmes with the following aims:

- the improvement of parental supervision
- enabling consistent, appropriate discipline
- improving levels of attachment within the family.

The importance of these interventions is further verified by research which notes the importance of parental support networks as a key protective factor for children, (McKeown et al 2000). Analysis of studies in this field indicates that effective support systems can enable parents to engage more effectively in therapeutic programmes, sustain healthier lifestyles, and reduce stress levels. Interventions which focus on the parent can therefore have an indirect, but positive impact on the child.

However, engaging the kind of parents who are least likely to possess positive parenting skills is extremely difficult, partly because they may have had previous hostile relations with or negative experiences of agencies and therefore regard any approach or invitation with suspicion. Making initial contact, gaining trust, and enabling participation are all crucial and skillful aspects of practice. This is inevitably long-term, labour intensive work.

Early interventions

It has been proposed that "the best protection children apparently have in the long term is parental interest in and enthusiasm for their education" (MacDonald and Roberts 1995:28). It is therefore no surprise that many family support programmes focus on enabling both the parent and the child to engage in educational processes.

An evaluation of eighteen early home visit and pre-school education programmes found them to be largely promising in terms of the later prevention of criminal behaviour (Sherman 1997). The *Syracuse Family Development Programme* (Lally et al 1988) provided pre- and post-natal advice and support to low income women, largely of African-American background. By the age of fifteen only 6 %

of the experimental group had convictions, and these tended to be for minor offences, compared with 22% of the control group. There was also a 73% reduction in probation referrals amongst the participating group by this age.

One of the longest running interventions is the American *Headstart* programme. Initiated in 1965, this is a pre-school intervention for children growing up in poverty, and has demonstrated impressive short to medium term benefits, including greater use of preventive health care such as immunisation; improved cognitive ability; greater educational achievement and motivation, and less likelihood of being held back in school or receiving special education (Reynolds et al 1997).

The Irish *Early Start* programme is based on this model, providing one years' pre-school intervention for three year olds from areas of social disadvantage (Department of Education and Science 2000). Additional funding is provided for similar interventions specifically targeting traveller children. An evaluation of *Early Start* found "no differences" in the cognitive, motor and language skills of the *Early Start* children compared to non-*Early Start* children during the first year of primary school (Educational Research Centre 1998). Whilst this may appear to be disappointing, it should be noted that the children participating in *Early Start* would necessarily have been disadvantaged, so to have been regarded as "no different from" the other pupils may in fact be positive. Furthermore, teachers were found to perceive the *Early Start* pupils as more advanced in terms of social and emotional maturity, concentration, motivation, and readiness for school.

Despite its narrow remit, the best known family support programme is probably the *High-Scope Perry Pre-School Programme*, which targeted fifty-eight black children and their families, all of whom were low-income. The two-year programme provided the children with a high quality, structured pre-school programme, which emphasised the children's involvement in choosing and planning activities, as well as reviewing their achievements. Ratios were favourable, with no more than ten children per teacher. In addition, parental involvement was encouraged, with weekly home visits, and regular classroom invitations. In comparing the experimental group with a matched control group, it was found that the experimental group were more likely to perform better in school and adult education; to graduate, and to obtain employment. They were about half as likely to have a teenage pregnancy and, at age nineteen, arrest rates were 40% lower. By the age of twenty-seven, those who had participated in the programme were more likely to have completed their education and be earning more than $2,000 per month. Seven percent of this group had been arrested five or more times, compared with 35% of the control group (Schweinhert and Weikart 1993). An analysis of cost benefit demonstrated that for every $1 spent, there was a long term saving of $7 to the welfare, justice and other public services.

Parent training

Parent education and training programmes aim to improve the knowledge and skills of parents so that they in turn can improve their child's development (McKeown 2000). Reviews of such programmes have demonstrated them to be "remarkably effective in improving the behaviour of pre-adolescent children" (Lloyd 1999: 72). In an American study which focused on enabling parents to set clear rules, negotiate effectively and give positive affirmation, the programme led to a 50% reduction in offending rates (Alexander and Parsons 1973). The Parent-Link (Davis and Hester 1998) programme in the UK provides thirteen sessions of two to three hours to groups of parents. An evaluation comparing participants with a non-participating matched group found that the programme had significantly improved "the behaviour of children ... the parent-child relationship, increasing the self-esteem of parents, and improving the relationship between partners" (McKeown 2000: 18). In the UK, both the Homestart and Newpin programmes befriend young families at risk, linking them with experienced parents in their area (van der Eyken 1982). Participants in both programmes report an improved ability to cope.

A review of therapeutic interventions with parents notes that the single most important factor is the client, and their belief in their capacity to resolve their own problems (McKeown 2000). The social supports available to the client both naturally and through intervention have an enormous bearing on client's belief in their own efficacy. This highlights the importance of tailoring interventions to the specific needs of the family.

With regard to parent education programmes, a large number of these are in place throughout Ireland, although when targeting the most at risk families literacy skills may well be a barrier to participation. In acknowledging the positive impact of these programmes, the need for comprehensive strategies is again highlighted:

> Overall, parent training courses do seem to be able to help parents respond more constructively, use discipline less harshly and more consistently and avoid situations which precipitate conflict. The most promising approaches combine parent training with other strategies, such as social and problem solving skills for the parents' children, and pro-active classroom management and peer-related strategies for older children (Goldblatt and Lewis 1998:12).

Two significant issues have been identified with regard to parent education. French (1998) has noted that few programmes are developed with disadvantaged parents in mind, and that low literacy levels can significantly impact on ability to participate. MacDonald and Roberts (1995) highlight the "predominant focus on mothers and the apparent invisibility of fathers" as a barrier to engaging the whole family on developmental work. Both these issues relate to service providers recognising and acting on their responsibility to engage their target group.

Family support

An important Irish initiative is the *Springboard* pilot projects, launched by the government in 1998. Based in disadvantaged communities and funded by the Department of Health and Children, these fifteen projects aim to provide supports and services for children aged seven to thirteen, with a central focus on increasing the family's ability to respond adequately to the needs of the child.

An interim report on the projects notes that there is a significant over-representation of single parent and traveller families; that fathers tend not to participate and are frequently absent, and that there are high levels of behavioural problems, particularly amongst the boys (McKeown et al 2000). The key methodology utilised by the Springboard projects is intensive group work. The projects also draw on a multidisciplinary team, which works with small case loads.

Despite the fact that the projects have only been operational for up to six months, some outcomes have been determined:

- there was a small reduction in "conduct problems, emotional symptoms, hyperactivity and peer relations" (*op cit*: 86)
- the projects are regarded positively by both children and parents, indicating that solid therapeutic relationships have been established
- a very small reduction in school absenteeism was noted, but a marked decrease in school lateness was identified, alongside a reduction in the numbers of children attending school hungry or without lunch
- parents developed improved support networks, particularly in terms of practical help and emotional support, and noted a significant reduction in stress.

Finally, it is noted that "it is too early to say if Springboard may have a preventive impact in terms of keeping children out of trouble with the law but there are some positive signs in terms of a reduction in the number of cautions from the JLO" (*op cit*:87).

These initiatives are important for their focus on family involvement, in conjunction with positive interventions with individual children, whilst the process of integrated evaluation and reportage of progress may provide invaluable lessons for support workers engaging with families facing a variety of difficulties.

Family group conferences

Family group conferences (FGCs) have arisen from the principles of restorative justice (see below) and were first utilised in New Zealand, where the over-representation of Maoris in the criminal justice system prompted consideration of the extended family as a source of support and informal control (Audit Commission 1996).

FGCs bring together the offender, family members and significant others, and members from the wider community, sometimes but not necessarily including the victim. Enabling the offender to understand and take responsibility for damage caused is central to this process, as is the collective involvement of all concerned in identifying measures which may prevent further offending. The ethos of FGCs is one of participation and empowerment (Audit Commission 1996) in which the family and community are meaningfully consulted and heard, rather than having a merely punitive involvement.

Family group conferences have been written into the Children Act 2001 as a youth crime prevention measure. In addition, Health Board personnel have taken on this model as a strategy for engaging families of children at risk, while the Probation and Welfare Service anticipates that FGCs will be a central strand of Court Probation Orders, following the eventual implementation of the Act. The Northern Ireland Probation Board, through its Watershed programme, has been using FGCs to good effect, and the underlying principles are expected to be further embedded in the juvenile justice system there following the current review (Breaking Through 2000).

Clearly FGCs have caught the imaginations of practitioners and policy makers alike, which is somewhat surprising given the cultural differences between Ireland and the family orientated Maori context and the fact that there is no convincing evidence of their effectiveness in preventing further criminality (Utting and Vennard 2000). Evaluations suggest that this process does enable families and offenders to make greater use of supports, but also notes that those interventions instigated by the process in order to prevent further offending are not always followed through. The process requires considerable supervision of the individual and the family which, given the inclusive philosophy of the approach, can create ethical dilemmas.

In terms of FGCs as a diversionary process, the responsibility for calling and mediating these conferences has been allocated to the Garda Juvenile Liaison Officers (JLOs). A number of JLOs have already received training and are piloting the use of FGCs as an additional aspect of cautioning. An evaluation is expected, although was unfortunately not built into the pilot stage. Allocating JLOs responsibility for FGCs, along with the proposed statutory status of the scheme, has led to some concerns that work will become focused on individual case work to the detriment of some of the more general preventive work which they currently undertake, such as the Garda Schools Programme.

There is a more fundamental issue, regarding whether or not the JLO is the appropriate person to take responsibility for this initiative. In other family group conference models, the chairing role is taken on by a more neutral figure, who represents the needs both of the community and the young person. In such models, the role of the police is to speak strictly from a law enforcement perspective.

Requiring the JLO to articulate the law enforcement element and maintain the balance between all interested parties could result in significant role conflict.

Furthermore, there is concern that extending the role of the JLO in this way could lead to "net-widening", whereby young people, for whom a caution might have been just as effective, are involved in FGCs. Once again this highlights the need for practitioners to ensure that participation in interventions does not in itself lead to the stigmatisation of young people.

SCHOOL-BASED PROGRAMMES

Truancy and school exclusion are key risk factors for later offending. Programmes which promote attachment to the school, which provide positive responses to behavioural problems and enable individual children to reach their educational potential, are of central importance. A key issue here pertains to the allocation of responsibility for children and young people whose behaviour is problematic or disruptive in the classroom. Although there are recent initiatives aimed at encouraging schools to develop positive interventions, schools have traditionally been reluctant to take responsibility for this minority of pupils, instead relying on both short- and long-term suspensions as the accepted response.

Rather than being excluded, some children choose not to attend school. Others are unable to do so due to family commitments (caring for younger siblings is a significant factor in non-attendance). Current practice in relation to these children emphasises a punitive approach, in which the gardaí carry out the role of the school attendance officer. Only the areas of Dublin inner city, Dun Laoghaire, Cork and Waterford have a professional truancy officer programme and do not call on the gardaí to operate in this way. Impending legislation may alter this situation significantly, with the Education (Welfare) Act 2000 proposing the "establishment of a single nation-wide authority with responsibility for the promotion of educational welfare and school attendance" (Minster for Education and Science 2000).

Parents may be prosecuted for failing to ensure that their child attends school, with a maximum penalty of £10. This situation has been regarded as unacceptable for many years by parents, teachers and the gardaí. Innovative, positive means of intervention in relation to non-school attendance are crucial to an effective crime prevention strategy. As the Audit Commission (1996: 70) argue "Reducing the number of pupils who are not attending school for reasons of truancy or exclusion could significantly reduce the number of young offenders in a local area".

Rutter has noted that schools which have a positive impact on children in terms of educational and employment opportunities (both key in terms of possible later offending), are characterised by the following:

- high expectations regarding work and behaviour

- clear guidelines for discipline, with an emphasis on encouragement rather than punishment
- teachers providing positive role models
- positive teacher-pupil relations
- opportunities for both parents and children to become involved in the organisation of the school
- pleasant environment and support structures for teachers (Rutter 1979).

A more recent evaluation of school based programmes which seek to reduce non-attendance found the most effective interventions included early preventive work by teachers at primary level, and in the first years of secondary school; making contact with parents on the first day of absence, and providing opportunities for all staff and pupils to be involved in developing policy on school attendance (Learmonth 1995).

Whilst there are clearly significant in-school factors which influence partici-pation, there are also a number of external factors which must be considered. The Education Act 1998 defined educational disadvantage as "impediments to edu-cation arising from social or economic disadvantage which prevent students from deriving appropriate benefit from education in schools" (Minister for Education and Science 1998). A number of initiatives are in existence in Ireland with the aim of offsetting such disadvantage. Unfortunately, none of the initiatives outlined below appears to have been evaluated, rendering this section largely descriptive.

Areas of designated disadvantage

Forty areas across the country have been designated disadvantaged by the Department of Education and Science on the basis of the socio-economic profile of the school feeder area and these areas qualify for special funding and programmes. Other factors, such as levels of early school leaving and educational attainment, were also considered. Both primary and secondary schools within areas of designated disadvantage have a guideline of a maximum of twenty-nine pupils per class. Additional teaching staff have also been allocated to provide non-teaching services, such as measures to improve links between the school, family and community, to develop parents' programmes, and to encourage families to see the school as a local resource. Activities may include adult literacy classes, family trips, outreach contact and morning classes for parents. Pre-school activities and after school homework clubs are also provided in these areas.

The presence of a school-based teacher who is not timetabled to classes is the key factor in the effectiveness of these developments. The home-school-community-liaison teacher is able to develop links with parents informally, and this process recognises that parents of children in difficulty have, very often, had a negative experience of school themselves. This scheme is, according to the

Department of Education and Science (2000), a "key element in the Department's strategy to combat educational disadvantage".

8-15's Early School Leaver Initiative

Another recent initiative of the Department of Education and Science, the *8-15's Early School Leaver Initiative* (ESLI), is a response to concern regarding levels of early school leaving in certain areas. Fourteen areas across the country have been targeted with the *8-15's ESLI*, based on the extent of early school leaving. Teachers within these areas have been seconded to non-teaching duties aimed at providing additional supports for those young people considered to be at risk of leaving school early.

These initiatives have introduced after schools groups and homework clubs, outdoor pursuits programmes, summer projects, additional help with literacy and basic skills, counselling and so on. While some activities take place outside school hours, targeted young people may also take part in special activities during school time.

This initiative marks an important shift in the role of the school, as teachers have become more pro-active in making contact with other agencies in the area and have also undertaken work outside the usual school hours, such as evening and summer work. The emphasis on inter-agency support arises from the understanding that schools alone cannot meet the needs of children in difficulty. The *8-15's ESLI* will provide some valuable lessons for both the formal education sector and alternative settings. Although the pilot projects are being evaluated, no written information was available at the time of writing.

There are several other measures which have been implemented in recent years with a view to reducing the levels of educational under-achievement. The *Stay in School Retention Initiative* is currently being implemented in over 100 second-level schools, focusing on the development of effective links between the school and community and establishing a multi-agency approach. The development of vocational certification programmes, such as the *Leaving Certificate Applied*, the *Junior Certificate School Programme*, and the broader educational remit of the Transition Year have all been seen to be positive, while the expansion of the personal development curriculum in schools (such as *On My Own Two Feet*, *Stay Safe*, *Walk Tall*), has broadened the scope of the teacher-pupil relationship. In addition, a number of specific interventions have been developed for traveller children, both within the formal education sector and separate from it.

This plethora of innovation has brought its own burdens. Teachers struggle to balance an overburdened curriculum; employers are confused by the new certification, and parents worry that these will be without value in the employment market. Practitioners remain concerned that strategies to prevent educational disadvantage tend to focus on the child as the problem, rather than seeing the school as part of the solution. Identifying positive ways to respond to non-attendance or discipline problems is very much the responsibility of the individual school, rather than a national requirement. The extent to which schools welcome and actively seek co-operative links with other agencies varies considerably and there is, perhaps inevitably, a reliance on the individual philosophies of the personnel concerned.

Teacher training does not include information about the role of key service providers, nor does it necessitate consideration of teaching as an integral part of a broader strategy. Inclusive approaches and effective methodologies which aim to enable school attendance are not a feature of teacher training despite the government's stated target to reduce early school leaving to minimal levels by the year 2005. Given the current policies and developments regarding early school leaving, it would appear that the burden of responsibility continues to lie with the child and his/her family.

INDIVIDUAL AND GROUP INITIATIVES

Youth service

In 1999, the youth work budget provided through the Youth Affairs Section of the Department of Education and Science was £15.44 million, a significant increase from the previous year. This funding is disseminated regionally and locally, largely through the four national youth work organisations (National Youth Federation; National Youth Council; Catholic Youth Council; Foroige) and a further youth service for Dublin City (City of Dublin Youth Services Board, or CDYSB). Only the latter is statutory, the remainder receiving government grants but working from a voluntary basis.

Youth work is generally regarded as having two distinct aspects: 1) main-stream activities, for all young people, frequently involving activity-based youth clubs and uniformed organisations such as the Girl Guides and Scouts; and 2) disadvantaged youth work, in which specific programmes are provided for targeted young people. Research has demonstrated that those young people who are most at risk of early school leaving, drug use and crime, are least likely to participate in youth service activities (Ronayne 1992).

The Youth Work Bill uses the following definition of youth work:

> a planned programme of education designed for the purpose of aiding and enhancing the personal and social development of young persons through their voluntary participation, and which is complementary to their formal, academic or vocational education and training, and provided primarily by voluntary youth work organisations (Minister for Education and Science 2000).

Three of the four national youth organisations fund projects based in disadvantaged communities, as does CDYSB. These projects employ professional youth workers to carry out a range of activities for young people at risk. These include:

- intensive group work programmes
- arts and activity based programmes
- training of local volunteers
- referral of young people with special needs, such as counselling, drug related issues, bereavement work, and so on.

There has been very little evaluation of youth work, either in Ireland or elsewhere. Meta-analysis does however demonstrate that outdoor pursuits and leisure activities can be effective when combined with a range of interventions which aim to bring about long-term behavioural change, while cognitive-behavioural approaches have been seen to be "among the most consistently effective community-based programmes in reducing recidivism among young offenders" (Utting and Vennard 2000: 48).

The Irish youth service has a strong tradition of volunteerism, with local people being centrally involved in both the management of projects and the delivery of interventions. The principle of empowering the local community to respond to its own needs is an admirable one, although it does create difficulties. With the increasing incidence of drug use amongst young people, the nature of this work is changing, and it is becoming significantly more difficult to engage volounteers. This is compounded by the many high profile cases of child abuse, which have left youth workers feeling vulnerable and aware of the need to protect both themselves and the young people. Furthermore, adults in the community tend to require high levels of support in order to be able to work effectively with young people in difficulty. The drain which this places on resources, in terms of time and energy, is not always recognised by funding agencies.

The significantly increased funding noted above has naturally been enthusiastically welcomed, but has also brought its own difficulties. The insufficient numbers of experienced, qualified youth workers to fill posts has prompted a growing awareness of the need for structured training and supports for new practitioners. How this is delivered will be a significant issue for the youth service over the next decade.

Garda special projects

The Department of Justice, Equality and Law Reform currently allocates funding for fifty-one community-based Garda Special Projects (GSPs) from the garda budget. These projects specifically aim to work with young people at risk of or known to be involved in criminal activity and were established in order to

- prevent crime through community and multi-agency co-operation and to improve the quality of life within the community

- divert young people from becoming involved in criminal/anti-social behaviour
- provide suitable activities to facilitate personal development and encourage civic responsibility
- support and improve garda/community relations (Bowden and Higgins 2000).

GSPs are all based in disadvantaged communities and managed by a local voluntary management committee with the support of the gardaí and the Youth Service. Whilst each project has evolved separately, reflecting the needs of the young people and local community, there are elements which are common to all. Most work with young people aged ten to sixteen years, with referrals coming from the Juvenile Liaison Officer (see below) or the Probation and Welfare Officer. As with the generic youth service, schools, youth workers and parents may also refer children, and some young people will initiate the contact themselves.

Projects tend to work with small groups of young people, combining group work programmes, such as *Copping On* (see below) with a range of arts and sports activities. An evaluation of the projects has recently been completed and the findings indicate that the young participants have made positive changes, particularly in relation to a reduction in offending and "unacceptable" behaviour and in terms of "development and acquisition of personal skills and abilities, and changes in lifestyles, outlook and socialising patterns" (Bowden and Higgins 2000:6).

The central factor in this reduction appears to be the nature of the relationship between the young people and the project youth workers. This relationship is valuable in itself, but also enables the young people to engage with the project contract which places limitations on their anti-social behaviour. In addition, the young people appear to develop a sense of ownership regarding the project and an awareness that their behaviour could reflect on public perceptions of the work undertaken by the youth workers. This provides an informal, but powerful source of social control.

A key aim of the projects is to improve the quality of relationship between the project participants and the gardaí. The evaluation (Bowden and Higgins 2000) indicates that this has not been achieved. While the young people may develop an easy rapport with those gardaí centrally involved in the project, this does not readily transfer to gardaí generally.

A central issue identified by the evaluation is the need for a clearly defined target group, both in terms of the young persons' level of involvement in crime and regarding the identification of priority communities, rather than the current targeting of "those loosely defined as *at risk*" (Bowden and Higgins 2000:9). Defining a clear target group enables evaluation of a project's ability to engage its identified audience and remains a major issue for all youth services. Furthermore, the study raises an ethical question regarding the involvement of young people in a crime prevention programme, if they have "no youth justice, police or criminal justice status. Apart from the ethics of this, it does not seem to make sense that children and young people who have never committed a crime should be recruited into a programme which aims to "divert them from crime and anti-social behaviour" (Bowden and Higgins: 156).

This indicates the need for clarity regarding intervention programmes (ie those aimed at specific groups of young people) and prevention programmes with a wider target group, as well as recognising the need for practitioners to ensure that young people are not further stigmatised by their very participation in activities.

Youthreach

Youthreach is a national programme for fifteen to eighteen year olds who have left school without any formal qualifications. The programme has been established for over ten years and there are currently over 150 centres across the country providing the full-time *Youthreach* programme, in which the young people receive a nominal training allowance.[1]

There are threes strands to the *Youthreach* programme: personal development, skills training, and preparation for work. These are incorporated into both the Foundation programme and the Progression element. The personal development aspect may include programmes such as assertiveness and communication; gender specific work; *Copping On* (see below); drugs awareness and sexuality programmes. The ethos promotes the concept that improving the young person's self-esteem is integral to all elements of the programme and is therefore as much the responsibility of the woodwork instructor as it is of the guidance counsellors.

All centres provide literacy, numeracy and basic skills programmes, and almost all include computer training. Other skills elements may include woodwork; metal work; catering; health and hygiene programmes; arts and crafts; creative writing; and outdoor pursuits/sports.

It is intended that all participants will gain work experience through the programme, and this is provided with support from centre staff. The centres also plan towards the young person leaving the programme and attempt to ensure that individuals go on to further education, training, or employment. The programme has been very successful in placing young people, with 80% of all participants achieving employment following their participation in the programme (European Social Fund Programme Evaluation Unit 1996).

Centres are encouraged to be innovative in their work, and there are many

---

[1] The Department of Education and Science funds seventy-four centres, with an additional forty-seven Community Training Workshops funded by the Department of Enterprise, Trade and Employment. FÁS and the Department of Justice, Equality and Law Reform provide six workshops, whilst the Department of Education and Science funds a further twenty-eight centres specifically for travellers

examples of exciting and empowering programmes which have developed within individual centres. In particular, there has been a range of highly effective arts based initiatives, such as drama projects, music and visual arts programmes, and photography activities.

Increasingly, *Youthreach* is integrating formal qualifications into its programme and while this is seen as a vital development in terms of improving employability, it has also raised concerns that the programme will become curriculum focused to the detriment of its established needs-based approach. Further issues are raised as a result of current economic growth, which has been accompanied by an "increase in early school leaving and a decrease in youth unemployment" (National Co-ordinators 2000:20). A change in economic climate could have serious implications for those without qualifications, as this group has been seen to be less likely to sustain employment even in a strong labour market (National Co-ordinators 2000). Furthermore, the draw towards the labour market for many early school leavers has changed the profile of those young people participating in Youthreach programmes, in that they are more likely to be characterised by multiple disadvantage. This has implications for staff training and support, resourcing of centres and appropriate referral mechanisms.

Copping on

Copping On is a national crime prevention initiative, funded inter-departmentally to provide training and support to locally-based, multi-agency groups working with young people at risk.[2] Training focuses on the delivery of a group work programme, which aims to improve young people's cognitive skills, encourage debate, challenge participants attitudes to crime, and provide accurate information regarding the justice system. The training brings together representatives of key agencies working in specific communities, with a view to encouraging inter-agency co-operation, and the development of a cohesive local crime prevention strategy.

Whilst *Copping On* developed within the *Youthreach* programme with the support of the gardaí, it now works with a wide range of organisations, such as the youth service, probation and welfare, the prisons, schools, drug programmes, and so on. All the programmes outlined in this section use *Copping On* as an aspect of their crime prevention strategy.

Juvenile diversion scheme

By far the most significant diversionary strategy in Ireland for young people beginning to get into trouble with the law is the Garda Juvenile Diversion Scheme

---

[2] Copping On is funded by the Department of Education and Science, the Department of Justice, Equality and Law Reform, FÁS, and the Department of Health and Children

(JDS), modelled on that developed in England. It has been in operation in Ireland since 1963, with a view to diverting young people from the courts and from criminal activity. Juvenile Liaison Officers (JLOs) are selected from the gardaí, usually for their interest in or experience with young people.

Young people are eligible for cautioning under the JDS if they are under eighteen years of age, admit the offence, and have not been cautioned before, although this latter factor is negotiable, depending on the offence and the individual. A caution is wiped from the records at age eighteen, in the event that no further offence has taken place. The parents must usually consent to the caution and the victim may be asked for his or her approval, although this is not required. Prior to 1991, the JDS related only to those aged under seventeen years. In raising the age to eighteen, the range of applicable offences was also broadened, although a number of serious offences must be referred to the Director of Public Prosecutions.

The high degree of discretion within the JDS is the subject of some criticism and is often linked with the scheme's lack of statutory status, an issue which may be resolved with the impending legislation outlined above. Despite this weakness in the scheme, it appears to be remarkably successful. Of the total number of young people cautioned through the JDS since its inception to the end of 1999 (110,611), 89% have been found not to re-offend before reaching eighteen years of age (Garda Commissioner 1999:86). However, a recent report found that one fifth of children "were prosecuted without ever having had the benefit of a diversionary alternative to prosecution" (McLoughlin et al 1999: 83). Unfortunately, the reasons for the exclusion of this 20% are not outlined, but this raises questions regarding the criteria used to decide who is cautioned, and suggests the need to examine the profile of those young people coming under the scheme, and those who are refused it.

A further issue is that, unlike the UK model, cautions are sanctioned by the Director of the National Office rather than by the local superintendent. Whilst this diminishes the scope for local prejudice, it does mean that there are generally delays of up to three months between the young person agreeing to the process, and the administration of a caution. This time lapse can be considerably longer for drug related offences, due to the delay in drug analysis.

Restorative justice

The principles of restorative justice may underpin both diversionary interventions and sanctions imposed by court order. The approach aims to:

- enable offender responsibility for harm caused
- involve, support and make reparation to the victim
- identify supports which will prevent further offending (Utting and Vennard 2000).

Restorative justice strategies will usually involve one or more meetings between the offender and the victim, with professional mediation. Evaluations have been largely inconclusive in terms of a reduction in recidivism (Hughes et al 1996) and some models have been criticised for their focus on the offender to the detriment of the victim (Davies et al 1989). However, the majority of both victims and offenders involved in restorative justice programmes have expressed satisfaction with this participation, while completion rates for reparation agreements have been seen to be significantly higher than those achieved through other means (Marshall 1998). In addition, there are cost benefits, with victim-offender mediation costs amounting to £150-300 per case as opposed to an average of £2,500 for court appearances (Marshall 1998).

Cognitive-behavioural training

Most of the initiatives outlined above include elements of cognitive-behavioural training, in particular the youth service, *Garda Special Projects* and *Youthreach*. The *Copping On* programme specifically aims to improve young people's cognitive skills, thereby enabling them to make positive choices. Evaluations of focused skills training programmes can highlight the essential elements of these interventions.

Interpersonal skills training carried out in Canada by Ross et al (1988) included reasoning and creative problem-solving, assertiveness and negotiating skills and social skills training. The logical reasoning training focused on enabling the young people to "stop and think before acting, to consider the consequences of their behaviour, to recognise alternative ways of solving their interpersonal problems, and to consider the impact of their behaviour on other people" (Farrington 1996:19). In just a nine month period, this programme resulted in a 74% reduction in offending amongst the small sample group.

COMMUNITY INTERVENTIONS

Identifying disadvantaged communities tends to include factors such as low income, proportion of social housing as opposed to privately owned homes, and the profile of residents (single parenthood, unemployment, level of educational attainment, and so on). There is however great difficulty in separating out these factors, because they tend to converge on particular communities, whilst research has not established a direct causal relationship between these factors and crime rates.

Farrington notes the importance of considering relative poverty, as opposed to absolute poverty, as there have been significant improvements in housing conditions and the levels of absolute poverty (Farrington 1996). The concept of relative poverty was first introduced by Peter Townsend, who defined this as experiencing a deficit in resources which resulted in the exclusion from "ordinary living patterns, customs and activities" (Townsend 1979:31).

The correlation between growing up in a disadvantaged community and later offending highlights the importance of targeting resources at those communities in need: "Targeting resources on deprived neighborhoods would help address factors associated with offending by young people, without rewarding criminal behaviour" (Audit Commission 1996:60-62). Community prevention strategies are based on the understanding that the profile and dynamics of the community within which we live have an impact on our behaviour, and changes to the former will also result in behavioural changes amongst residents. Initiatives in Ireland have tended to focus on anti-poverty strategies and interventions which enable active participation in educational, employment and social opportunities.

Early community crime prevention strategies were developed in the USA, the best known being Shaw and McKays' Chicago project. Based on the understanding that crime is a result of social disorganisation, they aimed to promote community organisation through physical improvements, better co-ordination of resources and provision of recreational facilities for young people (Farrington 1996). The project was never formally evaluated, nor outcomes determined.

Other examples of community crime prevention include "community organising; tenant involvement; resource mobilisation; community defence (both intentional organising and environmental modification); preserving order; and protecting the vulnerable" (Hope 1995:21). Hope goes on to note the importance of achieving a balance between those interventions which "support and control" young offenders and those which "protect the fearful, vulnerable and victimised". Without the latter, the most able and organised will move to safer communities, leaving behind those least able to make positive change, while interventions which focus only on the vulnerable will lead to the further alienation of young offenders.

Many of the approaches outlined above contain elements of community crime prevention. For example, areas of educational disadvantage improve the participation of all pupils through improved teacher-pupil ratios; the training and support of local volunteers by youth service organisations raises the skill level and confidence within a community.

Youth offender teams

Youth Offender Teams (YOT's) are a new development in England and Wales, established in the Crime and Disorder Act 1998 (Home Office 1998). Under this legislation, each local authority must establish a minimum of one YOT, with the secondment of at least:

- a probation officer
- a social worker from social services
- a police officer

- a health authority representative
- an education representative (Kelly 1999).

This is an important model of inter-agency co-operation, with a clear focus on developing comprehensive, holistic youth crime prevention strategies. Inevitably, the extent to which YOTs are able to deliver such an approach, depends on the understanding and commitment of the individuals involved and the level of support within each of the seconding agencies. It has been noted that the "principle obstacle to overcome will be ... the issues involved in establishing adequate resourcing and effective partnerships" (Towler 1998).

CONCLUSION

Currently in Ireland, there is an apparent openness to debate within the criminal justice system. Various sectors, such as the police, parliament, government departments and service providers have entered a period of reflection regarding juvenile justice. Preventative work is receiving more financial support than ever before; the government has engaged in a process of consultation regarding long-term strategies for responding to and preventing crime; and the existing system is undergoing a series of reviews and evaluations. However, the extent to which any of these processes will impact on the beliefs which underpin Irish responses, will significantly change funding and researching of crime prevention strategies, or will result in a more cohesive, inter-connected system, is uncertain. Whether the current process of engagement and dialogue will prove to be more than an exercise in rhetoric remains to be seen.

REFERENCES

Audit Commission (1996), *Misspent Youth: Young People and Crime*, Oxon: Audit Commission

Alexander and Parsons (1973), cited in Farrington, D. (1994), *Early Developmental Prevention of Juvenile Delinquency, Criminal Behaviour and Mental Health*, Vol. 4, pp 129-54

Bowden, M. and Higgins, L. (2000), *The Impact and Effectiveness of the Garda Special Projects*, Dublin: Department of Justice, Equality and Law Reform

"Breaking Through, 2000", *The Journal: Volume 2,* Maynooth: Breaking Through

Commission on the Family, (1998), *Strengthening Families for Life*, Dublin: Stationery Office

Communities that Care, (1999), *A Guide to Promising Approaches*, London: Communities that Care

Davies, G., Boucherat, J. and Watson, D. (1989), "Pre-court decision-making in juvenile justice", *British Journal of Criminology* 29: pp 219-235

Davis, H. and Hester, P. (1998), *An Independent Evaluation of Parent-Link: A Parenting Education Programme,* London: Parent Network

Department of Education and Science (2000), *Educational Initiatives to Combat Disadvantage*, unpublished

Department of Health and Children (1999), *Children First: National guidelines for the Protection and Welfare of Children*, Dublin: Stationery Office

Educational Research Centre (1998), *Early Start Pre-School Programme: Final Evaluation Report*, Dublin: Educational Research Centre

European Social Fund Programme Evaluation Unit (1996), *Early School Leavers Provision*, Dublin: ESF Programme Evaluation Unit

Farrington, D. (1996), *Understanding and Preventing Youth Crime*, York: Joseph Rowntree Foundation

French, G. (1998), *Enhancing Our Future: A Profile of Parenting Programmes in Ireland,* Dublin: Barnardos and the Department of Health and Children

Garda Commissioner (1993;1994;1996;1999), *Annual Report*, Dublin: Garda Headquarters

Goldblatt, P. and Lewis, C. (eds.) (1998), *Reducing Offending: an assessment of research evidence on ways of dealing with offending behaviour,* Home Office Research Study 197

Government of Ireland (1992), *First Report of the Select Committee on Crime. Juvenile Crime: Its Causes and Remedies,* Dublin: Stationery Office

Government of Ireland (1999), *National Development Plan 2000-2006*, Dublin: Stationery Office

Graham, J. and Bowling, B. 1995, *Young People and Crime: Research Study 145*, London: HMSO

Holthusen, B. and Schafer, H. (2000), "Prevention of Juvenile Delinquency in Germany and the Netherlands", in Bendit, R., Wolfganger E., Nieborg, S. and Schafer, H. (eds.) (2000), *Child and Juvenile Delinquency*, Munich: German Youth Institute

Home Office, (1998), *Crime and Disorder Act*, London: HMSO

Hope, T. (1996), "Community Crime Prevention", in Tonry. M. and Farrington D. *op cit*

Hughes, G., Pilkington, A. and Leisten, R. (1996), *An Independent Evaluation of the Northamptonshire Diversion Unit*, Open University

Kelly, M. (1999), "The Crime and Disorder Act and the Involvement of Young People in Community Safety", in *Copping On: Breaking Through: Young People, Crime and Disadvantage*, Maynooth: Copping On

Lally et al (1988), "More Pride, Less Delinquency: Findings from the ten year follow-up study of the Syracuse University Family Development Research programme", *Zero-to-three*, Vol. 8, No. 4, pp 13-18

Learmonth, J. (1995), *More Willingly to School?,* London: Department of

Education and Employment

Lloyd, E. (1999), *Parenting Matters: What works in parenting education?,* Essex: Barnardos

MacDonald G. and Roberts, H. (1995), *What Works in the Early Years? Effective Interventions for Children and Their Families in Health, Social Welfare, Education and Child Protection,* Essex: Barnardo's

Marshall, T. (1998), Restorative Justice: An Overview, unpublished paper for the Home Office, in Utting, D. and Vennard, J. *op cit*

McKeown, K. (2000), *A Guide to What Works in Family Support Services for Vulnerable Families,* Dublin: Department of Health and Children

McKeown, K., Haase, T. and Pratschke, J. (2000), *Does Family Support Make a Difference? Interim Evaluation of Springboard, January to May 2000,* Dublin: Department of Health and Children

Minister for Education and Science (1998), *Education Act,* Dublin: Government Publications

Minister for Education and Science (2000), *Education (Welfare) Bill,* Dublin: Government Publications

Minister for Education and Science (2000), *Youth Work Bill 2000,* Dublin: Government Publications

National Coordinators (2000), *Youthreach 2000: A Consultative Process,* Dublin: Department of Education and Science and Department of Enterprise, Trade and Employment

O'Mahony, P. (1997), *Mountjoy Prisoners: A Sociological and Criminological Profile,* Dublin: Department of Justice

O'Sullivan, D. (1979), "Social Definition in Child Care in the Irish Republic: Models of Child and Child Care Intervention", *Economic and Social Review,* Vol. 10, No 3. pp 209-229

O'Sullivan, E. (1997), "Restored to virtue, to society and to God, Juvenile Justice and the Regulation of the Poor", *Irish Criminal Law Journal,* Vol. 7, No. 2, pp 171-194

Reynolds, A., Mann, E., Miedle, W. and Smokowski, P. (1997), "The State of Early Childhood Intervention: Effectiveness, Myths and Realities, and New Directions", in *Focus: Newsletter of the Institute for Research on Poverty,* Vol. 19, No. 1, Summer/Fall, Madison: University of Wisconsin, pp 5-11

Ronayne, T. (1992), *Participation in Youth Service provision during the transition from School to the Labour Market: Gaps in Provision and the Policy Issues Arising. Summary Report,* Dublin: WRC Social and Economic Consultants Limited

Ross, R., Fabiano, E. and Ewles, C. (1988), "Reasoning and Rehabilitation", *International Journal of Offender Therapy and Comparative Criminology* 32, pp 29-35

Rutter, M. et al. (1979), *Fifteen Thousand Hours: Secondary Schools and their Effects on Children*, London: Open Books

Schweinhert, L. and Wiekart, D. (1993), *A Summary of Significant Benefits: the High/Scope Perry Pre-School Study through age 27*, Ypsilamnti-Michigan: High/Scope Press

Sherman, L. et al. (1997), *What works, what doesn't, what's promising*, Washington DC: US Department of Justice

Taoiseach (1998), *Implementation of the Integrated Services Project*, Dublin Castle, 4 December, Dublin: Government Information Services

Tonry, M. and Farrington, D. (1995), *Building a Safer Society: Strategic Approaches to Crime Prevention*, Chicago: Chicago University Press

Towler, K. (1998), "Establishing Youth Offender Teams in Wales", in *Youth Justice Matters*, September 1998

Townsend, P. (1979), *Poverty in the United Kingdom: A study of household resource and standards of living*, London: Penguin

Utting, D. (1996), *Reducing Criminality Among Young People: A Sample of Relevant Programmes in the United Kingdom*, Home Office Research Study No. 161, London: HMSO

Utting, D. and Vennard, J. (2000), *What Works with Young Offenders in the Community?*, Essex: Barnardo's

van der Eyken (1982), *Homestart: A Four Year Evaluation*, Leicester: Homestart

39

Offender Rehabilitation Programmes for Imprisoned Sex Offenders – Grounds for Optimism?

Paul G. Murphy

The concept of rehabilitation in prisons has a long and chequered career. However, it is an ideal that has been pursued in various forms since the establishment of prisons themselves. Historically, it has focused on "correcting a certain moral "abeyance"" (Foucault 1967, p 59) through varying degrees of work, education, religious instruction, and, above all, discipline. While some of the methods used are truly shocking by today's standards (eg the use of a "water cellar" in correctional houses in Amsterdam during the 1600s, in which obstreperous prisoners had to pump water continuously in order not to drown), the same concern about how to respond to crime and how to deal with offenders remains a very significant social and political issue.

To this day, punishment remains the primary official response to lawbreaking, with incarceration serving as the ultimate sanction. However, it is increasingly recognised that punishment, in and of itself, will not reduce offending. The evidence suggests, if anything, it has the opposite effect and increases the likelihood of recidivism (Bonta 1997). Consequently, over the last number of decades, considerable effort has focused on the development and implementation of intervention programmes for offenders, both within prisons and in the community, that effectively reduce re-offending. These efforts have led to considerable controversy in the criminal justice area and resulted in what has become known as the "what works" debate (McGuire 1995).

THE "WHAT WORKS" DEBATE

The belief that "nothing works" with offenders was very much fuelled by a paper written in 1974 by Robert Martinson. He had been commissioned by the prisons service in New York State to undertake a review of the available research to assess if time spent in prison achieved rehabilitative as well as punitive aims. The outcome of this review, which was based on 231 studies of rehabilitative programmes carried out in a variety of institutional and non-institutional settings over a twenty-two year period, was that, with few and isolated exceptions, the intervention programmes studied had no significant impact on further offending.

This pessimistic conclusion has been challenged in the intervening period (Gendreau and Ross 1980; Thornton 1987). More recently, the widespread use of the statistical tool of meta-analysis has yielded more specific information to support the efficacy of intervention programmes with offenders and clarify the types of programmes that do work (McGuire 1995; Bonta and Cromier 1999).

One of the most important messages emerging from contemporary writings on offender rehabilitation is the need to offer specific programmes designed to meet the needs of specific groups of offenders. Perpetrators of sexual crimes represent one particularly important target group within the prison population for such intervention. However, before considering the components of effective programmes for imprisoned sex offenders in more detail, it is essential to consider the broader social context within which such interventions take place.

SEX OFFENDING IN IRELAND

It is now generally accepted that as a society we have a very serious problem with sexual abuse and sexual violence. However, there remains insufficient empirical research to provide an accurate estimate of the prevalence of sexual offending in Ireland.

One important, albeit limited, source of hard data in this area is the Annual Crime Reports produced by An Garda Síochána.

As is apparent from Figure 1 the trend in indictable crimes reported to the gardaí (and recorded by them) over the last twelve years is a fairly smooth graph, at first continuously rising to the peak of 1995, but from then continuously reducing until 1999, the latest year for which figures are available. In 1999, 81,274 indictable crimes were reported to the gardaí, the lowest figures for the period covered.

Figure 1: trend in reported indictable crimes 1988-1999

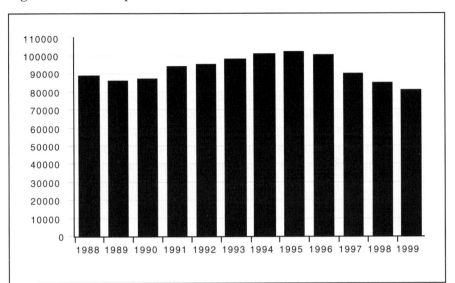

This graph stands in sharp contrast to the trend in reported sexual offences between 1988 and 1999 (see Figure 2), which shows a steady rise all the way through to 1997, when for the first time ever over one thousand sexual offences were reported to the gardaí. The Annual Crime Report for 1999 records 780 sexual offences reported to the gardaí up to the end of September. Prorating this figure for the whole year indicates that about 975 sexual offences were reported to the gardaí in 1999.

Figure 2: trend in reported sexual crimes 1988-1999

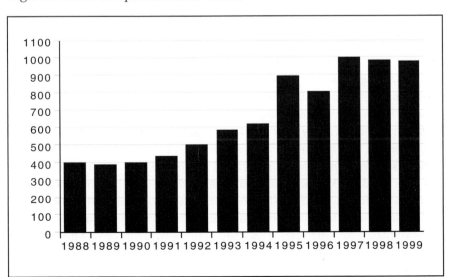

However, only a small percentage of the total number of sexual offences reported to the police result in the prosecution, conviction and imprisonment of the perpetrator. This is evident in Figure 3, which compares the number of sex offenders committed to prison to the total number of sexual offences reported to the police. For these former figures it is necessary to rely on the Annual Report on Prisons. A problem here is the latest comparable prisons statistical report produced was for 1994, so it only possible to make comparisons from 1988 through to 1994. It is not possible to discern, from the figures supplied in the Prisons Report covering the years 1995-1998, how many offenders were committed to prison to serve a sentence for a sexual offence. This is regrettable as such figures provide important, basic data about the nature of the prison population.

Figure 3: trend in the number of sex offenders committed to prison compared to the trend in reported sexual offences 1988-1994

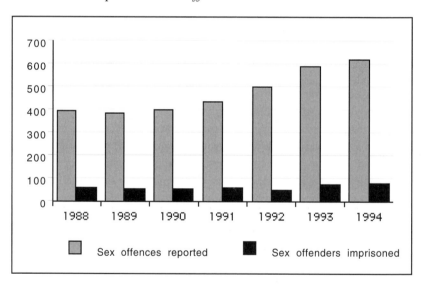

Notwithstanding these problems, probably the most striking feature about the above figures is that while there has been an increase in the number of sex offenders being imprisoned annually, it is a modest enough increase in absolute terms. When one considers that 619 sexual offences were reported to the police in 1994 (a figure that represents only a minority of the total number of sexual offences actually committed), it is apparent that only a very small number of the total sex offending population are being imprisoned. This has important implications. In particular, it suggests that reducing sexual victimisation in society will require a lot more in terms of social policy than simply focusing on imprisoned or indeed convicted sex offenders. This point is strongly reinforced by the results of recent epidemiological studies in Ireland (O'Reilly and Carr 1999; Lalor 1999).

O'Reilly and Carr's paper is a synthesis of two earlier studies, one carried out in the Republic of Ireland (McKeown et al 1989) and the other in Northern Ireland (The Research Team 1990). McKeown et al (1989) covered all confirmed or suspected cases of childhood sexual abuse in the Eastern Health Board Region in the Republic of Ireland, which were open or reported to Community Care teams during 1988. The Research Team study surveyed all newly reported cases of childhood sexual abuse in Northern Ireland in 1987. O'Reilly and Carr's review of these two studies indicated a number of important points:

- patterns of childhood sexual abuse were similar in Northern Ireland and the Republic of Ireland
- these patterns of abuse were similar to those reported in the international literature
- the ratio of females to males abused was 3-4 girls to 1 boy
- most children were under ten years of age when abused
- confirmed cases of abuse were more likely to be at the more serious end of the spectrum of abuse and to involve repeated penetrative abuse
- over 90% of abusers were related to or known to the victim
- one third of all sexual offences were committed by those in their teens or younger.

Lalor's (1999) study complements the above paper very well in that it provides important information on the extent of the problem of sexual abuse from a different perspective. Lalor surveyed unwanted sexual experiences, whilst under the age of sixteen, amongst 247 third-level students. The results of this survey indicate

- 31.8% of the female sample and 5.6% of the male sample had an unwanted sexual experience prior to the age of sixteen
- 10.3% of the female sample had endured unwanted sexual experiences over a period of months or years prior to their sixteenth birthday
- there was evidence of widespread sexual bullying of girls by their boyfriends. Six percent of females in the sample had had intercourse with their boyfriend despite requests on their part to stop, while 13.7% of them had had their genitals touched by a boyfriend, despite requests to stop.

While the issue is not discussed in the report of the study, it is likely that few, if any, of the abuses reported above were reported to the police, let alone prosecuted through the criminal justice system.

Studies like these go some way towards demonstrating both the nature and extent of sexual abuse in Ireland. They raise fundamental questions about the process whereby young people, particularly young men, are socialised to deal with sexuality, relationships etc. Above all they support the need to adopt a public health approach to the problem of sexual abuse, if this issue is to be addressed in a meaningful and comprehensive manner (Becker 1997). Thus, interventions need to be made at the primary (eg the Stay Safe and the Exploring Masculinities programmes), the secondary (eg early intervention programmes for children, adolescents and adults exhibiting sexual behaviour problems) and the tertiary levels of prevention (eg intervening with offenders with long-standing, chronic patterns of abusive behaviour).

Laws (1998), in an article arguing forcefully for the adoption of a public health approach to sexual offending, points out that most of our efforts at present are focused at the tertiary prevention level, where they are least likely to be effective. One of the reasons he sees for this is the public's perception of sex offenders and sex offending. People believe that sex offenders are somewhere "out there" – sexual crime is something that is happening to someone else, in another town, in another city. People do not believe sex offenders live on their street, belong to their social groups, work with them, teach their children, or interact with the public in ordinary ways. To get even a small grasp of its pervasiveness, the public needs to know that most sex offences are never reported and most sex offenders are never apprehended. This is why epidemiological studies are so important and why their findings need to form part of the discourse that shapes social policy in this area.

IMPRISONED SEX OFFENDERS

Imprisoned sex offenders, therefore, represent a particular subgroup of the total sex offending population. While this group will contain a heterogeneous mix of offenders varying in age, nature of offence and potential dangerousness, research shows that imprisoned sex offenders tend to be serious offenders whose offending is frequently characterised by one of two features – repetition and persistence or the use of violence or the threat of violence (Ellis 1989; Weinrott & Saylor 1991).

Table 1: a comparison between the number of offenders serving sentences for sexual offences in May 1997 and August 2000

	May 1997	August 2000	Percentage increase
Total sentenced male prison population	2,016	2,485	23.3%
Total sentenced for sexual offences	247	342	38.5%
Percentage of sentenced males imprisoned for sexual offences	12.2%	13.8%	

Table 1 indicates that there has been a significant increase in both the sentenced male prison population and sentenced sex offenders between 1997 and 2000. Overall, the percentage of the total sentenced male prison population serving sentences for sexual offences has increased from 12.2% to 13.8%. This trend in likely to continue in the coming years as more disclosures of abuse are made and more sexual offences are reported to the gardaí. These figures exclude a group of about fifteen offenders serving life sentences for murders which were committed in the context of a sexual offence. Classifying these as sexual offences increases the percentage of sex offenders in the prison system to 14.4% of the total sentenced male prison population.

Table 2: a comparison between sentence length and offender category for 1997 and 2000

	May 1997	**August 2000**
Average sentence length for total imprisoned sex offender population	6.4 years	6.24 years*
Percentage sentenced for offences against children**	53%	61%
Average sentence length – offences against children	5.3 years	6.08 years
Percentage sentenced for offences against adults**	47%	39%
Average sentence length – offences against adults	8.4 years	6.46 years

*   excludes one sentence of imprisonment for life imposed for a rape offence
** excludes a small group of offenders convicted of offences against adults and children

Table 2 indicates that the average sentence length being served by sex offenders as a total group has remained relatively unchanged in recent years. However, two important changes are discernible. First, the nature of the imprisoned sex offender population has changed, with the percentage of offenders serving sentences for offences against children having risen substantially. By August 2000, 61% of offenders were serving sentences for offences against children and 39% for offences against adults, almost exclusively against adult women. This indicates a very substantial proportion of recent committals are for offences against children, because the increase in their share of the total has occurred at a time when the total number of sex offenders has itself increased by almost 40%. Second, the average sentence length for child sex offenders and those who have offended against adults have converged. Sentences for child sex offenders have risen by almost a year, while those imposed on offenders against adults have reduced by almost precisely two years on average. However, these figures mask a wide range.

Sentences for child sex offenders in the 2000 sample range from six months to thirty-six years, while those for offenders against adults range from nine months to life imprisonment.

The distribution across type of offence has remained virtually unchanged in 2000 compared to 1997 (Murphy 1998). Of the 342 offenders in 2000, the vast majority are again serving sentences either for rape (47%) or sexual/indecent assault (39%). Smaller numbers are serving sentences for unlawful carnal knowledge (5%), buggery (4%), incest (2%), attempted rape (2%) and aggravated sexual assault (1%).

Table 3: the distribution of sex offenders throughout the prison system in August 2000

Institution	Number of sex offenders
Curragh Prison	98
Wheatfield Place of Detention	89
Arbour Hill Prison	83
Castlerea Place of Detention	42
Limerick Prison	13
Cork Prison	12
Mountjoy Prison	5
TOTAL	342

Sex offenders are widely distributed throughout the prison system, with the bulk of offenders being held in Curragh Prison, Wheatfield, Arbour Hill and Castlerea. Curragh Prison and Arbour Hill cater almost exclusively for sex offenders. The release dates for these offenders covers a wide range, as indicated in Table 4.

Table 4: the numbers of sex offenders due for release each year between 2000 and 2026

2000	2001	2002	2003	2004	2005	2006
41	84	69	65	24	22	20
2007	**2008**	**2009**	**2010**	**2011**	**2026**	**Life**
5	7	2	–	1	1	1

What table 4 confirms is that all of the 342 offenders now in prison are, with the exception of one offender serving a life sentence, serving finite sentences and will be released back into the community at some point in the future. Set against this background, it is clearly important that effective interventions with imprisoned sex offenders, aimed at reducing the risk such men present to the community on their release from prison, form part of any comprehensive social policy committed to a reduction in sexual victimisation.

However, this is not an easy task. Rather it is a difficult and complex challenge for the prison service, primarily for two reasons: a) the nature of the prison environment itself; b) the demanding nature of the therapeutic process offenders need to go through in order to have a realistic chance of effectively changing their behaviour.

The reality of life in prison for sex offenders

Coping with imprisonment can be very difficult for some offenders and particularly so for sex offenders. There are two major factors to be considered here.

a) The physical and psychological environment of prisons

Prisons are in the main bleak, artificial, male-dominated, secure environments. Offenders have to come to terms with the reality of their confinement and adjust to the restrictions placed on them. The daily routine is highly structured and repetitive, with offenders spending from 16 to 18 hours per day confined to their cells. Boredom is a major problem. Access to family and friends is limited, personal privacy is limited, and the scope for taking personal responsibility in any meaningful sense is severely restricted.

The Whitaker Committee (1985) put it succinctly when they stated:

> The greatest single obstacle to the personal development of prisoners, and to reducing the reconviction rate, is the nature of prison itself ... These conditions are so different from those prevailing in the outside world that they make it extremely difficult to prepare for life in that world. (p 90/91)

Critically, in the prison environment sex offenders are not exposed in any realistic way to the kinds of stresses, temptations or opportunities that present in the community and that may lead them to re-offend upon release.

b) The cultural environment

A further problem for sex offenders is that they are generally not tolerated by the dominant offender culture within prisons. Left on normal location, sex offenders are frequently subjected to physical and verbal abuse from other inmates. As a way of dealing with this problem it is, generally, the practice of the Irish Prison Service to hold sex offenders in designated institutions, segregated from other prisoners, eg Arbour Hill, Wheatfield and Curragh Prison. An exception is Castlerea Place of Detention, where sex offenders are integrated with other offenders.

The practice of segregating sex offenders has a lot to recommend it. It protects sex offenders from assault and gives them access to a reasonable prison regime.

However, it is also the case that holding large numbers of sex offenders together carries with it certain risks (Sampson 1992). In particular, there is a risk that offenders will support each other in their distorted views of their crimes – minimising personal responsibility for their offences, reinforcing victim-blame and legitimising their own behaviour. Within such an institution a pro-offending culture can develop, manifesting itself in extensive offender denial and limited motivation to change and to engage in the process of treatment. To counteract this process, active steps must be taken to manage the institution in such a way as to challenge offending attitudes and behaviour and to foster a pro-treatment ethos (Sampson 1992). Where such steps are taken (eg Arbour Hill, Curragh Prison) the potential for developing a pro-treatment ethos within the institution and for motivating offenders to address their offending behaviour is enhanced.

Thus, prison is far from an ideal environment in which to undertake intensive programmes with sex offenders. However, it is important to acknowledge these difficulties, firstly, so that the limitations inherent in attempting to effect change within the isolation of prisons is recognised and, secondly, so that efforts can be made to overcome the constraints that limit the potential contribution of sex offender programmes to reducing re-offending.

The nature of the change process

The second major obstacle to effecting change is the nature of the change process itself. In the 1980s James Prochaska and Carlo DiClemente developed a model of the process through which people pass in the long-term change of a behaviour (Prochaska and DiClemente 1982; 1983). Their early work focused on the process smokers go through in giving up cigarettes. However, their model has now been applied to many other behaviours including sexually abusive behaviours (Mann 1996). According to this model there are five stages through which sex offenders pass in effecting long-term change of their behaviour. The kind of approach which might be taken to support an offender in changing his behaviour depends on the stage of the change process in which he is located. Each of these stages will be considered in turn.

a) Pre-contemplation

Here the offender has no desire to change, either because he is unaware that he has a problem or because he chooses to ignore it.

A good many imprisoned sex offenders are currently at this stage and have not actively engaged in the change process. Probably the most helpful influence for sex offenders who are not actively contemplating change is exposure to a culture within the prison system that is actively supportive of change, eg institutions that are well resourced with therapeutic services, institutions where specialist prog-rammes are operating, contact with other offenders who are contemplating treatment, who are undergoing treatment or who have been through treatment and are working at maintaining the treatment gains they have made. A critical factor is that all staff working in such institutions are well versed in the dynamics of sex offending and in a position to encourage and support offenders in their efforts to change.

b) Contemplation

Here the offender is thinking about change. He may feel somewhat concerned about his behaviour, but he is still ambivalent and has not made a commitment to change. Contemplation can be a lengthy process. It requires the offender to move to accepting the problem exists at all, feeling some discomfort about it and taking some personal responsibility for bringing about change.

At this stage it is critical for the offender to have access to services that will help tip the balance towards him actively taking steps to effect change. Motivational counselling, aimed at strengthening the offender's belief that he is able to change, can play a very important role during this part of the change process.

c) Preparation

Here the offender becomes determined to change and makes a decision to do so, but he has not yet put the decision into practice. This may be triggered by a major event in the life of the offender and may be the result of a long process of contemplation. The offender is now more focused and purposive in planning how he will achieve the desired change.

The offender at this stage needs prompt and accurate responses to his requests for information about the options at his disposal for acting on his desire to change. He may also need help in determining what course of action may best suit his particular needs, eg individual counselling or a group programme. Access to individual counselling at this stage of the change process can be critical for offenders in supporting them in their commitment to change and in beginning the process of addressing their needs around their offending. Individual therapeutic work plays a very important role in preparing offenders for the demands of an intensive offence-focused group programme.

d) Action

This involves the offender in trying to change his behaviour by committing himself to a particular approach. It will, ideally, result in the offender attending a specialist offending behaviour programme.

Critically important here is access to intensive, structured, offence-focused therapeutic programmes. The easier the access to such programmes the greater the likelihood that offenders will participate in them.

e) Maintenance

This is a long-term process and involves the offender working at maintaining the changes he has made as a result of treatment. Failure to maintain these changes may result in re-offending.

In working with sex offenders, this is a critical component in effecting positive change. While efforts need to be made to support offenders in maintaining change while they are still in prison, even more importantly intensive support and supervision must be provided to sex offenders on their release if the treatment gains made in prison are to be generalised to life in the community. Currently, there are very few therapeutic services available to meet the needs of sex offenders released from prison.

It is clear that the process of change is complex and long term. Dedicated sex offender programmes play just one, albeit important, part in this process. There is, however, a real danger that the other critical elements necessary for effecting and maintaining change can be forgotten.

Features of effective rehabilitation programmes for offenders

Characteristics of offending behaviour programmes that reduce recidivism have been identified by a number of authors (eg Hollin 1993; Antonowicz and Ross 1994; McGuire 1995; Bonta and Cromier 1999). These critical success factors include the following.

a) Risk classification

Offenders need to be carefully assessed so that there is a match between their risk of re-offending and the nature of the intervention provided. More intensive programmes should be targeted at high risk offenders, while those at lower risk of re-offending should receive lower levels of intervention.

b) Targeting criminogenic needs

Criminogenic needs refer to those factors which contribute directly to criminal behaviour. Examples of these are anti-social attitudes, drug dependency, limited problem solving strategies and skills, employment problems. If the aim of the programme is to reduce re-offending, the focus should be on these needs and not on non-criminogenic needs. These latter needs refer to characteristics of offenders now known to be unrelated to or only distantly related to offending, eg low self-esteem, depression, anxiety, etc.

c) Responsivity

This refers to the need to match the teaching/presentation styles of programme delivery to the learning styles of offenders. Offenders gain most from structured, focused programmes that involve them in an active, participatory way in their own learning, eg role plays, guided self-discovery, peer review and feedback, etc. Such methods work better than either a didactic approach or less structured approaches, eg non-directive client-centred counselling.

d) Treatment modality

Programmes based on a cognitive-behavioural theoretical model have consistently been shown to be the most effective in reducing re-offending. Ideally programmes should address a range of offender's needs, include a cognitive component that focuses on the thinking, attitudes, beliefs and values that support offending and provide offenders with the opportunity to develop skills that make it easier to avoid criminal behaviour and to successfully engage in legitimate activities.

e) Programme integrity

Effective programmes need to be managed in such a way as to ensure that the programme is carried out in the manner intended by properly trained and committed staff. Essential components in this process are comprehensive training and support for staff involved in programme delivery, programme monitoring (eg video recording of programme sessions to ensure the accuracy and consistency of programme delivery) and programme evaluation (the application of rigorous research methods to assess the impact of the programme in respect of changes in individual attitudes and behaviour and, more generally, on reconviction rates). Carr (2000) gives a very clear outline of the methodological criteria that need to be met in the design of such evaluative research.

f) Throughcare

Although institutional programmes can be effective, this is more likely to be the case if every effort is made to promote a programme-supportive environment. Also, it is critical that prison-based programmes are structurally linked with community-based interventions. In the absence of this, there is a real risk that the therapeutic gains made in prison will not be maintained in the community.

These principles are consistently reflected in the specialist literature on programmes for sex offenders. Comprehensive cognitive-behavioural programmes, with a relapse prevention component (incorporating follow-up in the community), are now considered the approach of choice in this area (Blanchette 1996; Marshall and Pithers 1994; Marshall et al 1999; Laws et al 2000).

Recognising the need to intervene effectively with convicted sex offenders, a number of penal jurisdictions produced policy documents on the treatment of sex offenders in the early 1990s, informed by these principles. These included Canada (Solicitor General for Canada 1990), England and Wales (HM Prison Service

1991), and Australia (Victorian Prison Service 1995). In 1993, the Department of Justice produced similar proposals, representing the first politically driven commitment to implement structured, offence-focused work with imprisoned sex offenders (Department of Justice 1993). (For a full account of the history and development of work with sex offenders in Ireland see Geiran 1996.) The first programme directly informed by this policy was set up in Arbour Hill in 1994. A second programme, pursuing the same model, commenced in Curragh Prison in November 2000. There are also plans to initiate further rehabilitative programmes for sex offenders, which will see prison officers involved directly in delivering such programmes. This initiative is a very welcome one, as it holds out the prospect, in time, of making specialised programmes available to a far greater number of imprisoned sex offenders. However, implementing and maintaining such programmes will be a complex task and will present many challenges for the Irish Prison Service.

Sex offender programme, Arbour Hill Prison

a) Promoting a programme-supportive environment

Prior to setting up the programme, all staff working in Arbour Hill (prison officers, teachers, chaplains, etc) attended, in small multi-disciplinary groups, a one-day information/awareness seminar on sex offenders and sex offending. The objective of the day was to share information with staff about the new initiative for sex offenders, to clearly explain the logic behind it and, as far as possible, to get their support for it, with a view to fostering a pro-treatment culture in Arbour Hill.

Over the last six years the programme has generally been very well supported by management and staff. At a practical level this has manifested itself in the quality of facilities made available to run the programme, in support for offenders from prison staff, sometimes at critical times for them during the programme, and in the provision of flexibility around the time for ending group sessions. It is difficult to calculate the value of this contribution to a treatment programme for imprisoned sex offenders, but it is likely to be significant.

b) Recruitment of offenders for the programme

Current practice is to invite all sex offenders in the prison system to apply for a place on the programme when a new group is being set up. This requires little from the offender other than completing a written application form giving his name, offence and release date. Subsequent to this offenders go through an assessment procedure involving a prison review meeting, a clinical interview, and a psychometric assessment. A list of suitable offenders is then drawn up. Priority is given to those offenders who are closest to their release date and who still have sufficient time left to complete the programme.

Very few criteria apply for excluding offenders from the programme.

Offenders who are significantly learning disabled or who are considered seriously emotionally or psychologically disturbed, would be excluded from consideration. A key factor in assessing suitability is readiness to change. There are three broad criteria that apply (McGrath 1991):

a) the offender must acknowledge his having committed the offence
b) the offender must see his offending behaviour as a problem
c) the offender must agree to fully participate in the programme as outlined.

There are undoubtedly good reasons for working with well-motivated offenders in the early stages of a new therapeutic programme for sex offenders (Pithers 1994). The initial stages are critical in determining the acceptance or rejection of the programme by the offender culture. However, there are limitations to an approach that relies exclusively on the intrinsic motivation of offenders to seek treatment. Firstly, only a minority of sex offenders will be so motivated. Our experience over the last six years shows that only 15%-25% of sex offenders apply for a place on the programme. Secondly, there is no way of ensuring that those offenders most at risk of re-offending, and therefore most in need of treatment, in fact avail of it. If treatment programmes are to reach not only a greater number of sex offenders, but also the most dangerous offenders, some extrinsic motivators will be needed to entice offenders into treatment.

On this point Antonowicz and Ross (1994: p. 102), in their study of successful rehabilitation programmes for offenders, state that "only 8% of all successful programs actually were conducted with well-motivated clients. Since 92% of successful programs were actually conducted with offenders who were mandated into the program or enticed by promise of reduction in supervison/control, one must seriously rethink the notion of limiting rehabilitation programs to motivated offenders. Clearly, the offenders who are in greatest need of programs are those who are the least motivated."

c) Brief details of the programme

The current programme is a structured, offence-focused programme, employing a cognitive-behavioural approach, with a relapse prevention component. The design and structure of the present programme is a product of a number of contributions, particularly the programme set up in the UK in the early 1990s (HM Prison Service 1991) and by the programme that preceded it in Arbour Hill, run by the Probation and Welfare Service (Cotter, Geiran, Ryan and Tallon 1991). It has also benefited from more recent feedback from international experts in the area (Pithers 1994), as well as modifications introduced by the programme delivery team, based on its experience over the last number of years.

The aim of the programme is to reduce sexual victimisation in society. This is achieved through enabling offenders to gain increased control over their offending behaviour and thereby reducing the probability of re-offending. The programme is a group-based programme, catering for up to ten offenders at a time. It takes about one year to complete and participation is voluntary. The group meets three times a week for three two-hour group sessions. Group members complete extensive assignments in their cells and have access to individual counselling. Family members or concerned persons of the offenders are given the opportunity to attend a series of seminars as part of the programme.

The programme covers four main areas considered to make important contributions towards reducing re-offending. These are

    i)   Acceptance of responsibility/modification of cognitive distortions

        Here the offender is facilitated in taking full responsibility for his offending behaviour. The cognitive distortions that offenders typically use to justify or minimise their behaviour, and that serve to maintain offending behaviour, are challenged in a respectful and consistent manner. A key component in this process is getting the offender to share with the group the details of his offence(s), including the thoughts and feelings that accompanied it and the planning in which he engaged. Group members are encouraged to challenge what they see as any attempt to rationalise or justify the offence.

    ii)   Victim issues

        Work on victim empathy is aimed at sensitising the offender to the full impact of his abusive behaviour on his victim(s). Inputs from agencies working with victims of abuse are included as part of this process (eg Dublin Rape Crisis Centre; St Clare's Unit, Children's Hospital, Temple Street).

    iii)   Offence decision chain

        In completing his offence decision chain the offender has to outline the detailed sequence of decisions he made in order to commit his sexual offence. The objective is for the offender to be able to "own" this series of decisions that made offending inevitable. In doing this the planning (which frequently can be very subtle) that the offender engaged in is made explicit. It also becomes clear to the offender that, at each point in his decision chain, he could have made alternative decisions that would have enabled him avoid offending.

    iv)   Relapse prevention

        The main focus here is on the offender identifying those factors that put him at risk of re-offending in the future. Having identified them, the offender has to work out, with the help of the group members and group leaders, practical and realistic ways of coping with these factors, so as to minimise as far as possible the risk of re-offending. It is made clear that this is a long-term process involving lifetime change. An increasingly recognised imperative in this process is supporting the offender in identifying positive life goals that he wants to attain and in developing the skills that will be necessary for their attainment (Mann 1999).

DOES TREATMENT WORK?

Marshall et al (1998) commented, in the conclusion to their edited volume in 1998, that "it remains to be unequivocally demonstrated that treating sexual offenders produces reductions in recidivism, although our view is that there are good grounds for optimism." (p 478). In a more detailed review of treatment outcome for sexual offenders published the following year, Marshall et al (1999) reported some of the most encouraging results available to date on the impact of treatment on recidivism. In this review, Marshall et al limited themselves to a consideration of rigorous scientific studies that provide a satisfactory comparison group of untreated offenders. Leaving out studies that constitute appraisals of outmoded treatment approaches, Marshall et al found seven methodologically sound, positive evaluations of current treatment approaches, and one equally sound negative evaluation. Of particular importance, they report clear benefits resulting from prison programmes. These results, they conclude, "should encourage optimism in treatment providers and encourage governments to continue, or begin, to fund treatment programs" (p 162).

No comparable evaluative studies have yet been carried out on Irish sex offender programmes. It is critical that such studies are undertaken and in 1998 a collaborative study between the Psychology Department at University College Dublin and the Department of Justice, Equality and Law Reform was established to evaluate the effectiveness of treatment programmes for imprisoned sex offenders (O'Reilly et al 2000). Currently extensive data is being collected on each of the following three groups. Group one (Treatment Group) is comprised of men who are participating in a treatment programme and have been convicted of sexual offences against children and/or adults. At the conclusion of the study there will be a minimum of thirty men in this group. At present twenty men have completed pre- and post-treatment assessments. Group two (Motivated Untreated Group) are men suitable for participation in the treatment programme, who have applied to take part, but who are not currently participating in treatment due to the limited number of treatment places. These represent a waiting list control group. By the conclusion of the study there will also be a minimum of thirty men in this group. At present nine men in this group have fully completed assessments equivalent in time to pre- and post- treatment. Group three in the study (Unmotivated Untreated Group) is comprised of men who have never applied to take part in the treatment programme. In essence they are unmotivated to participate in treatment. By the conclusion of the study there will also be a minimum of thirty men in this group. At present six men in this group have fully completed assessments equivalent in time to pre- and post- treatment.

This carefully designed study will, in due course, yield a rich source of information on the effectiveness of current interventions with imprisoned sex offenders in Ireland. Certainly, such evaluations should be an integral part of all intervention programmes with sex offenders.

FUTURE DIRECTIONS

Some progress has been made over the last number of years towards meeting the needs of imprisoned sex offenders. There are now two dedicated sex offender programmes operating and there are plans to introduce a new rehabilitative programme for sex offenders to be delivered by multi-disciplinary teams, including prison officers. This should ensure, in time, that all sex offenders, who want treatment, will have access to it.

However, two important problems remain and need to be addressed. Firstly, there is the problem of enticing offenders into treatment, particularly those men who need it most. As long as the programme relies exclusively for its recruits on those who are intrinsically motivated to change their offending behaviour, only a minority of offenders will apply. It is difficult to see how this situation will change in the absence of some form of stimulus for offenders to take part in treatment. One such incentive would be to hold out the possibility of some form of supervised temporary release for suitable offenders who make therapeutic progress on the programme. Not only can programmes operating under these conditions be effective (Antonowicz and Ross 1994), but through the application of such incentives the Correctional Services of Canada have been able to recruit over 90% of sex offenders in federal penitentiaries into treatment programmes.

A second, related problem is the need to provide mandatory follow-up for sex offenders in the community after their release from prison. This is an important aspect of best practice in work with imprisoned sex offenders (Eisenman 1991; Marshall and Pithers 1994). However, the current practice in this jurisdiction of denying sex offenders access to temporary release under the 1960 Criminal Justice Act precludes this possibility. Thus, sex offenders are, effectively, detained in prison until the last day of their sentence, irrespective of whether or not they have made therapeutic progress. This has been the de facto situation for these offenders under all administrations for the last fifteen years. The blanket application of this policy to all sex offenders is flawed. As a consequence of this policy, agencies of the Department of Justice, Equality and Law Reform can have no influence over where an offender lives or works. Nor can they oversee the implementation of the relapse prevention plan drawn up with the offender while he is in treatment.

Many sex offenders serve long sentences and, having done so, adjusting to societal change, in addition to implementing a relapse prevention plan, is difficult. In the absence of mandatory support and supervision a lot of what has been learnt in prison may simply not be put into practice and, in this event, the risk of re-offending is increased. Finding some mechanism whereby treated sex offenders are provided with mandatory follow-up in the community is critical.

REFERENCES

Antonowicz, D.H. and Ross, R.R. (1994), "Essential components of successful rehabilitation programmes for offenders", *International Journal of Offender Therapy and Comparative Criminology* 38, 97-104

Becker, J. (1997), *Why do sex offenders offend?*, Paper presented at Northern Ireland Criminal Justice/NOTA Conference, Bangor, Northern Ireland

Blanchette, K. (1996), *Sex Offender Assessment, Treatment and Recidivism: A Literature Review,* Ottawa: Correctional Services of Canada

Bonta, J. (1997), *Offender Rehabilitation: From Research to Practice* (User Report 1997-01), Ottawa: Public Works and Government Services

Bonta, J. and Cormier, R.B. (1999), "Corrections research in Canada: Impressive progress and promising prospects", *Canadian Journal of Criminology* 41, 235-247

Carr, A. (2000), *What Works with Children and Adolescents? A Critical Review of Psychological Interventions with Children, Adolescents, and their Families,* London: Routledge.

Committee of Inquiry into the Penal System (1985), *Report of the Committee of Inquiry into the Penal System,* Dublin: Stationery Office

Cotter, A., Geiran, V., Ryan, T. and Tallon, M. (1991), *A Therapeutic Programme for Sex Offenders in a Prison Setting,* unpublished report, Probation and Welfare Service, Dublin

Department of Justice (1993), *A Proposal for a Structured Psychological Treatment Programme for Sex Offenders,* Dublin: Stationery Office

Department of Justice, *Annual Report on Prisons and Places of Detention 1988-1993,* Dublin: Stationary Office

Department of Justice, Equality and Law Reform (1998), *Prisons and Places of Detention Annual Statistics for 1994*, Dublin: Stationary Office

Directorate of Inmate Programmes, HM Prison Service (1991), *Treatment Programmes for Sex Offenders in Custody: A Strategy,* London: HMSO

Eisenman, R. (1991), "Monitoring and post-confinement treatment of sex offenders: An urgent need", *Psychological Reports* 69, 1089-1090

Ellis, L. (1989), *Theories of Rape: Inquiries into the Causes of Sexual Aggression,* New York: Hemisphere

Foucault, M. (1967), *Madness and Civilisation,* London: Tavistock

Garda Síochána, Annual Reports 1988-1999, Dublin: Garda Síochána

Geiran, V. (1996), "Treatment of sex offenders in Ireland – the development of policy and practice", *Administration* 44, 136-158

Gendreau, P. and Ross, R.R. (1980), "Effective correctional treatment: Bibliotherapy for cynics", *Crime and Delinquency* 25, 463-489

Hollin, C. (1993), "Advances in the psychological treatment of delinquent behaviour", *Criminal Behaviour and Mental Health* 3, 142-157

Irish Prisons Service (2000), *Report on Prisons and Places of Detention for the Years 1995-1998*, Dublin: Stationery Office

Lalor, K. (1999), "A survey of sexually abusive experiences in childhood amongst a sample of third level students", *Irish Journal of Psychology* 20, 1, 15-27

Laws, R.D., Hudson, S.M and Ward, T. (2000), *Remaking Relapse Prevention with Sex Offenders – A Sourcebook,* Thousand Oaks: Sage

McGrath, R.J. (1991), "Sex-offender risk assessment and disposition planning: A review of empirical and clinical findings", *International Journal of Offender Therapy and Comparative Criminology* 35, 328-350

McGuire, J. (ed.) (1995), *What Works: Reducing Re-offending – Guidelines from Research and Practice,* Chichester: Wiley

McKeown, K., Gilligan, R., Brannick, T., McGuane, B. and O'Riordan, S. (1989), *Child sexual abuse in the Eastern Health Board Area, Ireland, 1988: Volume 1: A statistical analysis of all suspected and confirmed child sexual abuse cases known to the community care teams in the Eastern Health Board and open at any time in 1988*, unpublished report, Dublin: Department of Health

Mann, R.E. (1998), *Relapse prevention? Is that the bit where they told me all the things I couldn't do anymore?,* Paper presented at 17th Annual Conference, Association for the Treatment of Sexual Abusers, Vancouver, British Columbia, Canada

Mann, R. (ed) (1996), *Motivational Interviewing with Sex Offenders,* Hull: NOTA

Marshall, W.L., Anderson, D. and Fernandez, Y. (1999), *Cognitive Behavioural Treatment of Sexual Offenders,* New York, John Wiley and Sons

Marshall, W.L., Fernandez, Y.M., Hudson, S.M. and Ward, T. (eds.), (1998), *Sourcebook of Treatment Programs for Sexual Offenders,* New York: Plenum Press

Marshall, W.L. and Pithers, W.D. (1994), "A reconsideration of treatment outcome with sex offenders", *Criminal Justice and Behaviour* 21, 10-27

Martinson, R. (1974), "What work? Questions and answers about prison reform", *The Public Interest* 10, 22-54

Murphy, Paul, (1998), "A therapeutic programme for imprisoned sex offenders: Progress to date and issues for the future", *Irish Journal of Psychology Special Issue: Understanding, Assessing and Treating Juvenile and Adult Sex Offenders,* 19 (1) 190-207.

O'Reilly, G. (2000), *A Robust Method for the Evaluation of Prison-Based Sex Offender Treatment Programmes,* Paper presented at CEP Conference, Dublin

O'Reilly, G. and Carr, A. (1999), "Child sexual abuse in Ireland: A synthesis of two studies", *Irish Journal of Psychology* 20, 1, 1-14

Prochaska, J.O. and DiClemente, C.O. (1983), "Stages and processes of self-change of smoking: Toward an integrative model of change", *Journal of Consulting and Clinical Psychology* 51, 3, 390-395

Prochaska, J.O. and DiClemente, C.O. (1982), "Transtheoretical psychotherapy: Towards a more integrative model of change', *Psychotherapy: Theory, Research and Practice* 19, 276-278.

Research Team, The, (1990), *Child sexual abuse in Northern Ireland: A research study of incidence,* Northern Ireland: Greystone Press.

Sampson, A. (1992), "Treatment programmes: From theory into practice", in Prison Reform Trust (ed.), *Beyond Containment: The Penal Response to Sex Offending,* London: Prison Reform Trust

Solicitor General of Canada (1990), *The Management and Treatment of Sex Offenders,* Ottawa: Solicitor General

Thornton, D.M. (1987), "Treatment effects on recidivism: A reappraisal of the 'nothing works' doctrine", in B. J. McGurk, D. M. Thornton and M. Williams (eds.), *Applying Psychology to Imprisonment: Theory and Practice,* London: HMSO

Victorian Prison Service (1995), *Statewide Sex Offender Strategy Framework,* Melbourne: Department of Justice

Weinrott, M.R. and Saylor, M. (1991), "Self-report of crimes committed by sex offenders", *Journal of Interpersonal Violence* 6, 286-300

40

Penal Policy and the
Adult Education of Prisoners[*]

Kevin Warner

1 INTRODUCTION

In the United States, Britain and to a lesser extent in some other parts of Europe, penal policy has of late been characterised by massive increases in the use of incarceration, by negative stereotyping of prisoners and by extremely vengeful attitudes. The essential point of this paper is that many of these linked and currently dominant penal approaches (which I title "Anglo-American"), as well as being destructive in themselves, severely narrow and distort the education of inmates. The solution to this problem can begin by connecting with penal perspectives that centre on human dignity, and also by linking correctional/prison education with the insights and practice of progressive adult education. (In this paper I will usually use the European term "prison education" to cover what in North America and elsewhere is called "correctional education".)

The paper begins by exploring in section 2 one perspective that is, in my view, coherent and credible in its description of the role of imprisonment, ie the philosophy inherent in the European Prison Rules (Council of Europe, Strasbourg 1987). The outlook in that European "policy document" complements very well the thinking in a further Council of Europe report, *Education in Prison* (1990), which is analysed in section 3 and which advocates an adult education orientation for the education of those held in custody. There are many earlier US works that

---

[*] A considerably revised version of a paper first published in the *Journal of Correctional Education* 49.3, 1998

can be drawn on to support these alternative views: eg John Dewey's general approach to education (Westbrook 1991), Austin MacCormick's (1931) prescription for correctional education, and Kenyon Scudder's (1952) account of a clear-headed and bold penal initiative at the California Institute for Men, among many others. Such American works will be touched upon rather than examined in detail in this paper, but they do offer powerful challenges to the state of things in American corrections today. The title of Scudder's story, *Prisoners are People*, neatly encapsulates the philosophy that underpinned his efforts and could just as well be used to summarise the European Prison Rules approach.

The underlying assumptions of these writings are greatly at variance with those of the "Anglo-American" approach to penal policy. The "Anglo-American" approach is analysed and criticised in section 4 and an argument made in section 5 that it is close to incompatible with genuine education. Prison education needs to detach itself from such destructive attitudes and practices. Those of us who work for the education of people held in custody have to also be advocates of humane and workable penal policies (bearing in mind that much of what happens at present in prisons is neither). Relating the thinking of adult educators such as Jack Mezirow (1990) to educational work in penal institutions offers guidance and encouragement, not just in the classroom but in how we might deal with the larger system as well; this is the theme of section 6. A concluding section 7 sketches suggestions for "a way forward".

2 PRINCIPLES FOR PENAL POLICY

The European Prison Rules (EPR) are far more than a set of rules or standards. They offer clear principles, and a policy framework, for the use of imprisonment. They represent an adaptation, to specific European conditions and aspirations, of the United Nations Standard Minimum Rules (SMR) for the treatment of prisoners. There is a clear assumption in them that, in general, *prison damages people and should be used as a last resort*, and, where used, the "suffering inherent" in imprisonment should be minimised (EPR 64,65). Tulkens (1998) says that the EPR, following the revisions in 1987, "explain, as it were : if you go on using imprisonment you have at least to try hard to make it as harmless and as positive as possible for the prisoners. Therefore: listen to them, take account of their opinions, make them co-operate and assume responsibilities; on the other hand, do not be over-ambitious as to what can be achieved or what can be promised, but offer prisoners consequently realistic and attainable opportunities, chances, activities and help which meet their needs and stimulate their interests".

Two other crucial characteristics of the EPR philosophy emerge in the above quotation. One is the idea that *there may be some scope in prisons to offer prisoners opportunities to develop themselves,* although this is not to deny "the detrimental effects of imprisonment", nor should the scope for such positive action be exaggerated – the over-riding fact is that prison is usually a destructive process. The other feature of the EPR to be noted is *the advocacy of serious self-administration by the prisoner-based on respect for his or her human dignity* (Rentzmann, 1996). Tulkens says, "What comes to the fore in particular is that prisoners should be listened to and their agreement or willingness ... should be sought in connection with decisions. This means that the prisoner should no longer be seen as an object of treatment but as a responsible subject".

These core features of the EPR may be found in three of the more important rules. The EPR begin with a statement of six principles, the third of which seems to me to go to the heart of the matter:

> The purposes of the treatment of persons in custody shall be such as to sustain their health and self-respect and, so far as the length of sentence permits, to develop their sense of responsibility and encourage those attitudes and skills that will assist them to return to society with the best chance of leading law-abiding and self-supporting lives after their release.

The idea of "treatment" here is clearly quite different from the narrower medical usage of this term. It has both defensive and more positive qualities; it recognises that the negative psychological, social and physical effects of imprisonment must be held in check as much as possible, while whatever openings there may be for personal development must be taken. This dual approach is seen in the elaboration of "treatment objectives" given in rules 64 and 65:

> 64. Imprisonment is by the deprivation of liberty a punishment in itself. The conditions of imprisonment and the prison regimes shall not, therefore, except as incidental to justifiable segregation or the maintenance of discipline, aggravate the suffering inherent in this.
>
> 65. Every effort shall be made to ensure that the regimes of the institutions are designed and managed so as:
>   (a) to ensure that the conditions of life are compatible with human dignity and acceptable standards in the community;
>   (b) to minimise the detrimental effects of imprisonment and the differences between prison life and life at liberty which tend to diminish the self-respect or sense of personal responsibility of prisoners;
>   (c) to sustain and strengthen those links with relatives and the outside community that will promote the best interests of prisoners and their families;
>   (d) to provide opportunities for prisoners to develop skills and aptitudes that will improve their prospects of successful resettlement after release.

3 EDUCATION IN PRISON

The European Prison Rules, then, developed thinking around this idea that the prisoner should be regarded as, in the words of Tulkens, "a responsible subject".

The prisoner's dignity is seen to be respected; the prisoner is seen as a citizen, a member of the community; and is allowed, as far as possible, scope to make choices and to seriously participate in shaping his or her life and activity within the prison. One logical outcome of this approach was to define a very strong role for education within regimes (EPR 77-82): there should be a "comprehensive education programme" in every institution; all prisoners should have access to education; and education "should be regarded as a regime activity that attracts the same status and basic remuneration within the regime as work".

It is interesting to note that while senior prison administrators were working out this policy in Strasbourg in the mid-80s, another Council of Europe "expert group" was, to a large extent independently, coming to conclusions in relation to prison education that are remarkably complementary to the ideas in the EPR. But that Select Committee, which produced the report, *Education in Prison* (1990), took its initial bearings largely from the world of adult education. This section notes how an adult education orientation to the education of prisoners supports and is supported by the "European" penal policy outlined above.

Education in Prison follows the EPR in asserting in its formal recommendation the rights of prisoners to education: "All prisoners shall have access to education ... Education should have no less a status than work within the prison regime ..." The introductory chapter to the fuller "explanatory memorandum" summarises the report: "... two overall complementary themes predominate: firstly, the education of prisoners must, in its philosophy, methods and content, be brought as close as possible to the best adult education in the society outside; secondly, education should be constantly seeking ways to link prisoners with the outside community and to enable both groups to interact with each other as fully and as constructively as possible". (1.5) Thus, the report is not just a statement about education but makes a major assumption as regards penal policy – that the person in prison is still a member of the wider community. In relation to Svenolov Svensson's (1996) crucial question, "Do we have citizens in prison or do we have prisoners?", it asserts, in line with general Council of Europe thinking, that the person incarcerated is still a citizen, still a member of society, and advocates using education to lessen the sense of separation from the wider community.

Seeing the fuller person rather than just the inmate is very much a part of the adult education approach. The Recommendation states, "Education in prison shall aim to develop the whole person, bearing in mind his or her social, economic and cultural context". Such a view contrasts with the one-dimensional perspective in which the student may be seen predominantly as an "offender" and the task then is to address the "offending behaviour"; or in which the focus is restricted to job-training. Aiming "to develop the whole person", on the other hand, greatly opens up the agenda. For a start, it implies a much wider curriculum so that artistic activity, social education, academic study less directed towards vocational outcomes, health and physical education, consciousness raising, can all have a more substantial and central role in the education programme available in prison.

But it is in the way learning is provided, in the adult education methods, that the Council of Europe approach may be most different from more restrictive "correctional" education. The key idea is that of participation, whereby the adult who chooses to study has a significant say as to what to learn, how to learn and in evaluating the experience of learning (Warner 1993). The significant say which an adult education student is entitled to in regard to his or her own learning connects clearly with the "self-administration" in one's own treatment advocated by Rentzmann and Tulkens. Clearly, mandatory education programmes which are increasingly common in US prisons are anathema to good adult education practice.

An adult education approach to the education of prisoners, then, fits very well with the "European" penal policy as outlined above. The two perspectives reinforce each other. This complementarity may be illustrated by looking at the aims of the Prison Education Service in Ireland (Department of Justice 1994), which are to help those under sentence

(i)   to cope with their sentences
(ii) to achieve personal development
(iii) to prepare for life after release
(iv) to establish the appetite and capacity for further education after release.

The first aim, enabling prisoners to cope with the destructive effects of being incarcerated, is fundamental, for the person overwhelmed by prison will be unable to progress in any other way. That aim corresponds very clearly with the EPR stipulation that regimes must seek to "minimise the detrimental effects of imprisonment" (EPR 65). The emphasis on personal development in the second aim is a wider and deeper aspiration than is often the case in other education (let alone penal) settings, but this reflects the adult education emphasis on working with "the whole person" that is also implicit in the EPR. The third and fourth aims, both of which look to the time beyond the sentence, are in tune with the EPR emphasis on developing "skills and aptitudes that will improve their prospects of successful resettlement after release" (EPR 65).

4 THE "ANGLO-AMERICAN" MODEL

But this "European" model of imprisonment is not the one most widely followed these days and would not even be recognised in many parts of Europe. Many prison educators have to grapple with a far less hospitable setting. I depict the alternative model as "Anglo American", and hope it will be understood that this is solely because the most vehement advocations and illustrations of this approach can be found in the United States and England in recent years. Strains of this model can be found virtually everywhere of course; and, on the other hand, there is much progressive practice, that runs counter to the dominant mood, to be found in Britain and the US, even at present.

The Anglo-American model can be characterised as having three key features:

(1) negative stereotyping of those held in prison
(2) vengeful attitudes
(3) massive increases in the use of incaceration.

The model is a set of such linked perspectives, and meshes with superficially simple policy slogans such as "zero tolerance"; "get tough on crime" and "prison works". Fear and the desire for vengeance drive the enormously costly expansion of the prison system. But this policy and the attitudes behind it are based on misunderstanding and misrepresentation of the facts about crime, about those sent to prison and about the effects of imprisonment. Prisoners are demonised, dehumanised, seen as "other" than "us". Grossly untenable presumptions are promoted about those we send to prison. Perceptions about prisoners in general are often inaccurately formed on the basis of a small number of untypical events or people. A critique of the "Anglo-American" model must, therefore, begin with a deconstruction of the hugely distorted perceptions of who are sent to prison.

One of the most obviously incorrect assumptions made about those sent to prison is that they are very violent people; at times the impression is given of unpredictable, irrational and even manic violence. Media and politicians contribute greatly to the promotion of this image. A very prominent Irish politician referred once to the general body of prisoners, saying "These fellows would cut your throat in church and walk off smiling" – a depiction probably true of none of the near 2,000 prisoners incarcerated in Ireland at the time. Whether in Ireland, England or the US, the facts show that only a minority of prisoners held in custody at any one time are sentenced for violent offences. For the US, Irwin and Austin (1994) give a figure of 29.9% of prison admissions (in 1988, based on 35 states) being found guilty of violent crimes. Seventy percent were sentenced for non-violent crimes such as burglary, drugs (possession and trafficking mainly), robbery and public order crimes. Comparable figures for England/Wales and Ireland are 12% and 9% respectively (O'Mahony 1997). Even where the "stock" rather than the "flow" of the prison population is looked at, those convicted of violence (which tends to be broadly defined) are still in the minority: 23% for England, 21% for Ireland and 47% for US state prisons (which figure would, presumably, be lower when county jails are taken into account) (O'Mahony 1997).

A further aspect to the stereotypical public perceptions of those who go to prison has to do with images of their personalities and lifestyles that are promoted by some politicians and by parts of the media. Those sent to prison may not just be presented as predominantly violent, but as "hardened criminals" (the adjective implying severe insensitivity and dehumanisation), or as "career criminals". This latter phrase is interesting in that, like "zero tolerance", it achieved huge usage in the United States before crossing the Atlantic and featuring prominently in the 1997 elections in Britain and Ireland. Perhaps the slavish copying, by Michael Howard and others, from America of even key phrases in their policy statements, well illustrates the paucity of critical thought that lies behind such presentations.

Indeed, like the presumption of violent tendency, Irwin and Austin have shown that the perception of most of those sent to prison as "career criminals" does not hold up to analysis either. In a study of 154 males randomly selected from the intake population of three US states, Irwin and Austin specifically tested the "career criminal" presumption. They found that 19% had engaged in a "crime episode or spree", but had "for an extended period ... lived a relatively conventional life". Fourteen percent were incarcerated for "one-shot crime", never having been "involved in serious crime before the current arrest". Six percent were classified as "derelicts", men who "had completely lost the capacity to live in organised society". Eighteen percent were people who, "though they avoid regular involvement as criminals, are at risk of being arrested because they are on the streets for many hours and police regularly patrol [their] neighbourhoods looking for street criminals". Thus, only a minority (43%) can be classified as "into crime", ie committing crime regularly. However, most (59%) of this group "were convicted of petty crimes ... rather than being vicious predators, most were disorganised, unskilled, undisciplined petty criminals who very seldom engaged in violence or made any significant amount of money from their criminal acts".

What emerges here is a picture much more familiar to educators and others involved in prison systems in many countries – a great proportion of those held in prison are victims of severe social and psychological neglect in the past. To acknowledge this is not to deny the appropriateness of criticising and addressing offending behaviour, but it does lead to a more complex picture than political and media slogans often allow: such acknowledgement is, in fact, a necessary part of the process (to borrow another slogan) of "being tough on crime and tough on the causes of crime". K.J.Lång (1993), the long-serving director of the Finnish prison service, depicted the mass of prisoners in most countries as people "deprived of all chances to develop and use what we can call their stronger parts ... [they] started with very low expectations of success ... experienced domestic and street violence in their childhood ... they are poorly educated and unskilled and have been unemployed for long periods or all of their lives. They live in sub-standard housing and have a wretchedly poor or deprived socio-economic and family background".

The reality then, even in US state prisons, points to no more than a quarter of those incarcerated being classifiable as "career criminals". That reality, as much as offending behaviour, is what educators and others concerned with crime need to focus on, so that real personal and social development can be facilitated. There is a challenge enough in that task, but the gross stereotyping of our clients, in relation to their propensity to violence and their lifestyle, as indicated above, confuses and complicates the picture. It is necessary for prison educators, and colleagues in related fields, to assert this awareness of a different reality.

We also need to be able to locate the negative labelling as part of wider social patterns. The stigmatising of prisoners often goes hand-in-hand with an exaggerated view of the extent of crime and, in particular, an exaggerated sense of things being out of control: a prominent political party in Ireland hyped the situation in its 1997 election literature – "crime is out of control in our cities, towns and countrywide" (in contradiction to any rational analysis of the evidence). It may not be just the offenders, but their families also, who are labelled: Vivien Stern, Secretary-General of Penal Reform International, noted, in the run-up to the British election in the same year, "the competition to scapegoat the families of the poor who cannot control their offspring".

In writings in the British paper, *The Observer*, Peter Beaumont provides analysis of a tendency in many commentaries to identify a new "Dickensian underclass", often, indeed, resurrecting nineteenth century phrases such as "vagabond" and "layabout" and depicting the "undeserving poor" and "dangerous classes". This tendency is evident in the treatment of groups other than offenders also, such as the homeless, single parents and asylum seekers. He quotes the criminologist, Rob Reiner, as seeing "a return to a pre-democratic view that regarded whole classes of society as effectively outlaws". This reverses "150 years of movement ... towards a more inclusive society in which everyone belongs, has equal citizenship and is guaranteed a minimum of rights". David Downes, a colleague of Reiner, speaks of the reintroduction of the "vocabulary of exclusion". He says, "The image that is being created is the lurking menace of the career criminal who lives by preying on society. These are old folk devils that have been resurrected to set alongside our own folk devils, like the mugger and the ram-raider. The label becomes all. Everything else – the causes crime, etc – is wiped out".

I identified such negative, and unfair, stereotyping of the prison population as the first of three key features of the "Anglo-American" model of imprisonment. The second feature – vengeful attitudes by politicians and the public towards those held in custody – follows directly from the first. Dehumanised images of the criminal or prisoner mesh with prejudice against the poor and other racial groups. They engender disdain and fear and allow, even foster, desires for revenge. Vindictive practices then become general within prisons, undermining the EPR principle of "minimising the detrimental effects of imprisonment". Stark illustrations of such attitudes were provided in Britain by the chaining of women prisoners in maternity wards and by the case of Geoffrey Thomas, who remained chained within three hours of his death from stomach cancer.

Such approaches, and the prison overcrowding that accompanies them, have been criticised in Britain not just by penal reformers, but by the very people charged with overseeing the justice system. Derek Lewis, the former director general of the Prison Service in England and Wales, accused the former Home Secretary, Michael Howard, of pandering to a populist "lynch mob mentality". (*The Observer* 29 October 1995). On the point of his retirement as Prisons Inspector, Judge Stephen Tumin warned, "that the Government's obsession with security in place of humanity was transforming the British prison system into something resembling Nazi concentration camps". (*The Observer,* 29 October 1995). Criticising Howard's policies of promoting longer sentences, mandatory sentences and generally greater use of incarceration, the Lord Chief Justice, Lord Taylor, pointed up the sheer ineffectiveness of Howard's approach: "I do not believe", he said, "that the threat of longer and longer periods of imprisonment across the board will deter habitual criminals. What deters them is the likelihood of being caught, which at the moment is small" (*The Independent* 13 October 1995).

Built on misleading stereotypes, fuelled by attitudes of vengeance and fear, the most dramatic outcome of the "Anglo-American" model is what I have called its third key feature – the massive increase in the use of incarceration. Prison populations are escalating throughout the US and, from a much lower base, throughout most of Europe. I wish to conclude the analysis of this model by dwelling on the sheer ineffectiveness of this expansion. Lord Taylor pointed this out in the above quotation in relation to its lack of deterrent effect. And yet the costs – in human, social and financial terms – of this policy are enormous.

In the discussion of the EPR, we noted that prison is inherently damaging to the individual and noted the wisdom of keeping such damage to a minimum. But current "Anglo-American" policies, both in their greater use of imprisonment and their promotion of more destructive forms of imprisonment, are creating far more bitter, alienated and damaged people. This contributes to a more divisive society, where crime and other social problems are likely to worsen. And the financial resources of society are swallowed up in such developments, as both the capital and running costs of even the worst of prisons tend to be great. Thus, the State of California now spends more on its prisons than on its universities. Irwin and Austin highlight, in particular, the destructive nature of the element of vindictiveness in this whole scenario: "Ultimately, vindictiveness erects barriers between people, isolates them, and prevents them from constructing the co-operative, communal social organisations that are so necessary for meaningful, satisfying human existence. Ironically, it is just these social structures that contain the true solution to our crime problem".

5 ISSUES FOR PRISON EDUCATION

Section 2 above presented what I believe is a coherent and credible penal philosophy, expressed through the European Prison Rules. Section 3 described an adult education approach to the development of those held in prison and I argued that this is very complementary to the outlook on prisons expressed in the EPR. Section 4 described an altogether different situation whereby penal policies are built on negative stereotyping of inmates, expressions of vengeance and excessive use of incarceration. Attempting to provide genuine education in this latter setting gives rise to enormous difficulties and dilemmas, and these are detailed in this section. Distortions of, and limitations to, the education of men and women held in prison may arise in several ways under the "Anglo American" model:

(i) a reduced concept of the incarcerated person, arising from the stereotyping, means that there is less recognition of his or her positive potential

(ii) a reduced concept of the community or society, which excludes rather than includes prisoners and others associated with them, hampers education that aims to integrate the learners with others

(iii) the content of education programmes tends to become narrowed due to a concentration on "criminogenic factors" and for other reasons; some of the very creative methodologies of adult education tend to become incompatible with the punitive attitudes – especially methodologies which respect the student, and his or her experience, allow "open spaces" and foster significant participation by students in shaping their own education

(iv) expanded prison populations restrict the education available to each prisoner as both space and resources become tighter.

These issues will be considered in turn.

The first two issues – a more narrow perception of the person held in prison, and seeing that person as "other" than us and not part of our society, arise directly from the stigmatising of the prisoner discussed earlier. We are invited to see the "offender" but not the "whole person"; to see one dimension, in terms of criminality, but not the more complex product of multiple social forces; to see the inadequate person but not the positive qualities and potential. Thus reduced in terms of his or her humanity, that person is all the more easily excluded from social membership. Yet, any concept of education worth its salt has at its heart some vision of full development of the person, and of that person in relation to the wider society. Such ambitions, so fundamental to genuine education, are clearly hampered in a climate of these penal policies.

A third way in which the Anglo-American outlook inhibits education is in the restriction of the content of education. Not only has education a less important role (and severe curtailing of prison education in England and the US in the 90s has been well documented), but the kind of education allowed is affected. A very dramatic illustration of this process is provided from Canada by Stephen Duguid (1997): renowned and clearly successful university courses in British Columbia federal prisons were terminated in 1993 by the Correctional Service of Canada in favour of "programming ... which more directly targets the criminogenic factors facing offenders", as the Deputy Commissioner put it. The criminogenic factors that were seen to lead to crime are summarised by Duguid as "substance abuse, anti-social and violent behaviour, illiteracy, mental illness, sexual deviancy and strong pro-criminal orientation". He quotes the Deputy Commissioner as saying, "Programming must be linked to meeting offenders' needs, and particularly those needs which if addressed will result in pro-social behaviour ... All programs should have a correctional orientation and correctional goals".

The most fundamental problem with this approach is that it fails to see education as a human right. A widely accepted expression of such a right is contained in the declaration which defined the right to learn at the 4th International Unesco Conference on Adult Education. The right to learn is

- the right to read and write
- the right to question and analyse
- the right to imagine and create
- the right to read about one's own world and to write history
- the right to have access to educational resources
- the right to develop individual and collective skills.
  (Quoted in *Education in Prison* 2.2)

If we see prisoners as members of our society we envisage them having such rights also, especially given the lack of educational opportunity most of them have had in earlier life. But, if we restrict our sense of them only to, or largely to, their image as "offenders", then we correspondingly restrict their education.

There are two further problems with such a policy. The first is that it represents very poor psychology. Even were one to be confined to "correctional goals" as described above, might there not be other ways of achieving them? Anger-management courses may be appropriate for some in prison, but might not art, for example, prove just as effective? Likewise, art or university study or any number of other subjects can be priceless "therapy" for many seeking to overcome substance abuse. It is a question of, at times, "by indirection finding direction out". Ideally, the direct and indirect methods – the anger-management or substance-abuse course and the art – should be available, to be pursued, alternatively or in combination, according as the prisoner-student judges his or her needs.

Duguid quotes T.A.A. Parlett as saying "to bluntly teach moral knowledge would be rejected by the inmates". One has to wonder just how effective many of the programmes with a "correctional orientation" really are, given that so many inmates are obliged or pressurised into following them. Many courses that seek to "address offending behaviour" seem far too frontal and morally directive in their approach, which must be seen as a poor technique in any adult teaching setting, let alone with adults deeply alienated from authority and given to low self-image such as prisoners often are. Parlett's point is asserted by Stephen Brookfield (1990) in relation to adult learners generally: "in assisting learners to explore their assumptive worlds, the last thing that educators should do is to ask learners directly what assumptions they operate under in various aspects of their lives. Such generalised questioning often confuses or intimidates. A far more fruitful approach is to work from the specific to the general".

One other problem with the Canadian Deputy Commissioner's narrow focussing in on "criminogenic factors" is that concentration on the personal, to the exclusion of the political or structural, dimension of criminal behaviour misses half of the picture. It is not a denial of personal responsibility, but rather an acknowledgement of part of the reality that prisoners often instinctively know, to explore in some way how violence or drug abuse or other anti-social behaviour is in part shaped by the power relations in society.

Some of the insights of Mechthild Hart (1990) in relation to consciousness raising by women, especially the capacity of the "personal" and the "political" to illuminate each other, may apply to prisoners also, in so far as they are a marginalised group in society dealing with great difficulties. She sees conscious-ness raising as a form of transformative learning "for social groups that have been considered marginal, that have been denied full social membership, and whose reality and experience is not reflected in mainstream analysis and theories. Consciousness raising is a process of reclaiming social membership .... The full cycle of consciousness raising therefore includes the actual experience of power on an individual level, a theoretical grasp of power as a larger social reality, and a practical orientation towards emancipatory action". Just as women needed to reject the dominant image in society as to who they were, as to what it meant to be a woman, likewise prisoners must (among other things) challenge and rise beyond the dominant image given by the "Anglo-American" ideology as to who they are. The wider and the freer the curriculum is, the greater is the chance that they will progress in that direction.

In analysing the effect of the "Anglo-American" approach on the content of prison education just now, the discussion, perhaps inevitably, also moved into the area of teaching methodology. The impact on methodology was the fourth issue listed earlier. Adult education is perhaps most distinguished by the way learning happens. Classically, real participation by the student in shaping the learning, a valuing of the student's life experience and a wide personal development aspect are among the key features of adult education. Each of these characteristics envisage "the whole person" and, in particular, imply genuine respect for the student. The penal approach being discussed, however, is manifestly lacking in such respect for its clients. Thus, there is inevitable tension between a genuine adult education approach and "Anglo-American" penal policies. There is inevitable pressure to adopt ways of teaching that are less respectful and less holistic – and, therefore, less effective.

Nowhere is the creative methodology of adult education more debased than in the practice of mandatory education courses, especially mandatory literacy programmes. An essential principal of adult education is that the student should have a real say in shaping his or her education, and that principle is affronted where the "education" is obligatory – all the more so in a penal context where the classes may then be seen as part of the punishment. Given that literacy difficulty among adults is as much a matter of negative self-image and sense of powerless-ness as it is to do with technical problems, a mandatory approach may well worsen things. If the education offered is even partly adequate, prisoners will opt for it in large numbers. Such is the experience in many European countries, at least. In Ireland, over 50% of all prisoners voluntarily take part in education. That figure reaches 60% or 70%, or even more, in prisons with good educational facilities.

Clearly, the more oppressive and demeaning the penal context in which education is offered, the more difficult will it be for that learning to be genuinely "transformative" and "emancipatory" ; but it is not impossible. Heaney and Horton (1990) state: "Even within hegemonic institutions, open spaces can be found wherein educators play upon the system's embedded contradictions and align themselves with movements for change". The Council of Europe report, *Education in Prison*, also advocates "a degree of autonomy for the education sector" within prisons. It asserts that it is appropriate that "some leeway or discretion be given to those involved in prison education in the way they approach their work."

The fifth way in which the Anglo-American model impacts negatively on education arises directly from the excessive use of incarceration. This happens in several ways. First of all, since building and running additional and enlarged prisons tends to be very costly, even in the most spartan of regimes, activities such as education often suffer in the competition for scare finance. In England, cost-cutting combined with an expanding prison system have been associated with severe cutbacks in prison education. (*Times Educational Supplement*, 20 October 1995). And even where the resources for education can be "ring-fenced", it is often extremely difficult to ensure education expands in pace with the increase in prison population. At times, the very accommodation used for educational activities will be diverted to use as living space for prisoners or for some other function to do with the administration of the prison. A less obvious, but none-the-less negative, impact of overcrowding is that it is far more difficult to learn when personal space – whether in a cell, a dormitory or recreation area – is reduced: in Ireland we have found that "doubling-up" in cells has resulted in heretofore serious students dropping out of university courses.

6 TRANSFORMATIVE LEARNING

Much has been made above of the richness offered by an "adult education approach". As with any other tradition, adult education may vary in its emphasis around fairly common core principles. Reference has already been made to Mezirow who, with associates, has contributed greatly in recent times to the theory of adult education. This penultimate section will briefly touch on some of that writing as an indication of the kind of issues with which I believe those concerned with the education of prisoners, like their colleagues in other adult education fields, should be centrally engaged.

A key concept for Mezirow (1990 a) is that of "meaning perspectives", that is the structure of presuppositions that we use to interpret experience. One's meaning perspectives are mostly uncritically acquired in childhood, but they may also be more formally learned. "Critical reflection" is a process in adult education (and outside education also) by which a person challenges the validity of his or her own presuppositions which may lead to "perspective transformation"; these can be individual, group or collective. Mezirow says:

> Perspective transformation is the process of becoming critically aware of how and why our presuppositions have come to constrain the way we perceive, understand, and feel about our world; of reformulating these assumptions to permit a more inclusive, discriminating, permeable, and integrative perspective; and of making decisions or otherwise acting upon these new understandings.

Fostering Critical Reflection in Adulthood is a text in which Mezirow and colleagues describe programmes and methods in a wide range of settings through which critical reflection can be developed and lead to "transformative learning". Because, as Mezirow says, we all find it difficult to free ourselves of bias, "our greatest assurance of objectivity comes from exposing an expressed idea to rational and reflective discourse .... No need is more fundamentally human than our need to understand the meaning of our experiences. Free, full participation in critical and reflective discourse may be interpreted as a basic human right".

In a prison education context, this concept of free discourse again implies "an open space" free from coercion and "a degree of autonomy within the education sector". An adult education approach will try to deliver such conditions. Approaches too close to, or too dominated by, what I have called "Anglo-American" penal policy will be less likely to ensure there is enough scope for imprisoned people to explore and change at the deep level envisaged by Mezirow.

Other features of the type of learning envisaged by Mezirow throw up similar interesting issues in a prison context. Mezirow expects educators to provide learners with "skillful emotional support and collaborate as co-learners" – again requiring a situation where there is mutual respect and a democratic spirit. Such conditions favourable to significant learning seem to me much more likely under regimes described by the EPR or by Scudder than under some of the current oppressive regimes that are built on attitudes that stereotype and which fail to respect.

For all their proclamations about seeking behavioural change, many "criminogenic"-focused courses, I suspect, lead to only superficial change: prisoners jump through the required hoops because life is more bearable for them if they do so. What adult education as envisaged by Mezirow is about is a process that leads to genuine change in the fundamental assumptions a person holds. Such growth, while brought about by educational aims, meets the kind of "correctional goals" referred to earlier in relation to Canada. My guess is that – because it is more respectful, more genuinely participative and works with people on a wider and deeper level – such adult education approaches beat the "criminogenic" ones even at the latter's own game.

Reference was made in the previous section to Hart's essay in Mezirow's book on consciousness raising among women as a form of transformative learning. I made the point that prisoners, as women did, need to challenge and rise beyond the established notion of who they are. Clearly, there are important differences between the situations of women or ethnic minorities and that of prisoners, not least the fact that men who are sent to prison can often themselves be oppressors, especially of women. Nevertheless, there can be illuminating parallels also, and those in prison often belong to other groupings for whom consciousness raising is seen as an appropriate process, such as ethnic minorities, the poor, and those with literacy difficulties.

Much imagery nowadays depicts people in prison one-dimensionally: as perpetrators of crime. This is true (although, as we have seen, often overstated), and this criminality is a reality that needs to be addressed. But it is not the whole truth and many in this population are oppressed people also, due to discrimination, poverty, educational and other injustice. Therefore the consciousness raising process is appropriate for them, so that they can have the opportunity, in Hart's words, of "re-evaluating and re-interpreting their own existence" and see that many difficulties are not a result of personal failure, but are "rooted in structures", in the "power relations" of society. Consciousness raising may begin with personal experience but this becomes "generative" of wider themes. As Hart says:

> It ignites around the theme of oppression, presupposes a certain view about knowledge and knowing that empowers rather than extinguishes the individual

knower, and calls for a relationship between theory and practice that begins with an, however vaguely felt or articulated, acknowledgment of power and finishes with a systematic understanding of the nature and complexity of the entire power-bound social reality. To "raise consciousness" means to arrive at such an awareness and to anchor the process of becoming aware in individual reality rather than in analyses and theories that were produced elsewhere.

A prison education, then, that is in touch with developments in progressive adult education out in the community will be grappling with such issues, asking how the creativity of such approaches may be tapped within prison settings, while also enabling the learners to grow in their capacity to take personal responsibility for their criminality, their oppression of others, their addiction problems. Indeed, addressing in education the "personal" and the "political" are not opposing emphases, but complementary aspects of the one transformation. For example, it is credible that education providers might help prisoners come to recognise "the futility of a criminal life " but at the same time respect and give a more legitimate outlet to aspects of the prisoner's culture that can be seen as positive, or at least acceptable, such as "a critical view of authority, anger at social injustice, solidarity with one another in the face of adversity, etc "(quotations are from the Council of Europe report, *Education in Prison*, 4.9). Drawing on the dynamic of good adult education outside the prison, and seeking to create the same energy within, raises issues that may take some working out. But this at least should be the focus of our work. The "criminogenic" focus, which is linked to the "Anglo-American" perspective, is far too narrow and distorting; its main fault is that it does not go beyond the personal to the social dimension in seeking to resolve problems, and it risks reinforcing negative self-image and being a disempowering process.

If we are to see the world within the prison as a part of that outside, then prison educators cannot ignore the linkages between the work they and their students are engaged in and larger social movements. To illustrate this point I will mention how I see some of the efforts in prison education in Ireland connecting with developments on the outside. Many of these linkages, I believe, will have parallels in other countries.

(i)   Many prisoners, especially in Dublin, are heroin abusers, and a considerable amount of educational effort is directed to helping them resolve their addiction problems. The heroin problem is mainly confined to the poorest communities, from which these prisoners come, but in recent years these communities have organised to resist pushers and build alternative outlets for their young people in particular. Obviously, this kind of community action can offer help, support and "vision" to the prisoner addicts.

(ii) Much "social education" in prisons is directed towards enabling men to change their role in relation to others, eg learning to share parenting and having more equal relationships with partners. This development may be seen as but a part of larger change in society in the respective roles of men and women.

(iii) Some education courses offer prisoners an alternative way to crime to express their opposition to the status quo in society. This is particularly true of sociology, political and social studies – even of art in some circumstances. Such study enables prisoners to feel an identity with particular political positions or social movements. And while prisoners tend to be anti-establishment in such expressions, connectedness with developments in society can also apply for those who learn to associate with more conventional views and thereby see ways of redirecting their energies – business studies students come to mind!

(iv) Growth in participation in adult education is often associated with wider social change. In some respects, adult education opportunities have expanded in Ireland recently, linked perhaps to many kinds of change in society. Prisons and prisoners are not immune to such developments and pro-education attitudes outside encourage and facilitate participation within prisons. This happens in many ways: family or friends engaging in education in the community may urge the prisoner to do likewise; on a wider level, education becomes "fashionable"; the fact that there are now more openings to continue learning after release encourages participation within.

In the "Closing Note" to his book Mezirow envisages adult educators "committed to encourage the opening of public spheres of discourse and to actively oppose social and cultural constraints that impede free, full, participation in discursive learning". The disconnection of the prison from society, and the prisoner from his or her humanity, which has been encouraged by the "Anglo-American" outlook, has contributed in some cases to a prison education that is not as in touch as it should be with "the public spheres of discourse", with happenings in general in the outside world and with developments in adult education. A narrow criminogenic approach to prison education, in particular, misses the opportunity to develop awareness and understanding of society at large; as such, this approach represents one of those impediments to "free, full participation in discursive learning". The work of Mezirow and colleagues was explored here to suggest the issues to which prison or correctional education may not be giving enough attention.

7 CONCLUSION : A WAY FORWARD

In this brief conclusion, I touch upon the main themes of this paper by pointing to four areas where it is necessary to develop attitudes and action if we are to meet the challenge posed by the penal policies I have criticised and ensure authentic education within humane and effective regimes.

One, prison or correctional educators cannot remain isolated or neutral in the face of current debates about penal policies. We must assert, in the penal context, those values consistent with good education and, inevitably, that will entail challenging the misrepresentations and destructiveness inherent in many current policies and practices.

Two, we must actively work from an inclusive concept of society which regards those in prison as still being members of the community at large. Education offers enormous scope for promoting "interaction with the community", as illustrated throughout *Education in Prison*. The value of such interaction is two-fold. On the one hand, it provides for prisoners a measure of "normality" and validates their sense of being members of society and (where the contact has a specifically educational purpose) their sense of being learners like any others. On the other hand, people from outside prisons who engage in meaningful interaction with prisoners have much to learn themselves, not least in recognising that so many of the stereotypes about those incarcerated are perversions of the truth.

Three, the education of prisoners should be guided mainly by the values and practice of adult education. This is the view taken in *Education in Prison*: "... professional integrity requires teachers and other educators working in prisons, like those in other professions, to take their primary aims, the underlying orientation, from within their own professional field" – and, in that Council of Europe report, that field is seen as adult education. In the American context, Austin MacCormick (1931), one of the founders of the Correctional Education Association, strongly advocated a similar view many years earlier: "Education of prisoners is fundamentally a problem of adult education, taking the term in its European sense .... We need to stress the normality rather than the abnormality of our prisoner-students, to apply standard educational practice to the problem rather than to try to develop a special educational technique designed for the criminal". MacCormick states: "education for adult prisoners has an aim and a philosophy. Its philosophy is to consider the prisoner as primarily an adult in need of education and only secondarily as a criminal in need of reform. Its aim is to extend to prisoners as individuals every type of educational opportunity that experience or sound reasoning shows may be of benefit or of interest to them ...." It is the argument of much of this paper that the inversion of the MacCormick philosophy (seeing criminals before potential learners) has led to much confusion and damaging policies. Connecting with the insights and developments of adult education, especially as outlined by writers such as Mezirow, offers educators in prisons scope for very fruitful work. And, the values of adult education tend also to be those needed for a credible and ethical penal policy.

Four, (the corollary of the above point) educators of prisoners, and organisations and institutions of which they are part, need to maintain and build bridges with individuals, groups and organisations engaged in the most creative adult education work out in the community.

The approach outlined here is premised on the view that "prisoners are people", as Scudder says, and that, to quote Tulkens, they have the capacity to become "responsible subjects" and (to conclude with the words of MacCormick) "be fitted to live more competently, satisfyingly and co-operatively as members of society".

REFERENCES

Beaumont, Peter, "Rebirth of the dangerous classes", in *The Observer*, 11 August 1996

Brookfield, Stephen (1990), "Using Critical Incidents to Explore Learners" Assumptions", in Mezirow, Jack and Associates, *Fostering Critical Reflection in Adulthood* (Jossey-Bass, San Francisco, 1990)

Council of Europe (1987), *European Prison Rules* (Council of Europe, Strasbourg)

Council of Europe (1990), *Education in Prison* (Council of Europe, Strasbourg)

Department of Justice (1994), *The Management of Offenders,* (Stationery Office, Dublin)

Duguid, Stephen (1997), "Cognitive Dissidents Bite the Dust – The Demise of University Education in Canada's Prisons", *Journal of Correctional Education*, vol. 48, issue 2, June 1997

Hart, Mechthild U. (1990), "Liberation through Consciousness Raising," in Mezirow and Associates, *op cit*

Irwin, John and Austin, James (1994), *It's About Time: America's Imprisonment Binge* (Wadsworth, Belmont, CA)

Lang, K.J. (1993), "What kind of prisoners do we meet in the 1990s", in *Beyond the Walls*, Report from the EPEA European International Conference on Prison Education, Sigtuna, Sweden (Swedish Prison and Probation Administration, Norrkiping)

Mezirow, Jack (1990a), "How Critical Reflection Triggers Transformative Learning", in Mezirow and Associates, *op cit*

Mezirow, Jack (1990b), "Conclusion: Towards Transformative Learning and Emancipatory Education", in Mezirow and Associate, *op cit*

MacCormick, Austin H. (1931), *The Education of Adult Prisoners* (The National Society of Penal Information, New York)

O'Mahony, Paul (1997), *Mountjoy Prisoners; A Sociological and Criminological Profile* (Department of Justice, Dublin)

Scudder, Kenyon J. (1952), *Prisoners are People* (Doubleday and Co., Garden City, NY)

Stern, Vivien (1997), "Criminal Waste of Money", in *The Guardian*, 5 March 1997

Svensson, Svenolov (1996), "Imprisonment – A Matter of Letting People Live or Stay Alive? Some Reasoning from a Swedish Point of View", *Journal of Correctional Education,* vol. 47, issue 2, June 1996

Tulkens, Hans H. (1998), "The Concept of Treatment in the European Prison Rules", *Prison Information Bulletin*, No. 11, June 1988 (Council of Europe, Strasbourg)

Warner, Kevin (1993), "Working through an Adult Education Model: Prison Education in Ireland", *Yearbook of Correctional Education 1993* (Correctional Education Association/Center for the Study of Correctional Education, San Bernardino, CA)

Westbrook, Robert B. (1991), *John Dewey and American Democracy* (Cornell University Press, Ithaca, NY)

41

Restorative Justice

Bill Lockhart

WHAT IS RESTORATIVE JUSTICE?

Let me start with a true but much paraphrased story. Some years ago I met with a well-known solicitor to talk about restorative justice. He told me about how he had unwittingly strayed into restorative justice without really knowing it.

One night his up-market car was stolen, at some distress to himself. Some time later the car was recovered and the police informed him that they had caught one of the culprits. When told his name the solicitor realised that he knew the young man, in fact he had defended him in court on previous charges and knew quite a bit about his background. He decided that there was little point in this young man being brought to court again, so he contacted a probation officer and asked if she could arrange for a meeting between him and the young man to be facilitated. The meeting went ahead and after hearing about the impact of his crime on the solicitor the young man apologised for his behaviour and undertook to make some reparation and change his behaviour.

Some six months later the solicitor was at home one evening waiting for a "carry out" meal to be delivered. A taxi man rang his door bell. When he answered the door, he was asked by the taxi driver to confirm his identity. When he had done this the taxi driver said he had someone in his cab who would like to meet the solicitor. He then called forward an elderly woman who was holding the ordered "carry out" food. She offered the food to him and said she would like him to receive it as a gift from her family. She then explained that she was the grandmother of the boy who had stolen his car. She wanted to thank him for all that he had done for her grandson. She said that had her grandson gone to court he would almost certainly have gone to prison and would have continued down a slippery slope. But since the meeting with the solicitor he had really changed, he changed his friends and was now doing very well, much to the relief of his family.

The solicitor had stumbled into the field of restorative justice much to the benefit of all concerned!

There is no doubt that there has been considerable interest in the development of restorative justice worldwide in recent in recent years. Much of this interest stems from a disillusionment with traditional methods of dispensing justice – particularly the retributive system which is preoccupied with handing out punishment and often fails to meet the needs of the victim, the offender and the community. The retributive system is massively expensive and seen to be increasingly ineffective in reducing crime and giving participants a sense that justice is being done.

Much of the recent interest in restorative justice comes from North America, New Zealand and Australia, but other regions are showing increasing interest, including South Africa, many western European countries and also the UK and Ireland. This is evidenced by the Crime and Disorder Act of 1998 in England and Wales which introduced the reparation order as part of its youth justice reform package and in the Republic of Ireland by the new Children Act (2001) which brings in the concept of family conferencing as part of its youth justice procedures.

There is now a vast literature on restorative justice – including a growing research base. Seminal writers have been Howard Zehr (1990) in North America and John Braithwaite (1989) in Australia with his concept of "reintegrative shaming". Jim Considine from New Zealand has also written helpfully and inform-atively. In his book *Restorative Justice: Healing the Effects of Crime* (1995) he explains that restorative justice is not a new concept and traces its roots to the justice system of Maori and other indigenous peoples, to Celtic culture and to the biblical concept of justice (particularly that found in Deuteronomy and Leviticus). This he does in a rather romanticised and idealistic manner; but there is no doubt there is some force in his arguments.

"Restorative Justice" means different things to different people – its modern practice developed from the victim-offender mediation movement which began in Canada and the United States in the early 1970s, and is used to cover a variety of practices that seek to respond to crime in a more constructive way than the more conventional criminal justice approaches. It has been defined as a process "whereby all the parties with a stake in a particular offence come together to resolve collectively how to deal with the aftermath of the offence and its impli-cations for the future" (Marshall 1999). It concentrates on restoring and repairing the relationship between the offender, victim and the community at large.

It is worth spending a few moments going over some of the key distinguishing contrasts, which Howard Zehr (1990) makes in his book *Changing Lenses*, between retributive justice and restorative justice. He in fact lists thirty-four contrasts, but I have chosen just a few by way of example.

Table 1: understanding of justice

Retributive Lens	**Restorative Lens**
Blame-fixing central	Problem solving central
Focus on past	Focus on future
Needs secondary	Needs primary
Adversarial	Dialogue normative
Imposition of pain considered normative	Restoration and reparation normative
Restitution rare	Restitution normal
Offender denounced	Harmful act denounced
Justice as right rules	Justice as right relationships
Assumes win-lose outcomes	Makes possible win-win outcomes

There are a number of key attributes underpinning criminal justice-based restorative justice which tend to be absent from the more conventional approaches, namely

- the principle of inclusivity
- the balance of interests
- non-coercive practice
- problem solving orientation.

Restorative approaches are "inclusive" in that they take account of the interests of victims, offenders and, sometimes, the wider community in addition to the public interest in deciding how best to deal with a case; they extend the range of those who are entitled to participate in the process of dealing with the offender; and they extend the range of potential outcomes of the process to include restoration for the victim and reintegration of the offender into the community.

Restorative approaches are more sensitive to the need to strike an appropriate balance between the various interests at stake, including those of the victim and the offender, as well as the public interest. The restorative justice process is not itself a tribunal of fact: if guilt is disputed, it is for the court to decide. The final attribute of restorative justice is that it often involves a problem-solving orientation that is forward looking, aims to prevent future offending, and goes beyond dealing with the aftermath of the particular crime.

Although approaches differ, as a research digest (Dignan and Lowey 2000) makes clear, restorative justice is often based on three elements:

- engaging with offenders to try to bring home the consequences of their actions and an appreciation of the impact they have had on the victims of their offence
- encouraging and facilitating the provision of appropriate forms of reparation by offenders, towards either their direct victims (provided they agree) or the wider community
- seeking reconciliation between the victim and the offender where this can be achieved, and striving to reintegrate offenders within the community.

It is worth saying a few words about the main variants or approaches for delivering restorative justice. These include victim-offender mediation (VOM), sentencing circles and family group or community conferencing.

Victim-offender mediation is believed to have originated in Canada in 1974; it was heavily influenced by the Mennonite Christian denomination which promotes peace-building and conflict resolution. It involves the quest for reconciliation between victim and offender and a process of dialogue between victims and offenders relating to the offence in the presence of a trained mediator. It offers victims the chance to tell offenders about the physical, emotional and financial impact that their offence may have caused, and gives them an opportunity to put unanswered questions to the offender.

Outcomes can include: an apology to the victim for the harm caused, reparation of various forms, including financial recompense, work for or on behalf of the victim, specific undertakings in relation to behaviour (for example to take counselling or treatment), or a mix of all three.

Sentencing circles were developed in Canada (see Stuart 1997). They bring together victims and their supporters, offenders and their supporters, judge and court personnel, prosecutor, defence lawyer, police and all community members who have an interest. The aim is to work consensually to devise an appropriate sentencing plan to meet the needs of all interested parties. Sentencing circles have been tried in some Canadian provinces and in some US states, such as Minnesota.

Family group (or community) conferencing emerged in New Zealand and Australia in the late 1980s and early 1990s. It has a number of differences from victim-offender mediation. Firstly, whereas VOM participation is normally limited to the victim, offender conferencing encourages the participation of a much wider group, including those who are concerned for the welfare of the victim or offender, and those who may contribute to a solution to the problem presented by the offence. There are two principal variants of the conferencing model.

The first is the family group conferencing (FGC) approach which originated in New Zealand. It is now an integral part of the youth justice system there (applying to 14-17 year olds inclusive) and enshrined in legislation. It has a variety of goals, a number of which accord with a restorative justice approach. These include: an emphasis on young offenders paying for their wrong-doing in an appropriate way; the involvement of families and offenders in decision making arising from the offending; the participation of victims in finding solutions; and consensus decision making. There are both pre-prosecution and court level systems operating in New Zealand. The FGC has a central role in both systems.

The second main conferencing model grew from a scheme implemented in a police district of Wagga Wagga, New South Wales. It was much influenced by John Braithwaite's (1989) theory of "reintegrative shaming" . It was developed by Terry O'Connell of the New South Wales police. This model is very much police led, in that the police decide which cases are appropriate for conferencing, convene the conferences, and facilitate the conference. The conference itself is carefully scripted (unlike the New Zealand model); this is to help ensure consistency and to see that the restorative nature of the conference is maintained, even though those delivering it might have been unfamiliar with it and be relatively untrained. The police-led model tends to be very offence focused, whereas the New Zealand model tends to be more holistic and takes a wider view of the needs of the victim and offender. There has been much criticism of the police-led model – essentially this takes the form that the police have too much control of the process and are playing conflicting roles.

There have now been a number of evaluations of the family group conferencing approach. These include an attempt to review existing empirical evidence in relation to restorative justice approaches by Braithwaite (1997). He looked at such themes as

- victim and offender participation rates
- victim "restoration" measures
- victim satisfaction with restorative processes
- offender satisfaction with restorative processes and outcomes
- impact on re-offending
- "balance of interests"
- restorative justice and the community

Space does not allow me to go into his findings in any depth. However, a few points are worth noting. The available research consistently shows that a majority of victims are willing to meet with their offenders, *provided* that they are adequately informed of the arrangements and that these are convenient. Evaluations consistently report that a high proportion of cases result in an agreement being reached and that there are high levels of compliance with the agreement (ranging from 70-100 per cent; Marshall 1999). In general, evaluation studies show that a majority of victims are satisfied with both restorative processes and the outcomes they secure. Restorative justice evaluations invariably report exceedingly high satisfaction ratings for offenders, who are much more likely than victims to feel that the process and outcome were fair.

The question is often asked about re-offending rates. Frequently this presupposes that this is the most important outcome of the process. Yet many of us fail to ask about the reconviction rates after retributive processes such as imprisonment. It seems to me that satisfaction for both victim and offender, at an emotional and practical level, is as important and valid an issue as their perception that justice has been dispensed.

Nonetheless, Maxwell and Morris (1996) in their evaluation of family group conferencing in New Zealand conclude that the recidivism recorded in their follow-up of conferenced cases was "certainly no worse" than that of similar offenders prior to the conferencing reforms. This seems to be broadly in line with other studies of recidivism, although some more recent studies (see, for example, Hayes and Prenzler 1998) are giving more grounds for optimism. Moreover, a more sophisticated statistical analysis of the New Zealand data relating to the same cohort of conferenced offenders (Maxwell and Morris 1999) has suggested that what happens during a family group conference can have a predictive influence on the likelihood of subsequent re-offending frequently reducing that likelihood.

It is worth quoting some of the conclusions from Maxwell and Morris (1999). Interviews were carried out with young people and their parents six and a half years after a family group conference had taken place. The interviews explored issues such as early childhood experiences, the impact of the family group conference and subsequent life events. Re-offending was assessed on the basis of court records of convictions and the sample classified into groups of persistently reconvicted, not re-convicted and others. Multivariate statistical strategies were used to identify significant factors that predict those likely to be re-convicted.

They concluded:

> ... the analysis so far supports the view that re-conviction is not an outcome that is simply determined by early life events. What happens at the family group conference can be critical. And so too are the events that happen after the family group conference.
>
> There are important messages from these findings for the youth justice system. The first is that, as shown in other research, prevention of offending by successful early intervention is likely to be the most effective strategy. The second is that it is unrealistic to expect the youth justice system to be able to prevent all re-offending because both early life events and subsequent life events have a powerful impact. The third is that simply holding a family group conference is not enough – there are a number of critical elements that have to be present if the family group conference is going to make a difference to the probability of offending in the future and these are:

- seeming fair to the parents and obtaining the active involvement of the young people in the process and the decision-making
- avoiding leaving parents and young people feeling bad about themselves
- above all achieving a process that increases the chance that the young person will feel truly sorry for what they have done, show remorse to the victim and make amends for what has happened. (Quoted from Maxwell and Morris 1999, pages 11-12)

Maxwell and Morris mention one other set of potential outcomes of the family group conference which they believe may also be critical. This is whether or not measures are put in place to help the young person acquire skills or to remedy deficiencies such as psychological problems, drug and alcohol abuse and learning deficits. A number of effective characteristics have already been identified from previous research. For example, Andrews (1999) showed that programmes for young people are likely to be effective in reducing offending, if the young people are at risk as indicated by their involvement in offending, if the programmes address criminogenic needs such as alcohol and drug use, anger and aggression and so on, and if the programmes are responsive to the particular populations for whom they are offered and are provided in community settings rather than custodial institutions.

I believe that the provision of effective programmes to which young people can be referred as a result of a family group conference will be a crucial aspect of any system which we put in place . There is a real danger that we may set up a conferencing system but have no or few effective programmes to which we can refer young people.

Similarly, if restorative justice approaches are to integrated into the criminal justice system it will be important to have full evaluations carried out into such issues as victim participation rates, victim and offender satisfaction with outcomes and re-offending rates. Clearly we want a system which will be culturally appropriate and not something which we have cloned from New Zealand or elsewhere.

DEVELOPMENTS IN THE REPUBLIC OF IRELAND

The current government in the Republic of Ireland was elected in 1997 on a strong law and order ticket. In spite of Ireland having a low recorded crime rate compared to other European Countries there has been a lot of media hype about crime. The government was elected to follow a "zero tolerance" policy which included the building of an extra 2000 prison places at vast public expense. This includes a requirement to provide a separate secure detention centre for up to twenty juvenile female and ninety juvenile male offenders. The present Minister of Justice has been said to have a preoccupation for incarceration (O'Sullivan 2000).

However, in spite of this there is considerable interest in restorative justice. In this respect by far the most significant development has been the passing of the Children Act (2001). The purpose of the Act is to "... replace the Children Act 1908, and further enactments relating to juvenile offenders, to amend and extend the Child Care Act 1991, and to provide for related matters". The Act has a strong restorative justice flavour.

It is a complex piece of legislation but the main points can be summarised as follows (see Raferty 2000):

- age of criminal responsibility raised to twelve years (from seven)
- detention is seen as last resort (in spite of the creation of the extra custodial places mentioned above)
- emphasis on diversion and community disposal of cases
- introduction of family conferences (largely based on a restorative justice philosophy)
- establishment of a Residential Services Board.

The Act has been generally welcomed as a fairly radical and innovative piece of legislation (see, for example, O'Dea 2000). It has, however, been sub-jected to a number of criticisms, not least, the delay in introducing it into legislation.

The introduction of family conferences creates a new, key decision-making process in the juvenile justice system. Family involvement is largely novel for youth justice practice in Ireland (O'Dea 2000, p 17). The family conference has the potential to provide a framework to engage families and use their strengths. It also has the scope to provide a platform for the development of interagency services to assist them.

The Act allows for family conferences to be introduced at various stages in the criminal justice process. First, it provides for conferences administered by the Garda Síochána (police) at the pre-prosecution stage through the Juvenile Diversion Programme. This is for young people who accept responsibility for an offence. This can include a restorative caution – which will be a type of mini-conference where a full conference is not believed to be warranted. It means that, where a formal caution is being administered to a child offender who has been admitted to the Diversion Programme, the victim may be present. This should provide an opportunity to confront the child with the consequences of his or her offending in the presence of the victim and for the child to be invited to offer an apology or make reparation to the victim.

As part of the Diversion Programme a full family conference may also be directed. Here the facilitator (a trained member of the Garda) brings together the child, his or her parents or guardian, and other relevant persons, as well as other appropriate persons on behalf of the victim. Their collective purpose is to

- establish why the child became involved in the behaviour
- discuss how the parents or guardian, relatives or any other person could help to prevent similar behaviour
- review the child's behaviour since admission to the programme
- bring together the child and the victim, so that the child may be given the opportunity to understand the consequences of his or her actions
- formulate an action plan for the child
- uphold the concerns of the victim and have due regard to his or her interests.

Conferences will not be held unless the child and his or her parents or guardian indicate that they are willing to attend it. The aim is to provide an action plan stemming from the conference. An action plan may include provision for any one or more of the following matters:

a) an apology, whether orally or in writing or both, by the child to any victims
b) financial or other reparation to any victims
c) participation by the child in an appropriate sporting or recreational activity
d) attendance of the child at a school or place of work
e) participation by the child in an appropriate training or educational course or a programme that does not interfere with any work or school schedule of the child
f) the child being at home at specific times
g) the child staying away from specified places or a specified person or both,
h) taking initiatives within the child's family and community that might help to prevent commission by the child of further offences
i) any other matter that in the opinion of those present at the conference would be in the child's best interest or would make the child more aware of the consequences of his or her criminal behaviour.

When the action plan and its duration have been agreed the facilitator will produce a written record of the plan in language that can be understood by the child. The plan is then signed by the child, the chairperson and one of the other persons present. The chairperson shall, after consulting the other persons present, appoint a date for reconvening the conference to review compliance with the action plan (although the chairperson may reconvene the conference earlier if it has come to his or her notice that the child is not complying with any of the terms of the action plan). The conference may be reconvened on any number of occasions to discuss any aspect of an action plan.

Second, family conferences will also be available at the court level for children charged with an offence. In such instances the child must accept responsibility for his or her criminal behaviour, the court must believe that it is desirable that an action plan should be formulated at a family conference and the child, parents or guardian must agree to attend such a conference and agree to participate in its proceedings. In court-initiated conferences the Probation and Welfare Service will be asked to arrange and convene the conference. Otherwise the proceedings are very similar to those convened by the Garda Síochána under its Diversion Programme. The Act does set various time limits for things to happen. For example, the conference should be held not later than twenty-eight days after the date of direction by the court. The probation and welfare officer who facilitates the conference is expected to submit to the court the action plan formulated at the conference or explain why he or she has been unable to convene a conference or agree an action plan.

The court may approve the plan or amend it. It then orders the child to comply with the plan and be supervised by a probation and welfare officer while it is in operation. The court then appoints a date when it will review the level of compliance of the child with the plan. This should be at a time not more than six months from the date of the order. At any stage before the review the probation and welfare officer may apply to the court if he/she believes that the child, without reasonable cause, has failed to comply with the terms of the plan. In such cases the court may resume the proceedings in respect of the offence with which the child is charged. At the formal court review, if the court is satisfied that the child has complied with the plan, it may dismiss the charge against the child on its merits.

Concerns about the Act relate to the child's legal rights and representation at various stages in the conferencing and review process. It could also be argued that the Act allows a level of intrusion into a child's life which lacks proportionality in relation to the offence charged. The fact that the family conferences will be managed or facilitated by members of the Garda Síochána or Probation and Welfare Service has been criticised on the grounds of "good practice". It is felt that members of both agencies are not sufficiently independent to play an objective role in the mediation aspect of the conference. This has been countered by saying that both agencies are sufficiently integrated into the com-munity as to command respect and standing with regards to their role in the conference. It also does away with the need to set up a separate structure to organise the conferences and will thus lead to financial savings.

Other criticisms concern the actual operation of the conference. O'Dea (2000) argues that the Act allows family conferences to regulate their procedures as they see fit. It offers no legal protection to a family's "private time" in a conference as usually happens in the New Zealand model of family group conferencing. Good practice emphasises that the plan of action should come from the family. When the family meets privately to discuss and reach decisions and report back to the full group it means that they own their solution, invest in their solution and sustain their solution. Without the safeguard of "family time" there is a danger that families may become primarily observers of the process and not become true stakeholders in it.

A further major concern relates to the resources which will need to be made available to allow the family conference model to be effective. It is clear that both the Garda Síochána and Probation and Welfare Service will need significant additional personnel resources. The indications are that setting up a family conference, preparing victims, facilitating the conference(s), preparing reports and supervising the action plan will take a lot of time. The government will need to fully resource this initiative and also make additional finance available to allow the action plan to be carried out, eg to provide drug treatment, counselling and so on. This has been a major failing in other jurisdictions. There are historical grounds to believe that the Irish government may not make available sufficient resources as the Probation and Welfare Service already suffers from a significant lack of personnel. Indeed there is a serious question of whether sufficient appropriately trained personnel could be recruited in the short term, even if funding is made available.

While we await the actual implementation of the Children Act a number of initiatives have been taking place in the Republic over the last year or so. In anticipation of the Children Act the Garda Síochána has established a Steering Group which includes academic and Department of Justice, Equality and Law Reform representation. This has overseen the development of the initiative. A significant number of juvenile liaison officers have been trained in mediation and conferencing skills. Two pilot schemes have been in operation. The first has pioneered "restorative cautioning" and the second has developed full-scale family conferencing. Although these pilots are still at an early stage the anecdotal evidence on the operation has been very positive. There have been good levels of attendance of young people, parents and victims at the conferences and feedback from all three sources has been uniformly positive.

Conferences have been held in neutral venues such as community halls and hotels. There are concerns about the time implications for preparing and seeing through a conference. One estimate is that at least an extra ten juvenile liaison officers will be necessary. If possible, some officers should be dedicated to facilitating conferences as it is difficult to carry out this role as well as undertake other duties. In time, it may be possible to franchise out some of the conference organising to other agencies.

Two other restorative justice initiatives are underway with the help of the Department of Justice, Equality and Law Reform. In April 1999 the Minister of Justice, Equality and Law Reform announced three-year funding for the establishment of a pilot Victim/Offender Mediation Service. It is a pre-sentence model receiving referrals from the Tallaght and Naas District Courts. It is managed by an independent board representing the main stakeholders in the criminal justice system. Mediation is carried out by trained volunteers. They explore with victims and offenders to see if a form of apology, reparation or resolution can be agreed. The Mediation Service then reports back to the court where the judge makes the final decision.

The second scheme operates in the Nenagh area of Co Tipperary and is a Community Reparation Project. It is a twelve months pilot project managed by a local committee representing different community interests in partnership with the Probation and Welfare Service. It began on the initiative of a local judge who had visited New Zealand in 1998 and was very impressed with some of the projects there. The project receives referrals of offenders from the courts. They meet with a panel of people made up from representatives of the community, gardaí and the project co-ordinator. The victim and any supporters may also be present at the meeting. The offender is encouraged to admit guilt and express remorse at the meeting. Normally the offender explains the offence, why he/she acted in this way, his/her feelings at the time and feelings about it now. The offenders also discuss how reparation to the victim and/or the community can be made. A contract is drawn up in which the offender agrees to the form of reparation and any changes he/she needs to make in his/her life. This may include a meeting with or a letter of apology to the victim, paying back any money involved in the crime, getting a job or starting on a course of treatment for alcoholism if appropriate, or whatever seems appropriate in each individual case. The contract is usually for six months during which the offender has regular meetings with the probation officer. If the offender breaks the contract then the case goes back to court and proceeds in the normal manner. If the offender is successful during the six-month period then he/she has no criminal record as a result of the offence.

So far the project has had only a small number of referrals – all coming from the judge who initiated the project. This could be a problem for this type of pilot, which relies very much on a limited source of referral. In the past, many of these schemes elsewhere have failed to build up a sufficient number of referrals and critical mass to allow them to operate in the long term.

CONCLUSION

Nonetheless, the initiatives described above and the new approaches introduced by the Children Act 2001 suggest that there is considerable interest in restorative justice in the Republic. There are concerns in all of these initiatives in relation to human rights and the danger of over-intrusion into an offender's life disproportionate to the seriousness of the offence. This is a real matter for concern which will need to be closely monitored and evaluated. Equally, none of the schemes seems to put in place sufficient safeguards in terms of victim rights and needs. It is vitally important to the success of restorative justice initiatives that victims are given sensitive support before, during and after the process.

REFERENCES

Andrews, D. A. (1999), *What works in young offender treatment: A meta-analysis*, Forum on Corrections Research

Braithwaite, J. (1989), *Crime, Shame and Reintegration*, Cambridge: Cambridge University Press

Braithwaite, J. (1997), Restorative Justice: Assessing an Immodest Theory and a Pessimistic Theory, available at: http://www.aic.gov.au/rjustice/braithwaite.html

Criminal Justice Review Group (2000), *Review of the Criminal Justice System in Northern Ireland*, Norwich: Her Majesty's Stationery Office

Dignan, J. and Lowey, K. (2000), "Restorative Justice Options for Northern Ireland: A Comparative Review", *Research Report Number 10*, Norwich: Her Majesty's Stationery Office

Hayes H. and Prenzler T. with Wortley R. 1998, *Making Amends: Final Evaluation of the Queensland Community Conferencing Pilot*, Grittith University, Brisbane: Centre for Crime Policy and Public Safety

Marshall, T. F. (1999), *Restorative Justice: An Overview,* London: HMSO

Maxwell, G. and Morris, A. (1996), "Research on Family Group Conferencing with Young Offenders in New Zealand", in J. Hudson et al (eds.), *Family Group Conferences: Perspectives on Policy and Practice*, New York: Criminal Justice Press

Maxwell, G. and Morris, A. (1999), *Restorative Justice and Reoffending*, Institute of Criminology, Wellington, New Zealand. Paper sent to author as personal communication and based on an earlier version of the paper presented at Youth Justice in Focus Conference in Wellington, October 1999, and published as conference proceedings

Minister of Justice, Equality and Law Reform (2001), *Children* Act *2001*, Dublin: Stationery Office

O'Dea, P. (2000), "Family Conferences in the Children Bill 1999", in the *Children Bill 1999*, Papers from a seminar organised by the Children's Legal Centre, Dublin: The Children's Legal Centre

O'Sullivan, E. (2000), "The Children Bill 1999: Responsibility and Regulation", in the *Children Bill 1999,* Papers from a seminar organised by the Children's Legal Centre, Dublin: The Children's Legal Centre

Raferty, G. (2000), "The Children Bill, 1999: Opportunities and Challenges for Practice", in the *Children Bill 1999.* Papers from a seminar organised by the Children's Legal Centre, Dublin: The Children's Legal Centre

Stuart, B. (1997), *Building Community Justice Partnerships: Community Peacemaking Circles*, Ottawa: Department of Justice

Zehr, H. (1990), *Changing Lenses,* Scottdale: Herald Press

42

Social and Psychological Aspects of Drug Treatment and Rehabilitation within Irish Prisons

Paul O'Mahony

The prison, perhaps more than any other institution, concentrates in one place for prolonged periods large numbers of people with multiple, serious health and personal problems. These problems include HIV/AIDS, hepatitis, suicidal tendencies, illiteracy, difficulties with anger control, learning disability and drug dependence. In dealing with these kinds of problems, the penal system is faced with both major challenges and potentially valuable opportunities for treatment and rehabilitation. This paper focuses on the drugs problem, examines the institutional, psychological and socio-cultural constraints on drug treatment and rehabilitation in prison, and, in the context of the recent report of the Steering Group on Prison Based Drug Treatment Services (2000), discusses the forms of drug treatment and rehabilitation that are viable and worthy of investment in the prison setting.

Irish prisons, especially Mountjoy and Wheatfield, currently contain large numbers of inmates who are or have been users of opiates and other drugs (Allwright et al 1999; Hannon et al 2000) and who have been deeply involved in crimes of theft, sometimes of a violent or threatening nature, in order to feed their habit (Keogh 1997). According to Hannon et al, who examined a sample of 777 prisoners in 1999, 63% of male and 83% of female prisoners had used a drug other than cannabis in the previous twelve months. Allwright et al found that 43% of their sample of 1,188 prisoners from throughout the system and 58% of 712 from what they term high risk prisons had experience of injecting drugs. Fifty-two percent of their total sample had at some point used heroin and 38.5% showed evidence of either hepatitis B, hepatitis C or HIV infection. Nevertheless, the vast majority of Irish prisoners who use drugs have been convicted for non-drug-related crime and only about 4% of all prisoners have been convicted for drug-related crime (O'Mahony 2000). According to Keogh's (1997) survey of indictable crime in Dublin, 43% of the people arrested for indictable crime are hard drug users and are responsible for about two-thirds of all indictable crime in Dublin, mainly larceny, robbery and burglary.

It is also well known from survey evidence (Allwright et al 1999; O'Mahony 1997a) that a great deal of drug use, including intravenous use of opiates, occurs in Irish prisons. Allwright et al found that 45% of ever injecting prisoners, who had been in prison for more than three months, had injected within the last month. There are also numerous reports of people initiating opiate use or intravenous use in prison. Allwright et al found that 21% of prisoners, who had ever injected drugs, claimed to have first injected opiates in prison and almost 9% of their total sample of 1,205 prisoners from nine different prisons claimed to have injected for the first time in prison.

In this context, there would appear to be an enormous need for drug treatment and rehabilitation programmes of various kinds within the prison system. They are required in order to fulfill the authorities' statutory duty of care to prison inmates, but they would also appear to be justified on utilitarian grounds, since drug treatment and rehabilitation may represent a realistic opportunity to impact on some prisoners' lives in a way that would make future involvement in crime and self-destructive and socially disruptive behaviour less likely.

However, it is also possible to make a case for the opposite viewpoint – that the prison system can never be an appropriate setting for drug treatment and rehabilitation programmes because any attempt to reconstruct the system in order to provide meaningful programmes could not succeed without compromising the fundamental penal purpose of the institution. In fact, some people argue that the correct approach for the prison system is to fully enforce society's and its own strictly prohibitionist policy on drugs. This approach is epitomised by the statement of the 1991 Mountjoy Visiting Committee report that "there should be endless efforts made to identify the sources of the supply, and elimination and punishment of suppliers". According to this strictly prohibitionist view, primary emphasis should be placed on preventing the use of drugs within prison by blocking the smuggling and distribution of drugs. Apart from offering limited detoxification and support programmes for drug using inmates on their initial committal to prison, this perspective contends that the problem of drugs and addiction should be left to the health authorities and others outside the penal system. The scandal of large numbers of prisoners beginning a serious drug habit in prison also argues that strong interdiction of drugs and stringent prohibition are what is required in the penal system.

The argument between those who recognise an urgent need for comprehensive drug treatment and rehabilitation in prisons and those who believe the correct response to the problem is a tougher regime that successfully stamps out drug use in prison can only be satisfactorily resolved if we have a clear understanding of the possibilities for and the limitations on both drug treatment and rehabilitation and prohibition within the prison system. After all, if there are no successful treatment modalities compatible with the prison setting, then perhaps a strictly enforced prohibitionist approach represents the best alternative for the prison system. On the other hand, if prohibition cannot be made to work, then treatment and rehabilitation are an obvious necessity. This paper focuses mainly on the cultural, social system and social psychological constraints on drug treatment and rehabilitation in prison. These are issues neglected by most treatment-oriented approaches to addiction, which tend to focus almost exclusively on individual-centred psychological and physiological processes.

This paper is informed by the social learning theory that addiction is a learned excessive appetitive behaviour, involving profound change in the motivational system (Orford 1982). According to this perspective, the addictive process has a basis in the physiological effects of the drug, but many psychological, social and environmental factors also play a central role in the acquisition and maintenance of an addiction. Orford proposes a "balance of forces" model which states that a complex of conflicting motives and reinforcers governs addictive behaviour, some favouring, some opposing drug use. In the individual case, the addiction process cannot be fully understood nor effectively tackled without addressing the addict's social context, personal history and psychological make-up. Attention is drawn, in this paper, to the cultural, political, and social psychological determinants and constraints which have shaped the present reality of the drugs problem in Irish prisons and which will undoubtedly continue to influence future developments in the area.

Four different groups or levels of determinants and constraints relating to prison drug treatment and rehabilitation can be distinguished, the first three of which are essentially socio-cultural or psycho-social in character:

a) the dominant political ideology and social policy with respect to psychotropic drugs in wider society

b) the purpose and nature of the prison as an institution

c) the prisoner culture as it emerges in response to the institutional realities of prison

d) the specific condition, needs and history of the individual addict-prisoner.

These four levels can be usefully distinguished for the purposes of analysis, but undoubtedly intersect and interact in complex ways. They will, however, be examined separately and in turn.

THE CONSTRAINTS ON DRUG REHABILITATION IN PRISON

a) Socio-political policy

Social policies with regard to illegal drugs inevitably impact on the prison system. But Irish social policy on drug use for most of the last twenty years has not, by any standard, been either proactive, coherent or effective in the health, education, and criminal justice spheres. This fact, more than any other, accounts for the weakness of the penal system's response to its drugs crisis. Only in the latter half of the 1990s did efforts to confront the realities of drug use in Ireland generally begin to take on the urgency, energy, and clarity that the problem demands. This recent advance is evidenced by the publication of the Rabbite reports (1996 and 1997), by the establishment of the National Drugs Council, and by generally better resourced and more concerted action in the area of treatment and prevention since 1996.

In the past, important official statements on drugs have often seemed to articulate a rationale for inaction. For example, the Committee on Drug Education (1974) stated that while "education is central to any programme of prevention, it should be recognised that it is also an area in which great damage can be done. To quote one expert, 'only education enjoys the dubious privilege of having the power to make matters worse'". Political, media, and state agency interest in the drugs problem waxed and waned from 1979 to 1996, the period during which opiate addiction gained an ever tighter grip on susceptible young people in Dublin's disadvantaged areas and came to permeate and dominate the criminal subculture. A policy vacuum and general climate of fatalism and defeatism about drugs facilitated continuing inertia and official neglect of an insidiously spreading drugs problem.

During this time, sporadic attempts were made to develop co-ordinated policy between health, justice, social welfare, environment, and education agencies, including the Special Government Task Force on Drug Abuse (1983) and the Government Strategy to Prevent Drug Misuse (1991). However, these initiatives quickly faltered or failed to develop sufficient momentum and eventually petered out with little enduring benefit (O'Gorman 1998). According to Cullen (1998), there was widespread denial of the drugs problem and especially of its links to social deprivation. He states that "when it became apparent, even at an official level, that a serious drug problem was evident, and that it was most prevalent in a small number of working class communities, an official strategy was adopted to deny this and this fact was not properly conceded until the publication of the Rabbite Report ".

Social policy and action in response to illicit drugs has been inadequate, ineffective and confused in many respects (Butler 1991). International law enforcement approaches, driven largely by a prohibitionist US policy agenda, have been the primary influence on Irish political attitudes and criminal justice policy. Simplistic prohibitionist policies have been adopted in an uncritical manner, leading to a deleterious lack of coherence between the law enforcement, education and health service responses. Most significantly, the political stress on law enforcement, as the most appropriate response to the drugs problem, resulted for many years in a lack of serious attention to and proper funding of the areas of prevention and treatment.

Official social policy on drugs, in so far as it can be identified, was for many years characterised by an absolutist prohibition of drug-taking, aimed indiscriminately at all types of illicit drugs. As a consequence, there has been an unhelpful disregard for the important distinctions between various illicit drugs and types of addiction. State authorities have often attempted to liken the use of cannabis to the use of opiates in order to differentiate both from the legal use of alcohol or cigarettes. However, the most important similarity between cannabis and opiate use is precisely the fact that they are, while alcohol and tobacco are not, socially defined as illegal.

The limited amount of debate on decriminalisation that has occurred in Ireland (Murphy 1996) has almost always focused on cannabis solely. The decriminalisation of all drug use has been an almost unthinkable proposition. However, it is the criminalisation of so-called hard drugs that actually does most collateral damage to the social fabric by the creation of a highly organised and profitable, violent, criminal black market in drugs. Prohibition and an overemphasis on supply control measures appear to be seriously counterproductive, creating more drug abuse and more devastating types of drug abuse, as well as many forms of drug-linked criminality. History in Ireland and elsewhere tells us that an essentially repressive, prohibitionist approach tends to be futile and self-defeating, at least in Western style democracies. For example in the US about $30 billion is spent annually on domestic measures to suppress illegal drugs, but this is to little good effect since more than 20,000 people a year die as a result of illicit drug use and more than one million people a year are arrested for drug-related offences (Terry 1999). According to MacCoun (1998), the harm reduction critique of harsh enforcement policies is twofold; first, these policies have failed to eliminate drug use, "leaving its harms largely intact" and second, they are themselves a "source of many drug-related harms, either directly or by exacerbating the harmful consequences of drug use".

The danger of blurring the important distinctions between types of drug and ways of using is clearly illustrated by the Garda Síochána statement in the Crime Report for 1993 that "once again, the major drug of abuse in Ireland is cannabis resin". This utterly erroneous assessment reflected the reality of garda activity against illegal drugs and the official concern to equate cannabis with hard drugs rather than the reality of the drugs crisis itself, which was mainly linked to heroin. At that time and for many years previously, the vast majority of drugs offenders were arrested and charged by the gardaí for possession of cannabis. The drug-related offences of the very large number of opiate using offenders were largely ignored, since heroin using offenders tended to be proceeded against only for their crimes of theft. The head of the Garda Drug Squad, illustrating the inherent confusion of the official prohibitionist agenda, stated in 1995 that "we are committed to tough, unrelenting law enforcement, although it is very clear to us that something more effective is required."

The policy failure to clearly differentiate between the inherent dangers of various drugs and modes of use has impacted negatively on preventative programmes, especially educational campaigns aimed at young people. Programmes have been under-resourced and of questionable benefit. In particular, they have lacked credibility with young people, who have found it easy to dismiss them on the grounds that they typify adult, "straight" world hypocrisy about illegal drugs, since adult drugs of choice, such as alcohol, are freely available and condoned in spite of the very substantial harm they cause. One indication of the failure of educational prevention is the fact that Ireland has seen the experimental use of cannabis, despite its official characterisation as a hard drug or as an almost inevitable gateway to hard drugs, rise to the level of 37% of sixteen-year-olds (Morgan et al 1999), which is more than three times the average exposure to cannabis for this age group in the EU.

The lack of political will and lack of clarity in official thinking about addiction and the proper responses to it have also been a major factor in the inadequacy of treatment services. As recently as the mid-nineties, there were huge waiting lists for methadone maintenance treatment and a general paucity of other therapeutic and support services. For much of the eighties there were only a few dozen treatment places, of all kinds from detoxification to therapeutic community, available to cater for several thousand heroin addicts, many of whom were in their early or mid-teens.

From the late-eighties, the AIDS crisis began to exert increasing influence on certain practical aspects of Irish social policy on drugs. This influence instigated a process of gradual compromise of the fundamentally prohibitionist principles of official policy. According to Butler (1991), the growing awareness of the strong relationship between HIV infection and intravenous drug use ushered in an initially half-hearted, covert adoption of harm reduction approaches, such as methadone maintenance, outreach, counselling and needle exchange. These measures, designed originally to halt the spread of the HIV virus, had to coexist with a still dominant official focus on prohibition.

A strategy of pragmatic social defence in the health area, therefore, rather than any ideological or evidence-based commitment to the approach, inspired the new degree of partial support for harm reduction measures. At the political level, this stance has more recently been articulated as a two-pronged assault on the drugs problem via, on the one hand, *reduction of supply*, through tough drugs interdiction, and, on the other, *reduction of demand,* through prevention and treatment of addiction. These two approaches are depicted as complementary to each other and generally compatible with a harm reduction agenda. The internal contradictions of a policy that attempts to marry the ideology and practice of prohibition and criminalisation with the philosophy of harm reduction are ignored.

This newly articulated philosophy is ultimately founded on prohibitionist goals, since the major aims remain the elimination of illicit drug use and the permanent abstinence of all established users. Whilst the political rhetoric reflects a continuing attachment to prohibitionist ideals, in reality there is growing acceptance of the normative nature of drug use and increasing recognition of the fact that the effectiveness of harm reduction approaches is severely impeded by prohibitionist policies that work through the criminalisation and demonisation of drug use. In some respects, the inherent tension between the prohibitionist and harm reduction approaches has been highlighted in recent years by the greatly increased use of methadone maintenance as the treatment of first choice for opiate users in the community. Many thousands of former heroin users now daily receive, by medical prescription, an opiate drug, which it would otherwise be a criminal offence to possess. So, actual practice belies the policy commitment to the goal of abstinence by promoting on-going drug use, albeit of a hopefully more stable and less risky and disruptive nature.

Since 1996, however, policy on drugs has also been driven by public outrage at the murder of the investigative journalist, Veronica Guerin, and at the arrogance and seeming impunity of those involved in that killing and other drugs-related killings. Initiatives have included Operation Dochas, aimed at street level dealing and using, and other more active law enforcement approaches, such as the Criminal Assets Bureau and intensive customs operations, aimed at drugs interdiction and the disruption of organised drugs crime. There have also been related repressive legislative initiatives, such as the Criminal Justice (Drug Trafficking) Act 1996 and the Criminal Justice Act 1999, that have, respectively, introduced draconian rules for the detention, search and interrogation of suspected drugs dealers and mandatory sentences of ten years for certain drug dealing crimes. These measures have, then, emerged from and in turn reinforced the longstanding prohibitionist agenda.

A third strand of influence on recent Irish drugs policy has been the "community action against drugs" movement that flourished in many of the deprived, drug-infested areas of Dublin between 1996 and 1998. This protest

movement, of parents and families in drug damaged communities, involved mass
meetings aimed at galvanising politicians into a more helpful response to the drugs
crisis, street marches leading to the forcible eviction of alleged drug dealers,
community self-policing and other vigilante type activities (O'Mahony 1997b).
For a time the movement threatened to usurp garda authority in certain localities.
This movement helped provoke a more proactive and realistic official engagement
with the drugs problem and has been influential in ways that impact on both the
supply and demand reduction programmes. Partly in response to community
action, policing and law enforcement in drug-infested areas have been stepped up,
but treatment facilities and resources have also been considerably improved.

The most distinctive legacy of the anti-drugs activist movement, however, is the
current broader recognition of the role of social exclusion in the drugs problem.
This recognition has prompted the development of programmes expected to impact
positively on drug abuse through the implementation of measures to improve
standards in housing and local neighbourhoods and to empower disadvantaged
groups by way of education and training and the creation of employment
opportunities. Much of this work has been facilitated by social partnership
arrangements and inter-agency co-operation, including improved links between
the gardaí and local communities. However, the years of prevarication were
totally unjustified because the links between social deprivation and the heroin
epidemic have from the start been obvious, most especially within the penal
system (O'Mahony and Gilmore 1982). It is also evident that the present more
energetic pursuit of demand reduction has not weakened the general political
commitment to prohibitionist thinking.

The current seriousness of drug-related crime (Keogh 1997), the enormous
number of serious addicts in the prisons and the steady encroachment of the drugs
culture into prison life all stand as testimony to the confusion and failure of
official social policy and action on illegal drugs since 1980 and to the devastating
impact of these shortcomings on the prison system. The eleven drug-related
deaths in Irish prisons between 1990 and 1997, through overdose or choking on
vomit (National Steering Group on Deaths in Prisons 1999), which have gone
almost unremarked in the media, also testify to the gravity of a situation that has
never been properly addressed but has, on the contrary, been allowed to fester and
continuously deteriorate. Stark evidence of the failure of the health and criminal
justice authorities to take action on the prison drugs crisis is the fact that, as long
ago as 1977, the Misuse of Drugs Act made provision for the designation of
custodial treatment centres for drug abusing offenders. In 1980, the Central
Mental Hospital became a designated centre but, through all the crisis years, it
was not used as such, in spite of the existence at the hospital from 1986 of a
modern forty-bed facility, which remained empty and unused for many years.

The prison system failed to react to the unique concentration of the drugs problem within its walls and merely adopted the fatalistic attitudes and essentially laissez-faire policies prevalent in the general community. Indeed, the system continued with them even after 1996, when significant improvements were made to provision outside the prisons. The Director of Medical Services for the Irish Prisons Service stated in his 1999 report: "For a considerable number of years previous reports have lamented the failure to adequately address the problems associated with drug abuse among the prison population. The ongoing lack of adequate therapeutic resources allocated to tackling the problem within prisons has become more marked in the context of the large amount of resources being devoted to addressing the problem in the general community, most specifically to those communities which are particularly affected by drug abuse".

The penal system has been seriously remiss for many years in not providing even a basic level of suitable healthcare, drug rehabilitation and educational programmes for drug abusing inmates. The introduction of the drugs free zone concept (for up to 100 prisoners) and the establishment of a proper medical unit with the facilities to provide detoxification with professional supportive counselling (for a dozen prisoners every few months) did not happen in the Irish prison system until 1996 (Crowley 1999). Currently, such facilities still only provide assistance to a small fraction of the drug abusers in prison.

The persistent inaction of the prison authorities was undoubtedly facilitated by the relative statistical invisibility of drug abusers within the system, due to the fact that most of them were imprisoned for non-drug offences. However, it was clearly also linked to the inadequacy and equivocation of the Irish social response to drugs generally. In particular, the prisons drugs crisis and the inadequate reaction to it have been shaped by the dominance of prohibitionist thinking, the neglect of the links between social deprivation and drug use, the ambivalence towards the harm reduction approach, and the failure to provide in the community the necessary broad range of therapeutic and support services required by drug users.

b) The nature of prison as an institution

The nature of the prison as a social institution has also contributed to the crisis. The prison is what Goffman (1968) has called a "total institution", which isolates offenders from the rest of society as a way of punishing them and temporarily impeding them in their criminal activities. Prison life is a microcosm – a world apart – insulated from normal life and distinctive in its own culture. It is characterised by what Goffman calls binary management, that is a system which separates people into two castes – the inmates and those who look after and manage the inmates. This system leads to a "them and us" mentality on both sides of the divide. A fundamentally oppositional relationship between prison officers and prisoners is almost unavoidable. The prison is highly regulated and governed by strict discipline imposed by one side on the other, although the prison officers who enforce the rules are also subject to a very regimented and rule-bound code of behaviour. The prison relies on mechanical, batch-living solutions to everyday practical problems, like supplying nourishment and maintaining hygiene. Rigid prison rules and routines inevitably create a dehumanising way of life, especially for the inmates, who have little choice but to passively comply with the regime.

From the prison management point of view, the most immediate priorities arising from the presence of drug abusing inmates in a "total institution" are:

- first and foremost, the overriding objective of secure custody, in accordance with the basic purpose of the prison, which is to hold offenders for the period of time laid down by the sentence of the court
- secondly, the control and where possible prevention of drug abuse and associated risk such as HIV and hepatitis infection, suicide, overdose, and initiation into drug use within prison
- thirdly, the exploitation of the potential for treatment and drug rehabilitation during the period of imprisonment.

Prison authorities, then, tend to think defensively about drugs and to be interested in therapeutic systems and programmes for drug abusers, only in so far as treatment is compatible with the status quo of the penal regime, particularly with its need for order and its (in reality largely theoretical) emphasis on the prohibition of drugs. The main objectives of the prison system remain deterrence from crime, security and control. The tone and methods of the institution remain recognisably punitive and coercive. Most of the methods of drug treatment and rehabilitation, with the possible exception of the Twelve Step moral method aimed at total abstinence, are in some essentials alien to the prison environment. The punitive purpose of the institution and the adversarial relationship and normal modes of communication between the prison officer and the prisoner cannot easily encompass the therapeutic role. These facts undoubtedly contributed to the failure of the prison system to develop its own initiatives to tackle drug abuse and its propensity to ignore, whenever possible, the drugs issue and its longer-term implications for prisons and society.

The institutional structures of the traditional prison do not encourage and, indeed, provide little scope for innovative, client-centred, caring approaches to drug using prisoners. They are not generally conducive to harm reduction methods, which require an attitude of tolerance to what are by definition criminal behaviours. Where there have been therapeutic endeavours in prisons, they have often been subordinated to the institution's primary commitment to penal goals. As Wexler et al (1988) argue "most prison-based treatment programmes operate under so many bureaucratic and political constraints that they are programmed to fail from their inception". Prison authorities, however benign in outlook, cannot escape their primary law enforcement role and cannot escape the reality that drug use is criminal and, typically in current circumstances, highly criminogenic.

The Irish penal system has tended to rely on outside agencies, such as Narcotics Anonymous and the Coolmine Therapeutic Community, for the provision of internal drug rehabilitation services. These agencies, unlike the prison, are not stymied by conflicting penal and therapeutic objectives and can sometimes surmount the bureaucratic negativity that constrains internal prison efforts. However, they can be seriously hampered by their lack of experience of prisons and by the many everyday practical and attitudinal barriers which confront an outside agency operating within a prison. Their presence in the Irish system, while valuable for many prisoners, has been little more than token in the context of the overall problem.

Another aspect of the generally defensive and evasive reaction to the drugs problem has been the tendency to medicalise the problem and thereby disown it. If those in charge of social institutions define the drugs problem as a specialist issue and if the specialists focus exclusively on individual-centred processes, most especially biological processes, and thereby effectively avoid engagement with the social environment, then the social aspects of the problem will inevitably be neglected.

Apart from the fact that the nature and purpose of the prison as a total institution severely constricts management attitudes, goals and priorities for action, the prison has inherent social psychological features that are frankly anti-therapeutic in their effects on prisoners. These can be classified under three headings: 1) stereotyped forms of social interaction dictated by the structures and strictures of the penal institution; 2) negative aspects of the inmate's psychological adaptation to the prison experience; and 3) promotion by the total institution of an oppositional prisoner culture favourable to drug use.

Strict social division – often reinforced by the harsh language of mutual disdain (screws/scumbags) – social stigma, stereotyping and strained communication between prisoners and all others, represent some of the constraints on social interaction that can impact negatively on therapeutic programmes. The prison creates and maintains rigid hierarchy, discipline and social distance, all of which are intrinsically damaging to many forms of therapy and education.

Many disempowering psychological and social experiences flow from the penal nature of the prison – from the system of coercive binary management, depersonalised batch-living and painful and demeaning isolation from family and open society. Prison life is in a sense a suspension of real life with all its demands and opportunities. Prison tends to brand the inmate as inferior, to obliterate individuality, to restrict opportunities for the exercise of personal responsibility and to encourage dependency, resignation and passivity. All of these processes are inimical to the kind of drug treatment and rehabilitation that stresses confrontation of reality and personal commitment to change, self-management and self-control. These prisonisation processes (Clemmer 1940) undermine the motivation of inmates to engage in rehabilitation programmes and cast doubt over the meaningfulness of inmates' commitment to change, whenever they do participate.

Prisoners vary greatly in how they adapt to the prison environment. Jones and Fowles (1984) suggest there are four typical patterns of adjustment, comprising conformity, innovation, withdrawal and intransigence or rebellion. However, at the collective level the predominant tone and ideology of the prisoner culture is oppositional and intransigent. In the words of McCorkle and Korn (1954) "the inmate social system in effect permits the inmate to reject his rejectors rather than himself". The prison isolates the prisoner from society, but simultaneously creates a microcosm conducive to the bonding together of prisoners in opposition to institutional and societal values. Drugs are ideally suited to this oppositional culture because of their highly symbolic, contraband, rebel status, but also because of their inherent utility and significance to both the individual drug using prisoner and the prisoner social system.

c) The prisoners' drug culture

Reflecting the power of the oppositional prisoner culture, the current reality in some Irish prisons is what might be called a *silent accommodation* on the part of the prison authorities with the drugs culture. A certain amount of effort is put into drugs interdiction but not enough to seriously disturb the routine activities of the covert drugs culture within the prison. It is paradoxical that the appearance of an ordered prison world coexists with a prison life consumed by illicit drugs. On the surface all appears properly ordered but the authorities actually preside over and acquiesce in a prison life which is a travesty of its own basic goals of a "secure, safe, caring, law-abiding and rehabilitative" prison environment (Department of Justice 1994).

What has evolved over the last twenty years is a working balance between the objectives of prison management, which include prohibition of drugs and secure containment, and those of the oppositional, drugs-oriented culture of the prisoners. This is a compromise, which allows the prison authorities to claim that they maintain the law and institutional rules and run an anti-drugs establishment, forbidding and imposing sanctions for drug smuggling and use; but which, at the same time, allows many prisoners to live a drugs-dominated life within the prison.

This compromise is not the deliberate design of management but is rather a subversion of official order that has been achieved by the efforts of inmates, reacting against the inevitable repression of a total institution. Prisoners as a group are intent on besting the system, exploiting its weaknesses, and creating boundaries around areas of prison life within which they can operate more freely.

As a result, the reality of life for many prisoners in crucial ways fails to meet the basic criteria laid down by the Department of Justice (1994) for an effective, decent, humane prison system. In this nether world, prisoners deal in drugs, smuggle drugs, use drugs, share syringes, contract HIV and hepatitis, begin a drugs habit, begin injecting, and intimidate and coerce each other over drugs.

Many prisoners' lives revolve around drugs, not just using drugs, but smuggling and trading in them and incessantly thinking and talking about them (Redmond 2001). Some prisons, like Mountjoy, are totally dominated by a drugs culture embodied in prisoners' attitudes, values and behaviours. For the core drug-abusing group the total immersion in drug-related activities almost takes on the characteristics of cult membership – a form of idolatry of the drug experience that even entails a true believer's eagerness to recruit new members.

This means that the prisoner culture is not only largely indifferent or hostile to rehabilitative efforts but itself successfully propagates and perpetuates pro-drugs values and behaviours. The situation in some prisons has reached a point where even prisoners, who have no interest in or sympathy with drug-taking, cannot avoid the influence of the drugs culture or its associated dangers (Redmond 2001). They face daily the expectation of co-operation with the prisoner drugs culture and in the absence of such co-operation the real threat of harassment. Apart from pressures to take up the drug abusing way of life and the pervasive presence of the drug users' obsession with drugs, there are real risks of accidental harm. For example, in a recent survey of about one hundred prisoners (O'Mahony 1997a), two non-drug using prisoners claimed to have been pricked by used syringe needles, one accidentally, the other possibly by malicious intent.

A complete account of the drugs culture in prisons must include an empathetic approach to the prisoner's point of view and motivation. The multiple functions that addiction serves, uniquely for each individual, are critical to an under-standing of his or her predicament, as are the drug-using prisoner's personal value system and lifestyle outside the prison. But it is equally necessary and useful to examine the social and psychological realities of life in a penal institution and how these impinge on the addiction process.

It can be argued that drug use is directly valued by prisoners, as by all drug users, for

a)   intrinsic pleasure
b)   oblivious escape from boredom and coercion
c)   as a domain of personal control
d)   as a source of excitement
e)   as a shaper of meaning
f)   as a source of social affiliation.

However, the specific realities of prison life mean that, for many prisoners, drugs are never more attractive than when in prison. For example, the excessive idleness, boredom and ubiquitous coercion of prison life make the pleasure and oblivion of the opiate fix especially attractive. The acts of smuggling, trading, and drug-using in defiance of the rules are particularly challenging and exciting and afford a rare opportunity to achieve the admiration and gratitude of fellow inmates. The general lack of autonomy experienced by the prisoner sharpens the sense of personal control obtained from controlling one's own internal psychological environment through the use of drugs. In these sorts of ways the psycho-social context of the prison promotes drug use and the prisoner drugs culture that flourishes around it.

The drugs-related social and quasi-occupational roles (Sackman et al 1978) available to the prisoner are important because they supply important sources of esteem, power, social networking and social meaning within an alternative social matrix defined and controlled by the prisoners themselves. Drugs activities provide prisoners with "busyness" and a route to success of a sort. For example, dealing in drugs or owning a syringe or besting the system by smuggling in drugs or using drugs under the noses of the authorities provide a means to status for inmates. These more obviously social functions of drug use motivate and sustain the prisoner drugs culture just as much as the hedonistic and escapist, physiological and psychological pleasures of drug use. The whole enterprise of the drugs culture serves to activate and energise the prisoners involved, giving their lives considerable meaning in an environment which otherwise might seem designed to deprive their lives of meaning.

Finally, part of the attraction of the prisoner drugs culture is that the conscious, overt adoption of the role of drug user within prison serves important expressive functions. It conveys the message that the addict is different, daring, defiant, rejecting of straight values and, perhaps, utterly mysterious to ordinary folk such as prison officers and psychologists. Proudly taking on the deviant role of addict is a powerful way to affirm one's distinctive identity and reject institutional prison and mainstream social values that tend to denigrate and demean one.

d) The condition and needs of the individual addict-prisoner

Another important constraint on the provision of effective drug treatment and rehabilitation within the prison is the huge diversity of situations in which prisoners find themselves vis-à-vis drug use. It is important to remember that addictions have a natural history and that the psychology and motivation of the individual user is very dependent on the stage of addiction that he or she has reached. In the prison setting there are all sorts of addicts, including: young people in the first flush of excitement about drugs, perhaps just beginning to experiment with opiates or intravenous use in the prison and as impressed by peer pressure and the social symbolism of drugs as by the drug intoxication itself; long established addicts who are dying of AIDS and have no intention of giving up drug use; long-term abusers who have avoided serious illness and are now careful not to share syringes; intravenous users outside prison, who choose for reasons of convenience and personal control not to use intravenously in prison, occasionally smoking heroin instead; totally rash and uninhibited intravenous polydrug-users who will use any drug in any way regardless of the consequences to themselves or others; and users who feel desolate and destroyed by the drug experience and their prison life and who are close to suicide (O'Mahony 1997a).

Prisoner drug users will also have had varied experience of treatment programmes and various attitudes towards treatment. Partly out of a sense of alienation from and disaffection towards officialdom and "the system", many drug using prisoners have not had contact with treatment programmes outside the prison. Others have had some, perhaps partially successful, experience of treatment and yet others have exploited treatment programmes with which they have been involved, for example by selling prescribed methadone in order to obtain illegal heroin. Some prisoners may in fact be better off "going it alone". The exercise of personal willpower and the feeling of self-mastery that can be generated by it are often key contributors to the recovery process (O'Mahony 1990). Mobilising and strengthening such psychological processes is vital to the therapeutic process, but some prisoners have an urge to define and prove themselves independently of the system and find the strength in themselves to give up drugs, defiantly turning their experience of isolation to good effect.

The diversity of prisoner drug user situations with respect to stage of addiction and prior experience of treatment must be acknowledged in drug rehabilitation programmes alongside the equally important diversity arising from wide variation amongst prisoners in terms of personal resources, background and life circumstances. Background and personal characteristics, stage and type of addiction and the particular social and psychological functions the addiction serves for the addict all interact to create his or her complex motivational make-up. Each addict is in a unique predicament and presents a unique challenge to the system and the would-be therapist. The level of individualised treatment required is a severe challenge for the prison, which is founded on batch-living arrangements.

On the other hand, while the immense diversity amongst drug users and types of addiction is a crucial issue, which cannot be ignored by addiction treatment programmes, there are also significant commonalities between all drug users and all forms of addiction. Most fundamentally, research (Orford 1982) has shown that addicts are almost always profoundly ambivalent about their addiction, although this fact may be well hidden. They are aware of the destructive potential of their addiction and they normally harbour at some level both a strong desire and a sincere intention to eventually break their habit and return to a drug free life. It is essential for treatment programmes to tap into and bolster this positive motivation in addicts. There is clearly a requirement for a sophisticated and flexible response, which recognises individual needs but provides a variety of programmes tailored to various general categories of drug user.

While individual differences are critical, the powerful synergy between the prisoner drugs culture and institutional features of the prison means that effective attempts to provide drug treatment and rehabilitation in prison must take account of strong forces at the psychosocial and cultural levels. It is insufficient to merely tackle the addictive process per se, as defined by physical and psychological dependence on particular mood-altering substances. It is essential in addition to target the drugs culture, the negative influence of the institution, and the specific values and motives that drug using prisoners derive within the context of the prison and its drugs culture.

But there are other serious constraints on drug treatment and rehabilitation in prison. Physical facilities for running programmes are generally inadequate even in modern prisons. Prisoners are also very heterogeneous in respect of their status within the criminal justice system. Since most programmes require lead-in time for assessment and planning and continue for at least several months, a very large number of drug using prisoners spend too brief a time in prison to benefit from or indeed qualify for programmes. The remand prison, Cloverhill, contains many drug using prisoners, who are unconvicted and whose longer term presence in the system depends on bail applications and trial outcomes and is essentially unpredictable. Clearly, special strategies need to be developed for short-term and remand prisoners.

Furthermore, under the best of circumstances in open society, treatment for drug abusers is beset with problems and suffers from substantial failure and attrition rates. No treatment modality can credibly claim much better than a 30% success rate (Encyclopaedia of Psychiatry 1972). The progress of an addict towards abstinence is very often characterised by a series of setbacks. The recovery process often takes the form of a cycle of abstinence and relapse before permanent or long-term abstinence is achieved (Marlatt et al 1988). This means that, as the US Drug Abuse Council points out (1980), "the overall efficacy of treatment cannot be judged on the basis of a brief episode of treatment or by the immediate achievement of abstinence". Prison programmes and overall strategy must take account of these limitations, yet somehow construct a system of treatment and rehabilitation built on a solid foundation of purposefulness and realistic optimism.

POSSIBLE DRUG REHABILITATION STRATEGIES FOR THE PRISON SYSTEM

In response to the formidable array of difficulties facing prison drug treatment and rehabilitation, in July 2000 the Steering Group on Prison Based Drug

Treatment Services made its report. The main thrust of this report is that there should be a "commitment to planned prisoner throughcare and aftercare (positive sentence management). Interagency working relationships should be based upon multidisciplinary integrated service provision in terms of assessment, intervention strategies and measures to promote prisoner integration into the community. From a policy perspective one of the main conclusions is that the Prisons Service must replicate in prison to the maximum extent feasible the level of medical and other supports available in the community."

Despite its high count of jargon and buzz words, this is a profoundly disappointing and seriously flawed report. The self-contradictory notion of promoting "prisoner integration into the community" exemplifies its woolly thinking. The report's main recommendation is the vague and purely aspirational wish for equivalence of care between the prison and the outside community. This lacks realism for two reasons: first, because it fails to take account of the psycho-social and physical conditions of imprisonment that make replication of many community services impossible; and second, because it ignores the continuing inadequacy of community services. Provision of drug treatment and rehabilitation in the community is still far from optimal, even for well-motivated addicts who are not deeply involved in crime. It is hard to build model programmes within prisons when such programmes are for the most part lacking in the community.

The report's emphasis on the need for after-care and through-care for prisoners is valid. Effective treatment and rehabilitation programmes run the risk of being undermined if there is no continuity of care and treatment in the committal and post-release phases. However, the Steering Group does not address the general lack of a structure for after-care and through-care for prisoners and does not appear aware of the need for specialised services for the ex-prisoner group, who are not always amenable to or suitable for assimilation into mainstream services.

Only one brief passage addresses the core issue of the drugs culture in prisons and it states: "It is the view of the Steering Group that there is a need to challenge and change the inmate culture in some of the prisons vis-a-vis drug misuse and promote effective ways in managing drug addicted prisoners. This involves the provision of different types of clinical and psychosocial methods of drug treatment as well as the construction of regimes, which would support such methods." There is, however, no elaboration on the forms such action might take nor any clarification of policy on the rival claims of harm reduction and prohibition. Indeed, this acknowledgement of the power of the prison drugs culture is immediately followed in the report by a statement that the culture should be challenged and changed "without relaxing or reducing enforcement activity to prevent access to illegal drugs in the prisons".

In the section on training the report states that "in relation to drug misuse, there is a need to shift the culture from a more custodial model towards the treatment and rehabilitation approach .... The potential for conflict between care and control issues also needs to be addressed. Stimulating thinking and lifestyle change among prisoners requires the development of a sense of responsibility, hope and empowerment". These are indeed core issues but this cursory mention is the only attention they receive in the report. There is no acknowledgement of the fact that prisoners need to be empowered within and by the system in order to become more responsible and that this will require radical change to regimes and to the forms of social interaction encouraged in the prisons.

The only substantive and detailed contribution of the report is its recommendations on staffing levels. For example, it recommends that Mountjoy Male Prison, in order to deal with an estimated 250 drug users, should have: five professionally qualified drug counsellors, one further psychologist to train about fifty prison officers in "direct work with drug dependent prisoners" and a panel of eight nurses (in addition to the large number of nurses already employed in the main prison) so that the medical unit can be manned night and day. The two full time equivalent posts for GPs and the two sessions a week from a psychiatric consultant in substance misuse are considered sufficient.

The Steering Group clearly does not envisage a radical restructuring of either the prisons or the drug treatment and rehabilitation services within them. Recommendations in effect consolidate the current direction of services by planning for their expansion and for the provision of moderately better resources and staffing for them. The main emphasis is on medical approaches including detoxification and methadone maintenance, drug free areas within prisons, and vaguely described counselling and support services. It is even proposed that there should be so-called drug free zones where prisoners who are abstinent, and those who are on methadone maintenance, will mix. This is justified by the curious notion that such zones will be free at least of "illicit" drugs. However, the difficulty of maintaining the motivation of abstinent prisoners, who under this plan will continuously rub shoulders with prisoners receiving prescribed opiates, is entirely ignored.

In general, the report lacks any thought-through philosophy or explicit framework for policy capable of resolving the fundamental dilemmas of drug treatment and rehabilitation in prison. Most seriously, no position is articulated on the extent to which treatment and rehabilitation should be abstinence-directed as opposed to harm-reduction-directed or on how it might be possible to strike a balance between these two approaches. As a result, there is no discussion of the legal, practical and theoretical complexities of maintaining or not maintaining prohibition in the proposed system. The intention appears to be to casually mix harm-reduction and abstinence-orientated programmes, continuing all the while with the current unsatisfactory system of far from effective prohibition. The whole approach is founded on the hope that prisoners will be compliant and content either to be supplied with methadone or, alternately, supported in their choice of abstinence. No attention whatsoever is given to the essentially oppositional nature of the prisoner culture or to the paradoxical, double-edged effects on prisoner motivation of a coercive prohibitionist system, which tends, at one and the same time, to discourage and promote drug use.

The report clearly gives precedence to already established medical approaches, such as detoxification and methadone maintenance, without adverting to the considerable evidence that these approaches are of limited value in the search for abstinence. While many different drug treatment and rehabilitation approaches have been tried in the US and other prison systems with varying degrees of success (Peters 1993), there are often fundamental contradictions between the models underpinning these approaches. For example, abstinence-focused approaches, like the Twelve Step moral method, medical harm reduction measures, such as methadone maintenance, and psycho-educational, empowerment and skills-focused approaches, which stress self-directed change and which attempt to alter the balance of forces that impact on the individual's motivation through cognitive-behavioural techniques and environmental manipulation, are often fundamentally incompatible with each other. It is an indication of the medical bias of the report that counselling, educational and psycho-social approaches are clumped together as if they were all indistinguishable from each other.

Psycho-educational techniques, group methods and political and institutional change to the prison, which are central to any attempt to transform the prisoner drugs culture and the motivation of individual prisoners, are seen by the Steering Group as, at best, secondary. However, if the main emphasis in the prisons is to be on abstinence-oriented approaches, then institutional change and psycho-educational methods must be centre stage and detoxification and medical harm reduction methods must take a subordinate place as indispensable but relatively minor stepping stones in a broader, gradual and often recursive rehabilitation process. The report's vocabulary of "managing the drug using offender" tends to place him or her in the category of passive consumer, when most effective abstinence-based approaches stress the need to win the active and willing participation of the user and to treat him or her as the senior partner in the rehabilitation process.

The failure of the Steering Group to develop a philosophy which takes a clear position on the difficult issues results in many serious omissions and evasions. Most obviously, the report completely neglects to examine the harm reduction measures now being widely introduced in other prison systems. These measures include the provision of needle exchange, which has been pioneered in Switzerland (Nelles et al 1998), of cleansing tablets for syringes, which is recommended by the World Health Organisation (WHO 1993), and maintenance on injected heroin as opposed to methadone, which has also been initiated in

Switzerland (Nelles et al 1997). The report leaves the reader uncertain of the Steering Group's position on these and other clearly useful, if contentious, harm reduction measures, such as encouraging the smoking of heroin as a substitute for intravenous use. There is also no discussion of the role of urinalysis as a control and decision-making tool in prison drug treatment and rehabilitation programmes. Bird et al (1997) place the Steering Group's declared concern for equivalence of care in a new light with their statement that "if current limited access to harm reduction measures (in British prisons) is perpetuated it represents a serious gulf between the standards of health care and public health available to the same individuals in prison and outside. Prison medical service policy promotes equality but is short on delivery". In the even more parlous Irish case, the Steering Group, though also advocating equivalence of care, totally fails to address specific harm reduction measures and their absence in the Irish prisons.

Moreover, the Steering Group makes no mention of the special problems posed by short-term and remand prisoners and gives no attention to the crucial issue of classifying and separating prisoners according to their drug status. This is a serious omission since classification and separation are necessary to effective treatment and offer potentially the most powerful means to prevent the spread of drug misuse and disease in the prison. There is also no mention of the drugs courts and the important role they might play, especially with minor offenders and those currently receiving short sentences that rule out meaningful involvement in prison programmes.

Discussion of the therapeutic community, which is, according to Inciardi (2000), "unquestionably the most appropriate form of drug abuse treatment in correctional settings because of the many phenomena in the prison environment that make rehabilitation difficult", is relegated to the Matters Outstanding section of the report. This option is put on hold since it requires "in-depth consideration". The prison therapeutic community offers most promise in relation to challenging the drugs culture because it entirely reconstructs the relationships and ethos of normal prison life in order to create a supportive, anti-drugs environment and powerful group pressures which motivate the individual to become and remain abstinent.

Grendon Prison in England, for example, has been successfully run as a therapeutic community for several decades and is founded on the four fundamental principles of "Democracy, Tolerance, Communalism, and Reality Confrontation" and on a simple set of rules required to establish a safe environment and a level of basic trust – that there be "no violence, drug use, sex or confidences" (Newell 1997). The ethos of the normal prison, by contrast, is authoritarian; inspired by intolerance; hierarchical, individualistic and divided; and encourages dissociation from reality. The normal prison is a negative environment which promotes resentment, rationalisation of criminal behaviour, increasingly anti-social attitudes, and drug use, whereas the therapeutic community is a total treatment environment that provides a "24-hr per day learning experience in which a drug user's transformations in conduct, attitudes, values, and emotions are introduced, monitored, and mutually reinforced as part of the daily regime" (Pan et al 1993).

The successful experiment in Grendon Prison provides a durable model for an alternative to the rehabilitatively inert and often counterproductive forms of imprisonment that still dominate the Irish system. A fully fledged therapeutic community within the prison would undoubtedly be beneficial, but it is very exacting on everyone involved, requires a high degree of self-imposed discipline and would not by any means suit all prisoners. Furthermore, a therapeutic community is an insulated treatment modality that is able to create a more positive therapeutic environment precisely because it separates and distinguishes itself from the rest of the prison system.

However, important lessons can be learnt from the therapeutic community which have a more general application to the prisons. Using some of the principles of the therapeutic community in combination with greatly improved facilities and services, it is possible to construct intermediate regimes that abandon the methods and entrenched attitudes of the total institution and instead genuinely focus on the needs of prisoners, on their empowerment, on their development of a sense of responsibility to themselves and others, and on their active participation as senior partners in the rehabilitation process. The system needs to instill in prisoners the belief that they have the personal power to change the direction of their lives. Many prisoners come from highly deprived, dysfunctional families and are under-educated and lacking in basic problem-solving and interpersonal skills. These deficits are intimately connected with their susceptibility to involvement in self-destructive drug use. A purposeful system that targets these deficits as well as drug abuse and fully occupies and motivates the prisoner, by prioritising personal development, self-actualisation and the enhancement of employability, offers the best prospect of defeating the prisoner drugs culture.

On the other hand, there are always likely to be drug using prisoners who are not prepared to be abstinent or not yet ready to seriously engage with treatment and rehabilitation, even with the support of methadone maintenance. Assessment, classification and subsequent separation of prisoners according to their capacity to benefit from different types of intervention are clearly essential to the running of an effective system. Sections of the system, which house apparently intractable drug using prisoners, will continue to require a primary emphasis on harm minimisation. Unfortunately, the Steering Group has failed both to grasp the nettle of harm reduction, where that is required, and to promote a progressive vision of a radically reconstructed prison system with the potential to advance many hundreds of drug using prisoners towards both self-actualisation and abstinence.

REFERENCES

Allwright, S., Barry, J., Bradley, F., Long, J. and Thornton, L. 1999, *Hepatitis B Hepatitis C and HIV in Irish Prisoners: Prevalence and Risk,* Dublin: Stationery Office

Bird, A., Gore, S., Hutchinson, S., Lewis, S., Cameron, S. and Burns, S. 1997, "Harm reduction measures and injecting inside prison versus mandatory drugs testing; results of a cross sectional anonymous questionnaire survey", *British Medical Journal* 315, 21-24

Butler, S. 1991, "Drug Problems and Drug Policies in Ireland: A Quarter of a Century Reviewed", *Administration* 39, 210

Clemmer, D. 1940, *The Prison Community,* New York: Rinehart

Committee on Drug Education 1974, *Report,* Dublin: Stationery Office

Crowley, D. (1999) "The Drug Detox Unit at Mountjoy Prison – A Review", *The Journal of Health Gain* 3 (3), 17-19

Cullen, B. 1998, "Young People and Drugs: Critical issues for policy", Dublin: Children's Research Centre, Trinity College

Department of Justice 1994, *The Management of Offenders: a Five Year Plan,* Dublin: Stationery Office

Director of Medical Services for the Irish Prisons Service 1999, *Report,* Dublin: Department of Justice

Drug Abuse Council 1980, *The Facts about Drug Abuse,* New York: The Free Press

Encyclopaedia of Psychiatry 1972, *Encyclopaedia of Psychiatry for General Practitioners,* London: Roche Products

Garda Síochána 1993, *Report on Crime,* Dublin: Garda HQ

Goffman Erving 1968, *Asylums,* London: Penguin Books

Government Strategy to Prevent Drug Misuse 1991, Dublin: Stationery Office

Hannon, F., Kelleher, C. and Friel, S. 2000, *General Healthcare Study of the Irish Prisoner Population,* Dublin: Stationery Office

Head of the Garda Drug Squad 1995, Speech to A Conference on Drugs of the Irish Farmers' Association

Inciardi, J. and Harrison, L. (eds.) 2000, *Harm Reduction: national and international perspectives,* London: Sage

Jones, K. and Fowles, A. 1984, *Ideas on Institutions,* London Routledge and Kegan Paul

Keogh, E. 1997, *Illicit Drug Use and Related Criminal Activity in the Dublin Metropolitan Area,* Dublin: Garda Headquarters

Marlatt, G., Baer, J., Donovan, D., Kivlahan, D. 1988, "Addictive Behaviours: Etiology and Treatment", *Annual Review of Psychology* 39, 223-252

McCorkle, L. and Korn, R. 1954, "Resocialisation within walls", *Annals of the Academy of Political and Social Sciences* 293, 88-98

MacCoun, R. 1998, "Toward a Psychology of Harm Reduction", *American Psychologist* 53, 11 1199-1208

Morgan, M., Hibell, B., Andersson, B., Thoroddur, B., Kokkevi, A. and Narusk, A. 1999, "The ESPAD study: Implications for prevention", *Drugs; Education, prevention and policy* 6 (2), 243-256

Mountjoy Visiting Committee 1991, *Report,* Dublin: Department of Justice

Murphy, T. 1996, *Rethinking the war on Drugs,* Cork: Cork University Press

National Steering Group on Deaths in Prisons 1999, *Report,* Dublin: Stationery Office

Nelles, J. Dobler-Mikkola, A. and Kaufman, B. 1997, "Provision of syringes and prescription of heroin in prison", in Nelles, J. Fuhrer, A. (eds.), *Harm Reduction in Prison: Strategies against drugs AIDS and risk behaviour,* Bern: Lang

Nelles, J., Fuhrer, A., Hirsbrunner, H. and Harding, T. 1998, "Provision of Syringes: the cutting edge of harm reduction in prison?", *British Medical Journal* 317 270- 273

Newell, T. 1997, Speech in Proceedings of Conference, *Is Penal reform Possible?,* Dublin: IPRT

O'Gorman, A. 1998, "Illicit Drug Use in Ireland: An overview of the problem", *Journal of Drug Issues* 28 (1), 155-166

O'Mahony, P. and Gilmore, T. 1982, *Drug Abusers in the Dublin Committal Prisons: A Survey,* Dublin: Stationery Office

O'Mahony, P. 1990, "Abstinence in Treated and Untreated Opiate Abusers: a Study of a Prison Sample", *Irish Journal of Psychological Medicine* 7, 2, pp 121-123

O'Mahony, P. 1997a, *Mountjoy Prisoners: A Sociological and Criminological Profile,* Dublin: Stationery Office

O'Mahony, P. 1997b, "Community Vigilantism: Cure or Curse?", *Doctrine and Life* 47, 325-333

O'Mahony, P. 2000, *Prison Policy in Ireland; Social Justice versus Criminal Justice,* Cork: Cork University Press

Orford, J. 1982, *Excessive Appetites: A Social Learning Analysis of the Addictions,* Chichester: Wiley

Pan, H., Scrappitti, F., Inciardi, J. and Lockwood, D. 1993, "Some Considerations on Therapeutic Communities In Corrections", in Inciardi, J. (ed.), *Drug treatment and criminal justice,* London: Sage

Peters, R. 1993, "Drug treatment in jails and detention settings", in Inciardi J, (ed.), *Drug treatment and criminal justice,* London: Sage

Rabbite Reports 1996, *First Report of the Ministerial Task Force on Measures to Reduce the Demand for Drugs* and 1997, *Second Report of the Ministerial Task Force on Measures to Reduce the Demand for Drugs,* Dublin: Stationery Office

Redmond, L. 2001, *Drug Use Among Prisoners: an Exploratory Study,* Dublin: Health Research Board

Sackman, B., Sackman, M. and De Angelis, E. 1978, "Heroin Addiction as an Occupation: Traditional Addicts and Heroin Addict Polydrug Users", *International Journal of the Addictions* 13, 427-441

Special Government Task Force on Drug Abuse 1983, unpublished Report

Steering Group on Prison Based Drug Treatment Services 2000, *Report,* Dublin: Irish Prisons Service

Terry, W. C. III 1999, "Judicial Change and Dedicated Treatment Courts", in *The Early Drugs Courts* (ed. Clinton Terry W. III) London: Sage

Wexler, H., Lipton, D. and Johnson, B. 1988, *A Criminal Justice System Strategy for Treating Cocaine-Heroin Abusing Offenders in Custody,* Washington: US Department of Justice

World Health Organisation 1993, *Global Programme on AIDs: WHO Guidelines on HIV Infection and AIDS in Prisons,* Geneva: WHO

Table of Cases

IRISH

OTHERS

CANADA

ECHR

Table of Statutes

Table of Constitutional Provisions

Index